ACCESS NEW YORK CITY

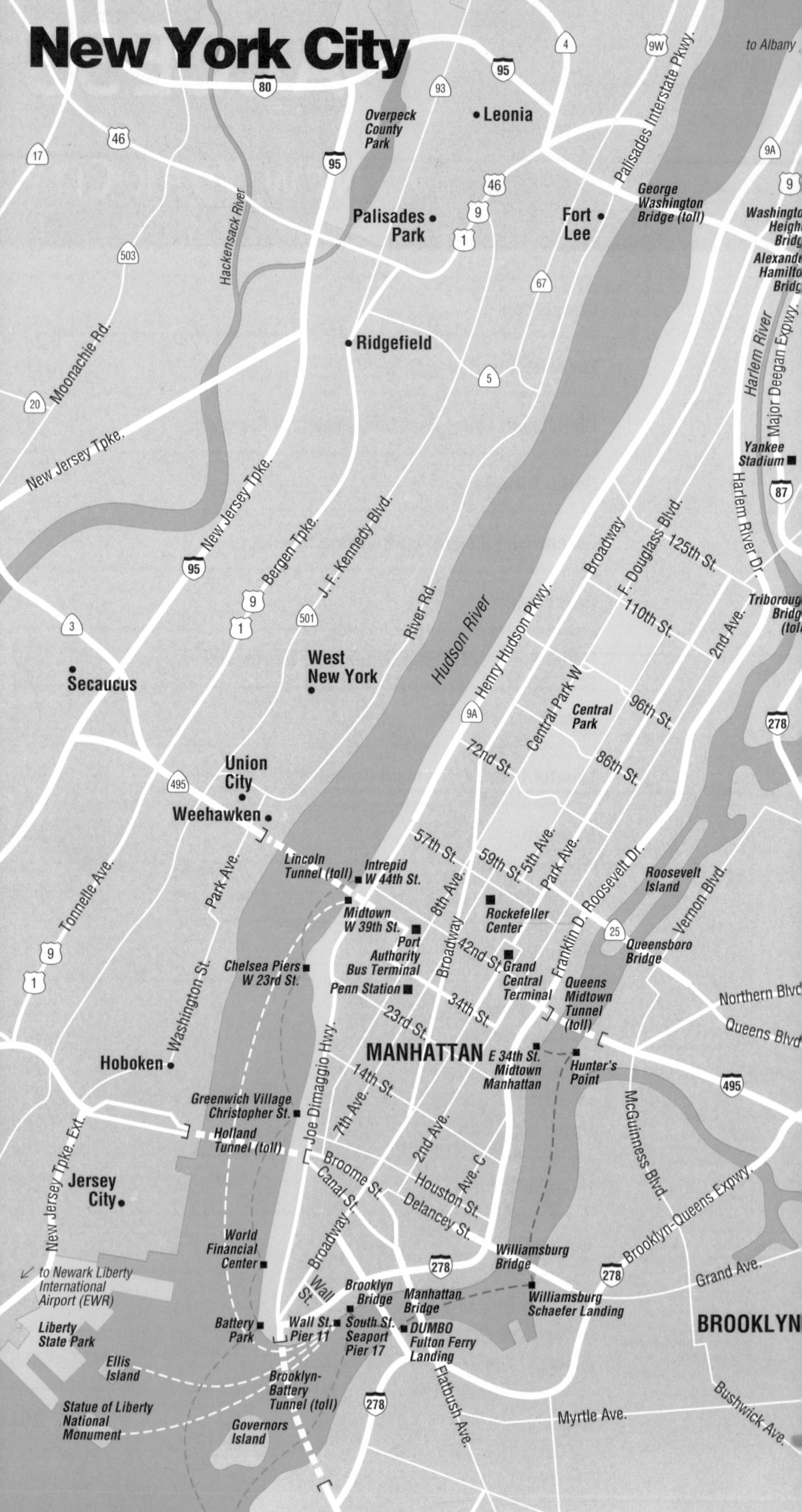

New York City
to Albany
Overpeck County Park
Leonia
Palisades Park
Fort Lee
Palisades Interstate Pkwy.
George Washington Bridge (toll)
Hackensack River
Moonachie Rd.
Ridgefield
New Jersey Tpke.
Bergen Tpke.
J. F. Kennedy Blvd.
River Rd.
Hudson River
Harlem River
Major Deegan Expwy.
Yankee Stadium
Harlem River Dr.
Broadway
F. Douglass Blvd.
125th St.
110th St.
2nd Ave.
Henry Hudson Pkwy.
Central Park W
Central Park
96th St.
86th St.
72nd St.
Secaucus
West New York
Union City
Weehawken
Lincoln Tunnel (toll)
Intrepid W 44th St.
Midtown W 39th St.
57th St.
59th St.
5th Ave.
Park Ave.
8th Ave.
Rockefeller Center
Franklin D. Roosevelt Dr.
Roosevelt Island
Vernon Blvd.
Queensboro Bridge
Tonnelle Ave.
Washington St.
Chelsea Piers W 23rd St.
Port Authority Bus Terminal
42nd St.
Grand Central Terminal
Queens Midtown Tunnel (toll)
Penn Station
34th St.
Northern Blvd
Queens Blvd
23rd St.
MANHATTAN
E 34th St. Midtown Manhattan
Hunter's Point
Hoboken
Joe Dimaggio Hwy.
14th St.
7th Ave.
Greenwich Village Christopher St.
Holland Tunnel (toll)
McGuinness Blvd.
Ave. C
Broome St.
Houston St.
Canal St.
Delancey St.
Jersey City
New Jersey Tpke. Ext.
World Financial Center
Williamsburg Bridge
Brooklyn-Queens Expwy.
Grand Ave.
to Newark Liberty International Airport (EWR)
Wall St.
Brooklyn Bridge
Manhattan Bridge
Williamsburg Schaefer Landing
BROOKLYN
Liberty State Park
Battery Park
Wall St. Pier 11
South St. Seaport Pier 17
DUMBO Fulton Ferry Landing
Ellis Island
Brooklyn-Battery Tunnel (toll)
Flatbush Ave.
Bushwick Ave.
Statue of Liberty National Monument
Governors Island
Myrtle Ave.

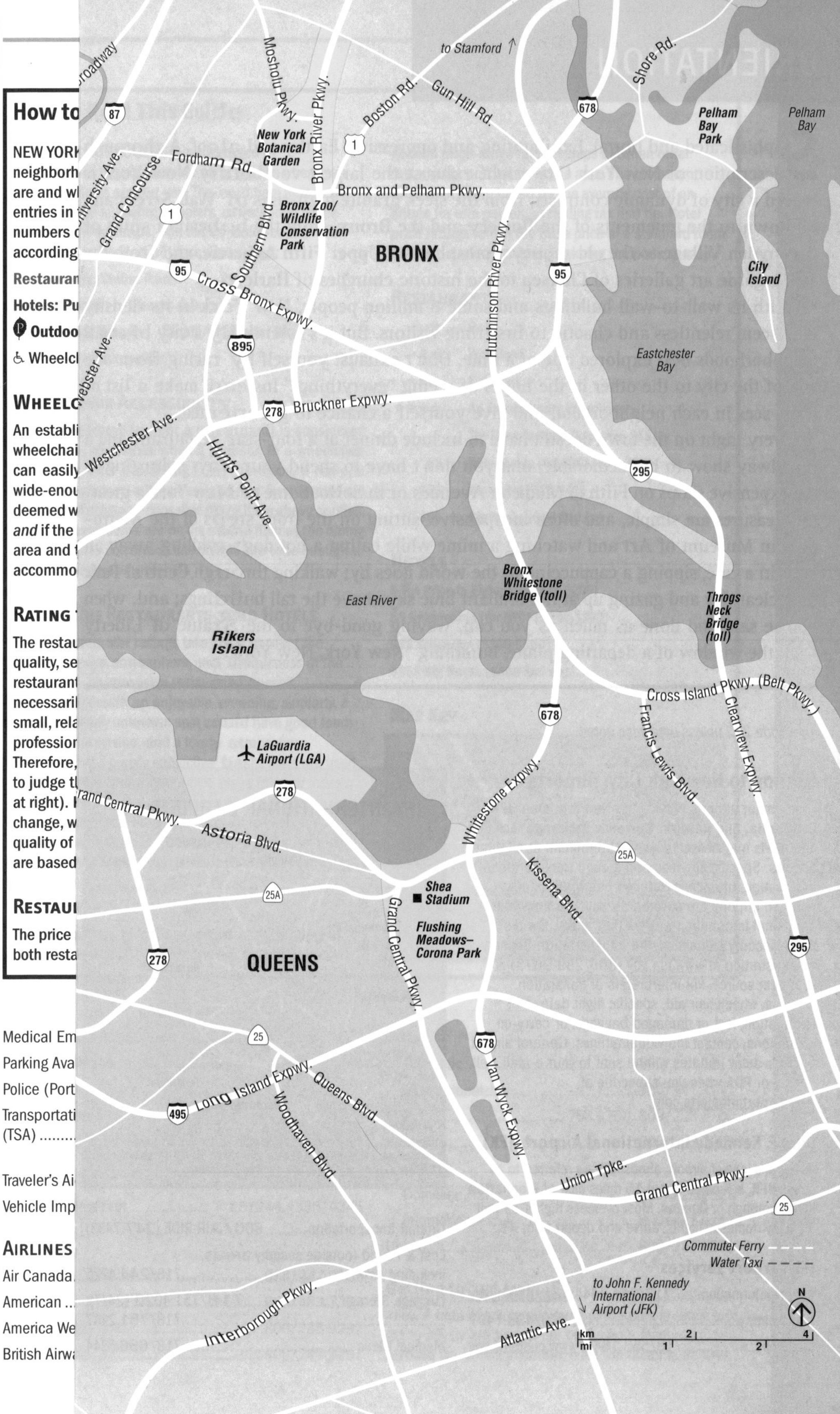

Broadway
to Stamford
Shore Rd.
Mosholu Pkwy.
Bronx River Pkwy.
Boston Rd.
Gun Hill Rd.
Pelham Bay Park
Pelham Bay
New York Botanical Garden
University Ave.
Fordham Rd.
Grand Concourse
Bronx and Pelham Pkwy.
Southern Blvd.
Bronx Zoo/ Wildlife Conservation Park
BRONX
Hutchinson River Pkwy.
City Island
Cross Bronx Expwy.
Webster Ave.
Eastchester Bay
Bruckner Expwy.
Westchester Ave.
Hunts Point Ave.
Bronx Whitestone Bridge (toll)
East River
Throgs Neck Bridge (toll)
Rikers Island
Cross Island Pkwy. (Belt Pkwy.)
Francis Lewis Blvd.
Clearview Expwy.
LaGuardia Airport (LGA)
Whitestone Expwy.
Grand Central Pkwy.
Astoria Blvd.
Kissena Blvd.
Shea Stadium
Grand Central Pkwy.
Flushing Meadows–Corona Park
QUEENS
Long Island Expwy.
Queens Blvd.
Woodhaven Blvd.
Van Wyck Expwy.
Union Tpke.
Grand Central Pkwy.
Commuter Ferry
Water Taxi
to John F. Kennedy International Airport (JFK)
Interborough Pkwy.
Atlantic Ave.
km
mi
N

OR

S
indee
Midt
Gree
avan
W
may
neigh
end c
must
Ev
Broad
the ex
est pl
polita
hour
on a
you'v
from

Area co

Getti

Three r
LaGua
and **AT**
airports
informa
betwee
additio
latest s
Admini
your be
service
informa
restrict
weathe
phone,
www.ai

John F

The are
simply
in the b
as man

JFK Ai

Airport
Compla
Custom

LOWER MANHATTAN

Lower Manhattan Island is bounded by **Chambers Street** and the **East** and **Hudson Rivers**. Here, at the confluence of these waterways, the earliest explorers—Giovanni da Verrazano, Esteban Gómez, and Henry Hudson—first touched land. And it was also here, in 1625, that the Dutch set up **Fort Amsterdam** to protect the southern perimeter of their settlement, called **Nieuw Amsterdam**.

The skyscrapers and canyons of today's **Financial District** stand where the tiny Dutch settlement, and later the prime residential enclave of post-Revolutionary New York, once flourished. The narrow alleys of the Financial District are a reminder of the scale of colonial America. However, except for a few fragments of old foundations, not a single building erected during the 40 years of Dutch rule remains. When the British Army withdrew in 1783 after seven years of occupation, the village of New York—which covered 10 blocks north from what is now **Battery Park**—lay almost totally in ruins. But once New York City pulled itself together and began to push north, the city grew swiftly. Two blocks of low-rise commercial buildings from this early surge of development have survived: the **Fraunces Tavern** block and **Schermerhorn Row**.

When **City Hall**—the one still in use today—was being built in 1811 on the northernmost fringe of town, its north side was covered with common brownstone instead of marble, because, despite all the growth, no one really expected the building to be seen from that angle. But by 1820 New York City had expanded another 10 to 15 blocks, and by 1850 the limits had pushed two miles north to 14th Street, and city planners began to assign numbers to the streets. A fire in 1835 leveled most of Lower Manhattan, but even that didn't halt the expansion of what had become the leading commercial center and port in the new country after the War of 1812. **Pearl Street** took its name from the iridescent shells that covered the beach at its location, the original shoreline of the East River. Landfill added **Water Street**, then **Front Street**, and finally **South Street** (by the 1820s a thick forest of masts congested the port; the **South Street Seaport Museum** evokes that maritime era). By 1812, lawyers, insurance companies, merchants, and financiers were crowding out families in what quickly became the Financial District, whose symbolic and geographic center was the intersection of **Broad** and **Wall Streets** (named for the wooden wall that served as the northern fortification of Nieuw Amsterdam). The construction of the **Merchants' Exchange** in 1836 speeded up the area's transition to a commercial district. Leap forward in time and we find the ultimate commercial–and residential–development, and the last big landfill operation that would change the shape of Lower Manhattan: the 1970s' building of the **World Trade Center** and, with it, **Battery Park City**.

In the limestone-and-glass caverns of Wall Street, only a few of the 18th- and 19th-century public structures remain: **Federal Hall**, the former **US Custom House** on **Bowling Green**, **Trinity Church** (an 1846 incarnation, several times removed from the original), and the even earlier **St. Paul's Chapel** (1766). The **Whitehall Building** is architecturally reminiscent of Dutch governor Peter Stuyvesant's mansion, which was on nearby **Whitehall Street**. Bowling Green, a cattle market in Dutch days and later a green for bowling and other recreation at the center of a desirable residential area, is now an egg-shaped park at the foot of **Broadway**; its 1771 fence is still intact. And the **Civic Center**, just north of the Financial District–a cluster of old and new government buildings, some handsome, some horrendous–was built mostly on land that is now recognized to be the extensive 18th-century **African Burial Ground**.

Firmly a seat of commerce and government through much of the 1900s with nary a resident in sight, a shift in Lower Manhattan's makeup began late in the century. As the dot-com boom heated up in the 1980s and 1990s, developers went crazy wiring the buildings with the latest Internet technology; unused commercial space was converted to residential, the better to serve the new 24/7 culture. Hotels, restaurants, shopping, and other amenities expanded to serve it as well.

But early in the new millennium the bubble burst, and a downturn was under way. Then, in shock from the events of 9/11, the whole city seemed to come to a stop. Today, though, a sense of stability–and progress–has taken root. The PATH station is once again servicing Financial District workers from New Jersey; **Hudson River Park** is complete, and along with **Battery Park** draws families and visitors from near and far for their cooling breezes, welcome greenery, and panoramic view of New York Harbor. Ferries to Liberty Island, Ellis Island, Staten Island, and even Governors Island jump off from here and nearby piers, and new museums, restaurants, and enclaves–like the **Stone Street Historic District** and the stretch of Front Street extending north from the Seaport area–are ready for discovery.

1 Jacob K. Javits Federal Building

The smaller building on the left houses the **US Customs Court**, and the taller one with the warp-and-weft windows is filled with government offices. Both buildings were designed by **Alfred Easton Poor** and **Kahn & Jacobs** in 1967. It was on the plaza fronting Javits that Richard Serra's "Tilted Arc" sculpture was installed—and aroused such controversy the Feds had it removed in 1989, an unusual fate for public art. Its replacement came in 1992 in the form of a benign installation by **Martha Schwartz Partners** involving a swarm of caterpillar-like swirls of greenery and benches dotted with dome-shaped misters. ♦ 26 Federal Plaza, Broadway (between Duane and Worth Sts)

2 African Burial Ground:

Startling news to many when the burial ground—now a National Historic Landmark and, as of 2006, a National Monument managed by the National Park Service—was uncovered in 1991 during foundation work for a new federal office building, the remains found here were those of some 20,000 Africans first brought to New Amsterdam in chains by late-17th-century Dutch; the slaves were provided to white settlers as part of the deal enticing them to come to the new colony. Trinity Church, the walls that comprised Wall Street, and other structures key to the development of Lower Manhattan were built by enslaved Africans who, according to recent studies, lived under conditions at least as grim as they were subjected to in the South.

On the grassy plot at the corner of Duane and Elk Streets—where 419 human ancestral remains were excavated, then re-buried after an appropriate tribute—a formal memorial has risen. Designed by architect **Rodney Léon** and opened to the public in 2007, the circular granite structure, *Ancestral Libation Chamber,* is a striking commemoration of an era that was almost lost to time. Completed in 1995, the adjacent **Ted Weiss Federal Building** (a noted design by **Hellmuth, Obata, Kassabaum**) houses related art installations and the National Park Service's **Interpretive Center**—its offerings include tours, a short film, and an oral history exhibit—in its lobby. As you enter the building, note the powerful darkly tinted concrete and fiber-optic homage *America Song,* by Clyde Lynds (1995). General Services Administration's Art-in-Architecture Program sponsored it along with the large-scale contemporary pieces inside—*The New Ring Shout* (1995, by Houston Conwill, Joseph De Pace, and Estella Conwill Majozzo-Poet), a circular metal-and-glass floor installation that fills much of the rotunda area; a devastating mosaic (untitled) by Roger Brown; Frank Bender's cast-bronze *Unearthed*; and *Renewal,* a 1998 mural by Tomie Arai, among them—that profoundly address the early African experience in New York. (The theme continues two blocks east, on Foley Square, with Lorenzo Pace's 2003 *Triumph of the Human Spirit*). ♦ African Burial Ground: Bounded by Broadway and Chambers, Duane, and Lafayette/Centre Sts. Memorial: Free. Daily, 9-5. Duane St (at Elk St). Interpretive Center and Installations: Free. M-F, 9-5 (expect to pass through security). Ted Weiss Federal Building, 290 Broadway (at Duane St). 637.2019. www.nps.gov/afbg; www.africanburialground.gov ♿

3 New York County Courthouse/NY State Supreme Court

A National Historic Landmark, this hexagonal building was designed by **Guy Lowell** in 1926. The Roman style of the building—particularly the Corinthian portico—works much better here than at the neighboring **United States Courthouse.** The building is not open to the public. ♦ 60 Centre St (at Pearl St)

4 United States Courthouse

Here's another Lower Manhattan structure trying to be a temple. Designed in 1936 by **Cass Gilbert** and **Cass Gilbert Jr.**, this civic building presents a traditional, stately image with rows of Corinthian columns as a base for a tower crowned with a gold pyramid. The building is not open to the public. ♦ 40 Centre St (at Pearl St)

5 St. Andrew's Church

This Roman Catholic church was established in 1842 to minister to the needs of Irish immigrants. Its mission has changed along with the neighborhood. The present church was designed in 1939 by **Maginnis & Walsh** and **Robert J. Reiley**. ♦ 20 Cardinal Hayes Pl (off Pearl St, between Park Row and Centre St). 962.3972

6 Tweed Courthouse

This magnificently restored building—the old **New York County Courthouse**—became known as the Tweed Courthouse because Tammany Hall chieftain William Marcy Tweed escalated its cost to 52 times the appropriated amount, most of which went into his own bank account. Because of the scandal, construction of the building (begun in 1861 and originally designed by

John Kellum) ceased for four years, during which time Kellum died. **Leopold Eidlitz** stepped in in 1876, adding Romanesque styling (colored brick, a dome ceiling) to Kellum's neoclassical cast-iron design. In 1984 the courthouse was given landmark status. Mayor Giuliani began an $85 million restoration, completed in 2001. Under Mayor Bloomberg's watch in 2002, the courthouse became the new home for New York City's **Department of Education** (formerly the **Board of Education**). The public may visit by appointment only: tours are offered jointly with City Hall tours, every Tuesday at 10AM and Friday at 2PM. ♦ 52 Chambers St (between Park Row and Broadway). Tour info and reservations: 311 (outside NY: 212/NEWYORK). www.nyc.gov/artcommission

7 City Hall

With a little help from periodic restorations (most recently in 1998), New York City is still doing business in the same building that was its headquarters in 1811, when construction was completed. This elegant scaled-down palace by **Mangin and McComb**, a winning entry in a design competition, successfully combines the Federal style with French Renaissance details. The central hall has a sweeping twin-spiral marble staircase under a splendid dome, making it the perfect setting for public functions and grand entrances. Kings, poets, and astronauts have been received here. Upstairs, the grand **City Council Chamber** and the **Governor's Room**—now a portrait gallery with paintings by Sully, Trumbull, Inman, and others—are worth a visit. There are always exhibits with historical or artistic themes. What is known today as **City Hall Park**—restored most sumptuously in 1999 by **George Vellonakis**—has always been the city's village green or town common; equally grand in scale, the park beautifully sets off the mass of City Hall. Tours, free: W, noon (first-come, first-served; sign up at the info kiosk on Broadway, at the south end of the park), and by appointment (offered jointly with Tweed Courthouse tours), Tu, 10AM; F, 2PM. ♦ City Hall Park, bounded by Broadway, Park Row, and Chambers St. Tour info and reservations: 311 (outside NY: 212/NEWYORK). www.nyc.gov/artcommission

8 Surrogate's Court

Monumental sculptures, including a pair by Philip Martiny at the entrance—one representing *Britannia* (an English soldier and a maiden), the other *America* (a Native American and a Pilgrim)—along with an array of cherubs, eagles, festoons, ship prows, and shields, let you know something important is going on here. The French Empire façade, reminiscent of the Paris Opera, is only the beginning. The interior has an Egyptian-tile mosaic ceiling with the 12 signs of the zodiac by William de Leftwich Dodge, as well as marble walls and floors and allegorical reliefs. The huge double stairway is yet another touch borrowed from the Opera. Intended to be the last resting place of important city records, the building, which was designed in 1911 by **John Rochester Thomas** and **Horgan & Slattery**, also serves as the Surrogate's Court. Over the years this became its primary function, as the need grew for more space to probate wills and administer guardianships and trusts. The building is not open to the public. ♦ 31 Chambers St (at Centre St)

Within Surrogate's Court:

Municipal Archives

What do you want to know about the city and its citizens? If it was ever documented, chances are it's here, in the NYC Department of Records' archives. Founded in 1950, the collection has the goods going back to the early 17th century—including coroner's records, census figures, and plans for the Brooklyn Bridge, plus maps, blueprints, moving images, sound recordings, and a wide range of historic photographs. ♦ M-F. 311; 212/NEW.YORK. www.nyc.gov ♿

9 Municipal Building

McKim, Mead & White created this neoclassical skyscraper—their first—in 1914 to house city government offices. The building straddles Chambers Street and coexists quite happily with neighboring, smaller **City Hall** without upstaging it. The almost Baroque confection is topped with a fanciful cluster of colonnaded towers capped by Adolph Weinman's 20-foot-high gilded statue, *Civic Fame.* Modern-day brides- and grooms-to-be flock here—often in full nuptial regalia—for the efficient, and official, four-minute weddings performed by the City Clerk's office. You might settle for a souvenir from the **CityStore** in the building's North Plaza area; stock up here on yellow-cab socks or skyscraper salt-and-pepper shakers. ♦ M-F. 1 Centre St (at Chambers St). 311 (outside NY: 212/NEW YORK)

10 Police Plaza

At three full acres, this is the largest public plaza in New York. On the south side is a prison window from the 1763 **Rhinelander Sugar Warehouse**, which was on this site until 1895. (The original building was used by the British to house American prisoners of war during the Revolution.) The five interlocking oxidized-steel disks, a 1974 creation by Bernard Rosenthal, represent the five boroughs of the city. Just beyond, an eight-foot waterfall marks the entrance to a multilevel parking garage under the plaza, which was designed in 1973 by **M. Paul Friedberg**. ♦ Park Row and Chambers St

11 Pace University

Originally founded as an accounting school, this university now offers courses in the arts and sciences as well as business, education, and nursing. The welded copper sculpture on the façade, by Henri Nachemia, is entitled *The Brotherhood of Man*. The building itself was designed by **Eggers & Higgins** in 1970. ♦ 1 Pace Plaza, Nassau St (between Spruce and Frankfort Sts). 346.1200. www.pace.edu ♿

12 Brooklyn Bridge

This milestone in civil engineering, built from 1869 to 1883 and designed by **John A. Roebling** and his son **Washington Roebling**, is an aesthetic, as well as a structural, masterpiece. The bridge gets its dynamic tension from the massive strength of its great stone pylons and Gothic arches contrasted with the intricate web of its woven suspension cables. In 1855, John Roebling's proposal for a bridge across the East River was met with derision, but farsighted residents of Brooklyn (then a separate city) pushed the idea after the Civil War. The Roebling family's fate was inextricably tied up with that of the bridge. John died as the result of an accident on a Brooklyn wharf before work on the bridge began, but his son, Washington, carried on, even when he got the bends during construction (he remained partially paralyzed for the rest of his life); his wife then took over the operation (plaques at both ends of the bridge commemorate the Roebling trio's dedication). The Brooklyn Bridge was the first to use steel cables. For 20 years it was the world's longest suspension bridge. The subject of many poems, paintings, paeans, and bad jokes, the bridge still gives a special lift to the bicyclists, walkers, and runners who cross it. If you care to venture across—and you absolutely should—the pedestrian entrance is just south of the Municipal Building, across from City Hall: The left side of the path is for foot traffic, the right for bikers. ♦ Between Adams St (Brooklyn) and Park Row

13 Bridge Cafe

★★★$$ This aptly named place is located in the oldest wood-frame building south of Canal Street, under the **Brooklyn Bridge** (it vies for the title of the oldest bar in the city as well!). The menu, featuring well-dressed staples such as savory buffalo steak and fresh soft-shell crabs, is one of the best in the **Seaport** area. The whitewashed room with tin ceiling, brick walls, and burgundy tablecloths is cozy by day and romantically candlelit at night; the service and ambience is always convivial. ♦ International ♦ M-F, lunch and dinner; Sa, Su, brunch and dinner. Reservations recommended. 279 Water St (at Dover St). 227.3344 ♿

14 Seaport Inn

$$ For the traveler who wants easy access to historic downtown Manhattan, or the businessperson who would rather walk to those early-morning Wall Street appointments, this handsomely restored 19th-century building houses 72 tastefully decorated rooms—all non-smoking, all with free high-speed Internet access—offering a warm and comfortable refuge. Some rooms have terraces with views of the Brooklyn Bridge. There is no restaurant, but a (very) small breakfast room offers continental fixings to get you started in the morning. ♦ 33 Peck Slip (at Front St). 766.6600, 800/HOTEL.NY; fax: 766.6615. www.seaportinn.com ♿

15 South Street Seaport Historic District

Back when sailing ships ruled the seas, New York's most active ports were along this stretch of the East River. With the coming of steamships, the deeper piers on the Hudson River attracted most of the seafaring traffic, and the East River piers fell into decline. In 1967, a group of preservation-minded citizens banded together to buy the run-down waterfront buildings and a collection of historic ships. Twelve years later, commercial interests moved in and provided funds to restore the old buildings and add some new ones. The result, thanks to the ingenuity of architects **Ben** and **Jane Thompson**, is a lively historic site that has revitalized the once-derelict neighborhood. Contributing to the historical air are the cobblestone streets paved with Belgian blocks and the **Titanic Memorial Lighthouse**, which greets visitors at Fulton and Water Streets. This lighthouse originally overlooked the harbor from the Seamen's Church Institute on Water Street at Cuyler's Alley. A memorial to the 1,500 who died when the **White Star Line**'s *Titanic* struck an iceberg in 1912, it was moved here in 1976 to mark the entrance to the seaport.

While modern Seaport development (and the crowd) still centers on the shops and restaurants off Fulton Street, you'll want to poke around the north end of the district. The strips of water on Front Street between Beekman Place up to the bridge attract galleries, restaurants, and some of the most interesting historic buildings in the area. ♦ Daily. Bounded by the East River and Water St, and

Taking Stock of Wall Street

Wall Street's west end is marked by the spires of **Trinity Church**, with its roseate façade and history-filled cemetery. Today's visitors, however, are far more intrigued with the less spiritual attractions of New York's Financial District. Whether the bulls (aggressive and expecting prices to rise) or the bears (more cautious, fearing falling prices) are in control, New York's financial center fascinates visitors both locally and from afar.

In 1653, a wooden wall was built as fortification against Indian and British attack, hence the name Wall Street. (The wall was demolished at the end of the century, never having been tested in actual battle). By the late 1700s, outdoor trading was entrenched in the area and some historians believe that the 1792 "Buttonwood Agreement"–among 20 or so stockbrokers and merchants–marked the beginning of the **New York Stock Exchange** (see page 29), the granddaddy of all trading enterprises in the city. However, the formal NYSE was not inaugurated until 1817; it was then known as The New York Stock and Exchange Board. (A bit of perspective: by the 1870s, one could buy an NYSE seat for about $4,000; by 2005 one could be had for $3.25 million.)

By the mid-1800s, though, the NYSE was far from the only trading institution in town. The **American Stock Exchange** (see page 27) was an 1842 start-up then known as the New York Curb Exchange, and commodity exchanges were soon well established (there were 1,600 of them in the city by the late 1800s). The **Butter and Egg Exchange** opened in 1872; it absorbed markets trading in eggs, poultry, and other edibles, and became the **New York Mercantile Exchange (NYMEX)** in 1882, merging with **COMEX** (metals, hides, rubber, and metal) in 1994 under the NYMEX name. Today, the **AMEX** specializes in small-to-midsize companies and is an independent entity owned by **NASDAQ,** which, when founded in 1971, was the world's first electronic stock market and is now the largest in the US.

The number 29 seems to have been a jinx for the stock market, as has the month of October. The infamous crash of 1929 took place on 29 October, when the market lost nearly a quarter of its value. The crash precipitated the creation of the Securities and Exchange Commission (SEC), which enforced a set of rules on how stocks could be represented and traded. In 1971 the NYSE was incorporated as a nonprofit organization, and in 1975 the ruling on fixed commission regulations was repealed, paving the way for discount brokerage firms. Standardization, supposition, and superstition remain a part of Wall Street's roller-coaster history. Right up to the present, both scandals and crashes continue to plague investors large and small. Interestingly, the last major "correction," as noteworthy declines are delicately referred to today, occurred in 1987–once again in the month of October. The influential Short Order Execution System, or SOES, legislation was borne of that crash. Meant to protect electronics-savvy independent traders in the event of future crashes, it also created the rough-and-tumble world of day-trading.

Lower Manhattan today is home to many of the world's most powerful investment firms, banks, and other financial institutions. While few are open to the public in this security-sensitive era, much can be gleaned from a

John and Dover Sts. 732.7678/SEAPORT. Special events: www.southstreetseaport.com

Within South Street Seaport Historic District:

Fulton Market Building

The 1882 building on this spot used to house a fresh produce and meat market, filled with merchandise brought from Long Island farms on the now-defunct *Fulton Ferry*, which connected Fulton Street in Manhattan with Fulton Street in Brooklyn. It now houses a predictable mix of chain shops (Gapkids/ Baby Gap) and a few stalls selling fresh food, including **Zaro's Bread Basket** and the **Fulton Market Retail Fish Market**. ♦ Daily. 11 Fulton St (at Front St)

Pier 17

Modeled after the recreation piers of the 19th century, this development was built directly over the water. In good weather, it's packed with people enjoying the pleasures of the waterfront. Good thing, because the mall stores inside could be in anytown USA, though **The Sharper Image** and **The New York Shell Shop** can be good for a browse. In summer, the pier becomes a venue for concerts and other special activities. The restaurants here offer spectacular scenery at spectacular prices; the food, however, is rarely better than average. ♦ Daily. South St. 732.8257 ♿

NY Waterway Cruises

A number of 60-minute sightseeing cruises of the harbor depart here daily March through December. ♦ Fee. Daily. Tickets available at Pier 16 kiosk. Pier 16, South St. 800/53-FERRY

16 Fulton Fish Market

Established in 1821, this venerable institution was based here from 1907 until 2005, walkabout outside the buildings, along with a nod to "ghost" sites where newer structures have replaced historically important landmarks.

Guided Tours and Public Exhibits

Federal Reserve Bank of New York (see page 26), where tours are offered and billions of dollars in gold bricks are on display. 720.6130. www.newyorkfed.org

Museum of American Finance (see page 29). This is the only American museum focusing on the country's financial development; it does so with a lively collection of exhibits and ephemera. 48 Wall St (at William St). 908.4110. www.financialhistory.org

NASDAQ's MarketSite. NASDAQ's immense zipper ticker is on view at its Theater District headquarters. No walk-ins, but opening- and closing-bell ceremonies may be viewed by advance arrangement. 4 Times Square, Broadway at W 43rd St. 646/441.5200. www.nasdaq.com

Skyscraper Museum (see page 32). This is where you can learn about the history and construction of Wall Street's towering icons of wealth and power. 39 Battery Pl (at First Pl). 968.1961. www.skyscraper.org

Notable Money & Commerce Sites (All closed to the public)

The former New York **Chamber of Commerce** (see page 26) at **65 Liberty Street** (between Broadway and Nassau Sts). Repurposed as the International Commercial Bank of China and hugely impressive as it now stands from the exterior, it has a dramatic Great Hall with an ornate, carved ceiling and a breathtaking skylight. Art Deco devotees should head to **70 Pine Street, American International Group (AIG) Insurance** headquarters, and **20 Exchange Place,** longtime **Hagedorn Insurance** headquarters and soon-to-be condos. Be sure to look up at the façades at both; aluminum and limestone details await on the first, and the latter will reward you (especially on its Beaver Street side) with what look like Easter Island heads rimming the top. The former **American Bank Note Company** at Broadway and Beaver Street is a Federal gem, and at **1 Hanover Square** (between Pearl and Stone Sts) lies the 1854 brownstone that once housed the **New York Cotton Exchange** (see India House page 31). The 1930 **U.S. Assay Office** has been gone since 1970, but its Emery Roth–designed replacement merits a stop for its street-level public art installations, and a moment of thought for the 55 million troy ounces of gold that were once stored here (**77 Water St** at **Old Slip**).

And of course the **New York Stock Exchange** (20 Broad St, between Wall St and Exchange Pl), the **American Stock Exchange** (86 Trinity Pl, between Rector and Thames Sts), and the **NY Mercantile Exchange** (World Financial Center, 1 North End Ave) all offer compelling façades.

Downtown Info Resources

Downtown Info Center: M-F, 9AM-6PM. Wall Street Rising, 55 Exchange Pl (between Broad and Williams Sts), Suite 401. 425.INFO. www.downtowninfocenter.org

Downtown Alliance: 120 Broadway, Suite 3340. 566.6700. www.downtownny.com

when it was moved lock, stock, and fish barrel to fancy-schmancy new quarters at Hunt's Point in the Bronx. It was given the name **Tin Building** by old salts who still remembered the wooden structure it replaced. The market was located here to conveniently receive the daily haul from local fishing boats, but by the late 20th century the catch (from cleaner waters) arrived via refrigerated truck. Local denizens found the market by day to be a quiet place, but it was positively frantic between midnight and 8AM. ♦ South St (between Fulton and Beekman Sts)

17 South Street Seaport Museum

New York's maritime heritage—and its economic, cultural, and historical impact as a world port—are explored in the museum's **Schermerhorn Row** home. Founded in 1967, the museum, which also maintains gallery space at its old location nearby on Water Street, moved in 2003 to this row of Federal-style warehouses and countinghouses. Built in 1812 by **Peter Schermerhorn** on landfill, at various times in their history the buildings were used as stores, taverns, rooming houses, and hotels. The landmark buildings were reconfigured by **Beyer Blinder Belle Architects** and designed to retain what they could of the aged interior. The renovation exposes historic walls, door frames, an original laundry room, and 156-year-old graffiti and retains the Greek Revival cast-iron storefronts that were added when the Fulton Ferry brought more stylish customers into the area. The mansard roof at the eastern end was added in 1868, when **2 Fulton Street** was the **Fulton Ferry Hotel**. The converted 30,000-square-foot, $21 million, five-story space opened with an exhibition that covered

New York's significant role in the slave trade; the permanent exhibition is entitled *World Port NY*.

Also part of the museum complex are the **Ships** at Piers 15, 16, and 17 (see below); and, near Battery Park, **New York Unearthed** (see page 35), the museum's urban archeology center. And two blocks away, on Water Street, the museum's **Walter Lord Gallery** features large models of the ships that brought turn-of-the-20th-century immigrants to America. Next door, the **Melville** and **Port Life** galleries have housed important shows like *All Available Boats*, an exhibit of photos and oral histories of the many people who offered support from the sea during the crisis of September 11. **Bowne & Co.** (see below) completes the group. A special branch of the **Metropolitan Museum of Art Shop** (below) serves as the museum's gift shop. Lectures and tours are available. ♦ Admission. Tu-Su. 12 Fulton St (between Front and South Sts). 748.8600. Galleries: 211-213 Water St (between Fulton and Beekman Sts). www.southstseaport.org ♿

Within the South Street Seaport Museum:

Metropolitan Museum of Art Shop

Besides being an outlet for the Met's lovely wares, this is New York's best source for fiction and nonfiction about ships of all kinds and the waters they sail. You'll also find rare prints, ship models, and otherwise hard-to-find books on New York City and its history. ♦ Daily. 14 Fulton St (between South and Front Sts). 248.0954 ♿

Bowne & Co. Stationers

Bowne & Co. is a fascinating, still-active print shop; the space—and its equipment—date back to the 19th century. They still do custom letterpress printing on-site and sell their beautifully printed cards there, as well as other print-related ephemera, from humorous broadside reprints to exquisite fountain pens and hand-crafted books. ♦ M, Tu, Th-Sa (days open may change seasonally). 211 Water St. 748.8651

The Ships

Ships visiting **Piers 15**, **16**, and **17** make this an ever-changing experience, but the South Street Seaport Museum's permanent collection includes two tall ships open to the public: the *Peking*, a steel-hulled, four-masted bark built in 1911 (and the second-largest sailing ship ever built), and the *Wavertree*, a full three-masted iron-hulled ship built in 1885. Also here is the *Ambrose*, the steel floating lighthouse that was anchored at the entrance to the harbor from 1908 until 1963, when she was replaced by a permanent tower. Tickets, available on Pier 16 (at the rear of the **Pier 16 Ticket Booth**) and at the **Visitors' Center** at the **South Street Seaport Museum** entrance at 12 Fulton Street, allow admission to the museum and daily changing events. Other ships in the South Street Seaport fleet include the working tugboat *W.O. Decker* and the schooner *Lettie G. Howard*. The *Pioneer*, a former cargo schooner, makes 90-minute daytime and twilight sails in the harbor from late March to mid-November. Hours vary according to season. Reservations can be made within 14 days of a sail; unreserved tickets are sold each day starting at 10AM at Pier 16 (669.9400). ♦ Admission. Daily. Pier 16, South St. 748.8600, 748.8659

18 127 John Street

A huge electric display clock designed by Corchia-de Harak Associates and colorful steel patio furniture add a touch of whimsy to the Water Street streetscape. ♦ View from Water St (between John and Fulton Sts)

19 TKTS

Score short-notice discount tickets to Broadway and Off-Broadway shows from this South Street Seaport branch of the well-known Theater Development Fund booth. Unlike at the Times Square location (see page 12), you can purchase next-day matinée tickets here as well as same-day tickets for evening shows. ♦ M-Sa, 11AM-6PM; Su, 11AM-4PM. Cash only, ♦ Front St (at John St). Also at Duffy Square, W 47th St (at Broadway). www.tdf.org/tkts ♿

20 Poets House

The largest open-access poetry collection in the country—some 50,000 volumes—expands horizons figuratively and literally: in the gorgeous reading room, with panoramic water-side views, you can look up from your free verse and see the Statue of Liberty. In a state-of-the-art green building (residential tower above, in-house wastewater treatment plant below) completed in 2008 by **Polshek Partnership**, Poets House occupies 11,000 square feet shaped by **Louise Braverman**—who also designed its former SoHo home—into a vibrant literary center. Public programs include readings, performances, master classes, and workshops; an annual Poetry Walk across the Brooklyn Bridge, and (with **City Lore**) the People's Poetry Gathering, a more or less biennial celebration of poetic traditions around the world. ♦ Tu-Sa 2 River Terrace (at Hudson River, between Vesey and Murray Sts). 431.7920. www.poetshouse.org ♿

21 Woolworth Building

One of the city's most dramatic skyscrapers and among the world's most ornate commercial buildings, this tower was designed by **Cass Gilbert** in 1913 as the headquarters of Frank W. Woolworth's chain of five-and-dime stores. Known in its day as a "cathedral of commerce," it is a Gothic celebration inside and out, with picturesque details enhancing the forceful massing and graceful vertical thrust, which culminates in a perfectly composed crown. Inside, the lobby features a soaring glass mosaic ceiling and marble walls awash with more Gothic detail. An added surprise are the caricature bas-reliefs, including one of Gilbert himself with a model of the building and another of Frank Woolworth counting nickels and dimes. The Woolworths were so pleased with the architect's work that they paid for it in cash ($1.5 million). It's well worth a visit–even just a peek from the entryway; security isn't likely to let you get much further these days. ♦ 233 Broadway (between Barclay St and Park Pl)

22 J&R Music & Computer World

Choosing the right door is the hardest part. Once you're actually inside one of the 15 separate stores that make up this 300,000-square-foot family-owned retail constellation facing City Hall Park, you'll find audio and video equipment, music and movies, cameras and optics, even kitchenware, and one of the city's largest selections of computer equipment and electronics–much of it at bargain prices, thanks to J&R's massive buying power. Don't let the motley effect put you off; do try to go on a weekday morning–the crowds are thinnest then. ♦ Daily. Park Row (between Ann and Beekman Sts). 238.9000

23 St. Paul's Chapel

Built in 1766 by **Thomas McBean**, this is Manhattan's only remaining pre-Revolutionary War church–it even survived 1776's Great Fire–making it the city's oldest public building in continuous use. The chapel is not only a rare Georgian architectural gem; it is also said to have been the most impressive church in the colony when built. It's humbling to consider that in 1750 this site was a wheat field; the cemetery once extended to the Hudson River, and George Washington came here to pray after his inauguration as the country's first president on 30 August 1789. McBean's plan for the edifice was much influenced by St. Martin-in-the-Fields in London, designed by his teacher, **James Gibb**. The interior, lit by Waterford crystal chandeliers, is one of the city's best. Come here for the concerts of classical and church music Monday and Thursday at 12:10PM (donation requested), or for services Sunday at 8AM. A place of respite for exhausted rescue workers after 9/11, the church's iron fence became a place of commemoration, tribute, and memory as people posted pictures of the missing at first, then mementos of the ones they'd lost. St. Paul's maintains an exhibit, *Unwavering Spirit*, of that time. Tours available ♦ Broadway (between Fulton and Vesey Sts). 602.0874 www.saintpaulschapel.org ♿

24 World Financial Center

More than eight million square feet of office, retail, and recreational space have been created on landfill produced by the construction of the **World Trade Center**, formerly across West Street. Designed by **Cesar Pelli & Associates** and completed in 1981, the complex includes four 33- to 50-story office towers (distinguished by the unique geometric form that caps each of them), two 9-story buildings designated as gatehouses, a four-acre plaza, and a vaulted and glass-enclosed **Winter Garden**. Severely damaged by the falling towers in 2001, a remarkably accelerated construction schedule–including an inspired redesign of its east-facing façade to allow direct street access–allowed it to reopen barely one year later. As spectacular as ever, one of its most dramatic features is a replacement set of 15 Washington robusta palm trees. The only ones of this size in the city, they are each a uniform 45 feet high. Services, meals, and snacks are found on the Winter Garden's first floor (street level)–**Ciao Bella Gelato, Godiva,** and **Barclay-Rex Tobacconists** are here–and its second floor (lobby level), where the upscale **Grill Room** (945.9400), **Columbus Bakery,** and **American Express Travel Service** are. Tenants in the lobby of WFC No. 2 include **Ann Taylor, Gap,** and **Urban Athletics**. The **Courtyard,** a two-level outdoor piazza, between WFC Nos. 3 and 4, houses–in addition to the restaurants listed below, branches of **P. J. Clarke's, Cosi Sandwich Bar,** and **Financier Patisserie**.

The **World Financial Center Plaza** is a stellar example of public space design: 3.5 beautifully landscaped acres of parkland on the Hudson River with twin reflecting pools. The center presents an ongoing series of music, dance, and theater events as well as visual arts installations, and is headquarters for the New York Mercantile Exchange and such companies as American Express, Merrill Lynch, and Dow Jones. ♦ Daily. West St (between Liberty and Vesey Sts). 945.0505 www.worldfinancialcenter.com ♿

Within the World Financial Center:

JOHNNEY'S FISH GRILL

★★$$ The dark green walls mounted with stuffed fish and black-and-white photos of fishermen plying their nets make you feel as if you were in a New England seafood house. The very fresh fish offered here reinforces this impression, and the rich New England clam chowder is another plus. Other standouts are clams on the half shell, Maryland crab cakes, grilled swordfish, and the fresh and artistically designed sushi. ♦ Seafood ♦ M-F, lunch and dinner. Courtyard, street level (between Nos. 3 and 4 World Financial Center). 385.0333 ♿

AU MANDARIN

★★$$ The authentic Mandarin menu served here–particularly the diced chicken marinated with minced garlic, ginger, and peppercorns; beef tangerine; and Peking duck–is especially popular among businesspeople seeking something a little different at lunchtime. ♦ Mandarin ♦ Daily, lunch and dinner. Courtyard, street level (between Nos. 3 and 4 World Financial Center). 385.0313 ♿

DONALD SACKS

★★$$ Three specials each day and six freshly made salads, including the signature curried chicken salad, are offered in this pleasant, casual spot. Heartier fare includes dishes such as duck-confit quesadilla and grilled rack of lamb served with roasted-garlic mashed potatoes and Port wine sauce. ♦ American ♦ Daily, lunch and dinner. Courtyard, street level (between Nos. 3 and 4 World Financial Center). 619.4600 ♿

25 WORLD TRADE CENTER

The **Twin Towers** of the World Trade Center, one of New York's most conspicuous symbols of commerce and prosperity, were destroyed by terrorist attacks on 11 September 2001 in a day of terrorist hijackings that also saw the destruction of a portion of the Pentagon outside Washington, DC, and the crash of a commercial airliner in rural Pennsylvania. In New York, nearly 3,000 people from all over the world were killed when hijackers commandeered two airliners into the towers, causing their collapse. The first plane, an American Airlines Boeing 767 with 92 passengers aboard, was hijacked en route from Boston to Los Angeles and deliberately slammed into the north tower (**1 World Trade Center**). Minutes later a hijacked United Airlines Boeing 767 with 65 passengers aboard slammed into the south tower (**2 World Trade Center**). Hundreds of New York City firefighters and police officers rushed to the scene after the collisions and were killed–along with remaining workers when first the south tower and then the north tower collapsed. The 47-story **7 World Trade Center** building collapsed later that afternoon, but had been evacuated before there were any casualties. All the structures around the base of the towers, including the **New York Marriott World Trade Center**, were also destroyed or severely damaged by falling debris.

Seven buildings, including the Twin Towers, made up this massive complex that was set on a semicircle around a five-acre plaza. Designed by **Minoru Yamasaki & Associates** and **Emery Roth & Sons**, the World Trade Center was begun in 1962 and finished in 1977. At 110 stories, the monolithic Twin Towers were the tallest buildings in the city and among the tallest in the world. There was an observation deck on the 107th floor of the south tower and an assortment of restaurants, including the celebrated **Windows on the World**, in the north tower. All the structures were connected underground by a concourse–a vast pedestrian mall filled with shops, banks, public spaces, and restaurants. Beneath it all were parking garages, where on 26 February 1993, a terrorist bomb went off in **1 World Trade Center**, killing six people, injuring many more, and causing millions of dollars of damage.

Post-9/11 rebirth has been hampered by politics (and economics), but New York's skyline got a much welcome addition in 2006 with the completion of the **David M. Childs (SOM)**-designed **7 World Trade Center.** Actually off the main site, just across Vesey Street to the north, it is best seen from the south end of the site, as its pale-blue shimmery lightness makes it seem to morph right into the sky. The lovely little park at its base is further brightened by the playful Jeff Koons sculpture Balloon Flower. Completion of the **Memorial** and **WTC Transportation Hub** are next, (see page 25), along with the planned cultural complex and controversial Freedom Tower. Until then, visitors seeking an opportunity to commemorate the events of 9/11 might want to stop at the **Tribute Center** at 120 Liberty Street (between Church and Greenwich Sts; 393.9160; www.tributewtc.org); donation suggested, exhibits and tours daily. And, around the corner on Greenwich Street–along the outer face of **FDNY Firehouse Ladder 10/Engine 10**–there is a memorial wall. ♦ Bounded by Vesey, Church, Liberty, and West Sts. www.wtc.com

26 WORLD TRADE CENTER MEMORIAL

Several years in the works–a period of civic soul-searching and often heated debate–the memorial to honor those killed in the terrorist attacks of 11 September 2001 and 26 February 1993 is scheduled to open on 11 September 2009. The design by **Michael Arad** and **Peter Walker**, called *Reflecting Absence*, centers on twin voids that occupy the original footprints of the Twin Towers, with walls of water cascading 30 feet from an eight-acre plaza into vast reflecting pools with the names of the dead inscribed around them. A lower level reveals remnants of the towers' box-beam columns and a section of the slurry wall. Nearby, there is a private contemplative space for victims' families. WTC site bounded by Church, Liberty, Vesey, and West Sts.

27 World Trade Center Transportation Hub

Where commuters once sprinted for trains beneath the Twin Towers, an elaborate new transportation complex is expected to be in place by 2009. A design partnership led by architect **Santiago Calatrava** (with **DMJM Harris** and **STV Inc.**) has envisioned a lofty Transit Hall roofed in glass, with ribbed steel arches that project dramatically above street level, to draw daylight to the interior. The hub will link the WTC PATH station with subway and ferry service. Church St (at Fulton St). www.panynj.gov ♿

28 The Millennium Hilton

$$$$ Fifty-five stories high, this sleek lodging has overlooked downtown Manhattan since it was built in the shadow of the former **World Trade Center** in 1992. Remarkably undamaged structurally by the towers' collapse, the hotel underwent a complete room-by-room renovation and reopened in 2003. It offers 561 nicely appointed guest rooms and suites done up in soothing neutrals, flat-panel TVs and high-speed Internet access in all rooms, Wi-Fi in all public areas, an indoor pool and health center, an executive business center, and other amenities. The hotel's restaurants include the coolly casual **Liquid Assets** lounge/café in the lobby and the contemporary design and American regional fare of the tasteful third-floor restaurant **Church & Dey.** ♦ 55 Church St (between Dey and Fulton Sts). 693.2001, 800/752.0014; fax 571.2316. www.hilton.com

29 195 Broadway

There are more columns on the façade of this building than on any other building in the world, with even more inside (the lobby is like an ancient Athenian temple). It was designed in 1917 by **William Welles Bosworth** as headquarters for the American Telephone & Telegraph Company. The ornamental panels over the Broadway entrance, as well as the bronze seals on the lobby floor and the other interior decorative elements, are by Paul Manship, whose best-known work in New York is the *Prometheus* fountain in **Rockefeller Plaza.** ♦ Between Dey and Fulton Sts

30 Fulton Street Transit Center

The MTA tore down a whole block of Broadway to make way for this high-concept subway station—except for **Francis H. Kimball**'s 1889 Corbin Building, which will be incorporated into the new hub in all its Romanesque Revival glory. Designed by the architectural firm **Grimshaw** and due to be done in 2010, the complex aims to replace a warren of dark tunnels with an easy-to-navigate network connecting 12 train lines, topped by a glass-and-steel cone that lets light all the way down to platform level. Good news for nostalgic types: century-old mosaics and terra-cotta tile in the old station are being preserved. ♦ Broadway, between John and Fulton Sts. 646/252.2670. www.mta.info ♿

31 Strand Bookstore

"Miles and miles of books" is the trademark description of this epic store, and its vast collection includes thousands of review copies of new books, hundreds of coffee-table books, and even more mass-market and trade paperbacks than at the main store (just south of Union Square), all sold at a generous discount. ♦ Daily. 95 Fulton St (between Gold and William Sts). 732.6070. Also at 828 Broadway (at E 12th St). 473.1452. www.strandbooks.com

32 American Numismatic Society

Located for decades up on Audubon Terrace at 155th Street, the American Numismatic Society relocated to this former bank building in Lower Manhattan in 2004. Its authoritative library is located here, but at least through 2012 its exhibits will be on view Monday through Friday in the **Federal Reserve Bank** (see page 26) nearby at 33 Liberty Street (720.6130). Featuring rare finds of the coin world, shows include "Drachmas, Doubloons, and Dollars: The History of Money." ♦ **Coin Research and Library**: Free. Tu-F, by appointment. ♦ 96 Fulton St (at William St). 571.4470. www.amnumsoc.org

33 Century 21

This place has three immense and constantly bustling floors of top-quality merchandise—everything from designer clothes and accessories for men and women to housewares and appliances. While some of the fashions may be from a season ago, the prices make them perennials. ♦ Daily. 22 Cortlandt St (between Broadway and Church St). 227.9092. Also at 472 86th St (between Fifth and Fourth Aves), Bay Ridge, Brooklyn. 718/748.3266

34 John Street United Methodist Church

Home to the oldest Methodist society in the US, this Georgian-style building, designed

by **William Hurry** in 1841, was erected on the site of a "preaching house" built by the congregation in 1766. On the lower level is the Wesley Chapel Museum, containing such early-days relics as a clock, an altar rail, and foot warmers. ♦ Museum: M, W, F, noon-4PM. 44 John St (between William and Nassau Sts). 269.0014

35 Chamber of Commerce of the State of New York

Designed by **James B. Baker** in 1901, and now long-abandoned by the Chamber (though its name carved across the front leaves no doubt as to its former occupancy), this ornate Beaux Arts edifice is ponderous, from its heavy stone base to its massive top, with Ionic columns adding to its almost predatory look. ♦ 65 Liberty St (at Liberty Pl): between Nassau St and Broadway

36 140 Broadway

One of Lower Manhattan's more successful modern-style steel-and-glass high-rises, it was designed in 1967 by **Skidmore, Owings & Merrill**. The sleek black building—formerly HSBC bank headquarters—is of an appropriate scale, largely due to a spandrel design that helps it fit into its older, more ornate surroundings. A vermilion cube by sculptor Isamu Noguchi enlivens the plaza on the Broadway side; the entrance, however, is on Liberty Street. ♦ At Liberty St ♿

37 Federal Reserve Bank of New York

This is the banker's bank, where the nations of the world maintain the balance of trade by the storage and exchange of gold, which is housed on five underground floors that occupy an entire city block. The unimaginable riches inside this Fort Knox are reflected in the building's exterior, modeled after a 15th-century Florentine palazzo, with Samuel Yellin's finely detailed ironwork adding to the serene beauty of the limestone-and-sandstone façade (designed by **York & Sawyer** in 1924). Free one-hour tours of the building and its gold vaults are available on weekdays; advance reservations are required. Joint exhibits with the **American Numismatic Society** may be viewed on a walk-in basis. ♦ Free. M-F, 10AM-4PM. ♦ 33 Liberty St (between William and Nassau Sts). 720.6130. www.newyorkfed.org ♿

38 One Chase Manhattan Plaza

Built in 1960 as a catalyst to revitalize the aging Wall Street area, the former Chase headquarters' aluminum-and-glass face rises an impressive 813 feet, and it is still a fittingly imposing base for the Rockefeller banking empire. The designers, **Gordon Bunshaft** (of **Lever House** fame) **Skidmore, Owings & Merrill**, gave the tower a trend-setting feature, its large plaza, which is home to *Group of Four Trees* by Jean Dubuffet (1972) and **Sunken Garden**, a 1964 below-grade water sculpture by Isamu Noguchi. ♦ Liberty St (between William and Nassau Sts)

39 LOUISE NEVELSON PLAZA

This small triangular park established in 1978 with large steel sculptures created by Louise Nevelson is a popular lunch spot. ♦ Bounded by Liberty St, Maiden La, and William St

40 EQUITABLE BUILDING

This massive structure is noteworthy not for any particular stylistic qualities but for its size, which changed the history of building in New York. The 40-story block contains 1.2 million square feet of office space on a site of slightly less than one acre. The public outcry when it was completed in 1915 by **Ernest R. Graham** led to the creation of the 1916 zoning laws, the first in the country, to ensure a minimum of light and air on city streets in the future. ♦ 120 Broadway (bounded by Broadway and Pine St, Nassau and Cedar Sts)

41 TRINITY AND US REALTY BUILDINGS

The **Trinity Building** by **Francis H. Kimball** replaced **Richard Upjohn**'s five-story 1840 building of the same name, which was the first office building in the city. After the present Gothic structure was built in 1906, its developer, US Realty Company, acquired a similar 50-foot plot next door and constructed an identical 21-story building for their own use, with a shared service core along Thames Street, which runs between them; high on their rooftops, an ornate—and narrow—metal bridge joins the two in the air. Fantastic creatures sporting lions' heads and eagles' wings watch as you approach the entrance to the Trinity Building. ♦ 111 and 115 Broadway (at Thames St, bounded by Broadway, Cedar St, Trinity Pl, and Trinity Church)

42 AMERICAN STOCK EXCHANGE

This building was known until 1953 as the "Curb Exchange," because before 1921 brokers stood at the corner of Wall and Broad Streets and communicated with one another through hand gestures. The present building was designed in 1930 by **Starrett & Van Vleck**; it is not open to the public. ♦ 86 Trinity Pl (between Rector and Thames Sts). 306.1000

43 BORDERS BOOKS & MUSIC

It's a Borders, but a particularly special one. Built here to replace its location lost when the World Trade Towers came down, it gave the city not only another thriving downtown business, but a full restoration of the 1895 **American Surety Building** that houses it. Original architect **Bruce Price**'s design was modernized a bit in 1975 by **Kajima International** when the **Bank of Tokyo Trust** occupied the building. Now Wi-Fi equipped and host to a **Dean & DeLuca** coffee bar outpost (as are all Borders' New York stores), the renovation highlights the spectacularly gilded period ceiling detail and historic wall treatments from the Surety era. On the outside, eight Greek ladies by J. Masse Rhind still guard the building from their perch on the third floor. Look farther up and you'll find more of them on an even higher level. ♦ Daily. 100 Broadway (between Wall and Pine Sts). 964.1988 ♿

44 TRINITY CHURCH

This historic architectural and religious monument has a strong square tower punctuated by an exclamation-point spire, and the good fortune to stand at the head of Wall Street. The shaded grassy cemetery, a welcome open space in this neighborhood, offers a noontime haven for office workers. The cemetery came first, and such notables as Alexander Hamilton, William Bradford, and Robert Fulton are buried here (their graves marked by placards that are especially helpful where gravestone inscriptions have worn away). This is the third church with this name on this site. The original was built in 1698, paid for by taxation of all citizens, regardless of religion, because the Church of England was the official religion of the colony. It burned in 1776; the second church was demolished in 1839. A small museum behind the main altar documents the church's history.

The present structure was designed in 1846 by **Richard Upjohn**; **Richard Morris Hunt**'s brass doors were added later. The **Chapel of All Saints**, designed by **Thomas Hash**, was built in 1913; and the **Bishop Manning Memorial Wing** by **Adams & Woodbridge** was erected in 1965. In 1993, work was completed on a time-consuming effort to restore the building to its original appearance. Workers steamed away a layer of paraffin that was applied to the building in the 1920s to keep it from crumbling; beneath the paraffin were layers of coal dust and pollutants that had made it blacker than many other historic buildings. The result of the cleaning process—rosy sandstone as Upjohn had intended—was quite a surprise to Wall Streeters who, every day for years, had been walking past what they believed to be a very dark building. Classical concerts are often given here on Sundays during the winter months. ♦ Services, daily. Tours, daily, 2PM. Museum, daily. M-F, 9-11:45AM, 1-3:45PM; Sa, 10AM-3:45PM; Su, 1-3:45PM. Broadway (between Rector and Thames Sts). 602.0800. www.trinitywallstreet.org ♿

45 The Bank of New York/ Mellon

Ralph Walker's only skyscraper was built in 1932 on what was called the most expensive piece of real estate in the world in the 1930s. He said his now landmarked design was one of superimposed rhythms, a steel frame draped outside with rippling curtains of stone. The dazzling gold, red, and orange Art Deco mosaics created by Hildreth Meière in the former (until 1989) Irving Trust Company banking room off Wall Street—just where the Dutch delineated New Amsterdam in 1653—makes one wish security didn't limit visitors to those with business here. ♦ 1 Wall St (at Broadway)

46 Bankers Trust Building

The pyramid on top of this gray granite 31-story neoclassical tower, built in 1912 by **Trowbridge & Livingston**, became the corporate symbol of Bankers Trust and remained its logo up until the day it was bought out by Deutsche Bank in 1998 (though Bankers had already departed this gigantic landmark back in 1963). The 25-story annex next door was by **Shreve, Lamb & Harmon,** who also built the **Empire State Building**. ♦ 14-16 Wall St (at Nassau St)

47 Federal Hall

This 1842 Americanization of the Parthenon is one of New York City's finest examples of Greek Revival architecture and a fitting National Historic Landmark. Designed by architects **Town & Davis**, it was the US Custom House until 1862; for the next 63 years it served as the US Subtreasury. An earlier building at this site (demolished in 1803) served as the United States governmental seat in the days when New York City was the nation's capital; it was here that the House of Representatives and the Senate first met. Today, Doric columns climbing 32 feet high extend across the building's face. John Quincy Adams Ward's 1883 statue of George Washington marks the spot where the Revolutionary War general became the country's first president. Its interior, which was originally designed by John Frazee and Samuel Thompson, was fully renovated in 2005. Exhibits chronicle the 1735 trial of John Peter Zenger and its impact on America's position on freedom of the press, as well as the site's role in the country's first inauguration in 1789, and other matters pertaining to the young country. Bookshop and National Park Service Visitors Center on-site. ♦ Free. M-F, 9AM-5PM. 26 Wall St (at Nassau St). 668-2561. www.nps.gov/feha ♿

48 Morgan Guaranty Trust Company

If ever a single man epitomized the American capitalist, J.P. Morgan (1837-1913) was that man. His son, John Pierpont Morgan Jr., took control of the empire in 1913, the year this building was constructed by **Trowbridge & Livingston**. Like his father, John Jr. was apparently not without enemies. On 16 September 1920, at the height of the lunch hour, a carriage parked on Wall Street suddenly exploded, killing 33 people and injuring 400. The marble walls of the building still have scars from the bomb, noticeable on the Wall Street side. No motive was ever determined, and the owner of the carriage was never found. The bank survived unscathed, as did Morgan, who was out of town at the time. ♦ 23 Wall St (at Broad St)

49 30 Wall Street

When this gilt and garland-detailed fortress-like structure was built as the gold-storing United States Assay Office in 1919 by architects **York & Sawyer**, the Greek Revival façade of its predecessor, the Branch Bank of the United States, designed in 1826 by **Martin E. Thompson**, was dismantled and eventually reconstructed in the **American Wing** of the **Metropolitan Museum of Art**. Originally three stories, a nine-story addition was made in 1955 by the firm of **Halsey, McCormack & Helmer**. ♦ Between William and Nassau Sts

49 40 Wall Street

Now **The Trump Building**, with all the gold leaf you'd expect, this tower was built in 1929, the same time as the **Chrysler Building** uptown, and was secretly designed by **H. Craig Severance** and **Yasuo Matsui** to be two feet higher, which, had they not been outfoxed by the Chryster folks, would have made it the tallest in the world at that time. This was the headquarters of the Bank of the Manhattan Company, which eventually merged with Chase National Bank. The Manhattan Company was founded in 1799 by Aaron Burr, who was blocked by political rivals when he tried to charter a bank. Instead he received legislative permission to establish a water company. In the charter's fine print, he was granted the power to loan money to property owners who wanted to connect their buildings to his wooden water mains. Before he had dug up too many streets, Burr abandoned the water business and became what he had always wanted to be: a banker. ♦ Between William and Nassau Sts

50 Museum of American Finance

The former headquarters of the Bank of New York, the oldest bank in the US, this is now home to the museum of American's monetary past (a Smithsonian affiliate, the museum reopened here on January 11, 2008 from the equally storied Standard Oil Building). The attractive Georgian building, built in 1927 and designed by **Benjamin Wistar Morris**, boasts tall arched windows and a broken pediment framing a handsome galleon lantern; the majestic banking hall holds exhibits on topics from empire building to entrepreneurship, innovation, technology, and more, such as little-known details about J.P. Morgan, the founding of Pan Am, and the history of the Nobel Prize. Don't miss the ancient, original Edison stock ticker always on display. Gift shop, tours, and public programs. ♦ Admission. Tu-Sa, 10AM-4PM. 48 Wall St (at William St). 908.4110. www.financialhistory.org ♿

51 55 Wall Street

One of the first buildings to be created in the area after the Great Fire of 1835 leveled 700 structures between South and Broad Streets, Coenties Slip, and Wall Street, this building was designed by **Isaiah Rogers** in 1836. It was built as a three-story trading hall for the **Merchants' Exchange** and later became the **Custom House**. In 1907, its height was doubled when it was remodeled and expanded by **McKim**, **Mead & White**, and it became the headquarters of First National City Bank. Briefly enjoyed as the luxe **Regent Hotel** in the late 1990s, it is now most frequently visited as an event space. ♦ Between Hanover and William Sts

52 74 Wall Street

The nautical decoration around the arched entrance of this solid-looking 1926 building by **Benjamin Wistar Morris** is a reminder that it was built for the Seamen's Bank for Savings, the second-oldest savings bank in the city. It was chartered in 1829 as a financial haven for sailors, who usually arrived in the port with their pockets full of back pay accumulated while they were at sea. The official address of the property was 76 Wall Street, but it was changed because superstitious seamen refused to leave their money there—the numbers added up to 13. ♦ At Pearl St

53 Wall Street Plaza

This 1973 white-aluminum-and-glass structure by **I.M. Pei & Associates** richly deserved the award it received from the American Institute of Architects for its classical purity, rather rare in the new buildings in this area. The 1974 sculpture in its plaza, by Yu Yu Yang, consists of a stainless-steel slab with an opening that faces a polished disk. It is a memorial to the **Cunard** liner *Queen Elizabeth,* whose history is outlined on a nearby plaque. ♦ 88 Pine St (at Front St)

St. MAGGIE'S CAFÉ

54 St. Maggie's Café

★$$ Young Wall Streeters come to this Victorian-style pub for such light fare as the Mulberry Street grilled chicken salad, and for seafood dishes, including Maryland crab cakes or Norwegian salmon in a sesame-and-ginger sauce. ♦ American ♦ M-F, lunch and dinner. Reservations recommended. 120 Wall St (at South St). 943.9050

55 New York Stock Exchange

The Exchange's giant portico, colonnade, and sculptures express austerity and security—key design goals in 1903, when this building was designed by **George B. Post**, as well as when the upper section was designed in 1923 by **Trowbridge & Livingston**. The solemn façade masks the leading-edge technology that drives the exchange today. That technology, integrated with the judgment and skills of the trading floor's professionals, provides investors with the broadest, most open, and most liquid equities market in the world. Before entering the glassed-in gallery that overlooks the frenzied action on the trading floor three floors below, the lucky visitor (only guests of NYSE members may come here) goes through an exhibition area that includes video presentations on the history and workings of the institution. More than two thousand companies deal on the exchange; it is the world's largest, with stock valued at more than $3 trillion. ♦ Not open to the public. 18 Broad Street (between Exchange Pl and Wall St). 656.3000. www.nyse.com ♿

56 Downtown Information Center (DNTN Info Center)

Created and run by **Wall Street Rising**—a nonprofit coalition of local businesses, cultural groups, and other neighbors—as part of its initiative to restore and rebuild commerce and culture in Lower Manhattan, the Info Center is a marvel of resources for everything from nearby events, where to eat, and basic transportation queries to building-specific historic research quandaries. Info is supplied by phone, online, or in person, where there are maps, plasma-screen touch stations, and personal guidance available. ♦ M-F; 9AM-6PM. ID necessary for entry to building. 55 Exchange Pl (between William and Broad Sts), 4th floor. 425.INFO/425.4636. www.downtowninfocenter.org

57 Battery Park City

This eclectic complex of 14,000 rental apartments and condominiums supports a population larger than that of Bozeman, Montana (the residential population is approximately 25,000). The total development cost of this 92-acre landfill site adjacent to the Financial District is estimated at $4 billion, including the privately financed $1.5 billion **World Financial Center**. The master plan devised in 1979 by **Cooper, Eckstut Associates** divides the blocks into parcels, with individual developers for each one, thus avoiding a superblock appearance. About 30 percent of the site is open parkland, with parks linked by the 1.2-mile landscaped waterfront. **The Esplanade** was designed by landscape architects Stanton Eckstut between Liberty and West Thames Streets; Eckstut, Susan Child Associates, and artist Mary Miss at the **South Cove**; and Carr, Lynch, Hack & Sandell between **North Cove Yacht Harbor** and Chambers Street; it extends the entire length of the site, providing a perfect place to relax and watch the river traffic. Access for the disabled has been incorporated into the overall design. Delightful—and thought-provoking—public art installations abound throughout the area. Andy Goldsworthy, Louise Bourgeois, Jim Dine, and Tom Otterness are just a few of the artists whose sculptures are on display.

The first completed section was **Gateway Plaza** (1982), a trio of 34-story towers and three 6-story buildings that provide 1,712 residential units. The structures, designed by **Jack Brown** and **Irving Gershorn**, were begun before the current plan was established.

The architects who worked on **Rector Place** (1988), the second phase of residential construction, included **Charles Moore**, **James Stewart Polshek**, **Gruzen Samton Steinglass**, **Ulrich Franzen & Associates**, **Conklin Rossant**, **Mitchell/Giurgola**, and **Davis, Brody & Associates**. Developed under the master plan, this nine-acre plot contains 2,200 apartments grouped around one-acre **Rector Park**, designed by landscape architects Innocente & Webel.

The third phase, **Battery Place**, consists of 2,800 residential units on nine parcels located between Rector Place and Pier A. The architects involved in the initial three buildings are **The Ehrenkrantz Group & Eckstut**, **Gruzen Samton Steinglass**, and **James Stewart Polshek & Partners**. The southern end of this area includes the **Ritz-Carlton**, the **Robert F. Wagner, Jr. Park and Café**, the **Museum of Jewish Heritage**, the **Skyscraper Museum**, and the three-acre **South Gardens** park designed by landscape architect Hanna Olin. ♦ Bounded by West St and the Hudson River, and Pier A and Chambers St. www.batteryparkcity.org ♿

58 Syms

Located in the heart of the Financial District, this famous discount house is primarily for men and women (and their kids) with conservative tastes. Sizes range from svelte and trim to portly, at discounts of 30 to 50 percent. But the greatest strength of this store is its menswear, especially the shirt department, which takes up nearly the entire first floor. ♦ Daily. 42 Trinity Pl (between Edgar and Rector Sts). 797.1199. Also at 400 Park Ave (at E 54th St). 317.8200

59 Delmonico's

★★★$$$ This cast-iron-and-steel landmark in orange brick and brownstone houses an old-fashioned steak house in the opulent space that was the nation's first fine restaurant—perfect for indulging robber-baron fantasies. While the menu has shrunk since the 1830s (veal 47 ways), you'll still find hearty cuts of meat as well as non-carnivore choices such as potato-crusted grouper. ♦ Steak house ♦ M-F, lunch and dinner; Sa, dinner. Reservations recommended. ♦ 56 Beaver St (at S William St). 509.1144

60 Stone Street Historic District

Wandering in and out of the twisty canyons of the Financial District, you suddenly happen on a low-slung cobblestone enclave, seemingly lost in time: the Stone Street Historic District (proclaimed so in 1996). The two-block district is bounded by Hanover Square on the east; remnants of the old street bed (known as "Hoog Straat" to the Dutch who first built it) march right into the lobby of 85 Broad Street on the west. Most of the three- to four-story brick buildings here date back to the great rebuilding of the city post the 1835 fire that demolished much of Lower Manhattan; their historic character has thankfully been preserved through the efforts of the Alliance for Downtown New York and a combination of public and private funding. Once a grim back alley (South William and Pearl Street buildings back onto barely 20-foot-wide Stone), improvements to the area—which includes the old **Coenties Slip** (now **Coenties Alley**) and tiny **Mill Lane**—were completed in 2000 and include landscaping, repaving (with rough-hewn granite blocks), historic lampposts, and new bluestone sidewalks. Now closed to traffic and a thriving destination for Wall Street lunchers and evening and weekend visitors, 19th-century

Stone Street is home to an international stew of restaurants and outdoor cafés. ♦ Broad St to Hanover Sq (between Pearl and South William Sts)

Within Stone Street Historic District:

Ulysses' Pub

Bloomsday in 2003 was opening day for Ulysses' Pub, and the spirit of James Joyce lives on in the black-and-white photographs that line the dark rough-wood walls of this large, friendly pub. When the weather's fair, picnic tables are set on the cobbles outside and you may enjoy one of their many beers or a range of Irish pub fare—like bangers and mash or fish and chips—or a selection of shellfish from the fresh raw bar. ♦ Irish pub food. M-Sa, lunch and dinner; Su, brunch and dinner. 58 Stone St (between Coenties Slip and William St). 484.0400

Financier Pâtisserie

Owned by nearby **Bayard's** restaurant founder Peter Poulakakos (also co-owner of **Ulysses' Pub** next door), this is a charming tile-lined French pastry shop and casual lunch spot. Light sandwiches (on baguettes of course), yummy little cakes, an espresso, or a bowl of latte are what you're here for. ♦ M-Sa. 62 Stone St (between Coenties Slip and William St). 344.5600. Also at World Financial Center

The Wall Street Inn

★★$$$ Just on the edge of the Stone Street enclave, this beautifully restored seven-story landmark building is home to a tastefully designed 46-room inn. Inspired but not overwhelmed by early American touches, the smallish rooms are up-to-date with all the tech a business traveler might want. There's an on-site health club, service is top-notch, and a complimentary continental breakfast is included. ♦ 9 S William St (at Mill La). 747.1500. www.thewallstreetinn.com

61 Hanover Square/British Memorial Garden

Named for the English royal family of the Georges, this was once a small London-style park at the center of a residential neighborhood. Homeowners included Captain William Kidd, who was considered a solid citizen in New York but something quite different by the British, who hanged him for piracy in 1701. The square was also the home of New York's first newspaper, the *New-York Daily Gazette,* established in 1725. In 2005, ground was broken here for something quite different. In honor of the 67 Brits who lost their lives at the World Trade Center on 9/11, a traditional English garden has been planted. The living memorial, designed by landscape architects **Isabel** and **Julian Bannerman**, opened to the public at the event anniversary in 2007. ♦ Bounded by William, Pearl, Beaver, and Hanover Sts. www.britishmemorialgarden.org

62 India House

Richard J. Carman built this beautiful brownstone (one of the largest in the city) as headquarters for the Hanover Bank in 1854. In the decades that followed, it was used as the New York Cotton Exchange and the main office of W.R. Grace and Co. ♦ 1 Hanover Sq (between Pearl and Stone Sts)

Within India House:

Bayard's

★★★★$$$$ This luxurious destination restaurant serves French cuisine with a taste of the New World in a suitably sumptuous setting: six fireplaces, a mahogany double staircase, rare nautical artwork, and resplendent chandeliers set the tone. For appetizers, try the trio of oysters or Maine lobster salad with artichokes, asparagus, and lemon vinaigrette. Standouts among entrées include braised beef short ribs with bitter chocolate, coriander carrot stew, and potato puree; and striped bass with mussel saffron *jus,* julienned vegetables, and fresh linguini. An extensive wine list features several rare vintages ranging in price from $25 to $2,750. ♦ French ♦ M-Sa, dinner. 514.9454

63 Elevated Acre

Take an escalator (hint: it's set back a bit between the two monolithic buildings on this block) and emerge, improbably, onto a lawn—complete with flowers, wild grasses, and a sweeping East River view. Here, among the many lovely **Rogers Marvel Architects** and **Ken Smith** (landscape) design features, are benches, a boardwalk, and a space for performances such as dance and film. Downtown's best-kept secret (unless you tell). ♦ Daily. 55 Water St (between Old Slip and Coenties Slip). www.elevatedacre.com ♿

64 Police Museum

Once up on East 20th Street, then down on lower Broadway, the Police Museum has finally settled into its current home in this mini–Renaissance Revival palazzo designed by **Hunt & Hunt** in 1909. Built originally for the 1st Precinct of the New York Police Department, it was considered the city's "first modern police station." Besides the expected "Hall of Heroes," the museum features historic items like a red 1912 Indian-brand motorcycle from the first fleet of the department's Motorcycle Squad, uniforms, a large mug-shot camera, and a posting of the 1845 rules and regulations. The museum shop carries every official NYPD-specific item imaginable. ♦ Admission. M-Sa, 10AM-5PM. 100 Old Slip (between South and Water Sts). 480.3100. www.nycpolicemuseum.org ♿

65 26 Broadway

This graceful giant, built in 1885 and altered in 1922 by **Carrère & Hastings**, actually curves along to follow the street line. The most important business address in the world for half a century, this was where John D. Rockefeller said that he had revolutionized the way of doing business "to save ourselves from wasteful conditions and eliminate individualism." Undeniably he accomplished his goal, and at the same time built one of the world's greatest fortunes behind these walls, the headquarters of Standard Oil. When the Supreme Court dissolved the trust in 1911, the building became home to Socony Mobil, one of the new companies that rose from Standard Oil's ashes. ♦ At Beaver St

66 Brooklyn-Battery Tunnel

In the early 1930s, builder **Robert Moses** announced that he was going to construct a bridge between Lower Manhattan and Brooklyn to connect his Long Island parkway system with his West Side Highway, which reached a dead end at **Battery Park**. Preservationists were appalled. City officials, noting that the city would lose $29 million a year in real-estate taxes, also opposed it. The battle raged until 1939, when President Roosevelt stepped in and denied federal funds for the project. The bridge became a tunnel, and Battery Park was saved. When the tunnel—engineered by Ole Singstad in 1949—finally opened, it carried more than 15 million cars in its first year. ♦ Between the Gowanus Expwy, Brooklyn, and West St

67 Bowling Green

In 1734, a group of citizens leased the space facing the **Custom House** as a bowling green for an annual rent of one peppercorn. In the process it became the city's first park. In 1729, the park was embellished with an equestrian statue of England's King George III, which was demolished by a crowd that assembled here to listen to a reading of the *Declaration of Independence* on 9 July 1776 (the park's fence dates to 1771). The statue was melted down to make bullets that, according to some contemporary accounts, were responsible for the killing of 400 British soldiers during the war that followed. ♦ Broadway (at State St)

At Bowling Green:

The Charging Bull

In response to the stock market crash of 1987, Arturo DiModica sculpted this 3.5-ton bronze bull to attest to the "vitality, energy, and life of the American people in adversity." It has been put up for sale; since the city is not allowed to buy works of art, they are half-heartedly looking for a patron.

68 Downtown Athletic Club

The arched ground-floor arcade and the window treatment of this orangey-brown brick Moorish-influenced Art Deco masterpiece, designed by **Starrett & Van Vleck** in 1930, are perfection itself. Built as the home for the 1926-founded Downtown Athletic Club, the upper floors were then dedicated as accommodations, the lower to the club's unstinting gym facilities. The original guestrooms, meant to evoke a 1920s ocean liner, were by Barnett-Phillips. For decades, and with much pomp, the Heisman Trophy was awarded here. In addition to an enclosed roof garden, the building originally contained a miniature golf course. 9/11 had its effects, and with bankruptcy looming, the club—off-limits to women until 1978—sold out in 2002. Now residential towers, it is no longer open to the public. ♦ 19 West St (between Battery Pl and Morris St). ♿

69 Museum of Jewish Heritage—A Living Memorial to the Holocaust

Housed in a dignified, tiered, hexagonal pyramid facing the water, this museum, including its newer wing opened in 2003, was designed by **Kevin Roche, John Dinkeloo & Associates**. First opened in 1977, the museum examines Jewish culture from the end of the 19th century to the present. The exhibits, featuring films, photographs, videotapes, and artifacts, give prominence to the Holocaust and its survivors and also include information on musicians, actors, writers, and philosophers. Besides adding 82,000 square feet of gallery space, the expansion made room for water-view dining (a kosher facility, **The Heritage Café.** 646/437.4231) and a very special Memorial Garden. Eighteen hand-chosen boulders, each planted with a single dwarf-oak sapling, have been placed just-so in this narrow space looking out to the Hudson; created by noted artist **Andy Goldsworthy,** it is called Garden of Stones. Shop; tours available. ♦ Admission; free W, 4PM-8PM. Closed Sa. Su-Tu, Th, 10AM-5:45PM; W, 10AM-8PM; F, 10AM-5PM. 36 Battery Pl (at First Pl). 646/437.4200; ticket info: 646/437.4202. www.mjhnyc.org ♿

70 Skyscraper Museum

Museum director Carol Willis's vision of celebrating New York's unique architectural heritage with a permanent museum dedicated to its skyscrapers finally came to fruition in 2004. Founded in 1996, the museum had a number of temporary homes, but with the donation of a spanking-new 5,800-square-foot ground-floor space on the north end of the **Ritz-Carlton**, (see below), the determined architectural historian was finally in business for good.

Coincidentally (the **Skidmore, Owings & Merrill (SOM)**-designed project was on the boards well before September 11), it and the **Museum of Jewish Heritage** (see page 32), just a block away, are seen as key to the reestablishment of this area as a cultural destination. A permanent exhibit, *Skyscraper/City*, offers a visual record of New York's commercial skyline through history. In an adjacent gallery changing shows explore architecture, construction, and development topics like Frank Lloyd Wright's high-rise designs. Within this one-story (plus mezzanine) space, using lots of polished stainless steel, SOM architects **Roger Duffy** and **Scott Duncan** (working pro bono) have evoked the sense of towering volumes of a real skyscraper. Bookstore/gift shop, lectures, and public programs. ♦ Admission. W-Su, noon-6PM. 39 Battery Pl. 968.1961. www.skyscraper.org ♿

70 The Ritz-Carlton New York Battery Park

★★★★$$$$ The Ritz is synonymous with luxury, and this one's no different. In fact, its waterfront location gives it even more panache. Opened in 2002, and designed by architects **Polshek and Partners** in collaboration with **Gary Edward Handel & Associates**, the 298-room, 39-story glass-and-brick tower (the top 25 floors are residences) features sleekly elegant interior décor (by Frank Nicholson) graced with a rotating selection of contemporary art originals, always by well-known New York–based artists (April Gornik, Ross Bleckner, and Jacqueline Humphries among them). The rooms—each one with a harbor view has a telescope, the better to see Lady Liberty with—are decorated in a sumptuous contemporary style. Its grand in size, fully teched-up (with high-speed Internet access in rooms, Wi-Fi in public areas as well, and an on-site business center), utterly comfortable . . . and quiet: the exquisite hush the lightly padded walls provide (in the halls as well) is an almost miraculous feat in New York. Soothing pale greenish teals and pale yellows reign in the rooms (always with the Ritz's signature cobalt blue as an accent); dark-marble bathrooms with all the amenities—even heated floors in some—have a Roman Empire feel. Locals and visitors flock to **Rise** for cocktails and light bites, with an array of Asian Fusion dishes; the 14th-floor aerie jumps to a techno-beat and has terrace seating looking out on the harbor action. Down on the lobby level is the acclaimed **2 West**, which, like the rooms, is sleek but totally comfortable; open for breakfast, lunch, and dinner, its innovative American-global menu offers the best in regional ingredients and a vast vintage wine list. The **Lobby Lounge** offers an afternoon "Power Tea," infused with vodka; you may also opt for a traditional tea with the usual scones and finger sandwiches. ♦ 2 West St (at Battery Pl). 344.0800. www.ritzcarlton.com

71 Whitehall Building

A 1930s real-estate guide says that the tenants of this 1903 building, which at the time included the Internal Revenue Service, Quaker Oats, and the Bon Ami Cleanser Co., had "an intimate relationship with the landlord," and no one ever moved out. There has been some turnover since the guide was written, but tenants are still (understandably) reluctant to give up offices boasting what may be the best views of New York Harbor. The original 20-story edifice was designed by **Henry J. Hardenbergh**; the 31-story rear section of this solid and pleasing Renaissance Revival structure was designed by **Clinton & Russell**, and added on in 1910. ♦ 17 Battery Pl (at West St)

72 United States Custom House

This 1907 building by **Cass Gilbert** has been called one of the finest examples of the Beaux Arts style in New York City, and the reason is instantly apparent. The granite façade is surprisingly delicate, despite an ornate frieze and Ionic columns with Corinthian capitals along the face. Four seated female figures, representing Africa, Asia, Europe, and North America, are Daniel Chester French pieces. Reginald Marsh painted the murals in the wonderful oval rotunda. ♦ State St and Bowling Green

Within the United States Custom House:

National Museum of the American Indian

The comprehensive collection of artifacts linked to the indigenous peoples of the Americas is part of Washington, DC's Smithsonian Institution. The artifacts were assembled over a 54-year period by George Gustav Heye, a New York banker, and had been housed at the Heye Foundation on 155th Street in Audubon Terrace. Opened in 1994, this facility, which features changing displays of the one million objects in its collection, also stages educational workshops, film and video festivals, and performances of indigenous peoples' dance and theater. Among the permanent exhibits on display are Navajo weavings and blankets; stone carvings from the Northwest; basketry and pottery from the Southwest; gold from Colombia, Peru, and Mexico; and jade objects from the Olmec and Maya cultures. The museum collaborates with tribes to present exhibitions that feature past and present traditions of indigenous culture. From Tierra del Fuego to the Arctic Circle, it works to represent all native peoples. ♦ Free. Daily, 10AM-5PM except Th, 10AM-8PM. 514.3700. www.americanindian.si.edu ♿

73 Fraunces Tavern

This Georgian brick building, erected in 1719, became a tavern in 1762, and was made famous when George Washington said farewell to his officers here on the second floor on 4 December 1783. Washington returned six years later to the old **City Hall**, five blocks away, to take the oath of office as the first president of the new nation. The building was refurbished in 1907 in the spirit and style of the period rather than as an accurate restoration. ♦ 54 Pearl St (at Broad St)

Within Fraunces Tavern:

Fraunces Tavern Restaurant

★$$$ Samuel Fraunces, George Washington's steward, opened a tavern on this site in 1763. Now, tourists (and a stray Wall Streeter or two) congregate here amid Colonial-era décor for seviceable fare such as beef Wellington, Maryland crab cakes, herb-roasted Cornish hen, and New York sirloin steak. ♦ American ♦ M-Sa, breakfast, lunch, and dinner. Reservations recommended. 968.1776

Fraunces Tavern Museum

Above the restaurant, permanent and changing exhibitions of decorative arts, period rooms, paintings, and prints and manuscripts from 18th- and 19th-century America are on display. Tours available. ♦ Admission. M-Sa, 10AM-5PM. 425.1778. www.fraunceestavernmuseum.org

74 New York Vietnam Veterans Memorial

So young, so many. From the head of this wedge-shaped plaza, where an inlaid map charts the theater of operations, a Walk of Honor lined with stone posts lists the names of New York's dead and MIA, leading toward the East River. There you find a glass-and-granite memorial wall designed by architects **William Britt Fellows** and **Peter Wormser** with writer **Joseph Ferrandino**, a veteran of the war. The quotes etched into the smooth, greenish surface—softly weathered like beach glass—include excerpts from soldiers' letters, poems, and journal entries: writes Specialist Fourth Class George T. Olsen, "You'd be amazed how much a man can age on one patrol." ♦ Vietnam Veterans Plaza, 55 Water St (at Coenties Slip). www.nyvietnamveteransmemorial.org ♿

75 Battery Park

The Dutch began rearranging the terrain the moment Peter Minuit bought Manhattan for trinkets valued at $24 from the Native Americans in 1626. When they dug their canals and leveled the hills, they dumped the dirt and rocks into the bay. Over the next 300 years or so, more than 21 acres were added to the tip of the island, creating the green buffer between the harbor and the dark canyons of the Financial District. The park takes its name from a line of British cannons that once overlooked the harbor in the late 1600s.

Planted in 1992, the 100,000-rose **Hope Garden** is a living memorial to those who have died of AIDS. A **World War II Memorial** and **Korean War Memorial** stand in the park, as does the haunting *American Merchant Mariner's Memorial* by Marisol Escobar (1991) and the horribly battered but remarkably intact *Sphere for Plaza Fountain* (1968-1971) sculpture by Fritz Koenig, which was the centerpiece of the grand fountain that had lain between the Twin Towers. By 2005, many years into a reclamation initiative for the park, the Battery Conservancy and Dutch landscape designer Piet Oudulf's master plan was clearly coming to fruition. The stunning **Battery Bosque** opened that year, and by 2007 next-phase plans were afoot for a **Frank Gehry**-designed playground and the *Sea Glass Carousel*, a fantasy ride of translucent resin and fiberoptics envisioned by the creative team of **Weisz** + **Yoes**.

Despite its bellicose moniker, the park has always been a place for those described by Herman Melville as "men fixed in ocean reveries" (Melville was born nearby at **17 State Street** in 1819). If those reveries make you hungry, you might enjoy the view while you're dining at the **Battery Gardens** restaurant at the south end of the park (daily, lunch and dinner; 809.5508). ♦ Bounded by State and Whitehall Sts and the Hudson River, and Upper New York Bay and Battery Pl. www.thebattery.org ♿

Within Battery Park:

Castle Clinton

Originally known as **South West Battery**, this structure served as a defense post housing 28 cannons within eight-foot-thick walls. It faced **Castle William** on Governors Island, and both were fortified to block the harbor from enemy attack. In 1811, **John McComb Jr.** designed the original building, which fell into disuse when no enemy appeared. In 1846 the Army gave the building to the city, which redesigned it as an entertainment venue called **Castle Garden**; the main hall was used for the American premiere performance of Swedish singer Jenny Lind, presented by showman P.T. Barnum. Beginning in 1855 it was the **Emigrant Landing Depot**, processing more than seven million immigrants before ceding that role to **Ellis Island** in 1892. In one of its final incarnations, from 1896 to 1941 the building housed the **New York Aquarium** (now at Coney Island in Brooklyn). Finally, as the need for repairs became apparent and its historical importance was realized, the building was designated a National Historic Landmark in 1950. It has since been restored as a fort and, now a National Monument, it is under the care of the National Park Service; 21st-century plans call for further restoration and expansion. A bookstore and museum are on site. It also serves as an information center and a ticket office for the ferry to the **Statue of Liberty** and **Ellis Island**. ♦ Daily. Just south of Battery Pl, near the water. 344.7220. www.nps.gov/cacl ♿

IRT Control House

One of two surviving ornate entrances to the original **IRT** subway (the other is at West 72nd Street and Broadway), this structure designed by **Heins & LaFarge** was built in 1905. The term "control house" was coined by engineers who designed them to control crowds coming and going in two directions at once. ♦ State St and Battery Pl

76 New York Unearthed

In 1990, a permanent archeological display (administered by the **South Street Seaport Museum**) opened in a courtyard behind 17 State Street. Visitors enter at street level, where they view 10 dioramas, created by graphic designer Milton Glaser, that hold such items as medicine vials, crucibles, cannonballs, and bottles, all excavated on or near this site. On the **Lower Gallery**, a glass-enclosed space reveals archeologists hard at work, while at the **Stratigraphy Wall**, visitors can view a three-dimensional cross-section of an archeological site. Museumgoers may also board the **Unearthing New York Systems Elevator**, which takes them on a simulated dig, four centuries back into New York history. ♦ Free. M-F, by appointment only. 17 State St (at Pearl St). 748.8753. www.southseaport.org ♿

77 Church of Our Lady of the Rosary

This pair of Georgian town houses, originally designed in 1800 by **John McComb Jr.**, was restored in 1965 as a shrine church dedicated to Elizabeth Ann Seton. Canonized in 1975 as the first American-born saint, Seton lived here with her family in the early 1800s. The exterior of each building, faithfully returned to its original condition with columns presumably cut from ship masts, provides a small reminder of the character of this fashionable residential neighborhood at the beginning of the 19th century. ♦ 7-8 State St. 269.6865

78 Statue of Liberty

Officially named *Liberty Enlightening the World*, the figure alone (supported by a steel skeleton engineered by **Gustave Eiffel**) is 151 feet high, not counting the pedestal, which adds another 89 feet. It is a full 30 feet taller than the Colossus of Rhodes, one of the Seven Wonders of the Ancient World. French sculptor Fréderic Auguste Bartholdi's original idea was to design a statue of a peasant woman holding the Lamp of Progress to Asia and place it at the entrance to the Suez Canal, an idea that was rejected by the sultan of Egypt. When Bartholdi came to the New World from France looking for a site for the statue, he traveled up and down the eastern seaboard and as far west as Salt Lake City, but he never for a moment seriously considered anyplace but **Bedloe's Island**, which he saw as his ship sailed into New York Harbor. It was finally placed on its pedestal, designed by **Richard Morris Hunt**, in 1886.

Bartholdi cleverly situated it so that when a ship rounds the Narrows between Brooklyn and Staten Island, the statue appears portside, striding forward in a gesture of welcome. As the vessel passes directly in front of her, she seems suddenly erect and saluting. It is truly one of the most impressive optical illusions in the world.

The island, which was renamed **Liberty Island** in 1956, was used as a quarantine station in

The Best

Rustie Brooke

Director of Operations, *Wall Street Rising*

Dance New Amsterdam: DNA sponsors on-site choreographers and teaching artists and offers performance programs, classes, and workshops in a wide range of dance forms to both professionals and nonprofessionals. 280 Broadway. 625.8369. www.dnadance.org

Lower Manhattan Cultural Council (LMCC): Organizes cutting-edge, contemporary performances, and exhibitions, plus gives grants and supports public art. In 2007, for three days at lunchtime, the Martha Graham Dance Company at the New York Stock Exchange was magnificent! 125 Maiden Lane. 219.9401. www.lmcc.net

PhotoGraphic Gallery: Intimate, sophisticated gallery near the Seaport inspired by the rich history of the neighborhood and featuring work about New York and its culture. Unusual themes and artists within changing and relevant exhibits. 252 Front St. 227.2287. www.photographicnyc.com

Poets House: A modern 50,000-volume poetry archive and meeting space, free and open to the public. Over 200 public programs are presented yearly, including poetry readings in libraries and parks. 2 River Terrace. www.poetshouse.org

Shooting Star Theatre: Offers enthusiastic and engaging year-round programs such as new play readings, established works, musicals and cabarets, historical reenactments, workshops, and special entertainments for kids and seniors. 40 Peck Slip. 718/852.7778. www.shootingstartheatre.org

3-Legged Dog (3LD Art and Technology Center): 3LD, a nonprofit theater and media group focusing on large-scale experimental artwork, was the first producing arts group to sign a lease in the Liberty Zone and the first to rebuild downtown. Unusual, thought-provoking, inventive! 80 Greenwich St. 645.0374. www.3leggeddog.org

Tribeca Performing Arts Center (TPAC): With multidisciplinary performances and a culturally diverse focus for underserved audiences, TPAC supports the growth of music and dance artists and emerging theater; it happily offers many family-friendly events. 199 Chambers St. 220.1460. www.tribecapac.org

Trinity Church: Classical and sacred musical selections by extraordinary artists performed in a refined setting. Concerts at One, The Trinity Choir, and some of the country's preeminent vocal ensembles—and the state-of-the-art digital Trinity organ—make their home at this historical church. 74 Trinity Place. 602.0800. www.trinitywallstreet.org

World Financial Center: The WFC and the waterfront Winter Garden provide highly original and fun (and free!) year-round showcases for the visual and performing arts—from the intimate to the spectacular. 3 World Financial Center. 945.0505. www.worldfinancialcenter.com

Ace Film Festival (www.acefest.com), **Culture Fest** at Battery Park (www.nycvisit.com), **Dine Around Downtown** at Chase Manhattan Plaza (www.downtownny.com), **J&R Music Fest** at City Hall Park (www.jr.com), Lower Manhattan Cultural Council **Sitelines** (www.lmcc.net), **Music Downtown** (www.musicdowntown.org), **Tribeca Family Festival/ Tribeca Film Festival** (www.tribecafilmfestival.org), and **River to River Festival** (rivertorivernyc.com)

the early 18th century. After 1811 it was the site of **Fort Wood**, which is the star-shaped structure that forms the pedestal's base. In the years between, it was a popular place to hang pirates.

The statue's restoration, completed in time for her centennial, made climbing the spiral staircase to its crown easier than it had been for the previous hundred years, but it still left 22 stories (300-plus steps) to climb, and in very close quarters. Visitors to the **National Park Service**-administered site today are limited to the museum and shop just atop the lady's pedestal. There you'll find a glass ceiling has been installed inside Miss Liberty, the better to appreciate her monumental infrastructure. The museum chronicles the full history of immigration to the New World, beginning with the arrival of the Dutch. It also contains exhibitions on the statue itself, including the original torch, which was re-created and replaced during the 1986 restoration.

♦ Time passes are necessary for entrance to the monument and museum. They may be ordered or picked up at the time ferry tickets are purchased. Be prepared for tight security. Ferry: Fee. Departs Battery Park every 30-40 minutes daily. Ferry Ticket Info: 877.523.9849 or www.statuecruises.com. Tickets may also be purchased inside Castle Clinton within the park. Museum and Statue: Free. Daily, 9:30AM-5PM (varies seasonally). 363.3200. www.statueofliberty.org; www.nps.gov/stli ♿

78 Ellis Island

On 1 January 1892, when a boat carrying 148 steerage passengers from the SS *Nevada* pulled into the new pier on **Ellis Island**, Annie Moore, a 15-year-old Irish girl, became the first immigrant to set foot on the island. More than 12 million souls followed in her footsteps before the island was closed. In 1907, its peak year, 1,285,349 people were admitted. The original station burned to the ground in 1897, and the **Ellis**

Island National Monument was erected by **Boring & Tilton** in 1898. The present complex of buildings was already decaying during the World War II years when German aliens were imprisoned there. When it finally closed in 1954, vandals moved in and did their best to destroy what was left. In 1990, after eight years of restoration (at a cost of $156 million, with much of the fund-raising spearheaded by Lee Iacocca), the main building opened as a museum. After years of litigation, the US Supreme Court ruled that the southern half of Ellis Island belongs to the State of New Jersey. ♦ Full ferry and ticket information are posted at the Statue of Liberty, above. As with the Statue of Liberty, be prepared for tight security both onboard and onsite.

On Ellis Island:

Ellis Island Museum of Immigration

Visitors can now follow the path their ancestors took upon arrival in America: from the **Baggage Room**, where they dropped off what were often all their worldly belongings, to the **Registry Room**, where they underwent 60-second medical and 30-question legal examinations, and on to the **Staircase of Separation**, which led to the ferryboats that transported the immigrants who were granted admittance (98 percent of those who arrived here) to Manhattan, New Jersey, or points farther west. Also on view are exhibitions tracing the immigration experience: *Islands of Tears* is a poignant film that documents the voyage to America; Treasures from Home contains personal property brought here by immigrants; the American Immigrant Wall of Honor is inscribed with the names of more than 420,000 American immigrants who were commemorated by their descendants through a donation to the Statue of Liberty-Ellis Island Foundation. This wall was later extended to accommodate an additional 75,000 names. In the **Oral History Studio**, visitors are given the opportunity to listen to immigrants reminisce about their experiences here. In 2001 the museum launched its much-lauded **American Family Immigration History Center**, a remarkable tool for researching family background. Shops, cafeteria. ♦ Free. Daily, 9:30AM-5:15PM (varies seasonally). 363.3200. www.ellisisland.org; www.nps.gov/ellis ♿

79 Staten Island Ferry/ Whitehall Ferry Terminal

Tourists and commuters alike enjoy the sparkling ambience of the rebuilt Whitehall Ferry Terminal, from which they embark (or return) for a trip to Staten Island. Designed by architect **Fred Schwartz**, the terminal, badly damaged by a fire in 1992, reopened in 2005 to much acclaim for its use of natural light and green technology. The adjacent **Peter Minuit Plaza** and neighboring subway entrances are targeted for a face-lift next. The ferry weaves through harbor traffic—from tug to sailboat, yacht to cruise ship—and travels past the **Statue of Liberty** and **Ellis Island** to the northeast edge of Staten Island, then back again. In the course of the 5.2-mile, 25-minute run, 65,000 riders a day get some of the greatest views in the world, and the greatest deal—it's free. Those who disembark in Staten Island will appreciate the redesigned **St. George Terminal**, which also reopened in 2005. ♦ Passengers and bicycles, free. (Service is suspended for vehicles.) Daily, 24 hours. South St and Peter Minuit Plaza. www.nyc.gov/dot ♿

80 Battery Maritime Building/ Governors Island Ferry

The sheetmetal-and-steel façade of this Beaux Arts ferry terminal has been painted green to simulate copper. Before the Brooklyn Bridge was built, there were 17 ferry lines between Lower Manhattan and Brooklyn. Until 1938, one of them operated out of this terminal, which was designed in 1906 by **Walker & Gillette**. Next door to the **Staten Island Ferry Terminal**, today it houses the small fleet of ferries that serves **Governors Island** (see below). ♦ 10 South St (at Whitehall St)

80 Governors Island

When the Dutch arrived here in 1624, they established their first toehold on what they called **Nut Island**. But even before the Dutch governor surrendered Nieuw Amsterdam to them in 1665, the British established their own governor here on the same island. In addition to the British **Governor's Mansion**, another historic landmark on the island is the 1840 **Admiral's House**, home of the commanding general of the army garrison stationed here from 1790 until 1966. For the next 31 years the Coast Guard headquartered their operations on the island. Granted National Monument status in 2001, the 173-acre island was placed under **National Park Service** management two years later. Access is a 7-minute ride away via **NY Water Taxi** ferry (742.1969. www.nywatertaxi.com), from the **Battery Maritime Building** (above), slip 7. ♦ Free. Open June-August only. Closed M, Tu. W-F, by guided tour only; Sa, Su, open access 10AM-3PM. Ticket and tour info: 825.3045. www.nps.gov/gois; www.govisland.com ♿

CHINATOWN/LOWER EAST SIDE/ NOLITA/LITTLE ITALY

In New York's early days, the swampy territory just northeast of City Hall was considered worthless. But as waves of immigrants began arriving in the middle of the 19th century, the former marshes became valuable to the real-estate developers who packed the newcomers into crowded tenements. The distinct ethnic flavors of China-

town, the Lower East Side, and Little Italy were established as each immigrant group settled the area roughly bounded by the **East River** and **Lafayette, Chambers,** and **Houston Streets.**

Nearly every part of New York has metamorphosed several times over the centuries. But in this area, it's mainly the populace, rather than the architecture, that has changed. During the 1860s, thousands of Germans arrived, forcing the long-settled Irish farther uptown. Between 1881 and 1910, 1.5 million Jews fled Romania, Hungary, and Russia, and settled here. Italians, Chinese, Poles, and Turks were among the other immigrants in this period. After 1943, when the Chinese Exclusion Act was finally ended, the next waves of newcomers followed the 1968 lifting of US immigration quotas. Today's heavily Chinese population, of late expanding with people from Fujian Province, is joined by a significant number of Latinos as well as Dominicans, Puerto Ricans, Vietnamese, Filipinos, and West Africans, not to mention young hipsters of all stripes.

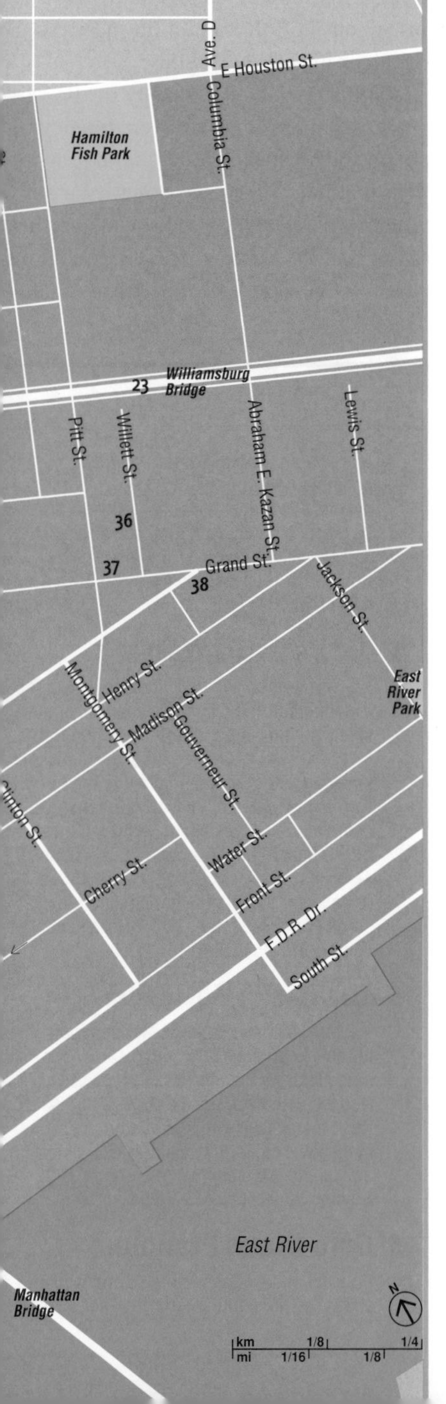

Once covering three square blocks and now 40 square blocks and growing, Manhattan's **Chinatown** is the largest Chinese community outside Asia, with more than 150,000 Chinese residents. Mostly centered south of Canal Street, Chinatown is a neighborhood that thrives on street life. Except for an occasional pagoda-style telephone booth, though, don't expect quaintness. What you'll find is a warren of shops, selling bok choy, lichees, and other native fruits and vegetables and low-cost clothing and housewares, along with many unassuming-looking restaurants, many of which prepare wondrous dishes. You will also find traditional herbal apothecaries, fine furniture and crafts (especially porcelain and other ceramics), and unusual paper goods. The largest crowds appear on Chinese New Year, which occurs in late January or early February.

The Lower East Side is pretty much bounded to the south by Canal Street and to the north by East Houston; the East River and the Bowery define its east and west extremes, respectively. It's now a mixed bag of (some shuttered) synagogues, Latino markets, cool new galleries, clubs, boutiques, and hot restaurants—all still tucked into seriously aging red-brick tenements. Old-style Jewish delicatessens (and pickle stores) survive too, as does that historic bastion of the shopping deal (though hardly the destination it once was), Orchard Street. In observation of the Sabbath, most secular sites on the Lower East Side are closed Friday afternoon and all day Saturday.

Since the late 1980s NoLita—bound by the Bowery to the east, Broadway to the west, Houston Street on the north, and Spring Street on the south—has carved an identity of its own. Cutting-edge designers priced out of SoHo and a bit of a restaurant scene have merged most comfortably with their historic surrounds.

Mulberry Street is the main drag of **Little Italy** (historically bounded by the Bowery and Lafayette, Canal, and Spring Streets), a bustling residential area filled with neighborhood stores, slews of restaurants, and old Italian social clubs—and a growing presence of shops that have moved north from Chinatown. The area was settled mainly between 1880 and 1924 by immigrant families, many of whom have moved on. But they too always come back—especially for the Feast of San Gennaro, a weeklong religious celebration held each September that is famous for its eating, drinking, and merrymaking.

---

1 Puck Building

This Romanesque Revival building reflects the influence of the Chicago School in its bold and vibrant use of brickwork. It was once the home of the humor magazine *Puck,* whose spirit remains in the two larger-than-life statues perched on third-floor ledges at the northeast corner. The interior of this great building, constructed in 1885 to the designs of **Albert Wagner**, has been renovated as commercial condominiums for art galleries, workshops, and design offices. The opulent rooms are also rented out for large-scale art events (such as the annual **Outsider Art Fair**, usually held in late January), weddings, and other celebrations. ♦ 295 Lafayette St (at E Houston St). 274.8900 ♿

2 Yonah Schimmel

★$ Jewish specialties, including at least 12 varieties of legendary knishes, clabbered milk (yogurt), and borscht, have been dished up in this old downtown storefront—which seems like it's barely changed since it opened at the turn of the last century. ♦ Eastern European/Jewish ♦ M-F, Su, breakfast, lunch, and early dinner. 137 E Houston St (at Forsyth St). 477.2858

3 Russ & Daughters

A shopping mecca for serious connoisseurs of bagels and lox with a schmear of cream cheese, this establishment is also not bad for take-out golden smoked whitefish, unctuous sable carp, tart and crisp herring, salads, dried fruits, nuts, and other items that belong to a category of food some native New Yorkers call "appetizing." ♦ Daily. 179 E Houston St (between Orchard and Allen Sts). 475.4880 ♿

4 Katz's Delicatessen

★$ This well-known delicatessen was made even more famous by the memorable deli scene shot for the 1989 movie *When Harry Met Sally.* Sit at a table and enjoy the whole experience, but only if you're not in a hurry. For counter service, take a ticket when you come in. Daily specials or pastrami or warm brisket on rye are always good. The famous salami, surprisingly, is not kosher. ♦ Deli ♦ Daily, breakfast, lunch, and dinner. No credit cards accepted. 205 E Houston St (at Ludlow St). 254.2246 ♿

5 The Hat/El Sombrero

★$ You won't find the best Mexican food here, but this popular neighborhood eatery has its defenders. Try the nachos *tradicionales* (topped with beef, beans, cheese, and salsa), wash them down with a margarita, and soak in the local color. ♦ Mexican ♦ Daily, lunch and dinner. No credit cards accepted. 108 Stanton St (at Ludlow St). 254.4188

6 Otto Tootsi Plohound

Unusual and well-made men's and women's shoes, as the name may or may not suggest.

♦ Daily. 273 Lafayette St (at Prince St). 431.7299. Also at 137 Fifth Ave (between E 20th and E 21st Sts). 460.8650

7 McNally Robinson

In the inviting, intelligently designed aisles of this 2005 addition to New York's independent-bookstore scene, knowledgeable staffers will guide you to serendipitous finds in areas from politics to poetry to popular fiction—or leave you to your own devices, which might include sitting in on an event in their fine reading series, or sipping a restorative cup at the teahouse on site. ♦ Daily. 50 Prince St (between Mulberry and Lafayette Sts). 274.1160. www.mcnallyrobinsonnyc.com ♿

8 Dö Kham

Sold here are clothing, jewelry, and accessories from Tibet and elsewhere in the Himalayas, some designed by the amiable store owner, Phelgye Kelden, a former Tibetan monk. Check out his chic fake and genuine fur hats. ♦ Daily. 51 Prince St (between Mulberry and Lafayette Sts). 966.2404. Also at other locations

9 Old St. Patrick's Cathedral

New York's first Roman Catholic cathedral, this wonderful Gothic Revival building was the original Cathedral of the Archdiocese of New York. (When the new St. Pat's at Fifth Avenue and 50th Street was consecrated in 1879, this became a parish church that would serve generations of European immigrants). Originally built by **Joseph Mangin** in 1815, the church was restored by **Henry Engelbert** after it was badly damaged in an 1866 fire. It was named a New York City landmark in 1966, a worthy appellation for a simple and moving place that immediately evokes the city's past. ♦ Church entrance: Mott St (at Prince St). Rectory: ♦ 264 Mulberry St (between Prince and E Houston Sts). 226.8075. www.oldsaintpatricks.com

10 Old St. Patrick's Convent and Girls' School

Built in 1826, the beautiful Federal doorway framed with Corinthian columns makes this unusually large Federal-style building a treasure. ♦ 32 Prince St (at Mott St)

11 New Museum of Contemporary Art

Art defies gravity in this asymmetrical stack of aluminum-mesh-clad boxes rising seven stories over the gritty Bowery, the first art museum ever built from scratch in downtown Manhattan. Designed by **Kazuyo Sejima + Ryue Nishizawa/SANAA** and opened here in 2007, this fitting home for the 1977-founded New Museum showcases the latest cross-media works of contemporary artists in floor-through, column-free galleries (see above re: gravity) and offers public programs in sleek event and educational spaces. Shop. Tours. ♦ Admission; free Th, F after 6PM. Closed M, Tu, W, Sa, Su, noon-6PM; Th, F, noon-10PM. 235 Bowery (between Rivington and Stanton Sts). 219.1222. www.newmuseum.org ♿

12 Off SoHo Suites Hotel

$$$ The 38 suites are large and the prices can be rock bottom (for their "economy standard"—and smallest—suites, that is). What's the snag? This isn't exactly Park Avenue, the 10 least expensive suites share a bath and kitchen, furnishings can be downright dowdy, and smoking is permitted everywhere (of course, that might be a plus for you). But very few others are recommended in this area east of SoHo (hence the name), with easy access to all mass transit. There's an onsite fitness center, and most suites have color TV, air conditioning, and an eat-in kitchen (with refrigerator, microwave, and cookware); high-speed Internet access in the lobby only (there is a dial-up line in the rooms). ♦ 11 Rivington St (between Chrystie St and Bowery). 979.9808, 800/633.7646; fax 979.9801. www.offsoho.com

13 Sammy's Famous Roumanian Restaurant

★★$$$ Though it's close to decrepit on the outside, locals still know that to step down into this basement-level establishment is like crashing a post-bar mitzvah party. People laugh, talk, joke, and hug all night long (when they're not grabbing the mike for an impromptu comedy set). For a main course, try the Roumanian tenderloin steak, fried breaded veal chop, or boiled beef with mushroom-barley gravy. Mashed potatoes with fried onions and kasha varnishkes (buckwheat groats with bow-tie macaroni) are old standards to order on the side. The food is authentically rich, so wash it down with an egg cream, the classic New York *digestif.* ♦ Eastern European/Jewish ♦ Daily, dinner; entertainment nightly. Reservations required. 157 Chrystie St (between Delancey and Rivington Sts). 673.0330

14 Congregation Adath Jeshurun of Jassy Synagogue

This 1903 building was also the home of the First Warsaw Congregation. Now abandoned, it still projects a rich and distinctive image with its collage of architectural styles. ♦ 58-60 Rivington St (between Allen and Eldridge Sts)

15 Economy Candy Company

People with a longing for old-fashioned penny candy will find it in this store, which has been selling candy of all kinds, as well as dried fruits, nuts, coffees, teas, and other delicacies, since 1937. Though the prices are good, a penny just doesn't go as far as it used to. ♦ Daily. 108 Rivington St (between Essex and Ludlow Sts). 254.1832 ♿

16 Streit's Matzo Company

A **Lower East Side** presence since 1925, this family-owned bakery is the only Manhattan producer of the unleavened kosher bread enjoyed during Passover, and year-round as well. Watch the huge sheets of matzos as they pass by the windows on conveyor belts, and buy some samples on your way out. (The shop is adjacent to the buildings where it's made.) ♦ M-Th, 9AM-4:30PM. Store: 148 Rivington St (at Suffolk St). 475.7000

17 Giselle Sportswear

This shop offers four floors of better American sportswear for women, organized by designer (like Escada) and well-discounted. ♦ M-F, Su. 143 Orchard St (between Delancey and Rivington Sts). 673.1900

17 Fine & Klein Handbags

The extensive collection of high-end handbags, briefcases, and accessories here includes designer knockoffs plus the latest from Carlos Falchi, Enny, and Lisette (sometimes Valentino and Givenchy, too). You'll find good discounts and gracious service at this Orchard Street institution. ♦ M-F, Su. 119 Orchard St (between Delancey and Rivington Sts). 674.6720

17 Altman Luggage

Brave the bargain-hunters en route to this Orchard Street institution (since 1920 the place for luggage, pens, and briefcases) and you'll find a large selection at good prices, purveyed by staff who know their stuff and will take the time to help you choose yours. ♦ Su-F. 135 Orchard St (between Delancey and Rivington Sts). 254.7275, 800/372.3377

18 Orchard Street

The old pushcarts are long gone, as is its more recent permutation as a designer discount mecca. But bargain hunters still roam this street and the adjacent thoroughfares—an indoor-outdoor bazaar of discounted dresses, coats, shoes, linens, fabrics, and accessories may still be found among the ever-fancier boutiques and upscale dining establishments. On Sunday, many of the streets are closed to traffic, the better to appreciate the designer knockoffs hawked from the sidewalks. Go weekdays if you can. Many stores close early on Friday and all day Saturday. ♦ From Canal to E Houston Sts

19 Essex Street Market

This block-square indoor market—one of the many created by Mayor Fiorello La Guardia to get pushcarts off the streets in the 1930s—is packed with open-air fruit and vegetable stands and a lively mix of sundries and services that reflect the diverse neighborhood. Eat your way through, and marvel at the superb quality of the produce... and its remarkably low prices (while they last; stalls are getting snazzier and dining is getting pricier). Starting from the north entrance, pick up a perfect carrot muffin at **Tra La La Juice Bar**, browse the myriad compact stalls like **Jose's Music and Memories** and **World Kitchen/Cocina Mundo**, get a trim at **Aminova's Barber Shop**, then move on to the tiny modern-art showcase in the far southern corner that's **Cuchifritos Gallery**, wind back around with a stop for a snack at **Shopsin's** or a New American bite at **Essex** or a panini at **Paradou**, sample some cheeses at the artisanal **Saxelby Cheesemongers** or **Formaggio Essex** or pastas at **Casa Tua**, and pick up the ripest mangoes at **Batista Grocery** or **Best Farm Fruits and Vegetables** or a few bottles of **Schapiro's Kosher Winery's** best on your way out. Schapiro's (M-F, 832.3176), a true remnant of the old Lower East Side, founded in 1899, was the first kosher winery in the country. Until just a few years ago they made their rich kosher wines right across the street from the market; they now make them upstate. ♦ M-Sa, 120 Essex St (between Delancey and Rivington Sts). 388.0449

20 Storefront for Art and Architecture

Fearless exhibitions that explore the latest thought on architecture, design, and planning are at the heart of this alternative gallery. Its façade—designed by **Steven Holl** with artist Vito Acconci—is as innovative as the gallery's programming: a series of panels that pivot on both the vertical and the horizontal axes in multiple conformations connect the inside with the sidewalk. This is all to the good, as the 100-foot-long triangular slice of a space is just 3 feet wide at its front end (it widens out to 20). Storefront's archives, which date back to its founding in 1982 and are a rare resource for experimental architecture and art, are open by appointment; its creatively curated bookshop is open during gallery hours. ♦ Free. Tu-Sa, noon-7PM. 97 Kenmare St (at Cleveland Pl, between Mulberry and Lafayette Sts). 431.5795. www.storefrontnews.org

21 Lower East Side Tenement Museum

This fascinating museum—its tour site, at 97 Orchard Street, is now a National Historic Landmark—is visited by folks curious about historic New York living—and working—conditions, but holds particular interest for descendants of immigrants who came to the US at the end of the 19th and beginning of the 20th centuries. The grim reality of the appalling hardships they faced is palpable here, where visitors on each of three guided tours see cramped living spaces in re-created tenement apartments and learn about the lives and occupations (notably in the garment trades) of actual residents: the Gumpertz family, German Jews of 1878; the Confino family, Sephardic Jews of 1916; and the Baldizzi family, Italian Catholics of 1935. Imaginative programs that focus on all facets of the immigrant experience include weekend walking tours of the Lower East Side, photographic and art exhibits, and living history events. The visitor center (where all tours begin) also houses a terrific book and gift shop, and a 25-seat theater with a running video on Lower East Side history from the 19th century to the present. ♦ Scheduled tours only. Admission. Daily. 108 Orchard St (at Delancey St). 431.0233. www.tenement.org

22 Blue Moon Hotel

$$$ Where pushcarts once clattered over cobblestones, visitors can sleep in comfort in this plushly renovated tenement's 22 atypically large rooms, all decorated with artifacts from local history and nicely restored detail. There's free Wi-Fi throughout; a continental breakfast is also on the house. The staff takes an interest, so ask for trip tips. ♦ 100 Orchard St (between Broome and Delancey Sts). 533.9080; fax 533.9148. www.bluemoon-nyc.com

23 Williamsburg Bridge

Built in 1903 by **Leffert L. Buck**, this is the second bridge to span the East River. Its construction changed Williamsburg in Brooklyn from a resort area to a new home for immigrants from the Lower East Side. The bridge is unusual in that there are no cables on the land side of the steel towers, robbing it of some of the soaring grace of a full suspension span. ♦ Between Broadway (Brooklyn) and Delancey St

24 Grotta Azzurra

★★$$$ In one of those New York twists-of-restaurant-fate, famed **La Grotta** (first opened in 1908) shut down in the late 1970s but was resurrected in this same spot in 2003. The underground grotto, once blue, is now a wine cellar; dining is now at street level. Like the décor, the Italian menu is a bit more contemporary than the homestyle it once was, but you can still expect your zeppoli to be served in the traditional brown paper bags. ♦ Neapolitan ♦ Daily, breakfast, lunch, and dinner. Prix fixe available at dinner. Reservations recommended. 177 Mulberry St (at Broome St). 925.8775

25 Caffè Roma

★$ Knowledgeable New Yorkers favor this lovely Old World bakery over all others. No redecorating was ever necessary to make this place look authentic—it just is. The cannoli, whether plain or dipped in chocolate, are perfect. ♦ Bakery/Café ♦ Daily. No credit cards accepted. 385 Broome St (at Mulberry St). 226.8413

26 The Police Building

A commanding presence with an imposing dome as a symbol of authority, this 1909 building by **Hoppin & Koen** was the main headquarters of the New York City Police Department for nearly 65 years. The new copper dome was crafted by French artisans brought here to restore the Statue of Liberty's copper flame, and the 1988 restoration was the work of **Ehrenkrantz Eckstut & Kuhn Architects**. The interior, by **dePolo/Dunbar**, has been converted into 55 cooperative apartments. ♦ 240 Centre St (between Grand and Broome Sts)

27 Benito I and Benito II

★$$ The original owners of this pair of small trattorie sold out and moved to Los Angeles. The restaurants are no longer related, except by name, but either one is a good choice for a hearty low-cost meal. ♦ Neapolitan ♦ Daily, lunch and dinner. Benito I: 174 Mulberry St (between Grand and Broome Sts). 226.9171. Benito II: 163 Mulberry St (between Grand and Broome Sts). 226.9012 ♿

28 Da Nico

★$ The décor is a tad more stylish—terra-cotta floors, hanging copper pots, brick walls lined with shelves of olive oil and wine bottles, a marble bar with antipasto platters—and the atmosphere a bit less raucous here than at surrounding neighborhood eateries. A backyard garden adds a romantic touch. It manages a full Italian kitchen with lobster, veal chops, and tons of pastas. ♦ Neapolitan ♦ Daily, lunch and dinner. Reservations recommended. 164 Mulberry St (between Grand and Broome Sts). 343.1212 ♿

29 Pho Bâng

★★$ Ignore the lack of décor and come here for authentic Vietnamese cooking, especially the excellent whole-shrimp summer rolls. A plate of exotic lettuces and an array of sauces accompany the meal. ♦ Vietnamese ♦ Daily, lunch and dinner. No reservations. No credit cards accepted. 157 Mott St (between Grand and Broome Sts). 966.3797. Also at 3 Pike St (at Division St). 233.3947

30 Italian Food Center

To the great delight of Italophiles, this long-running one-stop emporium is filled with domestic and imported Italian foodstuffs. More than a dozen kinds of breads are baked on the premises daily, and the vast array of Italian cold cuts is mouth-watering. Try the New York Special hero sandwich, a fresh pizza, focaccia, *bruschetta* (toast seasoned with garlic and oil), or one of the temptingly displayed spinach or sausage rolls. ♦ Daily. 186 Grand St (at Mulberry St). 925.2954 ♿

31 Alleva Dairy

Founded in 1892, the oldest Italian cheese store in the US is still family owned. Not a day goes by without a proud Alleva on hand to tend to the regular customers who come from far and near to shop for the mozzarella (fresh and smoked) made daily. There's also a small selection of noncheese items, including dried pasta, an excellent fresh tomato sauce packaged to go, and several types of smoked and cured meats. ♦ Daily. 188 Grand St (at Mulberry St). 226.7990

31 Piemonte Ravioli Company

Since 1920, the same family has been churning out freshly made pasta from old family recipes in this modest-looking store that is, in fact, one of America's major suppliers. The refrigerator and counter are freshly stocked with pasta of all types, colors, shapes, and fillings. The filled pastas such as ravioli and cannelloni, are favorites. Try the plump ravioli stuffed with cheese, spinach, or porcini mushrooms. ♦ Tu-Su, hours vary. 190 Grand St (between Mott and Mulberry Sts). 226.0475

32 Ferrara Café

$ Four generations into it, this Little Italy institution (it opened in 1892) is now a slick emporium and obvious tourist magnet. The café includes an extensive take-out department, and features a wide and reliable variety of Italian pastries, cookies, and small pizzas and panini. Expect the full gamut of coffees, of course, with spirits and without. In nice weather, the bar extends onto the sidewalk, where a counter dispenses Italian gelati. ♦ Bakery/Café ♦ Daily. 195 Grand St (between Mott and Mulberry Sts). 226.6150

32 E. Rossi & Co.

This old-fashioned, crowded, family-run store sells boccie balls, religious articles, pasta machines, cookbooks in both Italian and English, and a variety of kitchen gadgets, such as cheese graters. ♦ Daily. 193 Grand St (at Mulberry St). 966.6640

33 130 Bowery

The 1894 building designed by **McKim, Mead & White** is the former **Bowery Savings Bank**. Outside, the Roman columns attached to a Renaissance façade are somehow apropos on the edge of Little Italy. Inside, take a look, if you can, at the deluxe Beaux Arts details in this opulent multilevel space with its 65-foot ceilings, Venetian glass features, and marble mosaic floors. **Capitale NY** now runs the space for private, high-end special events. 130 Bowery (between Grand and Broome Sts)

34 Zarin Fabrics

Established in 1936 by Harry Zarin, decorator fabrics, trims, draperies, and now, furnishings all at super prices, are sold at this three-floor source that fills a full square city block. Find everything from opulent silk brocades to mattress ticking, upholsterer's tools, curtain rods and tie-backs, lighting, and sofas. This is one of the few spots in the area open on Saturday. ♦ Daily. 318 Grand St (between Orchard and Allen Sts). 925.6112 ♿

STAR DISCOVERIES

New York's attractions make it a glittering magnet for the rich and famous, and with more films than ever being made in the city, starstruck visitors are likely to strike it rich here. Celebrities—many of whom have residences in town—don't only shop at **Armani** and dine at **Nobu**; they also browse the museums and art galleries, soak up ballet and opera, go to jazz clubs and Broadway shows, and jog in Central Park. In fact, one of the charming aspects of New York City life is that you might unexpectedly glimpse a famous face almost anywhere. We've had the pleasure of spotting Paul Newman dining at a local Upper East Side restaurant, **Sarabeth's**; John Malkovich shopping at **Fairway** market on the West Side; Susan Sarandon and Tim Robbins at the Union Square Green Market; Diane Keaton at the movies in Kips Bay; and Julianne Moore strolling with her family in the Village.

Here are some of the best sites for celebrity sightings. Note that New Yorkers are fairly low-key when they come face-to-face with a well-known personality—a quick, appreciative glance is the sophisticated response.

The **Morgans**, **Royalton**, and **Paramount Hotels** are favorites of the hip and famous, as are the **Gansevoort**, **Rivington Hudson**, and **Maritime**. The venerable **Algonquin** appeals to British actors and followers of cabaret. The **Oak Room** remains one of the city's best rooms to see and hear top-flight singers. When Julie Wilson or Andrea Marcovicci are in the spotlight, the audience will probably be star-studded, too; the same thing goes at **The Carlyle** hotel when a popular chanteuse hits the stage. The **Four Seasons** is the hottest haven for show-biz business on parade. And the **Regency** has long been the favorite breakfast place of powerful business moguls.

Theater District restaurants such as **Sardi's** and **Gallagher's** are where many opening-night parties take place. And it's possible to catch a famous actor or actress eating a pre- or post-performance dinner or drink at these or other welcoming spots, like **Angus McEndoe**, in the neighborhood. Restaurants near **Carnegie Hall** and **Lincoln Center** are good bets for the same reason. Reserve early or late for the best chance to catch a dining diva.

The **Meatpacking District**, **SoHo**, and **TriBeCa** are popular neighborhoods with night owls from the worlds of entertainment and fashion; various nooks on the **Lower East Side** are also major draws for this crowd.

If you jog or racewalk around the **Reservoir** in **Central Park** or on any stretch along Hudson River Park, you might find yourself in step with any number of healthful "who" 's. Many show-business folks and their families live in and around these areas, and when the weather is good, they come out to play with their kids and walk their dogs.

And, it's a good bet that you'll find pro's enjoying others engaged at their own game: established rockers often drop in at local clubs to see what their next chart challenger might sound like, and star comedians regularly flock to the city's comedy clubs. When actors take the night off, many of them spend it catching shows both on Broadway and off. If you spring for orchestra seats, your fellow *Playbill* reader might well be someone you'll see on the other side of the footlights on your next outing.

35 The Pickle Guys

Once peopled by pickle purveyors by the peck, Essex Street is down to one shop—but it's the front line of the Pickle Wars. When the venerable **Guss' Pickles** moved a few blocks away (Su-F. 85-87 Orchard St, between Grand and Broome Sts; 917/701.4000), a splinter group stayed on to dispense sours, gherkins, and other puckery provender—made the old-fashioned way—from big red barrels in an open storefront. Savor the aroma while you wait in line. ♦ Su-F. 49 Essex St (between Grand and Hester Sts). 656.9739

36 Bialystoker Synagogue

Built in 1826 as the Willett Street Methodist Episcopal Church, this building was purchased by the Congregation Anshei Bialystok in 1905 and is the oldest structure housing a synagogue in New York. ♦ 7 Willett St (between Grand and Delancey Sts). 475.0165

37 Abrons Arts Center/ Henry Street Settlement

This complex for the performing and visual arts, built by **Prentice and Chan, Ohlhausen** in 1975, is part of the Henry Street Settlement, a social service agency that has operated on the Lower East Side since 1893. Its programs include arts workshops, professional performances, and exhibitions—all meant to help participants develop self-expression through the arts and an appreciation of the cultural diversity of New York City. The complex contains three theaters: the **Recital Hall**, the **Experimental**

Theater, and the 1912 Georgian Revival **Harry De Jur Playhouse**. Originally built for silent films and live performances, the 350-seat De Jur was restored in 1996. ♦ 466 Grand St (between Willett and Pitt Sts). 598.0400. www.henrystreet.org ♿

38 Ritualarium

In 1904, the former **Arnold Toynbee Hall** of the Young Men's Benevolent Association was converted to a mikvah (here formally known as the Mikvah of the Lower East Side), a ritual bath for Orthodox Jewish women, who are required to attend in preparation for marriage and on a monthly basis after that. Because the Scriptures command that the water be pure, rainwater is collected in cisterns. ♦ 313 E Broadway (at Grand St)

39 Museum of Chinese in America (MoCA)

In a former machine shop redesigned by **Maya Lin** around a skylit courtyard with an exterior of wood, concrete, and bronze, this gem of a museum—founded in 1980, and moved here in 2008—holds topical exhibitions and the nation's largest collection of oral histories, photographs, and artifacts relating to the Chinese-American experience. For an insider's view of Chinatown, join the walking tour on Saturdays at 1PM, led by a docent with roots in the neighborhood. An earlier location at 70 Mulberry Street (at Bayard St; 619.4785) houses the museum's archives. ♦ Nominal admission. Tu-Su, noon-6PM. 211-215 Centre St (between Howard and Grand Sts). 619.4785. www.mocanyc.org ♿

40 Taormina

★$$ With its blond wood and peach furnishings, exposed brick walls, large windows, and graceful tall plants, this is not the typical Little Italy restaurant. The stuffed artichokes are a favorite; the veal entrées are also quite good. Outdoor seating is available. ♦ Neapolitan ♦ Daily, lunch and dinner. 147 Mulberry St (between Hester and Grand Sts). 219.1007 ♿

At the corner of Washington Place and Greene Street, a plaque commemorates the deaths of 146 people in a 1911 fire at the Triangle Shirtwaist Company. The victims were predominantly young Jewish and Italian immigrant women. When the fire broke out, the workers were unable to escape because the owners locked them in the building during shifts, a common practice. The owners of the Triangle Shirtwaist Company were absolved of any responsibility for the deaths in a court of law. However, the fire brought attention to the despicable conditions of employment in the sweatshop industry, and the state enacted many reforms in the fire code and workplace safety regulations.

41 Angelo's of Mulberry Street

★★$$ An old Little Italy standby (it's over 100 years old) that is still a favorite for tourists and locals alike, this restaurant can be counted on for such consistently good entrées as veal *valdostana* (stuffed with cheese and ham) or veal parmigiana. ♦ Neapolitan ♦ Tu-Su, lunch and dinner. 146 Mulberry St (between Hester and Grand Sts). 966.1277

42 Sal Anthony's S.P.Q.R.

★$$ The multilevel room here is joined by sidewalk and patio seating. A menu of basic Italian standards is jazzed up a bit with items like linguine *veronelli* (seafood in tomato sauce) and shell steak sautéed with mushrooms. ♦ Neapolitan ♦ Daily, lunch and dinner. 133 Mulberry St (between Hester and Grand Sts). 925.3120

43 Holiday Inn Downtown

$$ The only hotel in Chinatown is technically in SoHo, but no matter. Contemporary in style, thanks to a complete renovation in recent years, its public areas and 227 guestrooms are essentially on par with any other contemporary hotel in Manhattan. Its prices, though, are lower. There is a fitness center and multilingual concierge on-site, and rooms all have large TVs and high-speed Internet access. ♦ 138 Lafayette St (at Howard St). 966.8898; fax 966.3933. www.hidowntown-nyc.com

44 Il Cortile

★★$$$ On weekends, the lines to get in may be too long, the rooms too noisy, and the waiters too harried, but the fresh food at this dining spot is well prepared and the room—especially the garden area—beautifully decorated. ♦ Neapolitan ♦ Daily, lunch, dinner, and late-night meals. Reservations recommended. 125 Mulberry St (between Canal and Hester Sts). 226.6060

45 Vincent's

★$$$ Choose the fresh seafood with a choice of mild, medium, or hot marinara sauce at this neighborhood institution, where, truly, sauce is the thing. Hot is for serious Italian pepper lovers, so beware. An expanded menu offers a variety of meat entrées, chicken, salads, coffee, and dessert. ♦ Neapolitan/Seafood ♦ Daily, lunch, dinner, and late-night meals. 119 Mott St (entrance on Hester St). 226.8133 ♿

46 CHINATOWN INFO KIOSK

Pick up free maps and guides under a neon pagoda roof in the heart of it all. ♦ Daily. Canal St (at Walker and Baxter Sts). www.nycvisit.com ♿

47 ORIENTAL PEARL

★$ Dim sum's the favorite, but other suggested items on the extensive menu at this large, plain restaurant are Peking spare ribs, steamed flounder, and shrimp with walnuts. ♦ Cantonese/Dim sum ♦ Daily, breakfast, lunch, and dinner. 103 Mott St (between Canal and Hester Sts). 219.8388 ♿

48 EASTERN STATES BUDDHIST TEMPLE

The sparkling gold mountain of Buddhas in the window beckons you into this temple, with more than a hundred statues of Buddhas and other religious articles in the back. Neighborhood worshipers come here to pay their respects and light incense. ♦ Daily. 64 Mott St (between Bayard and Canal Sts). 966.6229 ♿

49 ORIENTAL GARDEN

★★$$ Don't be surprised: The staff often seats strangers together at one table to accommodate the crowds, which seem to be ever present. But the seafood, particularly the golden walnut prawns, is good enough to make diners forget the feeling of being packed in like sardines. ♦ Cantonese/Seafood ♦ Daily, breakfast, lunch, and dinner. 14 Elizabeth St (between Bayard and Canal Sts). 619.0085 ♿

49 JING FONG

★$$ This place is immense and all about dim sum. It's a combination of every Chinese restaurant you've ever been to, replete with lanterns, lions on pedestals, fan-shaped windows, and dragons. ♦ Cantonese/Dim sum ♦ Daily, breakfast, lunch, and dinner. 20 Elizabeth St (between Bayard and Canal Sts). 964.5256 ♿

50 HSF

★$$ These folks are especially welcoming to westerners. It's easier than usual to order dim sum here, as the restaurant offers a photographic guide to the 75 available varieties. The *ha gow* (steamed shrimp dumpling) is always a winner. A full menu is offered at dinner but isn't especially recommended. ♦ Cantonese/Dim sum ♦ Daily, lunch and dinner. No credit cards accepted. 46 Bowery (between Bayard and Canal Sts). 374.1319

51 MAHAYANA BUDDHIST TEMPLE

Behind a faux pagoda façade, directly across from the entrance to the Manhattan Bridge, the largest Buddhist temple in New York is open to the public for visits and reflection. Services are held in a decorated hall dominated by a proportionally imposing golden statue of Buddha (it's some 16 feet high, blue neon halo included). ♦ Daily. 133 Canal St (at Bowery). 925.8787

52 MANHATTAN BRIDGE

The elaborate approach to the bridge from Canal Street is a shadow of its former self, but the quality still shows. Originally known as the **Court of Honor**, the bridge—a 1905 work by **Gustav Lindenthal**—was designed so that vehicles would pass under a triumphal arch designed by **Carrère & Hastings**. Brooklyn-bound streetcars were forced to go around the arch, and the subway was hidden underneath it. The Daniel Chester French sculptures (representing Manhattan and Brooklyn) that flanked the arch were moved to the front of the **Brooklyn Museum** in 1963.♦ Between Flatbush Ave Ext (Brooklyn) and Canal St

53 ELDRIDGE STREET SYNAGOGUE

The congregation of K'hal Adath Jeshurun Anshe Lubz built this as the first Orthodox synagogue in the area at a time when other congregations were transforming Christian churches for their own use. Constructed on grand scale in 1887 by **Herter Bros.**, the main sanctuary was an opulent room with brass chandeliers and an ark imported from Italy. The building fell into disrepair—although the congregation has never missed a Sabbath—and is now restored to its original splendor. Part of the building houses a center for the celebration of American Jewish history; there are special holiday events and tours available year round. Comedian Eddie Cantor spent his boyhood in a building across the street (he answered to the name Edward Iskowitz back then). ♦ Tu, Th, and by appointment on Su. 12 Eldridge St (between Division and Canal Sts). 219.0888. www.eldridgestreet.org

54 SEWARD PARK

Two blocks of tenement buildings were removed in the early 1900s to make way for this three-acre breathing space (named for American statesman William H. Seward). In its early days, the park—the oldest municipal playground in the US—was at the forefront of public reform programs eager to give kids a pleasant spot to play; it

Film Festivals in New York City

There's no doubt New York City is a film center. Besides the many movies that are filmed here (for a selection of those, see "**Hollywood on the Hudson**," pages (62-63), there is an abundance of films that are screened here—and quite often they are world premieres. Outdoor screenings have become quite the summer thing—there are an abundance of options in all five boroughs. But since New York's arts "season" begins in fall, so begins our list.

SEPTEMBER/OCTOBER

New York Film Festival

www.filmlinc.com

A grand international roster of premieres—big-studio and independents—and red-carpet glitz. It all takes place at Lincoln Center in late September or October, and usually offers a retrospective or two in its otherwise highly competitive lineup.

New York City Horror Film Festival

www.nychorrorfest.com

This relative newbie (born in 2003) is a downtown event, usually in October, featuring primarily new genre releases, heavy on the indies.

DocFest

paleycenter.org

Late October is the time for this annual new documentary roundup, held in Midtown at the former Museum of TV & Radio (now the Paley Center for Media).

NOVEMBER/DECEMBER

New York Film and Video Festival

www.nyfilmvideo.com

This fest is tops for underground, low-budget, and non-mainstream artists. It takes place in November, usually in a downtown venue.

Avignon Film Festival

www.avignonfilmfest.com

A November event, Avignon is indie all the way—but French and American films only, both premieres and retrospectives. Screenings are often at Hunter College's Kaye Playhouse.

Margaret Mead Film and Video Festival

www.amnh.org/programs/mead

Sponsoring international documentaries every November since 1977, the American Museum of Natural History has been at the forefront of the nonfiction form's boom.

JANUARY/FEBRUARY

NY Jewish Film Festival

www.thejewishmuseum.org

This world cinema festival, held at The Jewish Museum on the Upper East Side every January, is cosponsored by the Film Society of Lincoln Center.

MARCH

New York International Children's Film Festival

www.gkids.com

All about redefining the film scene for kids, this March event has an international roster of premieres, retrospectives, animations, and more—all in a distinctive non-Hollywood vein.

APRIL/MAY

Tribeca Film Festival

www.tribecafilmfestival.org

This springtime (usually in April or May) festival hosts big studio films and indies from around the globe. They're screened in an assortment of venues around town; a kids' series plus artist panel programming run concurrently.

African Film Festival

www.africanfilmny.org

also became a gathering place for immigrants looking for day work. Its 2003 centennial capped a restoration plan that refurbished its playgrounds and spray fountains, as well as the bronze statue of Togo, a heroic husky who toted anti-diphtheria vaccine to Nome in the 1920s (inspired by, as with other park details, Seward's Alaska purchase); later improvements added a lovely garden. ♦ Bounded by Canal and Essex Sts and East Broadway. www.nycgovparks.org ♿

55 The Educational Alliance

Built in 1891 by **Arnold W. Brunner**, this is the United States' first settlement house, founded in 1889 by so-called uptown Jews, who felt an obligation to help fellow Jews in the downtown ghetto and to stem possible anti-Semitism. It held classes to Americanize youngsters, provided exercise and bathing facilities, and gave assistance to women whose husbands had deserted them, which was common among immigrant families.

frican and African Diaspora cinema are featured in this ine-day-long noncompetitive event. New and previously eleased full-length and short-format works are resented along with panel discussions; the May festival creens in Brooklyn and Manhattan.

UNE

luman Rights Watch International Film Festival

ww.hrw.org/iff

ome June, it's time for a series of films and videos—ction, documentary, and animated—selected for their uman rights themes as well as artistic merit. At Lincoln Center's Walter Reade Theater.

he New York Lesbian, Gay, Bisexual & Transgender ilm Festival

ww.newfest.org

round since 1988, this annual NewFest series favors the est new releases in international LGBT film and video, and hows them at a variety of venues, often in the East Village.

ULY/AUGUST

sian American International Film Festival (AAIFF)

ww.asiancinevision.org

creening over a two-week period at IFC in Greenwich illage and Asia Society on the Upper East Side every uly is a comprehensive program of Asian artists' films—etrospectives, US premieres, animation, and shorts.

lew York International Latino Film Festival (NYILFF)

ww.nylatinofilm.com

atino filmmakers are featured in this July festival that howcases independent artists en route to Hollywood. lorence Gould Hall in Midtown is the usual screening enue.

UMMER OUTDOORS

ll are free and run in July/August unless otherwise ndicated.

IBO Bryant Park Summer Film Festival

ww.bryantpark.org

Monday nights, June through July, musicals and old favorites are featured. Get there early (films begin at dusk) and plan to picnic—the crowd gets deep fast. (Rain dates are Tuesday nights.)

Movies with a View, Brooklyn Bridge, Brooklyn

www.bbpc.net

Sponsored by The Brooklyn Bridge Park Conservancy, free popcorn accompanies this Thursday-night film program right under the Brooklyn Bridge. Pull up a beach chair; movies begin at sunset.

Music & Movies Series, Prospect Park, Brooklyn

www.brooklynx.org

The Prospect Park Bandshell is the place for this Celebrate Brooklyn! series, which takes place on Friday and Sunday nights; most screenings are accompanied by live music. Donation requested.

RiverFlicks, Hudson River Park, Manhattan

www.hudsonriverpark.org

Pier 46, on Fridays at dusk for family fare; Pier 54, at West 13th Street, on Wednesday evenings for quirky indies and other feature-length fare. Seating is available and the popcorn is free.

Outdoor Cinema, Socrates Sculpture Park, Queens

www.socratessculpturepark.org

Wednesday-night international film screenings amidst the sculptures begin at dusk, usually preceded by jugglers, dancers, or some other creative entertainment. Films—and swell views across to Manhattan—are free; food is available for purchase.

Rooftop Films, Brooklyn and more

www.rooftopfilms.com

An innovative program of underground movies shown on a citywide roundup of rustic (and not-so-rustic) rooftops. There is some seating, but it's best to bring your own mat. Tickets may be purchased ahead online.

Among the young people the organization served was Arthur Murray, who learned how to dance here. The alliance, known at this location as the **Downtown Community Center**, still offers the local community many of the same services today, and also has an active art gallery. ♦ 197 E Broadway (at Jefferson St). 780.2300. Also at 14th Street Y: 344 E 14th St (at First Ave). 780.0800. www.edalliance.org ♿

56 Shanghai Cuisine

★★$ Catering to the City Hall crowd, this is very much a local joint offering inexpensive lunch specials. The dinner menu is a bit more exotic, featuring soup dumplings (where it really shines), braised pork in brown sauce, and other Shanghai specialties. ♦ Shanghai ♦ Daily, lunch and dinner. No credit cards accepted. 89-91 Bayard St (at Mulberry St). 732.8988

57 Bo Ky

★★$ The specialty of this popular restaurant, owned by Chiu Chow people from Vietnam, are the big bowls of steaming hot rice noodles topped with shrimp, fish, shrimp balls, or sliced roasted duck. ♦ Vietnamese/Chinese ♦ Daily, breakfast, lunch, and dinner. No credit cards accepted. 80 Bayard St (between Mott and Mulberry Sts). 406.2292

58 Great N.Y. Noodle Town

★★$ Ever since the *New York Times* rhapsodized about the salt-baked crabs here, it's been virtually impossible to get a seat—which is not to imply that it was easy to get one before. The noodles with beef are deservedly popular, as are the various crisp roasted meats—such as the pig—and the softshell crabs in season. ♦ Cantonese ♦ Daily, breakfast, lunch, dinner, and late-night meals. No credit cards accepted. 28½ Bowery (at Bayard St). 349.0923

59 Criminal Courts Building

Called the "Tombs" after its Egyptian Revival ancestor across the street, this giant ziggurat is the third Manhattan jail, the last built before prisoners were housed at Riker's Island. Designed by **Harvey Wiley Corbett** in 1939, it is an elegant Art Moderne structure (you'll recognize Corbett's hand in **Rockefeller Center**). In its day, the Tombs' 835-cell jail set a standard for penal reform: Each cell housed only one prisoner. ♦ 100 Centre St (between Hogan Pl and White St).

60 Columbus Park

The only real open space in Chinatown provides a setting for ballplaying and outdoor entertainment and is a staging area for the dragon dancers during Chinese New Year. It replaced **Mulberry Bend**, once a red-light district and part of the 19th-century slum neighborhood known as **Five Points**. ♦ Bounded by Mulberry, Baxter, Worth, and Bayard Sts. www.nycgovparks.org

61 32 Mott Street

The eponymous store founded in 1891—as Quong Yuen Shing & Co., a vendor of medicinal herbs and silk brocades and other imports, it also served the community as a social center—was renamed **32 Mott Street General Store** when the founder's grandson took the reins in the 1980s. While it has since given way to a new tenant, Good Fortune Gifts, you'll still find traces of its venerable past inside, including an intricately carved arch above the counter and some original wooden cabinetry. The sign that once spanned the storefront's two box bays is held at the **Museum of Chinese in America**. ♦ 32 Mott St (between Pell and Mosco Sts)

62 Edward Mooney House

Built in 1789, the oldest row house in Manhattan led a checkered life, first as a home to Mr. Mooney (a "butcher" or a "wealthy wholesale meat merchant and racehorse breeder," depending on your source), then as a tavern, a store and hotel, a pool parlor, a restaurant, and now a bank. A little bit Georgian, a little bit Federal style, it was restored in 1971 to its full red-brick-with-white-trim glory. ♦ 18 Bowery (at Pell St

63 88 Palace

★$$ It helps to be Chinese in this large, garish restaurant (originally known as Triple 8 Palace)—the staff can be a bit surly to outsiders. If you can get your waiter's attention, try the steamed dumplings, fresh oyster pancakes, moist and tender soy chicken and abalone, and vegetable soups. Hordes of workers stop by at lunch, and it's crowded on weekends as well. ♦ Hong Kong ♦ Daily, breakfast, lunch, and dinner. 88 E Broadway, top floor (under the Manhattan Bridge). 941.8886

64 Peking Duck House

★★$$ As the name suggests, this is the place to come for Peking duck. The thoroughly crisped delicacy is carved tableside in what is called home-style (with the flesh clinging to the skin), rather than the usual banquet style (skin only), and is served with traditional accompaniments: thin pancakes in which to roll the duck, slivered cucumbers, and a scallion brush to swab the duck with hoisin sauce. Also great as an appetizer, one order serves six hearty diners. Or get steamed pork dumplings to munch on while you wait. ♦ Beijing/Szechuan ♦ Daily, lunch and dinner. Prix-fixe dinner available. 22 Mott St (between Park Row and Pell St). 227.1810. Also at 236 E 53rd St (between Second and Third Aves). 759.8260

65 Lin's Sister

Herbs, vitamins, and various traditional medicines are carried in this Chinese apothecary. If you're feeling especially poorly, stop in at their main location on Bowery for a detailed consultation and custom prescription from an herbalist, who might recommend a tea, capsules, or a poultice; acupuncture treatments are offered here as well. ♦ Daily. 4 Bowery (between Pell and Doyers Sts). 962.5417. Also at 18A Elizabeth St (between Bayard and Canal Sts). 962.8083.

66 Doyers Vietnamese

★★★$ Chef/owner Minh Ly offers diners over 200 menu choices including *cha gio* (Vietnamese spring roll), *mon canh* (soups), *do bien* (seafood dishes), and beef or chicken with lemongrass. Wash it all down with Hué beer from Hué City, the ancient capital of Vietnam. ♦ Vietnamese ♦ Daily, lunch and dinner. 11 Doyers St, downstairs (between Bowery and Pell St). 513.1521

67 Confucius Plaza

Just to the east of the open plaza, where a bronze statue graced—in both Chinese and English—with the wise sayings of the philosopher stands, is a clunky housing development that goes by the same name. Designed in 1976 by **Horowitz & Chun** and at odds with its smaller 19th-century neighbors, this massive building solved a pressing need for more living space; its construction was at the center of a groundbreaking effort to ensure onsite employment for local Asian immigrants and other minorities. It also houses a public school whose population is almost entirely first- and second-generation Chinese. ♦ Confucius Plaza: Division St (at Chatham Sq); Housing: Bowery (between Division St and Manhattan Bridge)

68 Chatham Square

The monument in the center of this square is the Kim Lau Memorial, designed by Poy G. Lee in 1962 and dedicated to Chinese-Americans who died in World War II. Now at the crossroads of Chinatown and the rest of Lower Manhattan, and ever a lively center, Chatham Square has been called "the Times Square" of the 1800s. ♦ Park Row (at Bowery), and bounded by Broadway, St James Pl, and Catherine St.

One man's junk is another man's treasure, and Canal Street between Broadway and Sixth Avenue has a history of being a source for both. While all sorts of electronic equipment, plumbing supplies, plastics, and other gadgets and hardware, once crowded the street, these days it's mostly about knockoff designer handbags and accessories. The street was originally a wide drainage ditch carrying polluted water from the Collect Pond (eventually filled to become the Foley Square area) over to the Hudson River. Citizen complaints about the stench and the mosquito problem led to the filling of the ditch—which the city preferred to call a canal—in 1820.

69 Golden Unicorn

★★★$$ This place is decorated in sleek black and peach with mirrors everywhere, and is as vast as they come. Always bustling, it is popular with families who come to sample the amazing variety of dim sum, so be sure to arrive early. Dinner is equally good, and interestingly enough, the nonspicy dishes are better than the hot ones. Start with tasty fried dumplings, then move on to egg foo yong, salt-baked shrimp, and chicken with black-pepper sauce. ♦ Cantonese/Dim sum ♦ Daily, breakfast, lunch, and dinner. 18 E Broadway (at Catherine St), third floor. 941.0911 ♿

70 William and Rosamond Clark House

Originally built in 1824, and now landmarked by the city, this red brick—and especially the entrance—would appear to epitomize all the elegance of the Federal style. But there is a twist: It is one of the few known to have four floors (two or three were preferred). ♦ 51 Market St (between Monroe and Madison Sts)

71 First Shearith Israel Cemetery

Located near Chatham Square, which it once covered, this is the surviving fragment of the Congregation Shearith Israel's first burial ground (there are two more), the oldest Jewish cemetery in Manhattan. The earliest gravestone is dated 1683. Shearith Israel was founded by early Portuguese and Spanish settlers in 1654 and is now located uptown at a synagogue on Central Park West. (see page 284) ♦ 55 St. James Pl (between James and Oliver Sts)

72 Mariners' Temple

Designed in 1842 by **Minard Lafever**, this brownstone Greek temple was originally called the **Oliver Street Church** and served sailors based at the nearby East River piers. It is now a Baptist church whose worshipers include a widely varied community. ♦ 12 Oliver St (at Henry St)

SOHO/TRIBECA

The name **SoHo** was coined to define the district **South of Houston Street**, not to honor the neighborhood in London. Combined with the wedge-shaped territory known as TriBeCa (the abbreviated description of **Triangle Below Canal Street**), it includes the area bounded by **Lafayette Street**, the **Hudson River**, and **Chambers** and **Houston Streets**.

The area was occupied by Native Americans during the 17th century, then by farms and estates that spread between old New York and the outlying suburb of Greenwich Village. Houses were built here in the early part of the 19th century (the oldest one still standing, at **107 Spring Street**, dates from 1806), and from the 1840s to 1860s this was the center of the city, boasting the first location of the department store **Lord & Taylor**, on **Grand Street**, as well as the city's principal hotel, **The American House** at **Spring Street** and **West Broadway**.

The architectural period referred to as American Industrial flourished in this area from 1860 to 1890. Businesses opened in prefabricated cast-iron buildings fashioned to look literally like temples of commerce. By the 1960s, light industry had moved on to new areas, and Robert Moses, the city's master planner, viewed SoHo as an industrial wasteland that he wanted to level and replace with the Lower Manhattan Expressway. When that plan was abandoned in the mid-1960s, artists looking for large cheap studio space flocked there. In 1973 the city proclaimed it the **SoHo–Cast Iron Historic District**; in recognition of "the highest concentration of cast-iron architecture anywhere in the world." It was granted National Historic District status five years later (for a short cast-iron tour see page 68). By the mid-1970s, **Dia Art Foundation** had large-scale installations in place; art galleries, one-of-a-kind boutiques, and expensive nouvelle cuisine restaurants soon followed.

By the early 1980s, SoHo had become the center of New York's avant-garde art scene. Midtown's 57th Street galleries had opened branches, or even relocated there completely. New galleries and new artists found a welcome home; the scene spread and spawned outposts in TriBeCa and even the East Village. The growth of course was tied into big money. And with that, a funky alternative to staid Midtown became one that artists could barely afford. By the late 1980s the art scene had begun to shift to Chelsea (and back to 57th Street). SoHo soon became more of a mainstream shopping and dining mecca. These days there are still a few galleries to be found, and the store mix, despite a growing chain presence (Ann Taylor, Sephora), is dominated by upscale and uptown, boutiques (Chanel, Vuitton, and Armani Casa).

TriBeCa, on the other hand, retains more of a down-to-earth, neighborhood quality. The area—and its impressive brick and cast-iron building stock—is distinguished by its historic role in the 19th- and early 20th-century markets, which specialized in the butter-and-egg trade. Set on the northern fringe of the Financial District, this area has become a residential draw with a mix of young families, people in the arts, and Wall Streeters. Mom-and-pop delis, Greek coffee shops, pet shops, used-book stores, and homely appliance stores nestle right next to the hottest restaurants and bars, photo galleries, high-end home furnishings boutiques and florists, and custom bike shops—all enlivening commercial streets otherwise little changed since the 1930s.

The economies—and the residents—of both SoHo and TriBeCa were gravely affected by the events of 9/11. TriBeCa suffered most directly, with many homes and businesses requiring extensive cleanup; many of the latter closed their doors forever. But New

Washington Square Park
New York University (NYU)
E 4th St.
W 3rd St.
E 3rd St.
GREENWICH VILLAGE
WEST VILLAGE
NOHO
SOHO
TRIBECA
LOWER MANHATTAN
LITTLE ITALY
Christopher St.
Grove St.
Barrow St.
Cornelia St.
Bleecker St.
7th Ave. S
Carmine St.
Bedford St.
6th Ave. (Avenue of the Americas)
Leroy St.
Walker Park
Clarkson St.
Downing St.
W Houston St.
E Houston St.
La Guardia Pl.
MacDougal St.
Varick St.
Hudson St.
King St.
Greenwich St.
Charlton St.
Vandam St.
Spring St.
Dominick St.
Broome St.
Watts St.
Sullivan St.
Thompson St.
W Broadway
Wooster St.
Greene St.
Mercer St.
Broadway
Crosby St.
Lafayette St.
Prince St.
Renwick St.
Holland Tunnel
Canal St.
Grand St.
Howard St.
Lispenard St.
Desbrosses St.
Washington St.
Vestry St.
Laight St.
Collister St.
Hudson Square
Hubert St.
Ericsson Pl.
Beach St.
Walker St.
Church St.
White St.
Franklin St.
Cortlandt Alley
Hudson River Park
West St.
Promenade
Pier 26
Pier 25
N Moore St.
Leonard St.
Worth St.
Harrison St.
Jay St.
Staple St.
Thomas St.
Duane St.
Reade St.
Centre St.
Foley Square
Washington Market Park
Chambers St.
Rockefeller Park
River Terr.
North End Ave.
Warren St.
Tweed Courthouse
Park Pl. W
Murray St.
City Hall
Park Pl.
Jersey City
km 1/8 1/4
mi 1/16 1/8
N
1 2 3 4 5 6 7 8 9 10 11 12 13 14 15 16 17 18 19 20 21 22 23 24 25 26 27 28 29 30 31 32 33 34 35 36 37 38 39 40 41 42 43 44 45 46 47 48 49 50 51 52 53 54 55 56 57 58 59 60 61 62 63 64 65 66 67 68 69 70 71 72 73 74 75 76 77 78 79 80 81 82 83 84 85 86 87 88 89 90 91 92 93 94 95 96 97 98 99 100 101 102 103 104 105 106 107 108 109 110 111 112 113 114 115 116 117 118 119

Yorkers are a resilient lot and with the jump-start effect of the first annual **TriBeCa Film Festival** in 2002, and other creative initiatives, people from far and wide were soon drawn back to the area.

Today, whether meandering the buzzing streets of SoHo or the ever-more-upscale but more quietly charming off-grid blocks of TriBeCa, there's always a reward in looking up and catching some of the most spectacular vintage architectural details in the city. (Keep in mind that many of the area's shops and restaurants don't open until 11AM or noon. And, while those venues are usually open daily these days, art galleries are almost always closed on Sundays and Mondays; in July and August it's always best to call ahead—they may be closed entirely, or available only by appointment.)

---

1 375 Hudson Street

Say the word "advertising" and Madison Avenue naturally comes to mind. But many advertising agencies have relocated downtown, including Saatchi & Saatchi, the world's largest ad agency holding company, which occupies this building. Check out the inspiring modern art in the lobby. Most of the building's neighbors are printing companies—or used to be. ♦ At W Houston St

2 S.O.B.'s/Sounds of Brazil

★★$$ Specializing in Bahian and other Brazilian food, this casual restaurant is better known for its late-evening showcase of salsa, samba, reggae, and whatever else is currently being imported from the Caribbean, South America, and Africa. The caipirinhas (Brazil's favorite cocktail, a blend of crushed limes, sugar, and sugarcane liquor) keeps them coming back. ♦ Brazilian ♦ Cover for music. M-Sa, lunch, dinner, and late-night meals. Reservations required for dinner. 204 Varick St (at W Houston St). 243.4940

3 Film Forum

This rare independent (and nonprofit) three-screen theater was designed by **Stephen Tilly** and **Jay Hibbs**. The agenda is the same as it was when it moved here from its Watts Street location back in 1990: very smartly programmed independent American and foreign films and retrospectives. Its small café serves up fresh-popped popcorn, espresso, and cakes. ♦ 209 W Houston St (between Sixth Ave and Varick St). 727.8110. www.filmforum.org ♿

4 Depression Modern

Owner Michael Smith likes to redecorate his shop, and does so every Saturday with the Moderne furniture of the 1930s and 1940s that he spends the rest of the week restoring to its original condition. ♦ W-Su. 150 Sullivan St (between Prince and W Houston Sts). 982.5699 ♿

4 Joe's Dairy

Today, only about three storefronts remain of the old Italian-American enclave along Thompson and Sullivan Streets. This store, with its checkered tile floor and sweating glass cases, is one of them; it specializes in creamy, delectable housemade cheese. Parmigiano-Reggiano is hewn from fragrant wheels, and sweet ricotta is drawn from moist, cool containers. Smoke pours from the basement door a few times a week, when mozzarella *affumicato* (smoked) is made. ♦ Tu-Sa; call ahead for weekend hours. 156 Sullivan St (between Prince and W Houston Sts). 677.8780

5 147 Wooster Street

Designed in 1876 by **Jarvis Morgan Slade**, the arched storefront decorated with bands of fleur-de-lis and other floral motifs is all hand-carved in marble. Only the cornice is iron. ♦ Between Prince and W Houston Sts

5 Dia Art Foundation

Since its founding in 1974, Dia (from the Greek word meaning "through") has played a vital role among art institutions both locally and internationally by producing projects in every artistic medium. While their fab primary facility roosts north of the city at **Dia:Beacon**, and the **Dia:Chelsea** location is shuttered, their two SoHo locations—dedicated to installations by Walter De Maria, both from 1977—remain. His transcendent *Broken Kilometer* fills the space on West Broadway; you'll find his *New York Earth Room* at the Wooster Street location. W-Su. 141 Wooster St (between Prince and W Houston Sts). Also at 393 W Broadway (between Broome and Spring Sts) 548 W 22nd St (between 10th and 11th Aves). (See also Hispanic Society of America pages 305-306.) 989.5566. www.diaart.org

6 Moss

Fashion entrepreneur Murray Moss's high-style design store comes across as a work of visual art, with glass cases and white platforms displaying sleek meetings of form and function (from china and flatware to an Edra pink leather sofa). The downtown-chic staff may look like part of the installation too, but you'll find them courteous and impeccably informed on the provenance, materials, manufacture, and, yes, actual function of the fabulous furnishings on offer. ♦ Tu-Su. 146 Greene St (between Prince and W Houston Sts). 226.2190

7 Distant Origin

This shop stocks an impressive selection of paintings, pillows, pottery, and furniture from around the globe and features unusual silk and blown-glass lamps inspired by the work of the renowned early 20th-century textile artist Mariano Fortuny. ♦ Daily. 153 Mercer St (between Prince and W Houston Sts). 941.0025

8 Housing Works Used Book Café

Housing Works, a nonprofit organization dedicated to helping homeless New Yorkers with HIV and AIDS, has locations around the city that recycle and sell clothing and home furnishings, with great finds to be had. This SoHo space, though, is unique among them, with its 45,000-title collection of new, used, and rare books as well as a plentiful selection of CDs, cassettes, and vinyl. The pleasant, well-organized mahogany-lined store feels like a cozy library. It features comfy chairs, a café with soups and sandwiches (and beer and wine), readings, and a monthly music series. ♦ Daily. 126 Crosby St (between Prince and Houston Sts). 334.3324 www.housingworksbookstore.org ♿. Thrift Shop locations: 143 W 17th St (between Sixth and Seventh Aves). 366.0820; 157 E 23rd St (between Lexington and Third Aves). 529.5955; and other locations throughout the city

9 Sean

The chic but unpretentious casual menswear at this shop, featuring French designer Emile Lafaurie, is much favored by fashion-conscious New Yorkers. ♦ Daily. 132 Thompson St (between Prince and W Houston Sts). 598.5980. Also at 224 Columbus Ave (between W 70th and W 71st Sts). 769.1489

10 Eileen Lane Antiques

Scandinavian, Biedermeier, and Art Deco furniture and lighting are the specialty of this shop. ♦ Daily. 150 Thompson St (between Prince and W Houston Sts). 475.2988

11 Soho Wine & Spirits

You won't encounter any wine snobbery in this well-organized, well-designed outlet. For a neighborhood that's short on spirit vendors, this one's especially notable for having one of the city's best selections of single-malt Scotch whisky. ♦ M-Sa. 461 W Broadway (between Prince and W Houston Sts). 777.4332

11 I Tre Merli

★★$$ The exposed brick walls and high ceiling give this restaurant with a wine bar a quiet charm. The food—especially a large selection of homemade pastas—is quite good. The seasonal menu might include garden vegetable salads, carpaccio (raw fish and meat varieties), veal scallopini sautéed with lemon and artichokes, grilled swordfish with red peppers and capers, and the fish of the day. Desserts are homemade and also delicious. ♦ Italian ♦ M-F, lunch, dinner, and late-night meals; Sa, Su, brunch, dinner, and late-night meals. Reservations recommended. 463 W Broadway (between Prince and W Houston Sts). 254.8699. Also at 183 W 10th St (at Seventh Ave). 929.2221

12 Betsey Johnson

For more than two decades, designer Johnson's fashion statements have been providing the youthful with a statement of their own. ♦ Daily. 138 Wooster St (between Prince and W Houston Sts). 995.5048. Also at 251 E 60th St (between Second and Third Aves). 319.7699; 1060 Madison Ave (at E 80th St). 734.1257; 248 Columbus Ave (between W 71st and W 72nd Sts). 362.3364 ♿

13 Kelley and Ping

★★$ The atmosphere is pure Southeast Asian noodle shop, with bare hanging lightbulbs, floor-to-ceiling wooden cases filled with Thai herbs and ingredients, and an open kitchen that allows a full view of the chef at work. Owned by Brad Kelley of **Kin Khao** (see page 60), this informal spot has been a neighborhood favorite since it opened. Try *yam woosen* (clear noodles with chicken, shrimp, scallions, and red onion), Malaysian curried noodles, and lemongrass chicken. ♦ Asian ♦ Daily, lunch and dinner. 127 Greene St (between Prince and

W Houston Sts). 228.1212. Also at 325 Bowery (at E Second St). 475.8600

14 Academy of American Poets

Since 1934, this little-known academy has been the city's—and the nation's—headquarters for American poets. The founders of an impressive roster of programs in support of US poets, their most visible public initiative is **National Poetry Month**, held every April. They sponsor sporadic readings around the city, and their web site features a wonderful walking guide, inspired by the writings of Walt Whitman, for the **SoHo Historic District**. Call or write for a reading schedule. ♦ M-F. 584 Broadway (between Prince and E Houston Sts), 274.0343. www.poets.org ♿

14 568 Broadway

A boon for art lovers is the proliferation of gallery clusters in fine old Broadway buildings, making life easy for the browser, rain or shine. This is where you'll find **Gallery Juno**, **Westwood**, **Susan Teller**, **Michael Ingbar**, and more. ♦ Between Prince and E Houston Sts

15 Cub Room

★★★$$$ Find upscale cuisine without unnecessary formality at this sleek (think legendary 1940s Stork Club) spot established by Henry Meer (formerly of Lutèce). Appetizers such as salmon tartare, pressed vegetable terrine, and Maine crab cakes are a treat. Sesame-crusted grilled yellowfin tuna, wood-grilled lobster fricassee, and chateaubriand (for two) with wild mushrooms and shallot Burgundy sauce are adeptly prepared. End the meal with a superb poached pear or crème caramel. The wine list leans toward American varietals. Lighter meals—featuring pizzas and pot pies—are offered on the less-pricey café menu. ♦ American ♦ M-F, lunch and dinner; Sa, Su, brunch and dinner. Reservations required. 131 Sullivan St (at Prince St). 677.4100 ♿

16 Erbe

All-natural herbal products from Italy for the face, body, and hair are sold in this intimate mini-spa shop. They customize their botanicals for each recipient of the superb facials and massages offered here, by appointment. ♦ Daily. 196 Prince St (at Sullivan St). 966.1445

17 Raoul's

★★$$$ This lovely old-fashioned bistro has wooden floors, an Art Deco bar, leather booths, and an antique stove in the center of the room. In pleasant weather, diners can sit in the garden room behind the kitchen. Try the pan-seared foie gras, steak au poivre and rare breast of duck with green apples. The extensive wine list includes French, Italian, Spanish, American, and Australian wines. ♦ French ♦ Daily, dinner and late-night meals. Reservations recommended. 180 Prince St (between Thompson and Sullivan Sts). 966.3518

17 Hans Koch Ltd.

Fine leather belts and handbags are featured in this shop, as well as jewelry, hand-beaded with semi-precious stones. If nothing suits your fancy, Mr. Koch will whip up something that does. ♦ Daily. 174 Prince St (between Thompson and Sullivan Sts). 226.5385

18 Milady's

★$ Opened in 1920, this is a refreshingly untricked-up basic neighborhood bar that is frequented by locals who come for beer and good conversation. The simple entrées include great burgers, sandwiches, and zesty salads, a jukebox and pool table provide entertainment. ♦ American ♦ Daily, lunch and dinner till 4AM. 160 Prince St (at Thompson St). 226.9340

18 Vesuvio Bakery

★$ A SoHo landmark, this charming storefront has been selling chewy loaves of bread, breadsticks, and addictive pepper biscuits since 1928. Passed on to close friends of the original owners in 2002, the onetime Dapolito family business has changed a bit, but all to the good: they added a small café serving tasty meals—usually including some of their incredible coal-oven-baked bread. ♦ M-Sa. 160 Prince St (between W Broadway and Thompson St). 925.8248

19 Aveda Esthetique

This national chain of beauty stores and salons sells environmentally and ecologically friendly products in a soothing, sumptuous SoHo space. As their slogan says, "It's a great day!"—Step in and enjoy. ♦ Daily. 456 W Broadway (between Prince and W Houston Sts). 473.0280. Also at locations throughout the city

20 Louis K. Meisel

Owner Meisel championed the photorealists—think John Baeder, Chuck Close, Richard Estes—back in the 1970s and has stuck to his convictions despite the art world's ever-changing tides. ♦ Tu-Sa (call first in summer). 141 Prince St (between Wooster St and W Broadway). 677.1340. www.meiselgallery.com ♿

21 Stuart Moore

Visit this jewelry shop if you are in the market for exceptionally well-made (and expensive) jewelry in 18K gold or platinum. Custom work is the specialty, and the markup on gemstones is claimed to be lower than elsewhere—though the high-quality metal they use may also be priced higher than at other jewelers. ♦ Daily. 128 Prince St (between Greene and Wooster Sts). 941.1023

21 Reinstein/Ross

This is a shop devoted entirely to exquisite jewelry created by Susan Reinstein. She works primarily with multicolored sapphires and 22K gold, often alloyed in subtle colors, most of which she has developed herself. ♦ Tu-Su. 122 Prince St (between Greene and Wooster Sts). 226.4513. Also at 29 E 73rd St (between Madison and Fifth Aves). 772.1901

22 Apple Store

The grand, clear glass stairway you encounter as you walk into the historic former post-office building that houses this Apple Computer store is just like the stairway to heaven. Or what we'd imagine it to be, especially for computer geeks of the Mac persuasion. It's bright and light—computers, monitors, keyboards, even the software boxes all seem to have a glow about them. From iPods to blazing-fast towers, it's one of the few places in New York where you can see all the latest and the best from Apple—all spread out and ready for you to test drive—and get your ailing equipment looked over (though they'll likely need to keep it a bit to fix it) while you wait. ♦ Daily. 103 Prince St (at Greene St). 226.3126 ♿. Also at 767 Fifth Ave (between E 58th and E 59th Sts). 336.1440 ♿

23 Fanelli's Cafe

★$ A holdover from the days when SoHo was a neighborhood of factories, this café has a tavernlike atmosphere. The ambience is the greater draw; except for the terrific hamburgers and fries, the food is adequate. ♦ American ♦ Daily, lunch, dinner, and late-night meals. No credit cards accepted. 94 Prince St (at Mercer St). 226.9412

24 Zoë

★★★$$$ The food is ever-changing and consistently improving at Thalia and Stephen Loffredo's stylish restaurant, where the crowd is the perfect mix of uptown types meeting downtowners. Don't pass up the crispy calamari with Vietnamese dipping sauce. For a hearty main course, choose from char-grilled Argentine natural beef with Linzano-glazed vegetable skewers and Chimichurri sauce, lightly smoked Chilean sea bass on grilled asparagus, endive, and trevisano salad with roasted grapefruit vinaigrette, and other savory surprises. ♦ Contemporary American ♦ M, lunch; Tu-F, lunch and dinner; Sa, Su, brunch and dinner. Reservations recommended. 90 Prince St (between Broadway and Mercer St). 966.6722. Also at **Zoë Townhouse,** 135 E 62nd St (between Lexington and Park Aves). 752.6000

25 Lure Fishbar

★★$$$ The large basement space under Prada (below) is home to this cavernous and strenuously stylish restaurant, which serves—no surprise here—fish in its many guises: raw shellfish, crudo, sautéed, poached, or grilled, all adorned with a special sauce or extravagant topping. Designed by **CAN Resources** into a teak-lined luxury yacht, Lure is a refuge from the clamor of the street above (claustrophobes worry not, there are big windows—porthole-shaped, of course—facing Prince Street). ♦ Eclectic ♦ Daily, lunch and dinner; Sa, Su, brunch. 142 Mercer St (at Prince St). 431.7676

25 Prada

What was once the Guggenheim's SoHo outpost became architect **Rem Koolhaas**'s NYC architectural statement of the early 2000s. From the outside windows you might think you're looking into a giant wave-ride, with mannequins surfing the crest. Of course they're clothed in Prada. The whole line is here at this flagship store—from the expected shoes to dresses, bags, and even objets d'home and skin-care items. ♦ 575 Broadway (at Prince St). 334.8888. Also at other locations throughout the city

26 Savoy

★★★$$$ Run by chef/owner Peter Hoffman and his wife, Susan Rosenfeld, this cozy place features an eclectic menu that follows the seasons. An interior face-lift for the new millennium made a smart switcheroo. The main floor is now mostly taken up with a sleek yet friendly bar and café; the remodeled second floor is a cozy aerie for fine dining. The creative menu may include such popular choices as salt-crust-baked duck with braised kale, blood oranges, and black olives, and monkfish with chickpea fritters, bacon-braised collard greens, and green peppercorn bordelaise. Desserts might feature warm chocolate cake with clementine sorbet and orange sauce, coconut panna cotta with rum-roasted pineapple, or a coffee hazelnut napoleon. The carefully chosen wine list spotlights artisan vintners. ♦ Continental ♦ M-Sa, lunch and dinner; Su, dinner. Reservations recommended. 70 Prince St (at Crosby St). 219.8570 ♿

27 280 Modern

Decorative arts are this gallery's draw, with an emphasis on designer furniture from the 1920s to the 1960s. There is also a small selection of original works by the late Piero Fornasetti of Milan. ♦ M-Sa; Su, by appointment. 280 Lafayette St (between Prince and Jersey Sts). 941.5825 ♿

28 WNYC

After more than 80 years at One Centre Street, WNYC New York Public Radio moved in 2008 to snazzy new headquarters with a street-level, public-welcoming broadcast and event space (formally, the Jerome L. Greene Performance Center). ♦ 160 Varick St (at Charlton St). 669.3333. www.wnyc.org ♿

29 Il Bisonte

These fine handcrafted leather goods are known for their casual style: Handbags, portfolios, luggage, and accessories come straight from Florence. ♦ Daily. 120 Sullivan St (between Spring and Prince Sts). 966.8773

Giovanni da Verrazano, an Italian-born navigator sailing for France, was the first European to see New York, when he discovered New York Bay in 1524. Henry Hudson, an Englishman employed by the Dutch, reached the bay and sailed up the river now bearing his name in 1609, the same year that northern New York was explored and claimed for France by Samuel de Champlain.

30 Omen

★★$$$ Quiet and attractive, this restaurant with exposed brick walls, light fixtures wrapped in filmy white fabric, and gleaming dark tables has cultivated a loyal following. The namesake dish, omen (Japanese noodles served with a variety of toppings and flavorings), is a perfect introduction to the authentic, traditional Kyoto-style menu, which includes a tuna steak with ginger, oysters-in-miso casserole, raw tuna with mountain yam and quail eggs, yellowtail and string bean teriyaki sautéed with sake, and seafood tempura. ♦ Japanese ♦ Daily, dinner and late-night meals. Reservations recommended. 113 Thompson St (between Spring and Prince Sts). 925.8923

30 Peter Fox Shoes

All Peter Fox designs for women, inspired by Victorian and medieval styles, are handmade (except for the stitching that attaches the sole to the rest of the shoe) in Italy. ♦ Daily. 105 Thompson St (between Spring and Prince Sts). 431.7426

31 Peter Hermann

This small shop provides the finest handbags, belts, and luggage in the world, mostly from Europe. It's also one of the few places in the US where you'll find Mandarina Duck, a hi-tech luggage line from Italy. ♦ Daily. 118 Thompson St (between Spring and Prince Sts). 966.9050

32 Detour

The accent is on a European sensibility in this collection of clothing for men and women. ♦ Daily. 425 W Broadway (between Spring and Prince Sts). 219.2692

33 Taschen Books

Philippe Starck gets design credit for this shoebox-shaped flagship of the high-style German art publisher, with jazzy floor-to-ceiling wall murals by Brazilian artist Beatriz Milhazes. A downstairs gallery, to which a staffer escorts you, displays works by Taschen artists. ♦ Daily. 107 Greene St (between Cana and Spring and Prince Sts). 226.2212. www.taschen.com

33 agnès b.

Classics for men, women, and children—such as V-necked sweaters and cotton T-shirts—are made modern with a twist by this French designer with a loyal following. ♦ Daily. 103 Greene St (between Spring and Prince Sts). 925.4649. Also, for women's apparel only, at 13 E 16th St (between Fifth Ave and Union Sq W). 741.2585; 1063 Madison Ave (between E 80th and E 81st Sts). 570.9333

34 Little Singer Building

This 12-story building, designed by **Ernest Flagg** in 1904 to accommodate offices and factory space for the Singer Manufacturing Company, exudes a jaunty appeal that's totally in tune with the neighborhood. For the façade Flagg made ample use of loft-style oversized glass panes, terra-cotta paneling, and tasteful cast-iron ornamentation. Note the lacy wrought-iron flourishes on the eleventh floor; they are reminiscent of the base of the Eiffel Tower, which was completed while Flagg studied architecture in Paris. The big Singer Building (in case you were wondering) was also designed by Flagg but no longer exists: The 41-story tower on lower Broadway was demolished by the U.S. Steel Corporation in 1967 to make room for a more commodious edifice. ♦ 561-563 Broadway (between Spring and Prince Sts)

35 560 Broadway

This fine old brick structure holds its own in a sea of cast-iron neighbors. It was remodeled to house an ebb-and-flow of distinguished art galleries. Usually open Tuesdays through Saturdays, among them are **Staley-Wise** (966.6223; www.staleywise.com), whose artistic roster is centered on masters of fashion photography, from Horst to Lillian Bassman, Bert Stern, Louise Dahl-Wolfe, and more; **Janet Borden**, whose stable of hard-hitting photographers includes the likes of Lee Friedlander, Larry Sultan, E.J. Bellocq, Fred Cray, and Robert Cumming (431.0166; www.janetbordeninc.com); and **David Nolan** (925.6190; www.davidnolangallery.com), who features prints, drawings, and paintings by contemporary artists Richard Artschwager, Alice Maher, and Jim Nutt. ♦ At Prince St

Within 560 Broadway:

Dean & DeLuca

The ultimate and original high-tech gourmet grocery is housed here in 9,700 square feet of space. Wonderful kitchenware, cookbooks, and samplings from the world's gastronomic centers are displayed with extraordinary panache. Added bonuses: a coffee/espresso bar, butcher, fish counter, and a full range of prepared take-out dishes. This place is a must for anyone passionate about food. ♦ Daily. Ground floor. 226.6800. ♿ Also at Borders bookstores and other locations throughout the city

36 Blue Ribbon

★★$$$ The acclaimed flagship of the Bromberg Brothers restaurant empire, the kitchen of this bustling spot stays open very late, which is one reason it's a favorite stop for chefs who arrive after their own shifts end. The other incentive is the eclectic menu, featuring such dishes as duck breast with orange sauce, paella *basquez* (with seafood and chicken), and shrimp Provençal. The wine list is small but well chosen, and desserts, such as the banana split, will transport you back to your childhood. ♦ Eclectic ♦ Daily, dinner and late-night meals. 97 Sullivan St (between Spring and Prince Sts). 274.0404. Also at Blue Ribbon Sushi, 119 Sullivan St (between Prince and Spring Sts). 343.0404; 278 Fifth Ave (between First St and Garfield Pl), Brooklyn. 718/840.0408; Blue Ribbon Bakery, 35 Downing St (at Bedford St). 337.0404

37 Mezzogiorno

★★$$$ Designed by architect and interior designer **Roberto Magris**, this airy restaurant opens onto the sidewalk during the warmer months. Highlights include wood-fired pizzas, vibrant salads, and wholesome homemade pasta specials. For starters, try the fresh tuna carpaccio or the eggplant croquettes. Then follow with a hearty entrée of *taglierini alla ciociara* (pasta with cherry tomatoes, prosciutto, peas, and mozzarella) or the pasta of the day. ♦ Italian ♦ Daily, lunch, dinner, and late-night meals. 195 Spring St (between Thompson and Sullivan Sts). 334.2112

38 Snack

★$ Greek snack, that is. Though you'd never guess it from the name, tasty Greek food is what this tiny restaurant serves to weary SoHo shoppers and loyal locals alike. The Greek salad is delicious, with just the right combination of tangy tomatoes, onions, cucumbers, and feta, as are standards like tzatziki and skordalia. Or try any of the sandwiches, pastries stuffed with chicken and olives, and vegetarian souvlaki. ♦ Greek ♦ Daily, lunch and dinner. No reservations. 105 Thompson St (between Spring and Prince Sts). 925.1040. Also at **Snack Taverna**, 63 Bedford St (at Morton St, near Seventh Ave). 929.3499

39 Paracelso

A moderately priced source for women's clothes made from natural fibers, this store features styles—many from India—that are casual and loose-fitting. ♦ Daily. 414 W

Broadway (between Spring and Prince Sts). 966.4232

40 Kin Khao

★★$$ Still a fun find for Thai fare, this cavelike restaurant offers decent versions of such traditional dishes as *pad thai* (sautéed noodles with shrimp, egg, and peanuts) or *por pia sod* (vegetable spring rolls). Flavorful *massaman kari* (beef, coconut curry, and potatoes with peanut sauce), *kwaytio ki mow* (sautéed spicy rice noodles with basil and tomatoes), and fresh *pla pow* (whole grilled fish in banana leaves) are great main dishes. ♦ Thai ♦ Daily dinner. No reservations. 171 Spring St (between W Broadway and Thompson St). 966.3939

41 Boom

★$$$ Innovative creations at this popular SoHo spot for "world cuisine" range from sesame-crusted rare tuna to avocado blini with lobster, osetra caviar, and crème fraîche. The candlelit setting is eclectic yet romantic. ♦ Eclectic ♦ Daily, lunch and dinner; Sa, Su, brunch and dinner. 152 Spring St (between Wooster St and W Broadway). 431.3663

42 Manhattan Bistro

★★$$$ Its charming French bistro look complements the classic and sometimes creative cuisine. For starters, try the salmon combo (cured, smoked, and poached). Entrées might include monkfish choucroute with a cabbage-stuffed pastry shell and vegetable breadcrumbs, and rack of lamb with braised fingerling potatoes. For dessert, indulge in the "chocolate molten" with home-made chocolate ice cream or a made-to-order soufflé. The wine list is good. ♦ French ♦ M-F, lunch and dinner; Sa, Su, brunch and dinner. Reservations recommended for dinner. 129 Spring St (between Greene and Wooster Sts). 966.3459

43 Judd Foundation

Designed by **Nicholas White** in 1870, this building displays a sensitive approach to the use of cast iron as complex ornament. It also happens to be the late sculptor Donald Judd's former New York home and studio, and the only remaining single-use building in the **Cast-Iron Historic District**. Judd's will decreed that it be preserved precisely as he left it: with the early works of his 1960s and '70s contemporaries—among them Dan Flavin, Carl Andre, John Chamberlain, and Frank Stella—placed just so, a reflection of Judd's own artistic aesthetic. Tours, every Friday at 11AM; reservations required. ♦ 101 Spring St (at Mercer St). 219.2747. www.juddfoundation.org

44 New York Open Center

Each year this education center offers hundreds of workshops, courses, lectures, and performances that explore spiritual and social issues, psychology, the arts—in short, all aspects of traditional and contemporary world culture. Check out the bookstore for the latest literature on all of the above. ♦ Bookstore: daily. 83 Spring St (between Crosby St and Broadway). 219.2527 www.opencenter.org

45 Balthazar

★★$$$ Even if celebrity restaurateur Keith McNally's brasserie wasn't filled with picture-perfect model types, it would still merit a visit because of the picture-perfect Paris bistro décor and surprisingly good food. French classics like onion soup and escargot share the menu with updated comfort cuisine like duck shepherd's pie and rabbit rillette with apricots. There's a good selection of well-priced wines, along with draft beers and traditional French aperitifs like Cynar (distilled from artichokes). Save room for the rich desserts, some of which can be bought at their adjacent bakery. If your name—or style—doesn't have star value you probably won't get one of the cozier booths or window tables, but the equalizing, frenetic bar at the entrance provides a perfect vantage point for star-spotting. Yen for their bread or pastries? Stop at their small bakery right next door. ♦ French bistro ♦ M-F, breakfast, lunch, and dinner; Sa, Su, brunch and dinner. Reservations recommended well in advance. 80 Spring St (between Crosby St and Broadway). 965.1414

46 Kate's Paperie

Kate's is a treasure of pulp-based finds: gorgeous handmade papers sold by the sheet, exquisite stationery (from the very proper to the properly craftily funky), and all the ribbons, pens, journals, rubber stamps, and everything else you might want to wrap—or write—the stuff of your dreams. ♦ Daily. 72 Spring St (between Lafayette and Crosby

Sts) 941.9816. Also at 8 W 13th St (between Fifth and Sixth Aves). 633.0570; 140 W 57th St (between Sixth and Seventh Aves). 459.0700; 1282 Third Ave (at W 74th St). 396.3670

47 Spring Street Natural

★$ The health-oriented menu is mostly vegetarian, but almost any appetite can be satisfied in this airy place filled with greenery. Line-caught fish and free-range poultry—especially stir-fry and the roasted chicken with honey-mustard glaze—are among the best nonvegan choices. ♦ American ♦ M-F, breakfast, lunch, dinner, and late-night meals; Sa, Su, brunch, dinner, and late-night meals. No reservations. 62 Spring St (at Lafayette St). 966.0290

48 The Ear Inn

★$ The building that houses this dark and dusty 1817 bar/restaurant near the river has been designated a landmark. Back then, the shoreline was only five feet from the entrance, and the place was filled with seafaring rowdies. Today, it offers poetry and other spoken-word events and serves crowds of landlubbers decent pub food, including burgers and sandwiches. ♦ American ♦ M-Sa, lunch, dinner, and late-night meals; Su, brunch, dinner, and late-night meals. 326 Spring St (between Greenwich and Washington Sts). 226.9060

49 New York City Fire Museum

The NYC Fire Department's own collection of apparatuses and memorabilia dating back to Colonial times is combined here with that of the Home Insurance Co. This is the largest exhibition of its kind in the country, and if you have youngsters in tow they won't complain a bit about the long walk west when they discover this is the destination. ♦ Admission suggested. Tu-Su. 278 Spring St (between Varick and Hudson Sts). 691.1303. www.nycfiremuseum.org ♿

50 Country Café

★★$ The rustic décor starts with the rooster sign outside and continues inside with pale yellow walls dotted with illustrations of farm animals, wood pumpkins on shelves, and dried flowers scattered artfully about. Just as earthy is the delicious food. Try the wild mushroom casserole, onion tart, Cornish hen with tarragon juice, hanger steak with shallot sauce, and the rich tarte Tatin. There's also a good, inexpensive wine list. ♦ French ♦ Tu-Th, dinner and late-night meals; F, lunch and dinner; Sa, Su, brunch and dinner. Reservations recommended. 69 Thompson St (between Broome and Spring Sts). 966.5417

51 Barolo

★★$$$ In inclement weather, the dining room provides a sophisticated setting; but once the weather warms up, the scene moves to the charming back garden. There's excellent pasta made daily on the premises, including a ravioli that changes daily. Standout main courses include a delicious grilled chicken breast stuffed with goat cheese, savory breaded veal chop topped with fresh tomato and arugula, and whole sea bass baked in salt. ♦ Italian ♦ Daily, lunch, dinner, and late-night meals. Reservations recommended. 398 W Broadway (between Broome and Spring Sts). 226.1102 ♿

52 Ceramica

Classic Italian patterns appear on imported linens, mosaics, and earthenware—the Rafaelesco, a dragon pattern Raphael used on many of his frames, is particularly beautiful. Everything is handmade, most of it hailing from Italy. ♦ Daily. 59 Thompson St (between Broome and Spring Sts). 941.1307

53 O.K. Harris Works of Art

A SoHo landmark since 1969, this gallery—one of the few that never fled—is a record-setter, with more than 60 artists represented and an average of 50 exhibitions each year in its 11,000-square-foot spread. Ivan Karp, an early champion of Pop Art, is the gallery's founder and chief point man. ♦ Tu-Sa; closed August. 383 W Broadway (between Broome and Spring Sts). 431.3600. www.okharris.com

54 Morgane Le Fay

The window at this women's clothing boutique is always austere and monochromatic. Featured inside is clothing designed by Liliana Ordas—flowing dresses, coats, capes, and skirts in a wide range of wool flannels, wool crepes, jerseys, and velvets. ♦ Daily. 67 Wooster St (between Broome and Spring Sts). 219.7672. Also at 746 Madison Ave (between E 64th and E 65th Sts). 879.9700 ♿

55 The King of Greene Street

Greene Street offers a concentration of the best of SoHo's surviving cast-iron architecture (see page 68 for a stroll up its entire five-block stretch) but even here this industrial palace is a standout. It is one of four on this street designed by **Isaac**

Hollywood on the Hudson

New York was a thriving film production city long before the sunny skies of Hollywood began to lure producers and filmmakers west in the early 1900s. D.W. Griffith loved to shoot here, and Mack Sennett's Keystone Kops ran rampant through Coney Island.

The city goes out of its way to court the film industry: There's a special mayor's office to act as an industry liaison, to provide police protection for stars and production crews, and even to help arrange scenes ranging from helicopter chases to historical location settings. Movie, TV, and commercial production ranks among the city's top growth industries: wander around town enough and it's likely you'll come across a film crew of some sort in action.

And it's no wonder that many visitors to movieland's Gotham get a feeling of déjà vu. Here are but a very few of the movies and locations you may remember:

Arthur (1981), in which Dudley Moore questions his date's (Liza Minnelli) profession just a bit too loudly in the **Oak Bar** at the **Plaza Hotel**.

Big (1988) stars Tom Hanks and Robert Loggia performing a charming impromptu musical number at **FAO Schwarz**.

Bonfire of the Vanities (1990), based on Tom Wolfe's novel, captures Sherman McCoy's world of **Upper East Side** privilege and debauchery. Courtroom scenes were filmed on location in the **Bronx**.

Breakfast at Tiffany's (1961), in which Audrey Hepburn and George Peppard find love on **Fifth Avenue**.

Bright Lights, Big City (1988) finds Michael J. Fox in the fast lane in the film adaptation of Jay McInerney's bestselling novel.

John Sayles's *The Brother from Another Planet* (1984) has low-tech space-traveler Joe Morton washing up on the shores of (soon-to-be-restored) **Ellis Island**, then moving on to **Manhattan**, with a stay on the streets of **Harlem**.

Crocodile Dundee (1987), in which Paul Hogan checks in at the **Plaza** while visiting from Down Under.

Desperately Seeking Susan (1984) portrays Rosanna Arquette as a suburban housewife and her unexpected adventures with Madonna in **Battery Park**.

Die Hard with a Vengeance (1995), in which Bruce Willis and Samuel L. Jackson track down a mad bomber (Jeremy Irons) on the streets of New York.

Dog Day Afternoon (1975) stars Al Pacino and two cohorts who turn a simple **Brooklyn** bank robbery into chaos.

First Wives Club (1996), in which Goldie Hawn, Diane Keaton, and Bette Midler wreak havoc and revenge on their ex-husbands in such places as **Café des Artistes** and **Barneys New York**.

Fort Apache, The Bronx (1981), in which Paul Newman fights the bad guys in this crime-ridden part of the **Bronx**.

The French Connection (1971) casts Gene Hackman as the unforgettable cop Popeye Doyle as he tracks drug smugglers in a spectacular car chase along Brooklyn's **Stillwell Avenue**.

Funny Girl (1968) has Barbra Streisand sharing the spotlight with the **Statue of Liberty**.

Ghostbusters (1984), in which Bill Murray, Dan Aykroyd and Harold Ramis move into (and blow the roof off) the **No. 8 Hook and Ladder Firehouse** in **TriBeCa** and finally come to terms with these supernatural beings at **55 Central Park West**.

The Godfather (1972), the first of the trilogy, stars Al Pacino, Marlon Brando, James Caan, Diane Keaton, and Robert Duvall in a little look at Little Italy (and the mob). Part I's survivors return in 1974 for Part II, with Robert De Niro.

GoodFellas (1990), a Martin Scorsese film in which Robert De Niro, Ray Liotta, and Joe Pesci rise in the mob ranks.

Hannah and Her Sisters (1986), Woody Allen's Manhattan-based family drama starring Mia Farrow, Barbara Hershey, and Dianne Wiest. Michael Caine, Carrie Fisher, Sam Waterston, and Allen add to the angst

Duckworth in 1873 and was called the "King of Greene Street" (the "Queen" is at **No. 28-30**). It is actually two buildings that pass as one, whose five-floor columned, cast-iron façade is a masterpiece of French Second Empire. ♦ 72-76 Greene St (between Broome and Spring Sts)

56 Bar 89

★$$ The clean white space is predictably SoHo, but the immense curved bar and skylit cathedral ceiling lend a dramatic sense of place to a surprisingly low-key atmosphere. Have a Manhattan, or order a light meal from the casual American menu. Incidentally, the high-tech, second-floor bathrooms here are not to be missed: It seems like the doors of the stalls are transparent, but thanks to some artful lighting, they (thankfully) are not. ♦ American ♦ Daily, lunch and dinner. 89 Mercer St (between Broome and Spring Sts). 274.0989

57 521-523 Broadway

Nothing but this section remains of the luxurious **St. Nicholas Hotel**, which was *he Lost Weekend* (1945), in which Ray Milland uffers the DTs at **Bellevue Hospital** after a three-day ender.

anhattan (1979), with Mariel Hemingway and Michael lurphy, is Woody Allen's perfect and beautiful black-nd-white valentine to New York. His 1977 *Annie Hall* is n especially charming slice of New York quirk and haracter.

anhattan Murder Mystery (1993) features Woody llen as a New York book editor, with Diane Keaton, as is wife, delving into the mysterious disappearance of eir neighbor.

ean Streets (1973), Martin Scorsese's slice of life in **ittle Italy** starring a young Robert De Niro and Harvey eitel.

idnight Cowboy (1969), in which Dustin Hoffman and on Voight stop traffic at **West 58th Street** and **Sixth venue**.

iracle on 34th Street (1947) is the classic tale that roves there really is a Santa Claus. A young Natalie ood costars with Maureen O'Hara.

oonstruck (1987) has Cher finding love with Nicolas age at the **Metropolitan Opera**.

ight Falls on Manhattan (1997), Sidney Lumet's rama about police corruption, starring Andy Garcia, akes its cast to the **Municipal Building**, the **US ustoms House**, and **Bowling Green**.

n the Town (1949), a musical by Leonard Bernstein, etty Comden, and Adolph Green, is the quintessential ew York picture, with Frank Sinatra, Gene Kelly, and nn Miller dancing from **Wall Street** to **Rockefeller enter**.

he Pawnbroker (1965) is Sidney Lumet's film of a ewish concentration camp survivor (Rod Steiger) unning a pawnshop in **Harlem**.

rince of Tides (1991) stars Barbra Streisand as a New ork psychiatrist who helps a high school football coach Nick Nolte) uncover his darkest secrets.

Ransom (1996), directed by Ron Howard, stars Mel Gibson as a distraught father trying to save his kidnapped son. Scenes include **Central Park**'s **Bethesda Fountain** and the **Heliport** at **61st Street** and the **FDR Drive**.

Rosemary's Baby (1968) highlights the **Dakota Apartments** (West 72nd St and Central Park West) in Roman Polanski's film, starring Mia Farrow and John Cassavetes.

Saturday Night Fever (1977) shows John Travolta's life as he tries to escape his dead-end career as a disco king. His identity crisis reaches a climax atop the **Verrazano-Narrows Bridge** when a friend falls to his death.

Serpico (1974) features Al Pacino fighting corruption in the NYPD, with location shots at **New York University**.

Sophie's Choice (1982) stars Meryl Streep and Kevin Kline, who reside in **Flatbush** at 101 Rugby Road.

Superman (1978) finds Clark Kent, the mild-mannered reporter for the *Daily Planet,* saving the world—and Lois Lane. The former **Daily News Building** is featured.

The Taking of Pelham One Two Three (1974) finds subway riders at the mercy of extortionists on the **IRT**'s No. 6 train.

Taxi Driver (1976), a Martin Scorsese film in which Robert De Niro discovers his talents for cleaning up New York's crime-ridden streets.

A Tree Grows in Brooklyn (1945), based on Betty Smith's novel, stars Dorothy McGuire and Joan Blondell in the depiction of a troubled family.

West Side Story (1961) pits two street gangs on the **West Side**. Director Robert Wise's opening scene takes place between Amsterdam and West End Avenues at West 68th Street.

When Harry Met Sally (1989) features a memorable scene in which Meg Ryan demonstrates to Billy Crystal the art of sexual deception as they share a meal at **Katz's Delicatessen** on the **Lower East Side**.

built in 1854 and once extended along Broadway, Mercer, and Spring Streets. Its original frontage on the three streets was 750 feet. Inside, the rugs, tapestries, crystal chandeliers, and beveled mirrors made it a tourist attraction even among visitors who couldn't afford to stay there. The bridal suite, filled with satin, lace, rich rosewood, and crystal, was considered the best place to begin a happy marriage. Today, purveyors of footwear for the feet are sold on street level: **Puma** (334.7861) and **Lady Footlocker** (965.0493) ♦ Between Broome and Spring Sts

58 495 Broadway

Proof that hope springs eternal, this handsome brick-and-stone structure with fine iron panels, designed by **Alfred Zucker** in 1893, replaced an 1860 cast-iron building at almost the same time the district began its decline. ♦ Between Broome and Spring Sts

59 Bloomingdale's

Canal Jeans was once the king of lower Broadway at this very same location. In a firm confirmation of the shopification of SoHo, Bloomingdale's created a southern outpost here, renovating this previously pedestrian interior and converting it into a palace. Bloomie's-style means six floors of retail, joined by a grand escalator. While you might find a quaint brick wall or two, and lots of windows uncovered for natural light, this is still the classic Bloomingdale's shopping experience—lots of buzz, lots of goods. ♦ 504 Broadway (between Broome and Spring Sts). 729.5900. Also at 1000 Third Ave (between E 59th and E 60th Sts). 705.2000

60 Joanne Hendricks Cookbooks

Behind a dubious wooden door in a crumbling landmark building, an admirable collection of books, kitchen antiques, and ephemera includes an LP of Alice B. Toklas reading from her own cookbook. On your way out, glance across the street at the flowing glass folds of Dutch architect Winka Dubbeldam's Greenwich Street Project. ♦ Daily. 488 Greenwich St (between Canal and Spring Sts). 226.5731. www.joannehendrickscookbooks.com

61 The Cupping Room Cafe

★$$ This tightly packed, brick-walled spot is where locals go for a great Sunday brunch. Everything from waffles and giant muffins to bagels with the fixings and terrific coffees is worth the visit. Noteworthy lunch and dinner selections include shrimp quesadilla and black-pepper fettuccine with homemade chicken sausage. There's live jazz every Wednesday and Friday night. ♦ Continental ♦ Daily, breakfast, lunch, and dinner; Sa, Su, brunch and dinner. Reservations recommended for dinner. 359 W Broadway (between Grand and Broome Sts). 925.2898.

62 59 Wooster Street

Originally a warehouse, this six-story building, designed by **Alfred Zucker** in 1890, dominates the corner where it stands. Its mass is relieved by arched, iron-rimmed windows on its Broome Street façade, and by highly sculptural reliefs scattered over its surface. The seemingly random play between the rough-hewn masonry, smooth brickwork and crenellated roofline (look hard and you'll see hand-size human faces way up top) somehow pulls the building together and gives it an oddly noble presence. It's best seen from the south side of Broome Street. ♦ At Broome St

Within 59 Wooster Street:

Brooke Alexander

In luxurious quarters designed by the English architect **Max Gordon**, this gallery features painting, sculpture, and American prints since 1960 by such contemporary masters as Ed Ruscha, Raymond Pettibon, Richard Tuttle, Jasper Johns, Roy Lichtenstein, and Donald Judd, as well as a selective inventory of works by younger American artists and Europeans. ♦ W-Sa. Second floor. 925.4338. www.baeditions.com ♿

63 Gourmet Garage

This produce emporium offers a wide variety of goods at decent prices. Whether you're looking for a supply of crusty breads, blood oranges, Portobello mushrooms, sun-dried tomatoes, kalamata olives, Parmigiano-Reggiano, English farmhouse cheddar, or one of several chutneys, this store probably has it. ♦ Daily. 453 Broome St (at Mercer St). 941.5850. Also at other locations throughout the city

64 Haughwout Building

Famous as the building that contained New York's first elevator (a reminder of which is a small rusting sign over the door just to the left of the main entrance), this cast-iron Italian palazzo was designed by **John Gaynor** and built in 1857. The building now houses a **Staples**. In its former life, it was E.V. Haughwout's cut-glass and silver store. ♦ 490 Broadway (at Broome St)

65 486 Broadway

Built in 1883 by **Lamb & Rich**, this titanic former home of the Mechanics Bank combines Romanesque and Moorish elements in brick, stone, and terra-cotta. Look up at the mansard roof with its projecting windows and small cupolas. ♦ At Broome St

66 L'Orange Bleue

★★$$ "The earth is blue like an orange," wrote the French poet Paul Eluard (in French, of course), and his rather luscious observatio

The Best

Elliott Kanbar

President, QUAD CINEMA

Conservatory Garden, Central Park. The closest you'll get to a stunning English garden without buying an air ticket.

Battery Park and Marina. Walking on the **Esplanade** on a warm summer night is simply heavenly. And don't forget about the view of the beautifully lit **Statue of Liberty** in the harbor.

Café at the 79th Street Boat Basin. Almost like being in Saint-Tropez.

Rooftop at the Metropolitan Museum of Art. A great spot for grabbing lunch while enjoying the breathtaking views of Central Park.

Grand Central Station. It was once close to being demolished, and after a major renovation. It's now perhaps the grandest railroad station in the world.

West 11th and 12th Streets between Fifth and Sixth Avenues. Tourist buses don't go here (much), but these two streets represent Greenwich Village at its best.

Federal Reserve Bank of New York. Take the tour. The highlight will be seeing the immense Gold Vault.

The Frick Collection. More than just a fascinating museum, it will give you a glimpse of how the rich and famous once lived.

Central Synagogue. Brilliantly restored after a devastating fire, it's now, perhaps, the most beautiful synagogue in the country.

New York Public Library Reading Room. Will take your breath away. After the visit, stroll in the adjacent and rejuvenated **Bryant Park** with its famous café.

applies as much to this romantically charged, appealingly louche edge-of-SoHo watering hole and eatery as it does to the planet at large. For here you'll find a Gallic-exotic ambience—think faintly lit deep orange walls, gorgeous North African lighting fixtures, and the Gipsy Kings—and French-Moroccan menu in uncommon harmony. Tagine and couscous dishes are uniformly generous and served in thickly glazed ceramic earthenware, which amplifies the earthy and large-group-pleasing vibe of the place. ♦ French/Moroccan ♦ M-F, dinner; Sa, Su, brunch and dinner. 430 Broome St (at Crosby St). 226.4999

67 Holland Tunnel

Built in 1927, this was the world's first underwater tunnel for vehicles, dipping nearly a hundred feet below the surface of the Hudson River. The tunnel is about 29 feet wide, with a 12-foot ceiling. Its north tube is 8,558 feet long, and its south tube stretches 8,371 feet. **Clifford M. Holland** was the man who masterminded this engineering marvel, and the feat secured his name in New York—and American—history. ♦ Between Watts St and Boyle Plaza (Jersey City, New Jersey)

68 Beau Brummel

Ralph Lauren began his career designing ties for this store. Today, most of the men's clothing and accessories sold here are by European designers. ♦ Daily. 347 W Broadway (between Grand and Broome Sts). 219.2666. Also at 287 Columbus Ave (between W 73rd and W 74th Sts). 877.3689

69 The Drawing Center

This elegant space, designed by **James Stewart Polshek** in 1986, is an important nonprofit exhibition space for unaffiliated artists, as well as for exceptional scholarly shows of works on paper from historical and contemporary periods. ♦ Tu-Sa. 35 Wooster St (between Grand and Broome Sts). 219.2166 www.drawingcenter.org. ♿

69 Performing Garage

This space is home to **The Wooster Group**, one of America's oldest experimental theater companies, founded in 1967 by director Richard Schechner. Under the direction of Elizabeth LeCompte, it redefines traditional notions of story line, thematic content, and performance structure. These days The Wooster Group also performs at **St. Ann's Warehouse** in DUMBO (718/254.8779). ♦ 33 Wooster St (between Grand and Broome Sts). 966.3651. www.thewoostergroup.org

70 Artists Space

One of the most original and certainly among the most successful of the alternative-space galleries, this perennial springboard for new talent maintains a file of about 4,000 artists from New York State and New Jersey, which is used by collectors, curators, and architects in search of an artist who falls into a specific category: conceptual, feminist, under 35, etc. ♦ Tu-Sa. 38 Greene St (between Grand and Broome Sts). 226.3970 ♿

71 Pearl River Mart

Any Sinophile's passion for clothing and housewares can be satisfied in this packed multilevel store. Choose from very well-priced cotton T-shirts, silk jackets, pillowcases, sheets, and bedspreads in pastel pinks, blues, and yellows, embroidered with flowers and animals. For Chinese cooking, an easy-to-use wok with a wooden handle is a great find. Serious furniture, at serious prices, fills the upper level. ♦ Daily. 477 Broadway (between Grand and Broome Sts). 431.4770 ♿

72 478 Broadway

Of all the cast-iron buildings in New York, this one, built in 1874 and designed by **Richard Morris Hunt**, was hailed by the magazine *Architectural Record* as the "most serious attempt to utilize the almost unlimited strength of the material." ♦ Between Grand and Broome Sts

73 Café Noir

★★$$ A relaxed European vibe, funky music, and late-night hours are the draws at this little bar-restaurant on the southern fringes of SoHo. The eats are just okay, but come for the fun of it. ♦ French ♦ Daily, 11AM-4AM; M-F, lunch and dinner; Sa, Su, brunch and dinner. 32 Grand St (at Thompson St). 431.7910

74 Lola

★$$$ Relaunched in 2007 with (ex-Le Cirque) chef Jennifer Printz at the stove, this former Chelsea favorite now calls these swell Tribeca digs—with an onyx bar and lantern-lit outdoor space—home. Try Lola's BBQ pork sliders, Prince Edward mussels three ways, and, of course, the onion rings. ♦ Caribbean/Soul ♦ M-F, lunch and dinner; Sa, Su, brunch and dinner. Reservations recommended. 15 Watts St (between W Broadway and Thompson St). 675.6700

75 Félix

★★★$$$$ Another player in the see-and-be-seen intersection of Grand Street and West Broadway, this place, like nearby **Lucky Strike**, attracts a cross-section of models, downtown hipsters, and trendy professionals who dine on such bistro fare as *moules du Père Tin-Tin* (steamed mussels in white wine), cassoulet, roasted chicken, and steak frites. The outdoor café is a good place to people-watch. ♦ French bistro ♦ Daily, lunch and dinner. Reservations required. 340 W Broadway (between Grand and Broome Sts). 431.0021

76 Lucky Strike

★$$ This very popular late-night hangout is a place people come to sit, talk, and eat. Bistro bites such as steak frites or lentil salad over arugula are served. ♦ French bistro ♦ M-F, lunch, dinner, and late-night meals; Sa, Su, brunch, dinner, and late-night meals. 59 Grand St (between Wooster St and W Broadway). 941.0772

77 IF

Inside this cavernous space you'll find high-end clothing for men and women, from the likes of designers Martin Margiela, Ivan Grundahl, Dries Van Noten, Comme des Garçons, and Vivienne Westwood—all cut from the same edge SoHo was known for in its earlier days. ♦ Daily. 94 Grand St (between Mercer and Greene Sts). 334.4964

78 Ingo Maurer

Ready to trade in your torchière for a Campbell's soup can on a wire? The staff of Munich-based Maurer will find you the lighting you need, be it a custom design or a starburst of broken crockery called *Porca Miseria!* ♦ Tu-Su. 89 Grand St (at Greene St). 965.8817

79 Yohji Yamamoto

Themes of recent collections by this talented Japanese designer have included turn-of-the-century Eastern Europe and haute couture with an asymmetrical twist. The prices are high, but the shop is worth a visit even if only to see the iron, rolled-steel, and bronze fixtures designed in London by Antony Donaldson. ♦ M-Sa. 103 Grand St (at Mercer St). 966.9066 ♿

80 Le Pain Quotidien

★$$ This airy bakery-restaurant began as Le Pain Quotidien and Communal Table, a reference to the oversized tables around which diners—solo and not—nibble at a variety of high-quality salads, sandwiches made with Euro-style breads, and baked goods. But this Belgian chain's noblest offering may well be its chocolate chip cookie, a crisp disk as thin and wide as a flapjack and bursting with flavor. ♦ Daily, breakfast and lunch (until 7:30PM). No reservations. 100 Grand St (between

Broadway and Mercer St). 625.9009. Also at other locations throughout the city

81 Ted Baker

Listen up, guys and gals: If Banana Republic and The Gap aren't quite cutting it anymore, and your wallet has fattened accordingly, check out the comfortably stylish threads at the New York outpost of this British designer. For men, cool shirts with innovative fabrics are a Ted Baker trademark, but there are great pants, sport coats, and accessories, too. Brit-o-phile women will appreciate the velvet tuffets and teapot décor on their side of this nook; clothes for her have simple wearable lines made special with unique detailing. Daily. 107 Grand St (at Mercer St). 343.8989 ♿

82 L'Ecole

★★$$$ This handsome restaurant with soft lighting and high ceilings is run by the students of the famed **French Culinary Institute**, which is located here. Alain Sailhac (formerly the chef at Le Cirque and Le Cygne) oversees as head chef and does double duty as Dean of Culinary Studies. The decently priced, three-course lunches and four- or five-course dinners change daily; selections might include classic French onion soup, country-style pâté, marinated venison stew, and sage-roasted rack of lamb. A short selection of wines by the glass is available. ♦ French ♦ M-F, lunch and dinner; Sa, dinner. Reservations recommended. 462 Broadway (at Grand St). 219.3300

83 443 Broadway

In a neighborhood of iron buildings pretending to be stone, this five-story building, designed by **Griffith Thomas** in 1860, is the real thing, and it's a real beauty, once you get past the altered ground floor. ♦ Between Howard and Grand Sts

84 Capsouto Frères

★★★$$$ The setting—a spacious multilevel room in a wonderfully neighborhood-dissonant 1891 landmark building—is calm and inviting, and provides a perfect backdrop for its fine contemporary French cuisine. Choose from among such entrées as ravioli St. Jacques aux Champignons (homemade ravioli with scallops and mushrooms), roasted duckling with a ginger and black currant sauce, red snapper in a nage of star anise broth and a confetti of vegetables, or steak au poivre. Soufflés here are legendary—chocolate, raspberry, pear, and pumpkin varieties may be offered, depending on the season—but all desserts are excellent, including the profiteroles, raspberry-laced napoleon, and "overstuffed" tarte Tatin with crème fraîche. The impressive wine list emphasizes French and Californian wines. ♦ Contemporary French ♦ M, dinner; Tu-F, lunch and dinner; Sa, Su, brunch and dinner. Prix-fixe available at lunch and dinner. Reservations recommended. 451 Washington St (at Watts St). 966.4900

85 Makor

Open to everyone, though geared mostly to the 20- and 30-something singles set, the Makor program of the venerable **92nd Street Y** (see pages 257-258) moved into this custom-designed space by **Kostrow Greenwood Architects** in 2008 after a stint on the Upper West Side. Offering a lively roster of cultural events by night, their growing Daytime programming is enjoyed by baby boomers on the flip side ♦ 200 Hudson St (between Vestry and Desbrosses Sts). 413.8867. www.92y.org ♿

SOHOGRANDHOTEL

86 SoHo Grand Hotel

$$$$ This stylish 15-story **William Sofield**-designed hotel sprouted here in the 1990s along with SoHo's surge to glam. The interior lobby and public areas reflect the art-influenced neighborhood with their combined Art Deco and modern design. Note the intricate work on the elaborate wrought-iron and glass stairway in the lobby. The 365 rooms are small, but boast amenities *du jour* like flat-screen TVs, iPods and Bose sound docks (on request), and Frette bathrobes. Top-floor rooms are more spacious and offer memorable skyline views. Their fitness and business centers, as well as room service, are available 24/7. The Grand Bar, opposite the lobby lounge, is a popular watering hole.

Until the late 1700s, the western area of what is today called TriBeCa was owned by Trinity Church (Broadway, between Rector and Thames Sts). Its most prominent parishioners, who were probably also those with the most generous wallets, had streets named after them: (John) Chambers, (James) Duane, and (Joseph) Reade.

The Best

Gregg Pasquarelli

Principal, SHoP Architects

Sitting on the steps beneath "Alma Mater" at **Columbia University** on any pleasant sunny afternoon in one of the grandest outdoor spaces in the city.

Strolling along **Roosevelt Avenue** in **Woodside** and **Jackson Heights** in **Queens**. One of the best places in New York to observe that the American dream of immigration remains alive and well and is not something relegated to the history books.

The front barroom at **Keen's Chop House** on **West 36th Street**, sitting under the spell of "Miss Keen's" when the Knicks are playing.

Evenings wandering around the side streets of the **Far West Village west of Hudson Street**—romantic historicism without nostalgia. Walking down dark streets and seeing the blue glow from television sets in apartment windows casting a ghostly spell all around you.

The remaining neighborhood shops and restaurants of **Arthur Avenue** and the **Belmont section** of **The Bronx**—the real Little Italy of New York City.

Walking in the park at the north end of **The United Nations** complex—modernist Corbusian splendor reminiscent of an era when New York believed in the power of the future.

The moment the uptown 4 train goes aboveground and the first sight of **Yankee Stadium** appears—as the el passes the right-field stands you can get a momentary glimpse of the playing field from the train, which is probably the only place in the country you can see professional sports while riding public transportation.

The sausage, black olive, and fresh garlic pizza at **Lombardi's** on **Spring Street**.

Late-night cab rides between bars in **Lower Manhattan** in the rain watching the urban kaleidoscope of neon reflecting off the droplets on the taxi's windows, especially holding hands with someone you love.

The Gallery restaurant on the parlor floor offers classic American cuisine (daily, breakfast, lunch, and dinner; Sa, Su, brunch. Reservations recommended. 965.3588 ♿). The hotel is pet-friendly—and guests can even order up a complimentary pet goldfish for the length of their stay. ♦ 310 W Broadway (between Canal and Grand Sts). 965.3000, 800/965.3000; fax 965.3200. www.sohogrand.com ♿

87 Greene Street Cast-Iron Tour

The five, mostly cobble-stoned blocks of Greene Street—from Canal Street north to West Houston Street—are in the heart of the SoHo Cast-Iron Historic District (designated in 1973), an area taken over by textile manufacturing and other light industry after the retail and entertainment center of the city moved north in the mid-19th century. The 50 cast-iron buildings still intact here were built between 1869 and 1895. Functionally, cast iron anticipated modern steel-frame building techniques, but decoratively, it was used to imitate styles and manners of traditional masonry construction. Designers particularly loved ornate Renaissance and neoclassical motifs, which they altered with a free and fantastical hand.

The instant you step into almost any of the shops that line this corridor, you'll see that solidly columned interiors remain intact. But for now, we'll just look at some superb exteriors. To begin, walk north from Canal Street, and, on your left, don't miss the detail at No. 31, by **George W. DaCunha** (1876). The two arguably most outstanding buildings on Greene—both are in excellent condition—are by **Isaac Duckworth**: Nos. 28-30 (1872; see pages 61-62), just across the street on this same block between Canal and Grand Streets, a magnificently mansarded 1872 representative of the Second Empire style with leafless Corinthian columns, and, one block north, between Broome and Spring Streets, Nos. 72-76. From 1873, it is also Corinthian, but here treated in an Italianate manner with a pedimented porch and porticoes all the way up the projecting center bays. This building was constructed for the Gardner Colby Company, whose initials appear on the pilasters. Noteworthy in the next block north, between Spring and Prince Streets, are the arched lintels and columns, with their egg-and-dart motifs, of **Nos. 114-120**, designed in 1882 by **Henry Fernbach** as a branch of a department store. The Ionic capitals turned sideways at **Nos. 132-134**, **136**, and **138** (1885) are worth a look while you're between Prince and West Houston Streets. Of course, not all of the buildings on Greene Street are cast iron. Several masonry buildings of the same period sport decorative ironwork as well—**Nos. 42-44**, **52**, and **84-86**, for example—and one is, well, paint. While you're walking uptown on Greene, raise your gaze above the street-level shops to your left as you approach Prince Street. The brick wall you'll see set back from the corner is graced by what remains of Richard Haas's now rather weathered trompe l'oeil mural (1975) of a cast-iron façade. ♦ Between Canal and W Houston Sts

88 F. ILLI PONTE

★★★$$$ A pan-Italian showplace, and as old school as they come, complete with downstairs bar, upstairs cigar lounge, wood-burning oven, French rotisserie, and a dining room that offers a panoramic view of the Hudson River. Main-course selections inspire and satisfy: Choose from pan-roasted chicken breast with baby artichokes, white striped bass and salmon on risotto, or flavorful veal chop with Marsala and black truffles. All pastas are homemade. Desserts are rich, and the wine list is formidable. ♦ Italian ♦ M-F, lunch and dinner; Sa, dinner. Prix-fixe available at dinner. Reservations required. 39 Desbrosses St (at West St). 226.4621 ♿

89 SCHOOLHOUSE ELECTRIC

As befits an outfit that makes its wares only from vintage molds, this Portland-based concern has found a historic building in which to set up New York shop. Among the early- to mid-20th-century designs with hand-blown shades, you'll find Deco, Arts & Crafts, and Mission-inspired styles. ♦ Tu-Sa. 27 Vestry St (at Hudson St). 226.6113 ♿

90 TRIBECA CINEMAS

A central site of the acclaimed **Tribeca Film Festival** also hosts premieres, performances, and private functions. ♦ 54 Varick St (at Laight St). 941.2001. www.tribecacinemas.com ♿

91 WHITE STREET

An eclectic range of styles reflects the history of the TriBeCa cast-iron district. There are more attractive streets nearby, but none more typical. Contrast the authentic Federal details of **No. 2**, which was originally built as a liquor store in 1809; the artful stonework of **No. 10**, which was designed by **Henry Fernbach** in 1869; and the mansard roofline of **No. 17**. The upper stories of **Nos. 8** and **10** are shorter than the lower floors—a favorite Renaissance Revival device that makes the buildings appear taller. ♦ Between Sixth Ave and W Broadway

91 MONTRACHET

★★★★$$$ It's a family venture back here, where it all started for brothers Drew and Tracy Nieporent. The low-key setting created by **Spanier & Daniels** is stylish, and the contemporary French cuisine, artfully prepared by Remi Lauvand, always excellent. Favorite entrées include roasted wild bass with flageolets and tomatoes and truffle-crusted salmon prepared with a red wine fumet. Desserts are also exceptional—especially the passion-fruit Bavarian with warm berries and banana-and-chocolate gratin on linzer crust. ♦ French ♦ M-Th, dinner; F, lunch and dinner; Sa, dinner. Reservations recommended. 239 W Broadway (between White and Walker Sts). 219.2777

92 LET THERE BE NEON

Founded by the late Rudi Stern, one of America's foremost neon artists, this gallery is now the front room for the eponymous neon (and diode-driven) signage fabricator. It features sensational clocks, chairs, windows, signs, stage sets, and interiors, all in neon or any number of cutting-edge lighting technologies. ♦ M-F. 38 White St (between Broadway and Church St). 226.4883. www.lettherebeneon.com

93 FRANKLIN STATION CAFE

★★$$ Edith Piaf croons in the background and there's a running slide show of artsy photographs in this airy, refreshing space dedicated to fresh Malaysian dishes with a French twist. Highlights of the delightfully illustrated menu include vegetable curry with coconut curry sauce, Rendang chicken with roasted coconut and ginger, and seafood laksa, a dish with fish, shrimp, and red clams in a coconut curry soup. Simple dishes such as mango curry shrimp and noodles in peanut satay sauce with pineapple, romaine, and tofu are equally flavorful, and icy fresh fruit shakes (try the mango) and homemade tarts add to the appeal. ♦ Malaysian French ♦ Daily, breakfast, lunch, and dinner. 222 W Broadway (at Franklin St). 274.8525

94 CHURRASCARIA TRIBECA

★★$$$ This downtown outpost of the famous **Churrascaria Plataforma** in midtown aims for the business dollar and delivers in spades. Tourists stumbling in should be forewarned that vegetarians—despite an extensive vegetable selection—need not apply. The banquet-style buffet features mouth-watering appetizers, before the main event—a nonstop orgy of delectable meats, including lamb, beef, chicken, ham, sausage, innards—is served at your table. Order a full pitcher of caipirinhas (a cocktail of sugarcane liquor and lime) to wash it all down and savor this version of the Brazilian experience. ♦ Steak house ♦ M-Th, dinner until late; F-Su, lunch and dinner until late. Reservations recommended. Prix-fixe. 221 W Broadway (between Franklin and White Sts). 925.6969. Also at **Churrascaria Plataforma**, 316 W 49th St (beween Eighth and Ninth Aves). 245.0505

95 SoHo Photo Gallery

Here you'll find the oldest and largest cooperative gallery for photographers in New York. There's always a fresh view to be had in this homey meandering space. ♦ Th evening, F-Su. 15 White St (between Sixth Ave and W Broadway). 226.8571. www.sohophoto.com

96 Tribeca Grand Hotel

$$$$ The sister hotel to the SoHo Grand a few blocks north, the Y2K-vintage Tribeca Grand caters to a similar entertainment-industry, hipster, and wannabe-hipster crowd. It even has a private, 98-seat movie screening room (its an occasional venue for the **Tribeca Film Festival**). As would be expected of a hotel in downtown Manhattan, attention has been paid to style—maybe too much. The lobby is a darkish mishmash of dark browns and orange, lodged underneath an eight-story atrium with wraparound hallways. The unlovely color scheme is fortunately not echoed in the 203 small but soundproofed guest rooms, but these too suffer from lack of warmth (though they do have a high-speed computer setup and other Grand amenties). However, if you really want to stay in TriBeCa and can't afford a loft, you don't have much choice. Take consolation in the staff, which is friendly, and your temporary pet goldfish companion. Their **Church Lounge** (drinks and light fare) fills much of the ground-floor atrium space. ♦ 2 Sixth Ave (at Church St). 519.6600, 877/519.6600; fax 519.6700. www.tribecagrand.com

97 Arqua

★★$$$ The poor acoustics in this pretty, peach-colored dining room with white, flying saucer-shaped light fixtures make conversation difficult. Concentrate instead on the food, especially the pappardelle with duck-and-mushroom sauce, gnocchi with tomatoes, and rabbit braised in white wine and herbs. ♦ Italian ♦ M-F, lunch and dinner; Sa, Su, dinner. Reservations recommended. 281 Church St (at White St). 334.1888

98 Tribeca Grill

★★★$$$ In 1990, Drew Nieporent teamed up with several celebrity partners, including actor Robert De Niro, to open this loftlike restaurant in the former Martinson Coffee Building. Enhancing the space are original artworks by De Niro's late father, Robert Sr., and custom-designed Tiffany chandeliers by David Rockwell. The menus change frequently but might include such contemporary offerings as pan-seared ruby red trout served with roast purple potatoes and citrus beurre blanc; herb fettuccine with caramelized cauliflower, wild mushrooms, and light Parmigiano cream; and roasted pheasant with chestnut stuffing and lingonberry sauce. For dessert, try a classic crème brûlée or the banana tart with milk-chocolate-malt ice cream. ♦ American ♦ M-F, lunch and dinner; Sa, dinner; Su, brunch and dinner. Reservations recommended. 375 Greenwich St (at Franklin St). 941.3900 ♿

99 Nobu

★★★★$$$$ Another venture by Drew Nieporent and Robert De Niro, this David Rockwell-designed spot is a wonderland of out-of-this-world sushi overseen by Los Angeles's star chef, Nobu Matsuhisa. The million-dollar fairy-tale forest setting features a copper-leaf ceiling, wooden floors with stenciled cherry blossoms, birch trees, and a wall of 50,000 black river pebbles. The food is as innovative as the décor. Try the Matsuhisa Specialty, black cod with miso, or the squid "pasta" (strips of seafood with mushrooms and asparagus in a garlic-flavored red-pepper oil). Desserts include a trio of pot de crème (green tea, ginger, and coffee custard) and The Bento Box, a warm chocolate soufflé cake with shiso syrup and green tea ice cream. For a casual version of the same (though no less pricey; the sushi's still the best), try waiting for a table at reservation-free **Next Door Nobu** at the same location (but call 334.4445). ♦ New Japanese ♦ M-F, lunch and dinner; Sa, Su, dinner. Reservations required. 105 Hudson St (at Franklin St). 219.0500. ♿ Also at 40 W 57th St (between Fifth and Sixth Aves). 757.3000

100 Urban Archaeology

Gil Shapiro's seemingly infinite collection of architectural ornaments and artifacts—mostly salvaged, some convincingly reproduced—is on view in this multilevel TriBeCa space (the uptown location is much smaller). Some of the city's hippest lodgings and restaurants get their lighting and plumbing fixtures here, so if you want your W.C. to look like a W Hotel, take a look. An entire floor is dedicated to a superb selection of glass and ceramic tile, shown in place, irresistibly, with the bath fixtures. ♦ M-F (also open Sa in winter). 143 Franklin St (between W Broadway and Hudson St). 431.4646, 431.6969. Also at 239 E 58th St (between Second and Third Aves). 371.4646

101 Chanterelle

★★★★$$$$ In the grandly high-ceilinged ground floor of the historic redbrick and limestone **Mercantile Exchange** (1872-1884), acclaimed chef/owner David Waltuck and his wife, Karen, provide an exquisite dining experience. Bedecked with prints, drawings, and lithographs, as well as stunning floral arrangements, the restaurant's lovely décor (and pretty yellow interior designed by Bill Katz) complements its original, artfully presented, and always delicious cuisine. Try the signature seafood sausage to start, followed by noisettes of venison or breast of moulard duck with citrus marmalade. Perfect endings include one-of-a-kind creations such as orange spiced crème brûlée with blood orange-Cointreau ice cream. The wine list is quite good; the service is flawless. ♦ French ♦ M-W dinner; Th-Sa, lunch and dinner. Reservations required. 2 Harrison St (at Hudson St). 966.6960 ♿

102 Puffy's Tavern

Renovated and reopened in 2005 after a tenuous hiatus, Puffy's managed to retain a bit of the atmosphere of a speakeasy, which it was during Prohibition. This pre-TriBeCa bar pulls you in from the street to have a beer, hang out, and listen to the jukebox with the after-work crowd and neighborhood regulars. ♦ Daily, 4PM-4AM. No credit cards accepted. 81 Hudson St (at Harrison St). 766.9159

103 Knitting Factory

An impressive if rather studiously avant-garde weekly roster of performances—everything from jazz to poetry readings to the latest performance art—are held in this lively two-level venue. ♦ Cover. Shows daily; call for schedules. 74 Leonard St (between Broadway and Church St). 219.3055

104 Harrison Street Row

Originally built in 1828 and restored in 1975 by **Oppenheimer**, **Brady & Vogelstein**, this row of impeccably restored Federal houses acts as an antidote to the massive apartment houses above it. ♦ 37-41 Harrison St (between Greenwich and West Sts)

105 Independence Plaza

Built in 1975 by architects **Oppenheimer**, **Brady & Vogelstein** and **John Pruyn**, this 40-floor middle-income housing project is a little off the beaten path but has great views of the river. ♦ Greenwich St (between Chambers and N Moore Sts)

106 A.L. Bazzini Company

While the nuts Bazzini has specialized in since 1886 are now roasted off-site (in the Bronx), you can still buy them in bulk here, as well as purchase a full array of gourmet treats, including breads, vinegars, preserves, pesto sauces, great coffee beans, and exotic condiments and spices. There are also a few tables at which to enjoy such homemade prepared foods as overstuffed peanut-butter-and-jelly sandwiches (among others), pastries, cookies, cakes, and muffins. ♦ Daily. 339 Greenwich St (at Jay St). 334.1280

107 American Telephone & Telegraph Long Lines Building

Designed by **John Carl Warnecke & Associates** and built in 1974, this almost windowless (except for the high, squared portholes) edifice houses a wealth of impressive electronic wizardry for communications. Texturized pink Swedish granite contrasts with vertical stripes of a beige granite used for decoration. ♦ Church St (between Thomas and Worth Sts)

108 Shoofly

At this retailer's cozy nook of a shop you may want to only admire—not actually buy—the adorable children's shoes, hats, tights, socks, and other accessories on offer, as many cost more than parents spend on themselves. The colorful Euro-shoes go up to US women's size 9, and are displayed on low shelves that children can reach (gulp!); the cunning chapeaux are either from Europe or made by local artisans. ♦ Daily. 42 Hudson St (between Duane and Thomas Sts). 406.3270

109 The Odeon

★★$$ Manhattan meets the Left Bank at this neon-lit space, a hot brasserie for the downtown art crowd when it first opened in 1980 and still going strong. Try the filet mignon au poivre with creamy potatoes dauphinois or homemade spinach-and-ricotta ravioli. Recommended on the lower-priced brasserie menu are the crab cakes and the steak frites. For desserts, you can't go wrong with the yummy profiteroles or cranberry-apricot bread pudding. ♦ American/French ♦ M-F, lunch, dinner, and late-night meals; Sa, Su, brunch, dinner, and late-night meals. Reservations recommended. 145 W Broadway (between Duane and Thomas Sts). 233.0507 ♿

110 Duane Park Cafe

★★★$$$ This comfortably elegant restaurant offers relative quiet in a pretty

NYC Goes Green: Gardens in the City

Beyond the grand parkscape treasures of **Prospect Park** (page 330) in Brooklyn, **The Greenbelt** in Staten Island (page 333), or **Central Park** (pages 262-264) in Manhattan, New York is a wonderland of hidden garden oases. Tucked between the tallest towers in Midtown or within winding Village streets, they offer a fine respite from the ceaseless thump of the city—and a sense of wonderment at their simply creative beauty. Here are just a small selection of these urban jewels:

Manhattan:

Hudson River Park, with its bikeway and walkway that run for five miles north from Battery Place to West 59th Street. Special stretches include the entire southern stretch up past the World Financial Center (including **Wagner** and **Rockefeller Parks**), and from Pier 40 (Clarkson Street) through Pier 54 (West 13th Street) in the West Village.

City Hall Park (page 18)

Battery Bosque & Park (page 34)

Abingdon Square (page 83)

Jefferson Market Garden (page 82)

Madison Square Park (page 119)

Gramercy Park (page 122)

Greenacre and **Paley Parks** (page 202)

Ford Foundation Atrium (pages 219-220)

Bryant Park (page 220)

Carl Schurz Park (page 225)

Conservatory Garden (page 265)

Heather Garden (Fort Tryon Park) (page 301)

Riverside Park (page 295)

Bronx:

Wave Hill (page 318)

Van Cortlandt Park (page 318)

New York Botanical Garden (page 319)

Queens:

The Noguchi Museum (page 323)

Queens Botanical Garden (page 325)

Brooklyn:

Brooklyn Botanic Garden (page 330)

Green-Wood Cemetery (page 331)

Staten Island:

Chinese Scholar's Garden (Staten Island Botanical Garden) (page 332)

Jacques Marchais Museum of Tibetan Art (page 333)

room with cherry-wood accents. Standouts include miso-marinated duck breast with arugula, crispy skate with ponzo and tempura vegetables, pan-seared yellowfin tuna and roast garlic potato gratin with eggplant caponata, and a delicious chocolate hazelnut strudel with homemade banana ice cream. ♦ New American ♦ M-F, lunch and dinner; Sa, Su, dinner. Reservations recommended. 157 Duane St (between W Broadway and Hudson St). 732.5555

Heroes have been honored with parades along lower Broadway since Colonial times. President Theodore Roosevelt was the first to be showered with ticker tape, as part of his welcome home from an African safari in 1910. Flags flew and paper cascaded from every window of every building, except one: The building at 26 Broadway, across from Bowling Green, didn't even raise a flag that day. It was the home of John D. Rockefeller, whose Standard Oil was involved in an antitrust suit instigated by the old "Rough Rider" himself. These days the tons of ticker tape that once filled the air have been replaced by shredded computer printouts.

111 Second Hand Rose

Antiques dealer Suzanne Lipschutz (a.k.a. Second Hand Rose) fills 5,000 square feet with treasures primarily from the 19th century, with an emphasis on Moorish designs. Her impressive stock ranges from custom-made leather furniture to a wide selection of unusual lamps and antique wallpaper and a rare representation of vintage rolled linoleum. ♦ M-F; Sa, Su by appointment only. 138 Duane St (between Church St and W Broadway). 393.9002 ♿

112 Bouley

★★★★$$$$ David Bouley's got a food complex: shopping, cooking, and dining (some of New York's finest), all within one short stretch of West Broadway. Under an atmospheric vaulted ceiling, the eponymous restaurant serves superbly executed New

French creations (foie gras with mango pearls and rosemary-apple purée, Maine day-boat lobster with vanilla baby bok choy, chocolate brioche pudding with prune-Armagnac ice cream) that combine with polished (not stuffy) service for a genuinely lovely experience. Want to try this at home? Across Duane Street, at **Bouley Bakery and Market**, you can buy ingredients prepped by Bouley's kitchen staff—diver scallops, vegetables, soup bases—as well as house-brand ice cream, aged prime meats, hundreds of cheeses, and 50 kinds of bread. The Bakery also offers light fare (panini, bento boxes) and seating (unreserved) for its eating. Above the Bakery, **Upstairs** serves as a cooking school by day, a modestly priced 30-seat (also unreserved) restaurant by night. ♦ New French ♦ Daily, lunch and dinner. Reservations required. Bouley, 120 W Broadway (at Duane St). 964.2525. Upstairs and Bouley Bakery and Market, 130 W Broadway (at Duane St). No reservations taken. 608.5829

113 Stuyvesant High School

Built in 1991 by **Alexander Cooper & Partners** to replace the overcrowded Beaux Arts location on East 15th Street, this is one of the most prestigious and progressive public high schools in the country. The building is not open to the public. ♦ 345 Chambers St (at West St)

114 Tribeca Performing Arts Center

Housed in Borough of Manhattan Community College, the center supports emerging artists and eclectic programs in theater, music, and dance. ♦ 199 Chambers St (between Greenwich and West Sts). 220.1460. www.tribecapac.org ♿

115 Washington Market Park

Progress has reduced the former **Washington Market** to this little park. In its day, the market extended up along the river from Fulton Street into this neighborhood. Even Washington Street, which once formed its spine, is now just a one-block thoroughfare between Vesey and Barclay Streets. (Though many New York households stocked their larders with goods from the old market, it was essentially a wholesale produce exchange—now centered at Hunt's Point in the Bronx.) The park that remains is one of Manhattan's better play areas for young children. It is clean, safe, and, from a kid's point of view, great fun. Look for outdoor music concerts in warm weather and a bit of the razzle-dazzle of the **Tribeca Film Festival** in the spring, as many of its events swirl around the adjacent **Tribeca Performing Arts Center** and the surrounding area. ♦ Between Chambers and Greenwich Sts

116 P.S. 234

Though this imaginatively designed school, built in 1988 by architect **Richard Dattner**, is not open to the public, be sure to study the fanciful blue-green iron fence by artist Donna Dennis that encloses the schoolyard. ♦ 292 Greenwich St (at Chambers St).

117 Ecco

★$$ Carved mahogany, beveled mirrors, and a high tin ceiling provide atmosphere for a crowd of Wall Streeters and art dealers; the pastas are recommended. ♦ Italian ♦ M-F, lunch and dinner; Sa, dinner. Reservations required. 124 Chambers St (between Church St and W Broadway). 227.7074

118 The Mysterious Bookshop

The amazingly informed staff here—headed by indefatigable proprietor Otto Penzler—will help you ferret out the book you're looking for among the thousands, both new and out of print, in this two-level shop. ♦ Daily. 58 Warren St (between Church St and West Broadway). 587.1011. www.mysteriousbookshop.com

119 Fountain Pen Hospital

Expert staff, top-notch repair, and the largest pen selection in the world. ♦ M-F. 10 Warren St (between Broadway and Church St). 964.0580 ♿

GREENWICH VILLAGE/MEATPACKING DISTRICT

Radical and old guard, quaint and glitzy, authentic and ersatz, Greenwich Village i anything but a homogeneous neighborhood. Bounded by **Broadway**, the **Hudso River**, and **West Houston** and **14th Streets**, America's birthplace of the bohemian spiri is home to students of **New York University** (NYU), actors in Off-Broadway theaters, jaz musicians, and more than ever an assortment of other, less-than-bohemian residents wh work elsewhere. Greenwich Village's eccentric personality starts with its layout. In th 1790s, the area's country estates were sold off in lots or subdivided and developed b large landholders. Weavers, sailmakers, and craftspeople moved into rows of modes homes along streets that followed the boundaries of the old estates and travelers' paths.

New Yorkers fleeing epidemics of smallpox, yellow fever, and cholera that ravaged th city in the 1790s and early 1800s settled in Greenwich Village, which was far remove from the congested city center. Hastily built houses and hotels arose to accommodate th newcomers. **Bank Street** is named for the Wall Street banks that opened here along with other commercial ventures during the severe epidemic of 1822.

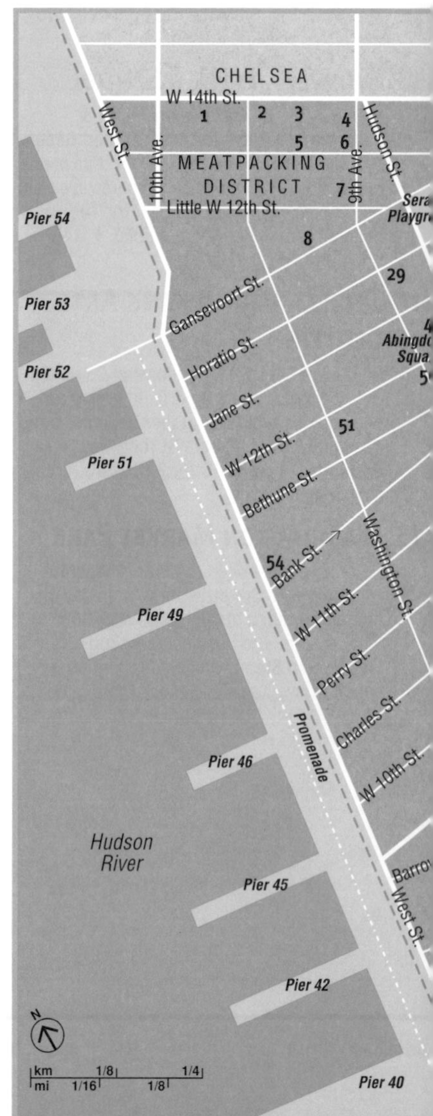

In the 1830s, prominent families began to build town houses at **Washington Square**, which had become a public park in 1828. New York society took over **Fifth Avenue** and the side streets from **University Place** to **Sixth Avenue** (more formally known as "Avenue of the Americas"). But the fashionable Washington Square elite soon gravitated to **Gramercy Park, Madison Square**, and upper **Fifth Avenue**, so that by the late 1850s the Village had turned into a quiet backwater of middle-class, old-line Anglo-Dutch families. Warehouses and industrial plants proliferated along the Hudson River, and commercial development began to the east and north. But the Village always retained its residential character. In the 1880s and 1890s, Irish and Chinese immigrants moved in, while Italians populated the tenements built south of Washington Square. Houses from all periods coexist in the Village, but only one brownstone still stands; they once lined Fifth Avenue from Washington Square to **Central Park** in what was called "Two Miles of Millionaires." Designed in the Italianate style, this lone survivor was built in 1853 at 47 Fifth Avenue for Irad Hawley, president of the Pennsylvania Coal 'ompany. The **Salmagundi Club**, the city's oldest club for art and artists (founded in 870), moved into the building in 1917 and still opens its doors for exhibitions from ıme to time. As the high rollers moved out, their large houses were divided into inex-ensive flats and studios and their stables transformed into homes. The cheap rents ap-ealed to such writers as Edgar Allan Poe, Horace Greeley, Walt Whitman, Mark Twain, nd Edna St. Vincent Millay, who at one time occupied the narrowest house in the city t **75½ Bedford Street**. The influx of creative energy continued, and Greenwich Village stablished itself as the seat of bohemia in the United States before World War I.

After the war, the Village continued to be a magnet for those seeking sexual freedom, adicalism, and revolt in politics and the arts. Upton Sinclair founded the Liberal Club on **MacDougal Street**; the **Washington Square Players** (later renamed the **Theater Guild**) ame into being in 1917; the **Provincetown Players**, the company that gave Eugene 'Neill his first chance, began performing at this time—first at **The Players Theatre**, then hree doors down at the **Provincetown Playhouse**, both on MacDougal Street.

Sharing the Village's streets with bohemians in the 1930s were families who had been here for generations, white-collar workers, and Irish and Italian blue-collar workers. After World War II, the Beat generation and then the hippies in the 1960s discovered the Village, as did entrepreneurs and developers. Although residents have fought hard to keep the community the way it was, apartment houses and high-rises have made inroads. Over the last two centuries, large landowners like Trinity Parish, and more recently, an aggressively growing NYU, have exercised their clout to great effect on local development. Robert Moses's reach as city planning commissioner nearly turned Washington Square Park into a bus turnaround. But it took Richard Meier's early-21st-century glass-faced high-rises on the Hudson to galvanize preservation efforts along the traditionally low-rise industrial and residential West Village river exposures. Today every style of 18th- and 19th-century architecture, culture, and history intermingles in Greenwich Village, from the gracious classical houses on the north side of Washington Square, where writers Henry James and Edith Wharton lived, to converted stables in **MacDougal Alley** behind them (where in the 1900s Gertrude Vanderbilt Whitney and actor Richard Bennett occupied houses), and all the way west to the crooked streets of Commerce and St. Lukes, where a midday stroll can make you feel as though you've come upon Brigadoon.

History is everywhere—in such places as the **Minetta Tavern** on MacDougal Street, filled with photos and memorabilia from earlier days, to **Golden Swan Park** nearby on Sixth Avenue. In addition to NYU's academic presence, the area is enhanced by the historically renowned **New School**. A walk on Christopher Street instantly puts one in mind of the travails of the **Stonewall** days. At the **Gansevoort Market** (now part of the officially landmarked historic **"Meatpacking District"**), the city's wholesale meat market, despite the swank shops and club scene, you can envision what the area was like when Herman Melville worked as a customs inspector for 19 years at what was then the **Gansevoort Docks**. Of course, the future finds its way into the Village as well, most markedly of late with the grand endeavor that is **Hudson River Park**—a remarkable reclamation of the decaying piers and public access areas along the full length of the West Side waterfront.

---

1 Meatpacking District/ Gansevoort Market Historic District

Begun as an outdoor market in 1884, by 1949 the area had become the city's wholesale meat district. Today a diminishing market presence continues to be housed in this collection of old brick buildings. But while the action still intensifies in the pre-dawn hours, the restaurant people that converge then to find the best meat to offer you for dinner are joined by late-night clubgoers who are stumbling out of the nearby boîtes that now thrive throughout this area. In the light of day, accompanied by the unmistakable scent of fresh meat, the cobbled streets of this now-official Historic District are trod by those in search of the latest new thing. You'll find galleries like **Bohen** (414.4575) for installation art; **Heller** (see opposite), for glassworks; the most modern furnishings at **Vitra** (see page 77) and **Design Within Reach** (see below); housewares at **Bodum** (367.9125); eccentric couture **à la McQueen** (645.1797), **McCartney** (255.1556), and **Jeffrey** (206.1272); and a hot dining scene, from **Pastis** (see page 77) to **Spice Market** (see page 77), **Matsuri** (243.6400), and **Florent** (see page 77). Bounded by Ninth Ave and West St, and Gansevoort and W 14th Sts

2 Heller Gallery

One of the most important representatives of the modern glass movement, this always interesting gallery usually has two solo shows and a monthly overview. ♦ Tu-Sa. 420 W 14th St (between Ninth Ave and Washington St). 414.4014, www.hellergallery.com ♿

3 Design Within Reach

The concept of Design Within Reach is to showcase the widest assortment possible of the sleekly modern furniture design available today—from lighting and floor coverings to office seating, home storage units, tables, and sofas—at prices that real people might actually be able to afford (remember, we said *might*). Carrying a number of pieces made by **Vitra** (especially much of its Prouvé collection), Design Within Reach is laid out in small tableaus, the better to see a real-use context for innovative works (reissues and new designs) like Le Corbusier's 1928 Glass Table or BLU DOT's 21st-century cantilevered shelving. ♦ Daily. 408 W 14th St (between Ninth Ave and Washington St). 242.9449. Also at 27 E 62nd St (between Madison and Park Aves). 888.4539; 142 Wooster St (between W Houston and Prince Sts). 475.0001; and other locations throughout the city

4 Vitra

This Swiss-based furniture manufacturer has always been forward thinking, having latched on to the designs of Americans Charles and Ray Eames, as well as George Nelson, early on. Launched in Europe in 1957 (Vitra was founded in 1950), the modern classic chairs and sofas caught on there and Vitra soon developed an international reputation for finely crafted, cutting-edge—and functional—office and home furnishings. Designers like Philippe Starck, Verner Panton, and Italy's Mario Bellini have had their work reproduced and distributed by Vitra. Their flagship New York store—a three-story, 12,100-square-foot showroom and gallery, it opened here in 2002—was designed by **Lindy Roy**. The beautifully lit open-space design shows off a selection of current chairs for sale and reflects the aesthetic of the designers represented, among them re-editions of pieces by Frank Gehry (who designed the **Vitra Design Museum** at company headquarters in Weil am Rhein, Germany, back in 1989), Jean Prouvé, Isamu Noguchi, and of course the Eamses. Design books and other related publications plus an inspired assortment of precision-made miniature chair reproductions—the mini Rietveld chair is a particular eye-catcher—are also for sale here. ♦ Daily. 29 Ninth Ave (between W 13th and W 14th Sts). 929.3626

5 Sperone Westwater

The New York home of Italy's most innovative artists, including Mario Merz, "the three C's" (Sandro Chia, Francesco Clemente, Enzo Cucchi), and Susan Rothenberg, this gallery also boasts an impressive roster of other European and American talents. ♦ Tu-Sa. 415 W 13th St (between Ninth Ave and Washington St). 999.7337. www.speronewestwater.com ♿

6 Spice Market

★★★ $$$ Star chef Jean-Georges Vongerichten's contribution to Asian/fusion, an instant hit with the beautiful people when it opened in 2004, manages to be accessible to the rest of us too (reservations, for example, aren't so hard to get if you don't mind dining on the early side). Designed by **Jacques Garcia** with rich woods, exposed beams, and sexy secluded niches, the two-level space—carved out of a Renaissance Revival warehouse—evokes one very sophisticated souk to match the reimagined "street food" on the Thai-Malay-based menu. You'll want to order (and share) several dishes, perhaps chili-garlic egg noodles with seared shrimp and star anise, deliciously crisp coconut monkfish with a tamarind glaze, spiced chicken samosas with cilantro yogurt, and, for a decadent dessert, a chocolate-and-Vietnamese-coffee tart with condensed-milk ice cream. ♦ Asian/Tapas ♦ Daily, lunch and dinner. Reservations required. 403 W 13th St (at Ninth Ave). 675.2322

7 Pastis

★$$ When New York restaurateur Keith McNally dropped anchor in the heart of the Meatpacking District, the then-ramshackle neighborhood found its place on the map. Like at his SoHo restaurant **Balthazar**, the formula is casual bistro French. Stick to basics like steak frites or Basque roasted chicken. The crowd (which is not nearly as hip as you might think) arrives early and the din gets correspondingly eardrum-aching as the night wears on. ♦ French ♦ Daily, breakfast, lunch, and dinner. 9 Ninth Ave (at Little W 12th St). Reservations recommended. 929.4844

8 Florent

★★$$ A diner-turned-hip-bistro, and one of the first on the scene at the Meatpacking District frontier, Florent Morellet's personality-plus enterprise is a welcome late-night spot for those seeking a complete meal. Despite the ever-diminishing number of meatpacking plants in the neighborhood, meat entrées continue to dominate the menu. The *boudin noir* (blood sausage) appetizer and the steak frites are both popular, but they also have a respectable chicken roulade and Louisiana crabcake, a grilled Portobello and goat cheese wrap, and a goodly range of other edibles for the non-carnivorous. After midnight there's an all-night breakfast menu. The late Tibor Kalman's M & Co. was responsible for the very stylish design, and to some extent, the layout of the restaurant itself. ♦ French bistro ♦ Daily, 24 hrs, breakfast, lunch, dinner, and late-night meals. Reservations recommended. 69 Gansevoort St (between Ninth Ave and Washington St). 989.5779 ♿

9 West 14th Street

Historically known as a magnet for bargain-hunters, this street continues to reinvent itself. Between Sixth and Seventh Avenues are the **Pratt Institute** and **McBurney Y**, both 2002 arrivals. This street is also home to a number of noteworthy loft buildings. Walk on the north side and look across at **Nos. 138-146** (1899), an ostentatious confection that drew on the 1893 Chicago World's Fair for its inspiration; and **Nos. 154-160** (1913), Herman Lee Meader's colorful glass-and-tile design that is literally grounded in Art Nouveau and aspiring to Art Deco. ♦ Between Sixth and Seventh Aves

10 Salvation Army Centennial Memorial Temple

This 1930 cast-in-place concrete building by **Voorhees, Gmelin & Walker** is one of the best Art Deco extravaganzas around, with an overblown entrance and unrestrained interiors that capture the exuberance and color of the era. Not open to the public, the building houses the executive offices and programs of the Salvation Army. ♦ 120 W 14th St (between Sixth and Seventh Aves). 337.7200 ♿

11 Integral Yoga Institute

All aspects of yoga are presented: Hatha yoga classes and workshops, meditation, breathing, relaxation, diet and nutrition, stress management, and chanting. The institute's store (next door) sells all kinds of macrobiotic groceries, natural body-care products, and other essentials. Vitamins, minerals, herbs, and homeopathic remedies are for sale across the street at the **Natural Apothecary** (No. 234). ♦ Daily. 227 W 13th St (between Seventh and Greenwich Aves). 929.0586. Integral Yoga Natural Foods: 229 W 13th St. 243.2642. www.integralyogany.org ♿

12 Village Community Church

This not-quite abandoned gem (condos lurk in the rear) is thought by architectural historians to be the best Greek Revival church in the city. The original design, dating to 1846, is attributed to **Samuel Thompson** and based on the Theseum in Athens. But the materials are the antithesis of the Doric model: The six huge columns and the pediment are of wood, and the walls are brick and stucco. ♦ 143 W 13th St (between Sixth and Seventh Aves)

"I should have been born in New York, I should have been born in the Village, that's where I belong."

—John Lennon

Edna St. Vincent Millay gained her middle name by virtue of being born in St. Vincent's Hospital.

13 Cafe Loup

★★$$ Cozy and comfortable, this French bistro, in business since 1977, serves solid fare. Chef/owner Lloyd Feit offers tasty grilled escargots for an appetizer. Smoked brook trout, Colorado lamb chops in a Cabernet sauce, grilled skirt steak in shallot sauce, and other classically prepared French dishes are among the excellent entrées. Desserts—rice pudding with Tahitian vanilla sauce, Valrhona double chocolate pudding, wedges of intense chocolate fudge, and lemon crepes—are luscious. ♦ French ♦ M-F, lunch and dinner; Sa, dinner; Su, brunch and dinner. Reservations recommended. 105 W 13th St (between Sixth and Seventh Aves). 255.4746 ♿

14 Bar Six

★★$ With its aged, yellow-ochre walls and mirrors, this bistro looks like it's been here forever. Not so, but the French, American, and Moroccan food is darn good. Best bets are the grilled spicy shrimp with warm lentil salad, lamb kabobs with lemon couscous, and chicken tajine. Ask for a table in the skylit back room—it makes a nice brunch even nicer. ♦ Bistro ♦ M-F, breakfast, lunch, and dinner; Sa, Su, brunch and dinner. 502 Sixth Ave (between W 12th and W 13th Sts). 691.1363

15 East West Books

This is an excellent source for books on Eastern philosophy, religion, cooking, medicine and health, and New Age lifestyles. There is a small café on their upper level; they also offer an assortment of classes, from chakra breath and dance meditation to pose-based programs. ♦ Daily. 78 Fifth Ave (between W 13th and W 14th Sts). 243.5994. www.eastwestnyc.com

16 Café de Bruxelles

★★$$ A sophisticated bar scene is the real attraction at this lovely spot, which made a name for itself as the first Belgian restaurant in the downtown area. Wash down the endless rounds of addicting frites with one of their 15 Belgian ales. Don't miss the rich *waterzooi* (Belgian stew) or ever-popular *moules* (mussels). ♦ French/Belgian ♦ M-Sa, lunch and dinner; Su, brunch and dinner. Reservations recommended. 118 Greenwich Ave (at W 13th St). 206.1830

17 Mxyplyzyk

Never mind saying the name. We pronounce this place a fun stop for browsers as well as a viable destination for shoppers who actually wish to *buy* design-forward gifts and home furnishings that range from snazzy to iconic and on to ironic, all with clean modernist lines: metal-mesh placemats, upholstered-cube ottomans, ceramic bowls, plus woven trash cans, sleek floor lamps, wind-up gizmos, a special section of bath items and another with children's toys, and more. ♦ Daily. 125 Greenwich Ave (at W 13th St). 989.4300

18 Tea and Sympathy

★$ Those enamored of bangers and mash, shepherd's pie, and other English specialties flock to this teeny spot. For traditionalists, there's a Sunday dinner of roast beef and Yorkshire pudding. Service can border on surly (charmingly eccentric, some might say), but the warm toffee pudding trumps all. ♦ English ♦ M-F, lunch and dinner; Sa, Su, breakfast, lunch, and dinner. No reservations (all members of your party must be present to be seated). 108 Greenwich Ave (between W 12th and W 13th Sts). 807.8329 ♿

19 Benny's Burritos

★$ After sipping one of Benny's high-octane margaritas, you'll understand why it gets so rowdy here. Any one of the foot-long burritos with a tempting choice of fillings at bargain prices is worth trying—just be sure to ask for your rice on the side if the San Francisco style (rice tucked inside the tortilla) isn't what you had in mind. So are the nachos, enchiladas, quesadillas, and chili. Expect a wait. ♦ Tex-Mex ♦ M-F, lunch, dinner, and late-night meals; Sa, Su, brunch, dinner, and late-night meals. No credit cards accepted. 113 Greenwich Ave (at Jane St). 727.0584. Also at 93 Ave A (at E Sixth St). 254.3286

20 Flight 001

True jet-setters come here for seriously stylish travel accessories: luggage and carry-ons, bag tags in neon rubber or printed toile, and all manner of groovy gadgets. If you're planning to circle the world in coach, you'll want to equip yourself from the selection of eye masks, pillows, buckwheat neck rests, and high-end in-flight survival kits. Other pampering package deals include aromatherapy, shaving, and snacking supplies, plus a "Mobile Foodie" kit with 19 spices and condiments, in case you're off to some desolate place where they don't have dill. ♦ Daily. 96 Greenwich Ave (between Jane and W 12th Sts). 691.1001

21 James Beard House

★★★★$$$$ Major chefs from New York and around the country prepare special dinners almost nightly here (in the late Mr. Beard's former townhouse) that are open to members and the public. Although it's pricey—this is an extravaganza for the truly deep-pocketed—considering the five or six courses that are served with almost as many wines, diners get their money's worth and more. Call ahead for a schedule and membership information. ♦ Eclectic ♦ One seating, at 7PM. Reservations required (call months ahead). 167 W 12th St (between Sixth and Seventh Aves). 675.4984. www.jamesbeard.org

22 The New School

The first building in the country developed specifically for adult education—designed in 1930 by **Joseph Urban** in high International Style—is home to this progressive institution for undergraduate and graduate studies in the arts, humanities, and social sciences, as well as highly regarded continuing-education programs that draw some 25,000 students a year. Founded in 1919 by a handful of free thinkers, among them Thorstein Veblen and John Dewey, the "university in exile" originally operated out of a cluster of rented Chelsea brownstones, attracting intellectuals fleeing Nazi Germany, along with such faculty as Lewis Mumford, Bertrand Russell, and John Maynard Keynes. Today, the university encompasses eight schools—including **The New School for Social Research** and **Mannes College** (now, formally, The New School for Music)—spread among more than two dozen buildings, most clustered nearby. Inside the main Urban building, on the ground floor (which is open to the public during the school's many lectures and special events), note the dramatic curves and surprising use of color in the egg-shaped **Tishman Auditorium** (which inspired the design of Radio City Music Hall) and the intriguing landscape of the **Vera List Courtyard.** Public access elsewhere in the building is limited, though the occasional event might allow a glimpse of Mexican artist José Clemente Orozco's murals upstairs in the **Orozco Room**. ♦ 66 W 12th St (between Fifth and Sixth Aves). 229.5600. www.newschool.edu ♿

Within The New School:

Parsons

This college, officially **Parsons The New School for Design**, holds a unique place in American education. Here, art and industry were for the first time linked on a large institutional level, even before Walter Gropius and the Bauhaus school. Founded as the Chase School in 1896 by painter William Merritt Chase, the institution was raised to its current position in the world of art and design education by Frank Alvah Parsons, who arrived in 1907 and, as the school's president, implemented his vision of art to influence both industry and everyday life. Under his direction, the school added programs such as interior architecture and design, fashion design, and advertising art. In 1970 it joined with The New School, and it now occupies space within its campus. The public is welcome at their gallery shows (2 West 13th Street, 66 Fifth Avenue). ♦ 66 Fifth Ave (between W 12th and W 13th Sts). 229.8910. www.parsons.edu ♿

23 Butterfield House

This 1962 edifice by **Mayer, Whittlesey & Glass** is an unusually sensitive apartment block. The fine seven-story, bay-windowed section on 12th Street is an in-scale counterpoint to a series of row houses. Beyond an interior courtyard and garden, the wing on 13th Street is taller, adapting to the stronger, larger scale of that block. Poet **Stanley Kunitz** lived here until his death in 2006. ♦ 37 W 12th St (between Fifth and Sixth Aves)

24 Forbes Galleries

The heart of the Forbes publishing empire is located in this 1925 **Carrère & Hastings** building. What's best here is the **Forbes Magazine Galleries** on the main floor. The wonderful displays delight both children and adults, and include more than 500 toy boats, displayed along with Art Deco fittings from the liner *Normandie* and models of the late Malcolm Forbes's private yachts. There is a collection of 12,000 toy soldiers, 250 trophies awarded for every accomplishment from raising Leghorn chickens to surviving a working lifetime in the corporate battlefields, and a display of historic Monopoly boards. American history is represented in a collection of presidential papers, historical documents, and a charming period kids' room. ♦ Free. Tu, 10AM-4PM; Th by reserved tour only. 62 Fifth Ave (between W 12th and W 13th Sts). 206.5548. www.forbesgalleries.com ♿

25 First Presbyterian Church

Joseph C. Wells modeled this fine Gothic Revival church with an imposing tower afte the one at Magdalen College at Oxford. The south transept, an 1893 addition by **McKi Mead & White**, includes an outdoor pulpit overlooking the inviting garden. The **Churcl House**, which adjoins the church on the uptown side, was designed in 1960 by **Edg Tafel** to perfectly match the 1846 building. ♦ 12 W 12th St (at Fifth Ave). 675.6150 ♿

26 Gotham Bar and Grill

★★★★$$$$ In this impressive, multilevel loft space—accented with massive overhea lights draped in white fabric, mustard-colored columns, and a statue of Lady Liberty—the master chef Alfred Portale continues to be in top form. His menu is superb: Try the striped bass with Manila clams, spinach, couscous, and Merguez sausage or rack of lamb with Swiss chard, roast shallots, and garlic mashed potatoes. Be sure to save room for one of the devastating desserts: warm chocolate cak served with toasted almond ice cream, wa apple tarte Tatin, or bittersweet chocolate tiramisù. ♦ American ♦ M-F, lunch and dinner; Sa, Su, dinner. Reservations required. 12 E 12th St (between University Pl and Fifth Ave). 620.4020

27 Bowlmor Lanes

The Nieuw Amsterdam Dutch introduced bowling to America, but their legacy seems be unappreciated in Manhattan, where the are only a handful of places to play the gan This one has become a huge scene and includes a bar and grill and a pro shop. ♦ Daily, till late. 110 University Pl (between E 12th and E 13th Sts). 255.8188 ♿

28 The Cast Iron Building

Designed by **John Kellum** in 1868, this building was converted from the **James McCreery Dry Goods Store** into apartments by **Stephen B. Jacobs** in 1973. In a city known for outstanding cast-iron structures (particularly in the SoHo neighborhood), this is one of the most representative examples, sporting layers Corinthian columns topped by arches. Unfortunately, the uppermost story added later is an insensitive mismatch. ♦ 67 E 11th St (at Broadway)

29 El Faro

★$$ A dark, minimally decorated den of a restaurant, this place has been around forever (since 1959, to be exact, or 1927 i you count the Spanish bar and grill that preceded it on this site) serving good-quality, full-flavored Spanish food. You car go wrong with the rich and fragrant paella, seafood stew, or other fish dishes. ♦ Spanish ♦ Tu-Su, lunch and dinner. No reservations 823 Greenwich St (at Horatio St). 929.8210

30 Tavern on Jane

★$$ This favorite Village gathering spot serves such basic tavern fare as fish and chips, homemade chili, burgers, pastas, salads, steaks and seafood, and daily specials. ♦ American ♦ M-F, lunch and dinner; Sa, Su, brunch and dinner. 31 Eighth Ave (at Jane St). 675.2526 ♿

31 'SNice

★$ At this friendly coffeehouse, the vegetarian menu includes many vegan choices (try a tempeh Reuben); other options include Thai salad and a tasty fontina panini. Free Wi-Fi makes for lots of laptop action; sit at a sunny table up front or in the brick- and art-lined back space. ♦ Café ♦ Daily, breakfast, lunch, and dinner. 45 Eighth Ave (at W Fourth St). 645.0310

32 Corner Bistro

★$ If strolling around the Village has whetted your appetite for a fat, juicy burger, this neighborhood standby is the place to go. You'll have plenty of time to check out the locals in this dark, cozy pub, because the crowds are thick and the service is slow. ♦ American ♦ Daily, lunch, dinner, and late-night meals. No credit cards accepted. 331 W Fourth St (at W 12th St). 242.9502

33 Li-Lac Chocolates

A Village institution since 1923 (they moved here from their longtime Christopher Street location in the early 2000s), Li-Lac makes impossibly indulgent chocolate the old-fashioned way. The results are on view in signature purple display cases stacked with milk and dark chocolate truffles, filled candies, raspberry jelly bars (dark chocolate version), and, for a really memorable (if short-lived) souvenir, a foot-high Empire State Building in 28 ounces of solid dark chocolate. ♦ Daily. 40 Eighth Ave (at Jane St). 242.7374. Also at Grand Central Terminal, Market Hall, Lexington Ave at E 43rd St. 370.4866

34 Chez Brigitte

★$ Come to this tiny counter-only eatery for inexpensive made-before-your-eyes food. While original chef Brigitte is long gone, the kitchen continues to serve simple, homey dishes with a bit of a French twist, such as a rich boeuf bourguignon, a hearty veal stew, omelettes, spaghetti, and soups; there's always a daily special. ♦ French ♦ M-Sa, lunch and dinner. No credit cards accepted. 77 Greenwich Ave (between W 11th and Bank Sts). 929.6736

35 St. Vincent's Hospital

The largest Catholic hospital in the United States, this modern monstrosity is the main building and proof that not every Village community protest is successful. But the medical facility now has a physician referral service (800/999.6266) and has served the community well in every other way since it was founded by the Sisters of Charity in 1849. ♦ Seventh Ave S (between W 11th and W 12th Sts). 604.7000

36 Nikos Magazine & Smoke Shop

This is a rare remnant of a dying breed of the neighborhood newsstands you go to when you want *McSweeney's*, a broad spectrum of literary, political and arts reviews, foreign newspapers, the odd travel magazine, and a full selection of the usual stuff—from *Newsweek* to the *New York Times*. Niko and Helen may not know your name, but they know you and are happy to help you find whatever periodical—obscure or not so—you've got in mind, and, if you're in the mood, to chat about the news of the day. ♦ Daily. 462 Sixth Ave (at W 11th St). 255.9175

37 Café Cluny

★★$$ This bistro cuz of **Odeon** can get noisy, but wide windows give a view of quiet streets. At brunch, have granola with yogurt and berries or poached eggs with short-rib hash; later on, try hanger steak or roasted cod. ♦ Bistro ♦ M-F, breakfast, lunch, and dinner; Sa, Su, breakfast, brunch, and dinner. Reservations recommended. 284 W 12th St (at W Fourth St). 255.6900 ♿

38 Le Fanion

This cozy storefront is alight with charm—first and foremost, in the form of Provençal chandeliers laden with jewel-colored crystal fruit. You'll also find French Country pottery and earthenware, antique furniture, fine art and folk art, and zinc by the sheet to outfit your own countertop or bar. ♦ M-Sa. 299 W Fourth St (at Bank St). 463.8760

39 Village Vanguard

This world-famous basement jazz club also features Dixieland, blues, avant-garde, and folk music. Monday nights' Big Band program has become an institution. ♦ Cover.

Two shows daily. Reservations recommended. 178 Seventh Ave S (at Perry St). 255.4037

40 Partners & Crime Mystery Booksellers

A Village stalwart, this indie bookseller serves the rapacious community of mystery- and crime-fiction lovers downtown, throughout the city, and beyond. A true neighborhood spot in spirit, Partners gets to know its customers and loves to match them with the latest find or rare volume. They're the largest such genre bookstore in Manhattan, and the selection here ranges from items like rare first editions of Walter Mosley's *Devil in a Blue Dress* to crossover titles like Jonathan Lethems's *Fortress of Solitude.* Come here for classics, out-of-print books, the latest paperback and cloth editions from publishers around the globe, readings, signings, and their live performances of mystery-themed Classic Radio Plays. ♦ Daily. 44 Greenwich Ave (at Charles St), lower level. 243.0440. www.crimepays.com

41 Cafe Asean

★★$ This warm and romantic café (named in recognition of the Association of South East Asian Nations) has a postage-stamp-sized outdoor dining space in the back, and features foods from Malaysia, Thailand, Vietnam, Indonesia, and Singapore. Start with *cha glo* (Imperial rolls with shrimp, chicken, and mushrooms), *sup mang cua* (crabmeat with asparagus soup), or Malaysian salad with squid, pineapple, and cucumber. Continue the feast with Singaporean fried rice noodles with shrimp and Chinese sausage, *bo lui* (Vietnamese beef rolls with garlic and onions), or *kari kapitan* (coconut curry chicken with potatoes). It's all well prepared and very affordable. ♦ Asian ♦ Daily, lunch and dinner. No credit cards accepted. 117 W 10th St (between Sixth and Greenwich Aves). 633.0348

41 Patchin Place

Like Milligan Place around the corner on Sixth Avenue (between W 10th and W 11th Sts), this cluster of small houses constructed in 1848 by Aaron D. Patchin was built as rooming houses for waiters and othe personnel from the now-converted-to-apartment-building **Brevoort Hotel** over on Fifth Avenue. It became famous in the 1920 as the home of poet e.e. cummings, among others. ♦ Off W 10th St (between Sixth and Greenwich Aves)

The annual Halloween parade in Greenwich Village—that once wound through the zig-zag side streets and is now a huge event—is the nation's largest night parade.

In the 1820s, a stagecoach ride from the Battery to Greenwich Village took one hour. By 1830, horse-drawn trolleys had reached 15th Street.

42 Jefferson Market Branch, NYPL

Frederick Clarke Withers and **Calvert Vaux** modeled this 1877 structure, built on the site of the old **Jefferson Market** and originally used as the **Third Judicial District Courthouse**, after Mad King Ludwig II of Bavaria's castle Neuschwanstein. It is the epitome of Victorian Gothic, with steeply sloping roofs, gables, pinnacles, sets of variously shaped arched windows, and stone carvings all set of by a rather unusual clock tower that served as a fire lookout. After the occupants moved out in 1945, the building sat idle until citizens pressured the city government to find a new user, and the public library agreed to move in **Giorgio Cavaglieri** handled the 1967 remodeling. During the Halloween Parade, a giant spider is often dangled down from the tower; its grand bell rings the time on the hour. ♦ M-Sa. 425 Sixth Ave (at W 10th St). 243.4334. www.nypl.org ♿

43 Jefferson Market Garden

Ⓟ A rare gem of an urban garden, the Jeff gets better all the time. Starting with the installation of its new and much-improved decorative iron gates in the late 1990s, then moving on to a completely rethought landscape scheme—created and overseen by the site-sensitive horticulturist **Susan Sipos**—this is a rare spot of solitude and beauty. Just under the shadow of the redbrick detail of the **Jefferson Market Library** and barely feet from the bustle of Sixth Avenue, you can sit in the sun—or shade—on the comfy wooden benches, listen to the birds and the trickle of the "waterfalls in the two small ponds, and admire the changing plantings—floral and woodland. ♦ No food, please. May-Oct only. Tu-Su afternoons, weather permitting. Enter on Greenwich Ave (between Sixth Ave and W 10th St). www.jeffersonmarketgarden.org ♿

44 Citarella

This is the site of the original family-owned version of **Balducci's**; mythologized as it was, it held this spot for decades until it sold out to corporate interests. Gone by 2003, it was promptly replaced by this outpost of the growing Citarella (fresh seafood's their claim to fame) empire. ♦ Daily. 424 Sixth Ave (at W Ninth St). 874.0383. ♿. Also at other locations

45 Village

★★$$ Village arrived on the scene in the early 2000s and was immediately embraced alike by local and nonlocal seekers of good, friendly dining. The warm atmosphere is enhanced by its large wooden bar and upfront café seating (with somewhat lower-price menu options); the intimate skylight-capped back dining room has a charming upper balcony. Favorites are the grilled tuna burger with wasabi mayonnaise, salmon on a bed of salsa-spiked posole, a perfectly dressed green salad, an irresistible warm apple crumble, and a special selection of foreign and domestic beers. Café menu items are available in the dining room as well. ♦ Bistro-Continental. ♦ Daily, dinner; Sa, Su, brunch. 62 W Ninth St (between Fifth and Sixth Aves). 505.3355

46 Patsy's Pizzeria

★★$ The downtown spin-off of the famous East Harlem pizzeria has more polish (formal seating and a good choice of pasta), but the pies are no less delicious. The salads too are exceptionally tasty—try the arugula—and service is friendly. There is a small wine list. ♦ Italian ♦ Daily, lunch and dinner. No reservations. 67 University Pl (between E 10th and E 11th Sts). 533.3500. Other locations throughout the city

47 Il Cantinori

★★$$$ Country antiques from Italy set the stage for an authentic Tuscan meal here. Begin with the assortment of grilled vegetables, then move on to *tonno al pesto* (grilled tuna steak sliced and served with pesto vinaigrette and diced tomatoes). For dessert, good luck trying to choose among the apple tart, various gelati, tiramisù, and double-layer chocolate cake. ♦ Northern Italian ♦ Daily, lunch and dinner. Reservations recommended. 32 E 10th St (between Broadway and University Pl). 673.6044

48 Knickerbocker Bar & Grill

★$$ Fascinating 19th-century artifacts and posters fill this casual yet classy bar and restaurant. T-bone steak, pork chops, and pan-roasted chicken are among the more popular dishes. (The café menu, available at the bar seating area only, is kinder on your wallet.) But the subdued atmosphere and live jazz (Wednesday through Sunday starting at 9:45PM)—often featuring name performers—are the main draws. There's a small cover charge added to meals during the shows. ♦ American ♦ M-Sa, lunch and dinner; Su, brunch and dinner. Reservations recommended. 33 University Pl (at E Ninth St). 228.8490 ♿

49 Abingdon Square

This pretty little square is named for Charlotte Warren, wife of the Earl of Abingdon and daughter of Sir Peter Warren, whose estate once covered this area. The statue at the uptown entrance, placed here in 1921, is a memorial to the American dead of World War I. ♦ Bounded by Bleecker St, Eighth Ave, and Hudson St, and W 11th and W 12th Sts

50 La Ripaille

★★$$ The cozy, warm atmosphere, much like a French farmhouse, makes this one of the most romantic dining spots in a neighborhood full of romantic dining spots. Chef/owner Alain Laurent takes pride in serving Provençal-style dishes such as duck *magret* with red currant and Port wine, shell steak in green peppercorn sauce, and Norwegian salmon in a light Champagne *velouté* (white sauce), which are consistently quite good. ♦ French bistro ♦ M-Sa, dinner. Reservations recommended. 605 Hudson St (between Bethune and W 12th Sts). 255.4406

51 Tortilla Flats

★$ This popular West Village eatery is known for its noisy atmosphere and inexpensive Tex-Mex eats—chicken, shrimp, or steak fajitas, enchiladas verdes (in a green-chili salsa), and chimichangas (deep-fried chicken and refried bean burritos)—made from natural ingredients. Monday and Tuesday are big-prize bingo nights, but don't bring along your mild-mannered grandma. ♦ Tex-Mex ♦ Daily, lunch, dinner, and late-night meals. 767 Washington St (at W 12th St). 243.1053 ♿

52 Biography Bookshop

As the name implies, this cozy bookstore has the best selection of biographies anywhere. It also carries a well-chosen selection of other nonfiction, and fiction as well. Its stock sometimes overflows to display tables—with special deals—outside. Feel free to browse. ♦ Daily. 400 Bleecker St (at W 11th St). 807.8655

53 White Horse Tavern

★$ Come here for the sense of history; the food is not the feature—with the exception of okay burgers and okay fries. They say poet Dylan Thomas drank himself to death in the corner of the bar, and the story still circulating is that his last words were: "I've had 19 straight whiskeys. I believe that's the record." ♦ American ♦ M-Sa, lunch, dinner, and late-night meals; Su, brunch, dinner, and late-night meals. 567 Hudson St (at W 11th St). 989.3956

54 WESTBETH

Built in 1897 by Bell Telephone Laboratories (then Western Electric), this was where the transistor was invented and the first TV pictures were transmitted. When Bell Labs moved to the suburbs in 1965, **Richard Meier Associates** renovated the 1900 **Cyrus Eidlitz**-designed building and turned it into a nonprofit residential building exclusively for artists of all kinds. Envisioned as a center for the arts with galleries and dance and sculpture studios, it is, in fact, merely subsidized apartments for anyone who happens to be an artist (and who has good genes: the waiting list is backed up 10 to 20 years). Just downstream a bit are Meier's three 21st-century glass towers. Those controversial structures also house a number of artists, but of the high-flying entertainment-world sort; they don't need help paying the rent. ♦ 463 West St (at Bank St)

55 MARY'S FISH CAMP

★★★$$ Though you may catch a whiff of the sea as you cross the threshold of this Village haunt, that roaring in your ears isn't the surf, it's the crowd. Mary's packs them in like sardines, but it's worth it to enjoy definitive versions of shore classics such as lobster rolls, steamers, and fried Montauk skate wings, as well as some unusual, delicious surprises. And if you really want to enjoy your lobster knuckles or shark BLT in peace, there's always takeout. ♦ Seafood ♦ M-Sa, lunch and dinner. 246 W Fourth St (at Charles St). 646/486.2185. Also at 162 Fifth Ave (between Douglas and Degraw Sts), Park Slope, Brooklyn. 718/783.3264

56 BONNIE SLOTNICK COOKBOOKS

Accessed through a narrow foyer, this tiny, eclectic sliver of a space holds an intelligently assembled collection of out-of-print, antique, sometimes wildly unusual cookery books. (One recent visit turned up a weighty tome on French pastry and a mid-20th-century pamphlet on butter rationing.) Depending on the season, owner Bonnie Slotnick may also showcase vintage kitchen gadgets, children's books, or Christmas ornaments. ♦ Open most weekdays; call ahead. 163 W 10th St (between Seventh Ave S and Waverly Pl). 989.8962

57 THREE LIVES & COMPANY

This warm, inviting wood-shelved village stalwart is impossible to enter without purchasing at least one book. Its windows feature the latest fiction and announce upcoming literary events. The shop carries a wonderful selection (particularly new fiction and literature, travel, photography, and othe[r] specialty books) and hosts occasional Thursday-night readings. The owners are knowledgeable and helpful. ♦ Daily. 154 W 10th St (at Waverly Pl). 741.2069. www.threelives.com

58 OSCAR WILDE MEMORIAL BOOKSHOP

This small shop offers a tasteful selection of books on gay and lesbian subject matter, including literary classics, rare editions, lega[l] guides, sociology, and periodicals. ♦ Daily. 15 Christopher St (between Greenwich Ave and Waverly Pl). 255.8097. www.oscarwildebooks.com

59 GAY STREET

Thought to be named after Sydney Howard Gay, the *New York Tribune*'s managing editor in the Civil War era, this block contains a well-preserved group of Greek Revival houses on the east side and Federal row houses on the west. **No. 14** is the location o[f] the basement apartment that was the setting for Ruth McKenney's play *My Sister Eileen*, which later was made into the musical *Wonderful Town*. ♦ Between Waverly Pl and Christopher St

60 EIGHTH STREET

The stretch of Eighth Street between Sixth Avenue and Broadway has gone through many a change over the years. In the 1920s up through the '40s and '50s it was art central; bookstores, movie theaters, and quaint clothing shops abounded. The 1960s and '70s saw headshops galore; it was in this period that Jimi Hendrix planted **Electric Ladyland Studios** here (it's still at 52 W Eighth, though the odd orange-tile hump tha[t] once marked it is gone). Sometime in there it became a street of shoe stores as well; by the 1990s it seemed that's all there was. Now that's pretty much over, and the diminished traffic these days has made the sidewalks easier to negotiate. The 21st-century selection of stores is meager, but there are signs of resurgence in the welcome mix of dining spots. ♦ Between Broadway and Sixth Ave

61 NEW YORK STUDIO SCHOOL OF DRAWING, PAINTING & SCULPTURE

The **Whitney Museum** was established here in 1931, founded by Gertrude Vanderbilt Whitney. (Tradition was already evident on the block, which was the heart of the Village art scene at the time. It began with the conversion of a stable at 4 West Eighth Street by **John Taylor Johnston** as a gallery for his private art collection. His friends were so impressed that they got together and founded the **Metropolitan Museum of Art** in 1870. When the Whitney moved north, the respected Studio School found its feet in its offering of art classes and lectures, a tradition it carries on today. ♦ 8 W Eighth St (between Fifth and Sixth Aves). 673.6466. www.nyss.org

62 Broadway Panhandler

This ex-SoHo resource serves both pros and home cooks with good kitchenware offered at a good range of prices. Pick up that sashimi knife or tatin pan you've been coveting, catch a demonstration, and find brands from All-Clad to Wearever, plus what may be the world's most ingenious pasta cutter. ♦ Daily. 65 E Eighth St (between Broadway and Mercer St). 966.3434

63 MacDougal Alley

Like **Washington Mews** (see below), this is a street of converted stables, with the advantage of trees but the same disadvantage of parked cars. **No. 7**, on the north side, was built in 1899 as a studio for a stained-glass artisan. **No. 75½** was converted to a home for Gertrude Vanderbilt Whitney in 1934. **No. 19**, on the south side, was built in 1901 as an automobile stable, and the 1854 stable that is **No. 21** was reconstructed in 1920 by architect **Raymond Hood**. ♦ Off MacDougal St (between Washington Sq N and W Eighth St)

64 Washington Mews

Some of these charming buildings behind the town houses on Washington Square North were stables in the early 1900s. But those on the south side of the alley, more uniform because they were all stuccoed at the same time, date from the 1930s. Most are now used by **NYU**. Their size and quaintness contribute to the small-scale, congenial atmosphere of the neighborhood. ♦ Between University Pl and Fifth Ave

65 August

★★$$ With artfully distressed walls, a cobblestone patio, and black pews for banquettes, this place has atmosphere to burn—along with a wood-burning oven that turns out smoky-crusty pizzas and raclette. Other choices on the seasonal menu may include a tuna tartare starter, linguine with cod, or baby back lamb ribs. ♦ Bistro ♦ M-F, lunch and dinner; Sa, Su, brunch and dinner. Reservations recommended. 359 Bleecker St (between Charles and W 10th Sts). 929.4774

66 Riviera Cafe

★$$ The people-watching here is probably the best in the Village and better than the casual menu, which includes burgers and salads. Sip some wine and enjoy the parade. ♦ American ♦ Daily, lunch, dinner, and late-night meals; Sa, Su, brunch. 225 W Fourth St (between Christopher and W 10th Sts). 929.3250

67 Christopher Park

Until the Parks Department put a sign near the entrance, everyone thought the park at this crazy intersection was Sheridan Square (see below). The confusion began when the IRT Sheridan Square subway stop (now called **Christopher Street/Sheridan Square**) was opened in 1918, and was compounded when Joseph Pollia's statue of the Civil War general was placed here (possibly by mistake) in 1936. Christopher Park goes back to 1837, but earned its place in history in 1969, when the mainly gay hangout the **Stonewall Inn** (which was just a few steps across Christopher Street, at No. 53) was raided by the police and the patrons fought back; that action, of course, was the start of the gay lib movement (the annual gay pride parade commemorates the event when it wends its way down this stretch every July). The park today is a respite from the general bustle of this area, at the crossroads of at least five different streets (you know you're in the West Village when you cross Seventh Avenue here). Take a gander at George Segal's wonderful life-size *Gay Liberation* sculptures (1980), and enjoy the well-tended garden—the result of an 1983 design by Philip Winslow. ♦ Christopher St (at Seventh Ave S; bounded by Grove, W Fourth, and Christopher Sts). www.nycgovparks.org ♿

68 Sheridan Square Viewing Garden

Sheridan Square is at the same time one of the best-known and hardest-to-find spots in all of Greenwich Village. The community garden in the center yielded rare archeological treasures when it was created in the

The residents of Greenwich Village named Waverly Place after Sir Walter Scott's novel *Waverley* to honor him the year after his death.

early 1980s. It was the only spot in Manhattan that hadn't been disturbed since Indians lived here. The small triangular plot is not square at all, but the high-fenced garden, designed by **Pamela Berdan**, is a lovely gem to peek at. ♦ Bounded by Barrow and W Fourth Sts and Washington Pl. www.nycgpvparks.org

69 St. Joseph's Church

The oldest Roman Catholic church building in Manhattan, this Greek Revival temple—a pleasant surprise on this retail-heavy thoroughfare—was built in 1834 by **John Doran**. It has a gallery inside, as well as delicate crystal chandeliers and a gilded sanctuary that contrasts with the simplicity of the Greek Revival exterior. The outside wall on Washington Place is made of Manhattan schist, the extremely hard stone that underlies the whole island. ♦ 371 Sixth Ave (at W Washington Pl). 741.1274

70 Washington Square Hotel

$$ Location trumps all with this longtime Village lodging. While most of its 160 rooms have undergone a 21st-century spruce-up ("deluxe" rooms are set up with high-speed Internet access), they're still small. That said, there is a fitness room (also small) on site, continental breakfast is included, and the joint has the cachet of being host to a long stream of artists and musicians—including, yes, Bob Dylan—dating back to the 'sixties, when it was known as the Hotel Earle. Ask for a room overlooking Washington Square. ♦ 103 Waverly Pl (at MacDougal St). 777.9515, 800/222.0418; fax 979.8373. www.washingtonsquarehotel.com

Within the Washington Square Hotel:

North Square

★★$ A cozy 50-seater, this restaurant has a relaxing atmosphere with friendly service. There's also some very earthy, satisfying food with a sophisticated twist, as well as a good-quality and affordable wine list. ♦ American ♦ Daily, breakfast; M-F, lunch; M-Su, dinner; Sa, Su, brunch and dinner. 254.1200

71 Babbo

★★★$$$$ Refined Italian regional cooking with uncommon flair is what packs them in nightly at one of the Village's most exciting restaurants. Chef Mario Batali changes the menu according to what's freshest at the market, but you can expect innovation in every bite. Antipasti might include organic lettuces with a black-olive blood orange citronette, or sweet pea "flan" with sweet pea shoots and a carrot marinade. The "Primi" portion of the menu features pasta dishes such as goat cheese tortellini with dried orange and wild fennel pollen (it's delicious) and spaghettini with spicy artichokes, sweet garlic, and a one-pound lobster. Follow with the likes of Spicy Two Minute Calamari "Sicilian Lifeguard Style" or any of the savory game or grilled meat dishes (in signature Batali fashion, this could mean boar or some other mealtime oddity). Desserts are the stuff sweet dreams are made of: saffron panna cotta with blood oranges and blood orange *sorbetto* and a devilishly divine chocolate pistachio *semifreddo* are standouts. The prix-fixe tasting menus are good deals, and Babbo's extensive all-Italian wine list is sure to please even the most discriminating oenophiles. ♦ Creative Italian ♦ Daily, dinner. Reservations required. 110 Waverly Pl (between Washington Square W and Sixth Ave). 777.0303

72 Washington Square North

At one time there were 28 of these exemplary Greek Revival row houses—home to the cream of New York society when they were built in 1831 and later the center of an artistic community. The first six constructed, **Nos. 21** to **26**, by **Martin E. Thompson**, remain intact. **Nos. 7** to **13** were gutted in the late 1930s, and the façades alone are left, fronts for an apartment complex owned by NYU. Of those demolished, **No. 1** was at one time or another the home of Edith Wharton, William Dean Howells, and Henry James, who set his novel *Washington Square* at **No. 18**, his grandmother's house; **No. 3** was where John Dos Passos wrote *Manhattan Transfer*; and **No. 8** was once the residence of the mayor. To the west of Fifth Avenue, the mock-Federal wing of the apartment tower at **2 Fifth Avenue** was a compromise by the builder, **Samuel Rudin**, in response to community objection to the original plan, which had the tower on the square. ♦ Between University Pl and MacDougal St

73 Washington Square Park

Village life centers around this square, especially the huge fountain that's its focal point. The area was a marsh, a potter's field, a venue for public hangings, and a military parade ground before it was claimed as a public park in 1828. Elaborate, fashionable houses soon appeared around it, and **NYU** appropriated the east side in the late 1830s. The **Washington Memorial Arch**, designed by **Stanford White** of **McKim, Mead & White**, was originally a wooden monument built in 1889 for the centennial celebration of George Washington's inauguration. It became so well-liked that six years later private funds were raised to rebuild it permanently in stone. In 1916, the now 77-foot-high monument was drunkenly scaled (via interior stairs, now closed to the public) by a motley group of freethinkers led by noted Ashcan School artist **John Sloan** and Dada king **Marcel Duchamp.** Once roosted atop, they lit up some Japanese lanterns and proclaimed the Village the independent state of "new Bohemia"; the mayor had to call in the militia to break things up. The sculpture, *Washington,* on the west pier was created in 1918 by Alexander Stirling Calder, father of Alexander Calder. By the 1950s the park had seriously decayed. The city transit authority was using the arch as a bus turnaround, and there was a proposal to run Fifth Avenue underneath it. Popular outrage blocked the tunnel, put a halt to the buses, and gave momentum to the movement to redesign the park—a community effort that was realized in the 1960s. The park made a great comeback after some druggie years in the '80s and '90s—so much so that it was a significant gathering spot for New Yorkers seeking solace after 9/11. Benefiting from a restoration completed in 2004, the gleaming white arch now presides over a haven for folks of all types—students, parents playing ball with their kids, musicians, dog walkers, chess players, and even a political rally or two. ♦ Bounded by Washington Sq E and Washington Sq W, and Washington Sq S and Washington Sq N. www.nycgovparks.org ♿

74 Pylones

As you browse the glossy, groovy goods at this Paris-based emporium, desire rapidly transforms into "need." Butterfly binder clips, a psychedelic blow dryer, a penguin thermos—everything from kitchenware to furniture is an explosion of color and whimsical form. ♦ Daily. 61 Grove St (between Bleecker St and Seventh Ave S). 727.2655 ♿. Also at 842 Lexington Ave (at E 64th St). 317.9822; 69 Spring St (between Broadway and Lafayette St). 431.3244

75 McNulty's Tea and Coffee Company

In business since 1895, this place has been selling exotic coffees (from China, Sumatra, and Indonesia) long before the trend for specialty coffees began in this country. The shop also stocks more than 250 varieties of tea. ♦ Daily. 109 Christopher St (between Bleecker and Hudson Sts). 242.5351

76 Lucille Lortel Theatre

Formerly the **Theatre De Lys**, this 299-seat house was a major boost to Off-Broadway in the 1950s, when a revival of the Brecht-Weill classic *The Threepenny Opera* was staged here. It was later renamed for its distinguished owner, Lucille Lortel, who produced *Brecht on Brecht* and *John Dos Passos's USA*. It was home to the hugely successful *Steel Magnolias* during its two-and-a-half-year run. **TheatreworksUSA** (performances for children) and **MCC** stage their productions here. ♦ 121 Christopher St (between Bleecker and Hudson Sts). 924.2817. www.lucillelorteltheatre.com ♿

77 Sweet Rhythm

★★$$$ When this club was still Sweet Basil, the giants of the jazz world would perform here regularly. They still do, but the club also features a wide roster of up-and-comers. Most people come to listen to music and have a drink, but the club also offers food, including good salads and stir-fry dishes. ♦ Cover. Two shows nightly, at 9PM and 11PM. 88 Seventh Ave S (between Grove and Bleecker Sts). 242.1785

78 One If By Land, Two If By Sea

★★★★$$$$ The onetime home of Aaron Burr, this candlelit restaurant boasts a working fireplace, a large bar, and a pianist who plays romantic tunes nightly. Chef Thomas Donnelly creates a seasonal array of dishes that may include roasted Maine lobster with crabmeat risotto, pan-seared sea scallops, spice-rubbed yellowfin tuna, and rack of Berkshire pork. For dessert, don't miss the warm apple Wellington. ♦ Continental ♦ M-Sa, dinner; Su, brunch and dinner. Prix-fixe or tasting menu only. Reservations required. 17 Barrow St (between Seventh Ave S and W Fourth St). 228.0822

79 Caffè Vivaldi

★$ This Old World Village favorite always pleases with its relaxed and cozy atmosphere—it offers a taste of turn-of-the-century Vienna, with dramatic arias playing in the background. Come here on a cold winter's day for a light lunch or sweets. ♦ Café ♦ Daily, lunch, dinner, and late-night meals. 32 Jones St (between Bleecker and W Fourth Sts). 929.9384

80 Surya

★★$$ Subdued lighting and trendy Indian techno music provide the decidedly (and successfully) Postmodern backdrop for inventive menu selections that draw on the spicy culinary traditions of Chettinand, the region of southern India around Madras. (Their popular backyard garden suits the food as well.) Try seafood dishes like crisp salmon varuval, fenugreek-scented salmon in a curry leaf, onion, tomato, and tamarind sauce, or sautéed halibut with ginger and coconut cream sauce. Most main courses are served with a nice mint rice, and the vegetarian menu is extensive. ♦ Indian. ♦ M-F, lunch and dinner; Sa, Su, brunch and dinner. Reservations recommended. 302 Bleecker St (between Seventh Ave S and Grove St). 807.7770 ♿

81 Ottomanelli & Sons

For years, the window display of stuffed rabbits and game birds here gave pause to even the least repentant of carnivores. Fortunately, this shop's reputation for fresh game is such that there is no longer a need to advertise quite so explicitly. All the meat is cut to order, and fans of the veal roast stuffed with prosciutto are legion. ♦ M-Sa. 285 Bleecker St (between Jones St and Seventh Ave S). 675.4217. *Note:* Other Ottomanelli locations in the city are separately owned.

82 Judson Memorial Church

This eclectic Lombardo-Romanesque church, erected in 1892 by **McKim, Mead & White**, was built as a bridge between the poor to the south of the square and the rich above it and has always had a full program of social activities. The best part is inside, where you can appreciate the fine stained-glass windows by John LaFarge. The church was named for Adinoram D. Judson, the first Baptist missionary to Burma. (**Judson Hall** and the bell tower above it are now NYU dormitories.) ♦ 55 Washington Sq S (between Thompson and Sullivan Sts). 477.0351. www.judson.org ♿

Hagop Kevorkian Center for Near Eastern Studies

Designed in 1972 by **Philip Johnson** and **Richard Foster**, this huge granite building fits snugly into its corner site and is highlighted by an interesting array of angled corner windows. ♦ 50 Washington Sq S (at Sullivan St). 998.8877 ♿

83 New York University (NYU)

More than 50,000 full-time students study at the Washington Square campus of New York's largest private university, composed of 14 schools, including the **Tisch School of the Arts** and the highly regarded **NYU School of Business and Public Administration**. The campus extends beyond the classroom and dormitory buildings and into the converted lofts and Greek Revival row houses common in Greenwich Village. When the old University Heights campus in the Bronx was sold to the **City University of New York** in 1973, the focus shifted here.

Architects **Philip Johnson** and **Richard Foster** were commissioned to make a master plan that would unify the disjointed collection of buildings and enable the campus to handle the increased activity. Their plan called for rebuilding some of the older structures, refacing the existing ones with red sandstone, and establishing design guidelines for future construction. Only three buildings were refaced before that plan was abandoned, and the campus continues to grow like Topsy. Notably, **Loeb Student Center**—a focal point in late '60s campus unrest—was torn down in 1999 to make way for the **Kevin Roche (John Dinkaloo Associates Architects)**-designed **Kimmel Center for University Life** (60 Washington Square S). Opened in 2003 as the new student center, it features the acoustically advanced **Skirball Center for the Performing Arts** (992.8484). ♦ Bounded by Mercer and MacDougal Sts, and W Third and E Eighth Sts. Main: 998.1212; University Info Center: 998.4636. www.nyu.edu ♿

Within New York University:

Elmer Holmes Bobst Library

Designed by **Philip Johnson** and **Richard Foster** to be the architectural focal point of the university, this stolid-looking cube is 150 feet high and clad in Longmeadow redstone (in the tradition of Washington Square), with a 12-story interior atrium around which the stacks and reading rooms are organized. Chevronlike stairways with gold anodized aluminum railings provide scale, and the design of the marble floor, influenced by Palladio's piazza for Venice's San Giorgio Maggiore, adds to the decorative interior detail that is the antithesis of the austere exterior. Aside from access to special collections (such as **Tamiment Library**'s comprehensive archives and displays pertaining to social labor issues; 10th floor, photo ID required. 998.2630), the building is not open to the public. ♦ 70 Washington Sq S (at La Guardia Pl). 998.2500 ♿

84 Twin Peaks

In 1925, **Clifford Reed Daily** transformed this conventional 1830 residence into a fairy-tale fantasy as a reaction against undistinguished Village architecture. Pseudo-

> In 1942, distressed by commercial publishers' lack of interest in her work, writer Anaïs Nin borrowed $175 and, with a friend, rented a loft at 144 MacDougal Street, purchased a used printing press, and went on to print three of her books.

Tudor details trim the stucco facing, and an unorthodox flap acts as a front cornice (there's an attic room behind it). It's not great architecture, but it is great fun. ♦ 102 Bedford St (between Grove and Christopher Sts)

85 Church of St. Luke in the Fields

James N. Wells designed this simple Federal-style building in 1822. Restored after a 1981 fire, it still has the feeling of a country church. It has a lovely garden that's open to the public and holds music programs on a regular basis. **St. Luke's School**, established in 1945, accepts children of all faiths and is one of the city's most highly respected private day schools. The thrift store next door is a tad more expensive than you'd expect, but it's well stocked. ♦ 487 Hudson St (between Barrow and Christopher Sts). 924.0562

86 Grove Court

Between 10 and 12 Grove Street, at the middle of what some consider to be the most authentic group of Federal-style houses in America, you can find one of the most charming and private enclaves in Manhattan. These six brick-fronted buildings were built in 1854 as houses for workingmen when the court was known as "Mixed Ale Alley." ♦ Between Bedford and Hudson Sts

87 Chumley's

$$ A speakeasy during the 1920s, this signless building has a convenient back door on Barrow Street, still used by regulars. Cozy and convivial, with working fireplaces and wooden benches deeply carved with customers' initials, it has atmosphere aplenty, but the food isn't terrific and the patronage is tourist-heavy. Nevertheless, it's a great place to stop for a drink, especially if you like ghost stories. According to local legend, the long-departed Mrs. Chumley comes back and rearranges the furniture in the middle of the night. *Note:* 2007 structural damage has closed the place for an indefinite period. ♦ American ♦ Daily, dinner. 86 Bedford St (between Barrow and Grove Sts). 675.4449

88 John's Pizzeria

★★$ Arguing about the best pizza in New York is something of a local sport, and this place, established in 1934, deserves at least honorable mention. No slices here, but the thin-crust pies are made in a coal oven—one reason they're so good. Another is the delicious toppings—fresh mushrooms, spicy sausage, or whatever you like. ♦ Italian ♦ Daily, lunch and dinner. 278 Bleecker St (at Morton St). 243.1680. ♿ Also at 408 E 64th St (between York and First Aves), 935.2895; 260 W 44th St (between Broadway and Eighth Ave). 391.7560

89 Pó

★★★$$ Whenever you visit this tiny, romantic place, you can count on such inventive, flavorful dishes as tomato ravioli filled with white beans in balsamic vinegar or marinated brown-butter quail with pomegranate molasses on a salad of *frisée* (curly endive). If you're having trouble making up your mind about which of the tempting dishes to select, a tasting menu is the way to go. ♦ Italian ♦ M, Tu, dinner; W-Su, lunch and dinner. Reservations recommended. 31 Cornelia St (between Bleecker and W Fourth Sts). 645.2189. Also at 276 Smith St (between Degraw and Sackett Sts), Brooklyn. 718/875.1980

89 Cornelia Street Café

★★$$ Started by artists in the dark ages of the late 1970s, this café has always been charming, with whitewashed brick walls, fireplace, and glass-paneled doors that in summer open onto the quiet street for alfresco dining. The menu changes seasonally and includes a tasty, crisp salmon with paella, zesty pepper-crusted yellowfin tuna with sweet garlic risotto cake, and grilled double-ribbed pork chop with spinach. Save room for one of the desserts baked on the premises—banana tarte Tatin with cocoa sorbet, for example. There's also live music that changes weekly and an acclaimed poetry program and other spoken-word events. ♦ Bistro/Café ♦ M-F, breakfast, lunch, and dinner; Sa, Su, brunch and dinner. Reservations recommended. 29 Cornelia St (between Bleecker and W Fourth Sts). 989.9319 ♿

90 Murray's Cheese Shop

Over 250 varieties of cheeses, many from Italy, France, and Spain, are sold at this expanded location, across the street from their old (and tiny) corner shop. Superior service keeps satisfied customers coming back, despite the ever-rising prices. All kinds of olives (pitted and non-), salads, and delicacies are also offered. ♦ Daily. 254 Bleecker St (between Leroy and Morton Sts). 243.3289. ♿ Also at Grand Central Terminal (off Lexington Ave and 43rd St). 922.1540

90 Aphrodisia

Herbs and spices rule at this longstanding Village institution, replete with overfed in-shop kitty. Whether seeking remedies or flavors, scoop your choice from among the 800 herbs and spices into a small paper bag and label it with the name and price. Those ready to turn over a new leaf could consult the wide selection of books for healthful living. ♦ Daily. 264 Bleecker St (between Sixth Ave and Seventh Ave S). 989.6440 ♿

90 Trattoria Pesce & Pasta

★$ Beginning with the bright red entrance and the windows displaying the catch of the day with an array of antipasti, this is one of the neighborhood's more welcoming places. Start with a fresh antipasti selection—marinated peppers, grilled fennel, marinated white beans, mozzarella—or *pasta e fagioli* (a broth rich with beans, vegetables, and macaroni). The fish specialties change according to market availability, but keep an eye out for the *zuppa di pesce* (an Italian bouillabaisse) or the mixed seafood grill. ♦ Italian ♦ Daily, lunch and dinner. No reservations. 262 Bleecker St (between Leroy and Morton Sts). 645.2993. Also at four uptown locations

91 Home

★★$$ This dining place was named in appreciation of the James Beard quote: "American food is anything you eat at home." Former Midwesterners David Page and Barbara Shinn have created a cozy spot, best described as an urban farmhouse, where they offer heartwarming entrées of peppered Newport steak, cumin-crusted pork chops, and grilled New York trout. Also memorable are the homemade ketchup, barbecue sauce, and thyme-mustard dressing. For dessert, try the creamy dark chocolate pudding. ♦ American ♦ M-F, breakfast, lunch, and dinner; Sa, Su, brunch and dinner. 20 Cornelia St (between Bleecker and W Fourth Sts). 243.9579

92 Blue Note Jazz Club

Top jazz artists perform here nightly at 8PM and 10:30PM (and sometimes again at 12:30AM), and on weekends for a jazz brunch and matinee at 1PM and 3:30PM. A reasonably priced continental menu is available. Grover Washington Jr., Abbey Lincoln, Milton Nascimiento, Clark Terry, Ron Carter, and Oscar Peterson have all made appearances here. ♦ Cover, drink minimum. Daily. Reservations recommended. 131 W Third St (between MacDougal St and Sixth Ave). 475.8592

93 La Lanterna di Vittorio

★★$ The menu at this quintessential old-school Greenwich Village café near NYU and Washington Square may be limited, but the pizzas and panini are tasty, the several varieties of lasagne satisfying, and the desserts and cappuccino downright praiseworthy. Good as it is, though, the draw isn't the food—it's the atmosphere: relaxing by day, dark and sexy by night, with fireplaces that set the mood for contemplating romance or Romanticism, depending on the circumstances. ♦ Italian/Café. ♦ Daily, breakfast, lunch, dinner, and late-night meals. 129 MacDougal St (at W Third St). 529.5945

94 Minetta Lane Theatre

This Off-Broadway theater presents revues as well as new plays in a more comfortable setting than many. Seats 378. ♦ 18 Minetta La (between MacDougal St and Sixth Ave). 420.8000 ♿

95 Bleecker Bob's Golden Oldies

The selection of records and CDs is voluminous, grouped according to genre (everything except classical and opera), not artist, but the knowledgeable staff knows the location of every last recording, and late-night browsing is an encouraged Village tradition. You might find yourself elbow-to-elbow with rock stars themselves. ♦ Daily, noon till late. 118 W Third St (between MacDougal St and Sixth Ave). 475.9677 ♿

95 Caffé Reggio

★$ Home since 1927 to one of New York City's oldest cafés, this fabulously bleak place is a great spot for deep conversation or journal writing, and the food offerings pass muster. Sip your coffee outside in nice weather. ♦ Café ♦ Daily, lunch and late-night meals. No credit cards accepted. 119 MacDougal St (at W Third St). 475.9557

96 Minetta Tavern

★$$ The caricatures and murals behind the old oak bar and elsewhere around this classical Italian restaurant will take you back to the Village of the 1930s (and it should—it's virtually unchanged since the day it opened in 1937). The menu offers standard northern-style Italian fare, which is nicely prepared, if not very exciting. ♦ Northern Italian ♦ Daily, lunch and dinner. 113 MacDougal St (at Minetta La). 475.3850 ♿

97 Peanut Butter & Co.

★$ You'll never look at a jar of Skippy the same way after feasting on one of the heavenly homemade peanut butter creations whipped up regularly at this unlikely eatery. Try the Elvis, a mouthful of sandwich made with peanut butter and sliced bananas drizzled with honey on thick toasted white bread. Like all the sandwiches, it's served with a side order of carrot sticks and potato chips. Unglue your smile with a Cherry Lime Rickey—or lots of water. There are peanut butter desserts too at this place that always seems to be manned by a young, friendly staff. ♦ American ♦ Daily, lunch and dinner. 240 Sullivan St (between Bleecker and W Third Sts). 677.3995

98 Il Mulino

★★$$$$ Behind the unassuming façade lies one of the most expensive restaurants in the city. It's an old-style Italian that doesn't put much stock in smarm or charm; its goal is to serve up plentiful portions and keep your wineglass filled and the courses coming. Space is tight—or cozy, depending on your perspective—and the dining room, with exposed-brick walls, has seen better days since it blazed onto the scene in 1980. Most appealing nowadays to an older bucks-to-burn crowd, it's still quite popular. Begin with something from the antipasto table—carpaccio, clams casino, or the crispy fried zucchini. Follow with chicken braised in wine and artichokes or rolled veal with wine, cream, and wild mushrooms. For dessert, the cheesecake or the poached pear topped with fresh cream is recommended. There's an extensive wine list. ♦ Italian ♦ M-F, lunch and dinner; Sa, dinner. Reservations required. 86 W Third St (between Thompson and Sullivan Sts). 673.3783

99 Village Chess Shop

Chess shops have been found on this strip of Thompson Street for decades, and this one goes way back. No slick emporium, the close quarters enhance the intensity of the game at hand. You can play chess from noon to midnight with another expert like yourself, or buy unique chess sets made from materials ranging from nuts and bolts to ivory and onyx. Diagonally across Thompson at No. 219 is **Chess Forum** (475.2369), with a more browsable space for viewing its hundreds of chess sets. Their annex next door offers timed games, both person-to-person and against a desktop computer. ♦ Daily, noon till late. 230 Thompson St (between Bleecker and W Third Sts). 475.8130 ♿

100 Stella Dallas

This shop is a good source for reasonably priced men's and women's retro rags from the 1940s to 1950s, collected by a fashion stylist and a clothing designer. ♦ Daily. 218 Thompson St (between Bleecker and W Third Sts). 674.0447

101 Center for Architecture/AIA

Designed by architect **Andrew Berman**, the innovative home of New York's chapter of the **AIA (American Institute of Architects)** opened to much ballyhoo in 2003. Heating and cooling are provided by two on-site geothermal wells; the eight-story structure also benefits from a clever use of natural lighting. The $2.5 million, 12,000-square-foot former industrial space includes galleries, a theater and lecture hall, a public resource center, and the **New York Foundation for Architecture**'s office space, as well as that of the AIA. ♦ M-Sa. 536 La Guardia Pl (between Bleecker and W Third Sts). 683.0023. www.aiany.org ♿

102 Ennio & Michael

★★★$$ Welcome to a well-run, cheerfully bustling trattoria. The large, airy dining room allows comfortable spacing between tables, and in fair weather you can sit outside in their pleasant (and rare) off-street plaza space. Among the hearty offerings are a *zucchini fritti* (french-fried shoe-string zucchini) appetizer and such satisfying main courses as *spaghetti puttanesca* (with tomatoes, capers, and olives) and *rigatoni amatriciana* (with fresh tomato sauce, prosciutto, and onions). ♦ Italian ♦ Daily, lunch and dinner. 539 La Guardia Pl (between Bleecker and W Third Sts). 677.8577 ♿

103 39 and 41 Commerce Street

This well-preserved pair of mansard-roofed houses with a central garden dates to 1831. An apocryphal but oft-repeated tale is that they were built by a sea captain for his two unmarried daughters, who were not on speaking terms. ♦ Between Barrow and Bedford Sts

104 75½ Bedford Street

Built in 1873, this 9.5-foot-wide building is thought to be the narrowest in the city and was the last New York City residence of Edna St. Vincent Millay and her husband, Eugen Boissevain. **No. 77** next door, built in 1800, is the oldest house in the Village. ♦ Between Morton and Commerce Sts

104 Cherry Lane Theatre

Built as a brewery in 1836, this building—on one of the Village's most charming and tucked-away historical blocks—was converted to a 184-seat theater (founded in 1924 by Edna St. Vincent Millay and pals) for avant-garde productions. *Godspell* had its world premiere here. ♦ 38 Commerce St (between Bedford and Barrow Sts). 989.2020. www.cherrylanetheatre.org

105 Hudson Park Branch, NYPL

The original 1905 building by **Carrère & Hastings**, who also designed the main branch up on Fifth Avenue, was expanded in 1935. **The Early Childhood Resource and Information Center**, a facility for parents, teachers, and caregivers, is located here; call for their special hours. ♦ Tu-Sa. 66 Leroy St (at Seventh Ave S). 243.6876

106 Church of Our Lady of Pompeii

The gilded marble interior of this 1927 church designed by **Matthew Del Gaudio** gives the impression that this structure might have been moved intact from the hills of Italy. Restored itself in recent years, its benevolent façade looks upon a freshly beautified **Father Demo Square.** The 2007 completion of work here anchors this remnant of the old Italian enclave in Greenwich Village. Some services are still conducted in Italian. ♦ 25 Carmine St (between Bedford and Bleecker Sts). 989.6805

107 House of Oldies

Here is an incredible collection of rare and out-of-circulation rock 'n' roll and R&B LPs (some barely, if ever, played), including 10,000 rock 'n' roll 78s and over a million 45s. Additional stock is sent up from the basement via a dumbwaiter. ♦ M-Sa. 35 Carmine St (between Bedford and Bleecker Sts). 243.0500

108 1 Minetta Street

DeWitt Wallace and his wife, Lila Acheson, published the first issue of the *Reader's Digest* from a basement apartment here in 1922. ♦ At Sixth Ave

109 Porto Rico

Opened in 1907, this old-time coffee store isn't even one of the Village's oldest, but the long lines of caffeine-oholics on Saturday mornings are evidence that it's the uncontested favorite. Three reasons: the quality of the beans, the price, and the abs lutely heavenly scent that fills the air (the beans are measured out from open burlap sacks). The store also has a huge selection of teas, both caf and herbal; all sorts of coffee and tea brewing devices; and a tiny coffee bar so you can pick up an espresso and biscotti to keep you occupied while you're on line. ♦ Daily. 201 Bleecker St (between MacDougal St and Sixth Ave). 477.5421. Also at 40½ St. Marks Pl (between First and Second Aves). 533.1982; 107 Thompson St (between Prince and Spring Sts). 966.5758

They're all over New York, but rooftop water tanks seem more visible in the Village than anywhere else. Their average height above sea level is about the same as a five-story building, and any building higher than that needs to pump water to its upper floors. The tanks are made of western yellow cedar and have a life expectancy of about 30 years. The two-inch boards, which are as strong as 14 inches of concrete, are held together with steel bands around the outside, and the water inside swells the wood to a tight fit. The insulating properties of wood prevent freezing in winter and keep the water cool, if not cold, in summer.

110 Le Figaro Café

★★$ In the old days, this place was a Beat hangout, with underground shows downstairs. But that, as they say, is history. Toda this high-volume beanery caters to the weekend blitz of young tourists on Bleecker Street. ♦ Bistro/Café ♦ M-F, lunch and dinner; Sa, Su, brunch, dinner, and late-nig meals. No credit cards accepted. 184 Bleecker St (at MacDougal St). 677.1100 ♿

111 Ponte Vecchio

★$$ This bustling white dining room decorated with posters is one of the old reliable Italian places in the neighborhood, and it offers a large, traditional menu. Try th calamari with marinara sauce; asparagus topped with Parmesan; spaghetti amatriciana; rigatoni with sausage and cream; fettuccine with sun-dried tomatoes and arugula; chicken with white wine, artichokes mushrooms, and peppers; and old-fashione cheesecake. ♦ Italian ♦ Daily, lunch and dinner. Reservations recommended. 206 Thompson St (between Bleecker and W Thir Sts). 228.7701 ♿

112 The Bitter End

Since 1961, this small room has served as a springboard for numerous high-octane musical (and comedy) careers—think Bill Cosby, Bob Dylan, Mimi Farina, Linda Ronstadt, Stevie Wonder, Norah Jones—but now features mostly once-famous folkies and/or young hopefuls performing rock, folk country, and occasionally comedy. But you never know . . . ♦ Cover, drink minimum. Nightly, 7:30PM or 8PM till late. 147 Bleecker St (between La Guardia Pl and Thompson St). 673.7030

113 University Village

This 1966 high-rise housing complex is noteworthy in a city where high-rises are the norm, thanks to **I.M. Pei & Partners**' deft handling of scale, a result of the well-articulated façade. The concrete framing an recessed glass clearly define each apartment unit and provide a straightforward, unadorned exterior pattern (the same treatment Pei used in his Kips Bay apartments on East 30th Street). Because of a pinwheel apartment plan, the inner corridors are short, and apartments are unusually spacious. Two towers are owned by **NYU**; the third is a co-op. A 36-foot-high sculpture in the plaza between the towers is an enlargement of a cubist piece by Picasso. ♦ 100 and 110 Bleecker St (between Mercer St and La Guardia Pl); 505 La Guardia Pl (at Bleecker St)

14 Caffè Dante

★$ Although Italian is spoken here, this place is really made authentic by the strong coffee and the let-them-sit-as-long-as-they-want attitude. Treat yourself to the cheesecake. ♦ Café ♦ Daily, 10AM till late. No credit cards accepted. 79 MacDougal St (between W Houston and Bleecker Sts). 982.5275

15 Da Silvano

★★$$$ An interesting menu features Tuscan fare. Start with chicken-liver *crostini* (croutons), followed by rigatoni focaccia in a sauce of butter, cream, garlic, sage, rosemary, tomato, and double-smoked bacon or quail in a Barolo wine sauce with radicchio. The elegantly rustic rooms attract a handsome, affluent, celebrity-riddled clientele. The service is correct, and the wine list well chosen. ♦ Italian ♦ M-Sa, lunch and dinner; Su, dinner. Reservations recommended. 260 Sixth Ave (between W Houston and Bleecker Sts). 982.2343 ♿

16 Sullivan Street Playhouse

This 153-seat theater had long been home to the longest-running production in American history, *The Fantasticks*, which opened in May 1960 and finally closed in 2002 (only to reopen elsewhere in the city just a few years later). In honor of this feat, Sullivan Street along this block has been dubbed "Fantasticks' Lane" by the city. ♦ 181 Sullivan St (between W Houston and Bleecker Sts). 674.3838

17 MacDougal-Sullivan Gardens Historic District

These 24 houses date from 1844 to 1850. To attract middle-class professionals, **William Sloane Coffin** (heir to the W.J. Sloane furniture fortune) modernized them in 1920 and combined their gardens to make a midblock private park. ♦ Sullivan and MacDougal Sts (between W Houston and Bleecker Sts)

Within the MacDougal-Sullivan Gardens Historic District:

Chez Jacqueline

★★$$ This popular bistro owned and run by lively Jacqueline Zini specializes in dishes from her native Provence, including one of the best fish soups in town and a delicious beef stew cooked in red wine. Other winners are the rack of lamb with fresh herbs and sautéed veal kidneys with braised onion. Try the tarte Tatin (caramelized upside-down apple tart) for dessert. ♦ French ♦ M-F, lunch and dinner; Sa, Su, dinner. Reservations required. 72 MacDougal St. 505.0727 ♿

118 Raffetto's

Fresh pasta is made daily (witness the alchemy next door), and, just as it's been done since 1906, it's cut into a variety of widths before your eyes. Stuffed versions—including ravioli and tortellini—are also for sale, as are sausages and imported Italian products that will help you create first-rate dishes. ♦ Tu-Sa. 144 W Houston St (between Sullivan and MacDougal Sts). 777.1261 ♿

119 Cable Building

This 1894 **McKim, Mead & White** building was once the headquarters and powerhouse of the Broadway Cable Traction Company, which operated streetcars propelled by underground cables in the 19th century. The home furnishings giant **Crate & Barrel** (308.0011) now occupies the ground-floor level; art and design businesses predominate in the converted upper-level offices. ♦ 611 Broadway (at W Houston St)

Within the Cable Building:

Angelika Film Center

Big commercial hits as well as a selection of independent and foreign films are shown in this ballyhooed but essentially flawed six-screen cinema. The subway rumble from below is an inevitable part of your film's soundtrack; alas, so is the gunfire from the action-flick screening next door, not to mention the noise from the lower-level concession stand that backs onto four of the theaters. But location counts, and the café, a good spot for reading the paper or writing in a journal, serves snacks until midnight. ♦ Mercer and W Houston Sts. 995.2750, 777.FILM

EAST VILLAGE

The East Village is counterculture central, where shaved heads, tattoos, pierce body parts, and whatever's next are as common as is the designer-clad crowd o Madison Avenue. In this neighborhood bounded by the **East River, Broadway**, an **East Houston** and **East 14th Streets**, many of the galleries, boutiques, clubs, and res taurants represent the northern fringe of downtown style—East Side–wise.

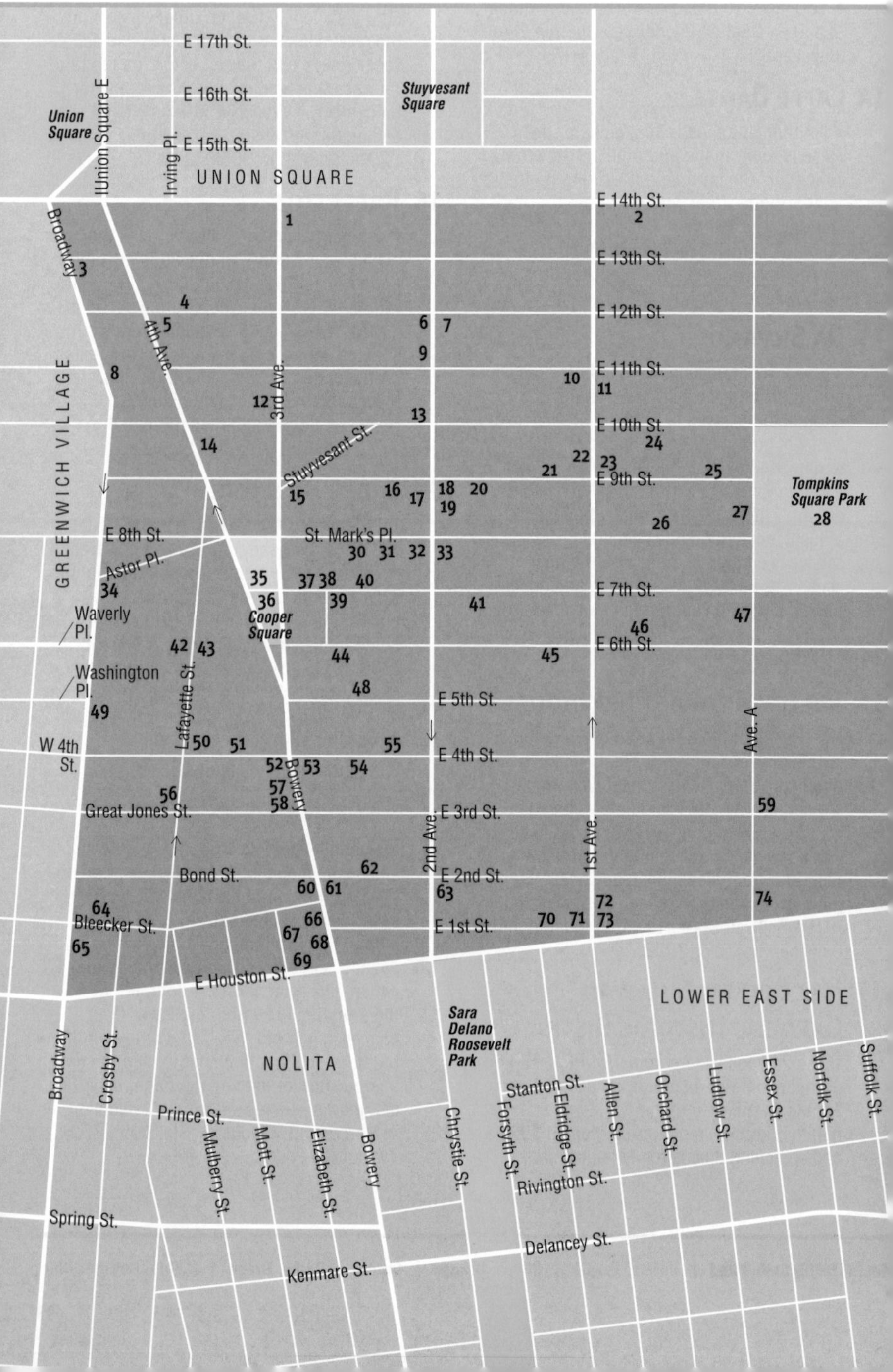

Believe it or not, this bastion of bohemia was once the grandest part of Greenwich illage. Governor Peter Stuyvesant's estate originally covered the area from the presnt **Fourth Avenue** to the East River and from **East 5th** to **East 17th Streets**. He is uried beneath his chapel, now the site of **St. Mark's-in-the-Bowery Church** (built in 799), today known as much for its ministry to the disadvantaged and its far-out regious services as for its historical significance.

In the 1830s, the houses of the Astors, Vanderbilts, and Delanos lined **Lafayette treet** from **Great Jones Street** to **Astor Place**. Almost nothing is left from those times except the old **Merchants' House** (now a museum) on **East Fourth Street** near Lafayette Street and the remaining homes of **Colonnade Row** (also known as "LaGrange Terrace"), where John Jacob Astor and Warren Delano, FDR's grandfather, lived. Astor Place was once the scene of the **Vauxhall Gardens**, where people went in the summer to enjoy music and theater. It was replaced by the popular **Astor Place Opera House**, which is remembered chiefly for the 1849 riot between rival claques (hands hired to applaud a certain performer or act) of the British actor William Macready and the American Edwin Forrest, in which 34 people were killed (or 22, depending on which account you read) before the militia brought the crowd under control. Astor Place was named for the first John Jacob Astor, who arrived from Germany in 1789 at the age of 21 with $25. Before his death at the age of 85, he had made a fortune in fur trading and Manhattan real estate. The 1853 **Astor Library**, built with a bequest from John Jacob Astor, is now the home base of **The Public Theater**, an enterprise where something exciting is always on the boards. Other architectural survivors from the 1850s are the Italianate **Cooper Union**, the country's first coeducational college and the first open to all races and creeds.

Waves of immigration in the late 1800s through the early-to-mid 20th century brought many Eastern and other Europeans to this area, which was then considered part of the Lower East Side. Yiddish theaters abounded along **Second Avenue**, tenement buildings became common, and a reputation for welcoming a population interested in social and political change (includin radical anarchist Emma Goldman, who lived on East 13th Street) took root. By the earl 1960s, the East Village had firmly taken on its own identity as an enclave of countercu ture; hippies crowded into Dayglo-painted "digs," spending nights with the Gratef Dead at such clubs as the **Fillmore East** and the **Electric Circus**; newspapers like the *Ea Village Other* thrived. Though geographically connected to its gentrified western neighbo Greenwich Village, the East Village today remains a younger, less manicured communit But things are hardly as gritty as they once were. The streets of **"Alphabet City"** (Avenue A, B, C, and D), once seedy and drug infested, have been lined with restaurants and bou tiques since the 1990s, though don't expect Madison Avenue either. Architecturally th area—aside from, yes, a creeping chain store or two—is still recycling old housing an commercial spaces. Run-down charm (and early 1900s details) is still the byword.

And the East Village is more than ever a melting pot. A strong Italian influence i still visible in the old-fashioned *pasticcerie* on First Avenue. The stretch of **East Sixt Street** between **First** and **Second Avenues** contains at least 20 Indian and Pakistar restaurants. Near Astor Place at **Cooper Square (Third Avenue)** and **East Sevent Street** is **Little Ukraine**—a world of Byzantine churches with onion domes, shops wit Slavic music and painted eggs, and restaurants serving pierogi and stuffed cabbage. A Japanese enclave centers on **St. Mark's Place** and **Stuyvesant Street** between Secon and Third Avenues, with restaurants, markets, and more.

Multiethnic, yes. Flamboyant, absolutely. Happily, everyone seems to coexis peacefully in what is one of the most colorful niches of New York City today.

1 Kiehl's

Located at the historical **Peter Stuyvesant Pear Tree Corner** since 1851, this vintage establishment produces handmade cosmetics and 118 essences (including four kinds of patchouli oil), using natural ingredients and extracts according to centuries-old formulations. A 2003 expansion gave the place more of a modern look, though it happily provided lots more space for potions—and quicker checkout—as well as a mini café. And despite rumors to the contrary since their sale to L'Oréal, the white-coated staff is extremely helpful and generous with samples. Adding to the unique atmosphere is an impressive collection of new and vintage motorcycles. All in all, it's an East Village must. ♦ M-Sa. 109 Third Ave (between E 13th and E 14th Sts). 677.3171. Also at 154 Columbus Ave (between W 66th and W 67th Sts). 799.3438

The New York City Transit Authority provides nearly 40 percent of America's total mass transit with a fleet consisting of 5,917 subway cars.

2 Immaculate Conception Church

Now a Roman Catholic church, this 1894 building designed by **Barney & Chapman** was originally an Episcopal mission of **Grac Church**, which included a hospital and social service facilities arranged in a cloisterlike setting punctuated by the elaborate tower. ♦ 414 E 14th St (between Ave A and First Ave). 254.0200 ♿

3 Forbidden Planet

This is the city's headquarters for science fiction, horror, and fantasy books, comics, models of your favorite characters—includir the latest creatures from Japanese anime—and related merchandise. ♦ Daily. 840 Broadway (at E 13th St). 473.1576 ♿

4 Footlight Records

Collectors of vintage LPs, rejoice! Here is the world's largest selection of film soundtracks and original Broadway cast albums as well as top vocalists (Sinatra, Crosby, Merman), jazz greats (Django Reinhardt, Bix Beiderbecke), and out-of-print records of all sorts. In most cases, you may listen before buying. ♦ Daily. 113 E 12th St (between Third and Fourth Aves). 533.1572

5 Utrecht Art & Supplies

This major manufacturer of professional art and drafting supplies offers a wide range of materials at excellent prices. Mail-order catalogs are available at the store or by calling 800/223.9132. ♦ Daily. 111 Fourth Ave (between E 11th and E 12th Sts). 777.5353. ♿ Also at 237 W 23rd St (between Seventh and Eighth Aves). 675.8699

6 Village East Cinemas

Built in 1926 as a Yiddish theater, this is now a five-plex, with its share of smallish screening rooms and a mostly indie lineup. The special draw here is the atmospheric upstairs space, where the original stage was set. If the action on the oversized screen doesn't hold your attention, sit back in the comfortable stadium seating and take in the ornate Moorish details of the auditorium's beautifully restored interior and soaring dome, replete with crystal chandelier. Call ahead to check whether the movie you want to see will be screening there. ♦ 181 Second Ave (between E 11th and E 12th Sts). 529.6998

7 Angelica Kitchen

★$ Named after an herb believed to bring good luck, there's enough old-hippie atmosphere to this place that you can catch a glimpse of the East Village circa 1976, when it opened. The seasonal macrobiotic menu (no dairy products or sugar) changes with the solstice and equinox. The vegan fare, such as lentil-walnut pâté, *norimaki* (rolled vegetable sushi), or three-bean chili (lentils, kidney beans, and black beans), and all of the homemade breads, spreads, and salads are made with organically grown ingredients. Vegan ♦ Daily, lunch and dinner. No reservations. No credit cards accepted. 300 E 12th St (between First and Second Aves). 228.2909

7 John's of Twelfth Street

★$$ This place could have been the model for every little Italian restaurant that was ever lit by candles stuck in wine bottles. It's one of the city's oldest and was once a favorite of Arturo Toscanini. The menu is red-sauce traditional, the special salad—big and bursting with a rare variety of fresh ingredients—outstanding. ♦ Italian ♦ Daily, dinner. Reservations recommended. No credit cards accepted. 302 E 12th St (between First and Second Aves). 475.9531

8 Grace Church

The fascinating spire atop this white marble church (the very one in which Tom Thumb got married), which is sited at a bend of Broadway, provides a focal point for any southern approach. **James Renwick Jr.** won the right to design the Episcopal church in a competition. He worked with copybooks of the Pugins, the English theorists, to produce a Gothic Revival structure in 1846 that many consider to be the city's best. **Heins & LaFarge** designed an enlargement for the chancel in 1900. Renwick's rectory, next door at **804 Broadway**, is another marvel—a restrained foil for the more fanciful church. Tours available on Sundays at 1PM. ♦ 800 Broadway (between E 10th and E 12th Sts). 254.2000

bar veloce

9 Bar Veloce

This is New York's most stylish panini bar. Gracious owner Fred Twomey mans a bar that serves nothing but Italian wines by the glass and delectable Italian panini sandwiches, served with a variety of gourmet fillings. Discreet pegs under the bar conceal coats and bags, leaving you free to flirt, nibble, or watch one of the black-and-white Japanese or Italian films playing on the small movie screen in the rear. A great place for a light meal, pre-dinner aperitif, or late-night libation. ♦ Daily, dinner only. 175 Second Ave (between E 11th and E 12th Sts). 260.3200. Also at 176 Seventh Ave (at W 20th St). 629.5300

10 Veniero's Pasticceria & Cafe

★$ Mirrors and chandeliers decorate this century-old bakery/café. But customers generally don't notice the décor; they're hypnotized by the desserts. Try the biscotti; creamy pastries; fluffy, golden ricotta cheesecakes; and fabulous fruit-topped custard tortes and tarts. There's also a seating area that is often crowded with locals and tourists, where cappuccino goes well with a *sfogliatelle* (a flaky cheese-filled pastry). ♦ Bakery/Café ♦ Daily. 342 E 11th St (between First and Second Aves). 674.7070

11 De Robertis Pasticceria & Café

★$ If you can get past the display counters filled with traffic-stopping cheesecakes, pies, cakes, and biscotti (among the best in the city), you'll find a wonderful tin-ceilinged and mosaic-tiled coffeehouse that hasn't changed a bit since it began serving frothy cappuccino back in 1904. ♦ Bakery/Café ♦ Tu-Su. 176 First Ave (between E 10th and E 11th Sts). 674.7137

12 NY Central Art Supply

In business since 1905, this art store has knowledgeable staff ready to help you choose brushes, colors, canvases, textile and printmaking supplies, and more. Upstairs, the famous paper department offers thousands of papers from around the world, from Australia to Bhutan. ♦ M-Sa. 62 Third Ave (between E 10th and E 11th Sts). 473.7705

13 St. Mark's Church-in-the-Bowery

Erected in 1799 on the site of a garden chapel on Peter Stuyvesant's estate, St. Mark's has always been held in high regard as a neighborhood church, and its stately late-Georgian style encourages this congenial attitude. As its membership grew, a Greek Revival steeple designed by **Ithiel Towne** was added in 1828, giving the church a more urban image; and a cast-iron Italianate portico was added to the entrance in 1854. This mélange does not mesh successfully, but it does reflect the parishioners' concerns about preserving the church's early history. A fire nearly destroyed the building in 1978. Architect **Herman Hassinger** took charge of the restoration, which included rebuilding the steeple according to the original design. The interior was gutted and redesigned in a simple and straightforward manner, typical of the pre- and post-Revolutionary War period. The stained-glass windows on the ground floor, designed by Hassinger, use themes similar to the original windows. ♦ 131 E 10th St (at Second Ave). 674.6377. www.stmarkschurch-in-the-bowery.com

Within St. Mark's Church-in-the-Bowery:

St. Mark's mission has long embraced support of the arts. To that end, three nonprofit groups housed here have made significant contributions to the lively state of independent productions and artistic development throughout the city.

Danspace Project

Commissioned works and works-in-progress from adventurous contemporary choreographers stand out against the church's elegant white interior. 674.8112. www.danspaceproject.org

Ontological-Hysteric Theater

Founded in 1968 by Richard Foreman, this company stages works of "compositional theater," drawing on many facets of 20th-century thought and art–philosophy, psychoanalysis, digital video–to startle us into new modes of perception. 533.4650. www.ontological.com

The Poetry Project

Programs on this experimental scene (site of Allen Ginsberg's only joint reading with Robert Lowell) include three readings series–Mondays, Wednesdays, and late-night Fridays–plus lectures, special events, and a New Year's Day marathon. 674.0910. www.poetryproject.com

14 Bussola Bar & Grill

★★$$$ In honor of the card game *briscola* played in Italy, the walls here are decorated with cards. But who cares about playing cards when you can feast on such authentic Sicilian specialties as artichokes with mint; tagliatelle with sausage, peas, and cream; bucatini with sardines; and swordfish carpaccio? ♦ Italian ♦ M-Sa, dinner. 65 Fourth Ave (between E Ninth and E 10th Sts). 254.1940

15 St. Mark's Bookshop

This popular independent bookstore–with wide aisles, natural woods, great lighting, and an airy, modern design–is home to an eclectic selection of titles. Besides literary fiction and nonfiction, they specialize in items you're not likely to find in the chains, such as journals on African culture, feminist issues, socialism, and cultural theory. ♦ Daily. 31 Third Ave (at Stuyvesant St). 260.7853. www.stmarksbookshop.com ♿

15 Sunrise Mart

Need a rice cooker? Octopus tentacles? This Japanese part supermarket, part community center above **St. Mark's Bookshop** has both, plus health and beauty aids, fresh delicacies, and good prepared foods. ♦ Daily. 4 Stuyvesant St (at E Ninth St), second floor. 598.3040. Also at 494 Broome St (between W Broadway and Wooster St). 219.0033

16 The Cloister Café

★ $ A delightful neighborhood spot for escaping the city, the inside is dark and encrusted with stained glass, while the outside is a beautiful grapevine-canopied bower. Gigantic salads, good challah French toast, and fresh fish entrées are featured. In hot weather, the yogurt ambrosia (made

All That Jazz

azz may have been born in New Orleans, but New York ity was its ultimate destination. In the heyday of jazz uring the 1940s and 1950s, musicians knew they adn't really made it until they'd played the Big Apple. nd play they do: Everything from fusion to Dixieland ontinues to flourish in locations throughout the city.

he Clubs

he clubs listed below regularly host big names in the azz world. Cover charges vary, depending on the club nd the performer, but you can almost always lessen he bite by listening from the bar.

irdland Having enjoyed its first heyday in the 1950s, hen it was located nearby on Broadway at West 52nd treet, and such luminaries as Charlie Parker and Dave rubeck ignited the stage, this **Theater District** spot now osts stars of today like the Chico O'Farrill Afro-Cuban Jazz rchestra, Diana Krall, John Pizzarelli, and Jessica lolaskey. The Django Reinhardt Festival lands here nnually in November. ♦ 315 W 44th St (between Eighth nd Ninth Aves). 581.3080. www.birdlandjazz.com

lue Note Big names—think Brubeck, the Clark Terry uartet, Cassandra Wilson—appear regularly at this remier jazz showcase, a must for jazz buffs. There are sually two shows on weeknights and three on weekend ights, and their Sunday jazz brunch in an institution in this ntimate room. ♦ 131 W Third St (between MacDougal St nd Sixth Ave). 475.8592. www.bluenote.net

Iridium Located along a busy stretch of Broadway, this is one of the city's most popular venues featuring well-known talent like Benny Carter, Jimmy Scott, and the Mingus Big Band. Les Paul on Monday eves is not to be missed. The cozy space has two sets on weekdays, three sets on weekends. The food menu has a southern slant, featuring items like chicken dumplings and crab cakes. ♦ 1650 Broadway (at W 51st St). 582.2121. www.iridiumjazzclub.com

Sweet Rhythm The jazz goes on in this one time Sweet Basil space, often with a world beat these days. As always, this small wood-and-brick space fills early, helped by their moderate cover charges. A Tuesday-night vocal series joins the usual two shows per weeknight and three on Friday and Saturday evenings. Weekend jazz brunches are a **Village** ritual. ♦ 88 Seventh Ave S (between Barrow and Grove Sts). 255.3626. www.sweetrhythm.com

Village Vanguard Since 1935, this landmark club has hosted jazz greats. Monk played here; so did Miles. Today the Vanguard Jazz Orchestra fills the house on Monday nights, and jazz virtuosos like the Jim Hall Trio, the Cedar Walton Quartet, the Joe Lovano Quintet, Bill Charlap, and Paul Motian pack them in the rest of the week. There are two sets nightly throughout the week, and a third usually added on Saturdays. ♦ 178 Seventh Ave S (at Perry St). 255.4037. www.villagevanguard.com

with fresh fruits and nuts) and a refreshing glass of iced mint tea are the next-best thing to air conditioning. ♦ American ♦ M-F, lunch, dinner, and late-night meals; Sa, Su, brunch, dinner, and late-night meals. No credit cards accepted. 238 E Ninth St (between Second Ave and Stuyvesant St). 777.9128

17 Ottendorfer Branch, NYPL

Anna Ottendorfer, founder of the German-language newspaper *New York Staats Zeitung,* founded this beautiful terra-cotta building, which was built by **William Schickel** in 1884. Before becoming a branch of the **New York Public Library**, it was the home of the **Freie Bibliothek und Lesehalle**, a German-language library and reading room. ♦ M-Sa. 135 Second Ave (between St. Mark's Pl and E Ninth St). 674.0947. www.nypl.org

18 Veselka

★$ An amazing array of Eastern European fare—pierogi, kielbasa, blintzes, and stuffed cabbage—is turned out at bargain-basement prices in this cozy establishment. A presence in the East Village for decades, it's more café now than its original counter style, but service is swell, décor a bit classier, and the food always satisfying. For pierogi on the go, stop at their corner kiosk on the brink of the Lower East Side. ♦ Ukrainian/coffeehouse ♦ Daily, 24 hours. 144 Second Ave (at E Ninth St). 228.9682. Also at **Little Veselka**, 75 E First St (at First Ave)

19 Ukrainian East Village

★$ Located within the **Ukrainian National Home** community center, this place brings on the borscht (the Red Lithuanian is served cold; Ukrainian-style is hot). Home-style sauerkraut with mushrooms, *varenyky* (pierogi), *nalesnyky* (blintzes), and *letcho* (Hungarian goulash)—and lots of it—top the old-world menu. Or try the pierogi-blintzes-stuffed cabbage combo platter. ♦ Ukrainian ♦ Daily, lunch and dinner. No credit cards accepted. 140 Second Ave (between St. Mark's Pl and E Ninth St). 614.3283 ♿

20 Dinosaur Hill

Adults will enjoy the fanciful toys, clothing, and gifts on offer here every bit as much as the children for whom they're ostensibly intended. Rattles in cherry wood or walnut prove that it's never too early to teach good design; the selection also includes one-of-a-kind quilts from Guatemala, a Noah's Ark on wheels, and alphabet blocks in 12 languages. ♦ Daily. 306 E Ninth St (between First and Second Aves). 473.5850

21 Enchantments

Local and visiting witches stop at this dimly lit, incense-laden (but not unfriendly) shop for the tools of their craft: herbs, oils, tarot cards, caldrons, and ceremonial knives (used to cut air and create a sacred space), plus candles, handmade soap, jewelry, books, and calendars. ♦ Daily. 341 E Ninth St (between First and Second Aves). 228.4394

22 Theater for the New City

Located in what used to be an indoor market, this offbeat, roots-in-the-1960s troupe has managed to keep its period ambience and point of view. The productions are hit-and-miss. Each of the four theaters seats between 60 and 100. ♦ 155 First Ave (between E Ninth and E 10th Sts). 254.1109. www.theaterforthenewcity.net ♿

23 P.S. 122

If the cutting edge can have institutions, this renowned space housed in a redbrick former public school building gets high marks as a landmark of avant-garde dance, theater, and performance art, providing creators with rehearsal space and critical feedback as well as production opportunities. Artistic director Mark Russell, who spent his 21-year tenure fostering the careers of such scene-makers as Eric Bogosian and Spalding Gray, stepped down in 2004; his replacement, **Vallejo Gantner** (formerly of the Dublin Fringe Festival), carries on with a commitment to works that leave audience "arguing about what the whole thing was about." ♦ 150 First Ave (at E Ninth St). 477.5829. www.ps122.org

Inside the doorway of the Public Theater are two white columns. "May Peace Prevail on Earth" is written on each in Japanese and English. The columns were sent to the late Joseph Papp by the Society of Prayer for World Peace, an organization that does not aim to convert lost souls, but is dedicated to planting as many peace poles as possible.

24 Russian & Turkish Baths

The last remaining bathhouse in a neighborhood that once was full of them still gets its steam heat the old-fashioned way: Enormous boulders are heated up in the sub-basement and when they're red-hot, water is thrown on them, releasing what the owners claim is true, penetrating wet heat—not mere steam heat. And if you've never had a *platza* rub, try it. Softened oak branches are tied together in the old Russian style to form a natural loofah-like scrub, soapy and tingly and very refreshing. There's also a Turkish bath (sauna). Upstairs are cots if you're overwhelmed, and a small food and drink bar. ♦ Daily, till late. Women only W; Men only Su AM; co-ed all other times. 268 E 10th St (between Ave A and First Ave). 674.9250. www.russianturkishbaths.com

25 Giant Robot

Giant Robot magazine, the influential watcher of Asian and Asian-American pop culture, spawned this shop/gallery offshoot (in two side-by-side shoebox spaces). Visit the shop to stock up on anime-inspired toys, plush dolls, T-shirts, magazines, graphic novels, and such icons as the cuddly/savage Gloomy Bear; step next door to see the work of the artists you've read about in the mag. ♦ Daily. 437 E Ninth St (between Ave A and First Ave). 473.4769. www.grny.net

26 Cafe Mogador

★★$ Deeply satisfying Moroccan cuisine is prepared here without fanfare. Lamb, beef, and *merguez* (sausage) kabobs, tagines, and several varieties of couscous follow a selection of appetizers brought to your table on an enormous tray. The spicy carrots are out of this world, and the steaming *bastilla* (fresh chicken and herbs in a puff pastry) is one of the best entrées on the menu. Top it off with tea or authentic Turkish coffee for dessert. In fair weather, enjoy this neighborhood favorite's outdoor seating. ♦ Middle Eastern/Moroccan ♦ M-F lunch and dinner; Sa, Su, brunch, dinner, and late-night meals. 101 St. Mark's Pl (between Ave A and First Ave). 677.2226

27 Flea Market Café

★★$$ French Bistro fare, from steak frites and duck confit to rabbit and sometimes even wild boar, is served in a setting apropos to the name. The *raviolio* is quite good, a break for vegetarians. Flea Market is a good choice when you've got the patience for the oft-abrupt service—and a seat near the front; the floor-to-ceiling windows overlook Tompkins Square Park. ♦ French bistro ♦ M-F, breakfast, lunch, and dinner; Sa, Su, brunch, dinner, and late-night meals. 131 Avenue A (between St. Marks Pl and E Ninth St). 358.9282

28 Tompkins Square Park

The original plan for this 16-acre park called for extending it all the way east to the river. It was to be a farmers' market, and part of the plan was to cut a canal through the middle to give easy access to Long Island farmers. But the land became a parade ground instead in the 1830s. In 1874 it was the site of America's first labor demonstration, when a carpenters' union clashed with club-wielding police. Among the injured was Samuel Gompers, who later became president of the American Federation of Labor. The little Greek temple near the center covers a drinking fountain placed there by a temperance organization in 1891. The park gained its modern-day notoriety in the 1960s, when it served as the grounds for "love-ins" and "be-ins," and more recently, in the 1980s and early 1990s, when it was the site of a violent confrontation over real-estate speculation in the area and unsuccessful efforts to enforce a nighttime curfew. While real-estate issues (in the form of higher and higher rents) continue to plague the area, Tompkins has been traversed by a lively neighborhood cross-section ever since it was purtied-up thanks to a turn-of-the-21st-century megabuck renovation. ♦ Bounded by Aves A and B, and E Seventh and E 10th Sts. www.nycgovparks.org ♿

29 Jacob Riis Houses Plaza

The large number of people who actually use this park is a tribute to **M. Paul Friedberg**'s careful and creative 1966 plan. Both adults and children find it a pleasant alternative to the streets, with its amphitheater, clever playground furniture, and plenty of room in which to roam. ♦ Bounded by FDR Dr and Ave D, and E Sixth and E 10th Sts

30 St. Mark's Place

In the 1960s, this extension of Eighth Street from Third Avenue to **Tompkins Square Park** was the East Coast capital of hippiedom. The sidewalks were crowded with flower children, and the smell of marijuana was everywhere. Among the shared interests of the street's denizens was the famous rock club **The Electric Circus**, which was in a former Polish social club at **No. 23**. Then, in the 1970s, the street became the punk boardwalk, and multicolored Mohawks predominated. It is quieter these days, but the crowds are still colorful, proving that the street's far from dead. ♦ Ave A to Third Ave

30 St. Mark's Sounds

A true music-lover's store (up one flight, in the historic **Daniel Leroy House**), it doesn't have the conveyor-belt feeling of of the chains, and they sell new and used CDs (and records) in excellent condition. ♦ Daily, till late. 20 St. Mark's Pl (between Second and Third Aves). 677.3444

31 Khyber Pass

★$ A former judge of the Supreme Court in Afghanistan runs this restaurant boasting handsome antiques and offering native music. Knowing you're in good hands—though you could do better on overall food quality and authenticity—just sit back on a throw pillow and get ready to enjoy *aushak* (scallion dumplings) as an appetizer, and entrées such as chicken kabob with *kabuli palow* (carrots, raisins, almonds, and rice). ♦ Afghan ♦ Daily, lunch and dinner. 34 St. Mark's Pl (between Second and Third Aves). 473.0989

32 B & H Dairy

★$ Once upon a time the initials "B & H" stood for owners Bergson and Heller, and the clientele comprised the cast and crew of the Yiddish theater productions along Second Avenue. This tiny restaurant (its official name, B & H Dairy and Vegetarian Cuisine Restaurant, is bigger than the space itself) has been refurbished several times since then, as has the menu—it includes tasty vegetarian offerings—but thank goodness the challah recipe is still the same. The French toast here is heavenly. ♦ Vegetarian ♦ M-F, breakfast, lunch, and dinner; Sa, Su, brunch and dinner. 127 Second Ave (between E Seventh St and St. Mark's Pl). 505.8065

33 Orpheum Theatre

This theater has been around since 1908, when it was the scene of many Yiddish theater hits. *Little Mary Sunshine* had a long run here. In recent decades it has hosted such winners as *Little Shop of Horrors*, the comedienne Sandra Bernhard's one-woman show, and *Stomp!*, the high-energy percussion performance from England.

The Best

Linda Fairstein

Crime Novelist and Former Prosecutor

Like my fictional counterpart in my series of murder mysteries, Alexandra Cooper, when I wasn't at work in the **Criminal Courthouse**, I was—and am—happiest spending time in my favorite places on Manhattan's **Upper East Side**.

I love to wander through the **Frick Collection** to see which paintings are on display, or study the fascinating exhibits at the **Metropolitan Museum of Art**'s **Costume Institute**. If kids are along for the day, the Met's collections of mummies and armor keep them riveted.

If it's a beautiful afternoon, pick up a novel at **The Corner Bookshop** and walk over to one of the city's best-kept secrets, **Central Park**'s **Conservatory Garden**, for a quiet read.

Then, wander down the length of **Madison Avenue**, and daydream at the magnificent window displays—everything from antiques to paintings to jewels to the chicest clothes in town.

♦ 126 Second Ave (between E Seventh St and St. Mark's Pl). 477.2477

34 Astor Place Hair

Considering all there is to do in New York, it may seem strange that watching haircuts became a spectator sport on Astor Place, but look at the pictures on the walls of the far-out styles and you'll understand why. The prices at this vintage 1947 basement barber shop are extremely low, too. (One of the signs in the window says they also do regular haircuts, but don't count on it.) ♦ Daily. 2 Astor Pl (near E Eighth St and Broadway). 475.9854 ♿

35 Cooper Union

Founded by multimillionaire Peter Cooper and built in 1859, this is a full-tuition-scholarship private college. The inventor and industrialist, so brilliant with problems of application in the country's young iron and rail industries, spent his entire life ashamed that he'd never learned to spell or read, and the opening of this school was his attempt to help underprivileged young men and women get the education they deserved but couldn't afford. It was the nation's first coeducational college, the first open to all races and creeds, and the first to offer free adult education courses.

Architect **Frederick A. Petersen** used T-shaped rails Cooper produced in his ironworks in the college's construction. This building is considered by some to be the oldest extant structure in America framed with steel beams, and was declared a National Landmark in 1962. Two other breakthroughs in the building were the use of an elevator and the placing of vents under each of the 900 seats in the **Great Hall** auditorium—in the basement—through which fresh air was pumped.

The Great Hall has, since the school's founding, been the scene of open expression on crucial issues of the day, from suffrage to civil rights. Abraham Lincoln delivered one of his most eloquent speeches here shortly before he was nominated as a presidential candidate. Both the NAACP and the American Red Cross were started in the building. When architect **John Hejduk** gutted and renovated the building in 1974, he provided pristine classrooms, offices, and exhibition space—all with a high-modern Corbusian vocabulary. Leo Friedlander, Milton Glaser, Alex Katz, and Seymour Chwast were graduates of the art school. The college still sponsors provocative lectures and many other events under its Great Hall Programs, which are open to the public. And, though no longer free, several classes are offered at night at nominal fees, to accommodate those working in the daytime. ♦ The Great Hall/The Foundation Building: 7 E Seventh St (between Third and Fourth Aves). 353.4100. Hewitt Building/Administrative offices: 41 Cooper Square (between E Fourth St and Astor Pl). www.cooper.edu

36 Cooper Square

The statue of inventor and industrialist Peter Cooper seated in this triangular park is by Augustus Saint-Gaudens, a Cooper Union graduate. Its base is by **Stanford White**, who spent his boyhood in this neighborhood. ♦ Bounded by Third and Fourth Aves and E Fourth and E Seventh Sts

37 The Fragrance Shop New York

Don't be put off by the densely packed front window; inside it's bright, the huge selection of fragrance and body-care products is well-arranged, and owner Lalita Kumu and her congenial staff love to get to know their customers and share their knowledge. They'll introduce you to the store's own line, which includes facial and skin-care products, body oils, and shampoos, and show you the products they offer from other companies, including Crabtree & Evelyn and J.R. Ligget. They'll even help you create your own scent, then apply it to the perfume, salts, and soap. ♦ Daily. 21 E Seventh St (between Second and Third Aves). 254.8950 ♿

38 McSorley's Old Ale House

Not so long ago, this saloon, which has been here since 1854, had a men-only policy; not surprisingly, it was among the first targets of the women's liberation movement in 1970. The current clientele, which includes women, is made up mostly of college students, but except for that, the place hasn't changed much since its early days. ♦ Daily, 11AM-1AM. No credit cards accepted. 15 E Seventh St (between Second and Third Aves). 473.9148

39 St. George's Ukrainian Catholic Church

An Old World cathedral with modern touches, this 1977 church designed by **Apollinaire Osadea** is the anchor of a Ukrainian neighborhood of more than 1,500 people. ♦ 16-20 E Seventh St (at Taras Shevchenko Pl). 674.1615

40 Surma

This charming, family-owned Ukrainian specialty shop carries (and plays) traditional music, along with ceramics, clothing, small finds, cards, and books, plus "Surma's own" egg-decorating kits and honey. ♦ M-Sa. 11 E Seventh St (between Second and Third Aves). 477.0729 ♿

41 Via della Pace

★$ This warm and unpretentious little café, detailed with delicate ironwork gates, is a few steps up from the street, and has good cappuccino and a very rich tiramisù. Head downstairs for a separate bar scene. ♦ Café ♦ Daily, lunch and dinner. No credit cards accepted. 48 E Seventh St (between First and Second Aves). 529.8024

42 Indochine

★★★$$ This spot survived its own mid-80s hype and can still boast excellent French/Vietnamese food, served in a softly lit tropical-themed room filled with an attractive, well-dressed crowd. Try the delicate spring rolls, a spicy salad of fillet of beef with Asian basil and shallots, crispy duck with ginger, and a delicious whole sea bass with lemongrass. ♦ French/Vietnamese ♦ Daily, dinner. Reservations recommended. 430 Lafayette St. 505.5111

42 Toast

★★$$$ Big overhead fans and palm trees lend a decidedly tropical feel to this space, where the food features the likes of squid ink pasta, Louisiana crab cakes, and other multicultural seafood dishes. ♦ Eclectic ♦ Daily, dinner. Reservations recommended. 428 Lafayette St (between E Fourth St and Astor Pl). 674.4066

42 Colonnade Row

The city's business and social leaders—the Astors, Vanderbilts, and Delanos—once occupied the homes along this row, also known as "LaGrange Terrace." Only four of the nine built in 1833 by **Seth Greer** remain. The streetfront Corinthian colonnade was used to give the row a sense of unity and solidity. Despite designation as a New York City Landmark, these unique and historic structures remain in disrepair. ♦ 428-434 Lafayette St (between E Fourth St and Astor Pl)

42 Astor Place Theatre

Across the street from the more artistically ambitious **Public Theater**, this 298-seat Off-Broadway venue has long runs (*The Foreigner*) and interesting musicals (*Tent Meeting, Meeting, Middle of Nowhere*) that click with the theater crowd. *Blue Man Group: Tubes* got its start here and has been entertaining audiences for about a decade now. ♦434 Lafayette St (between E Fourth St and Astor Pl). 254.4370

43 The Public Theater

Most commonly referred to as, simply, **The Public** (though its full, official name is the **Joseph Papp Public Theater**) the landmark home of **Shakespeare in Central Park** celebrated its 50th anniversary in 2005, and today comprises six theaters. Between the **Newman** (seats 299), the **Anspacher** (seats 299), the **Martinson** (seats 1,650),

After numerous attempts at private incorporation to build a city subway system, the city secured the passage of the Rapid Transit Act in 1891, under which the system was finally built.

The Best

Geraldine Ferraro

Former U.S. Congresswoman

Find out that New York City is more than just Manhattan by:

Taking a ride on the **Staten Island Ferry**.

Visiting the **Bronx Zoo**.

Catching the R subway to the **American Museum of the Moving Image** in **Queens**.

Enjoying the beauty of the **Brooklyn Botanic Garden**.

Attending early-morning Mass at **St. Patrick's Cathedral** (you needn't be Catholic).

Watching a parade (any parade) on **Fifth Avenue**.

Taking a car ride across the **59th Street Bridge** from Queens to Manhattan to see the most beautiful skyline in the world.

Eating your way through a street fair.

Riding the tram to **Roosevelt Island**.

Taking a toddler to the **Children's Museum of Manhattan** to meet the Cat in the Hat.

Bringing a blanket and enjoying **Shakespeare in the Park** at the **Delacorte Theater**.

Sitting in on an auction at **Christie's**.

Visiting **Ellis Island** and listening to the taped voices of those who came to this great country around the turn of the century.

Seeing a Knicks game at **Madison Square Garden** (if you can get tickets!).

Watching the opening of the **New York Stock Exchange**.

Joining the early-morning crowd at **Rockefeller Center** and appearing on *The Today Show*.

Food cruising on **Broadway** and stopping at **H&H Bagels** for the best bagels in the "bagel capital of the world" and **Zabar's**, the quintessential deli!

the **LuEster** (seats 135), the **Susan Stein Shiva** (seats 100), and the **Little Theater** (seats, 90), there's seating for over 2,500. The redbrick and brownstone "Round Arch"-type Romanesque Revival building that houses them was originally the Astor Library (the city's first public—and free—one), built from funds left as a bequest from John Jacob Astor. Built in three stages, its architects were **Alexander Saeltzer** (south wing, 1853), **Griffith Thomas** (center, 1859), and **Thomas Stent** (north wing, 1881). The building later served as the Hebrew Immigrant Aid Sheltering Society. These structures were on the verge of being demolished in the mid-1960s, when that dynamic man of the theater Joseph Papp (after whom the theater was renamed) came to thse rescue with the New York Shakespeare Festival, and by 1976 architect **Giorgio Cavaglieri** had fully converted the structure into a theater complex. Today, The Public not only manages to continually mount superb presentations but always seems to find the money needed to avert financial crises. The list of extraordinary shows that originated here and went on to Broadway includes *Hair* by Gerome Ragni and James Rado, *That Championship Season* by Jason Miller, Michael Bennett's *A Chorus Line* (which won three Pulitzers), David Rabe's *Sticks and Bones*, Caryl Churchill's *Serious Money*, and Rupert Holmes's *The Mystery of Edwin Drood*. In addition to summertime's Shakespeare in the Park (which takes place off-site, at the **Delacorte Theater** in Central Park), The Public mounts about 25 theatrical productions each year. Film viewings were introduced in 1981 and have been on again-off again ever since. Cavaglieri, who also renovated the **Jefferson Market Courthouse**, did an admirable job salvaging much of the interior: Many of the theater spaces are impressive, and the entrance and lobby still include the original Corinthian colonnade. ♦ 425 Lafayette St (between E Fourth St and Astor Pl). Current programs and productions, including Shakespeare in the Park: 539.8500. www.publictheater.org

Within The Public Theater:

Joe's Pub

★★$$ Joe's Pub honors Public Theater founder Joe Papp, not just in name but with a beautifully designed bar and fine classic Italian restaurant that features an eclectic range of first-rate entertainments, from caberet and swing to spoken word, classical, and rock. This is one smart room and a great place to get close to the music, without losing your shirt. It often hosts special late-night events. Cover charge after 8PM. ♦ Daily, 6PM-4AM. 539.8777. Late nights: 539.8778

44 The Ukrainian Museum

After nearly three decades in tiny quarters, this immigrant-founded institution finally has a space grand enough to show off its impressive holdings. Opened in 2005 with an assertive show of the works of the 20th-century modernist Ukrainian sculptor Alexander Archipenko, the three-story brick-and-glass structure, designed by **Sawicki Tarella Architecture+Design**, has spacious galleries to house impressive collections of folk art (including *pysanky*, the intricately patterned Easter eggs), fine art, and archival photographs and documents, as well as innovative installations for traveling exhibitions. There's also a café, a library, and a small gift shop offering books, art objects, textiles, make-your-own-*pysanky* supplies, and some lovely posters. ♦ W-Su, 11:30 AM-5PM. 222 E Sixth St (between Second and Third Aves). 228.0110. www.ukrainianmuseum.org

45 Mitali

★$ The running gag about the Indian restaurants on and around Sixth Street is that one central kitchen supplies them all. However, the meals prepared at this dimly lit eatery are a notch or two above the others. Try the *murgha tikka muslam* (chicken barbecued over charcoal and then cooked in a sauce of cream and almonds) or any of the tandoori specialties. ♦ Indian ♦ M-Th, lunch and dinner; F-Su, brunch and dinner. Reservations recommended. 334 E Sixth St (between First and Second Aves). 533.2508

46 Caravan of Dreams

★★$$ The food in this funky eatery is 100% vegan, mostly organic. Though the "live" category on the menu may seem counterintuitive, it simply indicates raw-food dishes, such as almond and Brazil nut meatballs; some choices are cooked, including burritos, paella, and a ginger curry stir-fry. There's often live music, and yoga classes offered on site. ♦ Vegan ♦ Daily, brunch, lunch, and dinner. 405 E Sixth St (between Ave A and First Ave). 254.1613

47 7A Cafe

★$$ The modern atmosphere here is defined by copious quantities of metal, aluminum, and post-industrial fixtures. The restaurant attracts a young crowd, who appreciate the diner prices and 24/7 hours, not to mention the tasty sandwiches, burgers, and breakfasts. ♦ American ♦ Daily, breakfast, lunch, dinner, and late-night meals. 109 Ave A (at E Seventh St). 475.9001

48 Degustation Wine & Tasting Bar

★★$$$ Score one of the 16 seats in this tiny, scene-y place and watch—side by side with your fellow diners at the U-shaped counter—as your envelope-pushing tapas are prepared in full view: perhaps squid stuffed with short ribs or crispy sweetbreads with yogurt and dill. ♦ French/Spanish ♦ M-Sa, dinner. 239 E Fifth St (between Second Ave and Bowery). 979.1012

49 Shakespeare & Co. Booksellers

Though not related to its Paris namesake, this bookstore is a favorite among New Yorkers. One of the last of the great independents. ♦ Daily till late. 716 Broadway (between E Fourth St and Washington Pl). 529.1330. Also at 939 Lexington Ave (at E 69th St). 570.0201; 1 Whitehall St (at Broadway). 742.7890; 137 E 23rd St (at Lexington Ave). 505.2054. www.shakesandco.com

50 Astor Wines and Spirits

A huge selection and good prices (plus a strong selection of organics and biodynamics) are the draws of this vast wine and liquor shop, moved in 2006 from its longtime Greenwich Village home to the 1885 landmark DeVinne Press building (**Babb, Cook & Willard**). ♦ Daily. 399 Lafayette St (at E Fourth St). 674.7500. www.astorwines.com

51 Merchant's House Museum

This outstanding example of an 1830s Greek Revival town house remains intact, with interiors and furnishings just the way they were when wealthy merchant Seabury Tredwell and his family lived here, thanks to Tredwell's daughter, Gertrude. Rumor has it Gertrude was the inspiration for Henry James's novel *Washington Square*, although museum staff staunchly deny any such connection. Paintings, furniture, china, and books reflect their tasteful and conservative style. ♦ Admission. Th-M, noon-5PM. Call for information about group tours. 29 E Fourth St (between Bowery and Lafayette St). 777.1089. www.merchantshouse.org

52 B Bar & Grill

★$$ A former gas station, this dining room flaunts its roots with an haute garage motif, from photos of car engines to displayed truck parts. The area where the pumps once stood is now enclosed with a vaguely translucent shed-like structure; it's not heated in winter, but attendance rises as soon as the temps do. The all-season section is dim but spacious, and has been known to draw a celeb or two. Food can be secondary here—the large tables appeal to a convivial drinking crowd. We like their fish tacos,

The Best

Gerry Frank

Author, *Where to Find It, Eat It in New York*

Taking in an afternoon game at **Yankee** or **Shea Stadium** on a warm summer day.

Visiting the **Museum of Immigration** on **Ellis Island**.

Sitting on one of the 7,674 benches in **Central Park** on a glorious spring day . . . or taking a boat trip on the lake there on a summer day.

Wandering through the **Frick Collection**.

Enjoying a leisurely and luxurious weekend at the **Four Seasons Hotel**.

Sipping an espresso or cappuccino in **Little Italy**.

Watching a favorite episode of a favorite TV show at the **Paley Center for Media**.

Visiting the **Federal Hall National Memorial** (26 Wall St), where George Washington took oath as the first US president.

Dancing at the **Rainbow Room**.

Exploring the towering beauty of the **Cathedral Church of St. John the Divine**.

Watching the lights on the **Statue of Liberty** while walking along the promenade at **Battery Park**.

Enjoying the Spring Flower Show at **Macy's**.

Visiting **Theodore Roosevelt's birthplace** and **George Washington's headquarters** (65 Jumel Terrace).

though, and you can get a perfectly acceptable grilled salmon, roasted free-range chicken, seared yellowfin tuna, and for dessert, a banana split or a brownie with ice cream. ♦ American ♦ M-F, lunch and dinner; Sa, Su, brunch and dinner. Reservations recommended. 40 E Fourth St (at Bowery). 475.2220 ♿

53 Phebe's Tavern & Grill

During the 1960s, this was a popular hangout among Off-Broadway playwrights Sam Shepard, Robert Patrick, and Leonard Melfi. Today it continues to attract the East Village arts crowd; beer and burgers pull in the college students, too. ♦ Daily, till late. Sa, 5PM-4AM. 361 Bowery (at E Fourth St). 358.1902

54 La MaMa E.T.C.

First called **Cafe La MaMa**, this theater has been in the vanguard of the Off-Broadway movement since 1961; in 2004 their stature was honored when the city landmarked the theater row La MaMa is housed in. Under the direction of Ellen Stewart, La MaMa has been instrumental in presenting both American and international experimental playwrights and directors to this country. Stewart nurtured playwrights Sam Shepard, Lanford Wilson, Ed Bullins, Tom Eyen, Israel Horovitz, and Elizabeth Swados, among others. Directors Tom O'Horgan, Marshall Mason, Wilford Leach, Andrei Serban, and Peter Brook have helped to stage many extraordinary productions here. ♦ Main box office: 74A E Fourth St (between Second Ave and Bowery). 475.7710. www.lamama.org

55 Cucina di Pesce

★$ Since 1987 this friendly restaurant wit a huge bar has been serving reasonably priced Italian dishes. The comfort food packs them in, especially for the downright retro-priced early-bird special, but don't come expecting more than the basics. Try the spinach penne with asparagus and sur dried tomatoes in cream sauce, or the tun steak grilled with sautéed sweet peppers, capers, olives, and onions. There's outdoo garden dining during the warmer months. ♦ Italian ♦ M-F, dinner; Sa, lunch and dinner; Su, brunch and dinner. 87 E Fourth St (between Second Ave and Bowery). 260.6800 ♿

56 376-380 Lafayette Street

This richly ornamented warehouse is most notable because it was designed by **Henry J. Hardenbergh** in 1888, several years afte he designed the **Dakota** apartments uptow on West 72nd Street. ♦ At Great Jones St

57 Marion's Continental Restaurant & Lounge

★$$ This was *the* supper club during the 1950s, when senators, presidents, and movie stars were all regulars. It closed in th early 1970s, but Marion's son and a business partner reopened it in 1990 with much of its signature décor intact. The food is good, with such favorites as Caesar salad and steak au poivre topping the menu. Com for the inexpensive vodka Gibsons, old-fashioneds, and Manhattans. ♦ Continental ♦ M-Sa, dinner; Su, brunch and dinner. Prix fixe pre-theater menu available. 354 Bower (between Great Jones and E Fourth Sts). 475.7621

58 Great Jones Café

★★$ Blackened fish, sweet-potato fries, gumbo, and other good, reasonably priced eats are served in a cozy but lively neighborhood café atmosphere. The daily specials are probably a lot like your mom used to make. Too bad they don't take reservations. ♦ Cajun/American ♦ M-F, dinner; Sa, Su, brunch and dinner. 54 Great Jones St (between Bowery and Lafayette St). 674.9304

59 Two Boots Pizza

★$ This family-oriented original serves Louisiana cuisine with an Italian twist—you may have to squint a bit to get it, but the boots refer to the shape of both country and state. The pizzas come with a cornmeal crust; the toppings are as far from New York traditional as you can get. They serve salad and sandwiches too. Delivery available. ♦ Creole/Italian ♦ M-F, dinner; Sa, Su, brunch and dinner. 42 Ave A (between E Third and E Fourth Sts). 254.1919. Also at 74 Bleecker St (at Broadway). 777.1033; 201 W 11th St (at Greenwich Ave). 633.9096; and other locations throughout the city.

59 Two Boots Pioneer Theater

Around the corner from **Two Boots Pizza,** this 100-seat theater has been screening a mix of classic revivals and independent premieres since it opened in 2000. Its screen may be tiny, but the seats are comfy, with an old-timey feel. You can feel just like a mini-mogul while you're there. ♦ Daily. 155 E Third St (between Aves B and A). 591.0434

60 Bouwerie Lane Theatre

In 1874, when the lower end of the Bowery was a theater district, **Henry Engelbert** built this fanciful cast-iron building as a bank. The unusually deeply detailed Second Empire Baroque structure is now landmarked; it was first converted to a theater in 1963. The **Jean Cocteau Repertory** was resident here through 2006, when its founder passed away (the re-formed troupe relocated to Theater Row, and now performs as The Exchange). ♦ 330 Bowery (at Bond St). 677.0060. www.jeancocteaurep.org

☆CBGB&OMFUG

61 CBGB/OMFUG

Long after everyone has forgotten what the initials of this Bowery dive stand for (Country, Bluegrass, Blues, and Other Music for Uplifting Gourmandizers), they will remember it as the birthplace of punk rock, or the house that the Ramones and television made. As it did for more than three decades (Hilly Kristal launched the joint back in the dark ages of 1973), the long, dark bar illuminated by neon beer signs played host to an array of groups under a wide banner of styles until its final chord was struck in 2006 (Patti Smith was the last act, on October 15); Mr. Kristal passed on less than a year later, in 2007. Their retail store lives on in the 'hood, though no longer at the club. ♦ 315 Bowery (between E First and E Second Sts). CBGB (shop), daily: 19-23 St. Marks Pl (between Second and Third Aves). 982.4052. www.cbgb.com

62 New York Marble Cemetery

Located on the inside portion of the block (enter from an alley on Second Street), this early-1800s cemetery was one of the first built in the city and is among the very few left in Manhattan. The burial vaults are underground, and the names of those interred are carved into marble tablets set into a perimeter wall that surrounds a small grassy area. Down the block (52-74 East Second Street) is the **New York City Marble Cemetery**, started in 1831 along the same nonsectarian lines but with aboveground vaults and handsome headstones. Genealogists can trace New York's early first families—the Scribners, Varicks, Beekmans, Van Zandts, Hoyts, and one branch of the Roosevelts—from tombstone information. Burial here is restricted to the descendants of the original vault owners, but no one has applied since 1917. ♦ E Second St (between Second Ave and Bowery)

63 Anthology Film Archives

Opened in 1970 in **The Public Theater**, and now located in the renovated former **Second Avenue Courthouse** building, this two-theater center for the preservation and exhibition of film and video works holds daily screenings—of both repertory and the rarely seen—that are open to all. Only students, scholars, museums, and universities have access to the archives and library, though there are usually a smattering of exhibits of interest to buffs in Anthology's public spaces. ♦ Admission. Daily; call for schedules. 32 Second Ave (at E Second St). 505.5181. www.anthologyfilmarchives.org

64 Bayard Condict Building

The only **Louis Sullivan** building in New York is hidden among the industrial high-rises on Bleecker Street. The structure (formerly the **Condict Building**) was already an anachronism when it was completed in 1898, because the Renaissance Revival style that followed the 1893 Chicago World's Fair turned popular taste away from the elegant, quintessentially American designs of Sullivan and the Chicago School. The intricate cornice filigree and soaring vertical lines of the terra-cotta-clad steel piers are Sullivan trademarks; the six angels at the roofline were applied under pressure from the client. ♦ 65 Bleecker St (between Lafayette St and Broadway)

65 New York Mercantile Exchange

Not to be confused with the also viewing-worthy 1886 **New York Mercantile Exchange Building** in TriBeCa (at Harrison Street)—or the current one in 5 World Financial Center—this merc precedes both. A cast-iron jungle with bamboo stems, lilies, and roses complemented with Oriental motifs, it was designed in 1882 by **Herman J. Schwartzmann**. The Exchange, obviously no longer here, was once headquarters for all the big butter-and-egg men and wholesale dealers in coffee, tea, and spices. The ground floor is currently occupied by **Urban Outfitters** (475.0009), clothier to many a university student. ♦ Daily. 628 Broadway (between E Houston and Bleecker Sts).

66 Bowery Poetry Club

A Lite-Brite portrait of Walt Whitman looks on as innovative poets—heavy hitters and newcomers alike—work their words in this forum run by Bob Holman, formerly of the Nuyorican Poets Café. Drop in for a daytime reading or workshop, stay for an evening slam, and check out the changing exhibitions on the Art Wall behind the sound booth. Light fare is served, along with drinks both soft and hard. ♦ Daily; drink minimum for some events. 308 Bowery (between Bleecker and Houston Sts). 614.0505. www.bowerypoetry.com ♿

67 Classic Kicks

Feet, do your stuff! This is the place for hip sneaks to up your street cred: turquoise Pumas, tweed Nikes, pixel-patterned Vans hightops, silver metallic Chuck Taylors. The selection of clothing includes windbreakers from Reine & Roi and Classic Kicks' own terry hoodies. ♦ M-Sa. 298 Elizabeth St (between E Houston and Bleecker Sts). 979.9514

68 Patricia Field

No points for guessing why Ms. Field won an Emmy as costumer for the *Sex and the City* gals. Trendsetting fashions are this store's forte, great for those who live by their own dress code. Unless you work in a most uncorporate job, you probably won't get to wear your purchases to the office. Still, the music's great, the clientele colorful, and the vibe (after a 2006 move from SoHo) hipper than ever. ♦ Daily. 302 Bowery (between E Houston and Bleecker Sts). 966.4066

69 Billy's Antiques & Props

Is it a yard sale? Is it trash day? Look close and you'll see that the furnishings ranged along the sidewalk are not only viable but, in some cases, very fine. Inside (it's a large green tent), you may find a mid-century armoire, a gilded mirror, or a skeleton in a dress. In the age of gentrification, this indoor/outdoor carnival of the beautiful, the broken-down, and the bizarre gives a glimmer of the Bowery's grittier past. ♦ Daily, weather permitting. 76 E Houston St (between Bowery and Elizabeth St). 917/576.6980. www.billysantiques.com

70 Prune

★★★ $$$ This tiny space draws crowds for braised escarole and beans with salt cod, whole grilled fish, and stewed pork shoulder. Brunch is a standout, with 11 kinds of Bloody Mary (but no reservations). ♦ American ♦ M-F, breakfast, lunch, and dinner; Sa, Su, breakfast, brunch, and dinner. Reservations recommended. 54 E First St (between First and Second Aves). 677.6221

70 City Lore

In a gentrified brownstone just off First Avenue, a group of serious folklorists explore New York cultural traditions through photo and tape archives, oral histories, discussion groups, music and film festivals, and their web-based historic documentation initiative **Place Matters.** ♦ Call for an appointment M-F. 72 E First St (between First and Second Aves). 529.1955. www.citylore.com

71 Boca Chica

★★$$ Discerning patrons come to enjoy delicious and fresh Latin American cuisine—*pollo asado havanero, camerones a la ajilo,* plantains, various curry-infused fish dishes, ceviche, and the like—at reasonable prices, in a casual setting. Dine early to avoid the decibel crush—the enthusiastic crowd has been known to break out in wild dancing. Could be the margaritas . . . ♦ Pan-Latin ♦ M-Sa, dinner; Su, brunch and dinner. 13 First Ave (at E First St). 473.0108

72 Lucky Cheng's

★$$$ At this popular-with-tourists spot, the waitresses in their tight silk dresses are not what they seem—they're actually men in a sort of lighthearted version of *M. Butterfly.* The food appears as dramatic as the servers; unfortunately it's not all that tasty. Indonesian chicken or beef satay, grilled mahimahi in a tangy Vietnamese sauce, Chinese five-spiced chicken with roasted chestnut-scallion pancakes, and spicy Japanese pepper sirloin with sun-dried shiitake mushrooms are some of the choices. You'll be so distracted by the raucous goings-on—or so inebriated by drinks like the Fishbowl or the Pink Pussy—you may not notice how indifferent the food is. ♦ Pan-Asian ♦ Daily, dinner. Drag shows nightly. 24 First Ave (between E First and E Second Sts). 473.0516

73 Lucien

★★$$ This French-to-the bone place is small and cozy, with close-set tables that would spell crowded in a less appealing restaurant. There are daily fish specials as well as such traditional bistro classics as bouillabaisse and cassoulet, along with roasted squab and linguini with whole lobster. Service is welcoming and properly attentive. ♦ French bistro ♦ M-F, lunch and dinner; Sa, Su, brunch and dinner. 14 First Ave (at E First St). 260.6481

74 Esashi

★★$$ This low-key sushi place won't charm you into sitting and lingering over sake, but it won't empty your wallet either. Decent sashimi and a good selection of beers make for a pleasant evening. ♦ Japanese ♦ Daily, dinner and takeout. 32 Ave A (between E Houston and E 2nd Sts). 505.8726

UNION SQUARE/FLATIRON/GRAMERCY/ MURRAY HILL

All cobbled from privately owned Colonial-era farmland, these three neighborhoods Union Square, Flatiron, Gramercy, and Murray Hill—cover **14th to 39th Street** from **Sixth Avenue** to the **East River.** Land that Elias Brevoort owned in the earl 1700s would become, by the early 1800s, the heart of the Union Square neighborhoo Named Union Place in 1811—for the spot where the Bowery intersected Bloomingdal

oad (now Broadway)—**Union Square Park** was established there in 1831, thus anging the name for good. By then, the area was filled with grand mansions, eaters, and concert halls, setting the scene for the **Ladies' Mile** shopping district at followed during the Civil War era. The Civil War also found Union Square a cal point for workers' rallies and political protests, traditions that are alive and well day. Seedy and run-down by the mid-20th century, the park and surrounding area ere well into a welcome renaissance by the late 1980s.

Running from higher Midtown rents, publishers, photography studios, and other ecialized companies renovated and moved into the many abandoned industrial fts sandwiched between 14th and 23rd Streets. At the north end, the **Flatiron istrict**, between Union Square Park and similarly revived **Madison Square Park**, d adjacent to the famous **Flatiron Building** on 23rd Street and Fifth Avenue, came a particular draw. Fashionable stores, restaurants, and condos have accompa-ed this rebirth, firmly establishing the now residential and service-oriented ighborhood for the 21st century.

Gramercy Park was established in the 1830s by lawyer and landowner Samuel iggles. To make one of his tracts more valuable, he sacrificed 42 potential building ts to create this London-style park. Then he set aside more land for a wide avenue orth of the park (which he named **Lexington**, for the Revolutionary War battle) and r **Irving Place** south of it (which he named for his friend Washington Irving, who eated "Father Knickerbocker," one of the symbols of New York).

The land that Ruggles owned was once part of a huge estate that belonged to Peter uyvesant, the last Dutch governor-general of Nieuw Amsterdam, who retired there ter the British took over. His original 1651 deed noted a valley created by a creek lled Crommessie, a combination of two Dutch words meaning "crooked little knife" or the shape of a nearby brook). The name was eventually altered to Gramercy to fall ore easily off English-speaking tongues. Stuyvesant's name lives on in the neighbor-ood east of Gramercy, and in another London-style park that straddles Second Ave-ie, **Stuyvesant Square**.

After the Stuyvesant family sold part of their estate to the Delanceys in 1746, it as developed into a working farm known as **Rose Hill**. It is a quiet residential area day, but into the early 1900s the notorious Gas House Gang ruled the neighborhood, eraging an estimated 30 holdups every night on East 18th Street alone. (The gang ok its name from factories along the East River that produced the gas needed to il-minate the city then.) The original Gas Housers' territory included another residen-l neighborhood, Murray Hill, which extends north from **34th** to **39th Streets**, and st from **Sixth Avenue**. The stretch near Second Avenue between 23rd and 34th reets is often called **Kips Bay**, after a farm established by Jacobus Kip in 1655. By e end of the 19th century, when J. Pierpont Morgan moved to the area, a gentle-en's agreement had been established restricting the streets of Murray Hill to private uses. Until the invasion of high-rise hotels and apartments in the 1920s, it was a ighborhood of elegant mansions, many of which still stand.

Today, where gas storage tanks once sprouted east of Stuyvesant Square, thousands people occupy middle-class apartments in the **Stuyvesant Town** and **Peter Cooper llage** rental complexes (both built in the late 1940s and attacked for being purely nctional and without ornamentation), and in **Waterside** (high-rises built in 1974 on e East River between **East 25th** and **East 30th Streets**).

1 W New York—The Court

$$$$ The 198 rooms here—43 of which are one-bedroom suites—are sunny and quiet, and the staff is enthusiastic. In-room amenities include luxurious pillow-top beds with 250-thread-count sheets and goose down comforters, high-speed Internet access, flat-panel TVs, and CD players. The hotel's lobby "Living Room," with its rich reds and mahoganies, opens up to the **Wetbar** watering hole and the contemporary American restaurant, **Icon**. Pets are welcome. ♦ 130 E 39th St (between Lexington and Park Aves). 685.1100, 877-WHOTELS; fax 889.0287. www.whotels.com ♿

1 W New York—The Tuscany

$$$ This is a slightly smaller alternative to the adjacent **W New York–The Court**. The 122 guestrooms are 480 square feet on average and feature similar upscale amenities, including high-speed Internet access and a 24/7 fitness center. Rover may join you, though perhaps not at **Audrey**, where you'll find a lounge at night and lattés by day. ♦ 120 E 39th St (between Lexington and Park Aves). 686.1600, 877.WHOTELS; fax 779.7822. www.whotels.com

2 Lord & Taylor

This store has made a specialty of stocking clothing by American designers. Its shoe department is legendary, as is the caring quality of its sales help, which is quite a rarity these days. The department store is also justly famous for its Christmas window displays, without which the holidays in New York wouldn't be the same. The store was the first in the history of retailing to devote its window displays to anything but merchandise during the holiday season. The custom began during the unusually warm December of 1905, when customers didn't seem to feel Christmasy. The management got them into the proper mood by filling the store's windows with a snowstorm the likes of which New Yorkers hadn't seen since the famous Blizzard of '88. While they no longer serve coffee to customers who arrive before the doors open in the morning, a white-gloved aide will find you a cab when you leave. **An American Place** occupies the fifth-floor dining spot; the restaurant serves lunch and light meals during the day. You'll find **Café 424** on the sixth floor and the **Soup Bar** on the main floor. ♦ Daily. 424 Fifth Ave (between W 38th and W 39th Sts). 391.3344 ♿

3 Jolly Madison Towers Hotel

$$ Completely modernized (it's in a historic 1920s building), this sleekly understated addition to the Italian boutique hotel group is both tastefully decorated and comfortable. The hotel offers meeting facilities and 242 rooms, all with high-speed Internet access and Frette linens. A small fee gives guests access to the **Oriental Spa**, an in-house health club with sauna and gym. Ask for a room with a view of the **Empire State Building**. The **Whaler Bar** is a favorite meeting place. ♦ 22 E 38th St (at Madison Ave). 802.0600, 800/225.4340; fax 447.0747. www.jollymadison.com

4 70 Park Avenue Hotel

$$$$ **The Kimpton Group** reopened the totally renovated and refurbished 212-room former **Doral Park Avenue Hotel** in 2004 as an exclusive and lushly upscale boutique accommodation. Guests will find high-speed Internet access, 42-inch flat-panel TVs, custom linens, and original artwork in all rooms; **Silverleaf Tavern**, for your imbibing pleasure, is on site. ♦ 70 Park Ave (at E 38th St). 687.7050; fax 973.2497. www.70parkave.com ♿

5 The Kitano New York

$$$$ Designed with the business traveler in mind (so you know the tech is up to speed), this understated and contemporary hotel offers its guests peace and quiet in a Park Avenue address on the southern cusp of Midtown. There are 149 soundproofed guest rooms, all done up in mahogany and cherry furnishings, along with eight suites and an authentic Japanese tatami suite replete with a tea ceremony room. Bathrooms are exceptionally clean and modern. You can enjoy the Japanese fare on offer at **Hakubai Restaurant**, in its main room or one of three private tatami rooms. 66 Park Ave (at E 38th St). 885.7000, 800/457. 4000. www.kitano.com ♿

6 Church of Our Savior

This perfect example of Romanesque Gothic architecture was built by **Paul C. Reilly** in 1959, a time when architects were tossing off glass boxes with the excuse that there were no craftsmen left to do this kind of work. The interior of this Roman Catholic church proves that there must have been at least a few in New York in the 1950s. ♦ 59 Park Ave (at E 38th St). 679.8166 ♿

Getting to the top is the literal object of the annual Empire State Building Run Up, a marathon race of unusual proportions. Entrants must negotiate the building's 1,575 steps. People from around the globe enter the event, held each February. Average winning time is 12 to 14 minutes, with winners and losers alike earning a splendid view from the 86th floor and an elevator ride down.

6 Rossini's

★★$$$ The hot antipasto Rossini—clams oreganata, shrimp scampi, and mozzarella *in carrozza* (wrapped in bread and fried)—is a specialty at this casual, friendly restaurant. Entrées include chicken *romano* (stuffed with spinach and roasted veal). A pianist performs on Monday and Friday, an electric keyboard player plays Tuesday through Thursday, and an opera trio serenades on Saturday. ♦ Italian ♦ M-F, lunch and dinner; Sa, Su, dinner. Reservations recommended. 108 E 38th St (between Lexington and Park Aves). 683.0135

7 M&J Trimming

Though this well-known chockablock trimmings store looks like the kind traditionally open to the trade only, it has always been a retail shopper's dream—and now it's twice as large. Countless buttons, tassels, pipings, frogs, and decorative borders will transform the most nondescript garment into an award-winner. Aspiring and professional designers come here for inspiration, resourcefully using buttons and beads for everything from jewelry to shoe decoration, kitschy to elegant. ♦ Daily. 1008 Sixth Ave (between W 37th and W 38th Sts). 391.6200

8 West Marine

Most of the stores on this block sell trimmings and ribbons, but if you need a stout coil of rope, you'll find it at this amazing emporium (formerly **E&B Goldbergs'**). New York is America's biggest seaport, but it still comes as a surprise to discover a place selling anchors, depth finders, fishing equipment (including the tournament reels that are so much more expensive in Europe), and other gear for yacht enthusiasts and sailors. It is a perfect store for the shoes and foul-weather clothes and other outfits you need if you want to look like you belong to the yacht club set. ♦ Daily. 12 W 37th St (between Fifth and Sixth Aves). 594.6065 ♿

9 Morgans

$$$ Hotel impresario Ian Schrager (known for the **Hudson** and **Gramercy Park** hotels, among others) runs this trendy hotel, with rooms and furnishings created by renowned French designer Andrée Putman. The hotel prides itself on getting you whatever you want—if the urge for sushi strikes at midnight, no problem. All 112 rooms have Wi-Fi Internet access, CD players, blackout shades on the windows, and phones in the bedrooms and bathrooms. Guests have access to a sports club facility nearby. There's also the gorgeous Philippe Starck-designed restaurant on the premises, **Asia de Cuba** (726.7755) featuring Asian and Cuban cuisine in the sleek—and snooty—two-level dining room. ♦ 237 Madison Ave (between E 37th and E 38th Sts). 686.0300, 800/606.6090; fax 779.8352. www.morganshotel.com

10 The Morgan Library & Museum

Financier J.P. Morgan began collecting books, manuscripts, and drawings in earnest in 1890, and eventually had to construct this magnificent small palazzo to house his treasures. Located at 29 E 36th Street, the **Morgan Library** was designed in 1906 by **Charles Follen McKim** of **McKim, Mead & White**. The building itself is a treasure, and the 1928 annex on the Madison Avenue side complements it perfectly—as does **Renzo Piano**'s 2006 design, bridging these buildings with the once free-standing mansion at the northwest corner of the current site. Built at 231 Madison Avenue in 1852 for banker Anson Phelps Stokes, that brownstone structure was bought by J.P. Morgan for his son in 1904.

The 2006 changes introduce a dazzling use of natural light for the spaces within, and provide not only an enlarged bookstore and shop, but more significantly, expanded exhibition space, an updated performance space, a state-of-the-art reading room, a welcoming—and more accessible—new entrance, as well as a restaurant and café. The Morgan Library and office remains intact, preserved exactly as it was when Morgan died in 1913.

The collection includes more than 1,000 illuminated medieval and Renaissance manuscripts, the finest such collection in America. It also contains the country's best examples of printed books, from Gutenberg to modern times, as well as an extensive collection of fine bookbinding. And its collection of autographed manuscripts, both literary and musical, is considered one of the best in the world. Art historian Kenneth Clark summed it all up perfectly when he said,

"Every object is a treasure, every item is perfect."

Tours are available. Public programs range from musical events to lectures, readings, and more; the gift shop is highly recommended. **The Morgan Dining Room** serves lunch, Tu-Su; dinner, F only. **The Morgan Café** is open during museum hours. Call 682.2130 to reach either dining facility. ♦ Admission free F after 7PM. Closed M. Tu-Th, 10:30AM-5PM; F, 10:30AM-9PM; Sa, 10AM-6PM; Su, 11AM-6PM. 225 Madison Ave (between E 36th and E 37th Sts). 685.0008. www.themorgan.org ♿

11 Scandinavia House

This sleek 2000 building by **Polshek Partnership** is home to the American-Scandinavian Foundation and its cultural and educational programs, including film series, concerts, language courses, and historical exhibitions. As you might expect, a Nordic cool prevails, from the zinc and spruce panels on the façade to the classic modern furnishings inside. Visit the not-for-profit shop for home goods, jewelry, art glass, and other design-driven wares. Access to **The Shop** and **AQ Café** (both, M-Sa) and **Library** (W, Th-Sa) are free. ♦ **Gallery:** Admission. Tu-Sa, noon-6PM. 58 Park Ave (between E 37th and E 38th Sts). 879.9779. www.scandinaviahouse.org ♿

12 The Corinthian

This 1987 taupe brick apartment tower, designed by **Der Scutt** and **Michael Schimenti**, is distinguished by deep fluting that creates fully rounded bay windows (many side by side, so that one fears for the occupants' privacy). ♦ 330 E 38th St (at First Ave)

13 Sniffen Court

This charming and unusually well-preserved mews of 10 carriage houses was built shortly before the Civil War (1850-60) and was designated a Historic District in 1966. ♦ 150-158 E 36th St (between Third and Lexington Aves)

14 Church of the Incarnation Episcopal

Built in 1864 by **Emlen T. Littel**, this modest church seems to be trying to hide the fact that it contains windows by Louis Comfort Tiffany and John LaFarge, sculpture by Daniel Chester French and Augustus Saint-Gaudens, and a Gothic-style monument designed by **Henry Hobson Richardson**. Fortunately, the church provides a folder for a self-guided tour. ♦ 209 Madison Ave (between E 35th and E 36th Sts). 689.6350

15 Complete Traveller Bookstore

This small store has an impressively large selection of rare and out-of-print travel books and maps—enough to satisfy even the most jaded traveler, armchair or otherwise. While it no longer carries currer travel guides, a browse or a buy here, at o of the older bookstores in the country, is headily inspirational. ♦ Daily. 199 Madiso Ave (at E 35th St). 685.9007. www.ctrarebooks.com

16 Science, Industry, and Business Branch (SIBL), NYP

This extensive library is located on several floors of the former **B. Altman** department store. NYPL/SIBL occupies more than 16,000 square feet of space in this grand Renaissance Revival building designed in 1906 by **Trowbridge & Livingston.** (**CUNY Graduate Center**, entered on the Fifth Avenue side of the block-square site, occupies much of the rest of the building.) The expansion, and attractively modern interior redesigned by **Gwathmey Siegel** in 1996, helped to relieve the overcrowded main library (on 42nd Street) of more than two million books and periodicals. It also gave SIBL state-of-the-art computer research facilities. ♦ M-Sa. 188 Madison Ave (between E 34th and E 35th Sts). 592.7000. www.nypl.org

17 Astro Gallery of Gems

With a collection of minerals and gems fro 47 countries, ranging from rare vanadinite crystals to zircons, this is a paradise for collectors and a good source of fine jewelr at decent prices. The huge (10,000-square foot) space is set up to show off everything from 2,000-pound amethyst geodes to museum-quality blue tourmaline from Braz and Mandarin-orange garnet crystals from Pakistan. ♦ Daily. 185 Madison Ave (at E 34th St). 889.9000

18 Empire State Building

Yes, Virginia, this is the once-upon-a-time World's Tallest Building (its ranking today i dubious in a world where structures like th Burj Dubai can attain a height over twice that of the Empire State), famous in fact a fiction, icon of New York City, and the first place from which to study the city. It (still) has an impressive collection of statistics: 1,250 feet to the top of the (unsuccessful) dirigible mooring mast; 102 floors; 1,860 steps; 73 elevators; 60 miles of water pipe five acres of windows; 365,000 tons of material—and it was under construction for only 19 months. Built by **Shreve, Lamb &**

Harmon in 1931, during the Depression, it was known for many years as the "Empty State Building," and the owners relied on income from the **Observation Deck** to pay their taxes. Oh yes—on a good day you can see for at least 50 miles. The architects must be lauded for the way in which they handled the immense and potentially oppressive bulk of this building. The tower is balanced, set back from the street on a five-story (street-scale) base. The subtly modulated shaft rises at a distance, terminating in a conservatively geometric crown. The limestone-and-granite cladding, with its steel mullions and flush windows, is restrained, with just a touch of an Art Deco air (compared to the exuberant ornamentalism of the **Chrysler Building**, for example). This is dignity. Belying the fears of the general public, the tower has not yet cracked or toppled, although it does sway quite a bit in high winds, and only once has a plane crashed into it (in 1945, when a bomber—accidentally—broadsided the 79th floor). There have been a few suicides, and a lot of birds have been knocked out of the sky during their migrating season, one of the reasons it always stays illuminated.

The site, too, has a lively history. Between 1857 and 1893 it was the address of a pair of mansions belonging to members of the Astor family and the center of New York social life. In the early 1890s a feud erupted, and William Waldorf Astor, who had the house on West 33rd Street, moved to Europe and replaced the house with a hotel—the **Waldorf**. His aunt across the garden, Mrs. William Astor, moved within the year, and had a connecting hotel—the **Astoria**—completed by 1897. The Waldorf and Astoria Hotels immediately became a social center and operated together as one hotel for many years, under the agreement that Mrs. Astor could have all connections between them closed off at any time. When the original structures were demolished in 1929, the **Waldorf-Astoria** moved uptown to Park Avenue. ♦ 350 Fifth Ave (at W 34th St)

Within the Empire State Building:

Empire State Observatory

There is an open platform on all four sides of the 86th floor, well protected with heavy mesh and metal bars. A few steps above it is a glass-enclosed area with food service and a souvenir shop. Alas, the 86th floor is as high as you can get these days—access to the enclosed 102nd-floor lookout ended in the late 1990s. But a visit here is still the quintessential not-to-be-missed way to end your evening on the town. Tickets are available on the concourse, one level below the street. ♦ Admission (combination tickets include **Skyride** admission). Daily, 9AM-midnight; last elevator at 11:30PM. 736.3100 ♿

19 3 Park Avenue

This brick tower structure is turned diagonally against its companions and the city. Compare this straight-up tower, built in 1976, and its stylized mansard roof with the careful, soaring composition of the **Empire State Building** two blocks away—they were designed by the same firm, **Shreve, Lamb & Harmon**. A plaque on the terrace wall at East 33rd Street marks this as the site of the 71st Regiment Armory. ♦ Between E 33rd and E 34th Sts

20 Affinia Dumont

$$$ All 250 rooms—be they studios or one- or two-bedroom suites—have their own kitchens. Efficiently fashioned for the business set, all accommodations offer high-speed Internet service, "executive-size" desks, and ergonomic chairs. A full-featured fitness facility and the pleasant **Barking Dog Café** round out the scene. ♦ 150 E 34th St (between Third and Lexington Aves). 481.7600, 866/246.2203; fax 889.8856. www.affinia.com ♿

21 St. Vartan Armenian Cathedral

This is the seat of the Armenian Church in America. Well-sited on a rise above Murray Hill, its elegant design—the pale gray stone face, soft angles, and striking dome are embellished tastefully and simply, with a restrained use of gold leaf—was inspired by a seventh-century church in Armenia. Built in 1967 by **Steinman & Cain**, their interior also offers a striking counterpoint to the more typical Gothic churches in the city: almost modern in appearance, its stained glass and wood details make the large space feel intimate. In summer, enjoy lunch, dinner, or weekend brunch on their lovely plaza (reservations: 213.4980). ♦ 630 Second Ave (between E 34th and E 35th Sts). 686.0710

22 El Parador

★★$$$ Opened long before traditional Mexican food came into vogue in Manhattan, this spot remains popular among aficionados as well as those looking for a good time. Among many estimable selections are the chicken Parador (marinated and steamed), grilled sirloin fajitas (braised strips of steak with red peppers and onions wrapped in tortillas), and *chilaquiles verdes* (stewed chicken with sour cream and green tomatillo sauce). ♦ Mexican ♦ Daily, lunch and dinner. Reservations recommended. 325 E 34th St (between First Ave and Tunnel Entrance St). 679.6812

23 Greeley Square

Alexander Doyle's statue of Horace Greeley, founder of the *New York Tribune,* was donated by members of the newspaper unions—which says something about Greeley's management style. The site across Sixth Avenue, now the home of the **Manhattan Mall**, is where **Gimbels** kept its secrets safe from **Macy's**, which is only a block away on **Herald Square**. ♦ Bounded by Broadway and Sixth Ave, and W 32nd and W 33rd Sts

24 Grolier Club (former)

Once an exclusive hideaway for the bibliophiles of the Grolier Club, then a private home, and most recently **The Madison**, a private club, this exquisitely proportioned, red-brick and brownstone turn-of-the-century landmark building now hosts and caters private parties. ♦ Closed to the public. 29 E 32nd St (between Madison and Fifth Aves). 679.2932

25 1 and 2 Park Avenue

When Fourth Avenue below East 34th Street had its designation upgraded to "Park Avenue South," **1 Park Avenue** and **2 Park Avenue,** across the street, kept their original addresses. Until 1925, when **York & Sawyer** built No. 1, the area wasn't considered upscale. In the 19th century, it was the location of Peter Cooper's glue factory and later of barns for the livestock and horsecars of the **New York and Harlem Railroad**. No. 2, by **Ely Jacques Kahn**, went up in 1927. Both are notable for their colorful Art Deco terra-cotta details, but Kahn's is the stronger of the two. ♦ Between E 32nd and E 33rd Sts

26 J.J. Hat Center

Put a lid on it with help from one of the professional "hat consultants" at this world-famous purveyor of porkpies, fedoras, homburgs, Stetsons, Stingy Brims, and more—the oldest hat shop in the city, in business since 1911 (when men knew how to wear hats). The fine men's headgear on offer includes Canadian Biltmores, Italian Borsalinos, Irish tweed, and the Montecristi *fino*, the gold standard of Panamas. (Don't miss the little shrine to IBM in the back—while put to perfect use for headgear, this space is virtually unchanged from the days when the electronic gearheads used this space for its first New York showroom back in the 1930s.) ♦ M-Sa. 310 Fifth Ave (between W 31st and W 32nd Sts). 239.4368 ♿

27 Hotel Wolcott

$ This 180-room hotel is efficiently run an popular with the young and young-at-heart because of its non-attitudy service and its reasonable prices. The façade and the hotel's polished-up Louis XVI-style lobby a turn-of-the-century, but the rooms have simple, tasteful décor meant to withstand heavy traffic: The hotel is always close to full. Perks include free coffee and muffins i the morning, a small business center with fee-based Wi-Fi, and a basic fitness room. ♦ 4 W 31st St (between Fifth Ave and Broadway). 268.2900; fax 563.0096. www.wolcott.com

28 Marchi's

★★$$$ Not much has changed since this restaurant hidden in a vine-covered brownstone opened in 1930. "No sign outside—no menu inside" is still the motto The Marchi family has served the same fixe menu with a European flair for nearly that long: an antipasto platter, homemade lasagna, deep-fried whiting with cold strin beans and beets in vinaigrette, roasted ve and roasted chicken with mushrooms and tossed greens, and a cornucopia of fresh fruit and *crema fritta* for dessert. You'll fin all either weird or charming; a seat in the garden enhances the experience. ♦ Northe Italian ♦ M-Sa, dinner. Reservations recommended. 251 E 31st St (between Second and Third Aves). 679.2494

29 Kips Bay Plaza

These twin 21-story slabs facing an inner, private park were—for better or for worse—the first exposed concrete apartment houses in New York. The complex, complet in 1965, was designed by **I.M. Pei & Associates** and **S.J. Kessler**. ♦ Bounded b First and Second Aves, and E 30th and E 33rd Sts

30 The Water Club

★★★$$$ Inside this glass-enclosed, skyli former barge, which is anchored at the rive edge, landlubbers are treated to views tha are among the best in town—the cocktail lounge opens into a terraced dining room with a panorama of the East River. Natural

seafood is the best choice—the lobster and the Dover sole win raves—but the traditional American cuisine ventures into carnivore-pleasing territory as well. On that side of the menu, pork tenderloin with orange-rosemary marinade, wood-grilled filet mignon, and rack of lamb with sweet garlic are good choices. Desserts range from a milk chocolate torte, to classic crème brûlée, to handmade sorbets and ice creams.
♦ American ♦ M-Sa, lunch and dinner; Su, brunch and dinner. Prix-fixe lunch and dinner available. Reservations required. E 30th St (at the East River; access from E 23rd or E 34th St). 683.3333

31 Church of the Transfiguration/The Little Church Around the Corner

When actor George Holland died in 1870, a friend went to a nearby church to arrange for the funeral. "We don't accept actors here," he was told, "but there's a little church around the corner that will." They did, and the Church of the Transfiguration—an Episcopal church built in 1849 and later expanded—got both a new name and a new reputation among actors, some of whom, including Edwin Booth, Gertrude Lawrence, and Richard Mansfield, are memorialized among the wealth of stained glass and other artifacts inside. During World War I and in the years following, the charmingly eclectic brick-and-timber village-like complex was the scene of more wedding ceremonies than any other church in the world. Built in phases from 1849 to 1926, not much is known about its various architects, but Gothic Revivalist **Frederic Clark Withers** is responsible for the lovely chancel. Colorfully polychromed here and there, and set around a lush little garden, the church and its grounds provide a surprising respite from the fray. ♦ 1 E 29th St (between Madison and Fifth Aves). 684.6770. www.littlechurch.org ♿

32 Marble Collegiate Church

This Gothic Revival church has not been changed since the day it was built in 1854 by **Samuel A. Warner**. Its clock is still wound by hand every eight days, and the cane racks behind the pews are still waiting to receive your walking stick. A Dutch Reform church (the oldest denomination in the city), established here by Peter Minuit in 1628, it has served under the flags of Holland, England, and the US. The most famous minister to use its pulpit was Dr. Norman Vincent Peale, author of *The Power of Positive Thinking*. ♦ 272 Fifth Ave (at W 29th St). 686.2770

33 Manhattan Fruitier

Owner Jehv Gold fills stupendous baskets with a varied selection of exotic seasonal fruits from all over the world. He can supply the appropriate arrangement, according to your needs, and will deliver your order throughout Manhattan. In addition to the beautiful fruit baskets, other exquisite food gifts include jars of fruit in maple syrup, chocolate truffles in beautiful boxes, European cookies, and New Hampshire honey. ♦ M-F. 105 E 29th St (between Lexington Ave and Park Ave S). 686.0404

34 Les Halles

★$$$ A re-creation of the type of hangouts that once surrounded the great wholesale food market in Paris, this place—the spawn of über-celeb Anthony Bourdain, who still occasionally attends, as chef-at-large—has been a success since it opened in 1990. Some of its loyal customers patronize the butcher shop next door (open daily; others head for the often noisy dining room in back for onion soup, garlicky sausage, steak served with *pommes frites* (french fries), or cassoulet. ♦ French bistro/steak house ♦ M-F, breakfat, lunch, and dinner; Sa, Su, brunch and dinner. Reservations recommended. 411 Park Ave S (between E 28th and E 29th Sts). 679.4111. ♿ Also at 15 John St (between Broadway and Nassau Sts). 285.8585

35 Museum of Sex

Opened with a blare of publicity in 2002, there's a high-minded mission ("to preserve, and present the history, evolution, and cultural significance of human sexuality") behind the exhibitions at this museum. Its first exhibition, "NYC Sex: How New York City Transformed Sex in America" (designed by the UK firm **Casson Mann**), ran for over a year; since then a show of sex toys—some as complex, and as large, as any Rube Goldberg invention—and one on cigars have drawn crowds. Their permanent collection (including gifts from the Whittington Collection, Harmony Theatre burlesque house, and The Lannan Foundation) often form the basis for the changing exhibits at this for-profit venture. Gift shop/bookstore.
♦ Admission; last tickets are sold 45 minutes prior to closing. Sa, 11AM-8PM; Su-F, 11AM-6:30PM. 233 Fifth Ave (at E 27th St). 689.6337. www.mosex.com ♿

36 Center for Book Arts

Master craftspeople offer hands-on instruction in all aspects of traditional and contemporary bookmaking—binding, letterpress printing, papermaking—in this large loft space. Small exhibitions showcase creative interpretations of the book as art. ♦ M-Sa. 28 W 27th St (between Broadway and Sixth Ave), third floor. 481.0295. www.centerforbookarts.org

37 New York Life Insurance Company

This 1928 Gothic masterpiece was designed by **Cass Gilbert**, the architect of the **Woolworth Building** and New York's **Federal Courthouse**. The square tower topped by a gilded pyramid—a style Gilbert called "American Perpendicular"—is dramatically lighted at night. Its lobby is a panorama of detail, from polychromed coffered ceilings to bronze elevator doors and ornate grilles over the subway entrances. While the building is not open to the public, you can catch a good glimpse of all the splendor when you come upstairs from the subway on the block-long structure's Park Avenue side (use the south exit of the No. 6 line's 28th Street station). ♦ 45-55 Madison Ave (between E 26th and E 27th Sts).

38 Hotel Giraffe

$$$$ If you're looking for luxurious lodgings away from the madness of Midtown and an easy walk from Union Square theaters and shopping, this boutique venue is worth investigating. Décor throughout is a sophisticated update of the Moderne period of the late 1930s and 1940s, with rich colors and textures creating an inviting atmosphere. There are 73 rooms, of which 21 are suites. All feature such amenities as CD and DVD players, high-speed Internet access, and access to the roof garden. ♦ 365 Park Ave S (at E 26th St). 685.7700; fax 685.7771. www.hotelgiraffe.com

39 I Trulli

★★★$$$ Nicola Marzovilla tried to re-create the trattorie of his childhood in Southern Italy's Puglia when he opened this warm, simple place. The dining room is dominated by a glassed-in fireplace and a whitewashed wood-burning oven that mirrors the distinctive beehive shape of *trulli*—ancient Pugliese houses. From here and from the kitchen emerge wonderfully earthy dishes, such as the clay casserole of potatoes, Portobello mushrooms, and herbs; baked oysters with pancetta; ricotta dumplings with tomato sauce; spicy chicken with vinegar and garlic; grilled free-range chicken and stewed baby octopus. For dessert, try the fruit poached in wine. There's also an extensive wine list with good choices at all price levels. In nice weather, sit in the garden out back. ♦ Italian ♦ M-F, lunch and dinner; Sa, dinner. Reservations recommended. 122 E 27th St (between Lexington Ave and Park Ave S). 481.7372

One year after New York City became the first capital under the Constitution in 1788, an official census of Manhattan's population registered 33,000. Exactly one hundred years later, the surrounding four boroughs joined Manhattan to create the world's largest city, with a population of 3 million. Today, the city is home to more than 8.2 million people.

40 Bellevue Hospital Center

Established in 1736, this municipal hospital cares for some 80,000 emergency cases per year. Its services are available to anyone, with no restrictions, including ability to pay. The medical center was a pioneer in providing ambulance service, in performing appendectomies and Caesarean sections, and in developing heart catheterization and microsurgery. It is not, as is often believed, solely a psychiatric hospital. The principal building was designed in 193[illegible] by the prestigious architectural firm **McKim, Mead & White** and underwent subsequent additions in 1939. In 2005, **Pei Cobb Freed & Partners** bridged the historic structures with a cool yet welcoming **Ambulatory Care Facility** that—situated between East 27th and East 28th Streets—also serves as the new entrance to the complex. ♦ 462 First Ave (between E 25th and E 30th Sts). 562.4141

41 Serbian Orthodox Cathedral of St. Sava

Built in 1855 by **Richard Upjohn** for **Trinity Church**, this chapel became a cathedral of the Eastern Orthodox faith in 1943. The beautiful altar and reredos inside are by Frederick Clarke Withers. The parish house was designed in 1860 by **Jacob Wrey Mould**. ♦ 15 W 25th St (between Broadway and Sixth Ave). 242.9240

42 Appellate Division of the Supreme Court of the State of New York

Here, in the busiest appellate court in the world, nine justices hear most appeals in civil and criminal cases arising in New York and surrounding counties. The building, designed by **James Brown Lord**—murals, statuary, and all—was finished in 1900 at $5,000 under budget, with a final price tag of just under

$644,000. It is one of the city's treasures, and the public may enter the lobby for a taste of the impeccable 21st-century renovation; if court is not in session, a guard may show you the impressive murals in the ground-floor courtroom. ♦ 27 Madison Ave (at E 25th St). 340.0400 ♿

43 69th Regiment Armory

Designed in 1905 by **Hunt & Hunt**, this is where the infamous Armory Show introduced modern art to New York in 1913—the most famous work in the show was Marcel Duchamp's *Nude Descending a Staircase.* When not fully engaged in armory business (it is still the National Guard's headquarters and training center for the "Fighting Sixty-Ninth"), the space is turned over to annual arts events like The Modern Show and the Gramercy Park Antiques show (www.stellashows.com). Note the gun bays overlooking Lexington Avenue, with the barrel-vaulted Drill Hall behind it. ♦ 68 Lexington Ave (between E 25th and E 26th Sts). 889.7249

44 Waterside

There are 1,600 apartments in these brown towers built by **Davis, Brody & Associates** in 1974 on a platform over the East River. They are a world apart, reached by a footbridge across FDR Drive at East 25th Street, or by the riverfront esplanade to the north. And yes, the river views here are spectacular. ♦ At the eastern end of E 25th St. 725.5374

45 Asser Levy Recreational Center

In 1906, right-thinking architects **Arnold W. Brunner** and **William Martin Aiken** finally used the overappropriated style of the Romans in its original manner—for baths (like Caracalla, or those of Diocletian). Until recently called the **Public Baths**, this formal structure now houses a fitness center with indoor and outdoor swimming pools. The pools are open to the public; membership required for other facilities. ♦ E 23rd St (at Asser Levy Pl). 447.2020

46 Worth Monument

This richly ornamented obelisk in a triangular plot separating Broadway and Fifth Avenue marks the grave of Major General William Jenkins Worth, for whom the street in Lower Manhattan and the city of Fort Worth, Texas, were named. After fighting the Seminole in Florida, he went on to become a hero of the Mexican War in 1846. The monument was designed in 1857 by **James C. Batterson**; the plot it sits on is appropriately named **Worth Square.** ♦ W 25th St and Fifth Ave

47 Madison Square Park

What once was a swampy hunting ground, then a pauper's graveyard, is now a quiet refuge in the midst of madness. The square dates from 1847, when it was a parade ground and only a small part of a proposed park that was laid out in the Randell Plan of 1811—the plan that created the city's grid street pattern. Like other squares in this part of town, it was the focus of a fashionable residential district that flourished in pre-Civil War days. After the war, the fancy **Fifth Avenue Hotel**, the **Madison Square Theater**, and the second home of **Madison Square Garden** all faced the square. (This incarnation of the Garden will always be remembered because **Stanford White**, who designed the building, was shot and killed in its roof garden by Harry Thaw, the jealous husband who thought White was paying too much attention to his wife, Evelyn Nesbit.) A favorite moment in the park's history, though, is the period from 1876 to 1892, when the Statue of Liberty's arm and torch were parked here as a fund-raising gimmick en route to her re-assembly. Today, the square is ringed by commercial buildings and a growing lot of residential condos; its carefully tended grounds lend an air of serenity to the neighborhood. The **Shake Shack** nested at the south end has become a seasonal institution, and a changing flock of large sculptures and a wealth of public programs—readings, music—add to the scene. ♦ Bounded by Madison and Fifth Aves, Broadway, E 23rd St, and Madison Sq N. www.madisonsquarepark.org ♿

48 Tabla

★★★$$$ Few restaurants in town have generated as much buzz—or praise—as this innovative Indian spot. The space may not exactly exude warmth, but go for the food. Why? Dinner entrées like coconut-spiced organic chicken with bok choy, watermelon radish, and kohlrabi, taro-crisped red snapper with white beans, a trio of mustard greens and ambot-tik sauce, and braised Nova Scotia lobster with toasted couscous, green beans, and coriander-coconut curry. For dessert, the vanilla bean kulfi with blood orange rosewater and pistachio crisp is a winner. Breads are great, and you can even save a few bucks if you dine at their ground-floor café, **Bread Bar at Tabla**; its outdoor seating area has a nice view out to **Madison**

NYC: Past and Present

Battery Park

Past: Located at the tip of Manhattan, this was a fortification used to block enemy attack. Later, it housed the **New York Aquarium**.

Present: Castle Clinton, with walls eight feet thick, still stands; this is where tickets can be purchased for the ferry to the **Statue of Liberty/Ellis Island**. The area is one of the prettiest promenades on the city's waterfront.

City Hall Park

Past: Formerly (in the 18th century, that is) **The Commons**, this park also served as a parade ground, a prison, and the site of public executions. The **African Burial Ground** lies just north of the park's border at Chambers Street.

Present: Between **Park Row** and **Broadway**, the beautiful grounds facing **City Hall** now serve as the site of many official city ceremonies–and more than a few demonstrations.

Flushing Meadows–Corona Park

Past: Nearly one-and-a-half times larger than Central Park, this was little more than a tidal marsh and garbage dump made famous by F. Scott Fitzgerald's *The Great Gatsby* as "the valley of ashes." In 1939 and again in 1964, the 1,255-acre site was home to the **World's Fair**.

Present: One of the city's largest parks, it offers a wide range of activities including golf, ice-skating, and roller-skating. Also here are the **Hall of Science**, the **Queens Museum of Art**, **Carousel**, **Queens Wildlife Center**, and **Queens Theater-in-the-Park**.

Fort Schuyler

Past: Located at the tip of **Throgs Neck** in the **Bronx**, it once housed a lighthouse to guide ships through the passage between the **Long Island Sound** and the **Eas River**.

Present: A refurbished Fort Schuyler is now the home the **United States Maritime College**, a branch of the **State University of New York**.

Mulberry Street

Past: The center of the Italian section of the **Lower Ea Side**, this area teemed with pushcarts, wagons, and tenements. Fire escapes were used for the storage of household goods and for drying clothes.

Present: The colorful, lively Italian influence can still b felt here, although the growth of **Chinatown** has made the neighborhood more diverse, with Chinese shops a restaurants.

Rockefeller Center

Past: This area was the city's first botanical garden.

Present: Today a city within a city, it boasts flora along the **Channel Gardens** (one side representing England, the other France). Its annual flower show, in April, features the artistic designs of area horticulturists; the lighting of its towering, sparkling Christmas tree officiall marks the start of the holiday season every year.

Park Avenue

Past: During the 1800s the New York and Harlem Railroad used the stretch from 46th to 96th Streets (then called **Fourth Avenue**) as a north-south rail link; was named Park Avenue in 1888. The avenue was line with brick and brownstone residences.

Present: The railroad tracks were covered and now run underground. Today, modern glass-and-steel office buil ings line the avenue. To the north, many elegant dowag apartment buildings lend touches of class; near its southern end the former Pan Am building (now **MetLif** silhouettes the sky.

Square Park. ♦ Indian Eclectic ♦ M-F, lunch and dinner; Sa, dinner. Reservations strongly recommended. 11 Madison Ave (at E 25th St). 889.0667 ♿

49 Duggal

Professional photographers bring their film and processing business to this retail outlet (open till midnight weekdays) of the innovative photo-imaging firm, with a continually changing photo exhibition on the wall out front. ♦ Daily. 29 W 23rd St (between Fifth and Sixth Aves). 242.7000 ♿

50 Stern's Dry Goods Store/ Home Depot

This restoration of **Henry Fernbach**'s 1878 building is possibly the most sensitive of an cast-iron building in New York. And after years of use as office and showroom space, in 2004 it became home to Manhattan's firs **Home Depot**. ♦ 32-36 W 23rd St (between Fifth and Sixth Aves)

51 Western Union Building

A reflection of the city's Dutch origins, this unassuming red-brick building was createc by **Henry J. Hardenbergh** in 1884, the same year as his **Dakota** apartment house overlooking Central Park. You can see the **Western Union** insignia of yore above the entrance, which is on the 23rd Street face of the building. ♦ 186 Fifth Ave (at W 23rd St)

52 Live Bait

★$$ At this long-run after-work destination, the bar is packed sardine-style, with a crowd downing oysters from shot glasses and sipping Rolling Rocks from bottles. The décor is pure fishing shack, and although a cheeky sign above the bar says, "If you want home cooking, stay home," the food is definitely Carolina home-style. The menu includes smothered pork chops, fried chicken, and plantation gumbo with andouille sausage, shrimp, and chicken served over creole rice. For dessert try the Mississippi mud, Key lime, or pecan pie. ♦ Southeastern ♦ Daily, lunch, dinner, and late-night meals. Reservations recommended. 14 E 23rd St (between Park Ave S and Broadway). 353.2400

53 Metropolitan Life Insurance Company

Originally, the 700-foot marble tower (adjacent to the main building) was decorated with 200 carved lions' heads, ornamental columns, and a copper roof. But its four-sided clock, which at 26.5 feet is 4.5 feet taller than Big Ben, hasn't changed since 1909, when the tower was built. The north building, across East 24th Street, was designed in 1932 by **Harvey Wiley Corbett** and **E. Everett Waid** and is surprisingly light for all its limestone mass. Note the sculpted quality of the polygonal setbacks, the vaulted entrances at each of the four corners, and the Italian marble lobby. This block was the site of the **Madison Square Presbyterian Church**. Completed by **Stanford White** in 1906, it was his last, and many say his finest, building. ♦ 1 Madison Ave (at E 23rd St)

54 Pearl Paint

Located as it is next to the **School of Visual Arts**, this branch of the discount art-supply emporium offers artists-in-training everything from pens and brushes to easels and portfolios. ♦ Daily. 207 E 23rd St (between Second and Third Aves). 592.2179. Also at 308 Canal Street (at Mercer St). 431.7932

54 School of Visual Arts

Working professionals teach more than 5,500 students the fundamentals of illustration, photography, video, film, animation, and other visual arts in buildings throughout the neighborhood. Frequent exhibitions in the main building on East 23rd Street are free to the public. The luminary faculty has included Milton Glaser, Eileen Hedy-Schultz, Ed Benguiat, and Sal DeVito. ♦ 209 E 23rd St (between Second and Third Aves). 679.7350 ♿

55 Bao Noodles

★★$ It can get crowded in this down-to-earth neighborhood spot, because neighbors have caught on to its tasty, complex, modestly priced (most dinner entrées are in the $10-$12 range) takes on traditional Vietnamese food. They're also big fans of the cozy brick-walled, tin-ceilinged room, with its small but friendly zinc-covered bar. The beer list–Tiger, Saigon, and a few more–is short, but just right for entrées like grilled chicken with lime zest, lemongrass tofu, or wok-seared flank steak. Not one of the pho or noodle dishes (such as Da Nang crabmeat noodle soup) tops $10, and baguettes (stuffed with pâté and Vietnamese cold cuts) are just $5.95. It's more of a scene down at Bao's twisted sister, **Bao 111**, in the East Village. ♦ Vietnamese ♦ Daily, lunch and dinner. 391 Second Ave (between E 22nd and E 23rd Sts). 725.7770. Also at Bao 111, 111 Ave C (between E Seventh and E Eighth Sts). 254.7773

56 NY Cake & Baking Supply

Pudding molds, brioche pans, wedding-cake dummies, gold dragées and sugar daisies, and a full line of gum paste equipment–this no-frills shop stocks all a serious baker needs. ♦ M-Sa. 56 W 22nd St (between Fifth and Sixth Aves). 675.2253

57 Flatiron Building

In 1902, when **Daniel H. Burnham** (of Chicago World's Fair fame) filled the triangular site where Broadway crosses Fifth Avenue in a most reasonable but unconventional manner–with a triangular building–he raised many eyebrows and made history. This limestone-clad Renaissance palazzo was one of the city's first skyscrapers, at 285 feet high, and it is one of Burnham's best. At the juncture between traditionalism and modernism, the structure, with its articulated base and strong cornice, looks like an ocean liner in a column's clothing. Built as the **Fuller Building**, it was soon dubbed the "Flatiron" for its shape, once people stopped calling it "Burnham's Folly." A variety of cosmetics and fragrance shops, including **Origins**,

M.A.C., and **Jo Malone**, occupy street-level (all with street access) space on the Flatiron's ground floor. ♦ 175 Fifth Ave (between E 22nd and E 23rd Sts)

58 Bolo

★★$$$ The décor is a manifestation of the vibrant energy at work here: vivid greens, reds, and golds, as well as collaged graphic images. This is the place where Bobby Flay takes on Spanish food and makes it hum. Try the warm octopus and sweet onion salad with sage and lemon vinaigrette, tenderloin of pork with walnut romesco and caramelized date shallot sauce, or curried shellfish and chicken paella. ♦ New Spanish ♦ M-F, lunch and dinner; Sa, Su, dinner. Reservations recommended. 23 E 22nd St (between Park Ave S and Broadway). 228.2200 ♿

59 Space Kiddets

This lively boutique features moderate to expensive clothing and accessories for boys and girls with an emphasis on trendiness and practicality. There's also a selection of toys and games, along with colorful "play" jewelry that fashion-conscious moms will borrow from their daughters. ♦ M-Sa. 26 E 22nd St (between Park Ave S and Broadway). 420.9878

60 Russell Sage Foundation Building

The foundation that set out to dispense $63 million for good works in 1906 did much of its own good work in this 1912 building by **Grosvenor Atterbury** before selling the building to Catholic Charities, which in turn sold it for development as apartments. ♦ 4 Lexington Ave (at E 22nd St)

61 Rolf's Restaurant

★$$ New York was once famous for its German restaurants, and this is one of the very few still operating. The walls and ceilings are covered with art, stained glass, and carved wood. Try the veal shank, shell steak, and excellent potato pancakes. For dessert, there's apple strudel and Black Forest cake. ♦ German ♦ Daily, lunch and dinner. 281 Third Ave (at E 22nd St). 473.4750

62 Calvary Church

This Protestant Episcopal church, designed in 1846 by **James Renwick Jr.**, the architect of **St. Patrick's Cathedral**, once had steeples, but Renwick had them removed in 1860 because, some critics said, they embarrassed him. If the exterior was less than perfect, the architect made up for it inside the church with the nave, which is exquisite. The Sunday-school building on the uptown side, also a Renwick design, wa[s] added in 1867. ♦ 61 Gramercy Park N (at Park Ave S). 475.1216

63 Gramercy Park/Gramercy Park Historic District

Established by **Samuel Ruggles** in 1831, this former marshland became the model of a London square ringed by proper 19th-century neoclassical town houses. It is the sole surviving "private park" in New York City—only surrounding residents have keys t[o] get in—but the perimeter is well worth a stroll.(Aficionados of Jack Finney's *Time and Again* will surely feel the ghosts of that era upon them.) Many notables have lived in thi[s] neighborhood, including James Harper, the mayor of New York City (1844), and Samuel J. Tilden, governor of New York State (1874–1886), who was an unsuccessful presidential candidate; his home (15 Gramercy Park S) is now the **National Arts Club** (below). The statue in the park is of actor Edwin Booth, who lived at **No. 16** Gramercy Park South until he had the 1845 building remodeled by **Stanford White** for **The Players Club** (also below) in 1888. **Nos. 34** and **36** on the east side are among the city's earliest apartment buildings, designed in 1883 by **George DaCunha** and in 1905 by **James Riles**, respectively. Note the magnificent ironwork on **Nos. 3** and **4** Gramercy Park West, attributed to **Alexande[r] Jackson Davis**, one of the city's more individualistic and energetic architects. The **Gramercy Park Historic District** extends in an irregular area out from the park, predominantly within a block to the east and west, and two blocks to the south. Of particular interest is the beautiful block between Irving Place and Third Avenue on East 19th Street (remodeled as a group by Frederick J. Sterner). Ian Schrager's 2007 venture, the **Gramercy Park Hotel** (2 Lexington Ave, at Gramercy Park N; 920.3300; www.gramercyparkhotel.com), lies across the street from the north side of the park, just beyond the historic district. ♦ Park: between Third Ave and Park Ave S, and bounded by Gramercy Park E and W, and Gramercy Park N (E 21st St) and S (E 20th St)

Within the Gramercy Park Historic District:

National Arts Club

Built in 1845 by **Calvert Vaux**, this building has housed the National Arts Club since 1906, but its colorful history began when politician Samuel J. Tilden, who gained fame by destroying the Tweed Ring, used the coup to become governor of New York. To protect himself in the topsy-turvy days of early unions and political machinery, Tilden installed steel doors at the front of this Victorian Gothic home and had a tunnel dug to East 19th Street as an escape route. ♦ 15 Gramercy Park S (between Irving Pl and Park Ave S). 475.3424

The Players Club Hampden-Booth Theatre Library

In 1888, founder Edwin Booth charged **The Players** with the task of creating "a library relating to the history of the American stage and the preservation of pictures, bills of the play, photographs, and curiosities." Small group tours and use of the library, which includes four major collections (from Edwin Booth, Walter Hampden, the **Union Square Theatre**, and William Henderson), are granted by appointment only. ♦ 16 Gramercy Park S (at Irving Pl). 228.7610

The Brotherhood Synagogue

This austere Greek Revival–style brownstone cube was designed in 1859 by **King & Kellum** as the **Friends Meeting House** and was remodeled in 1975 by **James Stewart Polshek** as a synagogue. ♦ 28 Gramercy Park S (between Third Ave and Irving Pl). 674.5750

64 Markt

★★$$ This upmarket Belgian brasserie now flexes its mussels in cozier quarters than its old Meatpacking District corner, but the feel is still authentic. Start off at the sizable raw bar, or order the aforementioned shellfish steamed in white wine or genuine Hoegaarden, the Belgian white beer (with a side of hand-cut *frites*). For something different, go for the *waterzooi,* a traditional Belgian stew with chicken and vegetables. The best dessert bet is also the simplest: the classic Dame Blanche, a generous serving of vanilla ice cream with fresh whipped cream, melted dark Callebaut chocolate, and a cookie. ♦ Belgian ♦ M-F, breakfast, lunch, and dinner; Sa, Su, breakfast, brunch, and dinner. Reservations recommended. 676 Sixth Ave (at W 21st St). 727.3314. ♿

65 Periyali

★★★★$$$ The friendly staff at this top-notch taverna is unabashedly proud of its traditional Greek menu. Giant white beans with garlic sauce, char-grilled octopus or shrimp, lamb chops with rosemary, anything in phyllo pastry, and fresh whole fish are all good picks. For dessert, there's homemade baklava and wonderful *diples* (thin strips of deep-fried dough dipped in honey). The extensive wine list includes a good selection of Greek wines. White stucco walls, wooden floors, and soft Greek music complete the experience. ♦ Greek ♦ M-F, lunch and dinner; Sa, dinner. Prix-fixe lunch available. Reservations recommended. 35 W 20th St (between Fifth and Sixth Aves). 463.7890

66 901 Broadway

Originally the **Lord & Taylor Dry Goods Store**, this 1869 **James H. Giles** building displays a romantic cast-iron façade with echoes of Renaissance castle architecture as a monument to the glories of this historic shopping neighborhood, before **Lord & Taylor** moved uptown along with its neighbors **W&J Sloane** and **Arnold Constable**. ♦ At E 20th St

67 900 Broadway

Chicago architects developed steel-framed office buildings with highly ornamental exteriors, and in the 1880s, firms such as **McKim, Mead & White** began developing their own variations on the theme, which they called "New York Style." Originally the **Goelet Building**, this redbrick and limestone structure with its polychrome arches is a prime example. ♦ At E 20th St

68 Theodore Roosevelt Birthplace

Teddy Roosevelt was born here in 1858 and lived in a house on the site until he was a teenager. The original house was destroyed in 1916, but was faithfully reconstructed seven years later by **Theodate Pope Riddle** as a memorial to the 26th president. The National Historic Site incorporates 26 East 20th Street, once the home of Roosevelt's uncle. The restoration contains five rooms of period furniture and an extensive collection of memorabilia, including teddy bears. ♦ Nominal admission; seniors, children free. Tu-Sa, 9AM-5PM. 28 E 20th St (between Park Ave S and Broadway). 260.1616. www.nps.gov/thrb

69 Gramercy Tavern

★★★★$$$ In a *New York* magazine cover story that preceded the restaurant's opening in 1994, owner Danny Meyer (of **Union Square Café** fame) stated his "modest" ambition: to reinvent the four-star restaurant. Together with founding chef Tom Colicchio, they pretty much got there; and now, in the post-Colicchio era, the standard is upheld. Superb selections from the seasonal menu include tuna tartare, ricotta raviolo with wild mushrooms, roasted cod with boulangère potatoes, loin of lamb with lemon confit, and roasted rabbit with olives, garlic, and rosemary. Excellent endings include oven-roasted pineapple with macadamia nut brittle and rum-vanilla ice cream, rhubarb cobbler, and a basket of warm cinnamon-sugar doughnuts. For those who want a less formal experience, the tavern room at the front of the restaurant offers more reasonably priced fare. ♦ American ♦ Daily, lunch and dinner; Su, dinner. Prix-fixe lunch and dinner available. Reservations required. 42 E 20th St (between Park Ave S and Broadway). 477.0777 ♿

70 L'Express

★★$$ Perfectly capturing the ambience of a French bistro, this charming café is one of the best places for friendly welcomes and hearty food. The 24-hour menu includes an omelette with Gruyère and ham, eggs Benedict, breast of duck with tomato chutney, and grilled salmon with lentils and mustard sauce. ♦ Bistro ♦ Daily, 24 hours. 249 Park Ave S (at E 20th St). 254.5858 ♿

71 Revolution Books

Before you start your revolution, stop here for inspiration from the masters of the art. The books cover political science, history, and social consciousness, with an emphasis on the radical. ♦ Daily. 9 W 19th St (between Fifth and Sixth Aves). 691.3345. www.revolutionbooksnyc.org ♿

72 Fishs Eddy

Sturdy ceramic hotel-ware (mostly reproductions these days and quite a bit pricier than in their early days) and glassware are the thing at this cozy emporium. Rough-hewn and dressed-down to look a bit old-timey to go with their wares, Fishs Eddy is a great place to stop whether you're into mix 'n' match or need a dozen of the same wide-edged white plates. Old Fred Harvey railroad dining-car patterns, swell green-glass mugs, and vintage hotel-logo coffee cups and creamers are just a few of the neatly displayed finds at this à la carte kitchen shop. ♦ Daily. 889 Broadway (at E 19th St). 420.9020

73 Arnold Constable Dry Goods Store Building

A glorious two-story mansard roof tops this skillful marriage of Empire and Italianate styles, designed by **Griffith Thomas** in 1877. Note the rare combination of marble and cast iron in the façade—the city's first use of cast-iron construction for retail space. ♦ 881-887 Broadway (between E 18th and E 19th Sts)

74 ABC Carpet & Home

The original owner of this 1882 building was **W&J Sloane**, which moved uptown and became one of the city's leading furniture dealers. It specialized in carpets and rugs when it was here, and the tradition is continued by one of Sloane's former competitors. Founded in 1987, this floor-covering emporium is one of New York's more reasonably priced sources of carpets of every description, from wall-to-wall carpeting to area rugs of every design, quality, and price, as well as various remnants and tiles. Most of ABC's carpet and floor-covering business is now located in the historic **Arnold Constable Building** at No. 881 across the street. Here now at No. 888 are six floors jammed with lushly styled home furnishings, including antique and reproduction rugs and furniture, plus bed, bath, linen, and lighting departments. The floor displays are so tasteful that apartment dwellers flock here on weekends just to look for ideas. ♦ Daily. 888 Broadway (at E 19th St). 473.3000. Also at 881 Broadway (at E 19th St); 20 Jay St, DUMBO, Brooklyn. 718/643.7400; 1055 Bronx River Ave, The Bronx. 718/842.8772

75 Craft

★★$$$ Master chef Tom Colicchio's order-by-numbers approach (a fish from column A, a braised or roasted meat from column B, perhaps a side dish of lamb's quarters or asparagus-lemon risotto from column C, and so on) may strike some as gimmicky, but it usually produces outstanding meals, assembled from flawlessly fresh, deceptively simple ingredients: Chatham cod, air-chilled Muscovy duck, ruby crescent fingerling potatoes. Around the corner, the more casual and affordable **Craftbar** offers the same quality on a lunch-and-dinner menu that's both more limited and more conventional (dishes come with accoutrements already assigned, as in baked wild king salmon with radicchio, peas, rhubarb, and summer truffles). ♦ American ♦ Daily, dinner. Reservations recommended. 43 E 19th St (between Park Ave S and Broadway) 780.0880 ♿ **Craftbar**: Daily, lunch and dinner. Reservations recommended. 900 Broadway (between E 19th and E 20th Sts). 461.4300 ♿

76 Friend of a Farmer

★★$$ The country cooking and on-the-premises baking might well take you back to your grandma's kitchen. The Long Island duckling and Cajun-style chicken are always good. ♦ American ♦ M-F, breakfast, lunch, and dinner; Sa, Su, brunch and dinner. Reservations recommended. 77 Irving Pl (between E 18th and E 19th Sts). 477.2188

77 Siegel-Cooper & Company

Originally **Siegel-Cooper Dry Goods Store**, this garish white brick and terra-cotta retail temple (fashioned by **DeLemos & Cordes** under the influence of the Chicago World's Fair of 1893) lived up to its slogan "The Big Store—A City In Itself" with 15.5 acres of space, 17 elevators, a tropical garden, and a smaller version of Daniel Chester French's monument *The Republic,* which had graced the Fair. (The fountain at the base of the statue became a favorite rendezvous for New Yorkers.) The store was located in the fashionable shopping district called "Ladies' Mile," but when **Macy's** and **B. Altman** moved uptown, it sold its inventory to **Gimbels** and the statue to Forest Lawn Cemetery in Los Angeles. The building was converted into a military hospital during World War I, and in recent years it has served as construction space for television scenery and home to garment manufacturing firms, as well as such traditionally "big-box" stores as **Bed, Bath & Beyond** and **Filene's Basement**. ♦ 620 Sixth Ave (between W 18th and W 19th Sts)

78 The City Bakery

★★$ Fresh ingredients from the nearby **Union Square Greenmarket** are turned into tasty dishes at this bakery/café/salad bar. Such hearty soups as lentil or potato with cumin, served with warm focaccia, are made on the premises each morning, as are the heavenly sweets, for which the bakery is well known. The tart-as-art follows the fruits of the season. Hot chocolate and lemonade festivals mark the seasons. Branches of City Bakery mastermind Maury Rubin's organic spin-off, **Birdbath**, have set down here and there; they're good stops for coffee and a special line of baked goods. ♦ American ♦ M-Sa, breakfast, lunch, and early dinner. 3 W 18th St (between Fifth and Sixth Aves). 366.1414. ♿ **Birdbath**: 145 Seventh Ave S (at Charles St) and other locations

79 Books of Wonder

If there are no children in your life, this store will make you wish there were—or at least make you fondly remember when you were a child yourself. Authors and illustrators make frequent appearances to read from their books and to sign copies. There is a half-hour storytime every Sunday at noon (except between Thanksgiving and New Year's). A branch of the kid (and adult) favorite **Cupcake Café** (456.1530) is here now also. ♦ Daily. 18 W 18th St (between Fifth and Sixth Aves). 989.3270. www.booksofwonder.com ♿

80 Barnes & Noble

Originally a purveyor of textbooks with branches at most major local colleges, this is where it all started. This is still the main store and it's still primarily about buying and selling textbooks, though there's also a good but smallish general selection. The closest superstore (the ones with cafés and full book, magazine, and music stock) is less than three blocks away on **Union Square**. It has the mega-chain's largest selection of university press titles. ♦ Daily. 105 Fifth Ave (at E 18th St). 807.0099. Also at 33 E 17th St (between Park Ave S and Broadway), 253.0810, and numerous locations throughout the city ♿

81 Paragon

This gigantic sporting goods store has three levels of gear and sportswear of all stripes—from bikinis to basketball, skiing, kayaking, and more—and all levels. Watch for their end-of-season sales, and, whatever your mission, avoid coming on weekends—the place gets packed. ♦ Daily. 867 Broadway (at E 18th St). 255.8036

82 MacIntyre Building

This 1892 **R.H. Robertson** Romanesque office building has obviously seen better days, but it hasn't lost its pride. You can tell by the way those beasts at the corners are sticking their tongues out at you. ♦ 874 Broadway (at E 18th St)

83 Old Town Bar

★★$ The popularity of this bi-level century-old tavern may be sufficient to keep it in business for another hundred years. Sit in the time-worn wooden booths and enjoy the famous chicken wings, a burger (served with fried onions on an English muffin), and an icy mug of draft beer; it's usually quieter upstairs. ♦ American ♦ Daily, lunch and

The Empire State Building is one of the world's eight wonders—and the only one constructed in the 20th century.

Tin Pan Alley, once located on West 28th Street between Broadway and Fifth Avenue, was the heart of the world-famous music publishing industry.

dinner. 45 E 18th St (between Park Ave S and Broadway). 529.6732

84 Pete's Tavern

★$$ One of several saloons that claim to be the oldest in town, this place also boasts that O. Henry did some of his writing in a corner booth. If the bar was as busy then as it is now, his powers of concentration must have been incredible. The food, which runs from standard Italian specialties to hamburgers, isn't exceptional, but the atmosphere is great, and the sidewalk café sits on one of the city's more pleasant streets. ♦ Italian/American ♦ M-F, lunch and dinner; Sa, Su, brunch and dinner. 129 E 18th St (at Irving Pl). 473.7676

85 Inn at Irving Place

$$$ One of the city's truly intimate hotels, this one is a gem, with 12 rooms handsomely appointed in *Age of Innocence* trappings in a 19th-century town house. Tastefully chosen period pieces might include big brass beds or oversized Victorian armoires—the kind of furniture seldom found on this side of the Atlantic. The inn's discreet albeit casual appeal extends to the lack of sign or awning or uniformed doorman, but within you'll find a small-but-swell martini lounge, **Cibar**, and the veddy proper, totally indulgent must-do treat that's **Lady Mendl's** tearoom. ♦ 54 Irving Pl (between E 17th and E 18th Sts). 533.4466; fax 533.4611. www.innatirving.com

86 Rothman's Union Square

For nearly seven decades (though at this location just since the 1980s) this discount retailer has been outfitting men in the know with labels from Canali, Hickey-Freeman, and Valentino. They stock a good selection of casual and dress shirts, and have a good eye for ties and other accessories. ♦ Daily. 200 Park Ave S (at E 17th St). 777.7400

87 W New York—Union Square

$$$ This W hotel, a 270-roomer, has the distinction of being the chain's fourth location in the city. Housed in the old 20-story Guardian Life Insurance Building, with its signature four-story mansard roof, the hotel looks over Union Square Park and its almost-daily Greenmarket. The place has, of course, been updated to typical W modern standards—high-speed Internet access, flat-screen TVs, and the gamut of upscale amenities—but the bright lobby lights, loud music, and walkie-talkie-toting security staff at the W hardly bespeak warmth and charm. Like other W hotels, this one is geared toward thick-walleted business travelers. ♦ 201 Park Ave S (at E 17th St). 253.9119, 877. WHOTELS; fax 253.9299. www.whotels.com

Within the W New York—Union Square:

Olives

★★$$$ Todd English's rich Mediterranean cuisine has proven popular with Manhattanites. The menu is large and creative; for appetizers (unless you fill up on the delicious home-baked breads), try the olive tart, made with marinated olives, goat cheese, caramelized onions, and anchovies, or the shredded artichoke salad on fontina risotto cake with artichoke silk and black truffle vinaigrette. For entrées, pan-seared snapper and roasted herb and garlic-basted chicken are good bets, as is the tortelli of butternut squash with brown butter, sage, and Parmesan—toothsome in any season. Desserts, from passion fruit flan to a "Very Vanilla Soufflé" (served with vanilla ice cream and vanilla sauce), are impressive. Warning: The restaurant gets very loud. ♦ American ♦ M-F, breakfast, lunch, and dinner; Sa, Su, brunch and dinner. Prix-fixe lunch available. Reservations recommended. 353.8345 ♿

88 St. Francis Xavier Church

This Baroque Roman Catholic monument to the Jesuit missionary would be right at home in his native Spain. The interior is the sort of thing American tourists go out of their way to see in Europe. ♦ 46 W 16th St (between Fifth and Sixth Aves). Wheelchair access: 55 W 15th St (between Fifth and Sixth Aves). 627.2100 ♿

89 Center for Jewish History/ YIVO Institute for Jewish Research

Composed of five major institutions of Jewish scholarship, history, and art—the **American Jewish Historical Society**, **American Sephardi Federation**, **Leo Baeck Institute**, **Yeshiva University Museum**, and **YIVO Institute for Jewish Research**—the Center opened here in 2000. Architecture firm **Beyer Blinder Belle**, well known for their sensitive and creative work with historic buildings, did the striking renovation of this strip of five now-interconnected brownstones. The complex showcases the unparalleled research facilities found in the beautiful **Lillian Goldman Reading Room** (and includes rare books, photographs, and genealogical resources); YIVO's historical collections, some shown in the **John and Gwen Smart Library Gallery**, which emphasize Eastern European heritage and the American Jewish immigrant experience; state-of-the-art performance space; and the stunning aluminum-and-bronze "Biblical Species" installation by Michele Oka Doner in the **Paul S. and Sylvia Steinberg Great Hall**. The largest repository documenting the Jewish experience outside of Israel, a six-story addition for their expanding archives, was completed in 2004. The center is host to a wide range of public programs, including film screenings, concerts, lectures, and seminars. ♦ M-Th. Shop: M-Th, Su. 294.8301. www.cjh.org. YIVO 15 W 16th St. 246.6080. www.yivoinstitute.org ♿

Also at the Center for Jewish History:

Yeshiva University Museum

Yeshiva's impressive holdings represent over 3,000 years of Jewish history from around the globe. Representing Jewish communities from Germany to Ethiopia, from Turkey to Morocco, from Birobidjan to Dubrovnik, and from Israel to the United States, the museum has endeavored to make Jewish history and culture accessible to audiences young and old since its founding in 1973. Archeological artifacts from the Bronze Age, illuminated manuscripts from the 15th century, silver and gold ceremonial objects and clothing dating from the 1700s, synagogue textiles and architecture, and the work of contemporary Jewish artists are just a few examples of the rich heritage that may be seen in the innovative exhibits here. Also here are a lovely outdoor sculpture garden, gift shop, and the kosher **Date Palm Café**. ♦ Admission. Tu-Th, Su, 11AM-5PM. **Date Palm Café**: closed summers. 294.8330. www.yumuseum.org ♿

90 Paul Smith

Rock stars and Wall Street bankers have been found here shopping for classic clothing with style. This is the eccentric Englishman's only US outlet for his handsomely made suits, sports jackets, and slacks, plus, occasionally, wacky playclothes. Unfortunately, prices can be out of touch, but the windows are always fun and worth a look. ♦ Daily. 108 Fifth Ave (at W 16th St). 627.9770. Also at 142 Greene St (at W Houston St). 646/613.3060

91 Mesa Grill

★★$$$ With its spacious setting and soaring ceilings (and wicked volume to go with them) this upscale Southwestern restaurant draws a crowd for celeb-chef/owner Bobby Flay's cooking. The menu includes such innovative dishes as goat cheese and fresh basil quesadilla; tomato-tortilla soup with avocado, white cheddar cheese, and cilantro; red snapper wrapped in a blue corn tortilla with fire-roasted poblano chili vinaigrette; and grilled baby lamb chops served with a preserved jalapeño sauce and sweet potato tamale. Save room for the blueberry cobbler with pecan biscuit and buttermilk custard sauce or banana ice-cream cake with pecan butter crunch. ♦ Southwestern ♦ M-F, lunch and dinner; Sa, Su, brunch and dinner. 102 Fifth Ave (between W 15th and W 16th Sts). 807.7400 ♿

92 Union Square Café

★★★★$$$ The very light, airy, modern space has rich cherry-wood floors and beige walls, wainscoted with hunter green and dotted with small brightly colored paintings. Chef Michael Romano's inventive dishes include gazpacho risotto with shrimp, cucumber, tomatoes, and peppers, and grilled marinated filet mignon of tuna. Be sure to save room for one of the delectable desserts. Can't get a reservation? Dine at their bar. Fact is, wherever you sit at this Danny Meyer classic, you are bound to walk out satisfied. ♦ American ♦ M-Sa, lunch and dinner; Su, dinner. Reservations required. 21 E 16th St (between Union Sq W and Fifth Ave). 243.4020

93 Coffee Shop

★$$ In pleasant weather, trendy "club kids" spill into the sidewalk café of this slick diner with a Brazilian flair. The menu includes the Sonia Braga chicken salad sandwich (rolled with papaya and cashews in a flour tortilla) and a traditional Brazilian *feijoada* (pork and bean stew) served on Saturdays. ♦ Eclectic ♦ Daily, breakfast, lunch, dinner, and late-night meals. 29 Union Sq W (at E 16th St). 243.7969

94 Union Square

Ⓟ In 1811, when the city fathers decreed that all of Manhattan's streets should follow a rigid grid pattern, Broadway was already in place, cutting an angle from southeast to northwest. Rather than change it, they turned it to the city's advantage by creating squares wherever Broadway crossed a north-south avenue. What may have

On 16 December 1835, fire engulfed Lower Manhattan, scorching everything south of Wall Street and east of Broadway. More than 650 buildings were burned. The flames took nearly 20 hours to bring under control; property damage was some $20 million.

inspired them was this already existing square, which grew up around the meeting point of Broadway, the post road to Albany, and the Boston Post Road, which later became Third Avenue. In the years before the Civil War, it was the heart of a fashionable residential neighborhood, surrounded by prestigious stores and theaters. When fashion moved uptown, the square became a center for labor demonstrations and rallies. It was landscaped and altered in 1936, when it was also raised a few feet above ground level to allow for the subway station under it. The pavilion at the north end was added at the same time. The redesign also forced Broadway to make a left turn at East 17th Street and share its right-of-way with Park Avenue South before getting back on course at East 14th Street. The landscapers came back almost 50 years later to begin a multiphase renovation to transform the area once again. (The park had become a gloomy hangout for drug pushers and derelicts.) Among their accomplishments is the replacement of the **Independence Flagstaff** at the center of the park, originally donated by Tammany Hall. The face-lift also included Art Deco–style subway kiosks, which flank the equestrian statue of George Washington, the masterpiece of sculptor John Quincy Adams Ward, which was placed there in 1856. Ward's collaborator was Henry Kirke Brown, who was responsible for the figure of Abraham Lincoln at the other end of the park. Nearby is a representation of the Marquis de Lafayette, created in 1876 by Frederic Auguste Bartholdi, who gave us the **Statue of Liberty** 10 years later. A statue of **Gandhi** is tucked off in the southwest fringe of the park. In summer, you can dine al fresco at the north end of the Square, in **Luna Park**. The chef changes each year, and there's always a crowd. ♦ Bounded by Union Square E and Union Square W, and E 14th and E 17th Sts

On Union Square:

Union Square Greenmarket

This location is the largest and arguably the most interesting of the city's greenmarkets.

During the peak years of immigration on Ellis Island, the record of languages spoken by a single official interpreter was 15. One interpreter was Fiorello LaGuardia, who would later become the most famous—and possibly the most beloved—mayor of New York City, responsible for cleaning up the corruption of Tammany Hall. He worked at Ellis Island for an annual salary of $1,200 from 1907 to 1910 and later was the first mayor to serve an until-then unprecedented three terms, from 1935 to 1945.

In addition to a huge variety of fresh seasonal and organic fruits and vegetables sold here (a regulation stipulates that all perishables must be sold within 24 hours o harvesting), fish, cheese, eggs, baked goods, honey, and plants are offered. Som locals make a beeline for the fresh flowers, and at Christmastime, for the freshest trees, wreaths, and garlands. ♦ M, W, F, Sa Union Sq W and E 17th St. 477.3220 ♿

95 Washington Irving High School

Though originally a technical high school for girls, the school expanded its curriculum to include a full range of subjects when it moved here from Lafayette Street in 1912. The huge bust of Irving at the East 17th Street corner was created in 1885 by Friedrich Baer. Not open to the public. ♦ 40 Irving Pl (between E 16th and E 17th Sts)

96 St. George's Church and Chapel

It's easy to believe that this imposing brownstone Romanesque Revival Episcopal church was where financier J.P. Morgan attended services. Dating from 1846, it was the design of **Otto Blesch** and **Leopold Eidlitz** and remains one of New York's overlooked treasures. In its shadow, just to the north at 4 Rutherford Place, lies its companion chapel. This lesser Romanesque structure was built in 1911 by **Matthew Lansing Emery** and **Henry George Emery**. ♦ E 16th St and Rutherford Pl. 475.0830

97 216 East 16th Street

Part of a row of striking Italianate houses built in the early 1850s, this building is still a joy to behold. The lower stories are brownstone, but brick is used on the upper floors, which, along with the wonderful windows, makes the building stand out. ♦ At Rutherford Pl

98 Friends Meeting House

This simple, two-story Greek Revival structure, built in 1860 by **Charles T. Bunting**, reflects the peaceful nature of the Society o Friends, whose meetings for worship are hel here. ♦ 15 Rutherford Pl (at E 15th St). 777.8866

99 Stuyvesant Square

Ⓟ Created in 1836 at the edge of the Gas House District (one of the city's poorest neighborhoods), this four-acre oasis, donated to the city by the Stuyvesant family, was the dividing line between rich and poor. In the center of the western half is a 1936 sculpture of Peter Stuyvesant by Gertrude Vanderbilt Whitney, founder of the **Whitney Museum**. ♦ Bounded by Nathan D. Perlman and Rutherford Pls, and E 15th and E 17th Sts

100 Stuyvesant Town

There are 8,755 mostly moderately priced rental apartments in this complex, which looks forbidding from the street (when it was built in 1947, Lewis Mumford called it "police state architecture"). The roadways within the complex are virtually free of cars. The tenants, many of whom are senior citizens and young families, lived a carefree existence for many years, thanks to good security and careful maintenance provided by the original landlord, the Metropolitan Life Insurance Company. In the blocks between East 20th and East 23rd Streets, the development is known as **Peter Cooper Village**, an upscale version of this complex, with larger apartments and higher rents. Newcomers to both Stuyvesant Town and Peter Cooper Village will still find a well-kept community; unfortunately, though, middle-income folks will find it harder to find a home here (in 2006 MetLife sold the property and there are no longer price-control guarantees for anyone). ♦ Bounded by Ave C and First Ave, and E 14th and E 20th Sts

101 Zeckendorf Plaza

There are more than 670 cooperative apartments in this 1987 building by **Davis, Brody & Associates**. Four illuminated pyramids sit atop the sprawling complex. Life here is self-contained, with such amenities as a health club and shopping facilities. At 108 East 15th Street is the 225-seat **Gertrude and Irving Dimson Theater**, the permanent home of the **Vineyard Theater Company**. The development is often cited as a key to the gentrification of the Union Square neighborhood, though many will never forgive the developers for so thoughtlessly blocking the west face of the Con Ed clock tower (below) with Zeckendorf's apartment towers. Bounded by Irving Pl and Union Sq E, and E 14th and E 15th Sts. 826.2900

102 Consolidated Edison Building

This massive structure, completed in 1929 by **Henry J. Hardenbergh**, has its critics, but everyone loves its clock tower, built in 1926 by **Warren & Wetmore**. It is softly lit at night, as it should be, considering that its owner is the electric company. The building, which fills nearly the whole block, replaced two structures that each had an impact on the city. **Tammany Hall**, which controlled City Hall for more than 100 years, was headquartered here in a large but unassuming brick building that had a spacious auditorium for public meetings, and a smaller one that became a profit center as **Tony Pastor's Music Hall**, which, in 1881, was the birthplace of American vaudeville. It was next door to a jewel box of a building known as the **Academy of Music**, the predecessor of the **Metropolitan Opera**, which in its decline became the scene of anti-Tammany rallies. ♦ 4 Irving Pl (between E 14th and E 15th Sts). 460.4600 ♿

The first slaves brought from Africa arrived in New York in 1625. The practice grew, and the first slave market was established at the foot of Wall Street in 1711; it was not until 1827 that slavery was abolished in New York. The *African Burial Ground*, just north of City Hall, was granted Monument status in 2006.

CHELSEA

Named for the estate acquired by Captain Thomas Clarke in 1750, Chelsea w originally bounded by **West 14th** and **West 25th Streets**, and **Eighth Aven** and the **Hudson River**. Today, the Chelsea area, which is broadly considered to exte north to **West 39th Street** and east to **Sixth Avenue**, is quite a mixed bag. Cleme Clarke Moore, who had inherited his grandfather's land, divided his family esta and laid out the neighborhood's original building lots in 1830, some of which he d

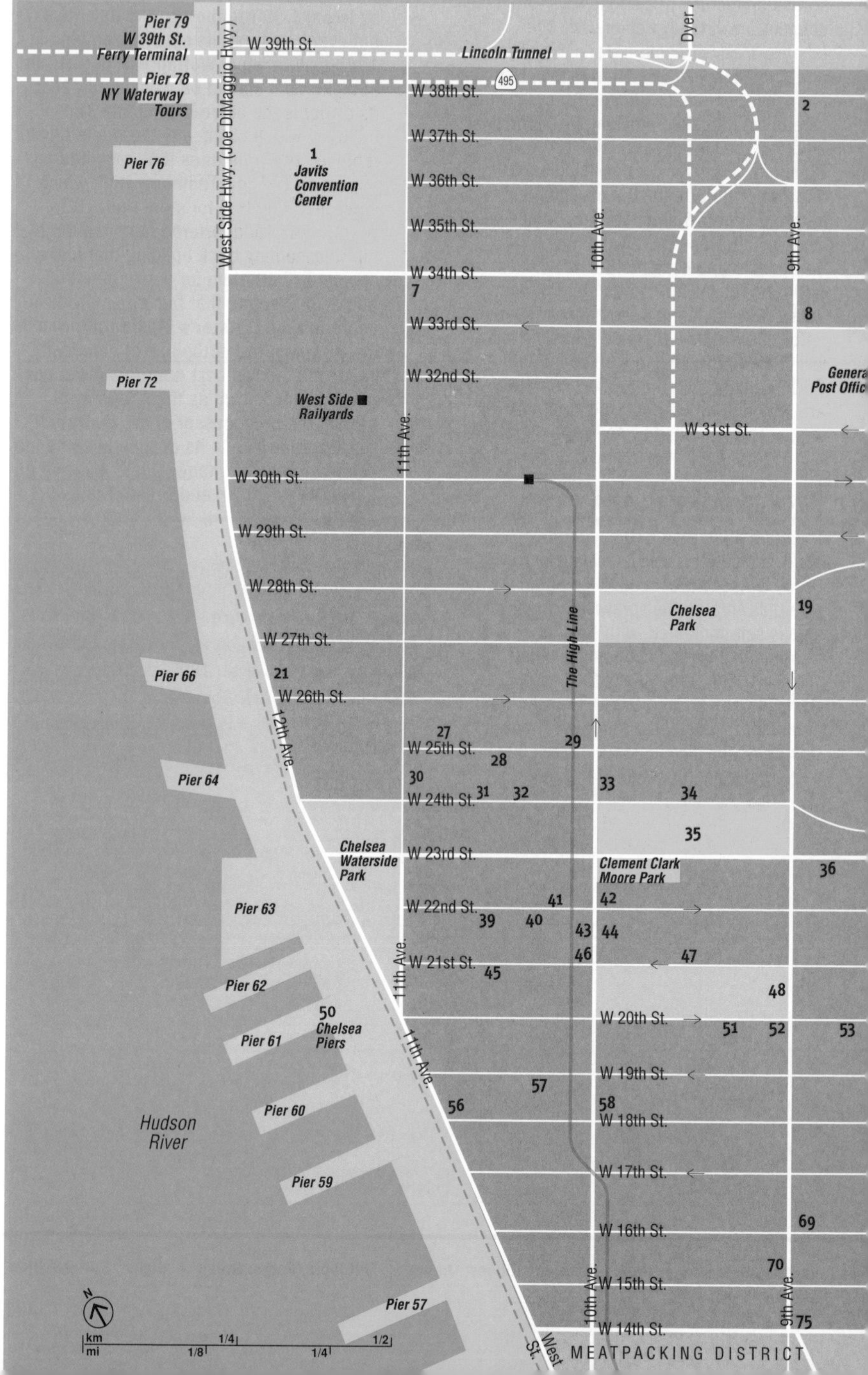

ated to the **General Theological Seminary**. The surrounding area was a flourishing middle-class suburb that never quite made it as a desirable address. Once the **Hudson River Railroad** opened on **11th Avenue** in 1851, it attracted breweries and slaughterhouses and their workers' shanties and tenements, which marked the beginning of the area's aesthetic decline. In the 1870s, the remaining westerly town-house blocks were invaded by the city's first elevated railroad, on **Ninth Avenue**.

Despite its industrial image, Chelsea became a creative retail center. As the gentry pursued their determined course uptown, so did fashionable stores. By the 1870s, West 23rd Street had blossomed, and the blocks on Sixth Avenue south of it became known as the "**Ladies' Mile.**" Giant dry-goods stores of limestone and cast iron lined Sixth Avenue and Broadway. And, as fashion retail grew, so did the garment-manufacturing trade. Before 1900, the garment trade was centered below East 14th Street on the Lower East Side. By 1915, it had moved north along Broadway and Sixth Avenue as far as West 30th Street, replacing part of the rough-and-tumble Tenderloin District. The merchant princes who were reestablishing their fine department stores along Fifth Avenue were distressed to find garment workers mingling with their affluent customers and formed a committee to put a stop to it. The committee's solution was to order the construction of two garment workshop buildings, Nos. 498 and 500 Seventh Avenue, at West 37th Street, a comfortable distance away. Not long after the 1921 completion of the loft buildings, Seventh Avenue came to be synonymous with American fashion and New York City's "rag trade": street signs today read "Fashion Avenue."

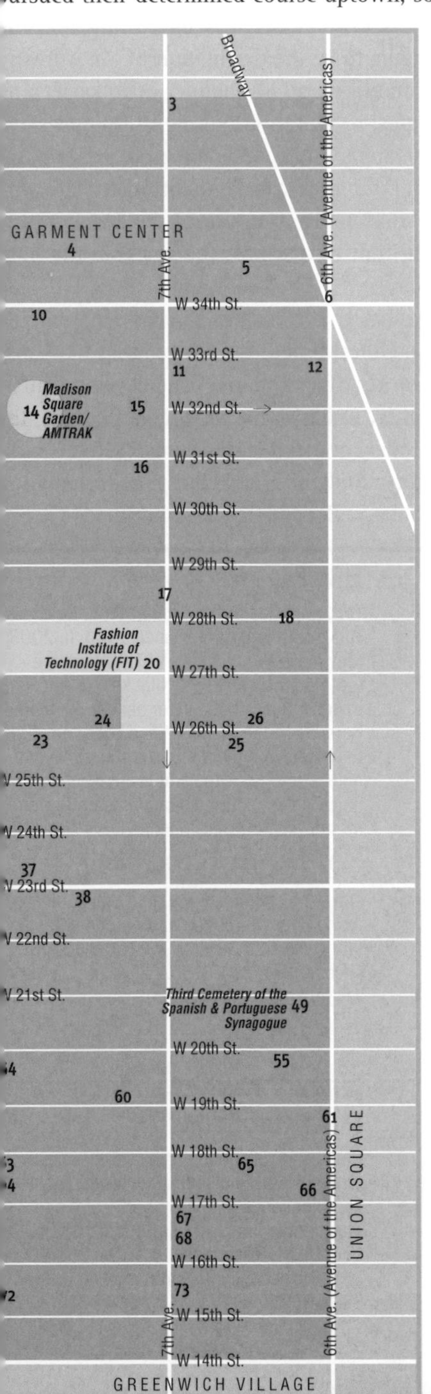

A flurry of theatrical activity took over West 23rd Street in the 1880s, and while short-lived—by 1892, Times Square had begun to beckon—it left behind a creative tradition and a resident population rich in artists and writers. (The **Hotel Chelsea**, which went up in 1884, housed many of them.) Fittingly, in about 1905, the country's motion picture industry got an early boost in Chelsea—it's arguably the home of the first US film studios.

Adolph Zukor's Famous Players Studio, which employed Mary Pickford and

John Barrymore, produced films here, and for a decade or so after film activity began in the area it flourished in old lofts and theaters used as studios. But the Astoria Studios in Queens built a better facility, and eventually balmy Hollywood beckoned. The film business also moved on.

In the 1930s, new industry found quarters in the area near the piers. The 11th Avenue railroad was replaced by the **High Line**, a less objectionable elevated train, and the Ninth Avenue line shut down. The clean sweep of 1950s and 1960s urban renewal replaced slum housing with housing projects, and renovation started on desirable Federal and Greek Revival town houses. With its lower rents and interesting housing stock, by the late 1970s and 1980s Chelsea came to be the destination of a northward immigration of Greenwich Village's gay community and all manner of folks seeking relief for their wallets and a new frontier. Shops, restaurants, and nightlife flourished and by the 1990s another change had become apparent as more and more art galleries fled SoHo (those rents again). The **Dia Center for the Arts Foundation** led the way when they moved to way-west 22nd Street in 1985. By the turn of the 21st century Chelsea was the new center of the art world (not to discount the key role the 57th Street–Madison Avenue area continues to play).

With its increased cachet, of course, Chelsea has gotten costlier. Dia has departed; the neighborhood's gay population is not quite so concentrated; the **Flower District** is disappearing; and the **Garment Center** is a shadow. But other initiatives and developments—the big-box chain restorations of the former Ladies' Mile buildings; hotels; the humongous **Chelsea Piers** sports facility; the lovely and expanding **Hudson River Park**; **Chelsea Market,** in the former Nabisco factory; and the High Line park reclamation project—ensure Chelsea's status as a most livable—and visitable—neighborhood.

1 Jacob K. Javits Convention Center

This huge facility—made almost entirely of glass—covers 22 acres between West 34th and West 39th Streets. Designed by **I.M. Pei & Partners**, it was called "the center at the center of the world" when it opened in 1986. The building appears opaque during the day, while at night the interior lighting makes the structure glow. ♦ 655 W 34th St (between 11th and 12th Aves). 216.2000. www.javitscenter.com ♿

2 Manganaro's

★★ $ Mouthwatering aromas prime the appetite for the prosciutto, sopressata, and other old-country delicacies hanging from the rafters high above the worn wooden floors of this little place, which seems unchanged since it opened in 1893. Bask in the eccentric service and retro décor and take out a sandwich and cookies or have a hot meal—they do an eggplant parmigiana hero that would make Parma proud. (What's up with—antiseptic, we think—**Manganaro's Hero Boy** next door? It *is* all in the family, but the two branches haven't spoken in decades.) ♦ Italian ♦ M-Sa, breakfast, lunch, and dinner; Su, breakfast and lunch. 488 Ninth Ave (between W 37th and W 38th Sts). 563.5331

3 B&J Fabrics

This store has been at the heart of New York's Garment Center since 1940. In 2003 they moved to this large (15,000-square-foot) location just three blocks from the building they'd been in for almost 50 years. Catering to the many set and costume designers in the area, B&J's superb layout and generosity with samples make it as much a destination for students and other up-and-coming designers as it is for those long established in the business. While the original Bob and Jack of "B&J" are long gone, it's still family-run, and still dedicated to the finest European and American fashion fabrics. ♦ 525 Seventh Ave (at W 38th St), second floor. 354.8150. www.bandifenbrics.com ♿

4 Jerry Ohlinger's Movie Material Store

Ohlinger's collection of current, classic, and rare movie art includes innumerable posters and thousands of stills in both color and black-and-white, including some 10,000 from Disney films alone. ♦ M-Sa. 253 W 35th St (between Seventh and Eighth Aves) 989.0869

5 MACY'S

Facing onto **Herald Square**, the Broadway building of this New York institution was built in 1901 by **DeLemos & Cordes**; the Seventh Avenue building was built in 1931 by **Robert D. Kohn**. Back to its earliest days down on 14th Street, Macy's has always seemed to have more of everything than any other department store. But it didn't really develop a fashion identity of its own until later in the 20th century. Today, the range of goods offers quality at a good range of price points. You can buy a Balenciaga or Dockers, get a manicure, mail a letter, have your jewelry appraised, buy a bed, and get your eyes checked, all without ever leaving the store. The place is immense—pick up a map as soon as you enter. ♦ Daily. Bounded by Broadway and Seventh Ave, and W 34th and W 35th Sts. 695.4400 ♿

6 HERALD SQUARE

Ⓟ During the 1880s and 1890s, this was the heart of the Tenderloin, an area of dance halls, bordellos, and cafés adjacent to Hell's Kitchen. New York City's theater and newspaper industries were once headquartered here. The square—which, like most of the squares in New York, is anything but—was named for the *New York Herald*. (Greeley Square, to the south at West 33rd Street, was named for the founder of the *New York Tribune*, Horace Greeley.) Time your walk-through to hear Stuff and Guff—two seven-foot bronze blacksmiths from the parapet of the original Herald building—strike the hour on the bell of the 1940 monument to publisher James Gordon Bennett Jr. (Thanks to a 2007 restoration, the bell is no longer being pummeled directly by the blacksmiths; softer, hidden mallets do the job). ♦ Bounded by Sixth Ave and Broadway, and W 34th and W 35th Sts. www.nycgovparks.org ♿

7 COPACABANA

In the 1940s and 1950s, you could be thrilled here by the Copa Girls and entertained by such personalities as Sammy Davis Jr. and Jerry Vale. Although nightclub shows like those are a thing of the past here, the latest incarnation of this club is still a hot spot for the 30-and-over crowd. Salsa and merengue rule the live music most nights after 10PM on the main floor. A DJ's the thing in the lower room, spinning disco, house, and R&B. In 2002 the Copa moved to this new glitz-o-dome post a 10-year run on W 57th Street. In its original glory days the Copa made hay on the East Side. ♦ M-Sa. 560 W 34th St (between 10th and 12th Aves). 239.2672

8 B&H PHOTO-VIDEO-PRO AUDIO

With a reputation for a knowledgeable staff and good, reliable service and equipment among the many professional photographers in New York (they do a huge Internet and mail-order business as well), B&H has grown and grown, taking up a good part of this block. Their solid camera stock has expanded to include the whole gamut of audio and video—including Mac and PC computers—that technology has to offer these days. And while they most definitely still service the pros, they're the place to go for an average Joe as well—especially one with an inkling of what he wants or needs. ♦ Su-F (closes early on Fridays). 420 Ninth Ave (between W 33rd and W 34th Sts). 444.6670. www.bhphoto.com ♿

9 TÍR NA NÓG

★$$ This lively spot in a restaurant-starved area is a good place to come for hearty portions of dishes the likes of shepherd's pie, Clonakilty roasted black pudding, or Irish salmon with warm corn blini, dill crème fraîche, and baby greens. The Corleggy goat cheese package with roasted beets and pepper cress salad is delicious. On the American contemporary side, go for the grilled mahimahi with artichoke potato purée and tomato confit basil or the Tír Na Nóg burger, made with Ballycashel Irish cheddar. One warning: The bar's popularity as an after-work hangout and sports-viewing venue can make dining a noisy experience. ♦ Irish/American ♦ M-F, lunch and dinner; Sa, Su, brunch and dinner. 5 Penn Plaza (Eighth Ave between W 33rd and W 34th Sts). 630.0249

10 1 PENN PLAZA

In 1972, **Charles Luckman Associates** designed this, the tallest of the complex of buildings that replaced the original **Pennsylvania Station**. ♦ 250 W 34th St (between Seventh and Eighth Aves)

11 HOTEL PENNSYLVANIA

$$ Originally designed in 1918 by **McKim, Mead & White** as the largest hotel in the world, it was named for the old **Pennsylvania Station**. In the 1930s, it was a hot stop for the Big Bands: Glenn Miller immortalized its phone number with his "Pennsylvania

> Only a handful of all the semiactuated signals (those chest-high buttons that pedestrians push to make the light change to green) installed on lightpoles around Manhattan actually work; most are located along West Street/12th Avenue.

6-5000." The lobby's been spruced up, but beware the rooms. While some of them (1,700 in all) have indeed been renovated (always ask for one), most are mediocre at best. Better to enter the lobby, sing the song, and retreat. **Globetrotter** restaurant serves breakfast only. ♦ 401 Seventh Ave (between W 32nd and W 33rd Sts). 736.5000, 800/223.8585; fax 502.8712. www.hotelpenn.com

12 Manhattan Mall

With eight floors with some 50 shops plus a food court, this place will make you feel like you're in a mall in the 'burbs—and a noisy, overcrowded one at that. While you'll find the expected chain stores like **The Body Shop**, **Brookstone**, **Victoria's Secret**, and **Steve & Barry's**, aside from the public bathrooms and a small tourist information kiosk, there's not much reason to stop here. ♦ Daily. 100 W 33rd St (at Sixth Ave). 465.0500 ♿

13 General Post Office

The monumental stairway and columned entrance were designed by **McKim**, **Mead & White** in 1913. Look up for that famous inscription about rain, snow, and the gloom of night that made it the first attraction of visitors arriving by train. Progress has been made, in fact, on a plan to convert the venerable old P.O. (or part of it) into a replacement for the much-loathed 1960s-era station across the street. A target date of 2010 has been set for renovations; when it comes out of its construction shroud it will take the name **Moynihan Station**. ♦ Daily 24 hours. Eighth Ave (between W 31st and W 33rd Sts). 800/275.8777. www.usps.com ♿

William Marcy "Boss" Tweed began his political career in 1848 as the organizer of the Americus Volunteer Fire Company, whose unusually large fire engine was painted with the head of a tiger. The fire company was associated with Tammany Hall (the Democratic political machine), and it was an easy step from one to the other. By 1853, Tweed had become a congressman; by 1867, he was powerful enough to overthrow Reform mayor Fernando Wood and put his own man, George Opdyke, in charge at City Hall. In 1868, he became Grand Sachem of Tammany Hall, which gave him backroom control over the state as well as the city. Attacks by cartoonist Thomas Nast in *Harper's Weekly* led to his downfall in 1873. He was convicted of "official embezzlement," but jumped bail and slipped away to Spain, where he was captured by police who recognized him from the Nast cartoons. Tweed died in prison three years later.

14 Madison Square Garden

America's premier entertainment facility, and the fourth home of Madison Square Garden, was designed by **Charles Luckman Associates** in 1968. It hosts more than 600 events for nearly 6 million spectators each year. Within the center are the 20,000-seat **Arena**, the 5,600-seat **Theater at Madison Square Garden**, and the **Exposition Rotunda** with a 20-story office building. It is home to the **New York Knicks** and the **New York Rangers**. Throughout the year, the facility hosts exhibitions and trade shows; giant truck competitions; boxing; rodeos; dog, cat, and horse shows; circuses; graduations; rock concerts; tennis, track and field, and gymnastics events; and an occasional presidential convention. ♦ Eighth Ave (between W 31st and W 33rd Sts). Enter from Seventh Ave (between W 31st and W 33rd Sts). Event info: 465.6741 ♿

15 Pennsylvania Station

New Yorkers will always lament the original station, lost to the wrecking ball in 1963. The good news is that that Beaux Arts architectural tragedy led to historic preservation laws that saved many another remarkable building in the city (including **Grand Central** terminal). Nondescript now (even with a **Maya Lin** sculpture to call its own), and wholly underground, here's where you come for connections to Long Island (and the **JFK AirTrain**) via the Long Island Railroad, for commuter service to the west and south (including **Newark Airport**) via New Jersey Transit, and for longer hauls to points north, south, and west via Amtrak. ♦ Bounded by Seventh and Eighth Aves, and W 31st and W 34th Sts. Main entrance: Seventh Ave (at W 32nd St); other entrances on all sides. Amtrak, 800 USA-RAIL, www.amtrak.com; Long Island Railroad (LIRR), 718/217.5477, www.lirr.org; NJ Transit, 800.772.2222, www.njtransit.com ♿

16 St. John the Baptist Church

Designed in 1872 by **Napoleon LeBrun**, this Roman Catholic church is noted for its white marble interior. ♦ 210 W 31st St (between Seventh and Eighth Aves). 564.9070 ♿

17 Fur District

It seems like yesterday when you could stroll in this area and not blink to see that the man you just passed *did* have a silver fox cape over his arm. He didn't steal it, and chances are that no one would have stolen it from him. Back in the day, before the rise of overseas piecework—and as recently as the 1990s—it was commonplace in the Fur District for thousands of dollars' worth of merchandise to be delivered in such a casual way. Rare now though it is, there are still small pockets of people who make and sell fur garments in this neighborhood. But, as with the rest of the garment district, you're more apt to see goods arrive here by truck, en route to a wholesaler. ♦ Bounded by Sixth and Eighth Aves, and W 27th and W 30th Sts

18 Flower District

The best time to smell the flowers here is the early morning, when florists from all over the city arrive to refresh their stock. If you're in the market for a large plant or a small tree, you'll find it here on the sidewalk soaking up the sun. While the co-ops and other commercial enterprises are encroaching on the rapidly withering district, and negotiations to relocate it are under way, we think there's life in the Flower District right here—at least for a few more years. The highest concentration of shops (many open only to wholesalers, but you can still sniff) is on the West 28th St strip now. Ironically, some of the best selection of intricately formed silk flowers are found here as well. Stop in at **Starbright Floral Design** (150 W 28th St) or **Designer's Garden** (136 W 28th St) for the real thing; try **PANY** (146 W 28th St) for the ersatz, and **B&J** (103 W 28th St) for supplies. ♦ W 28th St (between Sixth and Seventh Aves), and Sixth Ave (between W 27th and W 29th Sts)

19 Church of the Holy Apostles

The slate-roofed spire of this Episcopal church makes it a standout among the huge brick apartment houses all around it. Built in 1848 by **Minard Lafever** with 1858 transepts by **Richard Upjohn**, it's an unusual feature of the view to the west from the **Observation Deck** of the **Empire State Building**. ♦ 296 Ninth Ave (between W 26th and W 28th Sts). 807.6799 ♿

20 Fashion Institute of Technology (FIT)

If there were a competition for the ugliest block in Manhattan, the center of this complex on West 27th Street would win easily. All the buildings, built between 1958 and 1977, are by the same firm, **De Young & Moscowitz**, but obviously not by the same hand. The prestigious school, part of the **State University of New York**, was created by New York's garment industry to train young people in all aspects of the fashion business. ♦ Seventh Ave and W 27th St. 217.7999. www.fitnyc.edu ♿

Within FIT:

The Museum at FIT

Fashion fans will not want to miss the superbly designed (and manageably sized) Museum at FIT. Its shows are true gems, and may feature anything from a particular 1930s designer to automobile fabrics. ♦ Free. Tu-F, noon-8PM; Sa, 10AM-5PM. 217.4588. Tours: 217.4555. www.fitnyc.edu/museum ♿

21 Starrett-Lehigh Building

A pacesetter in its day, this rare American International-style collection of glass, concrete, and brown brick with rounded corners was built over the yards of the **Lehigh Valley Railroad**, and had elevators powerful enough to lift fully loaded freight cars onto its upper warehouse floors. It was designed in 1931 by **Russell G.** and **Walter M. Cory** and **Yasuo Matsui**. The dot-com-driven economic boom of the 1990s led to gutting and refurbishment of this mammoth NYC landmark. ♦ 601 W 26th St (between 11th and 12th Aves)

22 Penn South Houses

This 12-square-block complex of 2,820 apartments was built in 1962 by **Herman Jessor** as middle-income housing for members of the **International Ladies' Garment Workers Union**. ♦ Bounded by Eighth and Ninth Aves, and W 24th and W 29th Sts

23 Phyllis Kind Gallery

A late addition to the SoHo gallery diaspora, Kind's eclectic collection of contemporary paintings by American and international artists both with and without formal training joined the gang here in Chelsea in 2007.

♦ Tu-Sa. 236 W 26th St, fifth floor (between Seventh and Eighth Aves). 925.1200. www.phylliskindgallery.com

24 Chelsea Television Studios

The building originally on this site was an armory. It was also once movieland's **Famous Players Studio**, where, in 1915, Adolph Zukor paid Mary Pickford an unprecedented $2,000 per week as one of his most famous players. ♦ Television production is the thing today. Here's where Ricki Lake's show was taped; the post-prison *Martha Stewart Show* began to broadcast from here. ♦ 221 W 26th St, between Seventh and Eighth Aves. 727.1234

25 Lightforms

Whether you need an elaborate illumination system or a table lamp, the expert consultants here will help you. Brands on offer include Kovacs, Artemide, Lightolier, and Fabbian, and on the flip side of all that modernism and tech, a line of colorfully bejeweled and wonderfully whimsical finials is also available. ♦ M-Sa. 142 W 26th St (between Sixth and Seventh Aves). 255.4664. Also at 509 Amsterdam Ave (between W 84th and W 85th Sts). 875.0407

26 Burgundy Wine Company

OK, the first things you need to know are that red Burgundy is made from the Pinot Noir grape and white Burgundy is—*tada!*—from the Chardonnay. And that true French Burgundies are not named for the grape variety, but the village in which it was grown. Oenophiles of all levels will learn something here; the shop is small, the service attentive—and utterly unintimidating—and the selection, delicious. ♦ Tu-Sa. 143 W 26th St (between Sixth and Seventh Aves). 691.9092

27 P.P.O.W.

The adventuresome young partners Penny Pilkington and Wendy Olsoff (hence the gallery's name) pride themselves on their preference for individuals over trends. They show the work of David Wojnarowicz and Erika Rothenberg, as well as installation work (built environments) by TODT. ♦ Tu-Sa. 555 W 25th St (between 10th and 11th Aves), second floor. 647.1043. www.ppowgallery.com ♿

28 PaceWildenstein

The two Chelsea branches of this blue-chip gallery are each located in vast spaces that provide a dramatic backdrop for large-scale paintings and sculpture. ♦ Tu-Sa. 534 W 25th St (between 10th and 11th Aves). 929.7001; 545 W 22nd St (between 10th and 11th Aves). 989.4263. Also at 32 E 57th St (between Park and Madison Aves). 421.3292. www.pacewildenstein.com ♿

29 Klotz Gallery

Begun in 1977 as **Photocollect**, this gallery continues to build its reputation in fine 19th and 20th-century photography. Usually showing one or two artists' works at a time, their exhibits have ranged from modern photojournalist Jonathan Torgovnik's color-infused pieces on Indian cinema to the vintage black-and-white work of Berenice Abbott and Weegee. ♦ W-Sa, or by appointment. 511 W 25th St (between 10th and 11th Aves), seventh floor. 741.4764. www.photocollect.com

29 High Line

P One of the most evocative remnants of the city's old infrastructure, this 1.5-mile elevated railway, built in 1934 to carry freight to West Chelsea warehouses, fell into atmospheric disrepair after trains stopped running in 1980; the tracks that cut through blocks of industrial buildings were overgrown with wild grasses and even trees. Thanks to a campaign to save it (launched in 1999 and soon a cause célèbre), the southernmost section of the derelict roadbed will be opened in 2008 and transformed into an elevated park with plantings and walkways. Plans call for other portions to be opened to the public, but until then they're city property—no trespassing. ♦ From Gansevoort to W 30th Sts, between 10th and 11th Aves. www.thehighline.org

30 Edward Thorp Gallery

Owner Thorp's affinity for slightly offbeat landscapes is clear in the work of Hilary Brace, who has shown astonishing power in her charcoal miniatures done on Mylar. He also represents Deborah Butterfield, who sculpts small- and large-scale horses out of found objects. ♦ Tu-Sa. 21 11th Ave (between W 24th and W 25th Sts), sixth floor. 691.6565. www.edwardthorpgallery.com ♿

31 Charles Cowles Gallery

Contemporary painting joins sculpture and ceramics by a wide-ranging stable that includes many West Coast artists. ♦ Tu-Sa. 537 W 24th St (between 10th and 11th Aves). 925.3500. www.cowlesgallery.com ♿

32 Barbara Gladstone Gallery

Gladstone's space allows her to mount dual exhibitions from an ever-increasing stable of European and American artists. Vito Acconci, Anish Kapoor, Rosemarie Trockel, and Jenny Holzer are part of her distinguished roster. ♦ Tu-Sa. 515 W 24th St (between 10th and 11th Aves). 206.9300. www.gladstonegallery.com ♿

33 Bottino

★★$$ Art-world types from the nearby galleries rub shoulders (at tight tables) with neighborhood folks in this clean, modern space—dark wood floor, white brick walls, Eames—which opens into a lovely back garden, tented in winter. While the Tuscan menu doesn't overwhelm with choices, you could make a fine meal of the *fritto misto* and a plate of green ravioli. ♦ Northern Italian ♦ Tu-Sa, lunch and dinner; Su, M, dinner. 246 10th Ave (between W 24th and W 25th Sts). 206.6766 ♿

34 Gallery of Wearable Art

Since this most unusual clothier recently moved from East Side retail space to a townhouse atelier, you can no longer wander in off the street, but Bronnie Kupris's idiosyncratic togs aren't impulse buys anyway. In addition to the trademark coats and jackets—gorgeous and one-of-a-kind, elaborated with antique textiles and trims—evening and bridal gowns are available by special order. ♦ By appointment only. 437 W 24th St (between Ninth and 10th Aves). 425.5379

35 London Terrace Apartments

This double row of buildings with a garden in the center contains 1,670 apartments. It was built in 1930 by **Farrar & Watmaugh** at the height of the Depression and stood virtually empty for several years, despite lures such as an Olympic-size swimming pool and doormen dressed as London bobbies. It is the second complex by that name on the site. The original, built in 1845, was a row of Greek Revival buildings with wide front lawns on West 23rd Street. ♦ Bounded by Ninth and 10th Aves, and W 23rd and W 24th Sts

36 Negril

★★$$ Negril's décor attempts to whisk you away to the island of Jamaica. Try the codfish fritters with avocado salsa; ginger-lime chicken; a whole fried red snapper with onions, peppers, scallions, tomatoes, and thyme; the *callaloo* (Jamaican greens with onions and tomatoes); or any of the *rotis*. For dessert, the bread pudding in caramelized raisin sauce is hard to resist, and even harder to forget. ♦ Jamaican ♦ Daily, lunch and dinner. Reservations recommended. 362 W 23rd St (between Eighth and Ninth Aves). 807.6411. ♿ Also at 70 W Third St (between La Guardia Pl and Thompson St). 477.2804 ♿

37 F&B Chelsea

★$ This small but exceedingly cheerful place purveys a variety of "European street food" to the hungry and upscale Chelsea crowd. At breakfast time they come for the fresh-baked beignets (accompanied by a variety of dips), later in the day for the hot dogs: The Great Dane, a Danish wiener with remoulade, crispy roast onions, marinated cucumber slices, Danish mustard, and ketchup on a toasted bun, is one of the more popular choices. Vegetarians need not despair; any of the hot-dog creations can be ordered with a tofu dog. Wash your dog down with one of the fresh flavored lemonades or single-serving Champagnes (replete with straw). ♦ European ♦ Daily. 269 W 23rd St (between Seventh and Eighth Aves). 646/486.4441

38 Hotel Chelsea

$$$ When the hotel was first built in 1884 by **Hubert**, **Pirrson & Co**., it was cooperative apartments and Chelsea was the heart of the theater district, attracting creative people just as Greenwich Village would a decade later. It became a residential hotel in 1905, and in its early days the hotel was home to such writers as William Dean Howells and O. Henry, and later to Thomas Wolfe, Arthur Miller, Mary McCarthy, Vladimir Nabokov, and Yevgeny Yevtushenko. Sarah Bernhardt once lived there, and it is where Dylan Thomas spent his last days. In the 1960s and 1970s, it was a favorite stopping place for visiting rock stars, who shared the atmosphere with modern classical composers George Kleinsinger and Virgil Thomson. The Chelsea is still a mix of hotel rooms and rentals, and while the premises can be somewhat dingy, you may find it irresistible for the ghosts or its still-artsy atmosphere. Then again, with the 2007 ouster of the beloved Bard family as the hotel's management team (after six decades in charge), it is uncertain in what direction the accommodations will go. The basement is home to the swank, dimly lit bar **Serena**. ♦ 222 W 23rd St (between Seventh and Eighth Aves). 243.3700. www.hotelchelsea.com

39 Sonnabend Gallery

The Sonnabend draws in contemporary artists, including such Americans as Robert Morris, who shares the floor with an ever-growing list of distinguished Europeans, including Jannis Kounellis, Gilbert & George, and Anne and Patrick Poirier. ♦ Tu-Sa. 536 W 22nd St (between 10th and 11th Aves). 627.1018. www.sonnabendgallery.com ♿

40 Comme des Garçons

Rei Kawakubo's cutting-edge clothes for men and women are for sale in this suitably stunning showcase. Merchandise is displayed in a series of bright white rooms, which you enter through a futuristic ramp made of brushed aluminum. The overall effect is both unsettling and sassy, an interesting twist in a neighborhood often lacking in unadulterated fun. ♦ Daily. 520 W 22nd St (between 10th and 11th Aves). 604.9200

41 Max Protetch

The primary commercial outlet in New York for drawings by such distinguished architects as Louis I. Kahn, Frank Lloyd Wright, Michael Graves, Aldo Rossi, and Rem Koolhaas, this gallery also exhibits painting, ceramics, and sculpture. It's well worth a visit to these spacious quarters. ♦ Tu-Sa. 511 W 22nd St (between 10th and 11th Aves). 633.6999. www.maxprotetch.com ♿

EMPIRE

42 Empire Diner

★$ Refurbished in 1976 by designer **Carl Laanes**, this 1930s-style diner has retained the classic trappings of the original establishment—the Art Deco aluminum-winged clock near the entrance and the baked-enamel finish outside. Too bad the service has only gone downhill. Open around the clock, this diner *cum* coffee shop has a bar and its gallery-centric location (and outdoor seating) makes it an inevitable draw regardless. ♦ American ♦ Daily, 24 hours. 210 10th Ave (at W 22nd St). 243.2736

43 Printed Matter

This nonprofit art center specializes in books made by artists, both big name and new discoveries. "Book" can be loosely defined here: cards, flips, letterpress documents, and folios bound with everything from string to rubber bands and more traditional methods are among the inspired displays. Besides visual (and tactile) satisfaction, prices can start as low as $10 to $15—choose among 15,000 titles by 5,000 artists—placing them among the few affordable media in the art world. ♦ Tu-Sa. 195 10th Ave (between W 21st and W 22nd Sts). 925.0325. www.printedmatter.org ♿

44 192 Books

Tall, inviting windows pull light into this small, elegant space, arranged with intelligence and stocked for serendipitous finds. In addition to signings, discussions, and readings, the shop (co-owned by gallery pro Paula Cooper) presents art exhibitions—for example, a "reprise" of Baudelaire's *Fleurs du Mal*—alongside books that relate to the artists or the theme. ♦ Daily. 192 10th Ave (between W 21st and W 22nd Sts). 255.4022. www.192books.com

45 Paula Cooper Gallery

A pioneer in the area years ago, owner Cooper has built a formidable stable of modern artists, including Jennifer Bartlett, Jonathan Borofsky, Elizabeth Murray, and Carl Andre. ♦ Tu-Sa. 534 W 21st St (between 10th and 11th Aves). 255.1105 ♿

46 Guardian Angel Church

This little complex of Italian Romanesque buildings, designed in 1930 by **John Van Pelt**, surrounds what is known as the **Shrine Church of the Sea**. The name, which has nothing to do with the red-bereted "street guardians" that once walked the city, reflects the onetime presence of the busiest piers in the Port of New York, a short walk to the west. The church's Renaissance interior is even more impressive than the redbrick-and limestone façade. The priest in charge of this Roman Catholic church is designated Chaplain of the Port, with duties that include assigning chaplains to ships based here. ♦ 193 10th Ave (at W 21st St). 929.5966

47 West 21st Street

Almost all the 19th-century houses on the north side of this block at the heart of the **Chelsea Historic District** follow a period requirement of front gardens and street trees. In its earliest years as a residential community, all of Chelsea looked much like this. The building with the unusual peaked roof on the Ninth Avenue corner was built in the 1820s by **James N. Wells** and is the oldest house in the neighborhood. ♦ Between Ninth and 10th Aves

48 General Theological Seminary

You're welcome to enter this oasis through the library building on Ninth Avenue during public hours (below). Land for the Episcopal Seminary was donated by Clement Clarke Moore in 1830 (the writer and scholar had grown up here and inherited it from his grandfather) on the condition that the seminary always occupy the site. The **West Building**, built in 1835, is the oldest on campus, as well as New York's oldest example of Gothic Revival architecture. It predates **Charles C. Haight**'s renovation (1883-1900), which includes all the other Gothic buildings. In the center is the **Chapel of the Good Shepherd**, with its outstanding bronze doors and 161-foot-high square bell tower. **Hoffman Hall**, at the 10th Avenue end, contains a medieval-style dining hall complete with a barrel-vaulted ceiling, walk-in fireplaces, and a gallery for musicians. The other end is dominated by the new and very much out-of-place **St. Mark's Library**, built in 1960 by **O'Connor & Kilhan**, containing some 170,000 volumes, along with one of the world's largest collections of Latin Bibles. ♦ Grounds (self-guided tours available) and Library: Open to the public M-Sa, 9AM-3PM (except when school is in session and on religious holidays). 175 Ninth Ave (between W 20th and W 21st Sts). 243.5150. www.gts.edu ♿

49 Third Cemetery of the Spanish & Portuguese Synagogue

Enclosed on three sides by painted brick loft buildings, this private enclave is the third cemetery established by the first Jewish congregation in New York; tombstones date from 1829 to 1851. The Second Cemetery is in Greenwich Village, on West 11th Street (at Sixth Avenue); the first is in Chinatown (see page 51), just south of Chatham Square. ♦ W 21st St (between Sixth and Seventh Aves)

50 Chelsea Piers

The first major modern-day development en route to reviving and redeveloping the city's waterfront parklands, the Chelsea Piers complex sits within the lovely greenway that is now **Hudson River Park**. Here at Chelsea, historic Piers **59**, **60**, **61**, and **62** house a $120 million–plus sports facility with a golf driving range (**Golf Club**, 336.6400); a vast sports-fitness center, including an indoor running track, a spa, rock climbing, and a 25-yard swimming pool (**Sports Center**, 336.6000); twin indoor ice-skating rinks (**Sky Rink**, 336.6100); a marina (336.6600); and a 40-lane bowling complex (**AMF Chelsea Piers Bowl**, 835.2695). In addition, there are several restaurants, film and photo studios, and for all those sports enthusiasts, the **New York–Presbyterian Health Center** (336.5100) can help alleviate sprains and pains. Originally built in 1910 by **Warren & Wetmore**, the architects of **Grand Central Terminal**, as docks for the era's grand ocean liners, it was refitted by **Butler Rogers Baskett** in the mid-1990s for its new role as the West Side's luxury playground. ♦ Daily. W 23rd St off the West Side Hwy (on the Hudson River). 336.6666. www.chelseapiers.com ♿

51 406-18 West 20th Street

This row of extremely well-preserved Greek Revival houses was built by **Don Alonzo Cushman**, a dry-goods merchant who developed much of Chelsea and built these, in 1839-40, as rental units. The attic windows are circled with wreaths, the doorways framed in brownstone. Even the newel posts, topped with cast-iron pineapples, are still intact—how unfortunate the same cannot be said for 19th-century rents! ♦ Between Ninth and 10th Aves

52 La Bergamote

In a city of surprises, this French bakery in an unlikely spot (in a neighborhood on the edge of hip and next to a massive housing project) comes as a particularly tasty one. In addition to delicious fancy pastries and sandwiches, here you'll find some of the best croissants in town. ♦ Daily. 169 Ninth Ave (at W 20th St). 627.9010 ♿

53 St. Peter's Episcopal Church

The church and its rectory and parish hall are based on **James W. Smith**'s plan to build them in the style of Greek temples. The traditional explanation is that the plan was changed when one of the vestrymen came back from England with tales of the Gothic buildings at Oxford. The congregation

"There are two million interesting people in New York—and only 78 in Los Angeles."

—Neil Simon

"There are two million palm trees in Los Angeles and only 78 in New York—and they're all fake."

—Anonymous

decided to switch styles, even though the foundations were already in place. The rectory, built first, is in Greek Revival style; the church, however, is a roaring example of Gothic Revival design. The fence that surrounds this charming complex was brought here from **Trinity Church** on lower Broadway, where it had stood since 1790. ♦ 346 W 20th St (between Eighth and Ninth Aves). 929.2390

54 La Belle Vie

★★$$ The romantic interior is accented with dark wood paneling, beautifully etched glass walls, and earth-toned banquettes at this neighborhood standby; fare is classic French bistro, deftly prepared. ♦ French bistro ♦ M-F, lunch and dinner; Sa, Su, brunch and dinner. Reservations recommended. 184 Eighth Ave (between W 19th and W 20th Sts). 929.4320

55 Kleinfeld Bridal

When the country's largest designer wedding-gown retailer moved out of Bay Ridge, Brooklyn, in 2005 (after 64 years there), it left several blocks of related businesses—shoes, veils, tailoring, tuxedo rental—high and dry. But its 35,000-square-foot home on Ladies' Mile (named for the Gilded Age shopping district that stretched along Sixth Avenue in grand Beaux Arts edifices) pampers brides-to-be in more comfort than ever, with two ample floors where they can test-drive the tulle in some 1,500 sample gowns from 85 designers. By appointment only. ♦ Tu-Su. 110 W 20th St (at Sixth Ave). 352.2180, 646.633.4300

56 Gehry (IAC) Building

Looking a bit like a ship or a bit like an iceberg, depending on your frame of reference, this tower of concrete and glass—an energetic modular assemblage of curvy surface and sharp edge—is **Frank Gehry**'s first building in New York. The specially coated glass, treated with patterned ceramic particles for energy efficiency, gives the whole thing a bluish-white cast from the outside. You won't see inside the offices unless you have business with Barry Diller's InterActiveCorp, headquartered here, but check out the lobby with its 118-foot video wall. ♦ 527 W 18th St (at 11th Ave)

> "New York is a city of dreams."
>
> —Isaac Bashevis Singer
>
> New York Bay is really a tidal estuary and the world's southernmost fjord.

57 The Kitchen

The Kitchen defines interdisciplinary art. Founded in SoHo back in 1971, it's been pushing the proverbial envelope ever since its self-proclaimed role as a center for vide music, dance, performance, film, and literature. Think Laurie Anderson, Eric Bogosian, and Karen Finley in their earliest formative years—and then returning to try out all manner of later material—and you begin to get the range of programming four here. Programs are scheduled most evening and generally require that tickets be purchased in advance. ♦ 512 W 19th St (between 10th and 11th Aves). 255.5793. www.thekitchen.org ♿

58 La Lunchonette

★$$ The homey bar and open kitchen in thi very French bistro seem familiar enough, bu the free-range chicken with mustard, lamb sausage with sautéed apples, and pan-fried whole trout with wild mushrooms add interesting variations to a time-honored cuisine. ♦ French ♦ M-F, lunch and dinner; Sa; Su, brunch and dinner. Reservations recommended. 130 10th Ave (at W 18th St) 675.0342

J O Y C E

59 The Joyce Theater

Renovated in 1981 by **Hardy Holzman Pfeiffer Associates**, this is a theater for dancers and the people who love dance; it elegant, intimate, and deep in the heart of Chelsea. The building was once the decrepi and infamous **Elgin** movie house, but a 19 remodeling resulted in the current 474-sea venue, completely replacing the building's interior and re-Deco-izing the exterior. The theater is named for the daughter of the principal donor. ♦ 175 Eighth Ave (at W 19 St). 242.0800. Also at **Joyce Soho**, 155 Mercer St (between Prince and Houston Sts). 431.9233. www.joyce.org ♿

60 Dance Theater Workshop (DTW)

Along with **The Kitchen** (above), DTW was one of the earliest arts anchors in Chelsea. Programs here are relentlessly eclectic, always innovative, and often involve other media like audio, film, or animation; they also offer Saturday-afternoon kids' programs. Now officially known as **DTW's Doris Duke Performance Center,** this

The Best

Marie C. Wilson

Founder and President, **The White House Project**

A Day Uptown: Start at the **Metropolitan Museum of Art's Egyptian Galleries**, spending time at the **Temple of Dendur**. And don't forget the wonderful costume exhibit there. The gift shop is also a must for its variety of books and jewelry.

Walk south through **Central Park**, stopping at **The Carousel** if it is summer, or at **Wollman Rink** for ice- or roller-skating. At lunch or teatime, try the **Plaza Hotel**, then stroll down **Fifth Avenue** for window shopping (or more).

Walk a few blocks to **Times Square**, buy half-price tickets at the **TKTS** booth, In the summer months, you might consider getting a pre-theater bite at the **Bryant Park Cafe** in back of the library—great food and a great view. Afterwards, have a quick snack at **Joe Allen**, or a drink at **B. Smith's**.

A Day Downtown: If it's Monday, Wednesday, Friday, or Saturday, go to the **Union Square Greenmarket** for your breakfast (I'm particularly fond of the lemon poppyseed muffins). Walk north along **Broadway** through the Nesting District of New York, cruising the many floors of **ABC Carpet & Home**'s home furnishings. Pause to admire the design magnificence of the **Flatiron Building**, then walk west into the **Village**.

Stop at **Three Lives & Company** bookstore, where the selection is marvelous—and if you don't know what you want, ask anyone at the counter. Take a brief tour of the food displays in **Citarella's** on Sixth Avenue, and possibly buy a snack for later. Then walk the **Village** at night, a singular place for people watching, or make a reservation to see an **Off-Broadway** play. If you like jazz, make a reservation at **Sweet Rhythm**. After the music or the theater, go to **Caffè Vivaldi** for dessert and a hot drink. Then, if you just can't sleep, ride the **Staten Island Ferry** back and forth as the light comes up. It's amazing.

nonprofit, longtime supporter of experimental choreography began as a collective, located in a nearby loft, in 1965. In 1995 they bought the building on West 19th Street that they'd moved to, then launched a capital campaign—aided by a Doris Duke foundation donation of $2.5 million, hence its new name—and began a state-of-the-art rebuild. The beautiful new space—an 11-story brushed aluminum and light-colored brick structure designed by architect **Ed Rawlings**—is custom-suited to DTW's global approach to dance performance. Video hookups throughout allow live collaboration with Tokyo, Finland, and anywhere else they choose. The new performance space—inaugurated with the 2002-2003 season—is still known as the Bessie Schönberg Theater, but its audience capacity has doubled (to 192 seats), and it now has a curtain—and superb sight lines. Lucky passersby glancing into the floor-to-ceiling windows of the street-front rehearsal space may catch the dancers in action. ♦ 219 W 19th St (between Seventh and Eighth Aves). 691.6500; box office (daily): 924.0077. www.dtw.org ♿

61 Sixth Avenue Ladies' Mile

The grand old department stores of Ladies' Mile underwent a renaissance in the 1980s and '90s, and today it is again a vital center for shopping. Bargain hunters flock to **620 Sixth Avenue**, a Victorian-pillared landmark built in 1896 as the **Siegel-Cooper Dry Goods Store** (page 125), where such popular emporia as **T.J. Maxx** and **Filene's Basement** discount fashions and accessories. Also here is **Bed, Bath & Beyond**'s flagship megastore, featuring 80 patterns of bed linens, 132 colors and patterns of bath towels, 218 styles of place mats, as well as gadgets galore. **The Container Store** and **Staples** are nearby and a **Barnes & Noble** superstore is three blocks north, at 675 Sixth Ave (at W 22nd St); **Old Navy** is just south at 610 Sixth Ave (at W 18th St). The area's side streets are also treasure troves of poster and art shops, including **A. I. Friedman** (44 W 18th St) and **Sam Flax** (12 W 20th St). Hungry? **Petite Abeille** (107 W 18th St) is especially nice—and reasonable. ♦ Between W 18th and W 23rd Sts

62 Chisholm Larsson Poster Gallery

If you want to deck your walls with Italian travel posters, Chinese propaganda, or a World War I-era eyeful advertising "Tag Your Shovel Day," you've come to the right place. The collection here includes more than 35,000 classic advertising posters from as far back as the 1890s—a dizzying range, from travel and liquor ads to artifacts of the Spanish Civil War—plus more than 15,000 original movie posters. ♦ Tu-Sa. 145 Eighth Ave (between W 17th and W 18th Sts). 741.1703 ♿

The Best

Karen Brooks Hopkins

President, Brooklyn Academy of Music (BAM)

1. Opening Night at **BAM**. There is nothing more exciting than the crowd of 2,000 jamming the BAM lobby before the show. You can feel the energy as people pour into the historic 2,100-seat **Howard Gilman Opera House**. Showtime!

2. **Brooklyn Botanic Garden**. The Rose Garden in June is heaven on earth. Beautiful, fragrant, and peaceful.

3. **St. Ann's Warehouse**. Clearly the coolest theatrical destination in Brooklyn's newest and most unusual neighborhood—DUMBO.

4. **Park Slope brownstones**. Park Slope is the ultimate New York place to live: low density, great stores, wonderful architecture, a real sense of family and community resonates on every block.

5. Fountain at the **Brooklyn Museum**. WOW! The new outside public space at the museum embraces the fabulous fountain with its varying volumes of spray—itself an artwork.

6. **BAM Rose Cinemas**. With no commercials, four large screens, and comfortable surroundings, the BAM Rose Cinemas feature more art—less hype.

7. Last but not least, the **Brooklyn Bridge**. What could be more exciting than entering America's most diverse, progressive urban community than by making your way across the world's most famous bridge?

63 Gascogne

★★★$$ Rich, hearty foods from the southwest region of France are on the menu here, including a superb fish soup, foie gras, roasted duck, and an excellent cassoulet. Also featured are wines from the same region (there is a great selection of Armagnacs). You can't tell from the street, but the restaurant has a lovely garden in the back. ♦ French bistro ♦ M, dinner; Tu-F, lunch and dinner; Sa, Su, brunch and dinner. Prix fixe available. Reservations required. 158 Eighth Ave (between W 17th and W 18th Sts). 675.6564

64 Cola's

★$ You'll find a casual mix of Northern and Southern Italian cuisine served at this cozy restaurant. Hand-painted walls lend a gentle ambience to the small room, where a lively downtown crowd comes to sample such pasta dishes as penne with goat cheese and eggplant and heartier fare like pork chops in balsamic vinegar. The wine list offers many fine selections. ♦ Italian ♦ Daily, lunch and dinner. 148 Eighth Ave (between W 17th and W 18th Sts). 633.8020

65 Movie Star News

Millions of head shots, stills, and lobby cards fill the filing cabinets in this garage space, a popular source for collectors, newspapers, magazines, and TV. Paula Klaw and her family also stock movie posters, as well as a selection of books on theater and film. ♦ M-Sa. 134 W 18th St (between Sixth and Seventh Aves). 620.8160 ♿

66 Da Umberto

★★$$$ This casual and restful trattoria specializes in Tuscan dishes, especially wild game (hare, pheasant, and venison). The veal chop with cognac sauce is a favorite, and the antipasto selections are worth a try. ♦ Northern Italian ♦ M-F, lunch and dinner; Sa, dinner. Reservations required. 107 W 17th St (between Sixth and Seventh Aves). 989.0303

67 Rubin Museum of Art

Once the downtown headquarters of the Barneys department store, this five-story space carved from six adjoining circa 1880 row houses was overhauled in 2004 by Richard Blinder of **Beyer Blinder Belle Architects** to house Donald and Shelley Rubin's comprehensive collection of Himalayan art. Climb the sinuous steel-and-marble staircase to see changing exhibitions of mandalas, thangkas (Tibetan Buddhist cloth paintings), sculpture, and textiles; head to the lower level to attend a film, concert, or talk. There's also **Milton Glaser**'s fine lobby design to peruse and a pleasant café; the museum shop (connected to the museum, but with a convenient additional entrance a few doors to the east) has a particularly well chosen selection of objects old and new. ♦ Admission; free Friday after 7PM. Closed Tuesday. M, Th, 11AM-5PM; W, 11AM-7PM; F, 11AM-10PM; Sa, Su, 11AM-6PM. 150 W 17th St (at Seventh Ave). 620.5000. www.rmanyc.org ♿

)H, FOR A DOG'S LIFE IN THE CITY!

ır best friend, the canny canine, is an especially ·loved sight in New York City. While cat lovers erywhere are justifiably proud of their furry felines, ıgs—by virtue of their needs—are a far more ·mmon sight on the streets of the city. You see ıppies scrambling for your attention behind windows pet stores, or dogs dragging along their half-asleep vners in the wee hours, admonishing them for their ziness, or in a jovial pack on the combined leash of professional dog walker, their varying heights, eeds, and temperaments forming a veritable dog version of the United Nations. New Yorkers invariably stop to pet, scratch, and rub a stranger's dog on the street. In their neighborhoods, dog-owning folks may never learn each other's names, referring to them simply as "Fido's mom" or "Rover's dad." It's almost as if in the whirlwind bustle of everyday life, taking the time to admire and fraternize with a pretty poodle, lanky Labrador, bemused basset hound, pugnacious pug, golden retriever, or sympathetic schnauzer soothes the city dweller's soul—and rising to the challenge, the dogs oblige, forever best friends.

›8 Loehmann's

Don't expect much plushness or service on the inside. Instead, you'll find 60,000 square feet filled with discounted merchandise—mostly for women, but plenty for men as well. Skip the first floor altogether; the best clothes are in the "Back Room" on the fourth floor, with names like Bally, Donna Karan, and Kenneth J. Lane. As with all quality discounters, the labels and stock are constantly changing. One feature that hasn't changed from its formative Fordham Road days is the communal dressing rooms. ♦ Daily. 101 Seventh Ave (between W 16th and W 17th Sts). 352.0856. Also at other locations

›9 The Maritime Hotel

$$$ This building has been a Chelsea landmark since 1966, when the white 12-story monolith with its huge porthole-shaped windows was built for the National Maritime Union. Repurposed for Covenant House (a shelter for runaway teens), and then as a facility for the Chinese government, it's now in its fourth incarnation. Those remarkable windows—they're five feet in diameter, and all open—face out onto the Hudson River, and perhaps they were the inspiration for developers and designers **Eric Goode** and **Sean MacPherson** (better known for their clubs and restaurants on both coasts) to turn the structure into a 120-room luxury boutique hotel. Completely refurbished and opened as The Maritime in 2003, its location at the cusp of the Meatpacking District and the west Chelsea gallery scene was undoubtedly part of the decision to proceed as well. The private stateroomlike quarters are smallish and cozy (the four penthouse suites are more on the grand scale), in deep blues and white with dark wood trim, and properly teched up. The understated nautical theme runs throughout the large lobby, which faces out onto an equally large plaza and garden. **Matsuri**, a dramatic and upscale Japanese restaurant, is on the lower level (daily, dinner till late; reservations recommended. 243.6400) there's a more casual Mediterranean café on the plaza. ♦ 363 W 16th St (at Ninth Ave). 242.4300; fax 242.1188. www.maritimehotel.com

70 Chelsea Market

This 85-plus-year-old structure was once a Nabisco factory churning out cookies and crackers. Today, with much of its industrial interior of overhead pipes, oversized fans, remnants of the Highline track, and exposed brick walls still intact—and enhanced with fitting and witty stone artworks by Mark Mennin placed throughout the meandering halls, and a carefully engineered broken-pipe waterfall to boot—it's a uniquely Manhattan marketplace. Here strollers and shoppers can peruse a variety of goodies from a variety of merchants or pause for a bite at one of the cafés, or watch tango

Mother

Famous for its outrageous Jackie 60 drag events, this group hosts wildish parties at various locations around the city. Events include the now famous and outlandish Night of 1000 Stevies, an homage to Stevie Nicks. There is no direct number, but events are listed at www.mothernyc.com.

Fitness à la Carte

New York City offers so many culinary delights that it's easy to let your willpower wander while you spoon up that last delicious bite. If you want to eat your cake and keep your figure too, consider working out. Running, biking (most cycling shops will rent you one), and even kayaking are all viable sports on New York's truly not-so-mean streets and waterways. Many of the city's deluxe hotels offer their guests gyms with up-to-the-minute fitness equipment. New York City also has some of the best workout centers in the country—it's possible to swim in Olympic-size pools, climb simulated mountains, go cross-country biking, and even play team volleyball on a year-round basis. The health and fitness clubs below sell single-day passes.

Prices range from a reasonable $16 to a muscle-cramping $50; higher doesn't always mean better. Most facilities ask for a photo ID. Some allow you to take group classes on an availability basis. It's a good idea to call ahead for schedules. Some of the bigger clubs have numerous locations throughout the city, so when you call, ask which is nearest to your hotel.

Asphalt Green Housed in what was an actual asphalt plant on the East River, this is perhaps Manhattan's finest swim facility. Although it offers private memberships, it has become a popular community center, organizing team sports and swim meets. Besides the two indoor pools, there are two equipment-filled gyms and an outdoor track. Day passes are available for $25. ♦ 369.8890. www.asphaltgreen.com

Crunch This group of clubs has a hip sensibility—their local TV commercials feature people dressed as animals or men talking about working out in women's clothing (their slogan is "no judgments"). Most city locations offer one-day passes, which cost $16 to $24. Certain Crunch out-of-state memberships offer access to their facilities here. Locker-room facilities are a bit more spartan than at other clubs. ♦ 888.1310.6011. www.crunch.com

Equinox Another chain with a "downtown" attitude. You'll find more hard-body types sporting black workout gear at these locations than you will elsewhere. A number of their Manhattan locations—including Columbus Circle and Greenwich Village—offer pool and spa facilities. No day-pass plan is offered, but short-term memberships are available and "all-access" out-of-state members may use any New York Equinox gym. ♦ 774.6363. www.equinoxfitness.com

New York Health & Racquet Club One of the first health clubs in New York, this chain offers a day pass fo[r] $50. They have swimming pools at all of their locatio[ns] though some—like Whitehall, 56th Street, and 23rd Street—are grander than others; all have whirlpools, sauna, and steam rooms. They're all over town and are one of the few clubs with racquetball facilities and a clu[b] yacht. ♦ 797.1500. www.nyhrc.com

New York Sports Club With 40 locations within Manhattan and more in the boroughs, this is one of th[e] city's fastest-growing fitness centers. Most have complimentary steam and sauna in the locker rooms. One- and two-week trial memberships are availabl[e] (the latter may be accessed online only); no day passes are offered. ♦ 246.6700. www.mysportsclubs.com

92nd Street Y On a par with the better private clubs the **May Center for Health Fitness & Sport** at this Upper East side "Y" has a large pool and fitness equipment area, along with an elevated indoor track. Day passes are $35 for all facilities. There are locker rooms with steam and sauna. One caveat: the "Y" clos[es] for most Jewish holidays; call ahead. ♦ 415.5700. www.92y.org

The Sports Center at Chelsea Piers This state-of-th[e]-art facility is among New York's newest and largest. Da[y] passes cost $50. Facilities include a 25-yard indoor pool, a fitness center with aerobic equipment and weights, and a quarter-mile indoor track. There are als[o] boxing and volleyball. Rock climbing and spa services are available for an extra fee, and guests can use the café. ♦ 336.6000. www.chelseapiers.com

YMCA The YMCA has excellent facilities throughout t[he] five boroughs, with five locations in Manhattan. Nonresident day passes cost $25; members from out-of-state can use any New York location facilities for fre[e] within their membership limit. The West Side location West 63rd Street has a beautifully restored Art Deco–tiled pool; on West 14th, the McBurney Y's is a fine Olympic-style lap facility. All branches have classes a[nd] complete cardiac/aerobic machine and weights areas; indoor tracks and basketball courts may also be on si[te]. ♦ 630.9600. www.ymcanyc.org

classes in action (or partake) on weekends, and note the Food Network traffic (their studios are upstairs) bustling around. Check out **Fat Witch**, purveyor of delectable brownies; **Manhattan Fruit Exchange**, a wholesale/retail produce market; **The Lobster Place**, for seafood of every description; **Amy's Bread**, a haven for tasty breads, pastries, and sandwiches; **Hale & Hearty Soups**; **Chelsea Wine Vault**; **Sarabeth's Bakery**; the **Chelsea Wholesale Flower Market**, with a large space set up for wandering amid greener[y] and flowers from succulents to ficus tree[s] and orchids; **Bowery Kitchen Supplies**; and **Buonitalia**, an importer of select Italian pastas, cheeses, and olive oil. It's one-stop, glitz-free, and totally pleasant shopping—Manhattan style. ♦ Daily. 75 Ninth Ave (between W 15th and W 16th Sts). ♿

Within Chelsea Market:

Frank's

★★$$$ After moving less than a block to new digs within **Chelsea Market** in 2005, the Molinari family institution (it dates to 1912) is even closer to the source: If you enter from inside the market, rather than from 16th Street, you'll pass right by a fully operational meat locker and through a retail butcher shop (we suggest avoiding that route). Always extraordinary are the dry-aged shell steaks, a filet mignon weighing nearly a pound, and the loin lamb chops. All the pastas are made from scratch; try the fettuccine bolognese or the *paglia e fieno*. Basic, good-quality desserts include giant slabs of cheesecake. ♦ Italian Steak house ♦ M-Sa, lunch and dinner; Su, brunch and dinner. Reservations recommended. 410 W 16th St (between Ninth and 10th Aves). 242.6555

71 Port of New York Authority Commerce Building/Union Inland Terminal No. 1

The organization now known as the Port Authority of New York and New Jersey had its headquarters in this hulking Deco structure, designed in 1932 by **Abbott, Merckt & Co**. The top floors were designed for manufacturing, but the elevators can carry a 20-ton truck to any floor. ♦ 111 Eighth Ave/76 Ninth Ave (between W 15th and W 16th Sts)

72 Chelsea Ristorante

★$$ This pretty trattoria with peach walls and exposed brick is a reliable place for standard Italian fare. The osso buco and the fettuccine with artichokes, mushrooms, and tomatoes are especially recommended. ♦ Italian ♦ Daily, lunch and dinner. 108 Eighth Ave (between W 15th and W 16th Sts). 924.7786

72 Gerry's Menswear

This welcoming shop features a hip and reasonably priced range of men's casual wear from recognized labels as well as up-and-coming designers. You can walk out of a shop like this with a whole new look—especially if they're having one of their great clearance sales. ♦ Daily. Men's: 110 Eighth Ave (between W 15th and W 16th Sts). 243.9141. Women's: 112 Eighth Ave (between W 15th and W 16th Sts). 691.2188. Also at (men's only) 474 Sixth Ave (between W 11th and W 12th Sts). 691.0636

73 Jensen-Lewis

Two floors of creative, colorful merchandise, from sofas and beds to lamps. The focus is contemporary, the displays inspirational. Great deals on older goods can often be found on the lower level. ♦ Daily. 89 Seventh Ave (between W 15th and W 16th Sts). 929.4880

74 El Cid

★★$ This small and cheerful tapas bar with blue tablecloths and mirrored walls is an informal, fun place to come with a group to sample from among 32 varieties of tapas and a handful of meat and fish dishes, including a hearty *paella valenciana* (a casserole of chicken, Spanish sausages, shellfish, and saffron rice). The wine list showcases good, inexpensive Spanish wines. ♦ Spanish ♦ Tu-Su, dinner. 322 W 15th St (between Eighth and Ninth Aves). 929.9332

75 Old Homestead

★★$$$ Established in 1868, this is the oldest steak house in Manhattan, and huge steaks and prime ribs are served here the way they always have been. ♦ American ♦ Daily, lunch and dinner. Reservations recommended. 56 Ninth Ave (between W 14th and W 15th Sts). 242.9040 ♿

76 319 West 14th Street

A 20-year-old Orson Welles and his first wife, Virginia Nicholson, lived in a basement apartment here between 1935 and 1937, during which time he directed the famous all-black *Macbeth* for Harlem's **Negro Theater**. ♦ Between Eighth and Ninth Aves

THEATER DISTRICT/GARMENT CENTER/ HELL'S KITCHEN

The Theater District stands as the symbol of New York's impressive ability to rei vent itself on a regular basis. Neighborhood demographics shift and change, ec nomic tides may ebb and flow. But it is safe to say that no one familiar with t Theater District of the 1970s, '80s, and even the '90s could ever imagine the vibra world it is today.

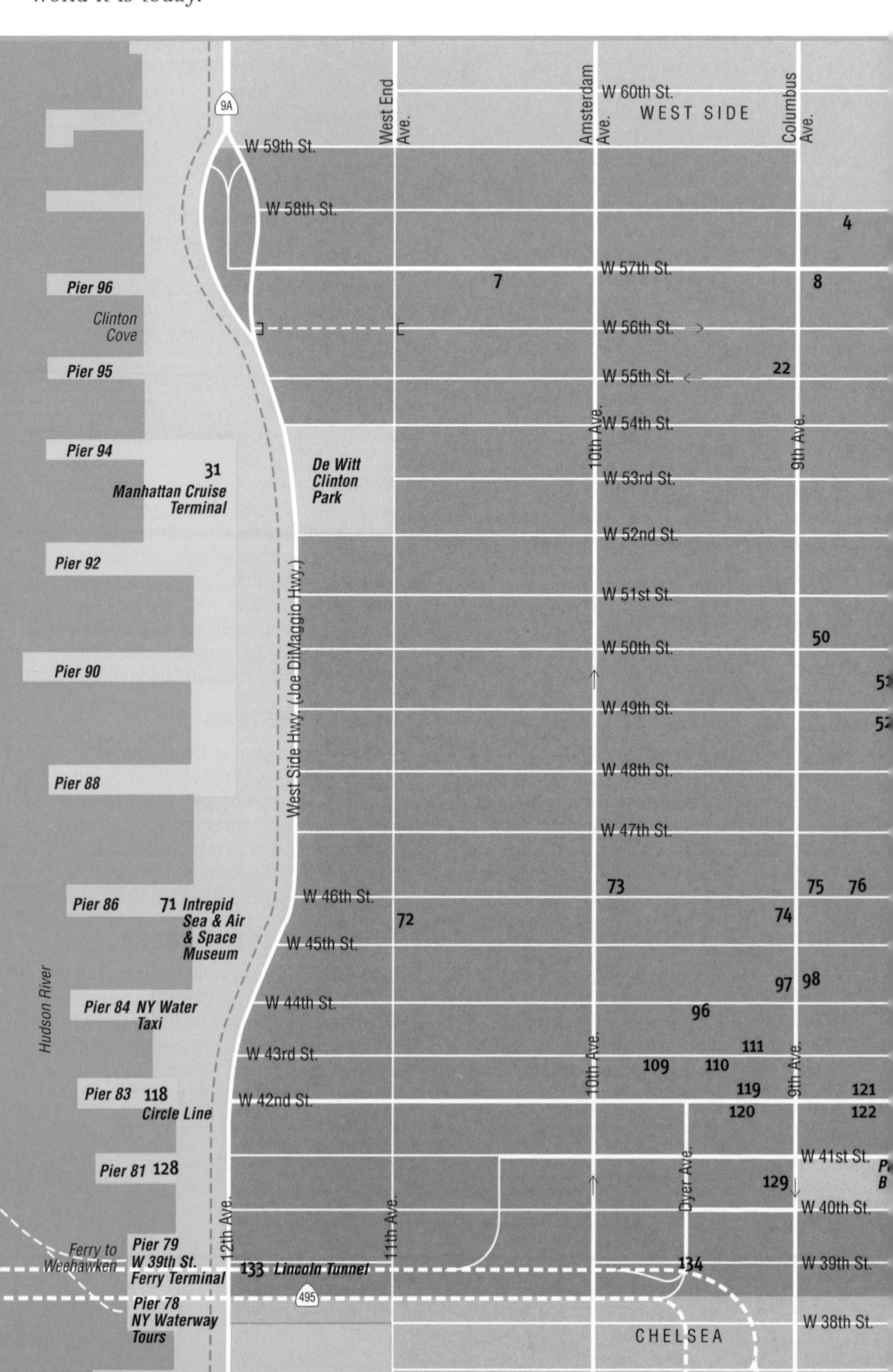

Theater and other entertainments of stage and screen—legit and otherwise—have, of course, a long history in New York. As with most other enterprises here, what started downtown rapidly moved up. When the **Metropolitan Opera House** opened at **West 39th Street** and Broadway in 1883, the **Floradora Girls** were already packing them in at the **Casino Theater** across the street. In 1902, **Macy's** new building at West 34th Street and Broadway replaced, among other buildings, **Koster & Bial's Music Hall**, where Thomas Edison first demonstrated moving pictures. By the early 1900s the theatrical quarter had made its way north to 42nd Street and beyond. In 1904, the *New York Times'* decision to build its new headquarters at the now iconic crossroads of Broadway and Seventh Avenue at 42nd Street helped clinch the matter. At the same time, theater owners banded together in a syndicate to gain more control over the artists they booked. This gave them control over the competition that remained downtown as well, and those theatrical enterprises were effectively put out of business. The syndicate's power increased greatly in 1916, when the three Shubert brothers began to build new theaters in the **Times Square** area (by then bounded by Sixth Avenue on the east and Eighth Avenue on the west), which the subway had put within easy reach of the entire city. Other entrepreneurs joined the rush, and their legacy is still with us.

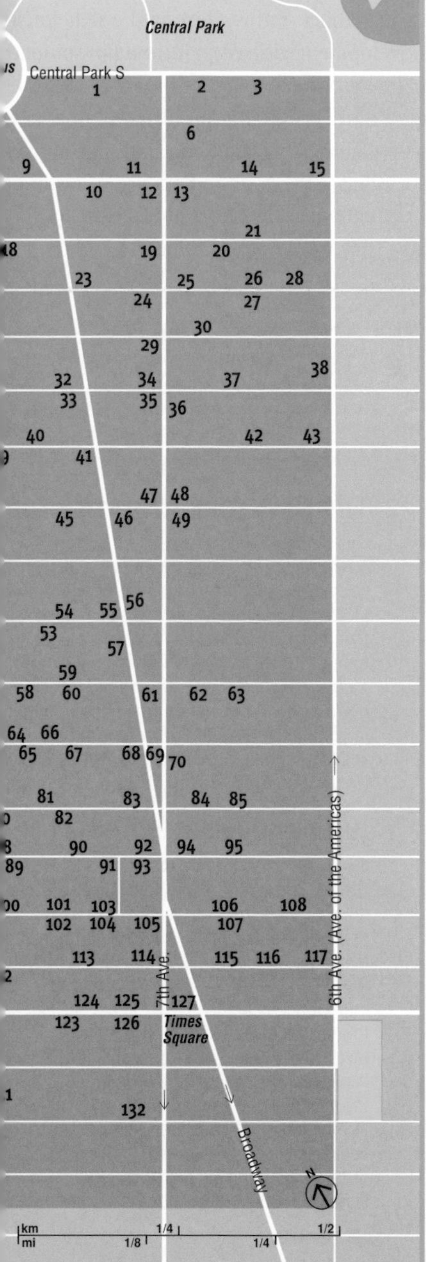

The far west section of this stretch from West 39th Street through West 59th extended from Eighth or Ninth Avenue over to the Hudson River, and had a somewhat different trajectory. By the 1880s the elevated railroad that had recently been built along Ninth Avenue drew thousands of immigrants to the neighborhood from downtown. Work was plentiful in the sawmills, slaughterhouses, warehouses, stone yards, and stables along the river. The area soon evolved into one of America's toughest neighborhoods. Known as **Hell's Kitchen** (these days gentrifiers often refer to it as **Clinton**), it likely got its moniker from one of the many gangs that ruled here then, all thriving on hoodlumism, extortion, and highway robbery. While gang warfare was notorious here well into the 20th century, today the area is chiefly inhabited by second- or third-generation immigrant families who have managed to hold on despite the rising rents, by aspiring actors yearning to be near the stage, and a growing gay population pushed north by the even higher prices in Chelsea. Restaurants abound, providing interesting alternatives just minutes away from the Times Square blare for pre- and post-theater dining. And as the waterfront continues its rebirth, inspiring hotel development, the expansion of Hudson River Park, and more, Hell's Kitchen is likely to benefit from visitors from that direction as well.

As for the Theater District today (now predominantly between Seventh and Eighth Avenues from West 42nd through West 50th **Streets**), it still has a sprinkling of adult movie houses and other dens of iniquity, but they're barely noticeable amid the other types of enterprise that now dominate the area. Along with the city, the Walt Disney Company played a key role in jumpstarting the renewal, with a megabuck renovation of the deliciously Nouveau 1903 **New Amsterdam Theatre**. New development soon crept in, and now modern architecture comes head-to-head with traditional restorations, the lights are truly brighter, and the area swarms not only with theater-bound tourists aplenty but office-bound folks as well. **Condé Nast**'s and **Reuters**' headquarters are here, The *New York Times* has moved into its spanking-new building, the old **Biltmore** is back, the historic Paramount Building theater marquee is restored, and—while some folks might miss the old-school steam-puffing billboards of yore—the neon is gaudy and exciting, like it was meant to be.

---

1 San Domenico

★★★$$$$ After captivating the palates of international food critics for 18 years in a suburb of Bologna, Gianluigi Morino transplanted his labor of love to New York in 1988, and began dazzling food critics here. The marble bar, terra-cotta floor imported from Florence, and smooth, ochre-tinted stucco walls applied by artisans from Rome provide a lovely, subdued environment. The meals, prepared at the artful hands of chef Odette Fada in the spirit of Italian *alta cucina*, can be—they do have off nights—equally delightful. End your repast with any of the innovative desserts—hazelnut chocolate soufflé or the napoleon made with orange *tuiles* (thin French cookies) layered with lime parfait—but don't overlook the quintessential tiramisù. The closer-to-affordable prix-fixe dinner can be a good deal if you don't mind eating early. ♦ Italian ♦ M-F, lunch and dinner; Sa, Su, dinner. Reservations required; jacket required. 240 Central Park S (between Seventh Ave and Columbus Cir). 265.5959 ♿

2 Gainsborough Studios

In 1908, **Charles W. Buckham** designed this apartment building—now one of the oldest in the city—as an artists' cooperative. It is worth passing by for a look at the frieze by Isadore Konti, across the second floor—a festival procession with a bust of Gainsborough at the center. In addition, the building has one of the city's best façades; this one was restored in 1992. ♦ 222 Central Park S (between Seventh Ave and Columbus Cir)

2 The New York Athletic Club

This 22-story building, designed by **York & Sawyer** in 1930, houses handball and squash courts as well as other exercise facilities, including a swimming pool. The club itself was founded in 1868 and has sent winning teams to many Olympic Games. There are guest rooms, but visitors who want to begin their day running in **Central Park** are not permitted to go through the lobby in jogging outfits. ♦ Daily, for members only. 180 Central Park S (at Seventh Ave). 247.5100

2 Jumeirah Essex House

$$$$ The original 1930 grand hotel by **Frank Grand** greeted the new millennium as a renovated **Westin Hotel** and rapidly moved on to become a gem in the Dubai-based Jumeirah hospitality group. The Art Deco details of the façade and the artful use of setbacks still make it one of Manhattan's more pleasing towers; the latest interior renovation is tastefully luxurious and top-of-the-line Deco-inspired. With Central Park as its front yard, the connection is further enhanced by its striking lobby art program, where specially commissioned works on that theme are on display along with historic photographs. Be sure to request a room with a park view. As

you might expect, all 515 rooms here are lushly appointed and include flat-screen TVs and 24-hour room service; high-speed Internet access throughout is a given; and workout and spa facilities are a must for the power set that stays here. Traditional afternoon tea is served daily. The elegant **Lobby Lounge** offers a New American menu for breakfast, lunch, and dinner daily; **The Restaurant at Essex House**, in the former Alain Ducasse room, is an appropriately hushed space for traditional dining (daily, breakfast, lunch, and dinner. 247.0300). ♦ 160 Central Park S (between Sixth and Seventh Aves). 247.0300, 888/645.5697; fax 315.1839. www.essexhouse.com ♿

3 Hampshire House

A hotel converted to elite cooperative apartments, this building, a work of **Caughey & Evans**, has a peaked roof of copper that has turned a marvelous shade of green, one of the highlights of the skyline bordering Central Park. Its lobby is a joy; when the cornerstone was put in place, it was filled with the best books and music of 1931. ♦ 150 Central Park S (between Sixth and Seventh Aves)

4 Hudson Hotel

$$$ Ian Schrager strikes again, this time bringing his unique brand of hip close to the edge of Central Park South. Access the lobby via an escalator aglow with lemon-yellow light; arrive to find a large greenhouse-type room strewn with fake leaves. (Designer **Philippe Starck** has also struck again.) The one thousand rooms are small but stylish, and really lucky single travelers may be able to snag one for an almost reasonable rate. The Hudson has Wi-Fi set up everywhere and a fitness center on site. For tasty basics like beef stew and pineapple upside-down cake, served at long communal tables, check out the **Hudson Cafeteria** around the corner from the front desk. ♦ 356 W 58th St (between Eighth and Ninth Aves). 554.6000; fax 554.6001. www.hudsonhotel.com

5 Museum of Arts & Design (MAD)

Over the years since it was founded in 1956, this museum has had, in addition to multiple name changes (it had a stint as the American Craft Museum), a commensurate share of curatorial identity pains. But with its redevelopment of the **Edward Durrell Stone**-designed Huntington Hartford Museum on Columbus Circle, MAD has committed itself to celebrating its impressive permanent collection of (mostly late 20th- through 21st-century) finely crafted objects in materials from glass, metal, and wood to ceramics, paper, and fiber. The controversial 2008 re-do of Stone's mid-sixties, "lollipop"-portholed marble façade is by **Brad Cloepfil/Allied Works Architecture**. A luminescent ceramic skin now guides you to the angular tower; the interior (triple MAD's former West 53rd Street space) is designed to draw in an abundance of natural light. A ninth-floor café overlooks Central Park. ♦ Admission; donation Th after 6PM. M-W, F-Su, 10AM-6PM; Th, 10AM-8PM. 2 Columbus Circle (W 58th St, between Broadway and Eighth Ave). 956.3535. www.madmuseum.org ♿

6 Petrossian

★★★$$$$ Whether you're in Paris or New York, this restaurant is the place to go for caviar. Many varieties of precious roe are offered at this high-class, Art Deco–influenced marble- and mink-trimmed room, with ornate gilded statuettes and enlarged etchings of Erté drawings. Try the sevruga, osetra, and beluga, the foie gras terrine, or the sampling of salmon—marinated, smoked, and spiced. Innovative and delicious dishes include lobster with winter vegetables, potato purée, and mushroom truffle sauce; and halibut with shrimp aioli. Desserts are similarly hard to pass up—especially the lemon tart with lemon custard and caramel. The wine list is excellent and the very best Champagnes can be ordered by the glass. There's a sublime prix-fixe brunch and surprisingly affordable prix-fixe lunches and dinners. Take-home delicacies are available in the adjoining shop (245.2217). ♦ Continental ♦ M-F, lunch and dinner; Sa, Su, brunch and dinner. Reservations required; jacket required. 182 W 58th St (at Seventh Ave). 245.2214

6 Alwyn Court

The terra-cotta dragons and other decorations that cover every inch of this 1909 apartment house by **Harde & Short** are in the style of a great art patron of the Renaissance, Francis I. His symbol, a crowned salamander, is displayed above the entrance at the West 58th Street corner. Although it is not open to the public, almost no one ever passes by without stopping for a lingering look. ♦ 180 W 58th St (at Seventh Ave)

7 CBS Broadcast Center

Currently operating as a TV production center and the headquarters of *CBS News*, and not to be confused with "Black Rock," where CBS corporate headquarters has its home (see page 196), this was originally the headquarters of a dairy, and CBS old-timers still refer to it as the "Cowbarn." ♦ 524 W 57th St (between 10th and 11th Aves).

8 Parc Vendome Apartments

This was one of the sites considered for a second **Metropolitan Opera House**. The scheme died when opera patrons were told that a skyscraper would be built to help support it. "We don't need that kind of help," they sniffed, and took their money elsewhere. The 570-unit apartment house, a 1931 creation of **Henry Mandel**, contains a private dining room, a gymnasium and pool, a music room, and terraced gardens. ♦ 340 W 57th St (between Eighth and Ninth Aves). 247.6990

9 Broadway Dance Center

Founded in 1984 to serve the needs of the dance community, this facility of studios has been the stomping grounds for some of the best and brightest stars in the pantheon of dance. Renowned instructors such as Finis Jhung, jazz/hip-hop choreographer team Glenn & Brian, and many others teach a range of classes that encompasses classical ballet, tap, modern dance, funk, and more. Individual and group classes are open to visitors, and observers are welcome at the discretion of the teachers. Big-time stars such as Mikhail Baryshnikov have been known to drop in on occasion. ♦ Daily. 221 W 57th St, fifth floor (between Broadway and Eighth Ave). 582.9304. www.bwydance.com

10 Lee's Art Shop & Studio

This venerable "Department Store for Artists" is appropriately located directly across the street from the **Art Students League**. The extensive materials department attracts artists and architects (at least those that can afford the uptown prices; the rest of us browse), and the pens, stationery, and picture frames make great gifts. **Lee's Studio**, one floor up, offers sleek, contemporary lighting fixtures and table and floor lamps like those you'd expect to find in Milan or at the Museum of Modern Art, as well as a carefully chosen selection of chairs, sofas, and accessories. ♦ Daily. 220 W 57th St (between Seventh Ave and Broadway). Lee's Art Shop: 247.0110. Lee's Studio: 581.4400 ♿

> **The New York City Council passed a bill requiring that photographic records be made of any building about to be razed. The photos become part of the municipal archives. Councilman Harry Stein, sponsor of the bill, said his only regret was that no one had thought of the idea 150 years before.**

10 Brooklyn Diner

★★$$ If your ordinary drab diner with drab processed food to match died and went to heaven, it might look something like this bright, boisterous, and dependable eatery where tastes are big and portions bigger. Deftly turned-out basics such as chicken soup and a hand-carved roast turkey sandwich with cranberry sauce and real mashed potatoes will put a smile on your face and a full feeling in your stomach—but if you can, save room for dessert: The cakes and pies are tasty, and the shakes and malts ain't bad either. ♦ American ♦ Daily, breakfast, lunch, and dinner. 212 W 57th St (between Seventh Ave and Broadway). 977.2280

11 Art Students League

The three central panels on this French Renaissance palace represent the Fine Arts Society, the Architectural League, and the Art Students League, all of which originally shared this facility and made it the scene of nearly every important exhibition at the turn of the century. Dating to 1892, this is a work of **Henry J. Hardenbergh**. ♦ 215 W 57th St (between Seventh Ave and Broadway). 247.4510. www.theartstudentsleague.org

11 The Osborne

Except for the removal of its front porch and the addition of retail stores, this wonderful apartment building has hardly changed since it was built by **James E. Ware** in 1885. Unfortunately not open to the public, the opulent lobby was designed by **Louis Comfort Tiffany**. ♦ 205 W 57th St (at Seventh Ave)

11 Cafe Europa

★$ Bright and pretty, with dreamy trompe l'oeil ceilings, this café is a convenient spot to have a sandwich (made with fresh ingredients) or such hot dishes as pizza and pasta. The muffins, tarts, and cakes accompanied by full-flavored coffees make great snacks. ♦ Café/Takeout ♦ Daily, breakfast, lunch, dinner, and late-night meals. 205 W 57th St (at Seventh Ave). 977.4030. ♿ Also at numerous locations throughout the city

12 Trattoria Dell'Arte

★★★$$$ According to the proud management of this colorful restaurant opposite **Carnegie Hall**, the world's largest antipasto bar resides here. Choose from the impressive assortment, which includes sun-dried tomatoes, roasted fennel, fresh mozzarella, various seasonal vegetables, and a separate seafood bar with lobster, shrimp and scallop salad, calamari, and smoked salmon. ♦ Italian ♦ M-F, lunch and dinner; Sa, Su, brunch and dinner. Reservations recommended. 900 Seventh Ave (between W 56th and W 57th Sts). 245.9800 ♿

13 Carnegie Hall

This landmark was built in 1891 by **William B. Tuthill**; **William Morris Hunt** and **Dankmar Adler** served as consultants. Peter Ilyich Tchaikovsky conducted at the opening concert, and during the next 70 years, the **New York Philharmonic** played here under such greats as Gustav Mahler, Bruno Walter, Arturo Toscanini, Leopold Stokowski, and Leonard Bernstein. Considered to have acoustics matched by few other concert halls in the world, it has attracted all of the 20th century's great musicians, and not just the classical variety; W.C. Handy brought his blues here in 1928, and was followed by Count Basie, Duke Ellington, Benny Goodman, and others. Nowadays, Carnegie hosts the **New York Pops** and a global roster of musicians, orchestras, and other performances. When it was announced in the 1950s that the Philharmonic would be moving to **Lincoln Center**, the landmark was put up for sale. Violinist Isaac Stern and a group of concerned music lovers waged a successful campaign to save it. Their efforts eventually resulted in a restoration, completed in 1986 by **James Stewart Polshek & Partners**, which rendered it as glorious visually as it is acoustically. The corridors are lined with scores and other memorabilia of the artists and composers who have added to the hall's greatness. The space above the auditorium contains studios and apartments favored by musicians and artists. The third floor is occupied by the **Weill Recital Hall**, used by soloists and small chamber groups. In 1991, **The Rose Museum**—featuring a fascinating timeline of Carnegie Hall history via artifacts, photos, and period ephemera—moved in on the second floor. But the newest jewel is in the basement. With its grand opening during the fall 2003 season, the 644-seat **Zankel Hall**—designed by **James Polshek** and built into bedrock—gave the city an intimate, acoustically perfect space for eclectic programming. ♦ Tours and Rose Museum, free. Tours: Daily, but times may vary when there are performances scheduled. M-F, 11:30AM, 2PM, and 3PM; Sa, 11:30AM and 12:30PM; Su, 12:30PM. Rose Museum: Daily, 11AM-4:30PM, and during performance intermissions. 154 W 57th St (at Seventh Ave). CarnegieCharge: 247.7800. www.carnegiehall.org ♿

14 The Salisbury Hotel

$$$ Most of the rooms here—all renovated at the millennium, and all non-smoking—have serving pantries (including refrigerator and microwave oven) and individual safes. Décor is basic floral, the rooms (119 standards, 81 one-bedroom suites, and 4 two-bedroom suites) are decent-sized, two-line phones are the norm, and high-speed Internet access is available. Guests receive a discount at nearby health clubs. ♦ 123 W 57th St (between Sixth and Seventh Aves). 246.1300, 888.NYC.5757; fax 977.7752. www.nycsalisbury.com ♿

15 Steinway Hall

Look through the concave window into the showroom of this prestigious piano company, housed, appropriately, in a domed hall with a huge crystal chandelier. The 12-story building, built in 1925, with a 3-story Greek temple on the roof, also includes a recital salon. The relief of Apollo over the central arch is by Leo Lentelli; the building is by **Warren & Wetmore**. ♦ Daily. 109 W 57th St (between Sixth and Seventh Aves). 246.1100

16 Hearst Magazine Building

The Hearst Magazine Building (originally known as the **International Magazine Building** when magnate William Randolph Hearst commissioned it from architect **Joseph Urban**) topped out at only six stories when the Depression caught up with it in 1928. Its design then had intended a tower to rise from the quirkily adorned (and NYC-landmarked) quasi-Vienna Secessionist base. Flashing forward some 75 years, we find Hearst—in a mission to consolidate its scattered office spaces—resuming construction. In 2005, Pritzker-winner **Norman Foster** (Foster & Partners) would see his first New York City building come to fruition. A 42-story glass-and-steel-faceted tower now sits atop Urban's earlier base, its surrounding obelisks metaphorically clasping the new structure. Officially opened in 2006, Foster's creation is designed with "green" in mind, one of the first fully environmentally sensitive office towers in

New York. Employing an innovative "diagrid" infrastructure, all steelwork is in fact exposed, which along with the four-story-tall panes of glass encase a hollow core. How users—and critics—view this combo landmark and chrysalis will be interesting to follow. Access for the general public, however, is limited to the lobby and atrium area (M-F, business hours only, plus the occasional weekend). ♦ 959 Eighth Ave (between W 56th and W 57th Sts)

17 Bricco

★★★$$ The captivating aromas from the wood-burning oven alone would lure passersby into this chic restaurant, and the well-prepared Neapolitan food lives up to the scent: broiled calamari with sautéed mushrooms; clams with white wine and garlic; veal chop with Portobello mushrooms; and outstanding pastas including linguine *puttanesca* (with olives, capers, and anchovies). Desserts are just as tempting, with a selection of sorbets and tiramisù topping the list. ♦ Italian ♦ M-F, lunch and dinner; Sa, Su, dinner. Reservations recommended. 304 W 56th St (between Eighth and Ninth Aves). 245.7160

18 Baluchi's

★$ Come to this city-wide franchise for reliable, if restrained on the spice-o-meter, curries and chicken *tikka* (marinated in yogurt and cooked dry—a boneless tandoori) in the neighborhood. ♦ Indian ♦ M-F, lunch and dinner; Sa, Su, dinner. 240 W 56th St (between Broadway and Eighth Ave). 397.0707 ♿ Also at numerous locations throughout the city

19 Park Central New York

$$ When the 1920s roared, a lot of the sound and fury echoed through these halls, which were a meeting place for bootleggers and small-time gangsters. The ghosts have all been exorcised, and the 1927 hotel by **Groneburg & Leuchtag** has a new lease on life. The 935 decently priced rooms attract groups and airline crews. Their higher-priced "Concierge Level" rooms and suites appeal to corporate guests, who are provided with high-speed Internet access and a business center. There's also a health club and a breakfast bistro and lounge. ♦ 870 Seventh Ave (between W 55th and W 56th Sts). 247.8000, 800/346.1359; fax 484.3374. www.parkcentralny.com ♿

Cats ran for 18 years on Broadway, having gone through 28,492 makeup brushes, 1.5 tons of yak hair, 25,457 wig caps, 321 Siamese cat swords—plus 824 pounds of coffee.

20 Joseph Patelson Music House

Musicians, from beginners to world-renowned maestros, have been coming to this former carriage house for their music needs (sheet music and books, orchestral and opera scores) ever since it opened in 1920. With the widest selection of music (mostly classical, with some jazz, pop, and Broadway) in New York, it's no surprise that this shop receives orders from as far away a Japan. ♦ M-Sa. 160 W 56th St (between Sixth and Seventh Aves). 582.5840 ♿

21 Le Parker Meridien

$$$$ When making a reservation, ask for a odd-numbered room above the 26th floor fo a wonderful view of **Central Park**. The 42-story hotel has 730 super-sleek rooms and suites, three restaurants, the plush **Gravity** spa (708.7340), a rooftop swimming pool with a jogging track, racquetball and squash courts, high-speed Internet access throughout, and a full-service business center (weekdays only). The 24-hour room service has a European flair, as does everything else about the hotel—even their burger joint (708.7414) in the lobby. ♦ 24-hour entrance: 119 W 56th St (between Sixth and Seventh Aves). Alternate entrance (closed after 9PM daily): 118 W 57th St (between Sixth and Seventh Aves). 245.5000, 800/543.4300; fax 307.1776. www.parkermeridien.com ♿

Within Le Parker Meridien:

NORMA'S

Norma's

★★$$ This sleek, airy restaurant offers an unusually creative breakfast menu even for New York. Begin with a signature "smoothie shot," such as pineapple-cantaloupe-honeydew or plum-watermelon-pineapple. Follow that with an egg-white frittata of shrimp, oven-roasted roma tomato, and spinach; red berry risotto "oatmeal" in a crispy wafer bowl; or the totally decadent and delicious molten chocolate French toast with pineapple compote. Portions at Norma's are uncommonly generous. Another plus: authentic French coffee. ♦ Daily, breakfast until 3PM. 708.7460

Seppi's

★★★$$ An upscale midtown crowd enjoys a downtown vibe and the creations of an innovative kitchen at this atmospheric bistro

There are faithfully re-created pressed-tin ceilings, framed old French beer ads, cushy booths—and an in-house tarot card reader. The menu draws on that of countries once traversed by the *Orient-Express* (France, Switzerland, Austria, Italy, and Turkey) and changes seasonally, but might include grilled daurade with cumin-scented root vegetables and red beet-sumac sauce and Ottoman vegetable rice with a rosace of grilled vegetables and tomato coulis, as well as such staples as steak *au poivre.* Desserts run the gamut from assorted homemade sorbets to such treats as a white chocolate soufflé with kirsch-marinated cherries; chocolate is the key ingredient for all dishes in their special Sunday brunch. ♦ French/ Mediterranean. ♦ Daily, dinner until 2AM. M-F, lunch and dinner; Sa, dinner; Su, brunch and dinner. 123 W 56th St (between Sixth and Seventh Aves). 708.7444

22 Alvin Ailey American Dance Theater: The Joan Weill Center for Dance

The remarkable Alvin Ailey dance troupe gives their season performances at **City Center** (opposite). Opened with the Spring 2005 season, the eight-story space is home to a 295-seat "black box" theater for smaller performances, as well as 12 dance studios, a state-of-the-art school, and teaching facilities. Designed by **Iu + Bibliowicz Architects LLP**, the cleanly modern glass-faced building is the largest resource in the US devoted to dance. ♦ 400 W 55th St (at Ninth Ave). 767.0590. www.alvinailey.org

23 MONY Tower

When built in 1950 by **Shreve, Lamb & Harmon**, this was the headquarters of the insurance company known as Mutual of New York, which later became MONY Financial Services. The mast on top of the tower is all about change of another kind: If the light on top is green, look for fair weather; orange means clouds are coming, and flashing orange signals rain; when it flashes white, expect snow; if the lights on the mast itself are rising, so will the temperature, and when they descend, it is going to get cold. ♦ 1740 Broadway (between W 55th and W 56th Sts)

24 Carnegie Delicatessen

★★$$ Indulge yourself at the classic kosher-style deli, a New York legend that became famous for sandwiches named after other New York legends. The menu is pricey, but wait until you see the size of the sandwiches—massive affairs that inevitably provide enough to share or cart home. Leave room, if you can, for the cheesecake. The downside: Getting people in and out—which translates into not providing gracious service or comfort—is the goal here, and after so many years it's become an honored tradition. ♦ Deli ♦ Daily, breakfast, lunch, dinner, and late-night meals. No credit cards accepted. 854 Seventh Ave (at W 55th St). 757.2245 ♿

25 Wellington Hotel

$$ This 1930s property is often overlooked, even though it has 85 one-bedroom suites with kitchenettes plus 515 guest rooms, a coffee shop (**Park Cafe**, open daily for breakfast, lunch, dinner, and after-theater), and a noted restaurant (**Molyvos**, below). Décor is light, simple, and pleasantly functional; wireless Internet access is available in rooms and the lobby, for a fee. ♦ 871 Seventh Ave (between W 55th and W 56th Sts). 247.3900, 800/652.1212; fax 581.1719. www.wellingtonhotel.com ♿

Within the Wellington Hotel:

Molyvos

★★★$$$ Cast aside all thoughts of soggy spinach pie and sticky-sweet baklava, for this large, lively dining room elevates Greek food to its rightful place in the pantheon of gastronomy. The mood of generosity and intense, sunny flavors begins with the appetizers, including a wonderful sampler plate of traditional Greek spreads—smoky eggplant, tangy fish roe, and pungent garlic yogurt—and perfect wood-grilled octopus. Entrées include heroic portions of lamb shanks baked in a clay pot, rabbit stew, and impeccable grilled whole fish. Attention to detail here ranges from making tender phyllo dough in-house for desserts (don't miss the custard-filled pastry called *bogatsa*, or the definitive baklava) to offering some 30 Greek wines on the well-chosen list—they're as good as they are unknown. The noise level is reasonable and the service is warm and enthusiastic. ♦ Greek ♦ Daily, lunch and dinner. Reservations recommended. 871 Seventh Ave (between W 55th and W 56th Sts). 582.7500

26 City Center

This somewhat unlikely Moorish-styled emporium was built as a Shriners' temple in 1924 by **H.P. Knowles** and converted to a theater in 1943. It was the home of the **New York City Opera** and the **New York City Ballet** before they moved to **Lincoln Center**.

Splendidly renovated, the 2,731-seat theater has improved sightlines, so audiences no longer have to strain their necks to see. Regular performers include **American Ballet Theatre** and the **Alvin Ailey**, **Paul Taylor**, **Martha Graham**, and **Merce Cunningham** dance companies. ♦ Box office, noon-8PM. 131 W 55th St (between Sixth and Seventh Aves). 581.7907. www.citycenter.org ♿

27 The Blakely New York

$$$ First opened in 1929, the 120-room former **Gorham Hotel** was Brit-ified and redone throughout, then re-flagged as the Blakely in 2004. Sleekly stylish and replete with boutique-hotel amenities, it is a lovely and convenient Midtown choice. Rooms are large and come with compact although fully equipped kitchenettes, feather beds, Wi-Fi, and upscale toiletries. ♦ 136 W 55th St (between Sixth and Seventh Aves). 245.1800, 800/735.0710; fax 582.8332. www.blakelynewwyork.com ♿

28 Worth & Worth

Hat lovers know top quality when they see it, and there are very few such purveyors left in town. In business since 1922, Worth & Worth are experts when it comes to handcrafted hats. The staff is knowledgeable, patient, and friendly, and the merchandise ranges from classic to cutting-edge, from bowlers and top hats to the rear-by-the minute hardwoven Montecristis. ♦ M-Sa. 101 W 55th St (between Sixth and Seventh Aves), sixth floor. 265.2887 ♿

29 Stage Delicatessen

★$$ Since 1937, this local spot for Damon Runyon characters is a classic Jewish delicatessen serving enormous sandwiches to locals, celebrities, and tourists alike. Most famous are the pastrami and corned beef, but don't overlook the cheese blintzes or chicken in the pot. ♦ Deli ♦ Daily, breakfast, lunch, dinner, and late-night meals. 834 Seventh Ave (between W 53rd and W 54th Sts). 245.7850

30 The London NYC

$$$$ The onetime Rihga Royal re-launched in 2007 under the LXR Luxury Resorts flag with a top-to-bottom top-of-the-line new look by Brit designer David Collins. To imagine The London's 561 spacious one- and two-bedroom suites, think clean, pale, and elegant, with soft and soothing jet-age curves everywhere, from rounded glass tables to kidney-shaped sofas. Assume amenities like Egyptian-cotton bedding, leather desks, dual rain showerheads for your bath, Wi-Fi access, iPod docks, flat-screen TVs, a 24-hour spa and fitness center, and, of course, room service from **Gordon Ramsay at The London** (see below). The appropriately named Vista Suites offer the best views; if you don't need to ask "how much?," the all-white mod elegance of the 2,200-square-foot Penthouse Duplex may be your ideal retreat. Concierge service is by Quintessentially, and other gustatory options include Mr. Ramsay's **Maze** (daily, lunch and dinner. 468.8889) and **The London Bar** (daily, English breakfast, afternoon high tea, evening cocktails. 468.8889). ♦ 151 W 54th St (between Sixth and Seventh Aves). 468.8888, 866/690.2029. www.thelondonnyc.com ♿

Within The London NYC:

Gordon Ramsay at The London

★★★$$$$ Master chef Gordon Ramsay's spin on his three-Michelin-star establishment in the UK is now a New York destination as well. Intimate (it seats but 45 diners), hushed (a notable counterpoint to Ramsay's reality-TV persona), and with flawless service, it offers both à la carte and tasting menus (with an unusual all-vegetarian option). Each subtly sauced New French starter and main course—with an emphasis on seafood—is perfectly married with a mélange of seasonal vegetables. Try the tarte Tatin or Bitter Chocolate Cylinder (with coffee granité and ginger mousse) for dessert. ♦ French ♦ Daily, lunch and dinner. Reservations required; jacket preferred. 468.8888 ♿

31 Pier Shows @ Pier 94

This is where the famous **Pier Antiques Show** takes place every year over a weekend in November, and again in March. Humongous with over 500 dealers, the range of stuff on display makes it feel like *Antiques Roadshow* heaven. Vintage apparel gets its own section; spillover runs onto **Pier 92**, where the "Others" Art show also runs in November. In January, Pier 94 hosts the 200-dealer "Americana Show." ♦ Admission. 12th Ave/West Side Hwy (at W 55th St). Stella Shows Management: 255.0020. www.stellashows.com ♿

31 Manhattan Cruise Terminal

New York is bullish on its waterways these days, and this storied West Side terminal is a big part of that movement. Many thought the ocean-liner era—when glamorous grand dames like the "Cunard Queens" (the SS *France* and USS *United States*) plied the seas—was ancient history. And indeed, by the time this terminal complex (Piers 88, 90, and 92) was finished in 1976, except for the *QE2*, only short-jaunt cruise ships called here regularly. In 2005, though, a landmark deal was drawn: the onetime "Passenger Ship Terminals" would undergo a 30-year phased renovation (and dredging, to accommodate bigger ships) and hereafter be known as the Manhattan Cruise Terminal, and the Red Hook section of Brooklyn would become home to **Brooklyn Cruise Terminal.** Completed in 2006, it proudly welcomed the *Queen Mary 2* on an inaugural visit. ♦ Entrance: 12th Ave (West Side Highway) at W 55th St. 246.5450. www.nyccruiseterminal.com ♿

2 Ed Sullivan Theater

This landmark theater, which was built by **Herbert J. Krapp** in 1927 and is full of Gothic details inside and out, has showcased vaudeville, music hall, stage shows, radio, and TV. It was a casino-style nightclub in the 1930s, then became the broadcast home of the Fred Allen radio show, and, from 1948 to 1971, the *Ed Sullivan Show.* Under its vaulted cathedral ceiling, American audiences got their first look at the Beatles, Elvis Presley, and Rudolf Nureyev. CBS bought and restored the theater in 1993; it is now home to the ever-popular *Late Show with David Letterman.* ♦ 1697 Broadway (between W 53rd and W 54th Sts)

33 Broadway Theatre

Ethel Merman filled this large 1,765-seat theater with sound and ticketholders as the star of *Gypsy.* Designed in 1924 by **Eugene De Rosa**, this is also where Barbra Streisand performed in *Funny Girl,* and where Yul Brynner gave his final performance in *The King and I. Miss Saigon* opened here in 1991 and held on until 2001. ♦ 1681 Broadway (between W 52nd and W 53rd Sts). Telecharge 239.6200. www.shubertorganization.com ♿

34 Maison

★$$ This 24-hour bistro and bar with a variety of lighter sandwiches, salads, soups, pastas, burgers, pizzettes, and pastries along with full meals (from steak frites to *fruits de mer*) is an ideal place to relax with your thoughts or a newspaper. Soft background jazz and small marble pedestal tables create an airy, laid-back environment. There's also a spacious palm-lined outdoor seating area that is delightful in nice weather—its heated umbrella takes over when the weather is not so fair. ♦ French bistro-American ♦ Daily, 24 hours. Enter from W 53rd St at Seventh Ave (1700 Broadway). 757.2233

35 NYC Official Visitor Information Center

An enterprise of the city's tourism and convention bureau—branded as NYC & Company—this 2,200-square-foot space is New York's official source for information on culture, dining, shopping, sightseeing, events, attractions, tours, and transportation. There are multilingual tourism information counselors on hand as well as electronic information kiosks, an MTA fare-card machine, and tons of brochures. ♦ M-F, 8:30AM-6PM; Sa, Su, 9AM-5PM. 810 Seventh Ave (between W 52nd and W 53rd Sts). 484.1222; 800/NYC.VISIT. Kiosks and other locations: Financial District (Federal Hall National Memorial, 26 Wall St, at Broad St), Lower Manhattan (City Hall Park, on Broadway at Park Row), Chinatown (at triangle of Canal, Walker, and Baxter Sts); and Harlem (Apollo Theater Lobby, 163 W 125th St, between Frederick Douglass and Adam Clayton Powell Blvds). www.nycvisit.com, www.officialnycshop.com ♿.

36 Sheraton New York Hotel & Towers

$$$ This efficient 1,700-room hotel has excellent convention facilities for its mainly corporate clientele. The classically contemporary rooms—expect boldly tasteful deep reds or blues, with leather accents in the seating—have good desks, high-speed Internet access, and often, a city view. The fully equipped Atlantis Fitness Center opens early and closes late, and is immense. Both a steam room and a sauna are available in addition to the array of cardio equipment and free weights. This Sheraton offers a business center and multilingual staff; it is also pet friendly. There are several restaurants and lounges, and room service is available around the clock. ♦ 811 Seventh Ave (between W 52nd and W 53rd Sts). 581.1000, 866/716.8115; fax 262.4410. www.sheraton.com/newyorkcity ♿

37 Remi

★★$$$ Fresh antipasti, Venetian-style ravioli filled with fresh tuna and crispy ginger in a light tomato sauce, and a selection of grilled meats and fish please the corporate dealmakers who lunch here, as well as some of the city's esteemed chefs, who reserve tables here on their nights off. The desserts are worth the splurge, especially the *cioccolatissima* (a warm chocolate soufflé cake with a cappuccino parfait) and the zabaglione *sarah venezia* (broiled zabaglione with fruit and vanilla ice cream). For those who like grappa, there are 45 varieties from which to choose. ♦ Italian ♦ M-F, lunch and dinner; Sa, Su, dinner. Reservations recommended. 145 W 53rd St (between Sixth and Seventh Aves). 581.4242

38 Hilton New York

$$$ The quintessential luxury convention hotel in town is this tower of more than 2,000 well-appointed rooms or suites, each with a minibar and offering such services for businesspeople as quick checkout, high-speed Internet access, and a multilingual staff. Executive rooms offer deluxe décor and a dedicated dining lounge. A battery of restaurants and cocktail lounges line the ground floor of the hotel. ♦ 1335 Sixth Ave (between W 53rd and W 54th Sts). 586.7000, 800/HILTONS; fax 315.1374. www.hilton.com ♿

39 Neil Simon Theatre

When this 1,455-seater, originally named the Alvin Theatre, was erected in 1927 by **Herbert J. Krapp**, Fred and Adele Astaire were in the first production, George and Ira Gershwin's *Funny Face. Annie* arrived here exactly 50 years later; another major success, *Hairspray,* hit in 2002. In honor of the playwright whose *Brighton Beach Memoirs* played here, the Alvin was renamed the Neil Simon Theatre in 1983. ♦ 250 W 52nd St (between Broadway and Eighth Ave). Box office (daily): 757.8646; Ticketmaster 307.4100. www.neilsimontheatre.com ♿

40 Roseland Ballroom

The legendary ballroom, which opened in 1919 and was once host to big bands and aspiring Fred Astaires and Ginger Rogerses, is now better known for rock, salsa, world music bands, and special events. These days you're as likely to find a Marilyn Manson gig—or Bob Dylan—here as you are a Versace fashion show. ♦ Admission. 239 W 52nd St (between Broadway and Eighth Ave). Concert information: 777.6800; Ticketmaster: 307.7171. www.roselandballroom.com ♿

40 August Wilson Theatre

Formerly called the Virginia, and before that the ANTA, this theater was built in 1925 by **C. Howard Crane** and **Kenneth Franzheim** for the **Theatre Guild**. Pat Hingle and Christopher Plummer starred here in Archibald MacLeish's *J.B.,* which won the Pulitzer Prize in 1959. Sir Thomas More was brilliantly played by Paul Scofield in Robert Bolt's *A Man for All Seasons* in 1961. *Jelly's Last Jam* had a good run in the early 1990s, and Lieber & Stoller's *Smokey Joe's Cafe* ran for five years, closing finally in 2000. In 2005, when Tony-winner *Jersey Boys* opened, the 1,240-seat theater had just been renamed after the late playwright August Wilson; his *King Hedley II* had a bri run here in 2001. ♦ 245 W 52nd St (between Broadway and Eighth Ave). Telecharge 239.6200 ♿

41 Novotel New York

$$$ Part of a large French chain, the hotel begins on the seventh floor of this 1984 building by **Gruzen & Partners**, and many its 480 rooms and suites look down into th heart of Times Square. High-speed Interne access is available, and pets are acceptab Room service runs until midnight. **Café Nicole** on the seventh floor offers brasseri dining and alfresco views. ♦ 226 W 52nd S (between Broadway and Eighth Ave). 315.0100, 800/221.3185; fax 765.5369. www.novotel.com

41 Gallagher's Steak House

★★★$$$ Even confirmed carnivores may flinch as they pass the glass-walled meat locker (also visible from the street) filled with raw slabs of beef, but it's been there since the restaurant first opened in 1927. Oak floors and knotty pine walls confirm th you're in one of New York's very serious ste joints. In fact, management claims that the original "New York Strip" (prime sirloin on t bone) was first served here. The dry-aged prime sirloin, filet mignon, and prime ribs a all satisfying and delicious. ♦ Steak house ♦ Daily, lunch and dinner. Reservations recommended. 228 W 52nd St (between Broadway and Eighth Ave). 245.5336 ♿

42 Ben Benson's Steakhouse

★★★$$$ This classic-style New York restaurant serves massive portions of meat including T-bones, aged sirloins, and triple-cut lamb chops—that few will be able to finish in one sitting. Other dishes, some meatless, are also impressive: Maryland crab cakes, Maine lobster, whole roasted chicken, and broiled fillet of sole are all superb. If you have any room left for desse try the cheesecake. Their outdoor café offe lighter fare—soups, sandwiches, salads, an pasta dishes—as well as a petite fillet au poivre, English cut prime rib, and grilled po tenderloin. Alfresco diners can also select items from the regular menu. ♦ American ♦ M-F, lunch and dinner; Sa, Su, dinner. Reservations recommended. 123 W 52nd S (between Sixth and Seventh Aves). 581.8888

43 Looking Toward the Avenu

Installed in 1989, the three enormous bronze Venuses (ranging in height from 14 f

23 feet) by artist Jim Dine are a humanizing presence amid the impersonal towers that surround them. ♦ 1301 Sixth Ave (at W 52nd St)

4 René Pujol

★★$$$ A truly old-fashioned bistro, this town-house dining room is filled with French country atmosphere and décor, including an exposed brick wall and pottery on display. Try the lobster bisque, roasted breast of duck, grilled steak, or rack of lamb. The crème brûlée and any of the soufflés are highly recommended. ♦ French ♦ Tu-Su, lunch and dinner. Reservations recommended. 321 W 51st St (between Eighth and Ninth Aves). 246.3023

5 Gershwin Theatre

Formerly the **Uris Theatre**, this 1,900-seat structure—built in 1972 by **Ralph Alswang**—presents lavish revivals of such well-loved musicals as *Showboat* and *Candide*, as well as original blockbuster productions, like 2004 Tony-winner *Wicked.* ♦ 222 W 51st St (between Broadway and Eighth Ave). Box office (daily): 586.6510; Ticketmaster 307.4100. www.gershwintheatre.com ♿

6 Ellen's Stardust Diner

★$ The burgers here won't win any awards, but they're delivered to the shake, rattle, and roll of 1950s music. The menu gets as fancy as grilled swordfish, but your best bet is a Velveeta cheeseburger and an ice cream sundae for dessert. Be prepared to wait. ♦ American ♦ Daily, breakfast, lunch, dinner, and late-night meals. 1650 Broadway (at W 51st St). 956.5151

6 Winter Garden Theatre

This beautiful theater, back to its original name after a few years as the Cadillac Winter Garden, was designed by **W.A. Swasey**, and opened with Al Jolson in 1911. Fanny Brice, Bob Hope, and Josephine Baker were featured in the Ziegfeld Follies revues here. Other hits were the original productions of *Wonderful Town*, *West Side Story*, *Funny Girl*, *Cats* and, beginning with the 2001 season, *Mamma Mia!* ♦ 1634 Broadway (between W 50th and W 51st Sts). Telecharge 239.6200. www.shubertorganization.com ♿

7 Sheraton Manhattan

$$$ A 50-foot heated indoor swimming pool, a sun deck, and a gym with modern equipment are features of this conveniently located, recently renovated 660-room hotel. It's pet-friendly and high-speed Internet accessible, and 24-hour room service is available from **Russo's Steak and Pasta**, which offers breakfast and dinner onsite daily. ♦ 790 Seventh Ave (between W 51st and W 52nd Sts). 581.3300, 866/716.8115; fax 315.4265. www.sheraton.com/manhattan ♿

48 AXA Equitable Center

A huge painting (*Mural with Blue Brushstroke*) created by Roy Lichtenstein for this 1985 building by **Edward Larrabee Barnes** brings you in off the street. Near it are other works of art—among them, pieces by modern notables Sol Lewitt and Scott Burton—but the famous Thomas Hart Benton murals, painted in 1930, have been moved one block east on 51st Street to **1290 Sixth Avenue**, whose lobby shows them to better advantage. The lobby is open to the public during business hours, M-F. 787 Seventh Ave (between W 51st and W 52nd Sts)

48 Le Bernardin

★★★★$$$$ The elegant wood-paneled room with a collection of maritime art is a gracious setting in which to appreciate the heady cooking of chef Eric Ripert, protégé of late owner Gilbert Le Coze. If you love seafood you can't go wrong on the near-poetic menu, but you might start with the crab and shrimp bouillabaisse aioli crab cake melting in a rich saffron lobster broth, with poached shrimp and croutons, or the now classic tuna carpaccio, and follow with the pan-roasted loin of monkfish studded with roasted garlic and rosemary, with lemon tagliatelli, toasted pine nuts, aged Parmesan, and parsley oil, or a whole red snapper baked in rosemary and thyme salt crust (a dish with a two-person minimum that requires 24 hours' notice). Pastry chef Florian Bellanger works his own kind of magic to create a frozen tangerine parfait on a meringue with nougat and tangerine sauces, a warm chocolate tarte with melting whipped cream and dark chocolate sauce, homemade ice creams and sorbets, and more. Service is as flawless as the food. ♦ French/Seafood ♦ M-F, lunch and dinner; Sa, dinner. Reservations required. 155 W 51st St (between Sixth and Seventh Aves). 554.1515

49 Michelangelo Hotel

$$$ The onetime **Taft Hotel** received a new lease on life when it was transformed into this 178-room marble-and-crystal Venetian palace that belongs to the much-lauded Italian Starhotels chain. Amenities include 24-hour room service, a concierge, a tiny on-site fitness center and access (for a fee) to a full-service health club across the street.

Striving for the ambience of an Italian villa, the larger-than-average rooms have TVs in hand-inlaid armoires (and smaller TVs in the marble bathrooms, which all also have generously deep soaking tubs). High-speed Internet access and valet parking are available. ♦ 152 W 51st St (at Seventh Ave). 765.1900, 800/237.0990; fax 541.6604. www.michelangelohotel.com ♿

Within The Michelangelo Hotel:

Insieme

★★★$$$$ Its name translates from Italian as "together," and its twin traditional and contemporary Italian menus offer diners an opportunity to mix-'n-match between, say, a satisfying and hearty *lasagne verdi Bolognese* and a more challenging *Mediterranean bass "Saltimbocca"* (with spring onion, savoy cabbage, prosciutto, and sage). Dessert might be a rich mascarpone cannoli or ricotta-and-orange cheesecake. Coolly modern, the space, airy as it is, appears to be inspired by a wine cellar; it does have a superb wine list. Both **Gramercy Tavern** alum, owners Marco Canora (chef) and Paul Grieco (sommelier) are the team that created the East Village's acclaimed **Hearth**. ♦ Italian ♦ M-Sa, dinner; M-F, lunch. Reservations recommended. 777 Seventh Ave (between W 50th and W 51st Sts). 582.1310

50 Chez Napoléon

★★$$ Tucked away at the edge of the Theater District is this intimate bistro, where the menu features such classic French dishes as onion soup, escargots, steak au poivre, *choucroute garni* (sauerkraut garnished with potatoes and pork), and chocolate mousse, and the kitchen does them all justice. ♦ French ♦ M-F, lunch and dinner; Sa, dinner. Reservations recommended. 365 W 50th St (between Eighth and Ninth Aves). 265.6980

51 Worldwide Plaza

Changes in zoning laws encouraged the construction of this mixed-use complex of residences and offices on the site of the second **Madison Square Garden** (1925-1966). The apartment towers were designed by **Frank Williams**; the office tower by **Skidmore, Owings & Merrill**. Both were b in 1989 in a slow but successful attempt bring commercial activity to this area of Eighth Avenue. Commercial occupants ha included Ogilvy & Mather and Polygram Records. ♦ Bounded by Eighth and Ninth Aves, and W 49th and W 50th Sts

52 Churrascaria Plataforma

★★$$ Begin your journey into the tangy, hearty world of Brazilian barbecue at this palm tree–studded spot with a *caipirinha,* bracing blend of crushed limes, sugar, anc Cachaça (sugar cane liquor), the national cocktail of Brazil. This is the land of all-yo can-eat prix-fixe barbecue, so bring a hea appetite for dishes like garlic beef, short ribs, crispy chicken thighs, and flank steak There is live music Thursday through Satur nights. ♦ Daily, lunch and dinner. Reservations recommended. 316 W 49th St (betwe Eighth and Ninth Aves). 245.0505. Also at **Churrascaria Riodizio Tribeca**: 221 W Broadway (between White and Franklin St

53 Eugene O'Neill Theatre

This 1925 work of **Herbert J. Krapp** was th site of Arthur Miller's first major success, *A My Sons,* which opened here in 1947 with Begley and Arthur Kennedy. The stage adaptation of the hit movie *The Full Monty* had a solid two-year run in this 1,075-sea after it opened to rave reviews in 2000; *Spring Awakening* collected a slew of Tony for its 2006 opening season here. ♦ 230 49th St (between Broadway and Eighth Av Telecharge 239.6200 ♿

53 The Time Hotel

$$ Downtown style meets **Times Square** madness at this decidedly unconventional hotel, where each guestroom is done up in primary color—red, yellow, or blue. In a blu room, you'll find not only blue furnishings b an artfully displayed blue fruit for the tasti and a "blue"-inspired scent in the bathroo Reserve a room according to your mood (o the mood you think you'll be in when you arrive). The hotel's public spaces have har any color at all. This wonderfully wacky stu is the brainchild of dashing young hotelier (and former *Vogue* model) Vikram Chatwal The gifted Transylvanian-born **Adam D. Tihany** designed this 1999 luxury property which has a 24-hour fitness center and 16 rooms and 28 suites, all with high-speed Internet access and 18-hour room service Have a martini at the second-floor lobby-level bar, the **02 Lounge**, or dine at the branch of Italian-casual **Serafina** that replaced Océo here in 2007. ♦ 224 W 49t St (between Broadway and Eighth Ave).

246.5252, 877/TIME.NYC; fax 242.2305. www.thetimeny.com

54 Ambassador Theatre

Built in 1921, this is yet another work of ubiquitous designer **Herbert J. Krapp**. In 1939, Imogene Coca, Alfred Drake, and Danny Kaye began their careers here in the *Strawhat Review*. The Savion Glover tap tour-de-force *Bring in 'Da Noise, Bring in 'Da Funk* stormed the stage here for three years, starting in 1996, after a successful Off-Broadway run. And, following its opening at the somewhat larger **Richard Rodgers Theatre**, then a stretch at the **Shubert**, the 1996 revival of *Chicago* landed here at the 1,100-seat Ambassador in 2003. ♦ 219 W 49th St (between Broadway and Eighth Ave). Telecharge 239.6200 www.shubertorganization.com

55 The Brill Building

At the turn of the century, publishers of popular songs were all located on 28th Street west of Broadway. The noise of pianos and raspy-voiced song pluggers gave the name "Tin Pan Alley" to the street. When the action moved uptown, the publishers moved to this building and brought the name with them. The bust of the young man over the door is a memorial to the son of the building's original owner, who died just before construction began. ♦ 1619 Broadway (between W 49th and W 50th Sts)

Within The Brill Building:

Colony Records

An institution for recordings and sheet music for soundtracks, shows, and jazz, this is a fun stop for post-theater browsing. ♦ Daily, 9:30AM-1AM. 265.2050 ♿

56 Caroline's On Broadway

This upscale venue is a major stop on the comedy club circuit for up-and-coming talent. Jerry Seinfeld, Jay Leno, and Billy Crystal all cut their teeth here. Dinner is served, but you can order just drinks. ♦ Cover; drink minimum. Multiple shows daily. Reservations required. 1626 Broadway (between W 49th and W 50th Sts). 757.4100 ♿

Which US city has the most historical places? No, it's not Washington. According to the National Register of Historic Places, New York has the most—723 officially registered spots. Philadelphia is second with 530, and Washington comes in third with 457.

57 Crowne Plaza, Times Square

$$$ The arrival of the contemporary chain's crown jewel in 1989 gave a major boost to the effort to revamp the Times Square area. The 770 rooms are ideally situated for sightseeing and theatergoing. For a view of Broadway, book a room on the east side; to see the Hudson River, book on the west side. Indulge in its popular restaurant, **Samplings**, and work off those calories at the onsite branch of the **New York Sports Club** (use of its lap pool is free; there is a small day charge to use the rest of the facility). A full-service business center with high-speed Internet access operates Monday through Friday. ♦ 1605 Broadway (between W 48th and W 49th Sts). 977.4000, 800/243.NYNY; fax 333.7393. www.manhattan.crowneplaza.com ♿

58 Pongsri Thai

★$$ A good local no-frills stand-by, the mostly traditional Thai dishes here tend to be toned down to an assumed wimpy American palate. The menu includes lobster stir-fry with basil leaf and chili paste, whole deep-fried red snapper with a hot and spicy sauce, and assorted vegetables with bean curd in red curry and coconut milk. ♦ Thai ♦ Daily, lunch and dinner. 244 W 48th St (between Broadway and Eighth Ave). 582.3392. Also at 311 Second Ave (at E 18th St). 477.4100; 165 W 23rd St (between 6th and 7th Aves). 645.8808; 106 Bayard St (between Mulberry and Baxter Sts). 349.3132

59 Walter Kerr Theatre

It took precisely 66 days for the Shubert Organization and designer **Herbert J. Krapp** to build the former **Ritz Theatre** in 1921. It opened with Clare Eames in John Drinkwater's *Mary Stuart* and left audiences spellbound in 1924 with Sutton Vane's eerie *Outward Bound,* starring Alfred Lunt and Leslie Howard. Soon after, its 1943 revival of *Tobacco Road* productions were confined to live radio and TV broadcasts; it returned to legitimacy in 1971 with the long-forgotten rock opera *Soon*. With just 975 seats, this gem of Italian Renaissance detail easily ranks as one of Broadway's most beautiful theaters; a top-to-bottom renovation in the 1980s did nothing but enhance it. Renamed for renowned critic and playwright Walter Kerr in 1990, productions here have made a mark in American theater history. Tony Kushner's unqualified hit *Angels in America,* the two-part AIDS epic (*Millennium Approaches* and *Perestroika*), ran here in 1993-1994. Many claim the powerful duo brought integrity back to Broadway drama. *Grey Gardens* (2006-2007), starring Christine Ebersole, and a bit of risky business as a musical itself, was another big hit. ♦ 219 W 48th St (between Broadway and Eighth Ave). Telecharge 239.6200 ♿

60 Longacre Theatre

In the 1930s, **The Group Theater** premiered three Clifford Odets plays here: *Waiting for Lefty, Paradise Lost,* and *Till the Day I Die.* Julie Harris appeared in *The Lark* and *Little Moon of Alban.* In 1960, theater of the absurd invaded Broadway with the brilliant Zero Mostel in *Rhinoceros* by Eugene Ionesco. In 1980, *Children of a Lesser God* won a Tony; an acclaimed revival of Eric Bogosian's *Talk Radio,* this time with Liev Schreiber at the mike, took the stage in 2007. Neoclassical in design, the 1,005-seat 1913 building is the work of **Henry B. Herts**. ♦ 220 W 48th St (between Broadway and Eighth Ave). Telecharge 239.6200. www.shubertorganization.com ♿

61 Renaissance New York

$$$ Opened in 1992, this Marriott-owned property boasts a Postmodern structure by **Stephen B. Jacobs** in the heart of Times Square. All 305 rooms sport new décor thanks to a top-to-bottom renovation in 2007. With a tailored contemporary look freshened by clever color accents, the all-nonsmoking accommodations include high-speed Internet access, multiple-line telephones, minibars, and, all-important, soundproof windows. Business-friendly and pet-friendly, you can also expect room service from their own panoramic-view restaurant. The top three Club Floors offer additional personal services. ♦ 714 Seventh Ave (at W 48th St). 765.7676, 800/HOTELS-1; fax 765.1962. www.renaissancehotels.com ♿

62 Sam Ash Music Store

For decades this block of West 48th Street has been a musicians' mecca. Orchestral and rock 'n' roll musicians—from those struggling at the bottom of the heap to those celebrating at the top of the charts—come here for state-of-the-art supplies and equipment. Wander in just to see who's buying. Find keyboards, recording gear, live sound, and DJ equipment at the main store location (No. 162) on the south side of the street; cross West 48th and head to No. 155 for guitars, No. 159 for drums, and No. 163 for brass, woodwinds, and sheet music. ♦ Daily. 162 W 48th St (between Sixth and Seventh Aves). 719.2299 ♿

63 Cort Theatre

Peg O' My Heart opened the giddily ornate **Thomas W. Lamb**-designed 1,000-seat Co in 1912, and many other fine shows have played on this stage (its many balconies an appliquéd details a harbinger of Lamb's late "atmospheric" movie palaces), including *Charley's Aunt* and *The Diary of Anne Frank,* by famed Hollywood writers Frances and Albert Hackett, which won a Pulitzer in 195 The theme of children and oppression returned here in the 1980s with *Sarafina!* I 1990, *The Grapes of Wrath* took the Tony fo best play. ♦ 138 W 48th St (between Sixth and Seventh Aves). Telecharge 239.6200. www.shubertorganization.com ♿

64 Biltmore Theatre

Built by the **Chanin Brothers** to a design by **Herbert J. Krapp** in 1925, the Biltmore wen dark in 1987, but came back to life in 2003 after a major overhaul by **Polshek Partnership Architects** for the Manhattan Theatre Club and their full season of productions. A freshly austere façade (styled after a dressed-down French palace) greets theatergoers at this 650-seat historic hous that ran Joe Orton's *Loot* in 1968, followed immediately that year by the five-year run o *Hair* (and its revival in 1977). In the 1930s was used by the Federal Theatre's Living Newspaper Project; its relaunch season opener was Richard Greenberg's *The Violet Hour.* ♦ 261 W 47th St (between Seventh and Eighth Aves). Telecharge 239.6200. www.mtc-nyc.org

65 Brooks Atkinson Theatre

The former **Mansfield**, designed by **Herbert J. Krapp** in 1926 as a sort of "Spanish palazzo" affair, was renamed in 1960 in honor of the *New York Times* critic. The fabulous chandelier that was removed around that time reclaimed its home in 2000, cleaned up and poised to dazzle into the next millennium. *Come Blow Your Horn,* the first in a series of Neil Simon comedy hits, opened at this 1,069-seater. Charles Grodin and Ellen Burstyn performed here fo three years in *Same Time Next Year.* ♦ 256 W 47th St (between Broadway and Eighth Ave). Box office (daily): 719.4099; Ticketmaster 307.4100 www.brooksatkinsontheater.com ♿

66 Ethel Barrymore Theatre

One of the great artists of her era, Ethel Barrymore opened this theater (designed, with the period's requisite filigreed dome and chandelier, by **Herbert J. Krapp**) in 1928 in *Kingdom of God.* The stage has see the start of many illustrious careers: Fred Astaire danced his way to stardom in Cole

Porter's *The Gay Divorce* (filmed as *The Gay Divorcée*); Walter Huston introduced the haunting standard "September Song" in *Knickerbocker Holiday;* and Marlon Brando first achieved prominence when he costarred with Jessica Tandy in *A Streetcar Named Desire.* A noted revival of Stephen Sondheim's *Company* filled the 1,100-seat theater in 2006-2007. ♦ 243 W 47th St (between Broadway and Eighth Ave). Telecharge 239.6200. www.shubertorganization.com ♿

67 Edison Café

★★$ Cheese blintzes, broiled chopped sirloin, open-faced roasted turkey sandwich plate, a nice whitefish salad platter, cherry lime rickey, and orangeade. . . . The Edison is somewhat decrepit, but where else will you find baby-blue and -pink plaster walls festooned with delicate white handcrafted floral trim in what is basically a traditional New York coffee shop? It's reeking with history—in the center of the Theater District, all manner of theater folk have had a seat here, and, while most of the many magic shops that were once in the area are long gone, its stalwart practitioners, the famed Magician's Table, still hold court here (that is, when they aren't at Maui Tacos down on Fifth Avenue). There are no airs at the Edison: there's a counter, a bunch of tables, and as close to a sense of the pre-Disney Theater District as you are apt to find. At great prices, yet. ♦ American ♦ M-Sa, 6AM-9:30PM; Su, 6AM-7:30PM; breakfast, lunch, and dinner. 228 W 47th St (between Broadway and Eighth Ave). 840.5000 ♿

68 W New York–Times Square

$$$$ Enter this W from W 47th Street (as you must) and you know immediately you're inside an alternate reality. Shimmering shadows from a moodily lit waterfall greet you in the entry foyer, and while there are no signs to help, intrigue sets in and you have no choice but to press the beckoning elevator button. Exit into the ambient-light-infused Asian-style **W Living Room** on the promenade level, perhaps have a cocktail, and find your way to the check-in desk (a well-lit and well-chosen gift shop is tucked behind the check-in area). The 509 guestrooms are crisply modern. Sliding translucent glass panels lead to the bathroom; desktops are glass as well. Luminous amber-resin bedside tables add warmth to the setting; views, if you can get one, are spectacular. Opened in late 2001, this W is a Starwood venture with Toronto design firm **Yabu Pushelberg** in charge of the almost hallucinogenic public spaces, and the cooler guestrooms as well. The hotel has its own fitness center and a multitude of other amenities. The **Whiskey** bar on the lower level draws a crowd. ♦ 1567 Broadway (at W 47th St). 930.7400, 877/946.8357; fax 930.7500. www.whotels.com

Within W New York-Times Square:

Blue Fin

★★★$$$ Steve Hanson's ultra-glam two-level Blue Fin is a solid wave-maker among New York's dining cognoscenti. It's a 400-seat scene—that means noisy—but the modern surroundings are fun, and the raw bar and other fishy repertoire (try the halibut or the grouper for a change) good; you can even get a decent steak. There's live jazz on the upper level. ♦ Seafood ♦ Daily, breakfast, lunch, and dinner; Sa, Su, brunch. Reservations recommended. 1567 Broadway (at W 47th St). 918.1400

69 Duffy Square

World War I chaplain of the Fighting 69th, Father Francis P. Duffy served as pastor of nearby **Holy Cross Church** and is honored in this triangle with a 1937 sculpture by Charles Keck at West 46th Street. He shares the honor with a 1959 statue by George Lober of George M. Cohan, the actor/producer/writer who wrote "Give My Regards to Broadway," among hundreds of other songs. ♦ Bounded by Seventh Ave and Broadway, and W 46th and W 47th Sts

On Duffy Square:

TKTS

Here at this snazzy booth the Theater Development Fund sells tickets to Broadway and Off-Broadway shows and **Lincoln Center** productions; tickets are sold at half-price (plus a service charge) for performances on the day of sale. Tickets are not available for every show, but a board tells you what is available. The selection may improve as curtain time approaches, when producers release unused house seats, and during bad weather, when fewer people venture out. ♦ Tickets go on sale 10AM for W and Sa matinees, 11AM for Su matinees and evenings, 3PM for M-Sa evening performances. No credit cards or personal checks accepted. W 47th St and Broadway. 768.1818. ♿ Also at South Street Seaport, at Front and John Sts. Tickets at the Seaport go on sale at 11AM daily, for same-day evening performances and next-day matinees.

70 DoubleTree Guest Suites

$$$ This modern 460-suite hotel has carved its niche as one of the family-friendliest: the rooms are large, the décor is comfy, and if you're a kid, you get a warm cookie on arrival. Built in 1990, the streamlined **Fox & Fowle** structure was built to sit atop and around the historic **Palace Theatre** (see below) already at this corner. The hotel is within easy walking distance of **Rockefeller Center**, Fifth Avenue shopping, and, of course, Broadway theaters. There's also a restaurant, the **Center Stage Cafe**. ♦ W 47th St (at Seventh Ave). 719.1600, 800/222.8733; fax 921.5212. www.doubletree.com ♿

70 Palace Theatre

"Playing the Palace" was the dream of every vaudeville performer from the theater's 1913 opening well into the 1930s. The advent of movies brought hard times, but the Kirchoff & Rose–designed 1,740-seat theater was renovated and reopened as a showcase for big musicals in 1966. *Sweet Charity, Applause, La Cage aux Folles,* and *The Will Rogers Follies* were among its long-running hits; its 2000 arrival, Disney's *Aida*, was one of the most extravagant and expensive musical productions ever to be mounted on Broadway. ♦ Seventh Ave (at W 47th St). Box office (daily): 730.8200; Ticketmaster 307.4100. www.palacetheateronbroadway.com ♿

70 Times Square Information Center

With its surprisingly subdued signage, you'd think the official Times Square Info Center might stick out more from the surrounding neon fury. Nevertheless, and despite the dully covered façade, the former **Embassy Theater** is a fine step back in time: the joint **Thomas W. Lamb** and **Rambusch Studio** design, vintage 1925, has been nicely restored and repurposed. In this domed and filigreed space you can purchase tickets for Broadway shows (look for the **Broadway Ticket Center**), book sightseeing tours and airport transportation, get cash or exchange currency, surf the Net, and obtain free brochures. There's also a video history of Times Square and that NYC rarity: public bathrooms. Daily, 8AM-8PM. Seventh Ave (between W 46th and W 47th Sts). www.timessquarenyc.org ♿

71 Intrepid Sea, Air, & Space Museum

The veteran World War II and Vietnam War aircraft carrier USS *Intrepid* is now a technological and historical museum. Other than the Air and Space Museum in Washington, DC, no other institution gives such a thorough picture of the past, present, and future of warfare and technology in air, space, and sea. And the museum gets more interactive all the time, with a "G-force" loops-and-rolls lunch-defying ride, for example, and flight simulators. The tamer **Pioneers Hall** features mock-ups, antiques, and film clips of flying machines from the turn of the century through the 1930s. Insights into the future as well as contemporary exploration of the ocean and space are shown in **Technologies Hall**, along with the artifacts of 20th- and 21st-century warfare: jumbo jets, mammoth rockets, and complex weaponry. More aircraft can be inspected on the *Intrepid*'s 900-foot flight deck. The most recent acquisitions are the guided missile submarine USS *Growler*, the Vietnam-era destroyer USS *Edson*, and a British Airways Concorde. Visitors can climb through the control bridges and command centers of the carrier, but spaces are cramped, and there is often a wait. Dress warmly in winter months. Besides the many souvenirs in the gift shop, the book selection is quite good for harder-to-find related ship, plane, and military titles. Note: Hauled off for repair while its docking pier was overhauled, the *Intrepid* is scheduled to be back home by fall 2008. Call ahead to confirm. ♦ Admission; under six and uniformed military free. Daily, Memorial Day to Labor Day; W-Su, Labor Day to Memorial Day. Pier 86, 12th Ave (four blocks north of W 42nd St). 245.0072. www.intrepidmuseum.org

72 Landmark Tavern

★$$ An old (vintage 1868) waterfront tavern, this once-rowdy place was miraculously resurrected in 2005 after a year or so of great uncertainty. The current owners, of nearby **Druids** Celtic pub and restaurant renown, have got it under control. ♦ American ♦ M-Sa, lunch and dinner; Su, brunch and dinner. Reservations recommended. 626 11th Ave (at W 46th St). 247.2562 ♿

73 Mud, Sweat & Tears

Not one of those paint-a-ceramic (from a mass-produced mold) places, this is a cheerful, neat pottery studio for both beginning and expert potters. The facilities include 10 electric wheels, spacious tables, hand-building supplies, glazes, a kiln, and a small retail area where the potters sell their wares. ♦ Daily. Call for information on classes. 654 10th Ave (at W 46th St). 974.9121. www.mstpottery.com

74 Zen Palate

★★★$$$ A vegetarian oasis, this place serves excellent cuisine in an upscale, minimalist setting. It's a bit pricey, but worth the culinary cultural adventure for such dishes as basil moo shu rolls (with nuts and vegetables), Zen Retreat (a squash shell stuffed with vegetables, beans, and tofu), Dreamland (pan-fried spinach noodles with shiitake mushrooms and ginger), and Mushroom Forest (an exotic combination of fungi, pine nuts, and vegetables on a bed of Boston lettuce). Alcoholic beverages are not served, but you can bring your own. ♦ Asian/Vegetarian ♦ Daily, lunch and dinner. Reservations recommended. 663 Ninth Ave (at W 46th St). 582.1669. ♿ Also at 34 Union Sq E (at E 16th St), 614.9345; and other locations throughout the city.

75 Hour Glass Tavern

★$ There's a homey, old-fashioned, laid-back feeling here, the better to savor the reasonably priced, prix-fixe and à la carte pre-theater dining options. Tasty entrées include a spicy grilled blackened shrimp or salmon fillet, homemade lamb sausage, and penne with hot sausage, chicken, and spinach. While an hourglass is no longer poised to swivel above each table, they will still get you in and out in 60 minutes if your curtain time requires it. ♦ American ♦ Daily, dinner. 373 W 46th St (between Eighth and Ninth Aves). 265.2060 ♿

76 FireBird

★★★$$$ Within two adjacent Restaurant Row brownstones is a luxe Imperial Russian flight of fantasy that's as much about theater as cuisine—perhaps more. Dining here is like eating inside the Hermitage Palace in St. Petersburg, circa 1912, from the pricey paintings and elegant chandeliers to original costumes from Diaghilev's famed Ballets Russes and museum-caliber Russian artifacts that pepper the sumptuous premises. The menu features such czarist savories as buttered buckweat blini and sevruga caviar with sour cream, seared Karski shashlik, and marinated boneless lamb with fruit and almond pilaf and red pepper salad. If this kind of food doesn't turn you on, however, consider stopping by for a vodka-laced libation pre- or post-theater. ♦ Russian ♦ Tu-Sa, lunch and dinner; Su, dinner. Reservations required. 365 W 46th St (between Eighth and Ninth Aves). 586.0244

77 Becco

★★$$ The Bastianich family, who own the felicitous **Felidia** restaurant on the East Side, are also the proprietors of this informal spot on Restaurant Row. A wide variety of flavorful Italian dishes, such as wild-mushroom risotto and roasted suckling pig, are featured. The prix-fixe lunch and daily menus are both good values. ♦ Italian ♦ Daily, lunch and dinner. Reservations recommended. 355 W 46th St (between Eighth and Ninth Aves). 397.7597

77 Lattanzi

★★$$$ Enjoy a taste of the Roman Jewish Quarter in a casual atmosphere. Baby artichokes sautéed in olive oil, homemade pastas, and grilled fish are all made to order. ♦ Italian ♦ M-F, lunch and dinner; Sa, dinner. Reservations recommended. 361 W 46th St (between Eighth and Ninth Aves). 315.0980

78 Barbetta

★★★$$$ Owner Laura Maioglio oversees every detail of this splendid Italian restaurant, first established by her father over 90 years ago. The two-story interior has been skillfully refurbished with 18th-century Piedmontese and American antiques. The menu is as classic as the décor: Examples include linguine al pesto with Yukon gold potatoes, roasted organic rabbit in white wine with savoy cabbage, and char-grilled squab with cranberry beans and foie gras. Always a sensation are the truffles that are used in a number of the dishes. Classic desserts—try the zuppa inglese—are superb, and the extensive wine list boasts many Italian varieties. ♦ Northern Italian ♦ M-Sa, lunch and dinner. Reservations recommended. 321 W 46th St (between Eighth and Ninth Aves). 246.9171

79 Orso

★★$$$ It's easy to relax at this Northern Italian bistro serving pasta, seafood, veal, and wonderful pizzas—try the pie topped with roasted peppers, sun-dried vegetables, provolone, and sage. The handsome marble bar is an inviting place to unwind either before or after the theater. ♦ Italian ♦ Daily, lunch and dinner. Reservations recommended. 322 W 46th St (between Eighth and Ninth Aves). 489.7212

79 Joe Allen

★$$ Here is an opportunity to gaze upon posters of Broadway shows, handsome waiters, a stagestruck clientele, and occasionally the stars themselves. A blackboard menu lists the basic fare—salads, chili, or grilled fish—but this venerable standby is famous for its hamburgers, meat loaf, and fries. ♦ American ♦ Daily, lunch and dinner. Reservations recommended. 46th St (between Eighth and Ninth Aves). 581.6464

80 Broadway Inn

$$$ Located in the heart of Times Square, this is one of the smaller guest houses in the city (40 low-frills rooms and suites, each with private bath; the suites are all non-smoking), and its friendly atmosphere is unusual. The inn's interiors are contemporary, with exposed brick walls in the cozy, Wi-Fi-equipped lobby, and foliage throughout. The suites—for which there is no extra charge for kids—all have microwaves, and dataports are included in every room; complimentary continental breakfast is served daily, and they'll even help you get discounted theater tickets. ♦ 264 W 46th St (at Eighth Ave). 997.9200, 800/826.6300; fax 768.2807. www.broadwayinn.com

81 Paramount Hotel

$$$ In a building erected in 1928 by **Thomas W. Lamb**, the Paramount lobby is reminiscent of the set for a movie, with a large silverleaf-covered staircase that looks as though it could lead up to a spaceship but goes only as far as the mezzanine, where **The Mezzanine** restaurant (see below) is. Bathrooms in the smallish "pop Nuevo"-styled white, gray, and black rooms (the less expensive rooms can be downright tiny, though each has its very own, very large, gilt-framed Vermeer headboard) contain futuristic Philippe Starck designs like silver cone-shaped sinks. Amenities include fitness and business centers, a 24-hour concierge, non-smoking floors, Wi-Fi in every room, a **Dean & DeLuca** gourmet shop, and the popular **Paramount Bar.** ♦ 235 W 46th St (between Broadway and Eighth Ave). 764.5500, 866/760.3174; fax 354.5237. www.nycparamount.com ♿

Within the Paramount Hotel:

The Mezzanine

★★$$$ Though you'll be able to watch the comings and goings of people down in the lobby from this perch, the food will make a bid for your attention, too. The varied menu ranges from grilled chicken and wild-mushroom salad to Salmon Agrodolce, a pan-seared fillet wrapped in spinach. It's also a good place to come for dessert—try the banana bread pudding. A three-course pre-/post-theater prix-fixe menu is available. ♦ American ♦ Daily, breakfast, lunch, and dinner. Reservations recommended. 764.5500

82 Richard Rodgers Theatre

This Corinthian-columned theater is where Gwen Verdon appeared in *Damn Yankees, Redhead,* and *New Girl in Town.* It is also where Olsen & Johnson began the long-running *Hellzapoppin'*, filling all of its 1,430 seats for many nights. Formerly the **46th Street Theater**, built in 1925 by **Herbert J. Krapp**, it was dedicated to Richard Rodgers in March 1990. ♦ 226 W 46th St (between Broadway and Eighth Ave). Box office (daily): 221.1211 Ticketmaster 307.4100. www.richardrodgerstheatre.com ♿

83 Lunt-Fontanne Theatre

Mary Martin and Theodore Bikel appeared here in *The Sound of Music,* and Marlene Dietrich performed here alone not long afterward. The 1,500-seat theater, a work of **Carrère & Hastings**, dates to 1910, when it was called **The Globe** and had a retractable roof. That Shakespearean detail went by the wayside in the late 1950s when the theater was rebuilt to its current configuration, and renamed as well. Disney's *Beauty & the Beast* began its long run here in 1999. ♦ 205 W 46th St (between Broadway and Eighth Ave). Box office (daily): 575.9200; Ticketmaster 307.4100. www.luntfontannetheatre.com ♿

84 I. Miller Building

Almost hidden behind advertising signs, on the West 46th Street façade of this rare low-profile 1929 building are sculptures of great women of the theater: Ethel Barrymore, Marilyn Miller, Rosa Ponselle, and Mary Pickford, none of whom would have thought of appearing onstage in anything but I. Miller

On 13 May 1890, Mrs. Andrew Carnegie laid the cornerstone for the new Carnegie Music Hall. Amazingly, it was opened one year later.

Macy's, which claims to be "The World's Largest Store," boasts over two million square feet of floor space.

shoes. The figures are by **A. Stirling Calder**, whose son was the renowned artist Alexander Calder. The shoe store is gone, but the ladies are still here—as is the banner architect **Louis H. Friedland** had carved in the stone facing above them: "The Show Folks Shoe Shop Dedicated to Beauty in Footwear"—at least for now. ♦ W 46th St (at Seventh Ave)

85 Actor's Equity Building

This is the union for all stage actors in America—from the virtually unknown to the most famous. It was founded in 1913 by 112 actors to protect the rights and establish good working conditions for professional stage performers and stage managers. If you're into stargazing, keep your eyes peeled. ♦ 165 W 46th St (between Sixth and Seventh Aves)

86 Triton Gallery

You'll find theater posters and show cards for current and past performances on Broadway and elsewhere in this shop that provides custom framing and mail order, too. Ask for a catalog. ♦ M-Sa. 323 W 45th St (between Eighth and Ninth Aves). 765.2472 ♿

87 Al Hirschfeld Theatre

Originally the **Martin Beck Theatre**, it was renamed in 2003 in honor of the late beloved theater illustrator and caricaturist Al Hirschfeld. In the 1930s, the famed **Theatre Guild Studio** used this 1924 Moorish-influenced work of **G. Albert Lansburgh**. Great performances soon echoed from the stage and filled in 1,215-seat house, including those of the Lunts in Robert Sherwood's *Reunion in Vienna,* Katharine Cornell in *The Barretts of Wimpole Street,* and Ruth Gordon in *Hotel Universe.* In the 1950s, Arthur Miller's *The Crucible* and Tennessee Williams's *Sweet Bird of Youth* played here. In 1965, Peter Brook's production of *Marat/Sade* gave audiences a new look at documentary theater. Liz Taylor came here for her Broadway debut in Lillian Hellman's *The Little Foxes* in 1981, and the 1992 revival of *Guys and Dolls* had a huge success here. ♦ 302 W 45th St (between Eighth and Ninth Aves). Telecharge 239.6200 ♿

88 Frankie and Johnie's

★★$$$ A former speakeasy and onetime celebrity hangout for the likes of Al Jolson and Babe Ruth, this joint is still popular and tends to get busy (and loud) at dinner. But the crowds continue to get a hearty meal along with nostalgia for their money—this old Broadway chop house turns out great steak, veal, and lamb chops. ♦ Steak house ♦ M, dinner; Tu-Sa, lunch and dinner. Reservations required. 269 W 45th St (at Eighth Ave). 997.9494. Also at 32 W 37th St (between Fifth and Sixth Aves). 947.8940

89 John Golden Theatre

One of the longest-running shows in history, *Tobacco Road* (1933), played this 800-seat 1927 house, one of the smallest of the many Theater District buildings by **Herbert J. Krapp.** Over the years, *A Party with Betty Comden and Adolph Green, At the Drop of a Hat, Beyond the Fringe,* and Victor Borge kept audiences laughing here; in 2003 Tony-winner *Avenue Q* took the stage and continued the legacy. ♦ 252 W 45th St (between Broadway and Eighth Ave). Telecharge 239.6200. www.shubertorganization.com ♿

89 Bernard B. Jacobs Theatre

Mae West kept house in this theater, built in 1927 as the **Royale**, for three years as the title character in *Diamond Lil.* The Herbert J. Krapp–designed house was used as a radio studio by CBS from 1936 to 1940. Laurence Olivier dazzled audiences with his appearances in *The Entertainer* and *Becket. Grease,* which was Broadway's longest-running musical at the time, settled here in the 1970s during its last years. Filling the 1,170-seat theater, Michael Frayn's *Copenhagen* was a hit here in 2000–2001. ♦ 242 W 45th St (between Broadway and Eighth Ave). Telecharge 239.6200. www.shubertorganization.com ♿

90 Imperial Theatre

Rosemarie and *Oh, Kay!* set the tone for this otherwise unremarkable 1923 1,417-seater by **Herbert J. Krapp**. Hit musicals have always found a home here: *Babes in Toyland, Annie Get Your Gun,* and the incomparable Zero Mostel performing "If I Were a Rich Man" in *Fiddler on the Roof.* The original US production of *Les Misérables*, better known as *Les Miz,* bid adieu in 2003 after a 16-year run. ♦ 249 W 45th St (between Broadway and Eighth Ave). Telecharge 239.6200. www.shubertorganization.com ♿

90 Music Box Theatre

Composer Irving Berlin commissioned this charming 1,010-seat Federal Revival–style theater to accommodate his *Music Box Revue of 1921.* Also presented at this 1920 house (designed by C. Howard Crane and E. George Kiehler) were the first musical to win a Pulitzer Prize, George Gershwin's *Of Thee I*

Sing; John Steinbeck's *Of Mice and Men;* Kurt Weill's last musical, *Lost in the Stars;* and Kim Stanley in *Bus Stop.* ♦ 239 W 45th St (between Broadway and Eighth Ave). Telecharge 239.6200. www.shubertorganization.com ♿

91 Gerald Schoenfeld Theatre

Abe Lincoln in Illinois, with Raymond Massey, opened not long after John and Lionel Barrymore appeared here together in *The Jest*; the original production of *The Odd Couple* came along in 1965. Known for years as the **Plymouth**, this 1,065-seat theater was built in 1917 by **Herbert J. Krapp**. ♦ 236 W 45th St (between Broadway and Eighth Ave). Telecharge 239.6200. www.shubertorganization.com ♿

91 Booth Theatre

Although this small-for-Broadway (just 700 seats) 1913 theater, created with an eye for flourish by **Henry B. Herts**, was named for actor Edwin Booth, actress Shirley Booth also made a name for herself here with Sidney Blackmer in *Come Back, Little Sheba.* ♦ 222 W 45th St (at Shubert Alley, between Broadway and Eighth Ave). Telecharge 239.6200. www.shubertorganization.com ♿

92 New York Marriott Marquis

$$$ You can't get much more in the center of Times Square than here. This all non-smoking hotel boasts one of the world's tallest atriums through which its glass-enclosed elevators zip up and down, serving 47 floors and 1,949 refurbished rooms. It has a Broadway theater on the third floor (see opposite). New York's largest ballroom, and its highest lobby (reached by a chain of escalators passing through floor after quiet floor of meeting rooms). The 4,000-square-foot fitness center has weight equipment, saunas, Jacuzzis, and a trainer, if you need a push. A full-service business center, valet parking, concierge, and several restaurants (including the famous **View**, described below) and lounges are also available in this pet-friendly 1985 creation of **John Portman**. ♦ 1535 Broadway (between W 45th and W 46th Sts). 398.1900, 800/843.4898; fax 704.8930. www.marriott.com ♿

Within the Marriott Marquis:

The View

★$$$$ This is New York's only revolving restaurant. It has a limited view, as do the revolving lounges above it, but when the turntable takes you past **Rockefeller Center** and the skyline to the east and uptown, you'll be glad you took a ride in that glass elevator. ♦ Continental ♦ Daily, dinner; Su, brunch. Reservations required. No sneakers or jeans. 704.8900

Marquis Theatre

When it opened in 1986, many expected the almost 1,600-seat house (also designed by **John Portman**) to suffer from its somewhat untheatrical surroundings—and the bad press caused by the demolition of several venerable historic theaters, including the original **Helen Hayes** (see page 168), to make way for it. The ill will faded, however, during the almost four-year run of the theater's first large-scale production, *Me and My Girl.* It has since hosted the successful revival of *Annie Get Your Gun* and the 2006 Tony-winner *Drowsy Chaperone*, among other major productions. ♦ 1535 Broadway (between W 45th and W 46th Sts). Box office (daily): 382.0100; Ticketmaster 307.4100. www.marquistheatre.com ♿

93 Minskoff Theatre

In 1973, Debbie Reynolds opened this Der Scutt-designed house with a revival of *Irene.* Capacious and modern, this 1,600-seater has housed such technically extravagant productions as *Sunset Boulevard* by Andrew Lloyd Webber; *Lion King* made a mid-run leap over here in 2006. ♦ 200 W 45th St (at Broadway). Box office (daily): 869.0550; Ticketmaster 307.4100. www.minskofftheatre.com ♿

94 Planet Hollywood

★$$ Owned (though not managed) by a trio of celluloid powerhouses (Sylvester Stallone, Bruce Willis, and Arnold Schwarzenegger), this eatery is forever loud and packed. It's also fun: The interior, a veritable museum of movie memorabilia, was created by the set designer for the first *Batman* film. The pizza and burger selections are OK; leave room for the apple strudel—it's supposedly made from Arnold's mother's secret recipe. A gift shop next door sells souvenirs that no trendy diner should be without. ♦ American ♦ Daily, lunch, dinner, and late-night meals. 1540 Broadway (at W 45th St). 333.7827

94 Virgin Megastore

Modeled after its London flagship sister, this perpetually mobbed multilevel store boasts more than 150,000 music titles (on CD and cassette), 15,000 video titles, and a well-stocked bookstore. Listening stations with headphones allow customers to hear before they buy. ♦ Daily. 1540 Broadway (between W 45th and W 46th Sts). 921.1020. Also at Union Square South (corner of E 14th St and Broadway). 598.4666

95 Lyceum Theatre

Producer Daniel Frohman built this theater in 1903. Now a city landmark, it is the oldest

New York house still used for legitimate productions. It opened with *The Proud Prince.* In 1947, Judy Holliday and Paul Douglas wisecracked through *Born Yesterday.* The A.P.A.–Phoenix Repertory made this home base for several seasons, and in 1980, and again in 2002, *Morning's at Seven* by Paul Osborn was revived here. A 950-seat neo-Baroque structure with banded columns and an undulating marquee, it was the first theater designed by **Herts & Tallant**. Frohman was such a theater fan that he had his apartment above it fitted with a trapdoor through which he could see the stage. ♦ 149 W 45th St (between Sixth Ave and Broadway). Telecharge 239.6200. www.shubertorganization.com ♿

96 The Actors Studio

It was in this former Greek Orthodox church that Lee Strasberg trained such stars as Marlon Brando, Dustin Hoffman, Al Pacino, and Shelley Winters. ♦ 432 W 44th St (between Ninth and 10th Aves). 757.0870

96 The New Dramatists

This company, which offers free readings, was founded in 1949 by a group of Broadway's most important writers and producers in an effort to encourage new playwrights; alumni include William Inge, John Guare, and Emily Mann. The nonprofit organization took occupancy of the building, formerly a Lutheran church, in 1968. ♦ 424 W 44th St (between Ninth and 10th Aves). 757.6960. www.newdramatists.org

97 Poseidon Greek Bakery

The Fable family has been turning out paper-thin phyllo-dough pastries in this tiny shop for 75 years. Try the sweet baklava, spinach pies, and tempting cinnamon-and-sugar almond cookies. For those who want to make their own delicacies, phyllo is for sale. ♦ Tu-Su. 629 Ninth Ave (between W 44th and W 45th Sts). 757.6173 ♿

98 Film Center Building

The pink and black marble in the lobby and the pattern of the orange and blue tiles on the walls helped attract some 75 motion picture distributors, who made this 1929 building by **Buchman & Kahn** their head-quarters. The stores on this block rent out movie-making equipment. ♦ 630 Ninth Ave (between W 44th and W 45th Sts). Lobby: 757.6995

99 Birdland

★$$ Relocated from its old uptown outpost, this jazz club and restaurant features live jazz every night. Big-band music from Clark Terry to Chico O'Farrill's Afro-Cuban jazz is often in the lineup. ♦ American ♦ Cover; drink minimum. Daily, dinner and late-night meals. Call for changing schedule of shows. Reservations recommended. 315 W 44th St (between Eighth and Ninth Aves). 581.3080

100 Milford Plaza

$$ Built in 1928 by **Schwartz & Gross**, this 1,300-room hotel was originally known as the **Lincoln**. It was built and first operated by the United Cigar Stores Co., which said it catered to the better element of the masses. A 2002 spruce-up brought the (all smallish) rooms up to snuff with basic online (via modem) access in each. There are two restaurants and a complete fitness center. ♦ 700 Eighth Ave (at W 44th St). 869.3000, 800/221.2690; fax 944.8357. www.milfordplaza.com

101 Majestic Theatre

The Music Man, Carousel, A Little Night Music, and *The Wiz* helped this 1,607-seat theater, built in 1927 by the prolific Mr. **Herbert J. Krapp**, live up to its name. *The Phantom of the Opera,* which has been playing since 26 January 1988, is carrying on the tradition. ♦ 247 W 44th St (between Broadway and Eighth Ave). Telecharge 239.6200. www.shubertorganization.com ♿

101 Broadhurst Theatre

It was here, in this 1918 work of Herbert J. Krapp, that Humphrey Bogart picked up his credentials as a tough guy when he appeared with Leslie Howard in *The Petrified Forest*. British import *History Boys* won Tony acclaim here; soon after, the seemingly endless saga of Jean Valjean carried on when the *Les Miz* revival launched in this 1,150-seater in 2006. ♦ 235 W 44th St (between Broadway and Eighth Ave). Telecharge 239.6200. www.shubertorganization.com ♿

102 St. James Theatre

At this 1927 Moorish-influenced work of **Warren & Wetmore**, Rodgers and Hammerstein's *Oklahoma!* was followed by *Where's Charley?* with Ray Bolger, which in turn was followed by, among others, the original productions of *The King and I, The Pajama Game,* and *Tommy.* The blockbuster musical *The Producers* enjoyed a six-year run here, packing 'em in to the 1,510-seat house well into 2007. ♦ 246 W 44th St (between Broadway and Eighth Ave). Telecharge 239.6200 ♿

102 Helen Hayes Theatre

This theater was constructed by **Ingalls & Hoffman** in 1912, as the **Little Theatre** (rightly so, it has but 590 seats). In 1965 it became home to the Merv Griffin and David Frost television shows. By 1974 it was running legit again; *Torch Song Trilogy* had its premiere here in 1982. A year later, when the original Helen Hayes Theatre at 210 West 46th Street was demolished to make way for the Marquis, the Little was rededicated to the "First Lady" of the American theater. ♦ 240 W 44th St (between Broadway and Eighth Ave). Information line (recording): 944.9450; Ticketmaster 307.4100 ♿

103 Shubert Theatre

It's hard to imagine anything but *A Chorus Line* here (the original run, that is), but that's what they said about Katharine Hepburn in *The Philadelphia Story* and Barbra Streisand in *I Can Get It for You Wholesale.* The theater seats 1,440 and was built in 1913 by **Henry B. Herts**. Its impressive plasterwork and other ornamentation appropriately complement the staging of *Spamalot,* which opened here in 2005. ♦ 225 W 44th St (at Shubert Alley, between Broadway and Eighth Ave). Telecharge 239.6200. www.shubertorganization.com ♿

103 Shubert Alley

The stage doors of the **Shubert Theatre** (on West 44th Street) and the **Booth** (on West 45th, at its north end) open onto this narrow, well, alley. So does the entrance to the offices of the Shubert Organization, making this a favorite spot for Broadway hopefuls to casually stroll up and down on the chance of being noticed by the right people. A gift shop, **One Shubert Alley**, open daily, specializes in merchandise related to Broadway shows. ♦ Between Broadway and Eighth Ave, from W 44th to W 45th St

104 Sardi's

★★$$$ Since it opened in 1927, this restaurant has been synonymous with theater and Theater District dining. Sentimental favorites, such as cannelloni au gratin and steak tartare, are joined on the menu by more modern palate-pleasers like jumbo lump crabcakes and pork chops brushed with pesto. Once in a while, you can spot a celebrity; otherwise, stargazers can content themselves with identifying the famous customers immortalized in the numerous caricatures gracing the walls. ♦ Continental ♦ Tu-Sa, lunch, dinner, and late-night meals; Su, lunch and early dinner. Reservations recommended; jacket required. 234 W 44th St (between Broadway and Eighth Ave). 221.8440

105 Carmine's

★★$$ Come hungry and bring at least one friend to share the huge portions of Southern Italian fare served here; all meals are meant for two or more. If crowd noise is an issue for you, albeit jovial, you might also want to bring ear plugs. ♦ Italian ♦ Daily, lunch and dinner. 200 W 44th St (between Broadway and Eighth Ave). 221.3800. Also at 2450 Broadway (between W 90th and W 91st Sts). 362.2200

MILLENNIUM
BROADWAY · NEW YORK

106 Millennium Broadway

$$$ This sleek and handsome executive-style hotel offers such business-minded amenities as Wi-Fi access in all public areas and high-speed Internet access, phone mail in four languages, and dual phone lines in each of its 752 rooms. The **Club Floor** affords guests a private lounge (where a complimentary continental breakfast, as well as evening cocktails and hors d'oeuvres, are served) and such other upscale conveniences as a concierge for Club guests and private check-in and check-out. In addition, there is a fitness center staffed with private trainers. The Millennium's special-events space, the 650-seat **Hudson Theatre**, is a superbly restored 1903 Beaux Arts landmark. Exquisite arrangements of richly hued turquoise and green Tiffany glass mosaic tiles were uncovered in the course of that work; that display alone makes wangling an invitation here a worthy endeavor. ♦ 145 W 44th St (between Sixth Ave and Broadway).

768.4400, 800/934.9953; fax 789.7688. www.milleniumhotels.com ♿

Within the Millennium Broadway:

Restaurant Charlotte

★★$$$ An informal yet elegant room is a fine setting for menu favorites that include grilled veal rib chops and Moroccan rack of lamb. Save room for the classic crème brûlée or silk chocolate cake. ♦ New American ♦ Daily, breakfast, lunch, and dinner. 789.7508

07 Virgil's Real Barbecue

★$$ The placemats at this mammoth barbecue restaurant detail the search for the perfect version of each dish–Texas for sliced brisket, North Carolina for pulled pork. The walls are a source of more information–a history of barbecue in articles and pictures. Although authenticity, by its very definition, can't be copied, this place does a pretty good job–especially when it comes to ribs, pulled pork, mashed potatoes, and greens. The portions here are huge, including such desserts as butterscotch and lemon cheese pies. ♦ Barbecue ♦ Daily, lunch and dinner. 152 W 44th St (between Sixth Ave and Broadway). 921.9494

08 Cafe Un Deux Trois

★$$ Crayons for doodling on the paper-covered tables provide a charming bit of bohemia for those who never venture downtown. The gimmick isn't really necessary, however, as the place delivers satisfaction with such simple but good food as scallops Provençale and steak frites. ♦ French ♦ Daily, lunch and dinner. 123 W 44th St (between Sixth Ave and Broadway). 354.4148

08 Belasco Theatre

The eccentric David Belasco, whose preferred style of dress was a priest's frock, wrote and produced *Madame Butterfly* and *The Girl of the Golden West* here. Both were later adapted into operas by Giacomo Puccini. Belasco's ghost is said to continue to visit backstage (his apartment there remains intact). With the capacity for 1,030 corporeal bodies, this redbrick and limestone-trimmed theater, dating to 1907, was a creation of **George Keister**. ♦ 111 W 44th St (between Sixth Ave and Broadway). Telecharge 239.6200. www.shubertorganization.com

09 Manhattan Plaza

These towers, built in 1977 by **David Todd & Associates**, provide subsidized housing for performing artists, whose rent for the 1,688 apartments is based on their income. Their presence pays dividends in the vitality they bring to the neighborhood. The public may join the superbly well-equipped **Manhattan Plaza Health Club.** Complete with 75-foot pool and sundeck, day passes (M-Th only) are available for visitors. ♦ 400-484 W 43rd St (bounded by Ninth and 10th Aves, and W 42nd and W 43rd Sts). Admission. Health Club: 482 W 43rd St (between Ninth and 10th Aves). 563.7001. www.mphc.com

110 Little Pie Company

The aromas here are glorious, and the all-natural pies are just like Mom used to make. Fresh fruit pies predominate in summer; sour cream-apple and pumpkin pies are highlights in fall. ♦ Daily. 424 W 43rd St (between Ninth and 10th Aves). 736.4780. ♿ Also at 407 W 14th St (between Ninth and 10th Aves). 414.2324

110 ESCA

★★★$$$ With a daily changing menu that always evokes a fresh catch from the Southern Italian seaside, Esca has proven itself a charming and reliable purveyor of fishy delights since it opened in 2000. Chef and co-owner (with equally formidable restaurateurs Mario Batali and Joseph Bastianich) David Pasternack has held sway here since the beginning, making a special mark with his *crudo* tasting menu. You might also select from an ocean of choices like branzino (whole Mediterranean sea bass) in a sea salt crust, or, for non-fish folk, *gnocchi di zucca* (roasted cheese-pumpkin gnocchi) with wild mushrooms, all complemented by a regional Italian wine list. ♦ Seafood ♦ M-Sa, lunch; daily, dinner. Reservations required; jacket preferred. 424 W 43rd St (at Ninth Ave). 564.7272 ♿

111 Westside Theater

For more than 20 years the two Off-Broadway theaters in this converted Episcopal church have presented award-winning productions such as *A Shayna Maidel* and *Extremities.* They seat 210 and 190. ♦ Call for performance schedule. 407 W 43rd St (between Ninth and 10th Aves). Box office (daily): 315.2244; Telecharge 239.6200

111 Le Madeleine

★★$$$ This especially charming French bistro features salads, pastas, fish, and such light meat dishes as grilled chicken breast with a Pommery mustard sauce. There's also a beautiful skylit, brick-walled garden room that serves outdoor meals year-round and is always booked for brunch. ♦ French ♦ M-F, lunch and dinner; Sa, Su, brunch and dinner. Reservations recommended. 403 W 43rd St (between Ninth and 10th Aves). 246.2993

112 The Westin New York

★★$$$ It seems like you can see this 2002 **Arquitectonica**-designed spectacle from just about anywhere in the Times Square area. The Miami-based firm created a façade to remember: 8,000 sheets of glass, in a 10-color crazy quilt (though copper and blue predominate) bisected by a curved beam of white light. The ground-floor entry's a little weird, but once you're upstairs, things are tamer—the huge, bright, open-space main lobby makes clear you've arrived, then it's on to one of the 863 (non-smoking) guestrooms or suites. Tasteful, tailored with a modern-classical look in whites and grays with touches of color to warm it all up, the rooms feature fresh flowers, superb beds, large flat-screen TVs, high-speed Internet access (or wireless), and smartly functional desk space (complete with Aeron chairs). Check the panoramic views from the 23rd-floor fitness center and health spa. Dining possibilities include **Bar 10** (for cocktails and sushi) and **Shula's Steak House** (201.2776). ♦ 270 W 43rd St (at Eighth Ave). 201.2700, 866/837.4183; fax 201.2701 www.westinny.com

113 The *New York Times* Building (Former)

In 1913, less than 10 years after moving to Times Square, the *Times* had grown so much that this annex was built by **Ludlow & Peabody** around the corner on West 43rd Street. Its size was doubled in 1924. The building was expanded again in 1945, and the original tower was eventually abandoned. The newspaper discontinued printing at this location in 1997; the presses are now in modern and expanded facilities in nearby Queens. And in 2007, the *Times* offices were moved into their new **Renzo Piano**-designed building (see page 175) on Eighth Avenue, across from Port Authority. ♦ 229 W 43rd St (between Seventh and Eighth Aves).

114 Paramount Building

Built in 1926 by **Rapp & Rapp**, with a lobby modeled on the Paris Opera House, the famous Paramount showcased theater, film, and music for 40 years, marking such milestones as Elvis Presley's first movie premiere (*Love Me Tender*, in 1956). The steel-and-bronze marquee was torn down in 1967 and the space filled in with offices. But a decade-plus project managed by **Tobin Parnes Design Enterprises** has restored the building to its former glory, from the skyline-stopping four-sided clock and glass globe at its pinnacle (painted over during World War to maintain blackout conditions) to the marquee itself, replicated from historical photos and postcards. ♦ 1501 Broadway (between W 43rd and W 44th Sts)

Within the Paramount Building:

Hard Rock Café

★★$$ Beneath the Paramount's majestic marquee, the Hard Rock, set with the same features as its former home on West 57th Street, attracts the young tourist with decent burgers and sandwiches, a gift shop stocked with logo apparel, and a memorabilia collection that includes Prince's purple jacket and Jimi Hendrix's guitar. ♦ American ♦ Daily, lunch, dinner, and late-night meals. 343.3355

115 Casablanca Hotel

$$$ The Casablanca Hotel achieves the near impossible: an oasis of calm and character just footsteps from Times Square. The 48 rooms and suites exude the updated colonial flavor in evidence when you first walk in: rich wood paneling, exotic antiques, and antique French architectural prints. Guest refrigerators are stocked with complimentary iced tea, mineral water, and Callebaut chocolates. The second floor of this boutique hotel is home to the cozy **Rick's Cafe**, where guests repair for complimentary continental breakfast or afternoon wine and cheese. There's also a small computer center with Internet hookup here, and a tiny outdoor terrace in the back. (Wi-Fi access is available throughout the hotel.) ♦ 147 West 43rd St (between Sixth Ave and Broadway). 869.1212, 888/922.7225; fax 391.7585. www.casablancahotel.com

116 The Town Hall

This 1921 landmark, the work of **McKim, Mead & White**, is an elegant building with excellent acoustics. Joan Sutherland made her New York debut here. Today, the hall is constantly in use for concerts and cultural events. This is where Garrison Keillor stages his *Prairie Home Companion* Christmas series. ♦ 123 W 43rd St (between Sixth Ave and Broadway). 840.2824. www.the-townhall-nyc.org ♿

17 International Center of Photography (ICP)

First opened in 1989, this former satellite location (known then as **ICP Midtown**) was completely revamped and expanded by **Gwathmey Siegel and Associates Architects** in 2001, and is now the main event. While its former Upper East Side town house location is missed, this 17,000-square-foot space, with its state-of-the-art lighting and other technical advances, is all the more suited to fulfill **Cornell Capa**'s vision for the museum when it was founded in 1974. With over 60,000 photographs in its permanent collection, ICP continues to grow; its archives include the entire works of Weegee, Robert Capa, and Roman Vishniac. The best and the brightest from photography's beginnings in the mid-1800s to the most contemporary of work—from Henri Cartier-Bresson to Cindy Sherman—finds a supportive home here. So do multimedia exhibitions in ICP's Art for Web and Wall Series, created especially for this space. An extensive museum store sells books, photo reproductions, and more; there is also a café. The museum's library is not the only research facility—a 27,000-square-foot **ICP School** (857.0001) is across the street in the **Grace Building** (1114 Sixth Ave). Designed by the Gensler firm and opened in 2001, it offers a full program of courses and lectures to both enrolled students and the general public. ♦ Admission; voluntary contribution Friday after 5PM. Closed Monday. Tu-Th, Sa-Su, 10AM-6PM; F, 10AM-8PM. 1133 Sixth Ave (at W 43rd St). 857.0000. www.icp.org ♿

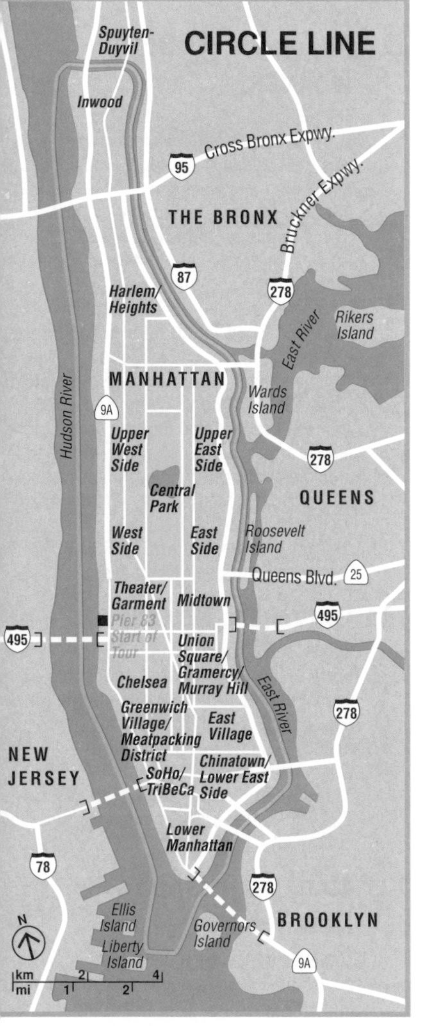

118 Circle Line

There is simply no better way to orient yourself to Manhattan's wonders. This well-narrated tour heads down the Hudson River, past the **Statue of Liberty**, up the East River to the Harlem River, through Spuyten-Duyvil, and back down the Hudson. The eight vessels are converted World War II landing craft or Coast Guard cutters. When you get on board, try to sit on the port side (left as you face forward and head south); that way, all your views are of Manhattan. During the summer, there are 12 three-hour cruises a day starting at 9:30AM. ♦ Fee. Daily. Pier 83, 12th Ave (just north of W 42nd St). 563.3200. www.circleline.com ♿

119 Ollie's

★$ Not haute cuisine, but the cold sesame noodles, scallion pancakes, and vegetable, pork, or shrimp dumplings are all favorites at this super-speedy bargain-priced Chinese restaurant. ♦ Chinese ♦ Daily, lunch, dinner, and late-night meals. 411 W 42nd St (between Ninth and 10th Aves). 868.6588. Also at other locations throughout the city

119 West Bank Café

★$$ This reliable Theater District standby (they will make sure you make your curtain) offers a satisfying assortment of chicken, fish, pasta, salads, and steak. Dine downstairs in their 80-seat **Laurie Beechman Theater**, where a small cover may be charged but you can enjoy a changing roster of readings, cabaret, and more musical events—often with surprise guests. Call ahead for performance schedule. ♦ New American ♦ M-Sa, lunch and dinner; Su, brunch and dinner. Reservations recommended. 407 W 42nd St (at Ninth Ave). 695.6909

120 Ticket Central

Sharing box-office space with **Playwrights Horizons** (see Theatre Row below), Ticket Central is a one-stop place to see what's on and purchase tickets for Off- and Off-Off-Broadway shows and other off-the-standard-radar performing events throughout the city. No service fees charged at box office; all tickets are full price (but way less costly than their Broadway brethren). ♦ Box office: daily, noon-8PM. 416 W 42nd St (between Ninth and Dyer Aves). 279.4200. www.ticketcentral.com ♿

120 Chez Josephine

★★$$$ In 1986, the ebullient Jean Claude Baker launched this unique restaurant as a tribute to his late adoptive mother, cabaret legend Josephine Baker. Years later, the place is still a great hit with critics and the public alike. Featured on the menu are lobster bisque, goat-cheese ravioli, and roasted duck à l'orange. A pianist playing bluesy tunes adds to the atmosphere. ♦ French ♦ Tu-Sa, dinner; Su, brunch and dinner. Reservations recommended. 414 W 42nd St (between Ninth and Dyer Aves). 594.1925

120 Theatre Row

Five small state-of-the-art theaters comprise this complex designed to showcase Off- and Off-Off-Broadway productions. It opened in 2002 as part of the 42nd Street revitalization plan that also brought the **Playwrights Horizons** (416 W 42nd Street, 279.4200) and the **Little Shubert** (422 W 42nd Street, 239.6200) theaters down the block (the old **42nd Street Playhouse**—a "live burlesk" house at the time—was demolished to make way for these new ventures). Here in Theatre Row, the 199-seat **Acorn** is the largest stage and so has the most commercial—as far as Off-Broadway goes—productions of the group. **The Beckett**, **The Clurman**, **The Kirk** (all 99-seaters), and **The Lion** (88 seats) often present works in development and that of emerging playwrights. Their annual Summer Play Festival (known as "SPF"), wi[th] its riot of readings, showcases, and chance-taking performances, has a perfect home here. ♦ Box office: daily, noon-8PM. 410 W 42nd St (between Ninth and Dyer Aves). 714.2442. www.theatrerow.org ♿

Bagels, from the Yiddish word *beygel*, are traditional Jewish rolls made from a yeast-based dough in the shape of a doughnut. Label Vishinsky, inventor of an early automatic bagel maker, claimed that the first New York bagel emerged from 15 Clinton Street in 1896.

121 Church of the Holy Cross

Although this was built in 1870 by **Henry Engelbert** as the parish church of a poor neighborhood, it has several windows and mosaics designed by Louis Comfort Tiffany. Father Francis P. Duffy, chaplain of the famous Fighting 69th Division in World War fought from the pulpit of this church to break up the gangs of Hell's Kitchen. He served here until his death in 1932. ♦ 329 W 42nd St (between Eighth and Ninth Aves). 246.4732 ♿

122 McGraw-Hill Building (former)

The original McGraw-Hill Building, this 35-story tower was commissioned when growth was expected in this area. Various occupants have come and gone since the publishing firm vacated years ago, but it is still known by that name (perhaps due to the distinctive Art Deco lettering carved into its stone face proclaiming it so). And, green and glorious, it still stands alone. Built in 1931 by **Raymond Hood** with **Godley & Fouilhoux**, it has the distinction of being the only New York building mentioned in *The International Style*, the 1932 book by Hitchcock and Johnson that codified modern architecture. In fact, this tower is not strictly glass-and-steel aesthetics but an individual composition with Art Deco detailing. Eminent architectural historian Vincent Scully called it "Proto-jukebox Modern." ♦ 330 W 42nd St (between Eighth and Ninth Aves)

123 Universal News

Finally, the crossroads of the world (Times Square) has a world-class newsstand. Here you can find out-of-town and international newspapers as well as just about every magazine under the sun. There is a good selection of guidebooks, too. ♦ 234 W 42nd St (between Seventh and Eighth Aves). 221.1809. Also at other locations throughout the city

123 Madame Tussaud's New York

London's legendary wax museum makes a splash in Times Square with 85,000 square feet and five floors filled with more than 200 life-size wax renditions of New York notables from the colonial to post-millennial periods. It's good, kitschy fun, but only you can decide whether it's truly worth $29 (and rising) per adult ticket. ♦ Admission. Daily till late (may close for special events. Call ahead). 234 W 42nd St (between Seventh and Eighth Aves). 512.9600. Info hotline: 800/246.8872. www.nycwax.com ♿

24 American Airlines Theatre

Now housing the renowned **Roundabout Theatre** company, the derelict 1918 former Selwyn Theatre (historic home to shows by George Kaufman, Cole Porter, and Noël Coward) was meticulously restored and reopened in 2000 for this group's classic repertoire. The 2005 Tony-winning revival of *Pajama Game* was staged in the 740-seater; George Bernard Shaw's *Heartbreak House* held audiences the next season. ♦ 227 W 42nd St (between Seventh and Eighth Aves). Tickets: 719.1300 ♿

25 Hilton Theatre

After years of neglect, two classic theaters—the **Lyric** (vintage 1903) and the **Apollo** (1920)—were resurrected in 1998 as a single 1,830-seat state-of-the-art complex. (Initially named the Ford Center for the Performing Arts, it was rebranded as the Hilton in 2005.) Much of the original ornate plasterwork found in both theaters was carefully restored, their distinctive yet complementary styles subtly "blended" by architectural team **Beyer Blinder Belle.** The debut production here was *Ragtime*; a revival of *42nd Street* had a good run in the early 2000s. ♦ 213 W 42nd St (between Seventh and Eighth Aves). Ticketmaster 307.4100

25 New Victory Theater

New York's oldest active theater was built in 1900 by Oscar Hammerstein as part of his plan to establish 42nd Street as the booming city's new theater district. Created by **J.B. McElfatrick and Sons**, the small gem's impressive interior boasted a large dome with plaster angels around its rim. Over the years productions here have run the gamut, from legit theater to burlesque shows to second-run and XXX films. In 1995, after an extensive restoration (by **Hardy Holzman Pfeiffer Associates**), the New Vic reemerged to herald the "New 42nd Street." Much of the original interior, including that beautiful dome, remains intact, as does the grand Venetian staircase. Family-oriented productions—including jugglers and clowns, classical ballet and modern dance, puppet shows, and films—are offered from fall through spring. **The Flying Karamozov Brothers**, **Le Carrousel Theatre Company**, and **Children's Television Workshop** are just a few of the headliners to be seen here. Note: the theater is usually dark in summer. ♦ 209 W 42nd St (between Seventh and Eighth Aves). Information: 646/223.3020; Tickets: 646/233.3010. www.newvictory.org ♿

126 New Amsterdam Theatre

Disney's much-heralded 1997 renovation of this 1903 showplace—originally designed by **Henry B. Herts** and **Hugh Tallant**—reflects the architectural talents of **Hardy Holtzman Pfeiffer Associates**, who restored and refurbished the elaborate interior to its original splendor, replete with ornate Art Nouveau-style flora and fauna. While it retains the best of its turn-of-the-century grandeur, the 1,750-seat landmark also sports a superb high-tech sound system. The New Amsterdam is now dedicated to Disney theatrical productions; *Mary Poppins* dropped in when *The Lion King* moved on. ♦ 214 W 42nd St (between Seventh and Eighth Aves). Ticketmaster 307.4100

127 Times Square

In April 1904, almost a year before the *New York Times* moved into what had been called Longacre Square, the mayor and the board of aldermen passed a resolution naming the area, bounded by Broadway, Seventh Avenue, and West 42nd and West 47th Streets, after the newspaper. It quickly became known as "The Crossroads of the World," partly in deference to the *Times,* which certainly could claim that title. Today, it is the heart of the Theater District and the site of some of the most spectacular electric advertising signs ever created. The square is one of a series of open spaces created by Broadway's diagonal cut across the north-south avenues, in this case Seventh Avenue. Standing at the base of the old Times tower and looking uptown, Broadway comes into the square on your right and leaves it on your left, having crossed Seventh Avenue at the intersection of West 45th Street. ♦ Bounded by Broadway and Seventh Ave, and W 42nd and W 47th Sts

127 1 Times Square

When this building was under construction as headquarters for the *New York Times,* even the *Times*'s arch rival, the *Herald,* grudgingly ran a story under the headline "Deepest Hole in New York a Broadway Spectacle," which said that the new Times tower was the most interesting engineering feat to be seen anywhere on Manhattan Island. The newspaper's pressroom was in the tower's basement, but because the building was being constructed over the city's biggest subway station, the basement had to be blasted out of solid rock 55 feet down. Designed by **Eidlitz & MacKenzie**, it was completed just in time for the last breath of 1904, on New Year's Eve. A fireworks display marked that first year, but 1907 saw the first dropping of a lighted ball down the flagpole on the roof. Aside from the period during World War II when blackout restrictions were in effect, the ball—ever more dazzling—has made the trip every year since. The Times vacated in 1913 (see page 170), then sold the building to Allied Chemical Co. in 1966; they replaced its original Italian Renaissance terra-cotta surface with marble. The 25-story former Times tower, though only about one-half the height of the skyscrapers that now surround it, still stands out. After it changed hands again in 1996, its current owners converted it from office space to use as a dedicated sign tower, juicing up its historic "zipper" news banner and leasing space for the giant ads that now slather its façade. ♦ W 42nd St (between Broadway and Seventh Ave)

127 Reuters and Condé Nast Buildings

Stand on 42nd Street between Broadway and Seventh Avenue and look up. How many buildings can you find? Believe it or not, you're looking at just *two* multifaceted, multimedia towers housing two media empires. As part of the ominous-sounding Times Square Master Plan for developing the district, architects **Fox & Fowle**—known for fitting form to context—distilled the chaotic energy of the "crossroads of the world" into exuberant, eco-friendly designs that present a different façade from almost every angle. The 2001 Reuters Building (3 Times Square), on the west corner of Seventh Avenue, alternates granite and terra-cotta with huge LED displays, a soaring glass curtain wall, and a colorful subway-entrance marquee that makes taking the A train feel like the piece of underground theater it is. The 48-story dynamically spired Condé Nast Building (4 Times Square), completed in 1999, anchors the east side of Broadway with eye-popping street-level signage, and businesslike dressed stone fronting its 42nd Street entrance. NASDAQ's ticker steals the show on No. 4's West 43rd Street façade at Broadway. ♦ Reuters, 3 Times Sq (W 42nd St, between Seventh and Eighth Aves); Condé Nast, 4 Times Sq (W 42nd St between Broadway and Sixth Ave)

128 World Yacht Cruises

★★$$$$ This five-yacht fleet offers romant[ic] year-round dinner cruises—including dancing—around New York harbor. The food (four courses, usually featuring a choice of salmon or beef entrée) is good; the scenery [is] better. ♦ Continental ♦ Daily, dinner. Reservations required; jacket required. Pier 81, 12th Ave (just south of W 42nd St). 630.8100

129 Cupcake Cafe

Laden with buttercream in fancifully colore[d] floral designs, the cakes that loyal customers flock here for may be considere[d] works of art. They moved (as Casa Cupcake[)] to far-less-funky digs than their original aluminum-clad spot two blocks south, but the flavors are as fab as ever: try lemon poppy cake, or chocolate, or carrot, topped with mocha, maple, orange, or vanilla crea[m]. Wedding and birthday cakes are specialties. There's a bit of seating at both locations, and a good cup of joe to go with your cake. ♦ Daily. 545 Ninth Ave (between W 40th and W 41st Sts). 465.1530. Also at **Books of Wonder**, 18 W 18th St (between Fifth an[d] Sixth Aves)

130 Port Authority Bus Terminal

Erected in 1950, the terminal was expande[d] in 1963 and again in 1982 by the **Port Authority Design Staff**. Actually two terminal buildings, "North" and "South," th[is] is the largest and busiest bus depot in the world, with three levels of platforms serving

The South Street Seaport Museum is home to the nation's largest private collection of historic vessels.

all of New York's long-distance bus lines and most of the commuter buses between New York and the New Jersey suburbs. A special section in the North building side also serves all three metropolitan airports. For people who prefer driving into Manhattan but not through it, a rooftop parking garage connects directly by ramp to the Lincoln Tunnel. As in any major transportation hub, exercise caution inside the terminal: be aware of your belongings at all times, and avoid isolated areas. ♦ Daily, 24 hours. Bounded by Eighth and Ninth Aves, and W 40th and W 42nd Sts. Main entrances are on Eighth Ave. Bus info: www.panyni.gov ♿ 564.8484

31 The *New York Times* Building

Architect **Renzo Piano** (Morgan Library re-do) adds another New York credit to his eclectic roster with this 52-story transparent glass tower, replete with high-tech shading system. The *New York Times* took possession in 2007; it is their first custom-built headquarters since they outgrew their original Times Square tower in the early 1900s (see page 170). The lobby is open to the public during business hours, M-F. ♦ 620 Eighth Ave (between W 40th and W 41st Sts)

The Drama Book Shop
Since 1923

32 Drama Book Shop

Established in 1923, this is one of the city's most comprehensive sources of books on the dramatic arts (the **Library of Performing Arts** at **Lincoln Center** is another; the sadly demised **Applause Book Theatre and Cinema Books** uptown was yet another). Subject areas include domestic and foreign theater, performers, music, dance, makeup, lighting, props, staging, and even puppetry and magic. ♦ Daily. 250 W 40th St (between Seventh and Eighth Aves). 944.0595. www.dramabookshop.com ♿

133 Lincoln Tunnel

The unusual three-tube tunnel, which is 1.5 miles long and 97 feet below the Hudson River, connects Manhattan with Weehawken, New Jersey; and more than 36 million vehicles use it every year. The 8,216-foot center tube was the first to be built. **Aymar Embury II** was the architect; **Ole Singstad** completed the engineering in 1937. It was joined by the 7,482-foot north tube in 1945, and the 8,006-foot south tube in 1957. Entrances (on the Manhattan side) are accessed from Dyer Ave, between Ninth and 10th Aves, from W 35th through W 40th Sts.

134 Hell's Kitchen Flea Market

Once upon a time (from the 1870s to the late 1930s), **Paddy's Market** found a home here, then resounding with the cacophony of the Ninth Avenue El running overhead. In 2003, Alan Boss—founder of the renowned and now defunct 26th Street Annex Flea Market—got city permission to close the block once again to weekend traffic. So now on Saturdays and Sundays year round you'll find a wondrous gamut of some 200 vendors selling goods from quality antiques to fresh farm products, vintage fabrics, doorknobs, aged periodicals, and all sorts of other stuff with eminent browse quality guaranteed to keep any urban archeologist happy. For a nominal fee, shuttle service is available between current locations. ♦ Sa, Su. W 39th St (between Ninth and 10th Aves). 243.5343. www.hellskitchenfleamarket.com ♿. Also at "Garage": 112 W 25th St (between Sixth and Seventh Aves); and 29-37 W 25th St (between Fifth and Sixth Aves)

The Ziegfeld Follies, the most beloved and long-lived of Broadway's musical revues, originated in Paris with the Follies of 1907 (patterned after the French Folies Bergère of the late 19th century). The Broadway extravaganza was named after its famed American producer, Florenz Ziegfeld Jr.

MIDTOWN

A sense of power pervades Midtown, the heart of Manhattan. Giant high-rises sta shoulder to shoulder, creating solid walls of concrete and glass that seem stretch to the sky. The area's weighty importance begins with a concentration of offi buildings around Grand Central Terminal; it extends beyond Rockefeller Center to t

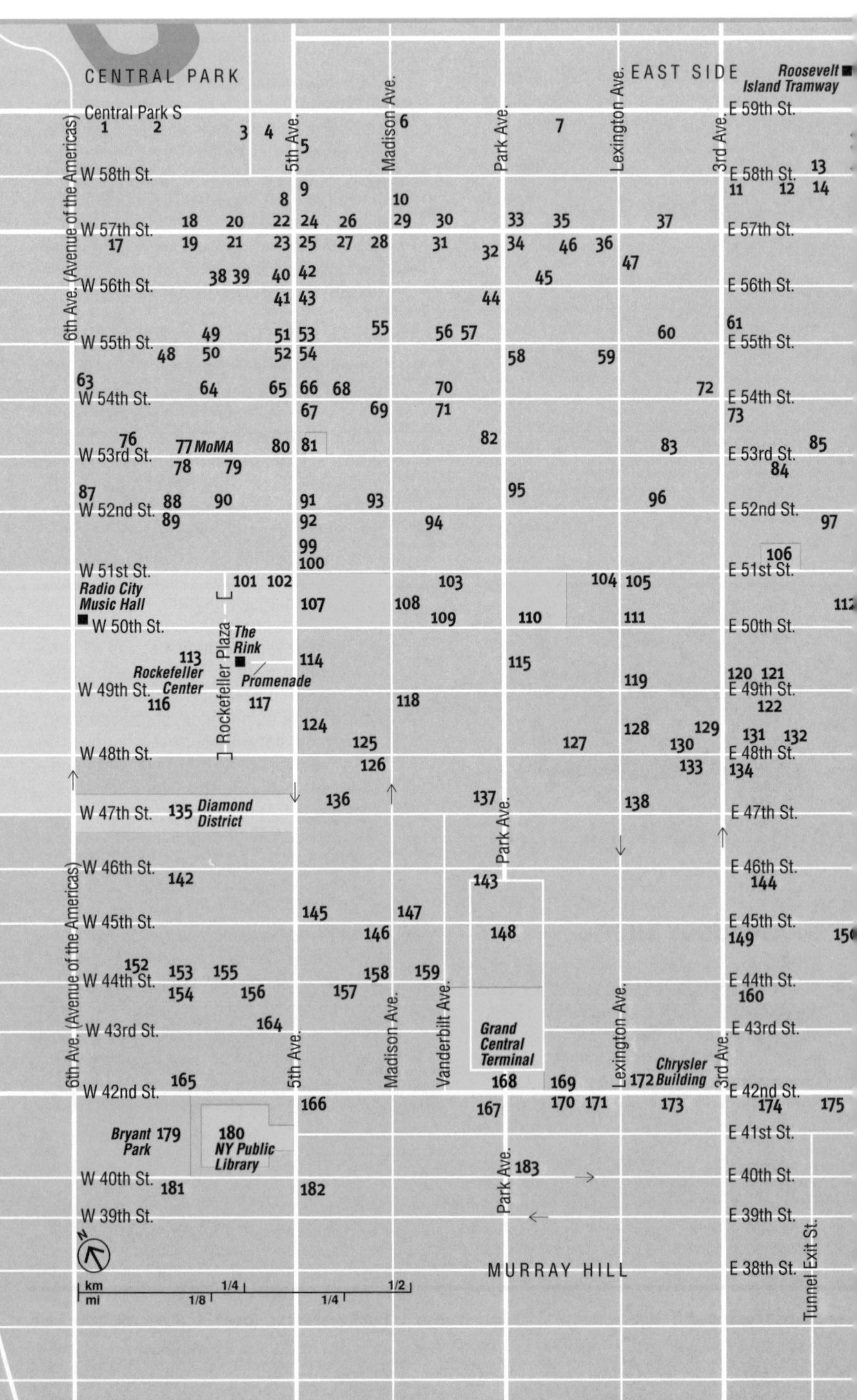

west, encompasses the headquarters of the United Nations to the east, and continues north to Central Park. The magnificent **Chrysler Building** soars here, as does the sheared-roof **Citigroup** building. On Fifth Avenue, the tote of choice is more often a classy shopping bag than a briefcase. The street is home to some of the world's most exclusive stores, including Cartier, the Romanesque Tiffany, and Bergdorf Goodman. Also within Midtown's boundaries (roughly 40th and 59th Streets, the East River, and Sixth Avenue) are world-class hotels (The Plaza, The Waldorf-Astoria, the Four Seasons, The Pierre, and The St. Regis), the many art galleries of East and West 57th Street, the monumental **New York Public Library,** beautiful **Bryant Park, Rockefeller Center,** and the incomparable Museum of Modern Art.

It's a good bet that 90 percent of the people who jam Midtown's streets live elsewhere. But the area is, infact, seriously residential. The possibilities include the huge **Tudor City** complex on First Avenue, across from the UN; **Turtle Bay,** with its blocks of brownstone houses in the 50s east of **Third Avenue**; and dozens of prewar apartment buildings standing proud throughout. **Beekman Place,** two blocks of town houses between the East River and **First Avenue,** is a hidden treasure. Ritzy **Sutton Place,** a longer residential street above **East 53rd Street** along the river, was part of a plan for English-style houses for the well-to-do developed in 1875 by Effingham B. Sutton. Morgans, Vanderbilts, and Phippses, among other notables, lived here.

But it wasn't always that way. When Sutton Place was built, it was in wild territory overlooking what was then called **Blackwell's Island** (now **Roosevelt Island**) in the East River, where the city maintained an almshouse, workhouse, prison, and insane asylum. Although a horsecar line ran along Second Avenue between Fulton and 129th Streets, Sutton's riverfront property was a long way from the mainstream. The neighborhood didn't become "acceptable" until J.P. Morgan's daughter moved here in 1921.

Before then, society folk generally stayed west of Park Avenue. In fact, in the 19th century anyone who suggested that **Fourth Avenue** would one day be called **Park Avenue** would have been laughed out of the city. In 1832, a railroad line was built in the center of the dirt road, and steam trains huffed and puffed their way in and out of New York past squatters' shacks with goats in the front yards and pigs out back.

Little by little, roofs were constructed over the tracks, but it wasn't until the present Grand Central Terminal was designed in 1903 that anything was done about covering the railroad yards that had grown up between **Lexington** and **Madison Avenues** from **East 42nd** to **East 45th Streets**. When the UN moved into the area in 1947, the cattle pens disappeared and **Midtown East** became a neighborhood in its own right.

From the day Fifth Avenue was established in 1837, the rich and famous began to arrive. Railroad tycoon Jay Gould was one of the first. He built a mansion at **47th Street** and Fifth Avenue and began taking important friends like Russell Sage, Morton F. Plant, and William H. Vanderbilt to business dinners at the nearby **Windsor Hotel.**

By the late 1800s, Vanderbilt had built three mansions on the west side of Fifth Avenue at 51st Street. His son, William K. Vanderbilt, built a fourth palace a few doors uptown. Another son, Cornelius II, tried to upstage them with an even grander house at 58th Street. In their quest to outdo one another, they ended once and for all the idea of the traditional New York row house with a brownstone front. Today, only a few reminders of the 19th-century mansions remain on Fifth Avenue, including two that house Cartier and Versace at East 52nd Street.

Except for the polychrome-domed St. Bartholomew's Church, the Deco-lite Waldorf-Astoria Hotel, and a few other notable holdouts, Park Avenue in this area of Midtown is now wall-to-wall office buildings, including important examples of the "glass box" genre built in the 1950s: the **Seagram Building** by **Ludwig Mies van der Rohe** and **Philip Johnson**, and **Lever House** by **Gordon Bunshaft** of **Skidmore, Owings & Merrill.** On Park Avenue north of East 59th Street, things turn decidedly residential.

Impressive office buildings and complexes on the other avenues range from the 19 buildings that comprise the Art Deco–period Rockefeller Center to the contemporary **Olympic Tower** and the **Sony** and **IBM** buildings. Madison Avenue above East 50th Street has seen an office-building boom, but it's Third Avenue in the 20-block strip from **39th Street** to 59th Street that has had the most sustained growth.

Houses of worship sprinkled throughout Midtown—including such landmarks as the modified French Gothic **St. Patrick's Cathedral,** the Moorish Revival **Central Synagogue,** and modern **St. Peter's Lutheran Church**—moderate the area's form and scale and contribute to its purpose. Secular monuments do as well, including of course, **Grand Central Terminal,** which was saved after a long citizens' battle spearheaded by the late Jacqueline Onassis.

And, unexpected pockets of distinctive apartment buildings and townhouses—often with a bit of streetside landscaping—continue to cling to the side streets of Midtown. In combination with small "pocket" parks such as Greenacre and Paley, they bring greenery and human scale to what at first glance might seem to be a solid concentration of masonry.

An incomparably vibrant mix, Midtown is the area where New York's strength and energy is most broadly displayed.

THE BEST

Chuck Scarborough

Broadcast journalist, NBC

'21.' When you visit this venerable old New York dining institution, be certain to ask the maître d' to give you a tour of the old Prohibition-era wine cellar. It was so cleverly hidden that the Feds never successfully raided '21' during Prohibition. Once you are shown the astonishing secret entrance, you will be allowed to browse through one of New York's most extensive wine collections, complete with the private stock of the rich and famous—past and present.

1 The Ritz-Carlton, Central Park

$$$$ In 2002, The Ritz came back to Central Park South, this time in the gloriously refurbished former **St. Moritz** hotel. Architect **Emery Roth** designed this landmark 33-story building in 1931; interior designer Frank Nicholson is responsible for the luxurious, historically sympathetic redo that increased the size of each room, for 277 rooms in all. The expected Ritz opulence is well represented in the soothing color palette, rich fabrics and Frette linens, original paintings (by American modernist Samuel Halpert), austere quiet, ultramodern technology, and the bounty of services—like Burberry raincoats for guests... and their pet dogs; in-room telescopes for viewing Central Park; a shopping limo and the on-site **La Prairie Spa.** The intimate **Star Lounge** with "New York Treasure" bartender Norman Bukofzer and chef Laurent Tourondel's **BLT Market** further enhance the elegant ambience. ♦ 50 Central Park South (between Fifth and Sixth Aves). 308.9100, 800/241.3333; fax 207.8831. Also at 2 West St (at Battery Pl). 344.0800. www.ritzcarlton.com

2 Mickey Mantle's

★$$ It's not surprising that sports fans of all ages love this place. They get to watch the day's big game or memorable moments in sports history on huge video screens, and they can study the restaurant's collection of uniforms and memorabilia. The basic American fare—gigantic burgers, ribs, hot-fudge sundaes—should please not-too-picky eaters; it's certainly a lot better than ballpark franks. ♦ American ♦ Daily, lunch and dinner. 42 Central Park S (between Fifth and Sixth Aves). 688.7777

2 Helmsley Park Lane Hotel

$$$ Designed by **Emery Roth and Sons** in 1971, this 46-story building has arches at the top that add interest to the block. Helmsley-empire developers Leona and hubby Harry Helmsley once picked this as their own home address. Its some 600 rooms are decorated in the grand European style—gilt, floral and striped prints, marble, and chandeliers abound—and the multilingual staff is eager to please. You can expect high-speed Internet access, plasma TVs, a well-equipped fitness center, and an international newsstand; and as long as your pooch (no kitties allowed) weighs less than 10 pounds, he or she is welcome too. In-hotel dining options include the **Room with a View** restaurant and the seasonal **Garden Court Café.** ♦ 36 Central Park S (between Fifth and Sixth Aves). 371.4000, 800/221.4982; fax 319.9065. www.helmsleyhotels.com

3 The Plaza Hotel

$$$$ Saved from total conversion to condos, this gloriously restored grande dame happily reopened in time for its centennial anniversary in fall 2007. The Plaza is a legend in its own time, a landmark that has hosted Teddy Roosevelt, the Beatles, and F. Scott Fitzgerald and his wife, Zelda (who, it's rumored, danced nude in the fountain out front). Solomon R. Guggenheim lived for years in the **State Suite** surrounded by fabulous paintings, and Frank Lloyd Wright made The Plaza his New York headquarters. The stylish Edwardian/French building dating from 1907 is considered one of architect **Henry J. Hardenbergh**'s masterpieces (he also did the **Dakota** apartments). **Warren & Wetmore** oversaw the 1921 addition. Located on a unique site with two sides of the building equally exposed, the dignified hotel has survived many years as the center of high social activity. With this latest development, part of The Plaza has been converted to exclusive private residences (182 of them); 282 amenity-laden Fairmont-run hotel rooms and suites comprise the public accommodations quota (about half of these are actually part-year owner-occupied "pied-à-terre" residences, but that won't be apparent to the guests who hang their hats there during the rest of the year). The elegant dining options endure (needless to say, the Midas wand has been passed over these as well): **The Oak Room** (woody, elegant, and

comfortable); the **Oyster Bar** with its sparkling fresh clams and oysters to order; the venerable, paneled **Edwardian Room**—always a fashionable spot for dining and dancing; and the fabled **Palm Court** in the lobby, particularly as a choice for tea. Look up for a surprise here: during renovation, workers discovered remnants of a stained-glass "laylight," or interior skylight; the developers promptly popped for the bucks to re-create this now lovely and luminous transparent ceiling. Of course, there's more: luxury shops, a spa, a lushly landscaped interior-courtyard garden, and a grand new entrance lobby on the West 58th Street side await. ♦ E 58th St (between Fifth and Sixth Aves). www.plazahotel.com ♿

4 Grand Army Plaza

One of the city's few formal pedestrian spaces, the plaza (bisected by **Central Park South**) acts as both a forecourt to the **Plaza Hotel** to the west and as an entrance terrace to **Central Park** to the north. The southern section is solidly anchored by the circular **Pulitzer Memorial Fountain**, which was built with funds provided in Joseph Pulitzer's will and designed by **Carrère & Hastings**. In 1903 the equestrian statue of *General William Tecumseh Sherman* (by *Augustus Saint-Gaudens*), displayed at the World Exhibition in Paris in 1900, was erected in the northern section of the plaza, where it still stands. Towering over the plaza from across Fifth Avenue is **Edward Durrell Stone** and **Emery Roth**'s 1968 **General Motors Building**.

Tradition survives in the horse-drawn carriages that congregate here. They were the limousines of another era, and in the 1930s, Hollywood loved to send romancing couples off in them for jaunts in Central Park. You can still take a romantic ride through the park in a carriage; many of the carriages still have top-hatted drivers. ♦ Fifth Ave (between W 58th St and Central Park)

5 General Motors Building

You may wonder what this immense and strictly linear tower is doing here, surrounded as it is by Beaux Arts beauties like the **Sherry-Netherland** hotel to the north, **The Plaza** across Fifth Avenue, and the **Bergdorf Men's** shop just to the south. But change is what New York is all about, and the old Savoy Hotel's time was up in 1964 when it was torn down to make way for this 50-story **Edward Durell Stone** (with **Emery Roth & Sons**) monolith. Completed in 1968, the pristinely white-marble-faced structure is set back and cleverly narrower on its Fifth Avenue side, allowing its broader mass to be tucked away on the cross streets. The sunken plaza that filled some of that setback is now covered over, and the two 2-story structures that flank the main building are now occupied by CBS's *Morning Show* in th onetime GM auto showroom, to the north, and **FAO Schwarz** (see below) to the south ♦ 767 Fifth Ave (between E 58th and E 59th Sts)

Also at the General Motors Building:

Apple

That crystal-clear 32-foot cube now sitting on the GM plaza is the entrance to Apple's second retail location in Manhattan. Rumored to have been designed by Steve Jobs himself, it's really quite a sight, particularly as the crowds start to thin and the streetlights come up in the dusky twilight. An echo, in its (much smaller) way of the **Hayden Planetarium**'s dramatically glassed-in space, Apple's presence still fe fresh in this part of town. While complete with Genius Bar and 24-hour service, the subterranean showroom may emphasize different products than the one in SoHo; it best to check ahead. ♦ 24/7. 767 Fifth Av (between E 58th and E 59th Sts). 336.1440. ♿ Also in SoHo at 103 Prince S (at Greene St). 226.3126; and Staten Isla Mall (2655 Richmond Ave, between Platinum Ave and Richmond Hill Rd, Staten Island). 718/477.4180 ♿

FAO Schwarz

Because this is the best-stocked toy store the United States, some parents never bri their kids here; the sight of so many toys c turn children into monsters of greed. The inexhaustible stock includes Madame Alexander dolls, Steiff stuffed animals (everything from parakeets to wallabies), LGB electric trains, outdoor swings, magic tricks, video games, meticulously detailed dollhouses of all sizes (if you're wondering what became of Manhattan Dollhouse in Murray Hill, they now make their home here and hundreds of other amusements. At Christmastime you may have to wait in line just to go inside. ♦ Daily. 767 Fifth Ave (at E 58th St). 644.9400 ♿

6 Baccarat

At the heart of Madison Avenue's "Crystal District" (**Steuben**, **Lalique**, **Daum**, and more are all nearby), Baccarat is more luxurious than ever. This is where to come for world-famous crystal, Limoges china, plus fine glassware and silver and a great expanded jewelry collection. ♦ M-Sa. 625 Madison Ave (at E 59th St). 826.4100

7 Argosy Book Store

Founded in 1925, few places in the United States have a better selection of historical pictures: photographs, posters, playbills, antique maps, engravings, lithographs, etchings, and woodcuts. ♦ M-Sa. 116 E 59th St (between Lexington and Park Aves). 753.4455. www.argosybooks.com

8 Bergdorf Goodman

In the most luxurious of the city's legendary department stores (although there is some moderately priced merchandise), the idea that living well is the best revenge reigns, partly because of the architecture (high ceilings, delicate moldings, arched windows) and partly because of the wares. All the merchandise bears the stamp of luxury, whether it's impeccable clothing from the best European designers or domestic stars Donna Karan and Calvin Klein, the iridescent jewelry of Ted Muehling, the aromatic scents from London's **Penhaligon**, delicate candies from Manon Chocolates, or glove-leather bags by Paloma Picasso. There is also a top-of-the-line beauty salon (**John Barrett**) and a café. Do not miss their Christmas windows—the tableaux are fantastical, the clothing and jewels unforgettable. ♦ Daily. 754 Fifth Ave (between W 57th and W 58th Sts). 753.7300 ♿

9 Bergdorf Goodman Men

According to the department store's chairman, Ira Neimark, this store is "for the sort of men who dine at the best restaurants, stay at the best hotels, and join the best clubs." What do these men wear? Shirts from Turnbull & Asser and Charvet; suits from Zegna and Brioni, Luciana Barbera, and St. Andrews; sportswear from Willis & Geiger. The couture also leans toward the cutting edge with names like Romeo Gigli and Dolce & Gabbana. ♦ Daily. 745 Fifth Ave (at E 58th St). 753.7300 ♿

9 McKee Gallery

This small but very smart gallery boasts an impressive list of youngish artists like sculptor Martin Puryear and painters Sean Scully and Jake Berthot, as well as the estate of the influential artist Philip Guston. ♦ Tu-Sa. 745 Fifth Ave (between E 57th and E 58th Sts), fourth floor. 688.5951. www.mckeegallery.com

9 Forum Gallery

Twentieth-century figurative American paintings and sculpture by names such as William Beckman, Chaim Gross, Odd Nerdum, and Gregory Gillespie are featured in this gallery. ♦ Tu-Sa. 745 Fifth Ave (between E 57th and E 58th Sts), fifth floor. 355.4545. www.forumgallery.com

9 Mary Boone Gallery

A much-publicized upstart among art dealers during the early 1980s heyday of neo-Expressionism, Boone moved here from SoHo in 1996 and has settled into the establishment with a solid roster of American and mid-career European artists. Eric Fischl, David Salle, Barbara Kruger, Jean-Michel Basquiat, and Ross Bleckner are among her successes. ♦ Tu-Sa. 745 Fifth Ave (between E 57th and E 58th Sts), fourth floor. 752.2929. Also at 541 W 24th St (between 10th and 11th Aves). 752.2929. www.maryboonegallery.com

10 Emporio Armani

The Italian designer's complete avant-garde ready-to-wear and couture lines for men and women are now under one roof. If you're hungry (and if you have any money left), ask for a table at the café, staffed by an army of beautiful people (what else?). ♦ M-Sa. 601 Madison Ave (at E 57th St). 317.0800. Also at 410 West Broadway (at Spring St). 646.613.8009 ♿

11 Boyd's Department Store

Long a Madison Avenue institution, Boyd's is now resettled in a three-story glass flagship a block from Bloomingdale's, where you can choose from the same international collection of feather powder puffs, rouges, combs, hair-brushes, and toothbrushes (as well as apparel and accessory offerings) that's supplied legions of well-known women, including Cher and the late Jackie Onassis. ♦ Daily. 968 Third Ave (at E 58th St). 838.6558

12 Dawat

★★★$$$ Actress and cookbook author Madhur Jaffrey is the guiding spirit behind this sophisticated Indian restaurant that's considered one of the best in town. Try *shami kabab* (finely ground lamb patty stuffed with fresh mint), samosas, or home-style *rogan gosh* (pieces of baby goat in a cardamom-flavored sauce). Desserts are first-rate. ♦ Indian ♦ M-Sa, lunch and dinner; Su, dinner. Reservations recommended. 210 E 58th St (between Second and Third Aves). 355.7555

13 Felidia

★★★$$$$ Chef Lidia Bastianich presides over this longstanding family-run restaurant. Two stories of golden yellow and mahogany-paneled walls await. Specialties from Lidia's native Istria (near Trieste) include *stinco di vitello* (roasted veal shank) in its own juices. Pastas are especially good, particularly the *pappardelle* (broad noodles) with porcini, or gnocchi with tomato sauce. The extensive wine list features some of Italy's top labels at equally high prices. ♦ Italian ♦ M-F, lunch and dinner; Sa, dinner. Reservations required; jacket required. 243 E 58th St (between Second and Third Aves). 758.1479

14 Paul Rudolph Foundation

Master architect **Paul Rudolph** died in 1997 leaving behind the Late Modernist gem that now houses this eponymous foundation, established in 2002. Charged with the protection and interpretation of Rudolph's unique work, the foundation occupies the multilevel upper floors that were his residence from 1989, when construction began, up until his death. The narrow structure, with its transparent façade hiding nothing from passersby, is a fine study in Rudolph 101. Once inside, his remarkable ability to break space into a complex of interlocking planes—a short flight of stairs here, another level-break there—makes movement through it more than a bit disconcerting, but the real trickery is that each functional space is its own oasis of calm. Painted almost entirely white inside, his personal assemblages of found objects—an army of white plastic robots and another of Moroccan textile combs among them—provide some of the few points of color. Rudolph's fine sense of lighting is apparent throughout, extending to the retail shop, **Modulightor**, on the ground floor. Custom spins on Rudolph's original work along with reproductions are available here. ♦ Call for open house and tour information. Modulightor: M-Sa. 246 E 58th St (between Second and Third Aves). 371.0336. www.paulrudolph.org, www.modulightor.com

15 Rosa Mexicano

★★★$$$ Forget about tacos and enchiladas; you won't miss them, because in their stead are complex regional dishes—platters of fresh seafood, *carnitas* (barbecued pork), shrimp in mustard-chili vinaigrette, and chicken wrapped in parchment. Be sure to sample the guacamole prepared tableside—and spiced to your pleasure. The frozen margaritas aren't bad, either. ♦ Mexican ♦ Daily, dinner. Reservations recommended. 1063 First Ave (at E 58th St). 753.7407. Also at 61 Columbus Ave (at W 62nd St). 977.7700; 9 E 18th St (between Fifth Ave and Broadway). 533.3350

16 Casa la Femme North

★★$$ While its "South" (SoHo) location is gone, this standby still defines sheik chic with tents straight out of an Arabian Nights fantasy and nightly gyrations by a belly dancer. The gauzy, rather gimmicky tents a available by special request; otherwise yo be seated more conventionally, and perha more comfortably, at an ordinary table or semicircular booth. Either way, you'll dine like a sultan on seriously fresh, well-executed Middle Eastern specialties. Popu appetizers include Egyptian grape leaves and *tamaya*, sautéed chickpea dumplings with fava beans and coriander, while don't miss entrées include succulent grilled chicken seasoned with sumac and oregan for dessert, go with the outstanding bakla ♦ Egyptian. ♦ Daily, dinner. 1076 First Ave (between E 58th and E 59th Sts). 505.00

17 Marlborough Gallery

One of New York's old-line establishments represents important names in European ar American art, including Red Grooms, Beverl Pepper, Richard Estes, Tom Otterness, and Magdalena Abakanowicz. ♦ M-Sa. 40 W 57 St (between Fifth and Sixth Aves), second floor. 541.4900. Also at 545 W 25th St (between 10th and 11th Aves). 463.8634. www.marlboroughgallery.com ♿

18 Rizzoli Bookstore

The ultimate bookstore, this is reminiscent an oak-paneled library in an opulent Italia villa, with classical music playing (CDs are for sale) and a hushed, unhurried atmosphere. Known for foreign-language, travel, art, architecture, and design books, the store also has an outstanding foreign and domestic general-interest and design periodical department. The building dates from the turn of the century, and was restored in 1985 by **Hardy Holzman Pfeiff Associates**. ♦ Daily. 31 W 57th St (betwe Fifth and Sixth Aves). 759.2424. www.rizzoliusa.com

19 J.N. Bartfield Galleries & Books

Nineteenth-century American and Europea art, including works by Remington, Russell and other masters of the American West, a displayed here, along with elegantly bounc antiquarian books by classic authors such Shakespeare and Dickens. ♦ M-Sa. 30 W 57th St (between Fifth and Sixth Aves), th floor. 245.8890. www.bartfield.com ♿

19 Marian Goodman Gallery

This gallery's stark but generous space is devoted to a host of weighty mostly impor talents, including the German painter Anse Kiefer and British sculptor Tony Cragg, as well as Gerhard Richter, Chantal Akerman, and Jeff Wall. Don't miss the gallery's publications display area. ♦ M-Sa, M-F in summer. 24 W 57th St (between Fifth and Sixth Aves), fourth floor. 977.7160. www.mariangoodman.com ♿

20 Addison on Madison

Subdued yet interesting men's shirts of fine single- and two-ply Egyptian cotton are offered in appealing, gentle stripes and checks, with a few bolder stripes; there is a good selection of ties to go with them. Addison is also a destination for custom-made shirts. Cut in the classic American style, as are the ready-mades, there are over 500 high-quality fabrics and patterns to select from. ♦ M-F. 29 W 57th St (between Fifth and Sixth Aves), ninth floor. 308.2660

21 Laurence Miller Gallery

Rotating works by important names in photography such as Helen Levitt, Eugène Atget, Duane Hanson, and Les Krims hang in this gallery beside those of younger shutterbugs, all chosen with Miller's customary discretion. ♦ Tu-Sa. 20 W 57th St (between Fifth and Sixth Aves). 397.3930. www.laurencemillergallery.com

21 MacKenzie-Childs

This purveyor of high-end home accessories is no place for the minimalist-minded. Designed and decorated with objets such as lamps, boxes, and frames that are hand-painted with spots, checks, stripes, and flowers, the charming street-level store is supplied by artisan workshops in upstate New York. Hand-painted dinnerware in myriad designs and mix-and-match possibilities is a particular strength. ♦ Daily. 14 West 57th St (between Fifth and Sixth Aves). 570.6050

22 Van Cleef & Arpels

When the late Shah of Iran needed a tiara made for his Empress Farah, he came here. The boutique department, where jewelry ranges from moderate to expensive, is actually in Bergdorf's main store next door, while gemstones that cost more are sold here. Jewelry can be custom-designed. Estate jewelry is also bought and sold. The guard is formidable, but the salespeople at least deign to acknowledge customers who make it past him. ♦ M-Sa. 744 Fifth Ave (at W 57th St). 644.9500 ♿

23 The Crown Building

At 26 stories, this was once the tallest building on Fifth Avenue above 42nd Street. Originally called the **Heckscher Building**, it was designed by **Warren & Wetmore** and built in 1922 as a wholesale center for women's fashions. In 1929, the **Museum of Modern Art** opened its first gallery here. The gold leaf on the façade and tower is late 20th century, as is the lighting of this entire intersection. ♦ 730 Fifth Ave (at W 57th St)

23 Bulgari

Elegantly nestled on the corner of one of the world's most expensive per-commercial-square-foot intersections is this three-story temple to the Rome-based jeweler of the privileged. Bold mountings offset the precious stones of vibrant colors for which this generations-old house is renowned. The intricate workmanship of some pieces is often an engineering and artisanal feat. ♦ Daily. 730 Fifth Ave (at W 57th St). 315.9000. Also at 783 Madison Ave (between 66th and 67th Sts). 717.2300

24 Burberrys

This rejuvenated stalwart has met great success with its more colorful—and *way* less staid—designs. Their classic raincoat has always possessed an incomparable style, but now the rest of the clothes for men and women—including hats, coats, jackets, trousers, and skirts—also appeal to a more adventurous clientele. ♦ Daily. 9 E 57th St (between Madison and Fifth Aves). 371.5010. ♿ Also at 131 Spring St (between Greene and Wooster Sts). 925.9300

24 Louis Vuitton

While Louis Vuitton corporate carries on in that striking glass tower down the block at 49 E 57th Street, Vuitton's retail flagship is here at the corner of Fifth. A big glassy cube itself, Marc Jacobs's modern ready-to-wear for men and women, along with watches, jewelry, and the luxe luggage and leather accessories adorned with that trademark LV signature, fill the store. ♦ Daily. 1 E 57th St (at Fifth Ave). 758.8877. Also at 116 Greene St (between Prince and Spring Sts). 274.9090 ♿

25 Tiffany & Co.

Built in 1940 by **Cross & Cross**, this store is so famous for quality and style that many of its well-designed wares have become classics, such as the all-purpose wineglass and Wedgwood china. Given as gifts, these items are further enhanced by the cachet of the signature light-blue box. In addition to table appointments, the store boasts a selection of fine jewelry, gems, stationery items, crystal, clocks, and watches in all price ranges. Salespeople are friendly and helpful. The window displays are worth going out of your way to see—especially at Christmas. ♦ Daily. 727 Fifth Ave (at E 57th St). 755.8000. Also at 37 Wall St (between Broad and Nassau Sts).

Christian Dior
PARIS

26 Christian Dior/Dior Homme

Mais oui, the complete haute couture and ready-to-wear collections. For women, John Galliano continues his rule as the designer du jour; for men, it's Hedi Slimane. ♦ Daily. Dior: 21 E 57th St (between Madison and Fifth Aves). 931.2950; Dior Homme: 17 E 57th St (between Madison and Fifth Aves). 421.6009

26 Chanel Boutique

This spacious world-class boutique showcases the increasingly popular Chanel fashions and accessories. The scent of Coco remains, but it is Karl "the Kaiser" Lagerfeld who now calls the sartorial shots from his Paris atelier. At the Madison Avenue location you'll find jewelry, bags, and shoes only. Super-hairstylist **Frederic Fekkai** maintains his salon on the fifth through ninth floors. ♦ M-Sa. 15 E 57th St (between Madison and Fifth Aves). 355.5050. ♿. Also at 733 Madison Ave (at E 64th St). 535.5828; 139 Spring St (between Greene and Wooster Sts). 334.0055

27 NikeTown

On a street with some of the most exclusive names in retailing, this cool five-story neo-1930s Italian-fronted building is what some consider the best entertainment in town. Everything you could possibly want in the way of athletic gear can be found here. From the amusing turnstile entrance on the street level to the rooftop garden, this is as much a high-tech amusement park as it is a merchandise mart. There are tons of sports memorabilia, interactive displays, big-screen videos, and an overall feeling of fun. Of course, buying is the real name of the game, and the store never lets you forget why you came here: Footwear is displayed on racks in a way that gives it the importance of fine art, and the brightly colored clothing catches the eye faster than a Michael Jordan slam-dunk once did. ♦ Daily. 6 E 57th St (between Madison and Fifth Aves). 891.6453

> The task of cleaning Rockefeller Center's rentable area of 15,000,000 square feet is equivalent to cleaning almost 11,000 six-room apartments. Some 65,000 people work in Rockefeller-built or operated buildings daily, and approximately 175,000 visit each day for business or pleasure, giving it a daily population of 240,000. Only 60 cities in the US exceed this total.

28 IBM Building

This 43-story sharply faceted black granite building, designed in 1982 by **Edward Larrabee Barnes**, rises dramatically over a high atrium containing a snack kiosk and tables and chairs for relaxing. Occasional art shows—usually of large-scale modern sculptures—help take your mind off Midtown's hectic pace. Now owned by a multinational corporation headed by developer and art collector Edward J. Minskoff, the building houses many private companies. IBM's former showroom space is currently **Tourneau Time Machine** (Daily. 12 E 57th St, between Madison and Fifth Aves. 758.7300), the watchmaker's flagship location. ♦ IBM: 590 Madison Ave (at E 57th St); enter the atrium from Madison Ave (at E 56th St)

Within the IBM building:

Dahesh Museum of Art

Set below street level (in the former Newseum space), this museum is dedicated to showing the lesser-known academic art of the 19th century. Along with a growing appreciation of this art form, the Dahesh gift shop and **Café Opaline** (daily. 521.8155) are proven crowd-pleasers. Admission. Closed Monday. Tu-Su, 11AM-6PM. 580 Madison Ave (between E 56th and E 57th Sts). 759.0606. www.daheshmuseum.org

29 Coach

Lovers of leather (not to mention tweed, suede, bouclé, and nylon) won't want to miss this affordable-luxe flagship carved into the corner of the spectacular Fuller Building (see below). Remodeled and expanded in 2005 to be the largest store in the Coach chain, it's the place to find bags, belts, briefcases, men's and women's shoes, accessories, and outerwear, plus, of course, wallets to replace the one you're wearing out. ♦ Daily. 595 Madison Ave (at E 57th St). 754.0041. Also at other locations throughout the city

29 Fuller Building

The identification over the entrance of this landmark black-and-white Art Deco tower, designed in 1929 by **Walker & Gillette**, is graced by a pair of figures by sculptor Elie Nadelman. The building is home to many art galleries, including the Zabriskie (fourth

THE BEST

Daniel Boulud

Chef and Owner, Daniel

The **Union Square Greenmarket** as it comes to life in springtime.

Pizza from the wood-burning oven at **Bella Blu** (Lexington and 70th St). My daughter's favorite! Sushi at **Nobu**.

Boxing matches at **Madison Square Garden**.

Men's shirts from the boutique **Sean** in SoHo.

floor, 752.1223), Peter Findlay (eighth floor, 644.4433), James Goodman (eighth floor, 593.3737), and Alexandre (13th floor, 755.2828). ♦ 41 E 57th St (at Madison Ave)

30 Four Seasons Hotel

$$$$ This 52-story (plus tower) world-class hotel was designed by **I.M. Pei.** The sparse limestone lobby with its 33-foot onyx ceiling and serene public areas has been compared to a soaring marble mausoleum, cool and Zen-like in its simplicity. But the 370 elegant and spacious (600-square-foot) rooms are considerably cozier and warmer, with Art Deco–influenced décor and wonderful views of the city and **Central Park**. Services befitting such a deluxe operation include 24-hour concierge, well-equipped fitness facilities, an executive business center, and a contemporary American grill/restaurant serving breakfast, lunch, and dinner. If you're not content with your room's 120-square-foot bathroom, look into the heart-stopping $7,000-a-night **Presidential Suite**. **L'Atelier de Joël Robuchon** is the much-lauded "New French" restaurant in residence (Reservations recommended. Daily, lunch and dinner. 350.6658). ♦ 57 E 57th St (between Park and Madison Aves). 758.5700, 800/332.3442; fax 758.5711. www.fourseasonshotel.com ♿

31 PaceWildenstein

Among the heaviest of the city's heavy hitters, this gallery represents a formidable roster of artists and artists' estates, including Jim Dine, Chuck Close, Louise Nevelson, Mark Rothko, and Lucas Samaras. Housed in the same building are the gallery's many offspring—**Pace Prints** (421.3237), **Pace Primitive** (421.3688), and **Pace/MacGill Gallery** (759.7999) for 20th-century photography. ♦ Tu-Sa. 32 E 57th St (between Park and Madison Aves), second floor. 421.3292. Also at 545 W 22nd St (between 10th and 11th Aves). 989.4263. www.pacewildenstein.com ♿

31 Buccellati

Italy's most opulent handcrafted silver, including flatware, is sold in this somewhat intimidating but appropriately elegant store. ♦ M-Sa. 46 E 57th St (between Park and Madison Aves). 308.2900

32 Suarez

High-end designer bags—most of them European and all top-of-the-line—at 20 percent (and more) below standard retail are the specialty of this well-stocked and smartly laid-out boutique. Some familiar labels are offered, but most of them are the "big names" without the logos. This is a store for people who care more about quality than status. The staff has its priorities in place, too; they are consistently friendly and helpful. ♦ M-Sa. 5 W 56th St (between Fifth and Sixth Aves) 315.3870

33 Ritz Tower

Emery Roth and **Carrère & Hastings** built this 42-story tower in 1925 as part of the Hearst apartment-hotel chain. Its stepped spire is still a distinctive mark in the skyline. ♦ 465 Park Ave (at E 57th St)

34 445 Park Avenue

Built just prior to the advent of glass curtain-wall construction, this 1947 structure—the former Universal Pictures building—by **Kahn & Jacobs** is noteworthy as the first office building on this previously residential section of Park Avenue and as the first to be built to the "wedding cake" outline of the then-current zoning regulations. ♦ 445 Park Ave (between E 56th and E 57th Sts)

Since 1931, the Rockefeller Center Christmas tree has been one of New York City's most beloved traditions. Today, the chosen tree is decorated with more than 27,000 7.5-watt, multicolored bulbs on five miles of wire. Sitting atop the tree is the 45-inch plastic star that has been used for more than four decades. It takes 15 to 20 people and an 80-ton crane to erect and move the tree. Since 1971, all trees have been recycled: The mulch has been used for trails at a Boy Scout camp in New Jersey.

35 The Galleria

This midblock tower, designed in 1975 chiefly by **David Kenneth Specter** and **Philip Birnbaum**, comprises luxury apartments above a health club, retail facilities, and a public through-block arcade. Also worthwhile is the individualistic silhouette created by a multigreenhouse quadriplex (considered one of Manhattan's most expensive apartments) custom-built for philanthropist Stewart Mott. Apparently Mott had such a passion for fresh milk that he wanted to keep cows on the roof, but the building's board turned him down. ♦ 117 E 57th St (between Lexington and Park Aves)

36 Habitat Hotel

$ This stylish yet inexpensive (by Manhattan standards) 330-room hostelry on the site of the former Allerton Hotel offers its guests modern furnishings, cable television, and Internet access. Rooms, while many have twin beds, range from singles and doubles to suites and studios, and there are both shared and private baths. ♦ 130 E 57th St (at Lexington Ave). 753.8841; 800/497.6028. www.habitatny.com

37 Royal-Athena Galleries

Ancient, European, Oriental, pre-Columbian, and tribal works of art are sold here. Each object is labeled and has a price tag, but the staff enjoys answering questions from browsers as well as from serious collectors. ♦ M-Sa. 153 E 57th St (between Third and Lexington Aves). 355.2034. www.royalathena.com ♿

37 Le Colonial

★★★$$ A glamorized Vietnamese bistro with white, black, and brown shutters, potted palms, ceiling fans, and pictures of Indochina during the French colonial years, this place has been packing them in since the day it opened in 1993. Choice dishes include delicate spring rolls, ginger-marinated roasted duck with tamarind dipping sauce, crispy fried noodles with stir-fried vegetables, and a tasty beef salad with lemongrass and basil. The lemon tart and crème caramel ice cream are good dessert choices. A large after-work crowd convenes for drinks in the lovely lounge upstairs. ♦ Vietnamese ♦ M-F, lunch and dinner; Sa, Su, dinner. Reservations required. 149 E 57th St (between Third and Lexington Aves). 752.0808

37 Hammacher Schlemmer

Unintentionally one of the funniest stores in the city, it can carry gadgetry to the limits of credibility with such items as a solar-powered ventilated golf cap, an electronic one-armed-bandit home casino, and an interactive talking chess game. On the practical side, it offers all manner of obviously useful home electronics and appliances (the best portable DVD player, the perfect coffee carafe); keep in mind it was the first store to introduce the steam iron, electric razor, and pressure cooker. Th mail-order catalog is a kick, too. ♦ M-Sa. 147 E 57th St (between Third and Lexingto Aves). 421.9000 ♿

38 Chambers

$$$$ If you're looking for a downtown vib with an uptown address, look no farther than this hip 77-room town-house-style hotel that lives and breathes modern art. The style starts the minute you walk in: A Macassar ebony and parchment check-in desk, alpaca couches, and leather-covere columns set a sumptuous but simple tone Both lobby and guestrooms double as showcases for more than 500 original wor of contemporary art—and that's in additio to the corridors on 14 floors that have bee done up by individual artists. The rooms themselves feature the latest tech, and furnishings made of gray-washed oak with details in hand-rubbed blackened steel; th platform beds are covered with fine linens cashmere throws, and thick Tibetan and Turkish rugs. Sleek bathrooms feature monolithic concrete floors inset with handmade iridescent glass tiles. As elsewhere in the hotel, no detail has gone unnoticed. The restaurant within is **Town**. Sleek and ultramodern, this *très* upscale bastion of fine New American dining also offers cocktails of the moment at its uppe level bar. 582.4445 ♦ 15 W 56th St (between Fifth and Sixth Aves). 974.5656 fax 974.5657. www.chambershotel.com ♿

39 OMO Norma Kamali

Kamali is the designer who, back in the 1980s, put many American women into hig fashion sweatshirt dresses, blouses, slit skirts, and cocoon wraps. The store today i sparkling white, perhaps better to complement Kamali's growing wellness and fragrance lines. The shop carries shoes, les expensive cotton and Lycra knits, her grand swimsuits, one-of-a-kind eveningwear, and a fine selection of vintage pieces. ♦ M-Sa. 11 W 56th St (between Fifth and Sixth Aves). 957.9797 ♿

40 DC Moore Gallery

Milton Avery, Arthur Dove, Charles Burchfield, and Romar Bearden, and othe masters of 20th-century art, as well as promising newcomers, are shown here. ♦ Tu-Sa. 724 Fifth Ave (at W 56th St), eighth floor. 247.2111. www.dcmooregallery.com ♿

40 Prada

The supple leather and industrial-nylon handbags and knapsacks sold here have become the accessories of choice for global customers who zealously follow this generations-old Milanese institution. Third-generation Miuccia Prada is responsible for the contemporary fashions displayed throughout the store, from shoes to separates. The E 57th Street location carries mostly shoes, bags, and other accessories. ♦ Daily. 724 Fifth Ave (between E 56th and E 57th Sts). 664.0010. Also at 45 E 57th St (between Park and Madison Aves). 308.2332; 841 Madison Ave (at E 70th St). 327.4200; 575 Broadway (at Prince St). 334.8888

41 Henri Bendel

The windows are among the most imaginative in New York, but don't stop there. Shopping here is an experience no one should miss. This exclusive store is filled with unique merchandise at moderate to eye-popping prices, including tabletop wares by Frank McIntosh, and it's still fun to kick up your heels and announce you just got those stunning shoes at Bendel's (be sure to say *Ben*-dls, as the natives do). The second floor's **Petite Cafe** and **Salon de Thé** are pricey but delightful. Take a moment to appreciate the unique Lalique etched-glass windows. ♦ Daily. 712 Fifth Ave (between W 55th and W 56th Sts). 247.1100

41 Harry Winston

The father of this world-famous seller of diamonds owned a little jewelry store on Columbus Avenue, but Harry went into business for himself while he was still a teenager and eventually established what may be the most daunting diamond salon in the city. It is the only store on Fifth Avenue that processes diamonds from rough stones to finished jewelry. ♦ M-Sa. 718 Fifth Ave (at W 56th St). 245.2000

42 Gucci

Having snagged the high-profile corner spot at the Trump Tower, the Gucci dynasty marches on. A staff that ranges from very pleasant to simply cool sells shoes and leather goods for men and women, exquisitely crafted by the generations-old Florentine family. Like most of the venerable older design houses, Gucci has infused its goods with a fresh breath of contemporary style—leather goods are joined by suits, topcoats, dresses, ties, and scarves. The famed red-and-green stripe and internationally recognized double-linked Gs are omnipresent on handbags, boots, and luggage. ♦ Daily. 725 Fifth Ave (between E 56th and E 57th Sts) ♿ Also at 840 Madison (between E 69th and E 70th Sts). 717.2619

42 Trump Tower

Offices fill the lower floors, along with a glitzy six-story atrium replete with a vertical waterfall along a soaring pink granite wall, though you likely know this building from the *Apprentice* television show. Retail on the ground level includes the fine pen store **Joon** (317.8466), high-end costume jeweler **Landau** (355.6349), and the **Trump Store**'s Signature Collection (head down to the garden level for their *Apprentice* stuff; both locations: 836.3226). There is informal lunchtime buffet dining on the lower level as well. Built in 1983, the knife-pleated glass tower was designed by **Der Scutt** of **Swanke, Hayden, Connell & Partners.** ♦ Daily. 725 Fifth Ave (between E 56th and E 57th Sts). 832.2000 ♿

43 Steuben

More like a museum than a store, engraved sculptures featuring Chinese calligraphy, animals, or even a forest of spreading pine are highlighted here. All are displayed in backlit glass cases in a gray-walled sanctuary. The State Department buys its gifts for heads of state here, and the hoi polloi find crystal in the shape of dolphins, elephants, and hippopotamuses. ♦ M-Sa. 717 Fifth Ave (at E 56th St). 752.1441, 800/424.4240

44 Mercedes-Benz Showroom

One of New York City's rare works by **Frank Lloyd Wright**, this 1955 design is a curious exercise in glass, ramp, plants, and fancy cars in a too-tight space. ♦ M-Sa. 430 Park Ave (at E 56th St). 629.1666

45 The Lombardy

$$$ Built in 1927 by **Henry Mandel** with the backing of William Randolph Hearst, this boutique-style hotel has 115 large rooms and suites, each with a different décor (though all in the realm of comfy, uncluttered, traditional style) and all with kitchenettes or wetbars and high-speed Internet access. About a third of the accommodations are secured by long-term residents who also enjoy the early-2000s face-lift to the lobby and other public areas. Within the Lombardy, there is a small fitness center, a beauty salon, and a 24-hour business center. ♦ 111 E 56th St (between Lexington and Park Aves). 753.8600,

800/223.5254; fax 754.5683. www.lombardyhotel.com ♿

46 Daffy's

Some swear by it, others revile it, but this large location (their SoHo location may be the largest) of the discount chain is jam-packed with designer clothes and accessories for men and women of every age group. We're not talking Calvin and Giorgio, but those with a discerning eye will always find some good pieces. ♦ Daily. 125 E 57th St (between Lexington and Park Aves). 376.4477. Also at 462 Broadway (at Grand St). 334.7444, and other locations throughout the city

47 Fitzpatrick Manhattan Hotel

$$$ A welcome attention to detail, 92 tastefully furnished rooms and public areas, marbled whirlpool baths, 24-hour room service, Internet access, a smiling top-hatted bellman, and Irish-inspired hospitality (this is the only US representation of a small Irish chain) make this a veritable oasis in the chaos of Midtown Manhattan. **Fitzers** serves an Irish grill including corned beef and cabbage on its Irish/New American menu, but the full Irish country breakfast gets the most plaudits. ♦ 687 Lexington Ave (between E 56th and E 57th Sts). 355.0100, 800/367.7701; fax 355.1371. www.fitzpatrickhotels.com ♿

48 La Bonne Soupe

★★$$ Soups, omelettes, a variety of chopped beef dishes, and daily French specials such as filet au poivre are good at this popular longstanding bistro. For a really retro experience, have a fondue. ♦ French ♦ Daily, lunch and dinner. 48 W 55th St (between Fifth and Sixth Aves). 586.7650

49 Menchanko-tei

★$$ Japanese businessmen frequent this cozy noodle emporium for hearty soups filled with a variety of ingredients. As authentic a noodle shop as can be found in Midtown, this place is great to duck into for a steamy broth. ♦ Japanese ♦ M, lunch, dinner, and late-night meals; Tu-Su, breakfast, lunch, dinner, and late-night meals. 43-45 W 55th St (between Fifth and Sixth Aves). 247.1585. ♿ Also at 131 E 45th St (between Lexington and Third Aves). 986.6805

49 The Shoreham Hotel

$$ Most of the hotels in this neighborhood are far grander than this. But the 174-room boutique-style hostelry has a soothing earth-tone décor and a service-oriented small-hotel sensibility. This, plus its excellent location, make it a favorite among denizens of the fashion world. Amenities include Wi-F throughout and a CD library. ♦ 33 W 55th S (between Fifth and Sixth Aves). 247.6700, 800/553.3347; fax 765.9741. www.shorehamhotel.com

MICHAEL'S

50 Michael's

★★$$ Sleek and airy, this is *the* place with Midtown business types for healthful breakfasts and lunches. The sunny, spare setting is punctuated with an impressive collection of modern art, and the light menu features imaginative California-style cuisine. The menu changes seasonally. Service, however, can be sometimes snooty and condescending to nonregulars.♦ American/ California ♦ M-F, breakfast, lunch, and dinner; Sa, dinner. 24 W 55th St (between Fifth and Sixth Aves). 767.0555

51 Fifth Avenue Presbyterian Church

When society moved uptown, this church, which had been at 19th Street since 1855 moved with it to this 1875 building designed by **Carl Pfeiffer**. Future president Theodore Roosevelt was one of the original parishioners, along with the Auchinclosses, Livingstons, and Walcotts. It was called the most influential congregation in New York. ♦ 7 W 55th St (at Fifth Ave). 247.0490

52 The Peninsula New York

$$$$ This hotel was built in 1905 by **Hiss & Weeks** and for many years, as the **Gotham Hotel**, was a favorite stopping place for movie stars. Then it briefly became **Maxim's** and was completely restored in the Belle Epoque tradition of the original Maxim's in Paris. These days the look is still opulent, but in a more contemporary vein. Its 241 guestrooms have luxe features like electronic bedside panels that adjust lighting, a flat-screen TV, and stereo and can even turn on a Do Not Disturb light. High-speed Internet service and special silent fax machines are also part of the scheme. Bathrooms in the larger rooms boast hand-free telephones and stereo speakers. Decorative touches are richly luxurious throughout, from silk bedspreads to Art Nouveau headboards, welcome vestiges from the Maxim's days. Unwind in **The Peninsula Spa**, perched atop the hotel's roof. Rare for New York, the hotel's deluxe health club also has a

pool. Multiple dining (and drinking) options include the Mediterranean **Fives** ♦ 700 Fifth Ave (at W 55th St). 247.2200, 800/262.9467; fax 903.3943. www.peninsula.com ♿

53 WORLD OF DISNEY

Three floors of mousely merchandise. Classic Disney characters from Bambi to Tinkerbell can be seen on T-shirts, jewelry (real and faux), dolls, luggage, and sportswear (in all sizes). The lower level features a travel department for those with an urge to visit Mickey's favorite theme park. ♦ Daily. 711 Fifth Ave (at E 55th St). 702.0702

54 THE ST. REGIS

$$$$ When **Trowbridge & Livingston** built the St. Regis for John Jacob Astor in 1904, Astor said he wanted the finest hotel in the world, a place where guests would feel as comfortable as they did in a gracious private home. Today this is still one of New York's finest—and most elegant—hotels. A recent $35 million refurbishment winnowed the original 500-room capacity to 256 sumptuous guest accommodations (including 74 suites); the remaining space has been converted to luxury residences. The spectacular Beaux Arts landmark exterior remains, with its stone garlands and flowers and its slate mansard roof. Its traditionally styled rooms are complemented by state-of-the-art technology, computerized phones, and other comforts. The hotel contains the deliciously old-world **Astor Court**, which serves light meals and afternoon tea, and the **King Cole Bar**; those familiar with the bar's beloved, but severely smoke-darkened, Maxfield Parrish *Old King Cole* mural of yore will be impressed with the results of its first scrubbing since the 1950s. A much-anticipated **Alain Ducasse** restaurant, the David Rockwell-designed **Adour** opened in 2008 in the former Lespinasse space. ♦ 2 E 55th St (between Madison and Fifth Aves). 753.4500, 800/759.7550; fax 787.3447. www.stregis.com ♿

55 THE SONY BUILDING

Known as the **AT&T Headquarters** until 1992, this pinkish granite structure designed by **Philip Johnson** and **John Burgee** in 1984 continues to be recognized by its broken-pediment top, often referred to as "Chippendale" in style. Primarily office space, the **Sony Wonder Technology Lab** (see opposite) is also here. At its glass-enclosed base, the building contains Sony shops, a café and newsstand, and a plaza with seating, open and free to the public. This building's profile is one of the more recognizable elements in Manhattan's urban fabric. ♦ Free. 550 Madison Ave (between E 55th and E 56th Sts).

Within The Sony Building:

SONY WONDER TECHNOLOGY LAB

Four floors of hands-on fun for kids . . . and the adults who must accompany them. They've got all the latest and greatest tech to help you design your own video, re-edit videos by rock's megastars, create your own computer racing game, explore medical imaging and robotic engineering, play in a television production studio, and more. Free; advance reservations are advised. ♦ Tu-Su. 550 Madison Ave (at E 56th St). 833.8100. www.sonywondertechlab.com ♿

56 FRIARS CLUB

This is the private club for actors who invented the famous roasts, in which members poke fun at celebrity guests. The five-story 1909 English Renaissance-style gem was originally built as a private residence; the Friars moved here in 1957. Designed by architecture firm **Taylor & Levi**, its steeply peaked roof is a visual complement to the gorgeously vaulted ceilings inside. Intricate stonework and leaded glass further mark this as a façade of interest. ♦ The building is not open to the public. 57 E 55th St (between Park and Madison Aves). 751.7272

AQUAVIT

57 AQUAVIT

★★★$$$$ Marcus Samuelsson's modern Scandinavian menu has such dishes as smoked salmon with buckwheat potato blini and goat cheese cream; gravlax with dill, flat bread, and espresso mustard sauce; tea-smoked duck with citrus risotto and seared sweetbreads; rare beef in beer and beef *au jus*; and sweet mustard-glazed Arctic char. Be sure to save room for the warm chocolate cake or hazelnut pancakes with blueberry ice cream. Coolly modern Arne Jacobsen "egg" chairs complete the bar and lounge décor. While you're there, try the "Aquatani"—a martini made with the restaurant's homemade Aquavit, the Scandinavian liqueur flavored with anise, caraway, fennel, or orange peel and typically served neat and very cold. Dining at their fine eponymous café won't put as large a dent in your wallet. ♦ Scandinavian ♦ M-F, lunch and dinner; Sa, dinner; Su, brunch. Reservations recommended; jacket requested. 65 E. 55th St (between Park and Madison Aves). 307.7311

58 WALTER STEIGER

This shoe salon features the newest silhouettes from Europe for men and women. Prices can be stratospheric; the same is true of their lovely selection of handbags. ♦ M-Sa. 417 Park Ave (at E 55th St). 826.7171 ♿

59 CENTRAL SYNAGOGUE

With the exception of its two green and gold onion domes perched on 222-foot towers, the relatively subdued brown and beige sandstone exterior of this 1872 Moorish Revival building (designed by **Henry Fernbach**, who was deeply inspired by the Dohany Street Synagogue in Budapest) belies the breathtaking polychrome detail to be found within. Despite a devastating fire in 1998, Central is the oldest Jewish house of worship in continuous use in New York City. Meticulously restored by **Hardy Holzman Pfeiffer** and **Dan Peter Koppel,** the national landmark reopened, remarkably, on 9 September 2001. Its superb rose window had survived, and the exquisite Maw & Co. encaustic tile floors, ornate Moorish- and William Morris–inspired wall and column stencils, and elaborate plasterwork were all repaired or re-created. The finishing touch was the specially configured world-class organ (it has 4,500 pipes and stops for both klezmer clarinette and trompette shofar) that was put in place when the original was found to be irreparable. Docent-led tours are offered every Wednesday; they are free and not to be missed. ♦ 652 Lexington Ave (at E 55th St). 838.5122 www.centralsynagog.org ♿

60 SHUN LEE PALACE

★★★$$$$ Owner Michael Tong collaborated with designer Adam Tihany to renovate this landmark Chinese restaurant. The result includes blue suede walls with gold-leaf panels, chandeliers of frosted glass, and mahogany cases displaying treasures of past dynasties. Try the unfortunately named dish Ants Climb on Tree (a combination of beef, Chinese broccoli, and cellophane noodles), steamed dumplings, orange beef, or whole poached sea bass with brown-bean sauce. The dessert menu includes such Western favorites as chocolate mousse cake in addition to Asian offerings. ♦ Chinese ♦ Daily, lunch and dinner. Reservations required. 155 E 55th St (between Third and Lexington Aves). 371.8844. Shun Lee West (595.8895) and Shun Lee Cafe (769.3888) located at 43 W 65th St (between Central Park W and Columbus Ave)

The United Nations has a peace garden that boasts more than 1,000 rosebushes.

There are 191 member states to the United Nations—the last being Switzerland and Timor-Leste, both admitted in 2002.

61 P. J. CLARKE'S

★$$ This 1884 joint was completely freshened up for the 21st century, and there are still few better places than this to witness rambunctious young professionals of Midtown getting slowly pickled during cocktail hour. Mysteriously, the hamburgers are famous, although habitués generally come here looking to meet, not eat meat. ♦ American ♦ Daily, lunch, dinner, and late-night meals. 915 Third Ave (at E 55th St). 376.1616. Also at 44 W 63rd St (at Columbus Ave). 957.9700; 4 World Financial Center (at Vesey St). 288.1500

62 THE MANHATTAN ART & ANTIQUES CENTER

More than a hundred dealers spread their quality wares over three large floors at Manhattan's specialized antiques "mall." One-stop shopping offers every imaginable item from the affordable to the exorbitant, from tiny pillboxes to magnificent chandeliers. The variety is extensive, the prices are competitive, and it's a fun place to browse. It's also a good place for appraisals and repairs. ♦ Daily. 1050 Second Ave (between E 55th and E 56th Sts). 355.4400. www.themaac.com ♿

63 WARWICK NEW YORK HOTEL

$$$ Rich in history, this 1926 apartment hotel was publishing magnate William Randolph Hearst's elegant residential retreat for his Hollywood friends (the Presidential Suite was once Cary Grant's private residence). At a cost of over $5 million, this building, designed by **George B. Post and Sons** and **Emery Roth**, was considered one of the two tallest apartment hotels in the world. It's still quite impressive with its graceful towers. Docent-led tours are offered every Wednesday; they are free and highly recommended. Pale, soothing tones contrast with elegant dark woods in the 359 spacious guestrooms and 67 suites. There are two-line phones and high-speed Internet access in all rooms, marble bathrooms in many, and a fitness center and 24-hour business center open to all guests. The restaurant **Murals on 54** is a lively spot with outdoor tables in warm weather. ♦ 65 W 54th St (at Sixth

Ave). 247.2700, 800/522.5634; fax 247.2725. www.warwickhotelny.com

4 Rockefeller Apartments

When John D. Rockefeller Jr. was assembling the site for **Rockefeller Center**, he lived on this block. By the end of 1929 he owned 15 of the block's houses, having joined his neighbors, most of whom were members of his family, in protecting the street from commercial use. But he wasn't above a little commercialism himself, and hired **Harrison & Fouilhoux** to design this building in 1936, a few months before he moved over to Park Avenue. Its bay-windowed towers overlook the **Museum of Modern Art**. ♦ 17 W 54th St (between Fifth and Sixth Aves)

5 University Club

Considered by many to be the finest work of **Charles Follen McKim** (of **McKim, Mead & White**), this 1899 building is an original composition with a bow to a half-dozen Italian palaces. When it was built, in the days before air conditioning, it had striped awnings in the windows, which made the pink marble exterior even more interesting. The interior is just as lavish. For decades, this private club set the style for all the others that followed. Despite its name, it is not linked with any particular university; it was open to men only through much of the 20th century. ♦ 1 W 54th St (at Fifth Ave). 247.2100

6 Takashimaya

Japan's largest retail conglomerate launched a unique venture in 1993 when it opened this elegant 20-story building designed by New York architect **John Burgee**. A distinctive array of East-meets-West design-sensitive products are sold on the third through fifth floors, ranging from home furnishings and fashion accessories to table and bed linens, specialty gifts, and objets d'art. The ground floor consists of a 4,500-square-foot gallery as well as a multilevel atrium, used as an exhibition space for contemporary Asian and American art and artisanal crafts. ♦ Daily. 693 Fifth Ave (between E 54th and E 55th Sts). 350.0100 ♿

Within Takashimaya:

Tea Box Café

★$ This soothing beige café in the store's basement is the perfect place for escaping the bustle of Midtown. Try one of the 40 varieties of tea, including apricot, lemon-grass, and *hoiji-cha* (a wood-smoked green tea), and a delicate sandwich—shrimp or cucumber on pressed rice, smoked salmon, or chicken with wasabi. ♦ Japanese ♦ Daily, lunch and afternoon tea. 350.0100 ♿

66 Elizabeth Arden Red Door Salon & Spa

Decorated by Clodagh, one of New York's most visually expressive interior designers, the famous red door leads to a world apart, filled with designer fashions, lingerie, sportswear, and a salon that has made pampering a fine art. The salon offers exercise facilities, massages, facials, hair styling, and more, all calculated to make you look and feel terrific. ♦ Daily. 691 Fifth Ave (between E 54th and E 55th Sts). 546.0200 ♿

67 Indonesian Pavilion

This is one of the few remaining buildings from the time when 54th Street east and west of Fifth Avenue was called "The Art Gallery of New York Streets." It was designed in 1900 by **McKim, Mead & White** and built by W.E.D. Stokes, who sold it to William H. Moore, a founder of the United States Steel and American Can companies. Note the massive balcony and strong cornices—evidence of **Charles Follen McKim**'s interest in Renaissance architecture. ♦ 4 E 54th St (between Madison and Fifth Aves)

67 Fortunoff

Time was, you would never expect to find a reasonably priced jewelry and silver store on Fifth Avenue, but here is one that offers good prices on strings of pearls; gold chains; hammered silver pitchers; urns; chalices; sterling silver; silver plate flatware by Oneida, Towle, and Reed & Barton; and stainless-steel flatware by Fraser and Dansk. The sales help is refreshingly courteous. ♦ Daily. 681 Fifth Ave (between E 53rd and E 54th Sts). 758.6660 ♿

68 Bice

★★★$$$ The long, curved white-marble bar, multilevel seating, bright lighting, and exquisite flower arrangements create a truly luxurious setting. The menu is just as pleasing. Try such main courses as roasted

> New York traffic engineers have not taken on the project of installing "Walk/Don't Walk" lights (a.k.a. "ped" lights) on Park Avenue between East 46th and East 56th Streets because of what lies barely eight inches below: the tunnels in and out of Grand Central Station.

rack of veal with new potatoes; baby chicken; grilled salmon, swordfish, or sole; and a delicious seafood risotto. Be forewarned: During lunch the noise level is thunderous. ♦ Italian ♦ Daily, lunch and dinner. Reservations recommended. 7 E 54th St (between Madison and Fifth Aves). 688.1999

69 San Pietro

★★$$$ Sister restaurant to the Upper East Side's **Sistina**, this place features dishes from Italy's Amalfi Coast. Try the shrimp with peppers and herbs, black sea bass baked on crushed sea salt or made to order, or grilled tuna steak with garlic and lemon. The sunny yellow setting—with jars of olives and sun-dried tomatoes, silver platters stacked with ripening tomatoes, and paintings of outdoor markets—manages to feel simultaneously elegant and homey. ♦ Neapolitan ♦ M-Sa, lunch and dinner. Reservations required; jacket and tie required. 18 E 54th St (between Madison and Fifth Aves). 753.9015 ♿

70 Bill's Gay Nineties

★★$$ Step into Bill's and get not only a whiff of the gay 1890s—the décor is dedicated to the second half of the 19th century, its walls plastered with posters (Buffalo Bill), photos (Ziegfeld girls), sports memorabilia, and playbills and other ephemera—but the Prohibition-era 1920s as well. While original owner Bill Hardy has passed on, the spirit of this onetime speakeasy is well-maintained. The original antique bar, the live nightly piano music, the know-how for a stiff pour, a pleasing menu (a good range of seafood, steaks, and salads), and a crowd with a 50-year age spread make this a neighborhood joint to reckon with. ♦ Continental. ♦ M-F, lunch and dinner; Sa, dinner. 57 E 54th St (between Park and Madison Aves). 355.0243. www.billsgaynineties.com

70 Oceana

★★★$$$$ When Rick Moonen, formerly of **The Water Club**, took charge of this kitchen already known for fine seafood, he proceeded to bring it up another level. Now diners in this pretty pastel room can experience such extraordinary dishes as oven-steamed spaghetti squash with vegetables and tomato *concassée* (reduction), crab cake with chipotle sauce, house-cured salmon gravlax with spicy black-bean cakes and cilantro crème fraîche, and grilled salmon paillard with asparagus in ginger-soy vinaigrette. ♦ Seafood ♦ M-Sa, lunch and dinner. Reservations required; jacket required. 55 E 54th St (between Park and Madison Aves). 759.5941

71 Hotel Elysée

$$$ Tallulah Bankhead used to be a regul here, as was Tennessee Williams. The hot still retains its old world atmosphere in sp of the modern buildings rising around it. Complimentary breakfast, on-site fitness facilities, and high-speed Internet access complement this elegant boutique, where each of the 99 rooms has its own persona ity; most go by names as well as numbers ♦ 60 E 54th St (between Park and Madis Aves). 753.1066, 800/535.9733; fax 980.9278. www.elyséehotel.com ♿

Within the Hotel Elysée:

Monkey Bar

★★★$$$ Whimsical monkey murals still decorate the bar, and the dining room ambience is still drop-dead glamorous, bu the kitchen—with Patricia Yeo at the helm has given up on steak and is now dishing New American cuisine with a decidedly As twist. ♦ New American ♦ M-Sa, dinner. Reservations recommended; jacket requir 838.2600. www.theglaziergroup.com

72 900 Third Avenue

The aluminum-faced section at the base of this brown stone and glass tower, and the proportion of its windows, are a direct reference to the neighboring Citigroup Cent (see page 195) across East 54th Street. Th arc drawn by the greenhouse near its top makes for another nice riff on complementa geometric forms. (You'll need to step acros Third Avenue to appreciate the two togethe Nine hundred Third was built in 1983, five years after Citigroup Center, by **Cesar Pelli Associates** with **Rafael Viñoly**. ♦ At E 54th

73 885 Third Avenue

This is the quirky elliptical-shaped "Lipstick Building," though some would say it remind them more of the bullet casing of a revolver An unappetizing shade of polished pink, an wrapped with a repeat pattern of silvery bands, this **John Burgee** and **Philip Johnso** structure from 1986 is all offices now that Lipstick Café has departed. But at the rear the building, with a separate entrance, **Von** prevails. ♦ Between E 53rd and E 54th Sts

Within 885 Third Avenue:

Vong

★★★★$$$ Superchef Jean-Georges Vongerichten and chef de cuisine Pierre Schutz weigh in with a wonderful interpretation of Thai/French cuisine in an elegant Eastern-influenced dining room. The menu reflects the two years Vongerichten spent in Bangkok: sautéed duck foie gras with ginger sauce and mango, raw tuna, and vegetables in rice paper with dipping sauce; lobster with Thai herbs; roasted baby chicken marinated with lemongrass and herbs; and black bass with wok-fried cabbage, water chestnuts, and hot chilies. The blend of fresh local and exotic ingredients, and an abundance of classic French ingenuity, make this a truly unique dining experience. ♦ Thai/French ♦ M-F, lunch and dinner; Sa, Su, dinner. Reservations required. 200 E 54th St (between Second and Third Aves). 486.9592

74 La Mangeoire

★★$$$ The atmosphere of this warm, rustic Provençal spot is so inviting that it would be worth coming here even if the food was less appealing. The stucco walls are enlivened with pottery, and dried and fresh flowers abound. The food more than complements the setting, with piquant spices and sunny flavors; try *pissaladière* (an onion, anchovy, and olive tart); penne with a sauce of tomato-olive purée; thyme-crusted rabbit; or beef daube with Swiss chard ravioli. ♦ French ♦ M-F, lunch and dinner; Sa, Su, dinner. Reservations recommended. 1008 Second Ave (between E 53rd and E 54th Sts). 759.7086

75 Sutton Place and Sutton Place South

Until colonized by Vanderbilts and Morgans moving from Fifth Avenue in the early 1920s, this elegant end of York Avenue was a rundown area. The town houses and apartment buildings are by such architects as **Mott B. Schmidt**, **Rosario Candela**, **Delano & Aldrich**, and **Cross & Cross**. Visit the park at the end of East 55th Street and the terrace on East 57th Street for views of the river and the Queensboro Bridge. Also peek in from East 58th Street, where **Riverview Terrace**, one of New York's last private streets, runs along the river lined with five ivy-covered brownstones. The secretary-general of the United Nations lives at **Nos. 1** to **3**. ♦ E 53rd to E 59th Sts

76 American Folk Art Museum

The best of American folk art from the 18th century to the present, including paintings, sculpture, textiles, furniture, and decorative arts, is displayed in the museum's 2001 building on West 53rd Street, where the museum was started in 1961. Designed by **Tod Williams Billie Tsien Architects**, the New York–based team has created a four-story jewel that utilizes natural light and rough-hewn stone and metal alloys, cherry wood, frosted glass, and softly polished chrome to perfectly complement the handwork of its collections. Venturing beyond traditional folk art, the museum has sought to expand its holdings to include contemporary self-taught or "outsider" artists. A small café, library, and gift shop complete the space, which also holds regular lectures and workshops. ♦ Admission; free Friday after 5:30PM. Closed Monday. Tu-Su, 10:30AM-5:30PM; F, 10:30AM-7:30PM. 45 W 53rd St (between Fifth and Sixth Aves). 265.1040. ♿ Also at the **Eva and Morris Feld Gallery**, 2 Lincoln Square (between W 65th and W 66th Sts). 595.9533. www.folkartmuseum.org

77 Museum of Modern Art (MoMA)

MoMA emerged from the most extensive rebuilding and renovation project in its 75-year history on 20 November 2004 and immediately reclaimed its position as one of the world's most dynamic showcases for modern and contemporary art.

When this museum was founded in 1929, a few days after the big stock market crash, the idea of a museum dedicated to the understanding and enjoyment of contemporary visual arts was novel. Founders Abby Aldrich Rockefeller (wife of John D. Jr.), Lillie P. Bliss, and Mrs. Cornelius J. Sullivan were joined by other collectors and philanthropists in the venture, and the collections have grown through the largesse of the early benefactors and others.

One of the institution's most important contributions to the art world is its embracing of disciplines previously considered unworthy of museum status, resulting in a collection that is not only strong in 20th-century painting and sculpture, but also photography, film, theater, music, industrial design, and architecture. When the museum's first director, Alfred H. Barr Jr., espoused this multidepartmental concept in 1929, the idea of including practical as well as fine art was considered radical. At first the museum displayed only paintings, but it soon began a slow and steady implementation of Barr's idea.

MoMA is strongest in art of the first half of the century—Impressionists, Cubists, and

Realists—but it also has good examples of post-World War II Abstract Expressionists through Conceptualists, including de Kooning, Rothko, Lichtenstein, di Suvero, and LeWitt. The photography galleries are well worth seeing, as are the galleries of architecture and design, where you will find such 20th-century classics as Thonet bentwood chairs, Tiffany glass, Bauhaus textiles, and Marcel Breuer furniture. Among the most important paintings in the collection are van Gogh's *Starry Night*, Mondrian's *Broadway Boogie Woogie*, Matisse's *Dance*, Picasso's *Les Demoiselles d'Avignon*, Andrew Wyeth's *Christina's World*, and Jackson Pollock's *One (Number 31, 1950)*.

The original sleek white horizontal building with its marble veneer and tile-and-glass façade was designed in 1939 by **Philip L. Goodwin** and **Edward Durell Stone** in the International Style—a striking statement by an innovative institution, practicing what it preached in a row of brownstones. There was (briefly) a plan to cut a street through the two blocks from **Rockefeller Center** leading directly to the museum (the Rockefellers controlled the land in the vicinity). **Philip Johnson**'s 1951 and 1964 additions, black glass wings to the east and west, not only expanded the gallery space and improved the **Sculpture Garden** (designed in 1953 by Johnson and **Zion & Breen**), but were an effective frame for the original front. The **Museum Tower**—residential condominiums at 15 W 53rd Street, directly to the west of MoMA's original entrance—was designed by **Cesar Pelli** in 1984. It fulfills its intent as a fund-raiser for the museum. The sublime design that doubles the capacity of the much-storied original building was created by architect **Yoshio Taniguchi**, and the soaring 110-foot-tall atrium bathed in natural light is already a haven for the area's office workers who welcome the return of this magnificent institution to their midst. New entrances on West 53rd Street (confusingly, the museum now wraps behind the Pelli tower at No. 15 to the west, so this entrance is No. 11—just as the old entrance was) and on West 54th Street lead to a block-wide lobby that opens onto a beautiful restoration of the beloved sculpture garden, now expanded to the east, west, and south while preserving Johnson's original 1953 design. A grand staircase leads up to the new contemporary art space on the second level, another block-wide expanse with 22-foot ceilings (and no columns to get in the way); higher floors hold galleries for other collections. At every turn, new vistas of space and light open up: through glass curtain walls above the garden, in quiet niches giving unexpected views of the street, from walkways above the atrium. On the lower level, the refurbished **Roy and Nina Titus Theaters** present MoMA's film and media program (note: the theaters also hav a dedicated lobby, accessed through MoMA's original main entrance); books and objects are for sale in the **MoMA Design and Book Store** off the lobby, **MoMA Book** on the second floor, and an exhibition shop on the sixth. And when "museum feet" sets in, patrons can choose from a range of restoratives, all created by golden-touch restaurateur Danny Meyer: **Café 2** for stylis cafeteria meals and **Terrace 5** for sweets (708.9400 for both), or the seriously acclaimed **Modern** and its more casual **Bar Room**, overlooking the sculpture garden, where chef Gabriel Kreuther's varied, vibran menus merit a visit all by themselves (M-Sa lunch and dinner. 333.1220; 9 W 53rd St, o through the museum). ♦ Admission; free Friday after 4PM. Closed Tuesday. Sa-M, W, Th, 10:30AM-5:30PM; F, 10:30AM-8PM. 11 W 53rd St (between Fifth and Sixth Aves). 708.9400. www.moma.org ♿

Also part of the Museum of Modern Art:

78 MoMA Design Store

Design-sensitive merchandise is inspired by the **Museum of Modern Art** collections across the street, including educational toys (Colorforms, kaleidoscopes, architectural blocks), furniture (designs by Frank Lloyd Wright and Charles Eames, plus a reproduction of the famous butterfly chair by Antonio Bonet, Jorge Farrari, and Juan Kurchen), housewares, desk accessories, and great gift ideas. ♦ M-Sa. 44 W 53rd St (between Fifth and Sixth Aves). 767.1050. Also at 81 Spring St (between Crosby St and Broadway). 646.613.1367

79 Donnell Library, NYPL

When he died in 1896, textile merchant Ezekiel Donnell left his estate to the New York Public Library to establish a place where youn people could spend their evenings away from demoralizing influences. Thanks to Donnell's legacy, this branch has the largest collection of literature in languages other than English in the entire NYC system, and one of the best collections of children's literature in the Unite States. It also has a fine film collection and occasional screenings. ♦ Each department has its own hours; call for specific times. Main floor: daily. 20 W 53rd St (between Fifth and Sixth Aves). 621.0618. www.nypl.org

80 St. Thomas Church

Cram Goodhue & Ferguson designed this picturesque French Gothic edifice on a tight corner in 1914. You have to wonder why a second tower wasn't included; the single one is rather awkward in an otherwise symmetrical composition. A dollar sign next to the "true lover's knot" over the Bride's Door is presumably a sculptor's comment on the social standing of the congregation. The Episcopal church's world-renowned boys' choir celebrated its 75th anniversary in 1994; it makes the services here a memorable experience from October through May. Call in advance for a schedule. ♦ 1 W 53rd St (at Fifth Ave). 757.7013 ♿

81 Samuel Paley Plaza

Named for the father of its benefactor, the late William S. Paley of CBS, this park is a spare, very welcome anomaly in the densest part of town. Good furniture and a wonderful waterfall provide the perfect spot to steal a moment's peace. The park was designed in 1967 by landscape architects **Zion & Breen** and consulting architect **Albert Preston Moore**. Just a few storefronts east on this side of the street is another tiny outdoor seating area, worth a visit to see the large graffiti-covered slabs from the Berlin Wall. ♦ E 53rd St (between Madison and Fifth Aves)

82 Lever House

Gordon Bunshaft was the partner in charge of this 1952 **Skidmore**, **Owings & Merrill** design. The first glass wall on Park Avenue, built when Charles Luckman was president of Lever Brothers, was, after a long battle, awarded landmark status and saved from possible destruction or disfigurement and was thoroughly spruced up in the early 2000s. The articulate building displays the tenets of orthodox Corbusian Modernism: It is raised from the ground on columns, it has a roof garden, and there is a free façade on the outside and free plan on the inside. With the **Seagram Building** (page 200) across the street (just south, at 375 Park Avenue), this is a landmark corner that changed the face of the city. ♦ 390 Park Ave (between E 53rd and E 54th Sts)

Within Lever House:

Lever House Restaurant

★★ $$$ Walk through a '60s futuristic white time tunnel to the Mark Newson honeycomb design of this 2003 New American restaurant tucked into Lever House. Elegant yet cozy, it features special desserts and greenmarket-fresh dishes. ♦ M-F, lunch; daily, dinner. Reservations required. Entrance on E 53rd St. 888.2700

83 Citigroup Center

Designed in 1978 by **Hugh Stubbins & Associates**, the rakish angle of the former Citicorp building's top was planned as a solar collector but is now nothing more than a vent for the cooling system, which provides a steamy effect for the night lighting. Also under the roof is a 400-ton computer-operated Tuned Mass Damper (TMD or "earthquake machine" to most of us). They don't expect an earthquake anytime soon, but the building is cantilevered on 145-foot columns that allow it to sway in the wind. Those 10-story stilts also make it possible for the structure to be the world's only skyscraper with skylights; they brighten its sunken floors, where occasional exhibits and live lunchtime piano performances take place in an open-seating area amidst a small group of shops and restaurants—**Barnes & Noble** (750.8033), **City Sports** (317.0541), and **Houston's** restaurant (888.3828) among them. ♦ 153 E 53rd St (between Third and Lexington Aves).

Within Citigroup Center:

St. Peter's Lutheran Church

This church is a major reason for the engineering and formal antics of Citigroup Center's design: The church refused to sell its air rights to Citigroup unless the bank agreed to build a new church clearly distinct from the tower, with the skyscraper perched on 10-story stilts above it. In contrast to the high-tech tower, the church is granite, with elegantly austere wooden furnishings and interior detailing by **Massimo and Lella Vignelli**. Within the church, the Erol Beaker Chapel was created by sculptor Louise Nevelson. Watch for jazz programming year round and musical vespers every Sunday at 5PM (the church is known as the city's jazz ministry). But the interior—with its chapel created by sculptor **Louise Nevelson** and works of art by **Kiki Smith**, **William Cordaroy**, and **Dale Chihuly**—is well worth a look at any time. ♦ 619 Lexington Ave (at E 54th St). 935.2200. www.saintpeters.org ♿

York Theatre Company at St. Peter's Church

Two productions that began in this excellent 165-seat space in the basement of Citigroup Center went on to Broadway: *Tintypes* and *The Elephant Man*. ♦ 935.5820. www.yorktheatre.org ♿

84 Solera

★★$$ Tapas and other Spanish delicacies top the list in this stylish town house. The soft lighting and colorful tiling create the ideal stage set for specialties that include empanadas, organic duckling breast with juniper-rosemary sauce, fillet of trout with Serrano ham, and sliced Atlantic salmon. Desserts are heavenly—favorites include coconut cheesecake with mango-pineapple salsa and vanilla poached pear with apple compote. ♦ Spanish ♦ M-F, lunch and dinner; Sa, dinner. Reservations recommended. 216 E 53rd St (between Second and Third Aves). 644.1166

85 Il Nido

★★★$$$ Owner Adi Giovannetti serves excellent Italian food in a rustic setting with timber beams and mirrors that are made to look like farmhouse windows. Try *malfatti* (irregularly shaped pasta squares filled with spinach and cheese), linguine *alla amatriciana* (in tomato sauce with onions and prosciutto), tortellini with four cheeses, baked red snapper with clams, or braised chicken in a white-wine sauce with mushrooms and tomato. ♦ Italian ♦ M-Sa, lunch and dinner. Reservations required. 251 E 53rd St (between Second and Third Aves). 753.8450 ♿

86 River House

This 26-story, twin-towered, limestone and gray brick cooperative, built in 1931 by **Bottomley, Wagner & White**, has always been one of the most exclusive apartment buildings in the city (when there was a dock on the river, only the best yachts used it). The lower floors house the **River Club**, which includes squash and tennis courts, a pool, and a ballroom. ♦ The building is not open to the public. 435 E 53rd St (at Sutton Pl S)

87 CBS Building

This is **Eero Saarinen**'s only high-rise building, although he didn't live to see its completion in 1965. Known as "Black Rock," the dark gray granite mass is removed from the street, and its surface is given depth by triangular columns. With the top the same as the bottom, the tower is the image of mystery—even the entrances are hard to identify—an intriguing and sleekly beautiful rendition of the monolith from *2001* right on Sixth Avenue. ♦ 51 W 52nd St (at Sixth Ave)

Within the CBS Building:

China Grill

★★$$$ This modern, airy space, though it can get noisy, is most stylish, with dark gleaming walls and light fixtures that resemble flying saucers hovering overhead. The cuisine—an amalgam of Asian, French, and California influences—is inventive and delicious; try the sake-cured salmon rolls with lemongrass vinaigrette or the grilled dry-aged Szechuan beef and chipotle mashed potatoes. Such desserts as pumpkin cheesecake and cream cheese mousse are also sure to please. ♦ Asian ♦ M-F, lunch and dinner; Sa, Su, dinner. Reservations required. 52 W 53rd St (between Fifth and Sixth Aves). 333.7788 ♿

88 31 West 52nd Street

In 1986, while designing this building, architects **Kevin Roche, John Dinkeloo & Associates** were also working on plans for the new zoo in **Central Park**. The zoo has covered walkways supported by columns with sliced edges, an effect called chamfering. The firm used the same idea here and put the building on similar columns. Changing contemporary art shows in the ground-floor lobby are open to the public. ♦ (between Fifth and Sixth Aves). ♿

89 Bombay Palace

★★$$ The crisp and light Indian breads, such as the nan stuffed with cashew nuts and dried fruits, are delightful, the curries mild, and the tandoori chicken properly moist and tender at this pleasant, subtly lit Indian restaurant with friendly service. Try the lamb *vindaloo* (cooked in a fiery vinegar-flavored sauce), followed by mango ice cream or Indian rice pudding—subtly flavored with rose water—for dessert. Don't miss the daily buffet; it's a best-bet bargain ♦ Indian ♦ Daily, lunch and dinner. 30 W 52nd St (between Fifth and Sixth Aves). 541.7777

90 '21'

★★★$$$$ Settle down to a savory '21' Burger, onetime favorite of Aristotle Onassis, or black mint-crusted antelope with roasted pearl onions, flageolets, and fava beans, and soak up the atmosphere of what is one of only a handful of genuinely legendary New York restaurants. Actually, "establishment" is the more apt word to describe '21,' which has been a magnet for the rich, famous, and powerful almost since its inception as a speakeasy during the Prohibition years. There's an unmistakable and mildly intoxicating buzz in the air here, generated as much by the legions of devotees past (Humphrey Bogart, Ernest Hemingway, and Salvador Dalí, to name a few) and present (it's David Letterman's favorite place for a steak) as by the uncommonly toothsome food. Chef John Greeley balances the classic and the contemporary with finesse, so whether you go for the "Speakeasy" steak tartare or crisp black sea bass with truffled potatoes and Champagne sauce, your palate is sure to be pleased. It will surely be overjoyed by dessert: All are champions, but the warm chocolate S'mores with chocolate peanut brittle ice cream should be declared a national institution. There are very reasonable prix-fixe lunch and pre-theater menus; if it's drinks and a lighter menu you're after, ask for a table in the fireplaced lounge. ♦ Continental ♦ M-F, lunch and dinner; Sa, dinner. Reservations required; jacket required of men at lunch, jacket and tie at dinner. 21 W 52nd St (between Fifth and Sixth Aves). 582.7200 www.21club.com ♿

90 The Paley Center for Media

Originally called the **Museum of Broadcasting**, then, through 2007, the Museum of Television and Radio, this museum and archive was established in 1965 by the late William S. Paley, the founder of CBS. At private viewing stations you can choose TV and radio programs from the museum's vast archives—everything from Edward R. Murrow to "Mr. Ed"—and screen or listen for hours if you wish. Changing exhibits and a lively range of public programs and screenings complement the archives. The entire permanent collection consists of more than 60,000 recordings, from commercials to documentaries. In 1991, the museum moved from its longtime home next to **Paley Plaza** on East 53rd Street into this $55 million, 17-story building designed by **John Burgee Architects** that more than doubled its size and added two theaters, a screening room, a gallery space, an expanded library with computer access to catalogs, and a museum shop. Docent-led tours are usually held at 12:30PM on Tuesday. ♦Admission. Closed Monday. Tu-Su, noon-6AM; Th until 8PM. 25 W 52nd St (between Fifth and Sixth Aves). 621.6600. Special events recording: 621.6800. www.mtr.org

Between March and August of 1946, 26 sessions of the United Nations Security Council were held in the Hunter College gymnasium in The Bronx. Other locations used included a building on the East River and another in Lake Success on Long Island.

91 La Grenouille

★★★$$$$ The annual budget for flowers here is close to $100,000, and the fresh daily arrangements show it. Mirrors sparkle everywhere, and the lighting is nearly perfect, making the "beautiful people" who frequent this place look even more so. There are wonderful traditional dishes on the menu such as Dover sole, rack of lamb, and cheese soufflé, but be prepared to spend big-time if you want a good wine to go with them. ♦ French ♦ Tu-Sa, lunch and dinner; closed mid-July through August. Reservations required; jacket and tie required. 3 E 52nd St (between Madison and Fifth Aves). 752.1495

91 Austrian Cultural Forum

Contemporary Austrian culture is the programming theme for this institution dedicated to advancing international communication through the arts. Built by the Austrian Ministry for Foreign Affairs, the slender tower that was constructed for this purpose immediately contributes to the streetscape. The 24-story building, only 25 feet wide at its base, tapers as it rises skyward. With its stepped and sloping glass-and-concrete façade that draws inspiration from the Secessionist era with its geometric window patterns, the 2002 **Raimund Abraham** design is both dramatic and inventive, and completely modern. Inside are equally tasteful exhibition galleries, a library, and a jewel-box theater along with the expected office space. ♦ M-Sa, 10AM-6PM. 11 E 52nd St (between Madison and Fifth Aves). 319.5300. www.acfny.org ♿

Cartier

92 Cartier

Lovely baubles for the body and the home, mostly at astronomical prices, are this shop's stock in trade. The creator of the

New York City in Print

Nonfiction

AIA Guide to New York City by Norval White and Elliot Willensky (Three Rivers Press, 2000). In the fourth edition of this stalwart guide to New York City's architectural history, the authors provide brief but superbly detailed information (including, in many cases, thumbnail photos) about key buildings throughout the city. Written from an architectural insider's point of view, as they guide you block-by-block the occasional offhand observation makes this especially enjoyable reading.

The Building of Manhattan by Donald A. Mackay (HarperCollins, 1989). This book answers the question "How did they build that?" Hundreds of archival photos and drawings trace the history of construction in Manhattan, from the early Dutch homes to the giant skyscrapers and the latest innovations in architecture and construction techniques.

Celluloid Skyline: New York and the Movies by James Sanders (Knopf, 2001). Everything you ever wanted to know, beautifully complemented with photos and production drawings, about New York City shooting sites . . . and the sets that understudy for them in Hollywood.

City in the Sky: The Rise and Fall of the World Trade Center by James Glanz and Eric Lipton (Times Books, 2003). How the World Trade Center was conceived—as "a city in the sky, the likes of which the planet had never seen"—through the results of its demise.

The Columbia Historical Portrait of New York by John Atlee Kouwenhoven, originally published 1953 (HarperCollins, 1972). A show-and-tell guide combining brief essays and 900 photographs accompanied by historical data.

Downtown: My Manhattan by Pete Hammill (Little, Brown, 2004). Journalist Hammill's beat here is downtown, meaning mainly below 14th Street. He provides a uniquely personal, and wholly memorable, visit to spots historic and architectural, of import to trade, to music, and more.

The Encyclopedia of New York City by Kenneth T. Jackson (Yale University Press/The New-York Historical Society, 1995). This massive illustrated volume contains encapsulated information, some of it highly detailed, on just about everything and everyone associated with New York City.

Forgotten New York: Views of a Lost Metropolis by Kevin Walsh (Collins, 2006). A wonderful companion on any New York walking tour, this guide covers all five boroughs and includes maps for each. Hidden gems from some 300 years of history—signage, sidewalk art streets to nowhere—and memory are brought to light for you.

Gotham: A History of New York City to 1898 by Edwin G. Burrows and Mike Wallace (Oxford University Press, 1998). A fascinating—and remarkably accessible—in-depth take on the history of our fair city. It seamlessly weaves together the historic characters and the events, bringing to life the period it covers so well.

Here Is New York by E.B. White, with a new Introduction by Roger Angell, originally published in 1948 (Little Bookroom, 2000). The elegant stylist shares his unique observations of the mid-20th-century city. His wit honed to its sharpest, White reveals the quintessential character of New York.

The Island at the Center of the World: The Epic Story of Dutch Manhattan and the Forgotten Colony That Shaped America by Russell Shorto (Doubleday, 2004). The less-known story of the city when it was in Dutch hands, but no less key to understanding how the city became the economic powerhouse it is today.

The Late, Great Pennsylvania Station by Lorraine B. Diehl, originally published 1985 (Four Walls Eight Windows, 1996). This illustrated oversized paperback traces the history and tragic end of one of New York's architectural wonders.

Lost New York by Nathan Silver, originally published 1982 (Houghton Mifflin, revised 2000). A beautifully photographed paean to buildings that are no longer with us—and a commentary on what their loss means to the fabric of this city. History of the buildings and neighborhoods of New York.

Low Life: Lures and Snares of Old New York by Luc Sante, originally published in 1992 (Farrar, Straus & Giroux, 2003). The underbelly of New York City, circa 1840–1919, fluidly revealed in Sante's depiction of that era's wayward street scene.

Manhattan '45 by Jan Morris, originally published in 1987 (The Johns Hopkins University Press, 1998). New York City in 1945 was a city of great promise, on the brink of great change. Morris begins with the return of our troops from World War II, as they arrive at New York's docks, and takes us on a memorable tour.

Manhattan Skyscrapers by Eric Peter Nash (Princeton Architectural Press, revised 2005). Everything you always wanted to know about the world's most famous skyline and its component parts, with plenty of photographs.

New York Enclaves by William Hemp, originally published in 1975 (Clarkson Potter, revised 2003). An illustrated gem covering 26 of Manhattan's hidden neighborhood treasures, from Patchin Place to Sniffen Court, Strivers' Row, and Treadwell Farm.

New York New York: The City in Art and Literature (Universe, 2001). This thick, attractive book draws from the Metropolitan Museum of Art's collection and pairs works of artists and writers who have drawn inspiration from the city over the years.

New York Streetscapes: Tales of Manhattan's Significant Buildings and Landmarks by Christopher Gray (Harry N. Abrams, 2003). Anecdotes and fine architectural writing accompanied by some 300 black-and-white photographs, many historic, tell the history of the city through some of its most remarkable buildings.

The Power Broker: Robert Moses and the Fall of New York by Robert A. Caro, originally published in 1974 (Vintage, 1975). A hefty tome about one of New York's all-time heavy hitters. Without Moses there would be far less parkland—or parkways. *With* him, urban-renewal issues arose that remain controversial today.

722 Miles: The Building of the Subways and How They Transformed New York by Clifton Hood (The Johns Hopkins University Press, 1995). Urban transportation buffs and social historians alike are apt to find themselves absorbed in this comprehensive illustrated narrative on the longest rapid transit system in the world—developed in New York City from 1904 through 1940.

Terrible Honesty: Mongrel Manhattan in the 1920s by Ann Douglas (Farrar, Straus & Giroux, 1995). The era is the Jazz Age, and Douglas covers the cultural history of that time in New York, presenting a provocative and fascinating picture of class, race, and the arts.

Waterfront: A Journey Around Manhattan by Phillip Lopate (Crown, 2004). The esteemed essayist dips into history, architecture, literature, and more as he circumnavigates Manhattan Island and regales us with fact-filled personal observations about its nature and development.

Writing New York: A Literary Anthology, edited by Phillip Lopate (Washington Square Press, 2000). The breadth of this impressive tome—with essays and poems from writers running the gamut from Henry James to Joan Didion to Vladimir Mayakovsky—may make it the definitive collection of writing on New York. More than a thousand pages, it makes for excellent reading before, during, and after a trip to New York City.

Fiction

The Age of Innocence by Edith Wharton, originally published 1920 (Modern Library Classics, 1999). An incisive but subtle attack on the mores and customs of upper-class society in turn-of-the-century New York. A richly detailed portrait of a world Wharton knew quite well, and disdained.

The Bonfire of the Vanities by Tom Wolfe, originally published 1987 (Picador, 2002). New York in the 1980s: greed was good, and the Bronx was burning. And Tom Wolfe absolutely nailed it.

The Catcher in the Rye by J.D. Salinger, originally published 1951 (Little, Brown, 1991). This once-controversial classic, about the adolescence of Holden Caulfield, a young runaway in New York, has been a touchstone for a generation or two.

Knickerbocker's History of New York by Washington Irving, originally published 1809; revised 1848 (Sleepy Hollow, 1981). A satirical and somewhat burlesque "history" of New York, written by Irving under the pseudonym Diedrich Knickerbocker (the same narrator as in *Rip Van Winkle*).

Ragtime by E.L. Doctorow, originally published 1975 (Random House, 2007). Doctorow has captured old(er) New York in print since (*Billy Bathgate, World's Fair*), but *Ragtime* stands alone for its mesmerizing synthesis of the Stanford White era, and the architectural goliath himself.

This Side of Paradise by F. Scott Fitzgerald, originally published 1920 (Scribner, 1998). A portrait of the "Lost Generation" in its college days, and yet another battle between true love and money-lust that ends in regret and cynicism.

Time and Again by Jack Finney, originally published 1970 (Touchstone, 1995). If you could go back in time—in particular, to 1880s New York City—and change the world, what would you do? Finney offers some suggestions.

A Tree Grows in Brooklyn by Betty Smith, originally published 1943 (Perennial, 2005). A sensitive child grows up in a rough neighborhood with a drunk but lovable father and a determined but sweet mother. Tender and moving.

Washington Square by Henry James, originally published 1880 (Signet, 2004). James grew up on Washington Square, the setting for this novel about the shy young daughter of a domineering and wealthy doctor who makes her life miserable. Made into a movie and a play titled *The Heiress* and, in 1997, a movie titled *Washington Square*.

tank watch is always coming up with original designs, and there are all those rings of diamonds, emeralds, and pearls. Don't miss "Les Must," the more affordable boutique collection of gifts, such as cigarette lighters. Once the residence of businessman Morton F. Plant, the Renaissance palazzo-style building is a rare survivor of the days when Fifth Avenue was lined with the private homes of such people as William Vanderbilt, who lived diagonally across the street. **Robert W. Gibson** designed the building in 1905; **William Welles Bosworth** supervised the conversion to a store in 1917. Note the detailing of the entrance and centralized composition catch it at Christmas, and enjoy the big red bows encasing the building then. ♦ Daily. 653 Fifth Ave (at E 52nd St). 753.0111. ♿ Also at 828 Madison Ave (at E 69th St). 472.6400

93 Omni Berkshire Place

$$$$ A plush European-style hotel, the Berkshire's 396 generously proportioned rooms boast high-speed Wi-Fi Internet access, faxes, two phone lines, and sitting areas; 44 spacious suites offer even more amenities. A full-service business center and health club are also on the scene. The adjacent **Fireside** restaurant (19 E 52nd St, 754.5011) is open daily for breakfast, lunch, and dinner . . . and cozy cocktails by their dramatic floor-to-ceiling fireplace. ♦ 21 E 52nd St (between Madison and Fifth Aves). 753.5800, 800/THE.OMNI; fax 755.2317. www.omnihotels.com ♿

94 Fresco by Scotto

★★$$ This family affair owned by Marion Scotto and her children Anthony Jr., Elaina, and Rosanna (the local newscaster) is both elegant and cheery. Colors abound, on the ochre walls with bold paintings by SoHo artists and in the complex floral displays. Try spaghettini with clams, garlic, basil, and roasted tomatoes; baked penne with *pancetta* (Italian unsmoked bacon), Parmesan, and cream; one of the homemade ravioli specials; rib-eye steak, or grilled veal chop. Desserts are irresistible—either the lemon tartlet or cinnamon ice-cream sandwich makes a perfect ending for the meal. ♦ Italian ♦ M-F, lunch and dinner; Sa, dinner. Reservations recommended. 34 E 52nd St (between Park and Madison Aves). 935.3434 ♿

New York is the only American city to house an American embassy, the United States Mission, located across the street from the United Nations.

95 Seagram Building

The ultimate representation of pure modernist reason, this classically proportioned and exquisitely detailed 1958 bronze, glass, and steel box by **Ludwig Mies van der Rohe** and **Philip Johnson** is the one everybody copied (see Sixth Avenue and other parts of Park Avenue)—but it's still the best. The building is set back on a plaza that was an innovative relief when it was conceived. ♦ 375 Park Ave (between E 52nd and E 53rd Sts)

Within the Seagram Building:

The Four Seasons

★★★★$$$$ One of the world's most celebrated restaurants, Seagram architect **Philip Johnson** dined here daily until his death in 2005. Its **Bar Room Grill** is power central at midday, when the top echelons of New York's publishing world gather to exchange notes and gossip. Featured in this casual space later in the day is one of the city's true fine dining bargains—an under-$59.50 three-course meal, including coffee or tea. The **Pool Room** next door, a more formal spot, has been going strong since 1958 and features such dishes as oxtail ravioli with sage, pumpkin bisque with cinnamon, carpaccio of tuna and salmon with ginger, foie gras with figs, and sea bass in an herb crust. ♦ Continental ♦ M-F, lunch and dinner; Sa, dinner. Reservations required; jacket and tie required. 99 E 52nd St (between Lexington and Park Aves). 754.9494

96 Nippon

★★$$$$ One of the first restaurants to introduce sushi and sashimi to New Yorkers, this gracious place maintains its overall high quality and continues to offer dishes unfamiliar to Western palates, such as *usuzukuri* (marinated fluke in very thin slices). There are also excellent versions of more familiar dishes, such as *shabu shabu* (beef and vegetables cooked at the table in a hot pot of soy broth) and tempura. ♦ Japanese ♦ M-F, lunch and dinner; Sa, dinner. Reservations recommended. 155 E 52nd St (between Third and Lexington Aves). 758.0226

97 242 East 52nd Street

With two UN missions on the north side of this block (Hungary's, at No. 227, is a grand Beaux Arts affair; at No. 237, Zambia's is a distinctive Italian Deco streamlined-meets-Bauhaus rarity), this stretch of East 52nd Street is already striking. Here on the south side, at No. 242, is a 1950 **Philip Johnson** design, which, like the **Lescaze Residence** (see page 209), is a quintessentially modern composition in a row-house lot. Commissioned by John D. Rockefeller Jr. as a guesthouse for the **Museum of Modern Art**, this rather petite, cube-isn structure was also used at one time by Johnson as a New York City pied-à-terre. More than a bit time-worn now—dare we say, oddly dumpy-looking—the base is Wrightian brick, the top Miesian steel and glass, and at one time the whole composition must have seemed almost Oriental in its simplicity and mystery. The buildings listed here are not open to the public. ♦ Between Second and Third Aves

98 Le Périgord

★★★$$$ A favorite haunt of UN ambassadors and celebrities, this formal but cozy French restaurant has been around since the mid-1960s. But the romantic room, with its pink banquettes, is still pretty, and owner George Briguet remains a charming host. Best choices are the crisp sweetbreads in a Sauternes sauce, goat cheese and vegetable tart with arugula and black olive paste, grilled Dover sole with mustard sauce, and fillet of beef in red wine. Save room for one of the soufflés, or choose the chocolate mousse or lemon tart from the pastry cart. ♦ French ♦ M-F, lunch and dinner; Sa, Su, dinner. Dinner is prix-fixe only. Reservations required; jacket and tie required. 405 E 52nd St (just east of First Ave). 755.6244

99 Versace

The late designer's New York boutique is a 28,000-square-foot renovated Vanderbilt mansion. The shop offers the popular—and sometimes flamboyant—Couture collection for men and women. For those with limits on their Visa Golds, there are also the mid-priced (for them) Versus and Istante labels. ♦ Daily. 647 Fifth Ave (between E 51st and E 52nd Sts)

00 Olympic Tower

This black glass box full of exclusive apartments was designed in 1976 by **Skidmore**, **Owings & Merrill**. The hospitable interior arcade is complete with a waterfall and a refreshment stand, plus a foreign currency exchange office. Reflections of **St. Patrick's** are a nice bonus. ♦ 645 Fifth Ave (at E 51st St)

01 Tuscan Square

★$$ Tuscany comes to New York in this popular, heavily themed Northern Italian brainchild of restaurateur Pino Luongo. Reservations recommended. ♦ M-Sa, lunch and dinner. 16 W 51st St (between Fifth Ave and Rockefeller Plaza). 977.7777

102 Façonnable

Replicating the Façonnable store on rue Royale in Paris, this shop is a destination for well-heeled and well-dressed men and women who will find a solid assortment of pricey, clean-cut Euro-prep wear, both tailored and casual. ♦ Daily. 636 Fifth Ave (at W 51st St). 319.0111 ♿

103 Tse Yang

★★$$$ Like the original Tse Yang in Paris, this stateside outpost offers outstanding Beijing cuisine and European-style service in a stunning Imperial setting of black mirrors, rich wood paneling, and hammered copper and brass appointments. Chef Yang Kui-Fah serves a tasty crab-leg salad, tea-smoked salmon, hot-and-sour soup, orange beef (served cold), and pickled cabbage. ♦ Chinese ♦ Daily, lunch and dinner. Reservations recommended; jacket required. 34 E 51st St (between Park and Madison Aves). 688.5447 ♿

104 General Electric Building

This 51-story tower was designed in 1931 by **Cross & Cross** to harmonize with the Byzantine lines of **St. Bartholomew's Church** (see page 203), and is still best seen with the church at its feet. But it's a beauty from any angle, lavishly decorated with what was possibly intended to be stylized lightning bolts in honor of its first tenant, the Radio Company of America, which moved soon after to the new **Rockefeller Center**. Take a peek at the lobby. ♦ 570 Lexington Ave (at E 51st St)

105 DoubleTree Metropolitan Hotel

$$$ Clad in seafoam-colored brick, **Morris Lapidus**'s 1961 plastic modern design for this hotel (originally **The Summit**, then **Loews New York**) stands as one of New York's rare tropical Deco moments. DoubleTree's millennial takeover and $35 million redesign freshened the 19-story building inside and out. Both its public spaces—complete with orange Arne Jacobsen scoop chairs—and the 755 guest-rooms maintain the spirit of Lapidus without overdoing it. High-speed Internet access, flat-panel TVs, and the gamut of modern amenities are offered along with a cardio fitness center, a business center, and the casual **Met Grill** (serving breakfast, lunch, and dinner) and the sleeker **Met Lounge.** ♦ 569 Lexington Ave (at E 51st St). 752.7000, 800/836.6471; fax 758.6311. www.metropolitannyc.com

The Best

Linda Wells

Former Editor-in-Chief, *Allure* magazine

Madison Avenue, from East 60th to East 93rd Streets, is the greatest shopping, people-watching, salon-stopping stretch in New York. Start at the **Calvin Klein** store for clean, modern, sleek clothes. Then go to **Barneys New York** for quirky, unusual beauty products, great children's gifts, stylish stationery, and a fashion editor's wardrobe. Try **TSE Cashmere** for luxurious sweaters; **Prada** for three floors of delicious fashion, shoes, and handbags; and **Polo Sport–Ralph Lauren** for the best weekend gear.

For a serious weekday breakfast, **The Carlyle Hotel** attracts the local moguls.

For a breather, duck into the **Frick Museum** and meditate by the fountain. **The Metropolitan Museum of Art** is wonderful for everything, especially the Frank Lloyd Wright room and the serene, hidden Chinese garden.

Run around the **Central Park reservoir** or skate at **Wollman Rink** at the southern end of the park. Both give an enchanted view of the city.

106 Greenacre Park

This "vest pocket park" is slightly larger and more elaborate than its cousin, **Paley Park**. Designed in 1971 by **Sasaki**, **Dawson**, **DeMay Associates**, it was a gift to the city by Mrs. Jean Mauze, daughter of John D. Rockefeller Jr. ♦ 217-221 E 51st St (between Second and Third Aves)

107 St. Patrick's Cathedral

Now dwarfed by its surroundings—particularly by **Rockefeller Center**—this church was considered too far out of town when **James Renwick Jr.** built it in the 1880s. (**Charles T. Matthews** added the **Lady Chapel** in 1906.) The 11th-largest church in the world, the structure is a finely detailed and well-proportioned but not very strict adaptation of its French-Gothic predecessors. There are no flying buttresses, for example, but there are pinnacles. The spires rise to 330 feet, and the rose window above the center portal is 26 feet in diameter. More than half of the 70 stained-glass windows were made in Chartres and Nantes. Renwick also designed the high altar. Docent-guided walking tours are available in summer; handouts for self-guided tours (when there is no service) are available year round. ♦ Fifth Ave (between E 50th and E 51st Sts). 753.2261 ♿

108 The Villard Houses

This collection of six houses was designed in 1884 by **McKim**, **Mead & White** to resemble a single Italian palazzo at the request of the original owner, publisher Henry Villard. They were later owned by the Archdiocese of New York, which sold them to Harry Helmsley in the late 1970s. In a precedent-setting arrangement, Helmsley—their owner until 1993—incorporated two of the landmark houses into the New York **Palace Hotel** (below.) ♦ 451-459 Madison Ave (between E 50th and E 51st Sts)

Within The Villard Houses:

Municipal Art Society

The Municipal Art Society (including **Urban Center Books**, below) occupies the north wing of The Villard Houses, where they frequently host talks on urban architecture and planning issues, and related exhibitions that are open to the public. They also offer an extensive selection of guided walking tours on fascinating and little-known details of the New York City-built environment. ♦ M-Sa. 457 Madison Ave (between E 50th and E 51st Sts). 935.3960. www.mas.org ♿

Urban Center Books

As you would expect, the emphasis here is on books, periodicals, and journals about architecture, historic preservation, and urban design. ♦ M-Sa. 457 Madison Ave. 935.3595. www.urbancenterbooks.org ♿

108 The New York Palace Hotel

$$$$ This elegant property incorporates part of the landmark **Villard Houses**, resulting in an uneasy but interesting marriage. The elaborate lobby in the old section (protected from alteration) is opulent—even excessively so—with the ornate woodwork, marble, frescoes, and fireplaces from the Gilded Age all intact. The 893 guestrooms, along with four triplex suites, are spaciously comfortable and thoughtfully appointed. Business-folk friendly, all accommodations include high-speed Internet service and fax/copy/scanner units. Guests staying on the **Executive Floors** are afforded complimentary food and beverage lounges. A fully equipped spa and fitness center, the **Istana** brasserie in the lobby (daily. Breakfast, lunch, dinner. 303.6032), and the fancier Euro-cuisine **Gilt** restaurant and bar (Reservations recommended. 891.8100) complete the picture. Don't miss the

whimsical animal topiary on the Madison Avenue-side outdoor terrace area. ♦ 455 Madison Ave (main entrance: E 50th St). 888.7000, 800/697.2522; fax 303.6000. www.newyorkpalace.com

09 Maloney & Porcelli

★★$$$ A prime destination for tender, prime meats. Chef Patrick Vaccariello's most popular entrée, the gigundo crackling pork shank served on a bed of poppyseeded sauerkraut with firecracker applesauce, is simply terrific. Other specialties include London broil and grilled rib eye, as well as such seafood dishes as lemon-crusted salmon steak and steamed lobster. Desserts are standard, with cheesecake topping the list. ♦ Steak house ♦ M-F, lunch and dinner; Sa, Su, dinner. Reservations recommended. 37 E 50th St (between Park and Madison Aves). 750.2233

10 St. Bartholomew's Church

This richly detailed Byzantine landmark with a charming little garden is a breath of fresh air on a high-rise-lined block. But it has been the object of a long-running battle between preservationists and church fathers, who wanted to sell off the **Community House** for commercial development (the plans were eventually nixed). The portico was a Vanderbilt-financed, **Stanford White**-designed addition (1903) to a church by **James Renwick Jr.** In 1919, **Bertram G. Goodhue** inherited the portico and designed the church—a confabulation handled with style that now, in addition to regular services, offers a wonderful range of Early Music programming. The site was a Schaefer brewery in the 1860s. Public tours on Sunday (378.0211). ♦ Park Ave (between E 50th and E 51st Sts). 378.0222. www.stbarts.org ♿

Within St. Bartholomew's Church:

Inside Park

★$$ The church's soaring Great Hall is a fine spot for year-round dining. But come spring (and summer), its outdoor terrace comes to life and the American fare is all the more special. A change of hands (and name, from Café St. Bart's) in late 2007 spruced the place up and renewed its focus on seasonal offerings. Reservations recommended. ♦ M-F, breakfast, lunch, and dinner. Sa, brunch and dinner, Su, brunch. 593.3333 ♿

11 The Benjamin

$$$$ Sumptuous and quiet, this hotel is a find. Most of the 200 accommodations in the hotel (reopened in 1999 and now run by the Affinia group; this 1927 **Emery Roth** building was formerly **The Beverly**) are suites or junior suites with quality desks and kitchenettes. Rooms feature Bose Wave radios, DVD/CD players, high-speed Internet access, aromatherapy bath products, Frette terrycloth robes, and baskets of potpourri. Other perks are complimentary daily newspapers and personalized business cards. Custom-made beds are very comfortable, and guests browse a pillow menu to select from eleven varieties—ask the resident Sleep Concierge (we're not kidding) for his or her recommendations. To revitalize after all that rest, head to **The Wellness Spa** (715.2517) or the 24-hour fitness center. Furry guests? The Benjamin's welcoming Dream Dog program awaits. Last, the lobby is small but has high ceilings and a gorgeous floral arrangement that changes daily; the **Benjamin Lounge** is located just upstairs. ♦ 125 E 50th St (at Lexington Ave). 715.2400, 888/423.6526; fax 715.2525. www.thebenjamin.com ♿

112 Zarela

★★$$$ Decorated with antique Mexican masks, colorful paper cutouts, and very bright fabrics, Zarela maintains a buoyant party atmosphere (ask to be seated in the upstairs dining area if you actually want to converse with your dining companions). Don't miss the special "call" tequila margaritas and famous red snapper hash. Also try chef Zarela Martinez's grilled marinated skirt steak with salsa, guacamole, and flour tortillas. But beware the all à la carte menu . . . and you might want to ask the price of that margarita you're about to order. ♦ Mexican ♦ M-F, lunch and dinner; Sa, Su, dinner. Reservations required. 953 Second Ave (between E 50th and E 51st Sts). 644.6740

113 Rockefeller Center

This is the largest privately owned business and entertainment complex in the world, with 19 buildings covering 21 acres. It all began in 1926 when John D. Rockefeller Jr. secured leases on land in the area to provide a setting for the old **Metropolitan Opera House**, which was going to move here from the Garment Center. The Great Depression changed the opera's plans and left the philanthropist with a long-term lease on 11.7 acres of Midtown Manhattan. He decided to develop it himself, and demolition of 228 buildings to make way for the project began in May 1931. The last of Rockefeller's original buildings (all clustered between West 49th and West 51st Streets and Fifth and Sixth Avenues), **Simon & Schuster**, at

1230 Sixth Avenue, was opened in April 1940. A second round of construction—this time all towers, mostly on the west side of Sixth Avenue—began in 1957, when Marilyn Monroe detonated the first charge of dynamite to begin excavation for the **Time & Life Building**, designed by **Harrison & Abramovitz**, at 1271 Sixth Avenue. 1211 Sixth Ave (Celanese), the **McGraw-Hill Building** at 1221 Sixth Avenue, and **Exxon** at 1251—all by H&A—soon followed.

Conceived by Rockefeller as the "Radio City," the original 14-building complex was designed by a trio of the era's most indomitable firms: **Reinhard & Hoffmeister**; **Corbett**, **Harrison and MacMurray**; and **Hood**, **Godley & Fouilhoux**. At its head, representing the Rockefeller interests, was John R. Todd of **Todd**, **Robertson & Todd Engineering Corp.** Their ideas included a north-south, midblock private street (**Rockefeller Plaza**) between West 48th and West 51st Streets, underground pedestrian and shopping passageways connecting all the buildings, off-street freight delivery 30 feet underground, capable of handling a thousand trucks a day, and a commitment to public artworks throughout.

The crown jewel of the original complex is "30 Rock," the 70-story **GE Building** (officially 30 Rockefeller Plaza; and formerly the RCA Building). Todd told the architects that no desk should be more than 30 feet from a window. They obliged him by placing all the rentable space no farther than 28 feet from natural light. The astonishing wealth of art that enhances the many lobbies and exteriors is the work of 30 of the finest painters and sculptors of the 20th century. Depicting Wisdom, **Lee Lawrie**'s limestone, glass, and gold entryway to 30 Rock never fails to dazzle; his *Atlas*, designed with **Rene Chamberlain**, stands in front of the **International Building** at 630 Fifth, across from St. Patrick's Cathedral. On the face of the former **Associated Press Building** (50 Rockefeller Plaza), **Isamu Noguchi**'s sculptural panel, *News*, presides. (For more, see tour information below).

About a quarter of Rockefeller Center's space has been left open—unusual for an urban development—and much of it has been landscaped. The star of the show—for the public, at least—is the **Channel Garden** on the **Promenade** off Fifth Avenue (across from **Saks Fifth Avenue**). The complex's gardeners are kept busy with more than 20,000 flowering plants that are moved periodically, and two acres of formal gardens on the rooftops, which on very rare occasions are open to the public.

Pronounced a National Historic Landmark in 1988 Rockefeller Center today is as much a process as a place, continually changing in one way or another. In 2001 the blocks of Rockefeller Plaza were made into pedestria malls—and a space for large-scale, witty ar installations like Jeff Koons's giant flowerin puppy and the helium anime of Takashi Murakami, as well as the annual Christmas tree and even a greenmarket—driving away the limousines that once used the street as their own parking and pickup locations. The year 2005 welcomed the return of the observatory atop 30 Rock. First opened in 1933, **Top of the Rock**, as it's called now, sits just above the **Rainbow Room** and is a delightfully Deco. ♦ Rockefeller Center guided tours: Daily (fee). 664.7174. Self-guided tours: Free brochures available at 3 Rockefeller Plaza, main desk. Rockefeller Center: Bounded by Fifth and Seventh Aves and W 48th and W 51st Sts. Information line: 632.3975. www.rockefellercenter.com Top of the Rock: Access by timed tickets. Daily (fee). 30 Rockefeller Plaza. 698.200 877/692.7625 (NYC-ROCK). www.topoftherocknyc.com ♿

At Rockefeller Center:

Radio City Music Hall

Since 1932, this Art Deco palace has maintained a tradition of spectacular entertainment. When it opened as a variety house operated by entrepreneur Samuel "Roxy" Rothafel, it was the largest theater in the world and included such features as a 50-foot turntable on the 11 foot stage, sections of which changed leve 75 rows of fly lines for scenery; a network of microphones; six motor-operated light bridges; a cyclorama 117 feet by 75 feet, and a host of other controls and effects. **Edward Durrell Stone** directed the Rock Center architectural team for this one; the glamorous and sophisticated Modernist interior spaces were designed largely by **Donald Deskey.**

The scale was overwhelming. "What are those mice doing onstage?" someone aske on opening night. "Those aren't mice, those are horses," his neighbor replied.

The opening of the hall in December 1932 drew such celebrities as Charlie Chaplin, Cla Gable, Amelia Earhart, and Arturo Toscanini. The premiere performance had 75 stellar acts, including Ray Bolger, the Wallendas, a the **Roxyetts** (later known as the **Rockettes**)

The hall was soon turned into a movie hous with stage shows, featuring the Rockettes, the **Corps de Ballet**, the **Symphony Orchestra**, and a variety of guest artists. Th premiere feature film was Frank Capra's *The Bitter Tea of General Yen* with Barbara Stanwyck. From 1933 until 1979—when the hall was granted NYC landmark status and restoration began—more than 650 features debuted here, including *King Kong, It Happened One Night, Jezebel, Top Hat, Snow White and the Seven Dwarfs, An American in Paris*, and *Mister Roberts*. In 1979, a new format was introduced. Musical spectaculars and pop personalities in concert are the current bill of fare, with major names such as Bette Midler and Stevie Wonder performing to sold-out audiences. The 57 Rockettes still make an annual appearance during the traditional Christmas and Easter shows. Three-quarters of a century after the theater's opening night on 27 December 1932, over 3,000 Rockettes have high-kicked their way across the 144-foot stage.

The 5,882-seat hall is now, with its impeccably detailed restoration completed, a glorious vision of its former self. (**Hardy, Holzer & Pfeiffer** can take the credit.) Its plush foyer rises 50 feet, overlooked by a sweeping stair and three mezzanine levels lined with gold mirrors and topped by a gold-leaf ceiling. The restrooms retain much of their fine Deco detailing—tilework, trim, and fixtures. Even the Stuart Davis mural *Men Without Women* that famously hung in a men's room here has been returned after a 25-year break at the **Museum of Modern Art**. The auditorium is everything a theater should be: a plaster vault of overlapping semicircles lit from the inside edge in a rainbow of colors, it provides sunsets and sunrises as the lights go down and up. ♦ Radio City "Stage Door" tours: daily (fee). In-person at box office; 307.1000 (Ticketmaster); or online. ♦ 1260 Ave of the Americas (at W 50th St). Box office (information only): 247.4777. www.radiocity.com ♿

The Rainbow Room

★★★★$$$$ First opened in 1934 to a post-Depression reemerging New York society, the legendary Art Moderne restaurant/supper club on the 65th floor of Rockefeller Center was taken over by Cipriani International (which operates the famous Harry's Bar in Venice) in 1998. The Rainbow Room, its famous revolving dance floor intact, is mostly used for private parties, while the former Promenade Bar on the south side has been reincarnated as the **Rainbow Grill**, open seven days a week. ♦ Italian ♦ **Rainbow Room**: F, Sa, dinner and dancing; Su, brunch. Reservations required; jacket and tie required. **Rainbow Grill**: Daily, dinner only. Reservations recommended; jacket required. 30 Rockefeller Plaza, 65th floor. 49 W 49th St (between Rockefeller Plaza and Sixth Ave), 65th floor. 632.5100. www.rainbowroom.com ♿

NBC Studio Tours

Tours of the radio and television facilities of the National Broadcasting Co. are offered. Children under six are not admitted. If you don't want to wait in line, walk over to West 49th and Rockefeller Plaza and see if you can catch sight of Matt Lauer, Meredith Vieira, and Al Roker, who do the *Today* show live from their street-level picture-window studio. ♦ Admission. Daily. 30 Rockefeller Plaza (between W 49th and W 50th Sts). 664.3700 ♿

The Rink

Under the year-round golden gaze of sculptor Paul Manship's Prometheus, the summer-time outdoor dining area becomes an ice-skating rink every October, staying slick and smooth right through April. Ice skates can be rented at the rink. ♦ Admission; additional fee for skate rental. Daily. Call for changing sessions. Lower plaza (between W 49th and W 50th Sts and Fifth and Sixth Aves). 332.7654

Rock Center Café

★★$$$ Upscale but casual American fare is served in the large renovated space that for years housed the popular **American Festival** restaurant. ♦ American ♦ Daily, breakfast, lunch, and dinner; Sa, Su, brunch. 20 W 50th St (between Fifth Ave and Rockefeller Plaza), lower plaza. 332.7620 ♿

The Sea Grill

★★$$$ Fresh seafood is served in a lush setting in the heart of all the action. Try the Baltimore crab cakes served with a mustard and scallion sauce, the buttery salmon with a Dijon mustard and roasted shallot sauce, or grilled Maine lobster with grilled vegetables. Request a window seat in winter so you can watch the ice skaters. ♦ Seafood ♦ M-F, lunch and dinner; Sa, dinner. Reservations required. 19 W 49th St (between Fifth Ave and Rockefeller Plaza), lower plaza. 332.7610 ♿

On the Promenade:

Metropolitan Museum of Art Gift Shop

At three floors and 6,000 square feet, this is the largest of the museum's gift-shop outposts. The merchandise, for the most part inspired by the museum's permanent collections and special exhibitions, includes prints and posters, stationery, jewelry, tabletop accessories, sculpture reproductions, and educational gifts for children.

Especially popular are the museum's signature items, which include William, a reproduction of the 12th-dynasty Egyptian hippo (the Met's unofficial mascot), and Venus earrings, one black and one white teardrop, worn by the goddess in Rubens's *Venus Before the Mirror.* ♦ South side of the Promenade, between W 49th and W 50th Sts. 332.1360. Also at other locations

Librairie de France/ Librería Hispanica

Home to a good selection of bilingual dictionaries, children's books, and audiobooks, this longtime family-owned (since 1935) bookstore provides one of the best—albeit expensive—selections of books in French and in English about France, with a smaller offering of Spanish-language titles. They also carry a selection of antique prints. ♦ M-Sa. 610 Fifth Ave (south side of Promenade, between W 49th and W 50th Sts). 581.8810. www.frencheuropean.com ♿

Teuscher Chocolates of Switzerland

Some of the city's best (and most expensive) chocolate bonbons are offered here. The spectacular window displays change with the season. ♦ M-Sa. 620 Fifth Ave (north side of Promenade, between W 49th and W 50th Sts). 246.4416. Also at 25 E 61st St (at Madison Ave). 751.8482

114 Saks Fifth Avenue

Fashionable and always in good taste, this New York institution has another asset few other stores can offer: service. Designer collections throughout the store will please any woman's sense of style, and the men's department is legendary. The selection for children is heaven on earth for parents and grandparents who enjoy seeing the little ones turned out in style. The small luxury selection of candies, liqueur cakes, and chocolates runs from the sublime to the decadent. The airy **Cafe SFA** on the eighth floor is a great spot for lunch, particularly if you come early and secure a window table overlooking **St. Patrick's Cathedral** or **Rockefeller Center**. If it's Christmastime, the window displays are a must-see. ♦ Daily. 611 Fifth Ave (between E 49th and E 50th Sts). 753.4000 ♿

The tradition of New York's Easter Parade is said to have begun in the 1870s when parishioners of St. Thomas Episcopal Church on Fifth Avenue walked up the avenue to deliver flowers to St. Luke's Hospital, which stood just a block to the north. The "parade" soon became an annual ritual of fashion.

115 The Waldorf-Astoria Hote

$$$$ Spruced up and renovated for the 21 century, the incomparable grande dame ha been home to permanent guests such as t Duchess of Windsor and the American representative to the UN, as well as temporary guests like King Faisal of Saudi Arabia and every US president since 1931. was moved here when the **Empire State Building** rose on its former site on lower Fifth Avenue. Taking up the entire block between Lexington and Park Avenues and East 49th and East 50th Streets, it has 1,215 spacious guestrooms. Together with the adjacent and slightly more expensive **Waldorf Towers**, with 118 guestrooms and 77 suites, the hotel is now administered by the Hilton chain. Designed by **Schultze & Weaver**, the building is considered by man to be the best on this stretch of Park Avenu The base is in proper relation to the surrounding buildings, while the unique tw towers are still noteworthy additions to the skyline.

The hotel epitomized the good life of New York in the 1930s, carrying on in the tradition of its fashionable predecessor at West 34th Street and Fifth Avenue. (The hotel's Tony guests often arrived underground in their private railway cars on a specially constructed spur off the tracks under Park Avenue.) The luxurious Art Dec interiors suffered some mistreatment and neglect over the years—the burled walnut elevator cabs, for example, were lined with brocade—but have been meticulously restored. Of particular interest are the Lou Rigel murals in the lobby and the Wheel of Life mosaic in the floor of the lobby. The **B and Bear** and the pretty **Peacock Alley** (freshly renovated and reopened in late 2005 after a four-year hiatus) are popular dining spots. **Plus One** is a complete fitne and spa facility. ♦ 301 Park Ave (between 49th and E 50th Sts). 355.3000, 800/925.3673; fax 872.7272. www.waldorfastoria.com ♿

Within The Waldorf-Astoria Hotel:

Inagiku

★★★$$$$ Few rooms capture a cool and peaceful ambience as well as this one, wh blends modern elements with traditional Japanese in its design. Diners can enjoy c Haruo Ohbu's tempura, sushi, or *shabu shabu* (thin slices of beef cooked in broth)

their table. Other top-quality dishes include excellent *hakata* (barbecued eel layered with shiitake mushrooms and spinach).
♦ Japanese ♦ M-F, lunch and dinner; Sa, Su, dinner. Reservations required; jacket required. 111 E 49th St (between Lexington and Park Aves). 355.0440

16 Christie's

The New York headquarters of the famous London auction house specializes in old masters, Impressionists, 19th- and 20th-century European and American art, and 22 other areas of art, including antiques and Chinese art. Tickets, available without charge a week or two before an auction, are required for evening auctions. Previews of items to be auctioned are held five days prior to the auction itself, and catalogs are available. ♦ Open to the public only during viewings before scheduled auctions. Call 636.2010, or check their web site, for schedule. 20 Rockefeller Plaza (W 49th St, between Fifth and Sixth Aves). 636.2000. www.christies.com ♿

17 Morrell & Company Wines

A playground for oenophiles, this large, well-organized store carries practically every worthwhile label, including many direct imports. Service is knowledgeable but occasionally impatient. ♦ M-Sa. 1 Rockefeller Plaza, W 49th St (between Fifth and Sixth Aves). 688.9370

Within Morrell & Company Wines:

Morrell Wine Bar & Café

With views onto the Rockefeller Center Rink, this is a great spot to sit back and expand your wine knowledge firsthand. The classic American cuisine offers a pleasing twist—most dishes include wine in their preparation. ♦ M-Sa, lunch and dinner; Su, brunch. Reservations recommended. 262.6547

17 Kinokuniya Bookstore

If your stroll through Rockefeller Center leaves you with a yen to read up on Zen or Tao, view a dubbed Kurosawa video, or learn to make sushi at home (or if your subway journey has made you wish you knew Aikido), you should find the resources you need in this well-stocked retail outlet of a top Japanese distributor. Among the 150,000 titles on tap are books on learning the language (try the *Japanese for Busy People* series) as well as books *in* the language. The stationery and cards upstairs are fun to browse as well. ♦ Daily. 10 W 49th St (between Fifth and Sixth Aves, in front of the Rockefeller Center skating rink). Also at 1073 Sixth Ave (between W 40th and W 41st Sts). 765.7766. www.kinokuniya.com

117 The Goelet Building

Don't miss the sleek Japanese patisserie, **Minamoto Kitchoan** (489.3747), on the ground floor of this crisp, early-modern structure, built in 1932 by **E.H. Faile & Co.** Also stop in the elevator lobby: The highly ornamented space is a hidden Art Deco gem all the way to the paneling of the elevator cabs. Note the lighting in the pilasters and cornices. ♦ 608 Fifth Ave (at W 49th St)

118 Ronin Gallery

This is the place to see Japanese art, including woodblock prints, ivory netsuke, and metalwork from the 17th through 20th centuries. ♦ Tu-Sa. 425 Madison Ave (at E 49th St). 688.0188. www.roningallery.com

119 W New York

$$$$ For the business traveler who seeks not just a respite but an all-out retreat from the concrete jungle, the **David Rockwell**-designed W New York is a great place to bed down. The former 722-room **Doral Inn** underwent a total transformation in 1998 to become the first in this chain of stylish business hotels. The nature theme—inevitably more Malibu than Midtown Manhattan—is at its most dramatic in the uncommonly airy lobby, with its light, earth-toned colors and fabrics and huge columns decked out in swaying, silkscreened translucent fabrics. The result is dramatic and different, if not exactly cozy. Guest-rooms are deliberately spare but comfortable, and feature such ostensibly restorative touches as sheets lined with inspirational sayings (such as "Dream with Lucidity" and "Sleep with Angels") and slender planters brimming with grass—along with watering cans. Flat-panel TVs and high-speed Internet access are in each room if you still can't sleep. The **Sweat Fitness Center** and **Bliss49 Spa** offer their own revivifying alternatives. The W is also a proud proponent of P.A.W. (pets are welcome).

You don't have to stay at the W to enjoy the dining and imbibing establishments that call it home. First there's **Whiskey Blue**, Rande Gerber's chic watering hole with its rich brown and heather hues, sensual lighting, and backlit mahogany bar. **Heartbeat** offers a modern, light health-oriented menu for breakfast, lunch, and dinner. (Daily). ♦ 541 Lexington Ave (at E 49th St). 755.1200, 877/946.8357; fax 319.8344. www.whotels.com ♿

120 Smith & Wollensky

★★$$$ Young corporate types favor this meat palace above all others. The décor is dramatic—black lacquered chairs, Chinese-lantern-style lights, and gargoyles perched on the sides of the banquettes—and the upstairs dining room has three skylights. The steaks and prime ribs are crowd-pleasers, and such basic desserts as Austrian strudel don't disappoint. For more casual and less expensive fare, try **Wollensky's Grill** (205 East 49th St, between Second and Third Aves, 753.0444). Both restaurants offer an extraordinary American wine list. ♦ American ♦ M-F, lunch and dinner; Sa, Su, dinner. Reservations required. 797 Third Ave (at E 49th St). 753.1530

121 Instituto Cervantes

A step off a busy Turtle Bay street takes you into one of Midtown's secret oases: the stone-paved, lushly planted garden of Amster Yard. Originally built in 1869, and believed to be the terminal stop of the Boston Stage Coach on its Eastern Post Road line, it was proclaimed a New York City landmark in 1966. **Carlos Jurado/MSL Architects** with **Thierry Noyelle-Victor** revamped the structure in 2003, beautifully blending its aged brick detailing with sleek sand-blasted glass and matte metal touches and readily adapting it to the needs of this nonprofit center, dedicated to promoting Spanish language and culture. You can benefit from this initiative through films, concerts, readings, and other programs; language classes taught by native speakers; courses on cinema, dance, art, or wine; and the free use of the **Jorge Luis Borges Library**, where you'll find Spanish periodicals, videos and DVDs, and a 40,000-volume contemporary literature collection. ♦ Office, M-F; library, Tu-Sa. 211-215 E 49th St (between Second and Third Aves). 308.7720. www.cervantes.org

122 Chin Chin

★★$$$ Chinese cuisine takes an innovative turn in this handsome, sophisticated restaurant with beige walls and recessed lighting. Try the country-style chicken with spinach, crispy sea bass, steamed salmon with black-bean sauce, or sautéed leg of lamb with leeks. ♦ Cantonese ♦ M-F, lunch and dinner; Sa, Su, dinner. 216 E 49th St (between Second and Third Aves). 888.4555

123 Beekman Tower Hotel

$$$ Originally called the **Panhellenic Hotel**, catering to women belonging to Greek-letter sororities, this deliciously Art Deco landmark is now an Affinia all-suite hotel (there are 174 in a range of sizes) favored by UN visitors looking for decently priced accommodations with fully equipped kitchens along with today's requisite high-speed Internet access. **John Mead Howell** designed the building in 1928. The once-swank, now a bit frowsy, **Top of the Tower** still a fine place to grab a drink and a 26-story-high view of the city. ♦ 3 Mitchell Pl (E 49th St, at First Ave). 355.7300; fax 753.9366. www.thebeekmanhotel.com

124 597 Fifth Avenue

The venerable original home of **Charles Scribner's Sons** bookstore, this 1913 **Ernest Flagg** structure has survived a spa of replacement retailers since Scribner's sold it in 1984. The current tenant is the cosmetics juggernaut **Sephora** (see below Respectful to the building's Beaux Arts heritage, the broadly glass-fronted façade retains its black iron detail, and the perio interior remodeling has always protected th fine railing-lined mezzanine that overlooks t main selling floor. The two-story-high vaulte plaster ceilings create a particularly light, a feeling. ♦ Between E 48th and E 49th Sts

Within 597 Fifth Avenue:

Sephora

With its cosmetics testers displayed in suc a way that confounds resistance, you migh as well give up and go on in. This chain's charm is in the immediate availability of a broad selection of wares from a multitude big-name make-up companies, the ones you'd normally find in high-end departmen stores. The difference here is you can dip right in—no salesperson required. ♦ Daily. 980.6534. ♿ Also at numerous locations throughout the city

125 Hatsuhana

★★★$$$ Sushi lovers give this bar top ratings for the freshest sushi, creatively rolled. Sit at a table or the counter, but definitely try to find a spot where you can watch the sushi chef in action. In additior the raw fare, good tempura and some skewered grilled dishes are available. The la carte items tend to add up quickly, so i you're on a budget, the prix-fixe lunch me is the way to go. ♦ Japanese ♦ M-F, lunch and dinner; Sa, dinner. Reservations recommended. 17 E 48th St (between Madison and Fifth Aves). 355.3345. Also

More than 1,200 people were killed in riots nea Tudor City in 1863, caused when the rich newcome to the area were permitted to buy draft exemptior that the poor could not afford.

237 Park Ave (E 46th St entrance, between Lexington and Park Aves). 661.3400

26 Crouch & Fitzgerald

This store is a venerable New York institution for luggage, handbags, and business cases. The emphasis is on traditional styling. Don't miss their legendary seasonal sales. ♦ M-Sa. 400 Madison Ave (at E 48th St). 755.5888 ♿

27 InterContinental The Barclay New York

$$$ Once known simply as the **Barclay**, this 686-room hotel designed by **Cross & Cross** in 1927 was the most luxurious of the hotels built by the New York Central Railroad. Now part of the InterContinental chain, it retains its elegance, with special amenities to make life easier for visiting businesspeople (24-hour room service, concierge, valet service and business center, high-speed Internet access in every room and Wi-Fi in all public spaces, health spa, and the **Barclay Bar and Grill**). ♦ 111 E 48th St (between Lexington and Park Aves). 755.5900, 800/782.8201; fax 644.0079. www.new-york-barclay.intercontinental.com ♿

28 New York Marriott East Side

$$$ Originally the **Shelton**, a club/hotel for men, this 34-story tower designed by **Arthur Loomis Harmon** in 1924 was the first major building to reflect the 1916 zoning regulations. Its set-back massing is admirable, and the design became particularly famous as the winner of architectural awards and as the subject of many paintings by Georgia O'Keeffe (she and husband Alfred Stieglitz, among other luminaries in the arts, once called the Shelton home). The hotel's 629 rooms and 17 suites were fully renovated at the new millennium; all accommodations are non-smoking and offer high-speed Internet access. Marriott amenities include a full business center, a fitness center, the **Lobby Lounge**, and the **Shelton Grill** for more serious dining. ♦ 525 Lexington Ave (between E 48th and E 49th Sts). 755.4000, 800/242.8684; fax 751.3440. www.marriott.com ♿

29 780 Third Avenue

Clad in a highly polished deep red Balmoral granite, this 50-story tower—the onetime **Wang Building**—is one of the nicest towers on this stretch of Third Avenue. A surprisingly warm **Skidmore, Owings & Merrill** design, it is set back from the street with a small tree-surrounded plaza that further enhances it; its concrete frame and central-core concept eliminate any interior columns that might break up floor space. Subtlety is the structure's key feature: a zig-zag pattern on its sides, and an "X" form on its front, are the result of the designers' application of pixel theory to the otherwise regimented windows that cover the exposed faces of the 1983 building. Where windows have been dropped, the granite facing extends, and *voilà,* the hidden diagonal bracing that supports 780 Third's structural walls is reflected on its façade. ♦ Between E 48th and E 49th Sts

130 Avra

★★$$ This stylish restaurant adds an upscale Greek option to Midtown's plethora of dining choices. Though there's no terrace or Mediterranean view, earth tones and billowy linen draped from the ceiling create a relaxed mood. Breads, salads, and appetizers are all high quality and delicious, as are the main courses, which feature big portions of classic Greek dishes such as moussaka and souvlaki and are given a somewhat more refined treatment than usual. Happiest diners seem to be those ordering seafood. ♦ Greek ♦ Daily, lunch and dinner. Reservations recommended. 141 E 48th St (between Third and Lexington Aves). 759.8550 ♿

131 Lescaze Residence

A rare, thoroughly Modernist find for the city. Glass block windows, white stucco, and industrial-pipe railings replaced the original brownstone front of this town house when Modernist architect **William Lescaze** converted it to his combination office/residence in 1934. Lescaze is well known as the co-designer of Philadelphia's extraordinary PSFS Building with George Howe. He also participated in the design of **1 New York Plaza** overlooking the harbor, and the **Municipal Courthouse** at 111 Centre Street. ♦ 211 E 48th St (between Second and Third Aves)

132 Turtle Bay Gardens

When planning began for the **UN** complex just east of here, these blocks were slated for demolition. Cooler heads prevailed, and this little development, dating from 1870 and remodeled in 1920 by architect **Clarence Dean**, was saved. The development, not open to the public, was created for Mrs. Walton Martin, who bought a back-to-back row of 10 houses on each street, then ripped out all the walls and fences behind them to create a common garden. She left a 12-foot strip down the middle for a path, at the center of which she installed a fountain copied from the Villa Medici in Rome. She redesigned the 20 houses so that their living rooms faced the private garden rather than the street and began attracting such tenants as Tyrone Power and Leopold Stokowski. It was still Katharine Hepburn's New York home when she died in 2003. ♦ 227-247 E 48th St and 226-246 E 49th St (between Second and Third Aves)

133 Helmsley Middletowne

$$$ Part of the Helmsley chain, but not of their better-known glitzy genre, this moderate 192-room hotel offers predominantly junior and large suites, some with kitchenettes, terraces, and fireplaces. ♦ 148 E 48th St (between Third and Lexington Aves). 755.3000, 800/221.4982; fax 832.0261. www.helmsleymiddletowne.com ♿

134 767 Third Avenue

This squeaky-clean curved office tower designed in 1981 by **Fox & Fowle** is high-tech, but clothed in brick and wood instead of aluminum and steel. A small, quiet courtyard on its East 48th Street side features an active story-high chessboard. Attached to the outside wall of the neighboring building, it was provided by 767 Third's developer, Melvyn Kauffman, and designed by **Pamela Waters Studio.** A new move is made on the board each week; ask the concierge at No. 767 for the bulletin and a short description of how to participate. ♦ At E 48th St. Concierge: 371.7767

135 Diamond District

On this tightly packed block of West 47th Street, anchored at both ends by diamond-shaped pylons that tower above the traffic, some of what glitters *is* gold. But most of it is stones of every cut, color, and carat weight in the windows and display cases of some 2,600 independent, often family-run merchants (many housed in warrenlike indoor "exchanges"). If you want to do more than window shop, you can choose from more than two million pieces of jewelry (not just diamonds but secondhand Rolexes and Victorian paste pieces), commission a one-of-a-kind engagement or wedding ring, or have your pearls restrung. Caveat: the street attracts the occasional less-than-reputable vendor, as well as hawkers inviting you to sell them your gold (at an incredible price, of course); as with any shopping experience, word of mouth is always your best guide. ♦ W 47th St (between Fifth and Sixth Aves)

136 The Mercantile Library Center for Fiction

Now best known for its wealth of open-to-the-public readings and other literary event "The Merc"—also a membership-only circulation library (predominantly fiction) and writers' room facility—has its roots in t New York that preceded a public library system. Founded in 1820 down on Fulton Street for the egalitarian purpose of makin books available to the average clerk, it became the second-largest private library i the city. Speakers like Mark Twain and Frederick Douglass made appearances, an its membership included Willa Cather and many other such lights. It moved to its current home in 1932. The eight-story bronze-trimmed classical white marble edifice was designed for The Merc by Henry Otis Chapman; in 1978 Beyer Blinder Belle stepped in and began a typically sensitive restoration. Its façade, punctuated with wic expanses of multipaned window, allows in a warm natural light that complements the interior's dark polished woods and pleasing period furniture. ♦ M-Sa. 17 E 47th St (between Madison and Fifth Aves). 755.6710. www.mercantilelibrary.org

137 JPMorgan Chase

This 53-story monster was built in 1960 by **Skidmore, Owings & Merrill** for **Union Carbide**, which has since moved to the suburbs. Railroad yards under the building made it necessary to begin the elevator shafts on the second floor, which is why the ground-floor lobby looks forgotten. ♦ 270 Park Ave (at E 47th St).

138 The Roger Smith Hotel

$$$ This historic (1929) boutique-ish hostelry offers 163 renovated rooms and suites and a spacious lobby that features mahogany and free-form bronze sculptures by hotel owner/artist James Knowles (his street-level **Lab Gallery** sponsors a changir roster of arts shows and events). Rooms come with their own refrigerator and coffeemaker, and most rooms on the **Concierge Floor** have granite bathrooms with Jacuzzis and other amenities. There's wireless access throughout, and a complimentary continental breakfast for all guests. ♦ 501 Lexington Ave (at E 47th St) 755.1400, 800/445.0277; fax 319.9130. www.rogersmith.com ♿

139 Japan Society

This wonderfully tranquil and elegantly modern 1971 building by **Junzo Yoshimura** near the **UN** houses Japan Society-sponsored historic and contemporary art

exhibitions, the Lila Acheson Wallace auditorium, and traditional Japanese gardens. Furnishings by master woodworker **George Nakashima** may be found throughout the facility. Exhibits like the provocative 2005 blockbuster curated by artist Takashi Murkami, "Little Boy," and "Yes Yoko Ono," "Isamu Noguchi and Modern Japanese Ceramics," "The New Way of Tea," and "Frank Lloyd Wright and the Art of Japan," and live shows that include Japanese puppet theater and *kyogen,* a "comic cousin" of traditional Noh theater, explore a broad range of Japanese culture. Its 14,000-volume **C.V. Starr Library** is open weekdays, and the **Japan Society Film Center** offers an ongoing calendar of Japanese films, from classics to experimental new works.
♦ Admission. Closed Monday. Tu-Th, 11AM-6PM; F, 11AM-9PM; Sa, Su, 11AM-5PM. 333 E 47th St (between First and Second Aves). 832.1155. www.japansociety.org ♿

40 Dag Hammarskjöld Plaza

A lovely block-long city park that serves both as a neighborhood respite (Katharine Hepburn and Kurt Vonnegut were just two of its well-known habitués) and a pleasant stop en route to the nearby **Japan Society** or the **UN.** Often a gathering spot for demonstrations, it was named after the UN secretary general whose legacy was cut short when his plane crashed on a peace mission to Congo in 1961. A simple plaza at the time, in 1997 some $2.3 million was invested in a redesign by NYC Parks architect **George Vellonakis.** Symmetrically spotted with six fountains and home to a changing selection of public art, the tree-filled plaza is further enhanced by the city's tribute to Kate: a prettily planted border along the south edge of the park formally known as the **Katharine Hepburn Garden**. ♦ Along E 47th St, bounded by UN Plaza (First Ave) and Second Ave. www.nycgovparks.org ♿

41 United Nations (UN)

This complex was designed in 1952 by an international committee of 12 globally renowned architects that included **Le Corbusier** of France, **Oscar Niemeyer** of Brazil, and **Sven Markelius** of Sweden; the committee was headed by American **Wallace K. Harrison**. The site—once the actual Turtle Bay where the Saw Kill ran into the East River—was a run-down area with slaughterhouses, light industry, and a railroad barge landing when John D. Rockefeller Jr. donated the money to purchase the land for the project. The complex, an enclave apart from the city (it is considered international and not American territory) and in formal contrast to it, has had tremendous influence on its surroundings as well as on the direction of architecture.

Housing the staff bureaucracy, the 39-story **Secretariat** was New York's first building with all-glass walls (these are suspended between slabs of Vermont marble), and is the only example that approaches the tower-in-the-park urban ideal of the 1940s. (To make way for the UN building, the city diverted the traffic on First Avenue into a tunnel under UN Plaza and created a small landscaped park, **Dag Hammarskjold Plaza** (see above). Measuring 544 feet high and 72 feet wide, this anonymously faced building is a remarkable sight seen broadside from East 43rd Street, where it was set in deliberate opposition to the city grid. The **General Assembly** meets in the limestone-clad, flared white building to the north under the dome.

Visitors enter through the north side of the General Assembly Building across from East 46th Street. Outside, flags of all 185 member nations fly in alphabetical order at equal height, the same order in which delegates are seated in the General Assembly. More than a million visitors come here every year to see the physical presence of this forum of nations, but also in search of the elusive spirit of peace it symbolizes. Taking a tour is a good idea if you want to explore more than the grounds (don't miss the gardens) and the Chagall stained-glass windows in the lobby of the General Assembly Building. But don't expect to witness more than real estate if the General Assembly isn't in session (regular sessions are from the third Tuesday in September through mid-December) and, due to post-9/11 heightened security, no meetings are open to the public until further notice.

Tours, conducted by young people from around the world, steer large groups through the elegant **Assembly Hall** (note the Léger paintings on the walls); the Secretariat Building; and the **Conference Building**, which houses media, support systems, and meeting rooms, including the **Security Council Chamber** (donated by Norway), the **Trusteeship Council Chamber** (donated by Denmark), and the **Economic and Social Council Chamber** (donated by Sweden). Tours of the General Assembly end at the basement **UN Gift Shop**, a great souvenir source with interesting handcrafted gifts representing all 185 member nations.
♦ Admission. Tours, daily (every half hour in

English), 9:30AM-4:45PM. First Ave (at E 46th St). General information: 963.1234; group tours: 963.4440; gift shop: 963.7700. www.un.org

Within the United Nations:

Delegates' Dining Room

★★$$$ The UN dining room is open to the public for lunch during the week. It offers an international luncheon buffet with a choice of 22 dishes, in addition to an à la carte menu that includes asparagus with lemon vinaigrette, lobster salad, barbecued salmon with ginger-honey sauce, loin of venison, and steak with shallot sauce. Try the chocolate terrine or frozen-raspberry soufflé for dessert. The view of the East River is the best of any restaurant in Manhattan. ♦ Continental ♦ M-F, lunch. Reservations required; jacket required. UN Conference Building. 963.7625 and 963.7626

142 Via Brasil

★★$$ This is one of the best places to sample *feijoada*, the country's national dish, or you might want to try one of the lighter grilled meat or poultry dishes, such as *frango ma brasa* (charbroiled breast of chicken); sirloin steak cubed and marinated in garlic, tomatoes, and onions; or a mixed grill of pork, chicken, beef, and Brazilian sausage. Down your meal with a *caipirinha*, the potent national drink made of rumlike cachaça, fresh lime juice, sugar, and ice. Diners are regaled with live music all evening, Wednesday through Saturday, and there's no cover charge. ♦ Brazilian ♦ Daily, lunch and dinner. Reservations recommended. 34 W 46th St (between Fifth and Sixth Aves). 997.1158

142 Ipanema

★★$$ On what is known as Brazilian row, this is a good backup choice if the wait at **Via Brasil** is too long. A modest little place, all entrées come with rice, salad, and beans, and you'll notice the clientele is mostly Brazilian, which is a good sign. Not as flamboyant as its neighbor, but still a good choice. ♦ Brazilian ♦ Daily, lunch and dinner. 13 W 46th St (between Fifth and Sixth Aves). 730.5848

Rockefeller Center, from West 47th to West 52nd Streets, is the world's largest privately owned business and entertainment complex. It is composed of 19 buildings and covers nearly 22 acres.

Articles for sale in the United Nations gift shop are duty-free because the UN is not officially in any country. The gift shop offers items from every member nation.

143 The Helmsley Building

Designed in 1929 by **Warren & Wetmore**, this fanciful tower was originally the **New Yo[rk] Central Building**, then **New York General**. A[n] example of creative, sensitive urban design, it was a lively addition to the architects' own **Grand Central Terminal** and the hotels that surrounded it. Built above two levels of railroad tracks, it essentially "floats" on its foundations—those inside feel nary a vibration. The gold-leafed building is worth a special viewing at night. Pause to appreciate the distinct separation of automobile and pedestrian traffic in the street-level arcades, and stop for a look at the wonderful rococo lobby. ♦ 230 Park Ave (entrance on E 46th St)

144 Sparks Steak House

★★$$$$ As at other great steak houses, excellent cuts of beef and fresh seafood are cooked to order at this big-men-in-business casual-attire joint. What makes this place different is the exceptional wine list—the extraordinary selection and fair prices make it a must for oenophiles. ♦ Steak house ♦ M-F, lunch and dinner; Sa, dinner. Reservations required. 210 E 46th St (between Second and Third Aves). 687.485

145 Fred F. French Building

The colorful glazed tiles in the tower call out from across the street. Answer the call; the lobby is worth a glance. The building was designed in 1927 by **Fred F. French Company** and **H. Douglas Ives**. ♦ 551 Fifth Ave (at E 45th St)

Within the Fred F. French Building:

THE STEAKHOUSE

Morton's, The Steakhouse of Chicago

★★★$$$ Among all the excellent steak houses in New York, especially in this part o[f] town, this Chicago original is one of the mos[t] popular. The extra-thick, extra-aged, extra-tender porterhouse is legendary. The lobste[r] cooked in butter and sage is as good as the beef. The baked potatoes? They're bigger than your head. Go hungry. ♦ Steak house ♦ M-F, lunch and dinner; Sa, Su, dinner.

Reservations recommended. Entrance on E 45th St. 972.3315

46 Paul Stuart

Classic, well-made clothing for the conservative gentleman (and woman) is the specialty. Look for jackets and suits in herringbone, Shetland, and tweed; handknit sweaters in alpaca, cashmere, and Shetland wool; and shirts of Sea Island cotton. Women have a reasonable niche to themselves on the mezzanine level, where there are tailored skirted suits, Shetland sweaters, and cotton shirts. If you're not the one shopping, a 17th-century Flemish tapestry and comfortable leather chairs make waiting quite pleasant. ♦ Daily; closed Su in summer. 10 E 45th St (at Madison Ave). 682.0320 ♿

47 The Roosevelt Hotel

$$$ Built in 1924 by **George B. Post and Sons**, this old hotel was prestigious when railroads were the main form of transportation and the location near **Grand Central** was highly valued. Reopened in the early 2000s after a $65 million renovation, it is managed by Interstate Hotels. All 1,033 rooms received a much-needed face-lift geared to the businessperson, so you can count on dual-line telephones and Internet access in the rooms and a full-service business center during the week. Guests also enjoy the Roosevelt's large 24/7 Fitness Center, and comfortable **Teddy's Table** restaurant and the **Madison Club Lounge**. ♦ 45 E 45th St (between Vanderbilt and Madison Aves). 661.9600, 888/TEDDY.NY; fax 885.6161. www.therooseveIthotel.com

48 MetLife Building

Formerly the **Pan Am Building**, this 59-story monolith set indelicately between the **Helmsley Building** and **Grand Central Terminal** started in 1963 as a purely speculative venture and became the largest commercial office building ever built, with 2.4 million square feet. Art in the lobby includes a mural by Josef Albers and a space sculpture by Richard Lippold. The shape of the tower is supposedly derived from an airplane wing section. The architects were **Emery Roth & Sons**, **Pietro Belluschi**, and **Walter Gropius**. Bauhaus founder and High Modernist Gropius could have done better. High atop the building, several peregrine falcons nest in its outdoor niches. ♦ 200 Park Ave (entrance on E 45th St, between Lexington and Vanderbilt Aves)

Within the MetLife Building:

Cafe Centro

★★$$$ This $5 million brasserie with marble inlay floors, gold-leaf columns, and etched Lalique-style chandeliers is reminiscent of the grand cafés in European train stations. Among the appealing entrées, don't miss the pan-seared calamari stuffed with basil and salmon, or the monkfish tagine with sweet potatoes, artichokes, olives, and dates. Leave room for the rich vanilla crème brûlée-chocolate tart with caramel sauce. The beer bar offers over 20 selections, 10 of which are on draft. At the bar you can order hamburgers, chicken wings, and potato skins—sans reservations. ♦ American/French ♦ M-F, lunch and dinner; Sa, dinner. Reservations recommended. Ground level. 818.1222 ♿

149 Bridge Kitchenware

The late Julia Child used to shop here. And now that it's moved a few blocks south of its original longtime location, the other pros still pick up their copper pots, knife sets, and pastry tubes at this exceptional store, which stocks a large selection of expensive specialty utensils at more affordable prices. Kitchen novices are welcome here too; the staff is knowledgeable and patient. ♦ M-Sa. 711 Third Ave (between E 44th and E 45th Sts), but enter on E 45th St (between Second and Third Aves). 688.4220

150 Palm

★★$$$$ Ranked among the city's best steak houses, this venerable dining room (opened in 1926, and still family-owned) serves huge portions of aged prime cuts, lobsters, and addictive cottage-fried potatoes. Caricatures of famous New York journalists are painted on the walls, but you're more likely to recognize faces at the next table. Across the street at No. 840 is its twin (23 years old); unlike the original, here you can still find sawdust on the floor. ♦ Steak house ♦ M-F, lunch and dinner; Sa, dinner. Reservations required. 837 Second Ave (between E 44th and E 45th Sts). 687.2953. Also at 840 Second Ave (between E 44th and E 45th

Sts). 697.5198; 250 W 50th St (between Broadway and Eighth Ave). 333.7256

151 Institute of International Education Information Center (IIE)

Secured in this blocky white box by **Harrison, Abramovitz & Harris**, vintage 1964, is the **Edgar J. Kaufman Conference Center**: the premier facility for the education and scholarship programs of the nonprofit IIE, and one of very, very few **Alvar Aalto**–designed spaces to be found in the United States. The attainment of Fulbright scholarships is just one way the IIE serves to help foreign nationals interested in studying in the US, and US nationals who wish to study abroad. ♦ Daily. 809 UN Plaza (between E 45th and E 46th Sts). 883.8200. www.iie.org

152 The Algonquin

$$$ Now owned (and refurbished) by Camberley Hotels, this property was built in 1902 by **Goldwyn Starrett**, and was a gathering place for literary types even before the famous Round Table of such writers as Alexander Woollcott, Robert Benchley, and Dorothy Parker began meeting regularly in the **Rose Room**. What the Round Table members had in common, besides their razor-sharp wit, was that they were contributors to *The New Yorker*, whose offices (at that time) at 25 West 43rd Street conveniently had a back entrance on West 44th Street. Few nearby places are as comfortable as the hotel's lobby, where you can summon a cocktail with the ringing of a bell. Guests find all the comforts and friendliness of a country inn here. A mural depicting the legendary Round Table writers was recently completed inside the hotel. (Of the 165 rooms, visiting writers favor Room 306, a suite whose walls are adorned with *Playbill* magazine covers.) ♦ 59 W 44th St (between Fifth and Sixth Aves). 840.6800, 800/555.8000; fax 944.1419. www.algonquinhotel.com ♿

Within The Algonquin:

Oak and Rose Rooms

★$$$ The dark paneling in the **Oak Room** contrasts with the brighter **Rose Room**. But the menu is the same in both, and the quality doesn't vary. The plate-size apple pancake topped with tart lingonberries is a perfect after-theater snack. The Oak Room provides top-notch supper club entertainment (like singer Karen Akers or pianist Paul Cincotti) after 8PM from Tuesday through Saturday. ♦ American ♦ Daily, breakfast, lunch, and dinner. Reservations recommended. 840.6800

152 City Club Hotel

$$$$ On the block known as Club Row (home to the Harvard, Penn, and New York Yacht Clubs, among others), hotelier Jeff Klein has converted a former private preserve of the city's power brokers into a sanctuary for travelers whose taste runs to classic forms and Frette linens. All 65 room (including three lavish duplex suites) are fitted out by designer **Jeffrey Bilhuber** with Honduran mahogany, feather beds, and chocolate-marble bathrooms, with high-speed Internet access and Dean & DeLuca delicacies in the minibars. Room service is from **db Bistro Moderne** (see below), and should you want to work off the indulgence, City Club guests have privileges at the New York Sports Club branch down the block. ♦ 55 W 44th St (between Fifth and Sixth Aves). 921.5500, 888.256.4100. www.cityclubhotel.com

Within the City Club Hotel:

db Bistro Moderne

★★★ $$$ Right off the City Club lobby is classical chef Daniel Boulud's wonderful db Bistro Moderne. Sample the famous db burger or enjoy any of the fresh and season offerings—they are all beautifully presented and delicious, in typical Boulud style. The bar crackles with energy, and there is alway a good pre-theater crowd (they're offered a exceptional prix-fixe deal). ♦ Daily, breakfa and dinner; M-F, lunch. Reservations recommended. 391.2400

153 Sofitel

$$$$ At street level, the Sofitel wears restrained limestone to blend in with such prestigious neighbors as the Harvard Club and the New York City Bar Association. But few floors up, the gloves come off: the rest of the building, completed in 2000 by **Brennan Beer Gorman**, is a curved glass tower rising 30 stories above West 44th Street, banded with a horizontal motif borrowed from Paris Moderne. Inside, the lobby sports South American teak paneling and a trompe l'oeil mural of New York and Paris monuments on the grand staircase. The 398 Art Deco–inspired rooms and suite are built around full-wall headboards of bird's-eye maple or rosewood, with plenty o luxe touches as well as high-speed Internet access. You can also log on free of charge (and of wires) while sipping a drink in the mezzanine lounge before a meal at **Gaby**, th hotel's Asian-accented brasserie. ♦ 45 W 44th St (between Fifth and Sixth Aves). 354.8844, 800.SOFITEL. www.sofitel.com

154 Royalton Hotel

$$$$ When it opened in 1988 (built on the bones of a classical 1898 structure by

Ehrick Rossiter), this hotel immediately made its mark with publishing trendoids and other midtowners with its ultradramatic Philippe Starck–engineered design. Given a top-to-bottom refurb in 2007, the Starck look is gone, and the rooms, many with working fireplaces, are completely redone, with every attention given to design and comfort. Amenities include 24-hour room service, high-speed Internet access, daily newspaper delivery, and valet parking. ♦ 44 W 44th St (between Fifth and Sixth Aves). 869.4400, 800/635.9013; fax 869.8965. www.morganshotelgroup.com ♿

55 The New York Yacht Club

This unusually fanciful, sculptured work was the creation of **Warren & Wetmore** in 1899. The highlight of the eccentric façade is the sailing-ship sterns in the three window bays, complete with ocean waves and dolphins. The setback above the cornice used to be a pergola. This was the home of the America's Cup from 1857 to 1983. ♦ 37 W 44th St (between Fifth and Sixth Aves). 382.1000

55 The Harvard Club

The interior of this 1894 Georgian-style building by **McKim**, **Mead & White** is much more impressive than its façade indicates. If you're not a Harvard alum, go around the block and see it through the magnificent window in back. If you are a club member, 60 rooms are available for your use. ♦ 27 W 44th St (between Fifth and Sixth Aves). 840.6600

56 The Mansfield

$$$ The 126 rooms here are small—particularly the bathrooms—but big on style. A few steps off Fifth Avenue and an easy stroll to most Broadway theaters, the location is an important draw, but so is the quiet, sophisticated ambience, perhaps inspired by the turn-of-the-last-century **James Renwick** Beaux Arts–style building in which The Mansfield is housed. Amenities include the **M Bar** in the lobby, a period club room, and a modern 24-hour business center; you'll find high-speed Internet access and flat-panel TVs in all rooms of this pet-friendly hotel. ♦ 12 W 44th St (between Fifth and Sixth Aves). 277.8700, 800/255.5167; fax 764.4477. www.mansfieldhotel.com

56 General Society Library of Mechanics and Tradesmen

More than 120,000 books of fiction, nonfiction, and history are stocked in this private library, which was first established in 1820. The comfortable, elegant surroundings—this is a century-old skylit landmark building—are worth the low membership fee. Within the library are the **New York Center for Independent Publishing** (formerly the Small Press Center; 764.7021, www.nycip.org), a nonprofit facility exhibiting books by independent publishers, and the **John M. Mossman Lock Collection**, where some 375 different locks—including antique padlocks, powder-proof key locks, and friction locks—are on display. ♦ Research by appointment. Circulation Library and Reading Room: M-F. 20 W 44th St (between Fifth and Sixth Aves). 921.1767. www.generalsociety.org

157 Chikubu

★★★$$$ This plainly decorated restaurant caters to a mostly Japanese clientele and is a good place for the delicate dishes of Kyoto. Specialties include *akabeko-ju* (rice with thin slices of grilled beef and broiled baby flounder) and *omakase* (a tasting menu of seven to eight courses, including appetizers, sashimi, steamed vegetables or fish, tempura, a noodle or rice dish, and dessert). ♦ Japanese ♦ M-F, lunch and dinner; Sa, dinner. Reservations recommended. 12 E 44th St (between Madison and Fifth Aves). 818.0715

158 Brooks Brothers

The home of the Ivy League look—the natural-shoulder sack suit, worn with an oxford cloth shirt and silk rep tie—this store is an American institution. Founded in 1818, it is the country's oldest menswear shop. And, after a 1990s foray into the world of more contemporary looks, we are assured Brooks is back to emphasizing its more traditional apparel. Some styles have become classics, such as the trench coats, Shetland sweaters, oxford shirts, and bathrobes of soft wool and cotton. Boys can choose from shirts, slacks, and sweaters, and women will find a feminine version of all the above on the fifth floor. ♦ M-Sa. 346 Madison Ave (at E 44th St). 682.8800. ♿ Also at 666 Fifth Ave (between E 52nd and E 53rd Sts). 261.9440; One Liberty Plaza (at Broadway). 267.2400

159 The Yale Club

In a neighborhood crowded with clubs waving the old school tie, this one boasts easy access to trains headed to New Haven for the overnostalgic. The building was designed in 1913 by **James Gamble Rogers**. Only Yalies are allowed in; a handful of rooms are available for their overnight use. ♦ 50 Vanderbilt Ave (between E 44th and E 45th Sts). 661.2070

160 East

★★$$ Part of a citywide chain, the service, prices, and quality of food are pretty darn good at all locations. Early dinner specials are unbeatably cheap—there isn't a Japanese place in town that can match these prices. ♦ Japanese ♦ Daily, lunch and dinner. No credit cards accepted. 210 E 44th Street (between Second and Third Aves). 687.5075. Also at other locations

161 Sichuan Palace

★★$$$ The Chinese menu here is one of the most interesting in the city and is popular with United Nations delegates. During lunch, regular customers tend to get preferential treatment, so be prepared. Chicken with mixed mushrooms, lemon chicken, ginger-and-scallion shrimp, scallops with peppercorn sauce, and crispy fish are all good choices. ♦ Chinese ♦ Daily, lunch and dinner. Reservations required for lunch, recommended for dinner. 310 E 44th St (between First and Second Aves). 972.7377

162 UNICEF House

The exhibitions here illustrate the international children's operation in action, highlighting the importance and potential of global cooperation among all races. **The Danny Kaye Center**, housed in the same building, runs *Within Our Reach*, a film about the challenges that face children all over the world. The center's retail shop has an extensive collection of UNICEF cards and a smattering of international gifts. ♦ Free. M-F. 3 UN Plaza, E 44th St (between First and Second Aves). 326.7000

163 1 United Nations Plaza

This combination office building, apartment house, and hotel with a striking glass-curtain wall was designed by **Kevin Roche, John Dinkeloo & Associates** in 1976. It was so successful that it was duplicated in **2 UN Plaza**, adjoining it to the west, in 1980. ♦ E 44th St (at First Ave)

Within 1 United Nations Plaza:

Millennium UN Plaza Hotel

$$$$ Beginning on the 28th floor of 1 UN Plaza, this contemporary hotel includes 428 rooms, a lounge and restaurant, an indoor tennis court, and a serious swimming pool and health club with a dazzling view. Complimentary limousine service to Wall Street, the Garment District, and theaters is also available, though the majority of diplomat guests need only stroll across the street for their day's business appointments ♦ 758.1234, 866/866.8086; fax 702.5048 www.millenniumhotels.com

Within the Millennium UN Plaza Hotel:

Ambassador Grill

★★$$$ This longtime New York stalwart offers such classical dishes as Dover sole, grilled double lamb chops with rosemary *jus*, steak frites with au poivre sauce, and grilled monkfish. On Sundays, stop in for the all-you-can-eat brunch. ♦ American ♦ M-Sa, lunch and dinner; Su, brunch and dinner. Reservations recommended. 702.5014

164 Century Association

McKim, Mead & White designed this 1891 Palladian clubhouse for men of achievement in arts and letters (McKim and Mead were members), which is not open to the public. The large window above the entrance was originally a loggia. ♦ 7 W 43rd St (between Fifth and Sixth Aves). 944.0090

165 Grace Building

With its sloping, ski-jump, wind-loading façade, the W.R. Grace Building (officially addressed at 1114 Sixth Avenue) is generally considered a poor interruption of the 42nd Street wall. Designed in 1974 by **Skidmore, Owings & Merrill**, it has a barren little plaza on the corner of West 43rd Street and Sixth Avenue—an alleged public amenity in exchange for which the developers were allowed extra floors. **Grace Plaza** is improved these days with the addition of the **International Center of Photography**'s glass-walled kiosk that serves as the entrance to its school. (The ICP museum itself is diagonally across Sixth Avenue; see page 171.) The architects built a doppelgänger of the Grace for a different client at **9 West 57th Street** at the same time. ♦ 41 W 42nd St (between Fifth and Sixth Aves)

166 Nat Sherman's

The longtime tobacconist to the stars (and captains of industry), the venerable 1930-vintage cigar shop abandoned its corner spot for this distinctively upscale, determinedly masculine, wood-lined emporium across the avenue. Everything a dedicated smoker could need, or imagine. ♦ Daily. 12 E 42nd St (at Fifth Ave). 800/692.4427 (MYCIGAR)

167 Whitney Museum at Altria

Ulrich Franzen & Associates' light gray granite-clad building, designed in 1983, is a glass box hiding behind a Postmodern/historicist appliqué of Palladian patterns.

The main façade, rather oddly, faces the Park Avenue viaduct. There's a bit of a seating area in the enclosed garden and lobby of the building and a satellite exhibition space of the **Whitney Museum of Modern Art** (www.whitney.org) is tucked into a corner on the 42nd Street side. The rest of the building is **Altria** (previously known as **Philip Morris** corporate headquarters). The site was originally the home of the Art Moderne **Airlines Building** (built in 1940 by **John B. Peterkin**). ♦ Museum: free. M-F. 120 Park Ave (between E 41st and E 42nd Sts). ♿

168 Grand Central Terminal

This extraordinary complex is a true jewel made even brighter with the extensive renovations completed in 1998. In 1913, **Reed & Stem**'s designs for the new terminal to replace the **New York Central** and **Hudson River Railroads**' Grand Central Station were chosen in a competition that included submissions by **Daniel H. Burnham** and **McKim, Mead & White**. The firm of **Warren & Wetmore** was hired as the associate architect and was largely responsible for the design of the elaborate public structure. Reed & Stem and railroad engineer William Wilgus devised the still-efficient multilayered organization of the immense amount of traffic that flows through the terminal: trains (on two levels), subways, cars, and people. The terminal was the centerpiece of a gigantic real-estate development that included eight hotels and 17 office buildings by 1934. When the railroad was forced to electrify, engineer Wilgus realized that if the trains were run underground and the tracks covered over, the air rights could be leased to developers. Thus Park Avenue was born.

The main, southern façade of the terminal is dominated by Jules Coutan's sculptures of Mercury, Hercules, and Minerva (*Glory of Commerce, Moral Energy,* and *Mental Energy*). At the center of the façade is a bronze figure of Commodore Cornelius Vanderbilt, founder of the railroad. The building's other major façade fronts Vanderbilt Avenue and what was a genteel residential neighborhood to the west; the tenements to the east were disregarded. In building the terminal, 32 miles of new tracks were laid, 18,000 tons of steel were used, and 2.8 million cubic yards of earth excavated.

The inner workings of the terminal are organized around the impressive **Main Concourse**. When entered by way of the arcades (**Lexington Passage** to the south, and **Graybar Passage** to the north) from Lexington Avenue, the soaring vault is particularly striking. But the space may be better appreciated as a whole from the marble stairs at the Vanderbilt Avenue end. The hall is 160 feet wide, 470 feet long, and 150 feet high at its apogee—larger than the nave of Notre-Dame in Paris. The ceiling, a plaster vault suspended from steel trusses, is decorated with a zodiac representing the constellations of the winter sky. Designed by Paul Helleu, the 2,500 stars were inadvertently reversed on installation. The floors of the Main Concourse are Tennessee marble, and the trim is Italian Bottocino marble. The great arched windows are 60 feet tall and 33 feet wide. Cleaned and restored in 1998 when **Beyer Blinder Belle** embarked on its top-to-bottom rehab of the entire terminal, they now let in massive amounts of light that augment the artificial light from enormous egg-shaped chandeliers.

The late-20th-century upgrade included a new grand staircase at the east end of the concourse (it was part of the original building plans), a new climate control system, and a new liquid crystal arrivals/departures display. The famous faux sky is more sparkling than before (though still reversed), thanks to fiber optics. With the new millennium, transportation has met retailing in a big way here: With new food court-style restaurants and upscale shops and food markets just about everywhere you look, Grand Central is now as much mall as train station. The super-chic **Campbell Apartment** cocktail bar (daily, on the balcony level at the 15 Vanderbilt Avenue entrance, 953.0409) is a major draw for local folks, as are the retail spaces in the Lexington and Graybar Passages and the specialty fresh-food shops in the **Grand Central Market**, all on the east side of the main concourse. **Vanderbilt Hall**—the grand old Main Waiting Room along the 42nd Street entrance—often features art installations and is home to a seasonal crafts show. ♦ Tours depart every Wednesday at 12:30PM from the Information Booth on the Main Concourse. Donation suggested. (Municipal Art Society, 935.3960, www.mas.org.) E 42nd St (between Lexington and Vanderbilt Aves). Metro North train information: 532.4900. www.grandcentralterminal.com ♿

Within Grand Central Terminal:

The Best

Zarela Martinez

Owner, Zarela's restaurant

I love:

Going to the **Copacabana** on Tuesday evenings for Latin and ballroom dancing and their all-you-can-eat buffet. It's a great place to learn to dance and to see dancing's old-timers.

Going to **Roosevelt Avenue** between 80th and 87th Streets in Queens to have really authentic Mexican tacos and to shop for Mexican and other Latin American products.

Visiting the **Isamu Noguchi Garden Museum** in Long Island City, with its beautiful sculpture garden that changes with every season.

Catching first-run and hard-to-find movies at the **Film Forum**, **Walter Reade Theater**, **Museum of Modern Art**, and **Anthology Film Archives**.

Having a drink and watching the sunset from the top of the **Metropolitan Museum of Art** Friday and Saturday evenings.

Watching the Rollerbladers near the **Sheep Meadow** in **Central Park**.

Oyster Bar & Restaurant

★$$$ Looking much like what it is—a railroad station with tables, though the winding counter seating and the vaulted white-tile ceilings have a special charm—this historic place offers nicely prepared and absolutely fresh seafood, including, of course, a large variety of oysters. Although the daily menu reflects the fresh catches of the day, you can count on delicious chowder and excellent oysters pan-roasted or fried, as well as smoked salmon, rice-battered shrimp, and a selection of clams on the half shell. Due to those nice tiled, vaulted ceilings, however, the lunch-hour crowd generates megadecibels . . . and service and quality can be uneven here. ♦ Seafood ♦ M-Sa, lunch and dinner. Reservations recommended. Lower level. 490.6650 ♿

NY Transit Museum

The perfect place to while away a minute or an hour between trains, this small (but always interesting) annex to the main **Transit Museum** in Brooklyn (see page 328) celebrates something most Americans and certainly most Manhattanites take for granted: transportation. The gift shop alone is worth a look. A host of subway- and train-related souvenirs are handsomely displayed beneath a contemporary mural by Brian Cronin. ♦ Daily, 878.0106. Also at Schermerhorn St (at Boerum Pl) in Brooklyn Heights, Brooklyn. 718/694.1600 www.mta.info/mta/museum ♿

Posman Books@GCT

At one time Posman had stores in various locations around the city, but like all independent booksellers as times got tough, the stores started shutting. But the Grand Central Posman's has been going strong since it opened in 1999 in the "shuttle passage" within the terminal. Could be its knowledgeable staff and smart selection of literature, the latest nonfiction, photo, and art books, depth in architecture and New York history, and unusual assortment of cards, journals, calendars, and other specialty stationery items have made this bookshop a keeper. ♦ Daily. 9 Grand Central Terminal (at Vanderbilt Ave and E 42nd St). 983.1111. www.posmanbooks.com

169 Grand Hyatt Hotel

$$$ The 1934 **Warren & Wetmore**-designed **Commodore Hotel** was remodeled beyond recognition in 1980 by **Gruzen & Partners**. A bustling commercial hotel reminiscent of Las Vegas with waterfalls and a soaring atrium, its dining and watering holes are on various levels, all visible from the lobby. The 1,311 rooms have undergone periodic refurbishment—flat-panel TVs and high-speed Internet included—and are stereotypically attractive, although some are small. The hotel has a business center and fitness facilities, both 24-hour. ♦ E 42nd St (between Lexington and Vanderbilt Aves). 883.1234, 800/223.1234; fax 697.3772. www.grandhyattnewyork.com ♿

170 110 East 42nd Street

Resembling a Roman basilica, this grand editice was originally the Bowery Savings Bank. The main banking room is 160 feet long, 65 feet high, the walls are limestone and sandstone, the mosaic floors are French and Italian marble, and the space is currently a private banquet facility: **Cipriani 42nd Street.** So while you can peek through the windows, your best shot at experiencing the inside is to get invited to an event there. The building was designed in 1923 by **York & Sawyer**. ♦ 110 E 42nd St (between Lexington and Park Aves).

171 Chanin Building

The headquarters of the Chanin real-estate empire is an Art Deco triumph built in 1929 by **Sloan & Robertson**. At the third-floor level is an exuberant terra-cotta frieze. The detailing of the lobby is extraordinary, particularly the convector grilles and elevator doors. ♦ 122 E 42nd St (between Lexington and Park Aves)

172 Chrysler Building

Built by **William Van Alen** in 1929 for the Chrysler Automobile Company, this tower, which many consider the *ne plus ultra* of skyscrapers, is an Art Deco monument. The building has many car-oriented decorative elements: abstract friezes depicting automobiles, flared gargoyles at the fourth setback resembling 1929 radiator hood ornaments, and the soaring spire modeled after a radiator grille. The lobby, decorated with African marble and once used as a car showroom, is another Deco treasure. Use the Lexington Avenue entrance and look up at the representation of the building on the ceiling. Try to peek into an elevator cab; alas, given post-9/11 security, that is as far as you will get unless you have business here. Another victim of security, the elite, top-of-the-tower Cloud Club, which closed in 1979, will not reopen to the public as was once hoped. But there is still much to appreciate. The lighting of the spire at night—with specially fitted lamps inside the triangular windows—was an idea of Van Alen's that was rediscovered and first implemented in 1981; set ablaze, it is a singular sight. The edifice was briefly the tallest building in the world until surpassed by the **Empire State Building** in 1931. The lobby is open to the public M-F only, 7AM-6PM. ♦ 405 Lexington Ave (at E 42nd St)

173 Mobil Building

The self-cleaning stainless-steel skin on this monolith is 37 thousandths of an inch thick—self-cleaning because the creased panels create wind patterns that scour them. The building was designed by **Harrison & Abramovitz** in 1955 for Mobil Oil's corporate headquarters; they vacated and sold the building in the late 1980s. ♦ 150 E 42nd St (between Third and Lexington Aves)

One of the waiting rooms in Grand Central Station was once known as the "Kissing Gallery" because it was there that travelers who had come long distances were met and kissed by kin and loved ones.

174 New York Helmsley Hotel

$$$ This 788-room property is geared toward the business traveler, and room service is available around the clock, as are a business center and fitness center. Other niceties include Wi-Fi in all rooms, **Harry's New York Bar** for drinks and **Mindy's Restaurant** for dining. ♦ 212 E 42nd St (between Second and Third Aves). 405.4300, 800/221.4982; fax 986.4792. www.newyorkhelmsley.com ♿

175 News Building

The former home of New York's most successful tabloid, the *New York Daily News* (the tabloid relocated in 1995 to larger quarters at 450 West 33rd Street), is a clean, purely vertical mass that was designed in 1930 by **John Mead Howells & Raymond Hood**, the pair responsible for the Chicago Tribune Tower (in all its Gothic wonder). The stringent composition even has a flat top—a bold step in 1930. The building, known as **The Daily News Building** back in the day, tells its own story in the frieze over the entrance and in the lobby, where a giant globe—shades of *The Daily Planet*—is the center of an interplanetary geography lesson. (When the globe was first unveiled, it was spinning the wrong way.) The 1958 addition on Second Avenue, by **Harrison & Abramovitz**, is not up to the original. ♦ 220 E 42nd St (between Second and Third Aves)

176 Tudor Hotel at the United Nations

$$$ This millennially renovated historic property (once notorious for having the smallest hotel rooms in the city) now boasts 300 expanded rooms, each with a marble bathroom, two-line telephones, and high-speed Internet access. Within the hotel are a restaurant, a bar and lounge, meeting rooms, conference and banquet facilities, a business center, and a small health club facility. ♦ 304 E 42nd St (between First and Second Aves). 986.8800; fax 986.1758. www.tudorhotelny.com ♿

177 Ford Foundation

This 1967 building by **Kevin Roche, John Dinkeloo & Associates** is probably the oldest and certainly the richest and least hermetic re-creation of a jungle in New York City. Though the building is small, with a rather typical entrance on East 43rd Street, the East 42nd Street side is much more extroverted. It appears as if a container had been opened, leaving the black piers barely restraining an overflowing glass and Cor-Ten steel box of offices that contains a luxuriant park inside a 12-story atrium. Although economically foolhardy and somewhat noisy, this building is handsome and very definitely not to be missed. The superb and off-the-grid garden (it's watered solely via a rainwater collection system) is open to the public M-F, 10-4. ♦ 320 E 43rd St (between Tudor City Pl and Second Ave). ♿

178 Tudor City

Soaring over East 42nd Street, this Gothic development on its own street was built in 1925 by the **Fred F. French Company** and **H. Douglas Ives**. It comprises 11 apartment buildings, a hotel, shops, a restaurant, a church, and a park. The complex's orientation toward the city seems ill-considered today, but when this enclave was planned, the East River shore below was a wasteland of breweries, slaughterhouses, glue factories, and gasworks. At the turn of the century, the bluff, known as Corcoran's Roost, was the hideout of the infamous Paddy Corcoran and the Rag Gang.
♦ Bounded by First and Second Aves, and E 40th and E 43rd Sts

179 Bryant Park

The only park in the city designed like a formal garden was named for the poet William Cullen Bryant, a prime mover in the campaign to establish **Central Park** and a champion of the Hudson River School of painters, which established the fashion for wild, naturalistic parks. Before becoming a park, the land was a potter's field, and in 1853 it was the site of America's first **World's Fair**, held in a magnificent domed pavilion of iron and glass known as the **Crystal Palace**. The building stood here until 1858, when it burned to the ground. After the ruins were cleared, the space was used as a parade ground for troops getting ready to defend the Union in the Civil War. When the war was over, it was dedicated as a public park.

In 1934, as the result of a competition to aid unemployed architects, the park was redesigned by **Lusby Simpson**, whose concept was executed under the direction of urban planning czar Robert Moses. In the Depression years, the area had been a gathering spot for the unemployed, and in the 1960s it became a retail space for marijuana peddlers. In 1980, the Bryant Park Restoration Corporation (Hanna/Olin Ltd.) went to work, and today the park is not only a safe spot, but a uniquely serene and beautiful one. With plenty of open-air seating, exquisite landscaping, fountains, footpaths, snack kiosks, and Le Carrousel a petite fantasy-creature ride for the little ones—the park brings a welcome bit of Paris to New York. A host of public events, such as live music and dance performances, outdoor movies in summer, and to-the-trade spectaculars like Fashion Week, complete the scene. At the library end of the park, a $4.2 million glass-and-steel pavilion designed by **Hardy Holzman Pfeiffer Associates** houses the **Bryant Park Grill** and the more informal **Cafe** (both are open daily, M-F, lunch and dinner; Sa, Su, brunch and dinner. 840.6500), which serve seasonal American fare. ♦ Bounded by the New York Public Library and Sixth Ave, and W 40th and W 42nd Sts. www.bryantpark.org

180 New York Public Library

Treat your soul to one of New York's greatest experiences, the grand entrance to the grandest public library we have. Officially the **Humanities and Social Science Library**, this icon—and outstanding repository and research facility—was designed in 1911 at a cost of $9 million by **Carrère & Hastings**. The familiar lions, *Patience* and *Fortitude*, are the work of Edward Clark Potter. But there is much more to see: the bases of the 95-foot-high, tapered steel flagposts (by Thomas Hastings) on the terrace; the lampposts; the balustrades; the urns; the sculpture high above by Paul Bartlett, George G. Barnard, and John Donnelly; and the fountains in front, both by Frederick MacMonnies (the one on the right represents Truth, the other Beauty). The library was built with the resources of two privately funded libraries, combined in 1895 with the infusion of a $2 million bequest from New York Governor Samuel J Tilden. John Jacob Astor's library, the first general reference library in the New World was enhanced by James Lenox's collection of literature, history, and theology. (In 1891, Andrew Carnegie donated $52 million for the establishment of 80 more branches in the New York Public Library system.) This grand building is completely dedicated to research, and none of its more than 6 million books or 17 million documents can be checked out; so vast is the collection that the original four floors of stacks beneath the building and behind the reading rooms have been supplemented by a space underneath **Bryant Park**, which can hold up to 92 miles of stacks.

Considered the repository of one of the largest research collections in the world, the building remains among the finest examples of Beaux Arts architecture. The main lobby, **Astor Hall**, contains the information desk, the bookshop, and an exhibition area. Marble from floor to ceiling, the hall is lavishly decorated with carved garlands, ribbons, and rosettes. The room directly behind Astor Hall is the **Gottesman Exhibition Hall**, which has the most beautiful ceiling in the city. The hall's changing exhibitions are thematic, covering a variety of subjects such as urban history, architecture, and photography. The exhibitions are based on materials drawn from the library's own holdings, demonstrating the richness of the research collections.

The **Third Floor Hall** and the rooms it serves are rich with carved wood panels and vaulted ceilings. The murals, by Edward Lanning, were executed as part of a WPA project. The library's art collection, including paintings by Gilbert Stuart, Sir Joshua Reynolds, and Rembrandt Peale, is displayed in the **Edna B. Salomon Room**. Directly across the hall is **Room 315**, the catalog room, where you can request books; it leads into the **Main Reading Room**, 51 feet high and one-and-a-half blocks long and totally refurbished with much-improved but period-sensitive lighting and laptop computer connections. History buffs will be especially pleased to know that the library's pneumatic-tube call-slip system is still intact, and counted on daily to whoosh your request down to the stacks with good speed.

The **Celeste Bartos Forum**, beautifully restored by the firm **Davis, Brody & Associates**, is distinguished by its 30-foot-high glass dome, which rests on steel pillars adorned with Corinthian ornamentation. It is used for lectures, concerts, films, and special events. The **Library Shop** is always worth a browse. ♦ Collections and Reading Room: Daily; closed Sunday in summer. Building tours (free): M-Sa, 11AM, 2PM; Su (except in summer), 2PM. Tours meet at the main information desk. Fifth Ave (between W 40th and W 42nd Sts). Reference service (free) 930.0830. www.nypl.org ♿

181 Bryant Park Hotel

$$$$ Inaugurated as the **American Radiator Building** in 1923, this New York Gothic icon is now gussied up inside thanks to a massive renovation in 2001 that transformed it into a luxury hotel. From the exterior you can barely detect the presence of windows in the 23-story black brick tower, an effect architect **Raymond Hood** devised to accentuate the gold ornamented top. However, the 130 rooms are surprisingly bright, and views from the upper floors over Bryant Park are nothing less than spectacular. Décor is more sleek than sumptuous, but the amenity-rich rooms (with DVD players, high-speed Internet, Jacuzzis, and more) are comfortable and quiet. And there's a health club, salon, bar, and restaurant, **Koi** (921.3330), on-site. ♦ 40 W 40th St (between Fifth and Sixth Aves). 869.0100, 877/640.9300; fax 869.4446. www.bryantparkhotel.com ♿

182 Mid-Manhattan Branch, NYPL

This branch, redesigned in 1981 by **Giorgio Cavaglieri**, once housed **Arnold Constable**, the department store that provided trousseaus for fashionable brides in the 1890s (you can see pictures of the brides in the library's collection of microfilm editions of old newspapers). This library has the largest circulating collection of any of the branch libraries. Free tours meet at the ground-floor information desk. ♦ Collections: M-Sa. Tours: M, W, F, 2:30PM. 455 Fifth Ave (at E 40th St). 340.0833. www.nypl.org ♿

183 101 Park Avenue

Designed in 1983 by **Eli Attia & Associates**, this speculative tower of black glass rises, angled and tucked, above a granite plaza on an awkward corner. Its slick outline and sheer height, which may be fun from the inside, are somewhat disturbing from the outside. ♦ At E 40th St

UPPER EAST SIDE
CENTRAL PARK
MIDTOWN
Neue Galerie
Metropolitan Museum of Art
Whitney Museum of American Art
Lenox Hill Hospital
Asia Society
The Frick Collection
Hunter College
The Arsenal
Roosevelt Island Tramway Station
5th Ave.
Madison Ave.
Park Ave.
Lexington Ave.
3rd Ave.
2nd Ave.
1st Ave.
E 86th St.
E 85th St.
E 84th St.
E 83rd St.
E 82nd St.
E 81st St.
E 80th St.
E 79th St.
E 78th St.
E 77th St.
E 76th St.
E 75th St.
E 74th St.
E 73rd St.
E 72nd St.
E 71st St.
E 70th St.
E 69th St.
E 68th St.
E 67th St.
E 66th St.
E 65th St.
E 64th St.
E 63rd St.
E 62nd St.
E 61st St.
E 60th St.
E 59th St.
25

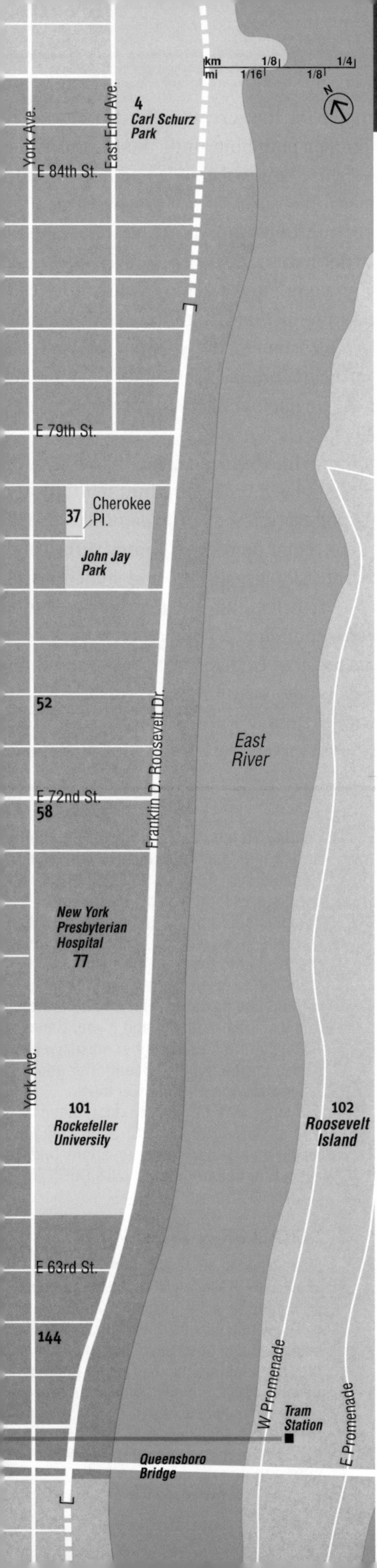

EAST SIDE

In the 1920s, the *New York Times* described the East Side as "a string of pearls: Each pearl is a double block of millionaires, and **Madison Avenue** is the string." Like everything else about New York, the East Side has been altered by time. But there are few places in the city where memory is as intact as in the blocks bounded by the **East River, Fifth Avenue,** and **East 59th** and **East 86th Streets.**

Until the close of the Civil War, this was the part of New York where the fashionable gathered to escape city summers—the counterpart of today's Hamptons on Long Island's South Shore. At the end of the 18th century, a necklace of mansions in parklike settings followed the shore of the East River all the way to Harlem. The **Boston Post Road,** now **Third Avenue,** made access to the city below Canal Street convenient, and summer residents with lots of leisure time traveled downtown on steamboats. By the late 1860s, the old summer houses were converted to year-round use for pioneering commuters, and, a few years later, the coming of elevated railroads on **Second** and Third Avenues opened the area to working-class people. The improved transportation brought summer fun-seekers as well. The area bounded by the East River, Third Avenue, and **East 66th** and **East 75th Streets** became **Jones's Wood.** It included such attractions as a beer garden, a bathhouse, an athletic club, and a block-long coliseum for indoor entertainment.

Society had its heyday on the East Side between 1895 and the outbreak of World War I. The state of American architecture was superb at the time, and the superrich had the financial resources to hire the best. Technology was very much in vogue then, and it was a rare four-story house that didn't have at least one elevator. Nearly every house had an elaborate intercom system, and all installed dumbwaiters, usually electrically operated, to make life simpler for the servants. But the showplac was the bathroom—no New York house had indoor plumbing until the **Croton Aque duct** began operating in 1842. Until the turn of the century, the style had been to bath in dark, wood-paneled rooms designed to conceal their use.

Up until 1900, any family sharing a house with other families (except servants, o course) was labeled déclassé. But when the barrier fell, the "best of the best" apartmen buildings appeared on the East Side, especially along **Park Avenue**, which after 191 became what one contemporary called "a mass production of millionaires." The hug apartment houses created a kind of leveling effect among the wealthy, as well as guarantee that this would remain their kind of neighborhood. They didn't even budg during the Great Depression, when armies of the unemployed took up residence acros the way in **Central Park.**

The 1960s brought construction of uninspiring white brick apartment houses to th area; many of the elegant town houses had already been broken up into multiple-un dwellings years before. The combination of a long-promised, *Brigadoon*-like Secon Avenue subway and housing overstock has kept rental (and co-op) rates surprisingl lower here than elsewhere in the city. Young professionals, singles, and students ofte find their first apartment on the East Side. Nevertheless, an air of privileged—ofte luxurious—lifestyle still prevails. And at the very mention of a stroll on New York's Eas Side, one still thinks of Madison Avenue and its roster of exclusive galleries and fashio boutiques brimming with European designer labels (along with those of American high end stars like **Ralph Lauren**, **Calvin Klein**, and **Donna Karan**). The neighborhoo continues to be what it has been for nearly a century: New York City's elite enclave.

---

1 Neue Galerie

This gallery is dedicated to German and Austrian fine and decorative art from the first half of the 20th century. The eponymous late owner of the Serge Sabarsky Gallery and collector Ronald Lauder found the ideal home to showcase their—and others'—collections of the era in this landmark 1914 onetime Vanderbilt home, built by **Carrère & Hastings** (of New York Public Library fame). Architect **Annabelle Selldorf** has done a masterful job of restoring the site to period, while ensuring it shows off the work—by artists from Secessionists Gustav Klimt and Egon Schiele to Blaue Reiter painters Paul Klee and Vasily Kandinsky, along with silver and furniture from design and craft masters Josef Hofmann and Koloman Moser—to best advantage. In addition to the **Design Shop** and **Book Store**, films, lectures, and chamber music events are offered. ♦ Admission. Closed T, W. M, Th, Sa, Su, 11AM-6PM; F, 11AM-9PM. **Bookstore/ Design Shop**: M, W-Su. 1048 Fifth Ave (at E 86th St). 628.6200. www.neuegalerie.org ♿

Within Neue Galerie:

Café Sabarsky

★★★$$ To step into this café is like taking a mini-trip to Europe—turn-of-the-19th-century Vienna, to be precise. The rich dark woods, period furnishings by Josef Hofmann and Adolf Loos, and 1912 upholstery fabric by Otto Wagner are complemented by the light and shadow from the grand windows that face across the avenue to Central Park. Expect Viennese specialties (it's hard to leave without having coffee and an authentic—and luscious—pastry), and if your timing's right, there will be chamber music (with help from the room's Bösendorfer grand piano) or cabaret while you dine. ♦ Viennese. ♦ M, W, breakfast, lunch through late afternoon; Th-Su, breakfast, lunch, and dinner. No reservations taken, except for cabaret nights. 288.0665 ♿

2 Schaller & Weber

Established in 1937, this family-owned shop—one of the few in the neighborhood from early Yorkville—is filled from floor to ceiling with cold cuts. Liverwursts, salamis, bolognas, and other savories (all of which they manufacture themselves, to international acclaim) are piled on counters, packed into display cases, and hung from the walls and ceilings. ♦ M-Sa. 1654 Second Ave (between E 85th and E 86th Sts). 879.3047

3 M. Rohrs' House of Fine Teas and Coffees

When Yorkville was as German as *apfelstrudel*, Mary Rohrs roasted coffee and sold exotic teas in her eponymous emporium, opened in 1896. In modern times, M. Rohrs' shared its tight quarters with an insurance company (it did business right amid the beans) until moving in 2007 to a separate space. Its coffee, by the bag or by the cup, is as compelling as ever—all the more so because few things in the neighborhood are as they used to be. ♦ Daily. 310 E 86th St (between First and Second Aves). 396.4456

4 Carl Schurz Park

Situated on land acquired by the city in 1891, the park was named in 1911 for the German immigrant who served as a general during the Civil War, was a senator from Missouri and secretary of the interior under President Hayes, and went on to become editor of the *New York Evening Post* and *Harper's Weekly.*

The park, which was remodeled in 1938 by **Harvey Stevenson** and **Cameron Clark**, is a delightful edge to the neighborhood of Yorkville. It is not very large, but its distinct sections and the varied topography make a walk here rewarding. The promenade along the East River above FDR Drive is named for John Finley, a former editor of the *New York Times* and an enthusiastic walker. **Gracie Mansion** (see page 260), the official residence of the mayor of New York City, occupies the center of the north end of the park.

Across the river is Astoria, Queens; spanning the river are the Triborough Bridge and Hell Gate railroad trestle; also visible are Wards Island and Randalls Island; and the little island that looks like an elephant's head is known as Mill Rock. This point of the river is a treacherous confluence of currents from the Harlem River, Long Island Sound, and the harbor—hence the name "Hell Gate." ♦ Bounded by the East River and East End Ave, and E 84th St/Gracie Sq and E 90th St/FDR Dr. www.nycgovparks.org ♿

5 Elio's

★★$$$ Wall Streeters and bankers mix with media types and celebs at this trendy neighborhood eatery, a spin-off of the ever-popular **Elaine's**. It's always crowded and noisy, and the food is always good. Order one of the specials, which seem to inspire the kitchen more than the regular menu does. But the pasta dishes and veal chops are also good picks. ♦ Italian ♦ Daily, dinner. Reservations required. 1621 Second Ave (between E 84th and E 85th Sts). 772.2242

6 Rosenthal Wine Merchant

Here you'll find a carefully edited selection of estate wines from California and Europe. Prices may be *un peu cher*, but staff is especially helpful. ♦ M-Sa. 318 E 84th St (between First and Second Aves). 249.6650 ♿

7 Church of St. Ignatius Loyola

The overscaled façade on Park Avenue was designed by **Ditmars & Schickel** in 1898. Its flat limestone late-Renaissance style looks very comfortable here—and it's a welcome change from all that Gothic. ♦ 980 Park Ave (at E 83rd St). 288.3588 ♿

8 Erminia

★★$$$ The crowning achievements here are the lushly sauced pappardelle tossed with artichokes, tomato, sausage, and porcini, and the excellent Tuscan lamb grilled over a wood fire. There are also a number of other roasted dishes, including veal chops. The romantic candlelight atmosphere makes this restaurant a popular place, so be sure to reserve in advance. ♦ Italian ♦ M-Sa, dinner. Reservations required. 250 E 83rd St (between Second and Third Aves). 879.4284

9 Girasole

★★$$$ A local, conservative crowd of East Siders favors this dependable, noisy Italian restaurant located on the ground floor of a brownstone. Poultry and game dishes—such as chicken sautéed with lemon, and grilled organic Cornish hens with peppercorns—are standards. ♦ Italian ♦ Daily, lunch and dinner. Reservations required. 151 E 82nd St (between Third and Lexington Aves). 772.6690

10 Le Refuge

★★$$$ Bare wooden tables, kitchen towels for napkins, American stoneware, and etched stemware generate a mood of romantic, rustic elegance. The ever-changing menu is prepared with carefully chosen fresh ingredients, all cooked and seasoned by the sure hand of chef/owner Pierre Saint-Denis. Try the vegetable terrine bathed in tomato coulis or the bouillabaisse, considered the best this side of the Atlantic. For dessert, go for the airy raspberry cheesecake, chocolate soufflé cake, or heavenly crème brûlée. ♦ French ♦ Daily, dinner. Reservations required. 166 E 82nd St (between Third and Lexington Aves). 861.4505. Also at **Le Refuge Inn**, 586 City Island Ave, Bronx. 718/885.2478

11 Kings' Carriage House

★★$$$ In a charming spot that looks as much like an Irish country cottage as you're apt to find on this side of the Atlantic, you'll find well-prepared food in a setting that will melt away those city blues and have you dreaming of *Ryan's Daughter.* The menu might include a buttery smooth salmon napoleon, chicken paillard over grilled vegetables and greens, or first-rate Gulf shrimp. Chocolate cake and crème brûlée are dessert winners. For afternoon tea, try the genteel scarlet room upstairs. ♦ Irish ♦ Daily, lunch and dinner. Prix fixe only. Reservations recommended. 251 E 82nd St (between Second and Third Aves). 734.5490 ♿

12 Primavera

★★$$$$ One of the great watering holes for the older, distinguished smart set, this sedate room has deep-colored wood paneling and upmarket, if not particularly attractive, oil paintings. The food is similarly dignified and usually of good quality. Try the chicken breast with Champagne sauce, pasta with truffles, or green-and-white pasta with ham. ♦ Italian ♦ Daily, dinner. Reservations required; jacket and tie required. 1578 First Ave (at E 82nd St). 861.8608

13 Metropolitan Museum of Art

Ten years after the first section of the Met was finished at the edge of **Central Park**, Frederick Law Olmsted, the park's designer, said he regretted having allowed it to be built there. He should see it now! From its first, original section—built in 1880 to a design by **Calvert Vaux** and **Jacob Wrey Mould**—museum has grown to 1.4 million square feet of floor space (more than 32 acres), with some 2 million works of art, making it the largest art museum in the Western Hemisphere. It seems to be expanding and getting better every day (much of this growth must be credited to director Philippe de Montebello). Founded in 1870 by a group of art-collecting financiers and industrialists who were on the art committee of New York's **Union League Club**, the museum's original collection consisted of 174 paintings, mostly Dutch and Flemish, and a gift of antiquities from General di Cesnola, the former US consul to Cyprus. Today, the museum has the most comprehensive collection of American art in the world, and excels in Egyptian, Greek and Roman, and European art. The list of priceless art and artifacts within these walls is almost impossible to comprehend. And the list of benefactors who have swelled the museum' holdings over the years reads like a Who's Who of the city's First Families—Morgan, Rockefeller, Altman, Marquand, Hearn, Bache, and Lehman.

The push to house the collection in style almost immediately resulted in additions and renovations to the Vaux and Mould base. A taste of the early changes that woul give the Met the basic form we know now includes the southwest wing in 1888, by **Theodore Weston**; north wing, 1894, by **Arthu Tuckerman**; central façade and Great Hall, 1902, by **Richard Morris Hunt**, **Richard Howland Hunt**, and **George B. Post**; and the Fifth Avenue wings, 1906, by **McKim**, **Mead & White.** The latter part of the 20th century and into the 21st produced the **Lehman Wing** (1975), which displays its collection of paintings, drawings, and decorative objects in rooms re-created from the original Lehman town house on West 54th Street; the **Sackler Wing** (1979) for the Raymond R. Sackler Far East Art Collection; the entire Egyptian **Temple of Dendur** (1978), given to the people of the United States for their support in saving monuments threatened by the construction of the Aswan High Dam;

One of the more colorful inmates at Roosevelt Island's New York City Lunatic Asylum was Mae West, who was locked up there for 10 days in 1926 and fined $500. She had been appearing locally in a play called *Sex* that raised one too many eyebrows. Upon her request, she was permitted to wear her silk undergarments beneath her prison uniform.

the **Egyptian Galleries** (1983) for the museum's world-class permanent collection; the **Michael C. Rockefeller Wing** (1982) for the art of Africa, the Americas, and the Pacific Islands; the **Douglas Dillon Galleries of Chinese Painting** (1983) and the **Astor Chinese Garden Court** (1980), with a reception hall from the home of a 16th-century scholar; an expanded and dramatically redesigned **American Wing** (1980); and the 1987 **Lila Acheson Wallace Wing** (20th-century art) with its incomparable roof garden, and which provides a dramatic contrast of high-tech glass curtain walls to the solid limestone Beaux Arts façade. Also here now are the beautiful **Andre Meyer Galleries** (1993), where you'll see the premier collection of 19th-century European paintings and sculpture in the world, rivaling the Musée d'Orsay in Paris; the **Arts of Korea** galleries (1998); and, well over five years in the works, the 2007-completed "New" **Greek and Roman Galleries** and the **Leon Levy and Shelby White Court**, which reclaimed the two-story atrium space that McKim, Mead & White had created for Roman art (1912-1926) and later became the museum's cafeteria and restaurant. These spaces feature over 5,300 objects of Hellenistic, Etruscan, and Roman art, many of which have never been seen publicly before.

The Met is a perpetual work-in-progress, and yet everyone seems to have a favorite section. Upstairs are the **Cypriot Galleries** (2000), which chart in glorious detail the chronological development of the art of Cyprus through a selection of major works from the Cesnola Collection. Always captivating is the colossal collection of historic arms and armor from around the world—all on the ground floor—and in particular the Japanese pieces from the samurai era. The **Costume Institute** (downstairs) displays its 35,000 articles of clothing in stylish themes, with special temporary blockbuster exhibits you won't want to miss. With the museum's 2005 acquisition of the Howard Gilman Foundation's world-renowned collection of over 8,500 photographs dating from 1839, the Met established itself as a major player in the representation of this relatively "modern" art.

The information desk in the center of the Great Hall has floor plans and a helpful staff to direct you. The staff also has information about concerts, films, and lectures in the museum's **Grace Rainey Rogers Auditorium** and will help you arrange for a guided tour, available in several languages. Tape-recorded tours of most of the exhibits are available for rental. Just off the Great Hall is the justly famous **Met Store** and a smaller satellite shop. (There are more small gift and book shops throughout the museum.) Members (depending on level) may gain exclusive access to the sophisticated and refined **Trustees Dining Room** (570.3975) and the antiques-filled **Patrons Lounge** (570.3999). The rest of us can comfortably snack at the **American Wing Café** on the first floor, overlooking the park and sculpture courtyard; eat at the aptly named **Cafeteria**; or go more upscale at the **Petrie Court Café** located in the **European Sculpture Court**, which enjoys park views as well. (Reservations recommended for the Petrie, 570.3964.) The **Iris and B. Gerald Cantor Roof Garden**, a lovely open-air sculpture garden with grand views from the roof of the museum, is open early May through late October and has a little café that sells coffee, cocktails, and light fare.

The Friday and Saturday evening hours have added a touch of civility and grace to the busy city scene. Many of the museum's guests take advantage of the tranquil twilight hours, when, beginning at 4PM, a string quartet or other live classical instrumentalists serenade from the **Great Hall** balcony, where a bar and candlelit tables are set up for relaxation. Guided tours available with admission. ♦ Admission (suggested). Closed Monday, except for holidays. Tu-Th, Su, 9:30AM-5:30PM; F, Sa, 9:30AM-9PM. 1000 Fifth Ave at E 82nd St. 535.7710. www.metmuseum.org ♿

14 998 Fifth Avenue

This 1912 apartment building in the guise of an Italian Renaissance palazzo was built by **McKim, Mead & White** when the bulk of society lived in mansions up and down the avenue. The largest apartment here has 25 rooms; it was originally leased by Murray Guggenheim. ♦ At E 81st St

14 1001 Fifth Avenue

Designed in 1978 by **Philip Birnbaum**, this average apartment tower has been upgraded with a limestone façade by **Philip Johnson** and **John Burgee**. Half-round ornamental molding relates horizontally to the neighboring **988 Fifth Avenue**, while the mullions struggle for a vertical emphasis, pointing at the mansard-shaped cutout roof. ♦ Between E 81st and E 82nd Sts

15 Frank E. Campbell Funeral Chapel

In this building, possibly the most prestigious funeral chapel in the world, we have said farewell to Elizabeth Arden, James Cagney, Jack Dempsey, Tommy Dorsey, Judy Garland, Howard Johnson, Robert F. Kennedy, John Lennon, J.C. Penney, Damon Runyon, Arturo Toscanini, Mae West, Tennessee Williams, and Peter Jennings, to name-drop just a few. ♦ 1076 Madison Ave (at E 81st St). 288.3500 ♿

16 E.A.T.

★★$$ Owned by Eli Zabar (of **Vinegar Factory** and **Zabar's** family fame), this informal eatery makes all its breads with a sourdough starter, including the famous *ficelle* (a super-crusty loaf, 22 inches long with a diameter barely larger than a silver dollar). Popular choices from the menu are linguine with broccoli rabe, the three-salad plate (choose three from a list of 12 salads), lamb sandwich, crab cakes, pot roast, and grilled chicken. For dessert try the chocolate cake or raspberry tart. The prices are high, but so is the quality. Plus, the people watching is pretty good; celebrities occasionally drop in. ♦ American ♦ Daily, breakfast, lunch, and dinner. 1064 Madison Ave (between E 80th and E 81st Sts). 772.0022

17 Beyoglu

★★$$ The hummus gets raves at this tastefully appointed neighborhood spot, where Mediterranean specialties are served up as *mezes,* small plates that exponentially increase the number of dishes into which you can dip. In good weather, grab a colorfully tiled outdoor table to make a meal of feta-stuffed filo, char-grilled octopus, cumin-spiced cured beef, and grilled sardines wrapped in grape leaves—and save room for the baklava. ♦ Turkish ♦ Daily, lunch and dinner. 1431 Third Ave (at E 81st St). 650.0850

18 Sistina

★★★$$$ Owned by brothers Giuseppe, Gerardo, Antonio, and Cosimo Bruno, this restaurant serves a pleasing mix of Northern and Southern Italian dishes. Try *pappardelle* (broad noodles) in veal sauce with mushrooms and tomatoes, grilled chicken with arugula salad, and sea scallops in a tarragon broth. For dessert, don't miss the almond cake with chocolate and vanilla sauces. ♦ Northern Italian ♦ Daily, lunch and dinner. Reservations required. 1555 Second Ave (between E 80th and E 81st Sts). 861.7660

19 The Comic Strip

This is a showcase club for stand-up comedy acts. Eddie Murphy, Jerry Seinfeld, Paul Reiser, Chris Rock, and Sarah Silverman all started here, and sometimes a big name will drop by. ♦ Shows most nights; reservations suggested. Cover, minimum. 1568 Second Ave (between E 81st and E 82nd Sts). 861.9386

20 Divino Ristorante

★★$$ Service and pasta are the high points of this unpretentious favorite of Italian expatriates. Specialties include good fettuccine with four cheeses, linguine with baby clams, breaded veal chop Milanese, and shrimp scampi. Top it all off with a wonderful cappuccino. ♦ Northern Italian ♦ M-Sa, lunch and dinner; Su, brunch and dinner. Reservations required. 1556 Second Ave (between E 80th and E 81st Sts). 861.1096

21 L'Occitane

Although the company's sensual bath accessories—soaps, perfumes, and creams—can be found in upscale department stores and boutiques throughout the city, making your purchase in one of their own shops is like stepping into a garden in Provence. No matter the weather outside, inside, you'll find a sunny world redolent of herbs, fruits, and fragrant flowers. Note that the essences are quite intense—a dab or two is all that's needed. ♦ Daily. 1046 Madison Ave (between E 79th and E 80th Sts), 639.9185. Also at numerous locations throughout the city

22 Junior League of The City of New York

One of a trio of perfect neighbors, this sophisticated 1928 Regency-style mansion by **Mott B. Schmidt** was built for Vincent Astor. The other two are Schmidt's Georgian house for Clarence Dillon (1930) at **124 East 80th Street** and the Federal-style George Whitney House (1930) at **120 East 80th Street**, by **Cross & Cross**. ♦ 130 E 80th St (between Lexington and Park Aves).

23 Parma

★★$$$ Owner John Piscina greets everyone at the door of this popular East Side trattoria, and a more hospitable atmosphere you won't find outside your grandmother's kitchen. All the homey favorites—gnocchi, lasagna, chicken parmigiana—are deftly prepared and generously portioned. In between courses of his own harried meal in the corner, Piscina will make sure you want for nothing. An extensive wine list features a number of good wines by the glass. ♦ Northern Italian ♦ Daily, dinner. Reservations required. 1404 Third Ave (between E 79th and E 80th Sts). 535.3520

24 Acquavella Galleries

One of the uptown heavy hitters, this gallery shows 19th- and 20th-century European masters and postwar American and European artists. ♦ M-F. 18 E 79th St (between Madison and Fifth Aves). 734.6300. www.acquavellagalleries.com

25 New York Society Library

Not part of the New York Public Library system, and often confused with the New-York Historical Society, this is New York City's oldest circulating library. It was founded in 1754 by a civic-minded group who believed that the availability of books would help the city to prosper. Housed since 1937 in a handsome Italianate town house built in 1917 by **Trowbridge & Livingston**, today it is a local landmark boasting a collection of more than 200,000 volumes, as well as first editions and rare books and manuscripts. The library's particular strengths are in English and American literature, biography, history, art history, and travel and exploration, as well as works relating to the Big Apple. There is also a children's section. ♦ M-Sa. 53 E 79th St (between Park and Madison Aves). 288.6900. www.nysoclib.org

26 Yorkville Branch, NYPL

This rather academic neoclassical building, designed in 1902 by **James Brown Lord**, is the earliest of what are known as the "Carnegie Libraries." There are 65 of these small branch libraries throughout the city, established by a donation from Andrew Carnegie. Later ones, similar in style, were designed by Lord and other distinguished architects such as **McKim**, **Mead & White**, **Carrère & Hastings**, and **Babb**, **Cook & Willard**. ♦ M-Sa. 222 E 79th St (between Second and Third Aves). 744.5824. www.nypl.org

27 James B. Duke House

A copy of an 18th-century château in Bordeaux, this mansion, designed in 1912 by **Horace Trumbauer**, was built for the founder of the American Tobacco Company. It was given to **New York University** in 1959 by Duke's widow and her daughter, Doris (who, along with Barbara Hutton, was known as a "poor little rich girl" in the 1930s), and is now **NYU's Institute of Fine Arts**. Many of the original furnishings are still here, including a Gainsborough portrait in the main hall. ♦ 1 E 78th St (at Fifth Ave). 992.5800

27 Cultural Services of the French Embassy

Created in 1906 by **McKim**, **Mead & White**, this Italian Renaissance mansion, built for financier Payne Whitney, is typical of upper Fifth Avenue at the turn of the 20th century, before the arrival of massive apartment houses. Since 1952 it has housed the cultural services component of the French embassy. The **Consulate General of France**, which may be helpful for those seeking information about visas and other services, is at 934 Fifth Avenue (606.3620). ♦ 972 Fifth Ave (between E 78th and E 79th Sts). 439.1400. www.frenchculture.org

28 La Maison du Chocolat

For chocolates of unsurpassed quality, New Yorkers in the know look no farther than this understated temple to the cocoa bean. French proprietor Robert Linxe treats chocolate with the earnestness and ardor of a true connoisseur. Try one of the dense ganaches, wedges of intense milk or dark chocolate with different fillings such as coconut and praline, or the pastries flown in fresh from Paris. The rear of the store is given over to a small tearoom, where you can experience true chocolate nirvana: a silky, ultrarich cup of Guayaquil (mild) or Caracas (bittersweet) hot chocolate. In summer there are equally indulgent chocolate sorbets and ice creams. ♦ Daily. 1018 Madison Ave (between 78th and 79th Sts). 744.7117. Also at 30 Rockefeller Pl (at W 49th St, between Fifth and Sixth Aves). 265.9404

28 Stuyvesant Fish House

Designed by **McKim**, **Mead & White** in 1898, this Renaissance palace was once the scene of the city's most lavish parties. It was owned by Stuyvesant Fish, who was president of the Illinois Central Railroad. He and his wife, Marion, were prominent social leaders. ♦ 25 E 78th St (at Madison Ave)

29 Missoni

The whole store is devoted to the Missoni signature Italian knits on what is a veritable "European Designers' Row." The recognizable

East Side, West Side . . . Detours Around the Town

First-time visitors to the city frequently stick to the main avenues of **Fifth**, **Madison**, **Columbus**, or **Broadway**. For those with a bit more time, there are some unusual clusters of side streets scattered throughout Manhattan and other boroughs. Many of these streets are specialty-interest areas catering to certain industries—did you know New York boasts a button district and a ribbon district? Other detours afford glimpses into the lives and customs of many of the city's ethnic communities. Most commercial areas are livelier during weekday business hours; on weekends and evenings, the deserted streets can be somewhat intimidating—and not particularly interesting, though many downtown side streets tend to have more after-dark activity, especially in the **East** and **West Villages**. Here are some off-the-beaten-path destinations worth a detour or two.

East Village

Start with **St. Mark's Place**. Here you'll find the ghosts of the 1960s in hole-in-the-wall vintage record stores, clothing stores, and inexpensive restaurants serving counterculture cuisine. While a few chain stores now intrude, the atmosphere is still tinged with patchouli. The surroundings become more exotic the farther east you venture. **East Sixth** through **East 14th Streets** are shot through with ethnic restaurants, from Ukrainian to Japanese and Indian (East Sixth Street between **First** and **Second Avenues** has a large number of similarly priced Indian spots; rumor has it that they're all owned by the same person), small galleries, and offbeat stores. Several spots cater to practitioners of the occult arts; you can buy herbs and charms to cast your own personal spells. This neighborhood is also home to Off-Off-Broadway theater companies; there's a cluster on East Fourth Street. Between **Avenues A** and **B**, the streets reflect the ever-growing gentrification of the area.

Greenwich Village

Bleecker Street, running diagonally from the West Village, then west to east from Sixth Avenue to the Bowery, cuts through the **NYU** campus and what's left of the old folk and rock clubs where people like Bob Dylan and Peter, Paul & Mary got their starts. Below **Washington Square Park** and north of Houston Street, **MacDougal**, **Thompson**, and **Sullivan** Streets are especially browsable (and especially nice on less-crowded weekdays). They retain the air of the '60s and '70s, as well as the Italian enclave it once was.

A bit farther uptown, **East Ninth** through **13th Streets**, from **Fourth Avenue** heading west, you'll find some of the most elegant and expensive antique furniture dealers this side of Paris or London. French Country, Louis XVI, and a smattering of European Retro are the primary styles. These are also some of the more genteel residential streets in the neighborhood.

Union Square, Chelsea, and Flatiron

The teens and twenties—mainly **15th** through **22nd Streets**—west of Union Square to **Ninth Avenue** are dotted with high-end vintage art poster galleries, photo and art supply stores, secondhand and specialty bookstores, and an endless number of trendy restaurants and night spots. These streets cut through the shopping areas of **Lower Fifth**, **Sixth**, and **Seventh Avenues**, hitting the big-box chains that now inhabit the former Ladies' Mile stretch on Sixth.

Garment and Flower Districts

The side streets of the **West 30s** from **Eighth Avenue** to **Fifth Avenue** are the lifeblood of New York's Korean population. There are dozens of tantalizing barbecue

blend of subtle color combinations and patterns is worked up in all kinds of dashing sportswear for men and women. ♦ M-Sa. 1009 Madison Ave (corner of E 78th St). 517.9339 ♿

30 Nara

This small but inviting shop that sells leather goods and costume jewelry is a good source for increasingly hard-to-find labels such as Koret, as well as French handbags. There is also a selection of ladies' leather belts. The staff is polite and helpful. ♦ M-Sa. 1132 Lexington Ave (between E 78th and E 79th Sts). 628.1577

31 Tiny Doll House

All the teeny, tiny furniture and accessories it takes to make a doll's home, including mini Degas paintings, handmade English houses, and furniture, are here under one roof. If you think you can make something better yourself, all the supplies you need are available. ♦ M-Sa. 314 E 78th St (between First and Second Aves). 744.3719

32 Leo Castelli Gallery

A must-see, Castelli's extraordinary gallery features a veritable Who's Who of Abstract estaurants (they can get rather smoky) where you grill our own meats and fire up your tongue with spicy ickled vegetables. The upper West 30s between Fifth nd Eighth Avenues are dominated by trimming and otion stores. Bridal veils and beading are a specialty, s are buttons, bows, and fanciful borders. The Flower District is small and mostly wholesale too, but the cents from its center on **West 28th Street** off Sixth Avenue are worth the stroll alone.

East Side

East 60th Street, between Second and **Third Avenues**, s an eclectic mix of elegant antiques shops and men's talian clothing boutiques. Designer Betsey Johnson has ne of her larger branches here. There's a startling store vindow filled with wigs, and a graceful Episcopal church vith a noteworthy stained-glass window that oddly esembles the Star of David. This block is also home to hat ice-cream warhorse, Serendipity, and other popular estaurants. It's a fine warm-up walk at the gateway to Bloomie's—or the 59th Street Bridge—and the rest of the East Side.

West Side

The **West 60s** and **70s**, between **Central Park West** and **West End Avenue**, are rife with romantic restaurants like Café des Artistes, impressive buildings like Christ and St. Stephen's Church and the Pythian Temple, where Buddy Holly recorded his later songs, and popular local shopping spots like Acker, Merrall & Condit (fine wines) and Top Shoes, located on opposite sides of the same busy block—West 72nd between Columbus Avenue and Broadway. While crosstown thoroughfares like **West 72nd** and **West 79th Streets** have the greatest density, don't ignore the less-explored and exploited streets in this thriving residential neighborhood.

Harlem

West 125th Street is the thriving heart of Harlem. Cultural landmarks like the **Apollo Theater** and the **Studio Museum** are on this famous street. In between are a growing number of familiar chain outlets, African-American boutiques, and a number of food stores and restaurants. Other Harlem cross streets of note are **West 138th** and **West 139th Streets**, between **Adam Clayton Powell Jr.** and **Frederick Douglass Boulevards**. Known as **Strivers' Row**, these two blocks of elegant late-19th-century houses were (and still are) home to many noted African-American professionals—and a growing population of professionals from other ethnic backgrounds as well. The **Mount Morris Park Historical District** is most interesting from **West 119th** to **West 124th Streets**, just west of Mt. Morris Park.

Queens

Jackson Heights is a heady mixture of Pakistani, Colombian, Argentinian, Korean, and Indian culture. At night, strolling outsiders may be viewed with suspicion, except at the area's many restaurants. The block of **74th Street** between **Roosevelt** and **37th Avenues** is replete with excellent—and relatively little-known—Indian restaurants, as well as dazzling jewelry and sari stores. **Astoria**'s side streets, jutting off from either side of the elevated subway around **Broadway**, **Steinway Street**, and **Astoria**, **Northern**, and **Ditmars Boulevards**, have rows of neat and tidy single-family homes, international and Mediterranean grocery stores, and lots of restaurants—Greek's the specialty here.

Downtown **Flushing**'s Main Street, running from **Sanford Avenue** to **Northern Boulevard**, mirrors Asian culture with herbal shops, greengrocers, and, best of all, some of the best Chinese, Korean, and Japanese restaurants in the city. This enclave of pan-Asian delights can be found at the end of the **No. 7** subway line.

Expressionist and Pop artists, many of whom have shown their work with Castelli since the early 1960s. Jasper Johns, Ellsworth Kelly, and Ed Ruscha are but a few of the gallery regulars. ♦ Tu-Sa. 18 E 77th St (between Madison and Fifth Aves). 249.4470. www.castelligallery.com

33 The Mark

$$$$ This elegant and intimate luxury hotel boasts rooms with original 18th-century Piranesi prints, feather pillows, marble bathrooms, terry-cloth robes, and heated towel racks—and just about any amenity you desire, including today's necessity, high-speed Internet access. Pets are welcome, and—but of course—there are on-site health club facilities. *Note:* Ongoing conversion to condos may limit room availability. ♦ 25 E 77th St (between Madison and Fifth Aves). 744.4300, 800/843.6275; fax 744.4586. www.themarkhotel.com ♿

34 Malia Mills

Mix and match tops and bottoms to create the perfect swimsuit at this unfussy but upscale boutique. Top sizes range from 30AA to 40DD, bottoms from 2 to 16; amid bandeaus and halters, colors and prints, high- and low-cut legs, and a selection of one-pieces, there's something for every body. ♦ Daily. 988 Madison Ave (at E 77th St). 249.2966. Also at 1031 Lexington Ave (between E 73rd and E 74th Sts). 517.7585; and other locations

35 870 Park Avenue

This 1898 town house has been completely remodeled. The tripartite division of the façade alludes to that era's tradition and the scale of the surrounding buildings. In terms of styling, this is the next step after Modernism (see the **Lescaze Residence**), and it holds its own. This structure was designed in 1976 by **Robert A.M. Stern** and **John S. Hagmann**. ♦ At E 77th St

36 Vermicelli

★★$ This spot is a local fave for that uptown rarity: good Vietnamese food, in a nice setting, and at good prices. Pho, Imperial shrimp rolls, a fiery green papaya salad, and an assortment of satay make for pleasing starters. For a main course, try the yellow curry vegetables over vermicelli or the grilled pork chop marinated in a spicy honey-garlic blend. ♦ Vietnamese ♦ Daily, lunch and dinner. Reservations recommended. 1492 Second Ave (between E 77th and E 78th Sts). 288.8868 ♿

36 Lusardi's

★★★$$$ This is one of several clublike uptown trattorie that attract a sleek, affluent crowd. The food here, however, is more reliable than at other places, and the service is more attentive. Try calamari with tomato sauce, sun-dried-tomato ravioli, pasta with white truffles (in season), or chicken with artichokes and sausage. ♦ Northern Italian ♦ M-F, lunch and dinner; Sa, Su, dinner. Reservations recommended. 1494 Second Ave (between E 77th and E 78th Sts). 249.2020

37 Cherokee Apartments

Built as model housing for the working class, these apartments are distinguished by the amount of light and air admitted by large casements and balconies—an unusual commodity in the days of "dumbbell"-shaped tenements; these were designed in 1909 by **Henry Atterbury Smith**. ♦ Faces onto Cherokee Pl between E 77th and E 78th Sts

38 The Surrey

$$$ This small apartment-hotel, part of the Manhattan East group, has 130 large and tastefully decorated rooms. The room service is from **Café Boulud**, a favorite spot of the staff of the nearby **Whitney Museum** and other art-world movers and shakers. You'll find high-speed Internet access in all rooms, and an on-site fitness center. ♦ 20 E 76th St (between Madison and Fifth Aves). 288.3700, 800/637.8483; fax 628.1549. www.affinia.com ♿

Within The Surrey:

Café Boulud

★★★$$$$ Renowned chef Daniel Boulud's casual (that is, no ties required) creation. The food here is as delectable as the sky-high prices would imply, and it's refreshingly unpretentious, too. The menu is divided into four categories: Le Voyage, inspired by world cuisines; La Saison, featuring courses in tune with the season; Le Potager, offering vegetarian dishes; and La Tradition, where classic French cuisine shines brightly. Choice selections, respectively, include potato gnocchi with country lentils and black truffle; roasted beef rib with carrots fondant and red wine shallots; root vegetable cassoulet; and chocolate-cinnamon mousse with a crisp red wine tuile. No matter what you order, make a point of trying one of Daniel's signature soups. Whether it's a curried cream of cauliflower and apple soup or chilled tomato soup with a basil guacamole, the combinations of ingredients are sure to be as unlikely as the results are light and delicious. ♦ French ♦ Tu-Sa, lunch; daily, dinner. Reservations recommended. 772.2600 ♿

39 The Carlyle

$$$$ At 38 stories, this hotel, designed in 1929 by **Bien & Prince**, soars above the East Side. Decorous charm and easy elegance pervade the 180 guest rooms and public premises; it is always at the top of someone's list of best New York City hotels and is one of the few hotels tolerated by those who are used to the grand European style. For them, the Tower apartments seem to fill the bill for short stays or as permanent residences. The Carlyle has been updated for Wi-Fi access throughout the hotel; the on-site health club facilities are fine. Pianist Bobby Short made the **Café Carlyle** famous; though he's passed on, we are certain his great warmth and spirit will inspire his successors to come. The more relaxed and less expensive **Bemelmans Bar** is named for illustrator Ludwig Bemelmans, who painted the murals here. **The Gallery** is recommended for people watching at teatime.

On a Clear Day You Can See . . .

verything looks better from a distance—and New York ity is no exception. Unlike the aging actress whose left rofile is better than her right, the Big Apple shines very which way, especially from the following vantage oints:

ircle Line Cruises

ier 83, 12th Ave and W 42nd St. 563.3200

mpire State Observatory

fth Ave and W 34th St. 736.3100

ort Tryon Park and The Cloisters

'est 190th St, Washington Heights

iberty State Park

ohnson Ave (east of Grand St), Jersey City, ew Jersey

rooklyn Heights Promenade

ear Clark and Montague Sts, Brooklyn

he Rainbow Room and **Top of the Rock**

0 Rockefeller Plaza (between W 49th and W 50th ts). Rainbow Room: 632.5000; Top of the Rock: 98.2000

River Café

1 Water St (at Old Fulton St, under the Brooklyn Bridge), Brooklyn. 718/522.5200

Riverside Church

490 Riverside Dr (at W 122nd St). 870.6700

Roosevelt Island Tram

Station: Second Ave and E 60th St

Staten Island Ferry

Battery Park, South St and Peter Minuit Plaza. 806.6940

Statue of Liberty

Liberty Island. 363.3200

The Terrace

400 W 119th St (at Morningside Dr). 666.9490

Triborough Bridge

Entrance at E 125th St and Second Ave

The View Restaurant (Marriott Hotel)

535 Broadway (at W 45th St). 704.8900

The **Carlyle Restaurant** serves fine Greek cuisine with a classical French accent in a romantic, elegant setting. ♦ 35 E 76th St (at Madison Ave). 744.1600, 800/227.5737; fax 717.4682. www.thecarlyle.com ♿

40 William Secord Gallery

William Secord, former director of the **Dog Museum** (now located in St. Louis), operates this gallery devoted to man's best friend. Exhibitions may also include cats and barnyard animals. ♦ M-Sa. 52 E 76th St (between Park and Madison Aves), third floor. 249.0075. www.dogpainting.com

41 Lenox Hill Hospital

A compound of modern buildings extends from the hospital's nucleus, the **Uris Pavilion**, built in 1975 by **Rogers**, **Butler**, **Burgun & Bradbury**. Ranked as one of the city's—and the nation's—best, this hospital is a forerunner in obstetrical and neonatal care (its **Prenatal Testing Center** is one of the most comprehensive in the country); cardiology (the first balloon angioplasty in the country was performed here in 1978); and sports medicine (the **Nicholas Institute of Sports Medicine and Athletic Trauma** was the first such hospital-based center in the US). ♦ 100 E 77th St. Bounded by Lexington and Park Aves, and E 76th and E 77th Sts. 434.2000. www.lenoxhillhospital.org ♿

42 St. Jean Baptiste Church

This Roman Catholic church, designed by **Nicholas Serracino** in 1913, was founded by French Canadians in the area. It is a little overwrought, in a French Provincial way, but charming nevertheless. Among its best features is the French-style organ, which is one of the finest in any New York church. ♦ Lexington Ave and E 76th St. 288.5082

43 Atlantic Grill

★★★$$$ A palace of all things piscine, fish here comes grilled, baked, broiled, poached, or raw, with accents as varied as citrus vinaigrette, porcini crust, mango chutney, and tamarind glaze. The menu offers a sweeping and tantalizing array of options, as the black-clad crowds that fill the two boisterous dining rooms nightly can attest. Enjoy one of the best by-the-glass wine lists in the city. ♦ Seafood ♦ M-Sa, lunch and dinner; Su, brunch and dinner. 1341 Third Ave (between E 76th and E 77th Sts). 988.9200 ♿

44 DELORENZO

Top-drawer furniture of the Art Deco era, sometimes including pieces by such eminent designers as Jacques-Emile Ruhlmann, Jean Dunand, and Pierre Chareau, is available here. ♦ M-Sa. 956 Madison Ave (between E 75th and E 76th Sts). 249.7575

45 WHITNEY MUSEUM OF AMERICAN ART

Sculptor Gertrude Vanderbilt Whitney founded this museum in 1931 to support young artists and increase awareness of American art. The nucleus of its collection was 600 of the works she owned by Thomas Hart Benton, George Bellows, Maurice Prendergast, Edward Hopper, John Sloan, and other American artists of the era. The present building, designed by **Marcel Breuer** with **Hamilton Smith** in 1966, is the museum's third home. Like the **Guggenheim**, the structure is more sculpture than building. A dark, rectilinear, Brutalist mass steps out toward the street, almost threatening those who want to enter. Only the drawbridge entrance seems protective. The museum, perched on the corner, is isolated from its surroundings by sidewalls. You can peer down into the sunken sculpture garden and see through to parts of the lobby. But otherwise, the interior's workings are a mystery—until you're inside, that is, where it all opens up—guarded by angled trapezoidal windows that refuse to look you in the eye.

A late-20th-century expansion added 7,600 square feet of space to the museum, greatly expanding the permanent collection's exhibition area. The vast gallery spaces are surprisingly flexible, and can be quite appropriate for a variety of types of art—an important quality for a museum equally dedicated to temporary exhibitions of contemporary art. The permanent collection, which has been increased to 10,000 pieces through gifts and acquisitions, includes works by Alexander Calder, Louise Nevelson, Georgia O'Keeffe, Robert Rauschenberg, Ad Reinhardt, and Jasper Johns, among others, and a portion of it is always on display. Special exhibitions often concentrate on the output of a single artist, which could be 1980s' video art by Nam June Paik, or 1930s' Realist paintings by Edward Hopper. The museum's regular invitational Biennial, which critics often pan, is a mixed bag of what's going on across the country. The museum, under the directorship of Adam D. Weinberg since 2003, has an aggressively independent series for American film and video artists and makes adventurous forays into the performing arts. For information on these and gallery lectures, check the information desk. Take a break in **Sarabeth**'s, which features a moderately priced lunch menu (until 4PM) of omelettes, pasta, salads, and sandwiches.

The museum operates two branches, one at Champion International Corp. in Stamford, Connecticut, and one at the **Altria Building** (Park Ave and E 42nd St). ♦ Admission; voluntary F, 6PM-9PM. W, Th, Sa, Su, 11AM-6PM; F, 1PM-9PM. 945 Madison Ave (at E 75th St). 800/944.8639, 570.3676. www.whitney.org. ♿

Perhaps the most distinguishing feature of the city's streets in the 1880s was the mass of telephone and telegraph wires overhead. After the blizzard of 1888 they were placed underground.

46 CANDLE CAFE

★★$ Vegetarians rejoice: This cheerful purple-and-gold neighborhood haunt serves organic foods fresh from farm to table. Try the Paradise Casserole (layers of sweet potato, black beans, and millet), the fat-free soy burger, or the charred seitan steak, complete with mashed potatoes and gravy. delectable array of desserts includes wonderful fruit pies and an amazing organic brownie. Should you find yourself requiring even more fiber, there's also a superb juice bar. ♦ Vegetarian ♦ Daily, lunch and dinner. 1307 Third Ave (at E 75th St). 472.0970 ♿

47 BARAONDA

★★$$$ The cheery, fanciful room is fitted with primary-color lanterns, caricatures on the walls, and streamers. Late at night there's even dancing on the tables. Before running completely amok, line your stomach with a good, simple plate of pasta, such as *tagliolini* (thin noodles) with tomato and basil; shrimp risotto; or an entrée—grilled salmon with wild mushroom sauce is a good bet. ♦ Northern Italian ♦ M-F, dinner; Sa, Su, brunch and dinner. Reservations required. 1439 Second Ave (at E 75th St). 288.8555

48 COCO PAZZO

★★$$$ A major glam spot, Coco Pazzo seemed to flag for a while there, but by the late 2000s it was having its own renaissance. The setting's elegant, the food more than fine—wild salmon roasted in rosemary, with warm lentils and beets; seared rib-eye steak marinated in herbs and olive oil. You may wish the service were warmer, though. ♦ Northern Italian ♦ Daily, dinner; Su, brunch and dinner. Reservations required. 23 E 74th St (at Madison Ave). 794.0205

49 Vivolo

★★$$ This quiet and cozy white-tablecloth trattoria features standard, well-prepared dishes that include eggplant rollatini, linguine with clam sauce, grilled panini sandwiches on homemade bread, and a host of appetizing salads. For dessert, try the peach or coconut sorbettos. ♦ Italian ♦ M-F, lunch and dinner; Sa, dinner. Reservations required. 140 E 74th St (between Lexington and Park Aves). 737.3533. Also next door at **Cucina Vivolo**, 138 E 74th St (between Park and Lexington Aves). 717.4700; and 222 E 58th St (between Second and Third Aves). 308.0222

50 Mezzaluna

★$$ This tiny restaurant with a distinct Tuscan flavor is popular among East Siders for pizzas baked in a wood-burning oven, as well as carpaccio, salads, and pasta specials. Pumpkin *tortelloni* (large tortellini) are among the favorites. ♦ Northern Italian ♦ Daily, lunch, dinner, and late-night meals. 1295 Third Ave (between E 74th and E 75th Sts). 535.9600.

51 Jan Hus Church

This 1914 Presbyterian church was founded by the Czech community, whose presence in the neighborhood led it to be known as Little Bohemia in the 1920s and 1930s. The parsonage is furnished to resemble a Czech peasant's house. ♦ 351 E 74th St (between First and Second Aves). 288.6743

52 Woodard and Greenstein American Antiques

At the city's premier shop for high-quality antique and early 20th-century quilts, you'll find sizes ranging from crib to king. Designs include stars, postage stamps, and "drunkard's path." ♦ M-Sa. 506 E 74th St (between FDR Dr and York Ave), fifth floor. 988.2906

53 Payard Patisserie & Bistro

★★$$$ The bistro menu features updated takes on regional French dishes, but the sweet stuff by pastry chef François Payard is without question the biggest draw here. Payard oversees the creation of a stunning array of toothsome French cakes, tarts, cookies, croissants, and traditional breads made with imported French flour. Nibble on the premises or select an assortment to go. There are handmade chocolates and macaroons too. ♦ French bistro ♦ Pastry shop, M-Sa. Bistro, M-Sa, lunch, tea, and dinner. Reservations recommended. 1032 Lexington Ave (between E 73rd and E 74th Sts). 717.5252

53 Il Papiro

Replenish your writing stock at this beautiful outpost of a Florentine firm specializing in fine papercraft. Variations on its signature hand-marbling technique may also be found on its custom photo albums and journals, which are all archivally bound. Small leather goods and hand-blown glass paperweights, and other irresistible objects both functional and decorative, round out the offerings in this small, well-edited shop. ♦ M-Sa. 1021 Lexington Ave (between E 73rd and E 74th Sts). 288.9330

54 Petaluma

★$$ This once-trendy café still attracts a decent crowd who flock to its bar or dine in the vast, pastel-colored Postmodern space. The food includes spaghetti primavera; zesty baby chicken in a light mustard sauce; osso buco; and swordfish with tomatoes, capers, and olives. Dessert fans shouldn't miss the Belgian chocolate cake. ♦ Italian ♦ M-F, lunch and dinner; Sa, Su, brunch and dinner. Reservations required. 1356 First Ave (at E 73rd St). 772.8800 ♿

55 Ralph Lauren

If you like the Polo look, you'll love the exquisite wonderland Ralph Lauren has created here in the **Rhinelander Mansion**. Designed in 1898 by **Kimball & Thompson**, the French Renaissance building was commissioned by Gertrude Rhinelander Waldo, a descendant of one of New York's most influential families. She lived here for a few months, but preferred to live across the street with her sister. She offered it to her son, but he preferred to live elsewhere too, and the house stood empty until it was sold in a foreclosure in 1920. Before Lauren moved in, it was the **Philips Auction Gallery**. Now it overflows with his highest-end "Black label" and "Purple label" designs for outerwear, sportswear, separates, and accessories for men, women, and children, along with an opulent home design section. It's well worth a visit even if you don't buy anything. The same might be said for their location, dedicated to infants and toddlers. It's across the street, at 872 Madison (434.8099), just south of Lauren's modern 10,200-square-foot activewear shop, which includes a boutique featuring Lauren's Double RL division of weathered classics: jeans, motorcycle jackets, flannel shirts, and the like (888 Madison Ave, 434.8000). ♦ All three locations open daily. 867 Madison Ave (between E 71st and E 72nd Sts). 606.2100 ♿

56 Evergreen Antiques

Scandinavian country furniture (white Swedish rococo armchairs from the 1770s) and items from Russia's "golden age" (intricately detailed late-19th-century metal and hardstone-inlay specimen boxes), as well as continental and Biedermeier furniture, are available here. ♦ M-Sa. 1249 Third Ave (at E 72nd St). 744.5664

57 Cafe Greco

★★$$ This lovely neighborhood stalwart knows its fish. Grilled or blackened salmon and Asian sautéed halibut are highlights of fare inspired by the Mediterranean's various shores. French, Italian, Spanish, and Moroccan dishes all find their way onto a menu that also includes grilled octopus and penne with black olives, tomatoes, and capers. Wrap it up with the lemon blueberry pie. ♦ Mediterranean ♦ Daily, lunch and dinner. Prix-fixe lunch and dinner available. 1390 Second Ave (between E 71st and E 72nd Sts). 737.4300

SOTHEBY'S

58 Sotheby's

The London-based Sotheby's is the largest and oldest fine-arts auctioneer in the world. Sales of international importance, exhibitions, and free seminars take place in this 10-story glass cube. Distinctive for its pleasing pale-green horizontal panes (**Lundquist & Stonehill**'s work went up in 1980; **Kohn Pedersen Fox** did the 1999 expansion), the building's a freshly modern respite from the predominantly nondescript hospital structures surrounding it. Admission to the more important auctions is by ticket only, but all viewings are open to the public. You can also do some upscale dining at Sotheby's top-floor restaurant venture (Daily, breakfast and lunch, 606.7070). ♦ Open for viewings before scheduled auctions. Call ahead for schedule. 1334 York Ave (at E 72nd St). 606.7000. www.sothebys.com ♿

> In 1882, Charles Henry Dow and Edward Jones, the namesakes of today's stock index, founded a financial news service that became the *Wall Street Journal* in 1902 when it was sold to C.W. Barron.

59 St. James Episcopal Church

Originally designed in 1884 by **R.H. Robertson**, this church was established on the East Side before the invasion of the millionaires, but its future was secured whe families such as the Schermerhorns, the Rhinelanders, and the Astors became members of its vestry. In 1924, the church was rebuilt by **Ralph Adams Cram**; the steeple was added by **Richard Kimball** in 1950. ♦ 865 Madison Ave (at E 71st St). 288.4100

60 131 East 71st Street

America's first interior decorator, **Elsie de Wolfe**, lived here and used the house as a showcase for her innovative and fresh combinations of colors, patterns, and textures. The house was built in 1867, but she designed the present façade in 1910 with **Ogden Codman Jr.** ♦ Between Lexington and Park Aves

61 Grace's Marketplace

It's no coincidence that this gourmet marke resembles the old original **Balducci's** on Sixth Avenue in Greenwich Village; Grace is the daughter of that now demised institution's founding family. (Foodies will surely note the resurgence of the Balducci's name on shops around town—they are the result o a licensing deal, and are not run by the family.) Similarly, this place has glorious produce, cheeses, breads, prepared foods, and cakes of the highest quality. But there's also a salad bar here and spectacular fresh pasta in colors seen only on tropical fish. ♦ Daily. 1237 Third Ave (at E 71st St). 737.0600

62 The Frick Collection

When the old Lenox Library was torn down, Henry Clay Frick, chairman of the Carnegie Steel Corp., bought the site, wanting a place to display his art. He had **Thomas Hastings** design the Beaux Arts house in 1914—one of the last great mansions on Fifth Avenue—with apartments for his fami and reception rooms for the art. In his will,

The Frick Collection

Frick decreed that his wife could continue living there until her death, at which time it would be renovated and expanded as a museum. **John Russell Pope**, who later designed the National Gallery in Washington, DC, designed in 1935 what is now the museum. He is responsible for its unique character, especially the glass-covered courtyard, a rewarding retreat from city anxieties if ever there was one. The east wing was added in 1977, designed by **John Barrington Bayley** and **Harry Van Dyke**; the great landscape architect Russell Page designed the garden. The **Frick Art Reference Library**, the elegant and comprehensive research arm of the museum, was founded in 1920 and is also open to the public.

Visiting the Frick is like being asked into the sumptuous private home of a collector who bought only the crème de la crème of the old masters. Treasures here include Rembrandt's *The Polish Rider,* Van Dyck's *Virgin and Child with Saints, and Donor,* Bellini's *Saint Francis in the Desert,* Titian's *Man in a Red Cap,* El Greco's *Saint Jerome,* Piero della Francesca's *Saint Simon the Apostle,* and a whole room of Fragonards. There are occasional free lectures and chamber music concerts. Absolutely worth a visit. ♦ Admission. Tu-Sa, 10AM-6PM; Su, 1PM-6PM. Children under 10 not admitted. 1 E 70th St (at Fifth Ave). 288.0700. www.frick.org ♿

63 Knoedler & Company

The oldest New York–based art gallery, founded in 1846 down on lower Broadway, handles modern greats such as Robert Motherwell, Frank Stella, Helen Frankenthaler, Sean Scully, Lee Bontecou, and David Smith. Located in a striking 1910 colonnaded building by **Thorton Chad**, the smart exhibits here often feature the New York School in the postwar period. ♦ Tu-Sa. 19 E 70th St (between Madison and Fifth Aves). 794.0550. www.knoedlergallery.com

64 Hirschl & Adler Galleries

Top-quality shows of 18th-, 19th-, and 20th-century American and European art appear in this gallery founded back in 1952. Also featured in its landmark town house are American prints and contemporary paintings and sculpture. ♦ Tu-Sa. 21 E 70th St (between Madison and Fifth Aves). 535.8810. www.hirschlandadler.com ♿

65 Yves Saint Laurent–Rive Gauche

Neighboring stores combine to offer the entire Saint Laurent line for men and women. Together, they have the city's largest variety of his collections, including hats, umbrellas, shirts, slacks, dresses, suits, and ball gowns. ♦ M-Sa. 855 Madison Ave (between E 70th and E 71st Sts). 988.3821. Also at 3 E 57th St (between Fifth and Madison Aves). 980.2970 ♿

66 45 East 70th Street

Originally the home of investment banker Arthur S. Lehman, this nondescript town house was designed by **Aymar Embury II**, who also designed the Triborough Bridge and the late, not-lamented, and also nondescript New York Coliseum; it was completed in 1929. Ironically perhaps, it later became the home of cosmetics queen Estée Lauder. ♦ Between Park and Madison Aves

67 THE EXPLORER'S CLUB

This ornate neo-Jacobean house, designed by **Frederick Sterner**, was built in 1912 for Stephen C. Clark, whose family owned the Singer Sewing Machine Co. Among his many interests was baseball—he founded the Baseball Hall of Fame at Cooperstown, New York. The former residence is now known as the Lowell Thomas Building, home of The Explorers Club. Its opulent interior, unlike most of its club brethren, may actually be glimpsed by the hoi polloi. All it takes is attendance at one of the venerable institution's renowned public lectures. With members past (the club was founded in 1904) including the likes of Ernest Shackleton and Sir Edmund Hillary, you get the idea of what sort of themes its presentations might cover. ♦ 46 East 70th St (between Park and Madison Aves). 717.1584. www.explorersclub.org ♿

68 ASIA SOCIETY

The permanent collection of Asian art assembled by John D. Rockefeller III between 1951 and 1979 was moved in 1981 to this austere yet appealing building designed by **Edward Larrabee Barnes**. A top-to-bottom renovation resulted in a grand reopening in 2001. It is known for its outstanding Southeast Asian and Indian sculpture, Chinese ceramics and bronzes, and Japanese ceramics and wood sculptures. Other galleries in this serene albeit extravagant building feature changing exhibits ranging from Chinese snuff bottles to Islamic books from the collection of Prince Aga Khan. The society also sponsors lectures here on Asian arts and adventures, as well as films and performances. The lovely atrium-like **Garden Court Café** and a wonderfully browsable gift shop and bookstore complete the scene. Tours daily. Note: On Sundays, a shuttle bus to the **Noguchi Museum** in Queens (see page 323) leaves from here (bus schedule and info: 718/204.7088). ♦ Admission; free Friday after 6PM. Closed Monday. Tu-Th, Sa, Su, 11AM-6PM; F, 11AM-9PM. 725 Park Ave (at E 70th St). 288.6400. Box office: 517.ASIA (2742). www.asiasociety.org ♿

69 107 EAST 70TH STREET

This Tudor Revival mansion, designed in 1921 by **Walker & Gillette**, was once home to Thomas W. Lamont, chairman of J.P. Morgan & Co. ♦ Between Lexington and Park Aves

69 123 EAST 70TH STREET

Designer **Samuel Trowbridge**, whose works include the **St. Regis Hotel** and other Beaux Arts gems, built this house for himself in 1903. The curved windows and finish work add a Nouveau feel to this interesting iron-trimmed structure. ♦ Between Lexington ar Park Aves

69 PAUL MELLON HOUSE

This French Provincial town house, right at home in New York, was built for the industrialist and art collector in 1965 by **H. Page Cross**. ♦ 125 E 70th St (between Lexington and Park Aves)

70 124 EAST 70TH STREET

Built for financier Edward A. Norman in 194 by **William Lescaze**, this International-style house was cited by the **Museum of Moderr Art** for its innovative design. ♦ Between Lexington and Park Aves

71 SETTE MEZZO

★★$$ Whitewashed walls and sandy polished wood floors and tables set the tone in this coolly understated trattoria. The neighborhood hangout is known for its earthy, flavorful pastas: saffron ravioli, orchiette with butter peas and capers, an capellini with grappa-spiked puttanesca sauce. ♦ Italian ♦ Daily, lunch and dinner Reservations recommended. No credit cards accepted. 969 Lexington Ave (between E 70th and E 71st Sts). 472.0400

72 154 E 70TH STREET

This Tudor house, built in 1907 by **Edward Casey** for Stephen H. Brown, governor of th New York Stock Exchange, was considered one of the area's showplaces before it was converted to a school in 1932. The private **Manhattan High School for Girls** is its 21s century occupant. ♦ Between Third and Lexington Aves

73 GRACIOUS HOME

The ultimate neighborhood hardware store: vacuum cleaners, TVs, woks, umbrellas, dishwashers, radiator covers, mason jars, and all the expected basics. At the store across the street (**No. 1217**), you will find a complete bath shop—everything from sinks and faucets to shower curtains and bath mats. **No. 1201** is the place for lighting an custom window shades. ♦ Daily. 1220 Thir Ave (between E 70th and E 71st Sts). 517.6300. Also at 1201 Third Ave (betwee E 69th and E 70th Sts). 517.6300; 1992 Broadway (at W 67th St). 231.7800

74 PRATESI

This is one of the more sybaritic bed-and-bath shops in town, selling sheets of linen, silk, and Egyptian cotton, as well as comforters filled with goose down or cashmere and covered in silk. ♦ M-Sa. 829 Madison Ave (at E 69th St). 288.2315 ♿

75 The Union Club

Designed in 1932 by **Delano & Aldrich**, this limestone-and-granite structure is a rather dry palazzo composition (compare with the **University** or **Metropolitan Clubs**) and, no doubt, looks the way you would expect the oldest men's club—it was founded in 1836—in New York City to look. ♦ The building is not open to the public. 101 E 69th St (at Park Ave).

76 First Reformed Hungarian Church

Hungarian-born architect **Emery Roth** gave us a taste of the old country in 1915 when he designed this ornamented white stucco church topped by an 80-foot, conical-roofed bell tower. ♦ 344 E 69th St (between First and Second Aves). 734.5252

77 New York Hospital/Cornell University Medical College

What appears to be a singular, almost solid, well-balanced mass is actually 15 buildings, designed in 1932 by **Coolidge**, **Shepley**, **Bullfinch & Abbott**. The strong vertical lines are offset by Gothic arches. ♦ York Ave (between E 68th and E 71st Sts)

78 9 East 68th Street

Designed in 1906 by **Heins & LaFarge**, this was formerly the **George T. Bliss House**. Four giant columns hold up nothing but that little balcony and a brave front to the world. Remarkably out of scale, the house is noteworthy because it is engaging and not overly pretentious. ♦ Between Madison and Fifth Aves

79 6, 8, and 10 East 68th Street

These three houses, designed by **John H. Duncan** in 1900, were bought by financier **Otto Kuhn**, of **Kuhn, Loeb & Co.**, in 1916, and altered in 1919 with a French Renaissance limestone façade designed by **Harry Allan Jacobs**. ♦ Between Madison and Fifth Aves

80 Joseph

The latest knits from London are here—some simple, some romantic, all representing the world of street chic. Also for sale are hats and leather bags. Shop for men at the SoHo store—it's women's-only here. ♦ M-Sa. 816 Madison Ave (between E 68th and E 69th Sts). 570.0077. ♿ Also at 106 Greene St (between Prince and Spring Sts). 343.7071

malo

81 Malo

If you have to ask how much these sumptuous cashmere items for men and women cost, you'd best not enter. This was the Italian company's first American boutique; it features their remarkably lightweight—if heavy-priced—items of ultimate luxury. ♦ M-Sa. 814 Madison Ave (at E 68th St). 396.4721. ♿ Also at 125 Wooster St (between Prince and Spring Sts). 941.7444

MaxMara

82 MaxMara

This upscale Italian women's clothing company purchased this six-story building and tastefully restored it to the tune of $1 million. Designed and built in 1882 in the neo-Greco style with Federal elements, the first two floors provide elegant retail space for the well-known manufacturer's stylish collections. ♦ Daily. 813 Madison Ave (at E 68th St). 879.6100. Also at 450 W Broadway (between Houston and Prince Sts). 674.1817

83 680–690 Park Avenue

A lively but not exceptional collection of brick and limestone neo-Georgian buildings, this ensemble is special because it is the only full block of town houses surviving on Park Avenue. No. 680: **The Americas Society** (see below), originally the home of banker Percy Rivington Pyne, was designed in 1909 by **McKim, Mead & White**; No. 684: **Spanish Institute**, the house of Pyne's son-in-law, Oliver D. Filey, was built in Pyne's garden in 1926, by **McKim, Mead & White**; No. 686: **Istituto Italiano di Cultura**, formerly the **William Sloane House**, was designed in 1918 by **Delano & Aldrich**; No. 690: **Italian Consulate**, originally the **Henry P. Davidson House**, was designed in 1917 by **Walker & Gillette**. ♦ Between E 68th and E 69th Sts

84 The Americas Society

In the late 1940s and early 1950s, this was the **Soviet Delegation to the United Nations**, which made this corner the scene of almost continuous anti-Communist demonstrations. The nonprofit Americas Society occupies it today. Founded to further understanding of political, social, and economic issues throughout the Western Hemisphere, their means are often cultural. Literature, music, and art are all represented in a rich mix of public programming. You'll find ongoing art exhibitions in the **Americas Society Art Gallery** (W-Sa, noon-6PM; 277.8361); for music, call 277.8359, and for readings and other literary events, call 277.8353. ♦ 680 Park Ave (at E 68th St). 249.8950. www.americas-society.org ♿

85 Council on Foreign Relations

This building, designed in 1920 by **Delano & Aldrich**, was built by **Harold I. Pratt**, son of Charles Pratt, a partner of John D. Rockefeller Jr. and founder of Brooklyn's **Pratt Institute**. The present owner is an organization that promotes interest in foreign relations and publishes the influential magazine *Foreign Affairs*. ♦ 58 E 68th St (at Park Ave). 734.0400

86 Hunter College

Founded in 1870 as a school for training teachers, this is one of the colleges of the **City University of New York**. Today the school emphasizes such practical disciplines as science, premed and nursing, and education. Hunter's **Sylvia and Danny Kaye Playhouse** on E 68th St (at Lexington Ave, 772.4000) is used for lectures, political forums, adult and children's theater, and music and dance programs. ♦ Bounded by Lexington and Park Aves, and E 68th and E 69th Sts. 772.4000. www.hunter.cuny.edu ♿

87 4 East 67th Street

This is an ornate Beaux Arts mansion with a mansard roof to reckon with, built for banker Henri P. Wertheim in 1902 and designed by **John H. Duncan**. It is now the residence of the **Consul General of Japan**. ♦ Between Madison and Fifth Aves

88 13 and 15 East 67th Street

This is a curious pair, particularly in contrast to the Modernist red-granite face at **No. 17**. **No. 13**, designed in 1921 by **Harry Allan Jacobs**, is an Italian Renaissance concoction that was built for theatrical producer Martin Beck. **No. 15**, a 1904 building by **Ernest Flagg**, now the not-open-to-the-public **Regency Whist Club**, was the **Cortland Field Bishop House**. Concocted of stone and restrained ironwork, this rather Parisian house was designed by the man who did the origina[l] **Scribner's Bookstore** at 597 Fifth Avenue. ♦ Between Madison and Fifth Av[es]

89 Emanuel Ungaro

Here is the location for this fabled designe[r] collection for women, including his opulent[ly] printed, jewel-toned fabrics—paisleys, stripes, florals, and checks. The shop also sells such accessories as boots, shoes, belts, and shawls. ♦ M-Sa. 792 Madison Ave (at E 67th St). 249.4090 ♿

90 Frette

This sleek Italian shop features extravagan[t] linens for bed and table, including piqué bedspreads, linen sheets, and damask tablecloths. ♦ Daily. 799 Madison Ave (between E 67th and E 68th Sts). 988.5221 ♿

91 660 Park Avenue

Architect **Philip Sawyer**, of **York & Sawyer** carved a reputation for himself as a designer of banks, but his work on the rustication of this handsome 1927 apartment building is worthy of any of them. ♦ At E 67th St

92 115 East 67th Street

Designed in 1932 by **Andrew J. Thomas**, this building is a happy place with owls, squirrels, and other animals in the decorative panels and huge arched entry. ♦ Between Lexington and Park Aves

93 Park East Synagogue

Designed in 1890 by **Schneider & Herter**, this Moorish extravaganza has a more sedate Victorian interior. But the modern Orthodox congregation, founded in 1888, does get to appreciate the spectacular "rose-style" circular stained-glass windows from the inside. ♦ 163 E 67th St (between Third and Lexington Aves). 737.6900

94 Solow Houses

Developer Sheldon Solow, who built the innovative office building at **9 West 57th Street** in 1983, created these 11 houses (designed by **Attia & Perkins**), the first new town-house row in the city since the end of the 19th century. The tannish granite façade, which binds them togethe[r] between flat and slightly bowed fronts, barely articulates each individual house. The front is fortresslike, hiding luxurious interiors. ♦ 222-242 E 67th St (between Second and Third Aves)

95 The Lotos Club

Designed by **Richard Howland Hunt** in 1900, this was once the home of William J

Schieffelin, head of a wholesale pharmaceutical firm and a crusader for civil rights at the end of the 19th century. The rusticated limestone base supports a redbrick midsection and a double-story mansard roof. A vigorous Second Empire composite on the verge of being excessive, it is now headquarters of an organization of artists, musicians, actors, and journalists. The building is not open to the public. ♦ 5 E 66th St (between Madison and Fifth Aves)

96 45 East 66th Street

Designed in 1900 by **Harde & Short**, this building displays a lacy pastry exuberance at an even higher level than the **Alwyn Court Apartments** (W 58th St and Seventh Ave) designed by the same firm. Note the Elizabethan and Flemish Gothic detailing and the sensuous ease of the round tower on the corner. ♦ At Madison Ave

97 Seventh Regiment Armory

Designed by **Charles W. Clinton** in 1880, this is a crenellated, almost cartoonish fort in an otherwise very proper neighborhood. The interiors were furnished and detailed by Louis Comfort Tiffany. The hall is immense: 187 feet by 290 feet. It is the site of the annual **Winter Antiques Show** (www.winterantiquesshow.com) and other huge events. ♦ Park Ave (between E 66th and E 67th Sts). 744.4107 ♿

98 Cosmopolitan Club

Cast-iron balconies give a New Orleans flavor to this 1932 Greek Revival building, designed by **Thomas Harlan Ellett**. It is the headquarters of a prestigious women's club for those interested in the arts and sciences. The building is not open to the public. ♦ 122 E 66th St (between Lexington and Park Aves)

99 Church of St. Vincent Ferrer

When New York's Roman Catholic elite make wedding plans, **St. Patrick's Cathedral** is their first choice; if the cathedral is booked, this is where they turn. It was designed by **Bertram G. Goodhue** in 1923. ♦ Lexington Ave and E 66th St. 744.2080

100 131–135 East 66th Street

The two apartment blocks, designed in 1905 by **Charles A. Platt**, are most noted for their dignified grandeur and Mannerist porticoes. ♦ Between Third and Lexington Aves

101 Rockefeller University

This collection of buildings was originally known as the **Rockefeller Institute for Medical Research**. The lovely site, which was a summer estate of the Schermerhorn family, was acquired in 1901; the first building, **Founder's Hall**, opened in 1903 as a laboratory. Most striking are the gray hemisphere of **Caspary Auditorium**, built in 1957, and the **President's House**, built in 1958, both by **Harrison & Abramovitz**. It's worth a visit. Ask the guard for permission to enter, and while you're here, stroll toward the river for a look at the gardens. ♦ York Ave (between E 63rd and E 68th Sts). 327.8000. www.rockefeller.edu ♿

102 Roosevelt Island

This island is separated from Manhattan by 300 yards and more than a few decibels, but politically it is very much a part of it. The community, built in the 1970s, is accessible from Manhattan by tramway and subway, and from Queens by a small bridge at 36th Avenue, Queens Plaza. The master plan for a series of U-shaped housing projects facing the river was designed by **Philip Johnson** and **John Burgee**. Only the southern section was built, and it's taller and denser than they recommended. Until the 1970s, when rental agents needed a name change, it was known as **Welfare Island** because of its many hospitals and sanitariums. Before 1921, it was **Blackwell's Island**, named for the family that farmed it for two centuries. A prison was built in 1828, and over the next several years a workhouse, an almshouse, and an insane asylum were added. A century later those institutions were swept away and hospitals were substituted. The present site has reminders of each of the island's former lives. The ruin at the southern end was the **Smallpox Hospital**, designed in 1856 by **James Renwick Jr.** Just above it are the remains of the 1859 **City Hospital**, and under the Queensboro Bridge is the Goldwater campus of **Coler-Goldwater Specialty Hospital**. Not far from the tramway station is the **Blackwell Farmhouse** (1796-1804). Nearby are the **Eastwood Apartments**, built for low- and middle-income tenants in 1976 by **Sert, Jackson & Associates.** On the Manhattan side are **Rivercross Apartments**, built in 1975 by **Johansen & Bhavnani**, for people who can afford to pay more. There are two more luxury complexes: **Westview**, built in 1976 by Sert, Jackson & Associates, and **Island House**, built in 1975 by Johansen & Bhavnani, which has a glassed-in swimming pool overlooking Manhattan.

Cars are not allowed on the island except in the garage complex known as **Motorgate**. Garbage is removed through vacuum tubes to the **AVAC (Automated Vacuum Collection) Building**—where it is sorted, sanitized, and packed for removal. Near this monument to a "Brave New World" is the **Chapel of the Good Shepherd**, originally built in 1889 by **Frederick Clarke Withers** and restored by **Giorgio Cavaglieri** in 1976, now used as a recreation center. Landmarks at the northern end include the **Octagon Tower**, an 1839 building by **Alexander Jackson Davis**, all that's left of the **New York City Lunatic Asylum**, and a 50-foot stone lighthouse designed in 1872 by James Renwick Jr. (According to an inscription on the lighthouse, it was constructed by John McCarthy, an asylum inmate who busied himself by building a fort to defend himself against the British but was persuaded to replace it with a more attractive lighthouse instead.) The hospital at the uptown end of the island is the 1952 former **Coler Hospital for the Chronically Ill** (now the second campus of **Coler-Goldwater**). A complex of 1,104 apartments, **Northtown II**, was completed by Starrett Housing in 1989. Talks recently began and they moved forward with a long-stalled development of a prime 14-acre site at the southern end of the island. Known as Southpoint Park, it could include the 2.8-acre FDR memorial **Louis Kahn** first conceived for Roosevelt in 1972. Transportation on the island is provided by bus, but probably the best way to enjoy it is by walking or bicycling on its riverside promenades. ♦ East River

103 Temple Emanu-El

Designed by **Robert D. Kohn**, **Charles Butler**, and **Clarence Stein** in 1929, this impressive gray limestone edifice on the site of a mansion belonging to Caroline Schermerhorn Astor is, in addition to being the temple of the oldest Reform congregation in New York, simply the largest synagogue in the world. Resembling only the nave of a cathedral, the structure has masonry-bearing walls. In style, it is Romanesque with Eastern influences; these are repeated on the interior with buoyantly colored painted Byzantine ornamentation and its exuberant stained-glass windows. The hall is 77 feet wide, 150 feet long, and 403 feet high; it seats 2,500—more than **St. Patrick's Cathedral**. Only the Dohany Synagogue in Budapest comes close to it in size. The **Herbert and Eileen Bernard Museum of Judaica** (744.1400) is within, on the second floor. Its 650 religious and historical objects date from the 14th centur through today. ♦ Free. Su-Th, 10AM-4:30PM. Docent-led tours available. 1 E 65th St (at Fifth Ave). 744.1400. www.emanuelnyc.org ♿

104 Julie: Artisans' Gallery

Clothes conceived as art to wear: Julia Hill's jackets of hand-painted silk, Linda Mendelson's scarves and coats knitted in geometrical patterns, and many other flight of fancy, all in gorgeously detailed cuts and eminently wearable colorways and textures. Julie also offers a well-matched selection o jewelry, including vintage Bakelite pieces and clever bangles by Nita Sax. ♦ M-F. 762 Madison Ave (between E 65th and E 66th Sts). 717.5959 ♿

104 Giorgio Armani

Here's the top of the line for discerning shoppers with big dollars. The four-story white cube makes the nearby **Calvin Klein** store seem cozy by comparison. What you'l find within these spartan surroundings are stunning (read: expensive) clothes and accessories for men and women. The staff i friendly and helpful. ♦ M-F. 760 Madison Ave (at E 65th). 988.9191

105 Cambridge Chemists

Housed in a charming old brick building with a little green awning capped jauntily with an oversized silver apothecary cup, you'll find top-of-the-line European products including Cyclax of London, Innoxa, Roc, and Vichy. ♦ M-Sa. 21 E 65t St (between Madison and Fifth Aves). 734.5678 ♿

106 Daniel

★★★★$$$$ Believe the hype: New York's most talked-about four-star restaurant, the creation of power chef Daniel Boulud, offe one of the finest dining experiences to be had anywhere. Housed in the onetime hom to the original **Le Cirque**, it is now resplendent with Venetian, ancient Greek and Roman, and Art Deco elements. Boulu recognizes that good service is as essentia an ingredient to an enjoyable evening as maximum flavor, and here it is as stellar as the food. For an appetizer, try the peekytoe crab salad in a green apple gelée with celery root remoulade. Boulud's signature dish, black sea bass in a crisp potato shel with tender leeks and a Barolo wine sauce, is as divine as ever. Other star entrées include his sea scallop and squab preparations. And, If the Idaho potato bake in sea salt, crushed, and covered with fres white truffle is on the menu, get it. Dessert come in both seasonal fruit and chocolate varieties. With flavors like raspberry-hibiscus and green apple, the sorbets are hard to resist. Daniel's wine list is, not surprisingly, superlative. ♦ French ♦ M-Sa, dinner. Prix fixe available. Reservations are required; jacket and tie required. 60 E 65th St (between Park and Madison Aves). 288.0033

.07 Roosevelt House

In 1908, when her son, Franklin, was married, Sarah Delano Roosevelt commissioned **Charles A. Platt** to design this pair of Neo-Georgian houses; one was for herself, the other for the newlyweds. The houses are identical, with a common entrance. Several of their rooms were connected by folding doors to make them larger when necessary, as well as to give interior access between the two houses. It was in the fourth-floor front bedroom of the house on the right that Roosevelt went through his long recovery from polio in 1921-1922. The future president's mother wanted him to go to their estate in Hyde Park, New York, but his wife, Eleanor, persuaded him to stay in the city. She felt he had a future in politics and needed to be closer to the centers of power, even though he was bedridden. Her decision doomed her to live under the thumb of her mother-in-law, not one of her favorite people. **Hunter College/CUNY** is the present owner; their thorough renovation, executed by **Polshek Partnership** and completed in 2008, created a home for their **Roosevelt House Public Policy Institute**. ♦ 47-49 E 65th St (between Park and Madison Aves). www.hunter.cuny.edu ♿

08 China Institute and Gallery

This gift of publisher Henry R. Luce, the son of missionaries to China, reflects his lifelong interest in Sino-American cultural and political exchange. Along with changing exhibitions on Chinese fine arts and folk traditions, the institute, housed in a 1905 building by **Charles A. Platt**, conducts educational programs. ♦ Donation suggested. Daily. 125 E 65th St (between Lexington and Park Aves). 744.8181. www.chinainstitute.org

09 Berwind Mansion

This Venetian Renaissance mansion was the home of coal magnate Edwin J. Berwind, who was the sole supplier of coal for America's warships. Today, the building, which was designed in 1896 by **N.C. Melton**, contains cooperative apartments. ♦ 2 E 64th St (at Fifth Ave)

110 Consulate General of India

This unusually wide (65 feet) mansion, designed by **Warren & Wetmore** in 1903, would be right at home on the streets of Paris. It was built for banker Marshall Orme Wilson, whose wife was Carrie Astor, daughter of the Mrs. Astor who lived around the corner. When the government of India bought it, it was often referred to as **New India House**, lest it be confused with the first **India House**, in Lower Manhattan. But this is where the Consulate General of India now has its New York offices. ♦ 3 E 64th St (between Madison and Fifth Aves). 744.0600. www.indiacgny.org

111 Emilio Pucci

This boutique for the Italian designer is in a house that was once owned by Consuela Vanderbilt Smith, daughter of William K. Vanderbilt. It was built in 1882 by **Theodore Weston**, with a 1920 façade by **Mott B. Schmidt**. Pucci, whose designs became popular in the 1950s, but whose '60s colorful kaleidoscope designs really left their mark, died in 1992. ♦ M-Sa. 24 E 64th St (between Madison and Fifth Aves). 752.4777. Also at 701 Fifth Ave (between E 54th and E 55th Sts). 230.1135

112 Wildenstein & Co.

In 1932, **Horace Trumbauer** designed the building housing this gallery, which is known for the depth of its collections of Old Masters and other major examples of European and American art, including contemporary paintings and objets d'art. Exhibitions often rival museum shows. ♦ M-Sa. 19 E 64th St (between Madison and Fifth Aves). 879.0500 ♿

113 726 Madison Avenue

A brick wall to the left of this Georgian bank, designed by **Morrel Smith** in 1932, conceals a colonial garden—a rare oasis on this busy street. ♦ 726 Madison Ave (at E 64th St)

114 Valentino

In this hushed and lavish setting, you can see the designer's ready-to-wear collection, including classic pants, beautifully shaped jackets, and luxurious dresses for day and night. ♦ M-Sa. 747 Madison Ave (between E 64th and E 65th Sts). 772.6969

115 Hotel Plaza Athénée

$$$$ Formerly the **Alrae Apartments**, designed by **George F. Pelham** in 1927, this intimate, ultra-classy hotel is modeled

after the famous Paris original. Its moderate size (149 spacious rooms and 35 suites) and residential location attract guests in search of serenity rather than the hustle of Midtown. The lobby is a combination of French period furnishings, Italian marble floors, and hand-painted mural tapestry walls. Amenities include 24-hour concierge and room service, kitchenettes, in-room safes (the hotel itself is extremely secure, with only one entrance), large writing desks, high-speed Internet access, and on-site fitness facilities. Pets are welcome. Each of the four duplex penthouse suites includes a terrace and solarium. The hotel's **Bar Seine** and **Arabelle** (606.4647), a swank, animal-printed restaurant featuring global cuisine, are well-appointed for diversion and dining. ♦ 37 E 64th St (between Park and Madison Aves). 734.9100, 800/447.8800; fax 772.0958. www.plaza-athenee.com ♿

116 Central Presbyterian Church

To build this former Baptist church, which was designed by **Henry C. Pelton** and **Allen & Collens** in 1922, John D. Rockefeller Jr. matched every contribution, dollar for dollar; he also taught Bible classes here. In 1930, the congregation moved to **Riverside Church**, also largely funded by Rockefeller. ♦ 593 Park Ave (at E 64th St). 838.0808

117 Edward Durell Stone House

Designed by **Edward Durell Stone** in 1956, the concrete grillwork covering the façade of the late architect's home is similar to the screen he used in his design for the American Embassy in New Delhi two years earlier. Now that his similarly clad museum tower on Columbus Circle has been resurfaced (by the **Museum of Art & Design**), this house may be the best remaining New York evidence of Stone's particular style. ♦ 130 E 64th St (between Lexington and Park Aves)

118 JoJo

★★★$$$ Hailed as a creative genius, chef-owner Jean-Georges Vongerichten was a forerunner in the movement to replace cream- and butter-based sauces with more healthful infused oils and vegetable juices. His casual bi-level spot spot, simply decorated with ochre walls, plain wooden tables and chairs, and a few vivid oil paintings, has been a hit since the day the sign went up. The limited menu offers Vongerichten's interpretations of bistro fare including tomato tart and cobbler; chicken roasted with ginger, green olives, and coriander juice; foie gras with quince purée and for dessert, a spectacular chocolate cake. The wine list spotlights good French wines, some at affordable prices. ♦ French bistro ♦ M-F, lunch and dinner; Sa, Su, dinner. Prix-fixe lunch available. Reservations required. 160 E 64th St (between Third and Lexington Aves). 223.5656

119 Jackson Hole

★$ Juicy hamburgers approaching the size of Wyoming are the specialty of this restaurant. Here, at the very first location of this little chain, you walk down a set of stoop stairs and enter through the small, genuinely retro feeling lunch-counter area, then with any luck find a seat in the garden beyond. Or just plunk down here. Any (or several) of 12 toppings can be requested to adorn the seven-ounce burgers; a side order of onion rings or french fries is an integral part of the experience. There's also a large selection of good omelettes. On weekends kids rule, and as could be expected, the noise level increases dramatically. ♦ American ♦ M-F, breakfast, lunch, dinner, and late-night meals; Sa, Su, brunch and dinner. 232 E 64th St (between Second and Third Aves). 371.7187. Also at numerous locations throughout the city

120 Maya

★★★★$$ Soft rosy walls, inlaid wood floors and colorful glassware add a touch of elegance to this room. But that's just the beginning: Chef Richard Sandoval's native Mexican dishes are outstanding. Some of the best include *mole poblano* (grilled chicken breast with cilantro rice and mole sauce) and *chilaquiles* (sun-dried tortillas served with grilled chicken, black bean purée, and tomatillo salsa). The sliced flambéed bananas with tequila and caramel sauce are the perfect ending to a satisfying meal. ♦ Mexican ♦ Daily, dinner. 1191 First Ave (between E 64th and E 65th Sts). 585.1818

121 820 Fifth Avenue

Designed in 1916 by **Starrett & Van Vleck**, this is one of the earliest luxury apartment buildings on Fifth Avenue. Among its first tenants was New York's governor Al Smith. ♦ At E 63rd St

122 Givenchy

For women who want their haute couture brought to their doorsteps, this boutique sends fitters from the House of Givenchy

Organized fire fighting began in New York in 1648 when the first Fire Ordinance was adopted by the Dutch Settlement of New Amsterdam.

(think Audrey Hepburn) in Paris to New York each spring and fall to measure their local clients. For others, there are blouses, skirts, sweaters, coats, suits, ball gowns, and hats from both ready-to-wear and couture adaptations, which feature the same styles as in the couture collection but in less expensive fabrics. ♦ Daily. 710 Madison Ave (at E 63rd St). 688.4338

23 The Lowell

$$$$ White-glove treatment is the norm in this small, charming, and notably discreet hotel. Many of the 65 rooms and suites in the 1926 building by **Henry S. Churchill** have serving pantries and wood-burning fireplaces, and some can accommodate formal board meetings. Room-service meals (available 24/7) arrive on a silver tray, or, if you prefer company, the second-floor dining room is both cheerful and serene. High-speed Internet access is provided in every room, as are flat-panel televisions; pets are welcome, and all guests are welcome to use the on-site fitness facilities. Definitely one of New York City's best. ♦ 28 E 63rd St (between Park and Madison Aves). 838.1400, 800/221.4444; fax 319.4230. www.lhw.com/lowellhotel.

Within The Lowell:

The Post House

★★★$$$$ Many New York steak houses are strictly for red-meat eaters, but this gracious establishment has some alternate food choice and, though it can get loud, a softer touch—subdued lighting, peach walls, 18th-century American folk portraits, and models of ship hulls. The menu offers crab cakes and lemon-pepper chicken in addition to some of the best beef in the city. ♦ American ♦ M-F, lunch and dinner; Sa, Su, dinner. Reservations required. 935.2888

24 Park Avenue Café

★★★$$$ After this East Side favorite was shuttered for a bit, it reemerged as a dedicated supplicant to the seasonal foods trend. Call it Park Avenue Summer when we're in that hot and humid time of year (and the food—and décor—will salve accordingly), but expect the reservations desk to call it Park Avenue Autumn when fall has rolled around. A market-fresh langoustine-laden roll may be on the lunch menu; a filet mignon sandwich (with some zippy horseradish cream) might replace it later in the year. Dinner creations (braised lamb shank with pistachios and saffron, quince-glazed quail) follow suit. Desserts are always standouts, and the wine list is broad. ♦ American ♦ M-F, lunch and dinner; Sa, Su, brunch and dinner. Reservations required. 100 E 63rd St (at Park Ave). 644.1900

125 Society of Illustrators

Built in 1875, this perfectly scaled tribute to American illustration features changing exhibitions of advertising art, book illustration, editorial art, and other contemporary work. ♦ Free. M-Sa. 128 E 63rd St (between Lexington and Park Aves). 838.2560. ♿ www.societyillustrators.org.

126 810 Fifth Avenue

Former residents of this 13-story limestone building designed in 1926 by **J.E.R. Carpenter** include William Randolph Hearst and Mrs. Hamilton Fish, one of the last of the grandes dames of New York society. Before he moved to the White House in 1969, Richard M. Nixon lived here. His neighbor on the top floor was Nelson Rockefeller, who had New York's only fully equipped bomb shelter. The building is not open to the public. ♦ At E 62nd St

127 The Knickerbocker Club

In the 1860s, some members of the Union Club proposed that its membership be restricted to men descended from the Colonial families of New York, known as the Knickerbockers. When their suggestion was rejected, they started their own club (though one of its most influential founders was August Belmont, a German immigrant). Today, the club is located in this 1914 building by **Delano & Aldrich**, which is not open to the public. ♦ 2 E 62nd St (at Fifth Ave).

128 Nello

★$$$ There's an ample supply of models, debs, and soap stars dangling designer shopping bags at this Euro-sleek trattoria, perfectly lit and covered with Peter Beard's magnificent photos of African fauna. As far as the menu is concerned, go for the arugula and fennel salad; grilled free-range chicken; baby calamari stuffed with shrimps, scallops, and salmon; or prime rib-eye steak. One diner was so pleased with his meal (and service) he left a $16,000 tip—on purpose. ♦ Italian ♦ Daily, lunch and dinner.

Reservations recommended; jacket required. 696 Madison Ave (between E 62nd and E 63rd Sts). 980.9099

129 Hermès

Back near the turn of the 21st century, Hermès moved into this fabulous 1928 Art Deco gem, keeping the brilliant atrium that its previous tenant, The Limited, added in a much-lauded renovation (by **Beyer Biinder Belle**) in the mid-'80s. Surprising for a **McKim, Mead & White** design (Beaux Arts was their usual thing), the building was originally built for the Louis Sherry restaurant. Nowadays the saddlery, scarves, and silk shirts Hermès is known for are sold at this quintessentially Parisian original. And of course it's still the home of the Hermès tie, the foolproof gift for the boss who has everything. ♦ Daily. 691 Madison Ave (between E 62nd and E 63rd Sts). 751.3181. Also at 15 Broad St (at Exchange Pl). 785.3030

130 Georg Jensen

Impeccably designed and crafted silver, including flatware and exquisite jewelry, and watches, is featured here: sleek, gleaming bangles and cuffs, Art Nouveau pins shaped like leaves and set with precious stones. This is also a good source for crystal glassware and the entire collection of Royal Copenhagen china. ♦ Daily. 683 Madison Ave (between E 61st and E 62nd Sts). 759.6457. ♿ Also at 125 Wooster St (at Prince St). 343.9000

131 The Colony Club

The building, which houses an exclusive club for society women, presents a solid, neo-Georgian redbrick face, settled on a limestone base. It was designed in 1924 by **Delano & Aldrich** and is not open to the public. ♦ 564 Park Ave (at E 62nd St)

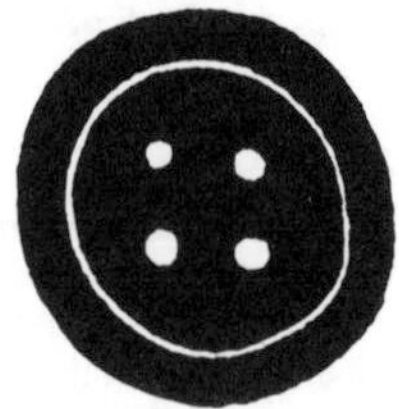

132 Tender Buttons

Featured at this charming, immaculate shop are millions and millions of buttons, new and antique, made of brass, stoneware, taqua nut, Lucite, wood, abalone, seashell, agate, plastic, silver—you name it. All are perfectly arranged and organized for browsing—and buying—pleasure. ♦ M-Sa. 143 E 62nd St (between Third and Lexington Aves). 758.7004

133 Il Vagabondo

★★$$ Robust Italian cooking, mostly Southern style, is one of the draws at this noisy, good-humored neighborhood trattoria. But the main reason to come here is to watch people play bocce at the city's only indoor court (ask for a courtside table). Specialties include homemade gnocchi, tuna steak, a fragrant veal stew, and fillet of sole. ♦ Italian ♦ M-F, lunch and dinner; Sa, Su, dinner. 351 E 62nd St (between First and Second Aves). 832.9221

134 800 Fifth Avenue

Until her death in 1977, Mrs. Marcellus Hartley Dodge, a niece of John D. Rockefeller Jr., lived here with her famous collection of stray dogs in a five-story brick mansion that was a mate to the nearby **Knickerbocker Club** (see page 245). In 1978, developer **Ulrich Franzen & Associates** promised they'd put up a tasteful replacement for it—one that would be a credit to the neighborhood. This 33-story building is how the promise was kept. The zoning law forced them to build a three-story wall along Fifth Avenue; unfortunately it isn't high enough to hide the building behind it. ♦ At E 61st St

135 The Pierre

$$$$ Designed in 1930 by **Schultze & Weaver**, the architects of the **Sherry-Netherland**, this is another of the grand old European-style hotels with many permanent guests and a loyal following of the rich and the powerful. A stretched mansard roof clothed in weathered bronze at the top of the tower gives the structure a distinctive silhouette; the Pierre and the Sherry, one block south (see page 249), make a romantic couple. Though at first glance it appears a bit intimidating, with all those limos in front and the miles of mural-lined lobby, the hotel offers the kind of luxury one could get used to: 202 enormous rooms and suites (with dramatic **Central Park** views from the upper floors; you can actually see the seals in the **Central Park Zoo**), with gleaming marble-and-tile bathrooms; 24-hour room service; an attentive, multilingual staff; high-speed Internet access (including Wi-Fi); fitness facilities; a full-service salon; twice-daily maid service; complimentary

There are nearly 17,000 restaurants dishing out everything from sweet breads to sweetbreads in the city that never sleeps.

The *New York World* printed the first crossword puzzle in 1913. The first comic strip serial, "The Yellow Kid," ran in an 1896 *New York Journal.*

shoe shine; and even an unpacking service. Afternoon tea is served daily in the **Rotunda**. ♦ 2 E 61st St (at Fifth Ave). 838.8000, 800/743.7734; fax 826.0319. www.lhw.com/thepierre ♿

Within The Pierre:

Café Pierre

★★★$$$ This sophisticated dining room may be mistaken for a French château with its tones of pale yellow and gray, imported silks, and ceiling murals. But the elegance doesn't rest there. Indulge in an equally classic menu of risotto with wild mushrooms, asparagus, truffles, and chervil; and roasted rack of lamb in herb crust with sautéed artichokes. The appealing desserts are tempting, including the white-and-dark-chocolate terrine with ginger chips and caramelized orange sauce. There's a fine wine list as well. ♦ French ♦ Daily, breakfast, lunch, and dinner. 940.8195

136 Barneys New York

This nine-story, 230,000-square-foot fashion temple designed by minimalist architect **Peter Marino** opened to much hoopla in 1993; it was the largest specialty store to be built in Manhattan since the Depression. Soon after, the Pressman family's original location in Chelsea—dating back to its start decades earlier as a discount suit store—shut its doors (the family sold off the entire shebang near the turn of the 20th century). The shop is light and airy, with large stretches of loftlike space. The women's side measures more than twice the size of its quarters in the former flagship. Men's contemporary sportswear has taken over the fourth floor. Chelsea Passage, with its wondrous finds, is on the ninth floor along with the views and **Fred's** (below). Don't miss the mesmerizing display of tropical fish in the main-floor jewelry department. ♦ Daily. 660 Madison Ave (between E 60th and E 61st Sts). 826.8900. Also **Barneys New York CO-OP** at 116 Wooster St (between Prince and Spring Sts). 965.9964; 236 W 18th St (between Seventh and Eighth Aves). 593.7800; 2151 Broadway (at W 75th St). 646/335.0978 ♿

Within Barneys New York:

Fred's at Barneys New York

★★$$$ Named for Fred Pressman, the late patriarch of Barneys, this bustling restaurant is a people-watching paradise. Try the assortment of marinated vegetables or a tasting of cheeses served with pears and Granny Smith apples. Also on hand are individual-size pizzas, and for hearty appetites, Baltimore crab cakes with homemade cole slaw and Belgian *pommes frites.* ♦ Northern Italian/American ♦ M-Sa, lunch and dinner; Su, brunch, late lunch. Reservations recommended. 833.2200 ♿

137 Aureole

★★★★$$$$ This is one of the most charming dining rooms in town. Chef Charlie Palmer's complex food, given a praiseworthy architectural presentation, is also among the most admired. Try the terrine of natural foie gras with pressed duck confit, applewood-grilled salmon with basil-braised artichokes, or slow-basted breast of guinea fowl with melted savoy cabbage and a ragout of morels. The desserts are spectacular, particularly the tower of dark-chocolate and praline mousse. ♦ New American ♦ M-F, lunch and dinner; Sa, dinner. Prix fixe available at lunch and dinner. Reservations required. 34 E 61st St (between Park and Madison Aves). 319.1660

138 The Regency

$$$$ This elegant hotel is the scene of some of New York's most important power breakfasts (**540 Park**), at which the city's movers and shakers get together to start their business day. Guests can take advantage of 24-hour room service for their breakfast, but it isn't as exciting. Other advantages include, as you might expect, high-speed and Wi-Fi Internet access everywhere, a full-service salon and well-equipped fitness center, and a large, multilingual staff. The hotel's luxurious feel is enhanced by French antiques in all 393 rooms. For added pleasure, **The Library** is a cozy spot for a drink or light meal. ♦ 540 Park Ave (at E 61st St). 759.4100, 800/23LOEWS; fax 826.5674. www.loewshotels.com ♿

139 Brio

★★$$ Thanks to its Italian-style home cooking, this attractive, wood-paneled trattoria is almost always full. The hearty polenta with porcini and the aromatic pesto-laden fusilli are two reasons to return again and again. ♦ Italian ♦ M-Sa, lunch and dinner; Su, brunch and dinner. Reservations recommended. 137 E 61st St (between Lexington and Park Aves) 980.2300

140 New York Doll Hospital

Even if your doll isn't sick, don't miss this experience. They buy and sell antique dolls and toys here, but what makes it so much fun (or creepy, depending on your point of view) is the collection of spare parts. ♦ M-Sa. 787 Lexington Ave (between E 61st and E 62nd Sts), second floor. 838.7527

141 Billy Martin's Western Wear

Yes, it's the late Billy Martin who used to pace the dugout at Yankee Stadium. This one-stop source of cowboy boots, fancy belts, and other expensive duds will make you look at home on the range. ♦ Daily. 1034 Third Ave (between E 61st and E 62nd Sts). 861.3100 ♿

142 Trump Plaza

This 1987 building by **Philip Birnbaum & Associates** is another attempt to immortalize the name of developer Donald Trump. The residential building is not open to the public, but don't pass up the waterfall or the open space to the left of the entrance that make it so pleasant. ♦ 167 E 61st St (at Third Ave)

143 Mount Vernon Hotel Museum & Garden

Abigail Adams Smith, the daughter of John Adams, for whom this 1799 house-museum was originally named, never even slept here. But she and her husband, Colonel William Smith, did own the land it was built on. They bought 23 choice acres on the bank of the East River in 1795 with the idea of building a country estate called "Mt. Vernon" (Colonel Smith served under George Washington). Because of financial reversals, they sold the estate in 1796. The stone stable that is now the museum was remodeled as a country day hotel in the 1820s, then used as a private dwelling until the neighborhood fell on hard times. The Colonial Dames of America rescued it in 1924, furnished it in the style of the Federal period, planted an 18th-century garden, and opened the house as a museum. It has since been refurbished to reflect the style of a 19th-century hotel. Colonial Dames members, well versed in the contents of the house (but not necessarily about antiques or the history of the period), show visitors the nine rooms. There are year-round concerts, lectures, and workshops for adults and children, and a gift shop. ♦ Admission. Tours. Tu-Su,11AM-4PM (last tour begins at 3:30PM). 421 E 61st St (between York and First Aves). 838.6878. www.mvhm.o

144 Bentley Hotel

$$$ Impossible though it may be to truly escape Manhattan's madding crowds, you do come pretty close at this office-tower-turned-hotel on island's edge. Guestrooms in this 21-story tower overlooking the East River are sleek and surprisingly spacious. There's an expansive glass-enclosed rooftop restaurant where complimentary continental breakfast is served. Request a room ending in "04" and you'll be treated to nighttime views of the **59th Street Bridge** that make your knees wobble; take a room on a low floor and you risk a vehicular serenade from FDR Drive. ♦ 500 E 62nd St (at York Ave). 644.6000; fax 207.4800. www.hotelbentleynewyork.com

145 Metropolitan Club

Designed by **McKim**, **Mead & White** in 1894, this is a good example of **Stanford White** in an enthusiastic mood. Note particularly the extravagant, colonnaded carriage entrance behind the equally extravagant gates of the château. An addition was built in 1912 by **Ogden Codman Jr.** The association was organized by J.P. Morgan for his friends who were not accepted at other clubs. The public, however, is not accepted here; the building is not open to the public. ♦ 1 E 60th St (at Fifth Ave)

146 The Harmonie Club

In 1852, wealthy German Jews, excluded from most other men's clubs, formed the Harmonie Gesellschaft, which was describe at the time as "the most homelike of all clubs" because its members made it a practice to bring along their wives. Today, this private club is located in a 1906 building designed by the ubiquitous **Stanford White** of **McKim**, **Mead & White**. ♦ The building is not open to the public. 4 E 60th St (between Madison and Fifth Aves). 355.7400

147 French Institute/Alliance Française

L'état, c'est vous—when you *parlez* your curiosity into cultural enrichment in this institution's wealth of public programs dedicated to all things francophone. Inside the Haussmann-like Beaux Arts building, yo can take part in book clubs, board games, acting workshops, lectures, and salons; vie the oeuvres of Truffaut and Godard (with or without subtitles); and, of course, learn French itself in the largest language center the US. ♦ 22 East 60th St (between

Madison and Fifth Aves). 355.6100. www.fiaf.org ♿

148 Calvin Klein

The trend-setting designs of one of America's timeless fashion icons (albeit in name only, now that Klein sold the business) can be seen here at this Madison Avenue megastore. The 22,000-square-foot retail space, built in 1928 to house the **Morgan Guaranty Bank**, offers shoppers the high end of his distinctive clothing collection, accessories, and home furnishings. ♦ M-Sa. 654 Madison Ave (at E 60th St). 292.9000

149 The Grolier Club

Named for the 16th-century bibliophile Jean Grolier, this Georgian structure, designed by **Bertram G. Goodhue** in 1917, houses a collection of fine bookbindings and a specialized library open only to scholars and researchers. Regularly changing exhibitions display books, prints, and rare manuscripts; an interesting roster of public lectures is programmed as well. ♦ Free. M-Sa. 47 E 60th St (between Park and Madison Aves). 838.6690. www.grolierclub.org ♿

150 Christ Church

Built in 1932 by **Ralph Adams Cram**, this is an interesting limestone-and-brick Methodist church. One of the best ecclesiastical structures of the 1930s, it was designed to look hundreds of years old. ♦ 520 Park Ave (at E 60th St). 838.3036

151 The Lighthouse Store/Lighthouse International

This small shop is entered through the rear of the headquarters of **Lighthouse International**, a nonprofit advocacy group for the vision-impaired founded in 1905. Housed in this understated 1994 **Mitchell/Giurgola**-designed tower (dedicated as the **Sol and Lillian Goldman Building** in 2005), this is the place to come for the latest tools and gadgets created to aid the blind, partially sighted, or otherwise vision-impaired consumer. Their wide selection of talking products and miniature GPS state-of-the-art technologies are of interest to the general public as well. All proceeds benefit the blind. ♦ Store, M-F: 110 E 60th St (between Lexington and Park Aves). 821.9384. Lighthouse International: 111 E 59th (between Lexington and Park Aves). 821.9384. www.lighthouse.org ♿

152 Le Veau d'Or

★★$$$ Longtime East Siders still flock to this somewhat faded but wholly traditional (vintage 1937) bistro for such well-prepared, basic French fare as steak au poivre, baby chicken with tarragon, and chocolate mousse. The service is unpretentious and efficient. ♦ French bistro ♦ M-Sa, lunch and dinner. Prix-fixe available, lunch and dinner. Reservations recommended. 129 E 60th St (between Lexington and Park Aves). 838.8133

153 Sherry-Netherland Hotel

$$$$ One of the grandes dames rimming **Central Park**, this hotel, designed in 1927 by **McKim**, **Mead & White** and built by Louis Sherry of ice cream fame, was once the centerpiece of an elegant trio, sitting between **The Pierre** and the **Savoy-Plaza** (whose site now hosts the **General Motors** tower). Its high-peaked roof sports gargoyles and chimneys like a Loire Valley confection. On the walls lining the entrance are panels rescued from a Vanderbilt mansion by **Richard Morris Hunt**. Service is continental luxury class, and the rooms are large, many with park views, and all 65 fully equipped with high-speed Internet access. There are a salon and fitness facilities on-site, and of course, Fifi and other pets are welcome. ♦ 781 Fifth Ave (at E 59th St). 355.2800, 800/247.4377; fax 319.4306. www.sherrynetherland.com

Within the Sherry-Netherland Hotel:

Harry Cipriani

★$$$$ If you can't get to the original Harry's Bar in Venice, don't think you can find it here. It's never been about the food, which is overpriced and consistently underwhelming, but rather the scene—which sprang right back in 2007 after a two-year hiatus. Try one of the raviolis, with fillings that change daily, and swing back a Bellini—a blend of peach nectar and dry Prosecco wine—while Ivana and Barbara Walters (possibly) do the same.

The Best

Cindy Adams

Syndicated Columnist for the *New York Post*

For jewelry watching: **The Diamond Center**, West 47th Street between Fifth and Sixth Avenues.

For kid watching: **FAO Schwarz**.

For view watching: **Rainbow Room**.

For lox/bagel/pastrami/salami watching: **Stage Deli**.

For window shopping: **Madison Avenue** going uptown from East 57th Street.

For shopping: **Trump Tower**.

For culture: **Lincoln Center**.

For color: **Greenwich Village**.

For architecture: **Seagram's Building** (supermodern glass and chrome), **Chrysler Building** (Art Deco), **Guggenheim Museum** (Frank Lloyd Wright).

For VIP high-rises, where people from Phil Donahue to me dwell: Walk **Fifth Avenue**.

For caviar: **Petrossian's**.

For seafood: **The Sea Grill**.

For steaks: **Gallagher's**.

For Japanese: **Inagiku** at the **Waldorf**.

For atmosphere: **The Water Club**.

For what's no place else in the whole world but in New York: **Statue of Liberty**, **Radio City Music Hall**, **United Nations**, **Rockefeller Center** skating rink, the **Theater District**, **Empire State Building**.

And read the *New York Post*.

♦ Northern Italian ♦ Daily, breakfast, lunch, and dinner. Reservations recommended; jacket required. 753.5566

154 Sherry-Lehman

One of the top wine merchants in the country, this place may have the most extensive retail inventory in the world—but smartly doesn't overwhelm its customers; it keeps only a tempting selection on display. Now ensconced in a wood-lined corner location, the easily browsable store specializes in French, California, and Italian wines, but also stocks German, Spanish, South American, and kosher labels. The courteous, expert staff will be glad to advise you. Catalogs are published five times a year—one each season, and an extra issue at Christmas. ♦ M-Sa. 505 Park Ave (at E 59th St). 838.7500. 838.7500

155 The Levi's Store

An icon in the annals of American fashion, the Levi's jean is here in every model, size, color, and interpretation imaginable. This spacious store is always filled with foreign shoppers having a field day. ♦ Daily. 750 Lexington Ave (between E 59th and E 60th Sts). 826.5957. ♿. Also at 536 Broadway (between Prince and Spring Sts). 646.613.1847; 25 W 14th St (between Fifth Ave and University Pl). 242.2128

156 Bloomingdale's

This store is show business. It caters to those who like to buy their clothes, food, and sofas in an atmosphere that is a cross between a designer showcase and a Middle Eastern souk. Once you get beyond the smiling and sometimes overzealous salespersons who threaten to squirt perfume at you, and TV screens showing endless tapes of designer fashion shows, you'll find the children's department, with layettes, strollers, Oshkosh overalls, and hand-knit sweaters. For women there is slinky knitwear by Missoni, seductive knits by Sonia Rykiel, the American chic of Ralph Lauren, and the luxe of Yves Saint Laurent and Chanel. For men, there are clothes by Donna Karan, Calvin Klein, and Armani. The sixth-floor **Main Course** is a cornucopia of kitchenware and gadgets. If it's all too much for you, special shopping services are extensive. ♦ Daily. 1000 Third Ave (between E 59th and E 60th Sts). 705.2000. Also at 504 Broadway (between Broome and Spring Sts). 729.5900

Within Bloomingdale's:

Le Train Bleu

★$$ A re-creation of the dining car on the long-defunct Calais-Méditerranée Express (*Le Train Bleu*), this welcome resting ground for worn-out shoppers has a spectacular view of the Queensboro Bridge and the Roosevelt Island Tramway. Not surprisingly, the food—such as steak au poivre, gemelli pasta with julienned fresh vegetables, and grilled chicken over Caesar salad—is simple and simply overpriced. ♦ Continental ♦ M-Sa, lunch; Su, brunch. Reservations recommended. Sixth floor. 705.2100

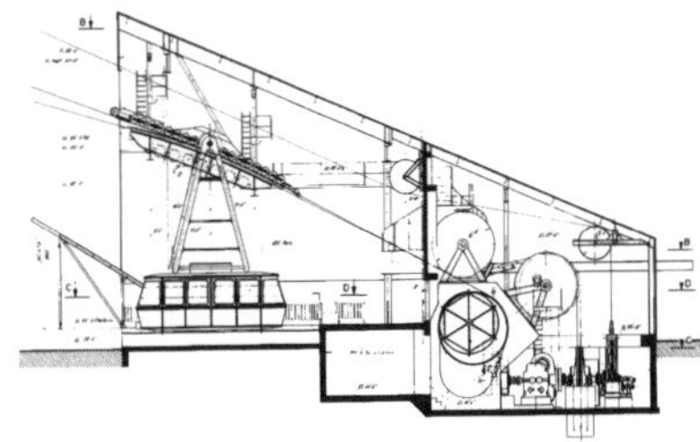

157 Roosevelt Island Tramway Station

This Swiss-made tram (see diagram), designed in 1976 by **Prentice and Chan, Ohlhausen**, would be more at home on a snow-covered mountain. It takes you across the East River's West Channel at 16mph and provides wonderful views of the East Side and the **Queensboro** (59th St) **Bridge** all for the price of one MetroCard ride. ♦ Nominal charge. Second Ave and E 60th St. 832.4543 ♿

158 Queensboro Bridge

Designed by engineer **Gustav Lindenthal** and built in 1909 by **Palmer & Hornbostel**, the distinctive triple span of this bridge is the image of a machine, an intricate web of steel that speaks of power, if not finesse. It is referred to by most locals, including Simon and Garfunkel, as the "59th St. Bridge." You may walk or bike across it on a decent-sized path. ♦ Between Queens Plaza (Queens) and Second Ave

159 The Conran Shop

This large home furnishings emporium has something of a high-end Ikea feel to it, crossed with MoMA Design store. Still, it comes as a refreshing alternative to places like **Crate and Barrel** and **Pottery Barn**. The ground floor of this sunlit glass cube has furniture, glassware, and an eclectic assortment of neatly arranged fun but can-do-without doodads, such as $16 airplane-shaped luggage tags and stylized plastic watches. The surprisingly poorly lit below-grade level is home to a comprehensive mélange of housewares, bed and bath furnishings, funky sofas, and a range of office accoutrements. The pleasantest browsing is to be had during the week. ♦ Daily. 407 E 59th St alongside the Queensboro Bridge, (between York and First Aves). 755.9079

159 Guastavino's

What's under the Queensboro Bridge? The East River, yes, but that's not all. The vast space beneath the roadbed on the Manhattan side is a designated city landmark, with soaring vaults—nearly 40 feet at their highest—illuminated by lofty windows. Once a marketplace, then a restaurant, now a private event space, it's named for the gleaming white tile that lines the vaults—a system of interlocking terra-cotta tiles following the curve of the roof, patented in 1885 by **Rafael Guastavino**, whose work graces sites from Carnegie Hall to the subway. ♦ 409 East 59th St (between York and First Aves). 980.2711 ♿

UPPER EAST SIDE

The upscale and largely residential Upper East Side, which is bounded by the **Eas** **River** and **Fifth Avenue**, and **East 86th** and **East 110th Streets**, has a heavy con centration of town houses, deluxe apartment buildings, elite hotels, and elegant man sions, interspersed with churches, museums, restaurants, gourmet take-out stores, an its fair share of tenements and neglect. Most of the great mansions of **Park** and **Fift** Avenues and the cross streets between them, the first constructions in this part of Nev York, were built between 1900 and 1920, when the classical tradition was in flower they all exhibit neo-Georgian, neo-Federal, neo-French, or neo–Italian Renaissanc styling. The original owners, families such as the Whitneys, the Astors, the Straight the Dillons, the Dukes, the Mellons, the Pulitzers, and the Harknesses, all moved her from downtown.

Construction of apartment houses and hotels began in 1881 and stalled in 1932. Almost all the churches were erected between 1890 and 1920 (the 1897 **Church of the Holy Trinity** on East 88th Street, near Second Avenue, is a fine example). Although there are still isolated blocks of row houses that date from the late 1860s to 1880s, as well as a few colonial relics and some contemporary buildings, the look, especially in the western part of the district, is generally more uniform than elsewhere in the city. The reason for the relatively late start in populating this area is that, except for the German village of **Yorkville** nestled along its eastern border, this was all open country. When work began on **Central Park** in 1857, the neighborhood consisted mainly of farms and squatters' shanties, and pigs grubbed on Fifth Avenue. Even after the park opened in 1863, steam trains chugging along Park Avenue made this an undesirable residential neighborhood. But in 1907, when the **New York Central Railroad** electrified the trains and covered the Park Avenue tracks, the Upper East Side became an attractive place for the well-to-do to live.

Museum Mile really defines this stretch of **Fifth Avenue** today. With the **Metropolitan Museum of Art** (at East 82nd Street) anchoring it on the south, and the forthcoming **Museum of African Art** capping it on the north (at East 110th Street), and at least six more majors in-between—the **Guggenheim** and the **Museum of the City of New York (MCNY)** among them—the area is a cultural force bar none. MCNY, at East 103rd Street, and **El Museo del Barrio**, one block north, together face the exquisite **Conservatory Garden** in Central Park. The **Neue Galerie, Cooper-Hewitt Design Museum**, and **Jewish Museum** are all housed in former mansions.

Madison Avenue above East 86th Street continues to serve the wealthy, but more in the realm of restaurants and smaller specialty shops than with the galleries and couture that mark its East Side extent. A pocket neighborhood around Madison in the East Nineties called **Carnegie Hill** has become an increasingly attractive magnet for young couples choosing to raise families in Manhattan. Park Avenue, with its landscaped center island (covered with thousands of tulips in the springtime and a forest of evergreen trees in the winter months) and legions of dignified apartment houses and old mansions (most of which are now occupied by foreign cultural missions or clubs), is still an address to conjure with.

Shops, restaurants, and singles bars line **Lexington, Third, Second,** and **First Avenues**, and, as you go farther north, more high-rise "people boxes" border these thoroughfares. The side streets are a mix of tenements—some gentrified, some not—and modest town houses. Yorkville, which extends from the East River to Lexington Avenue, from East 77th to East 96th Streets, continued to receive immigrants from Germany, and many from Hungary, over the first half of the 20th century. At one time, East 86th Street was filled with ethnic restaurants, beer gardens, and grocery, pastry, and dry goods stores. Now there are inexpensive chain stores and fried chicken and pizza parlors, and while the occasional new café or bake shop pops up, only a few of the old spots remain. It's always worth the venture east to the River, though—**Carl Schurz Park** is lovely, and amid it all sits Gracie Mansion, the official mayoral residence since the 1942 term of Fiorello LaGuardia, though more frequently than not these days, the city's mayors choose not to call it home.

1 Museum for African Art

This vibrant museum, one of a handful in the country specializing in sub-Saharan art, is sponsoring exhibits around the city while its new Manhattan home, by **Robert A.M. Stern**, is readied to open in 2009 at the top of Museum Mile. The museum's gift store remains in its Queens location for now; check the web site for updates. ♦ 1280 Fifth Ave (at E 110th St). Queens: 36-01 43rd Ave (between 36th and 37th Sts). 718/784.7700. www.africanart.org ♿

2 El Museo del Barrio

Located in the gracious neoclassical **Heckscher Building** at the north end of Museum Mile, El Museo is New York's only museum dedicated to Latino art. It was founded in 1969 as a community project in an East Harlem classroom and moved here in 1977. The 2007-2008 renovation (by **Gruzen Samton**) of their current space—including the courtyard and the addition of a café—gives it a facility to match its exhibitions. Mounting significant shows of Puerto Rican, Caribbean, and Latin American art—historic and contemporary—El Museo's impact today is global. From Kahlo and Rivera to ancient Taíno artifacts, video, painting, sculpture, photography, theater, and film are all represented. Permanent collections include pre-Columbian art and hand-carved wooden saints, one of the culture's most important art forms. The small but lovely gift shop features the work of Latino and Caribbean artisans. ♦ Suggested admission. W-Su, 11AM-5PM. 1230 Fifth Ave (between E 104th and E 105th Sts). 831.7272. www.elmuseo.org ♿

By the 1800s, Yorkville had become a haven for middle-class Germans, although the majority of Manhattan's Germans still lived on the Lower East Side in an area around Tompkins Square Park called "Kleindeutschland." By the turn of the century, many German families were leaving the southern part of the island to resettle in Yorkville in order to avoid the waves of immigrants from Eastern Europe and Italy. The single greatest event that originally brought New York Germans to Yorkville was the *General Slocum* disaster of 1904. This excursion steamer was filled with passengers, mostly women and children from Kleindeutschland. It burned and sank in the East River, killing more than a thousand people. The men of these families, who had not been on board because they could not get away from work that day, found their empty homes unbearable. They moved to Yorkville to help themselves forget.

3 The Museum of the City of New York (MCNY)

The story of New York City is told through contemporary and 20th-century themes, such as the history of the Broadway musica and in historical paintings, Currier & Ives prints, period rooms, costumes, Duncan Phyfe furniture, Tiffany silver, ship models, and wonderful toys and dolls, all handsome displayed in a roomy neo-Georgian building The structure, redbrick with white trim, designed by **Joseph Freedlander** in 1932, was built for the museum after it moved fro **Gracie Mansion**. Puppet shows are staged for children, concerts and lectures for adult ♦ Suggested admission; free Su, 10AM-noon. Tu-Su, 10AM-5PM, plus holiday Mondays. 1220 Fifth Ave (between E 103rd and E 104th Sts). 534.1672. www.mcny.org ♿

4 The New York Academy of Medicine

Built in 1926 by **York & Sawyer**, this charming combination of Byzantine and Romanesque architecture contains one of the most important medical libraries in the country. Its Historical Collections, housed in the exquisitely appointed **Malloch Rare Book Room**, contain over 50,000 items, from rare manuscripts (such as the Edwin Smith Papyrus, a 1700 BC Egyptian document on surgery of that era) to a circa 1829 Pepys Amputation kit to a first edition of Freud's work on dreams. The collection also includes 4,000 cookbooks, a gift of Dr. Margaret Barclay Wilson, who believed that good nutrition was the key to good health. ♦ Exhibits and Main Reading Room: M, Tu, Th, F, 9AM-5PM; W, 9AM-7PM. Malloch Rare Book Room: by appointment only. 1216 Fift Ave (at E 103rd St). 822.7300. www.nyam.org

5 Mount Sinai Hospital

The medical complex comprises three hospital towers in one grand pavilion. These facilities replace 10 older buildings—some dating as far back as 1904—all of which have been demolished. Also of architectural interest is the **Annenberg Building**, a 436-foot Cor-Ten steel box that gets its color fron a coating of rust that protects the steel from further corrosion. ♦ Bounded by Madison and Fifth Aves, and E 98th and E 101st Sts. 241.6500 ♿

6 Russian Orthodox Cathedral of St. Nicholas

Built in 1901-1902, this church is unusual in New York because, set above the polychromatic Victorian body, there are seven gilded

The Best

Fred Ferretti

Food writer and former columnist, *Gourmet* magazine

The cooking, on any day, in the very best of the city's French restaurants—such as at **Montrachet**.

There is nothing better than a hot dog, boiled on a street cart, served with a lot of mustard and a bit of sauerkraut, and eaten while sitting with General Sherman at the entrance to **Central Park**. Breakfast, lunch, or dinner, provided they have slabs of that rough country pâté, at **Café des Artistes**, just outside Central Park's western border.

The upper right-field stands of **Yankee Stadium** on a hot Sunday afternoon with a cold beer.

The best steak in the city at **Sparks** steak house, with a selection from what may well be New York's best list of American wines.

onion domes. You might say its history is unusual as well: originally funded by Czar Nicholas II, in the 1920s it became a political pawn between Bolshevik sympathizers and stalwart anti-communist factions. It was granted NYC Landmark status in 1973. ♦ 15 E 97th St (between Madison and Fifth Aves). 289.1915

7 Islamic Cultural Center of New York

A computer was used to ensure that this mosque precisely faces Mecca, as Islamic law requires. Its doors are open as the spiritual home to the 800,000 Muslims (as of 2007) living throughout the five boroughs. Built in 1991 by **Skidmore**, **Owings & Merrill**, it was New York's first major mosque. ♦ 1711 Third Ave (at E 96th St). 722.5234

8 Squadron A and Eighth Regiment Armory/Hunter High School

When the armory—a distinctly businesslike fortress built in 1895 by **John Rochestaer Thomas**—was on the verge of being torn down, community protest saved at least the façade on Madison Avenue. The school's architects, **Morris Ketchum Jr. & Associates**, marvelously incorporated it into their 1971 design, using it as both a backdrop to the playground and as a formal inspiration for the new building. ♦ Madison Ave (between E 94th and E 95th Sts)

9 Bistro du Nord

★★$$ This cozy little bistro with Parisian atmosphere serves haute versions of dishes you'd expect to find in this kind of place: smoked salmon, and baby rack of lamb with ratatouille. Steak frites and roasted codfish highlight the fare. ♦ French ♦ Daily, lunch and dinner; Sa, Su, brunch. Reservations recommended. 1312 Madison Ave (at E 93rd St). 289.0997

9 Pascalou

★★$$ Squeezed into a tiny two-level space (with a few sidewalk tables), this bistro serves a menu ranging from duck confit to Malaysian curry shrimp. ♦ French bistro ♦ M-F, lunch and dinner; Sa, Su, brunch and dinner. 1308 Madison Ave (between E 92nd and E 93rd Sts). 534.7522 ♿

10 The Corner Bookstore

Featuring a wide selection of books, over a third of them for children, this small but eminently friendly and helpful shop has an atmosphere conducive to browsing. Works on literature, art, and architecture are well represented. One of the last urban independents, Corner has a welcome roster of regular readings that often highlights debut works of notable fiction and nonfiction. ♦ Daily. 1313 Madison Ave (at E 93rd St). 831.3554 ♿

10 Island

★$$$ You might expect to find this sort of place on the West Side—a room full of young people wolfing down good, if slightly overpriced, pasta and dishes from the grill, including chicken paillard and pepper-roasted tuna. ♦ Continental ♦ M-F, lunch and dinner; Sa, Su, brunch and dinner. Reservations recommended. 1305 Madison Ave (between E 92nd and E 93rd Sts). 996.1200 ♿

11 Wales Hotel

$$$ This small European-style hotel is most welcoming, and ideally located if you plan to spend a lot of time on Museum Mile, shopping on Madison, or exploring jogging every morning in Central Park. All of the 86 suites and another 44 rooms were tastefully renovated for the millennium (which also happened to be their 100th anniversary), but ask for a large, bright room (preferably with views over the park) or you may end up with the opposite. The

good-size high-ceilinged rooms feature solid woods and classical décor (some with fireplaces), flat-panel TVs, and high-speed Internet access; complimentary continental breakfast is offered in their grand Victorian-era Pied Piper Room. A roof terrace, 24-hour cardio fitness center, and small business center are on-site; room service is from **Sarabeth's** (see below). ♦ 1295 Madison Ave (between E 92nd and E 93rd Sts). 876.6000, 800/428.5252; fax 860.7000. www.waleshotel.com

11 Sarabeth's

★★$$ Many a New Yorker has stood in line here for a weekend brunch of gourmet comfort foods: homemade waffles and pancakes crowned with fresh fruit; hot porridge; and warm-from-the-oven muffins (no reservations accepted for brunch). On your way out, pick up homemade brownies and cookies for a treat later. ♦ American ♦ M-F, breakfast, lunch, and dinner; Sa, Su, brunch and dinner. Reservations recommended for dinner. 1295 Madison Ave (between E 92nd and E 93rd Sts). 410.7335. Also at numerous locations throughout the city

12 56 East 93rd Street

This former home of showman Billy Rose was the last of the large, great mansions to be built in New York. Built for the William Goadby Loew family in 1932, the lovely limestone structure is in the delicate style of the 18th-century Scottish brothers Lambert and Nicholas Adam, who created some of the best houses in Edinburgh and London. This one, however, was designed by **Walker & Gillette**. The **Smithers Alcoholism and Treatment Center** (one of the first for the rich and famous) was its occupant from 1973 to 1995; the **Spence School** bought it in 1999 and recently moved in after a thorough restoration. ♦ 56 E 93rd St (between Park and Madison Aves).

12 60 East 93rd Street

After Mrs. William K. Vanderbilt divorced her husband, she leased an apartment on Park Avenue, only to discover that her ex-husband had one in the same building. She broke the lease and had **John Russell Pope** build this beautiful French Renaissance mansion in 1930. Occupied for a period in the late 20th century by the Lycée Française until 2002, it is once again in private hands. ♦ Between Park and Madison Aves

13 Russian Orthodox Church Outside Russia

Built in 1917 for Francis F. Palmer and renovated in 1928 by **Delano & Aldrich** for banker George F. Baker, this unusually large Georgian mansion has remained virtually unchanged, except for the introduction of exquisite Russian icons. A small cathedral occupies the former ballroom. ♦ 75 E 93rd St (at Park Ave). 534.1601

14 1185 Park Avenue

Designed in 1929 by **Schwartz & Gross**, this is the only East Side version of the full-block courtyard apartment house typified by the **Belnord**, **Astor Court**, and **Apthorp** across town. The Gothicized entrance adds needed levity to the otherwise traditional composition. ♦ Between E 93rd and E 94th Sts

15 Kitchen Arts & Letters

Books on low-fat cooking, regional American cooking, cooking with flowers, and cooking on boats, along with more traditional cookbooks—approximately 11,000 in all, new, rare, and out-of-print, and covering every aspect of food and wine—are displayed here. The staff is deeply informed and ready to help. Paintings and photographs of food, and reproductions of tin biscuit boxes and other culinary memorabilia, are on sale as well. ♦ M-Sa; summer hours are irregular, call first. 1435 Lexington Ave (between E 93rd and E 94th Sts). 876.5550. www.kitchenartsandletters.com

16 Corner Café & Bakery

★$$ Breakfast basics, salads, sandwiches, and comfort-food entrées are on offer in this bright space, formerly nabe favorite Yura. Order at the counter, then seat yourself or take out. ♦ American ♦ Daily, breakfast, lunch, and dinner. 1659 Third Ave (at E 93rd St). 860.8060. ♿

17 The Jewish Museum

This museum (illustrated on page 257) holds the country's largest collection of Judaica and mounts world-class shows of historic and contemporary art, from a major Modigliani retrospective in 2004 and one for Louise Nevelson in 2007 to provocative interpretations of the Holocaust experience. Besides permanent and rotating exhibits, it has classrooms, a delightful kosher café (**Café Weissman**, 423.3307; designed by architect **Kevin Roche**, it features specially commissioned stained-glass windows by artist Susan Stinsmuehlen-Amend), an attractive book and gift shop (**The Cooper Shop**), and, next door, a very modern design shop, **Celebrations**. Designed by **C.P.H. Gilbert** in 1908, the French Renaissance mansion was the home of financier Felix M. Warburg. Two annexes have been added: the first, in 1963, is by **Samuel Glazer**, and the second, finished in 1993, is by **Kevin Roche, John Dinkeloo & Associates**.

♦ Admission; free Saturday. Closed Friday. 11AM-5:45PM; Th, 11AM-8PM. 1109 Fifth Ave (at E 92nd St). 423.3230. Celebrations Design Shop: 1 E 92nd St (between Fifth and Madison Aves). 423.3260. www.jewishmuseum.org

18 1107 Fifth Avenue

Built in 1925 by **Rouse & Goldstone**, this was a perfectly ordinary apartment building except for a few anomalies on the façade—evidence of an era past. Marjorie Merriwether Post (at the time married to stockbroker E.F. Hutton) purchased a 54-room apartment here. The Palladian window near the top center of the façade opened onto the main foyer of this apartment. ♦ At E 92nd St

19 Night Presence IV

The intentionally rusty steel sculpture is by the late Louise Nevelson. The view down the avenue from here is picture-perfect. ♦ Park Ave and E 92nd St

20 120 and 122 East 92nd Street

Because fire laws made the construction of wooden houses illegal in the 1860s, there are very few of them in Manhattan. This pair (and the frame houses at **160 East 92nd Street** and **128 East 93rd Street**), built in 1850, are a reminder of what this neighborhood was like in the mid-19th century. ♦ Between Lexington and Park Aves

21 Sfoglia

★★★$$$ This cozy room with mismatched tables and dish-towel napkins books up weeks in advance. The bread is worth the wait, as are house specialties (try chicken cooked under a brick) and outstanding pastas. ♦ Italian ♦ M-Sa, lunch and dinner. Reservations required. 1402 Lexington Ave (at E 92nd St). 831.1402. www.sfogliarestaurant.com ♿

22 92nd Street Y

Founded in 1874 as a branch of the Young Men's Hebrew Association, the 92nd Street Y is now one of the city's cultural landmarks. Its **Tisch Center for the Arts** presents classical, cabaret, jazz, and world music, and **Kaufman Concert Hall** has become one of New York's best places to hear chamber music and recitals. The Y's **Jazz in July** program is an annual favorite; the Tokyo String Quartet is a regular here. The renowned **Unterberg Poetry Center** has

The Jewish Museum

offered readings by every major poet in the world since its founding in 1939. The **Harkness Dance Center** is sponsored by the organization, as are lectures featuring luminaries from the worlds of politics, literature, and more, plus seminars and workshops, and even unusual tours of the city. The **Makor** center—scheduled to be in its new home in TriBeCa in 2008—focuses on a 20-to-30-year-old crowd, with a nightclub, café, and movies (see page 67). ♦ 1395 Lexington Ave (at E 92nd St). 415.5562. www.92Y.org. ♿

23 The Convent of the Sacred Heart

Originally built in 1918 by **C.P.H. Gilbert** and **J. Armstrong Stenhouse**, this extravagant Italian palazzo was one of the largest private houses built in New York City, and the last on "Millionaire's Row." It was the home of Otto Kahn, a banker, philanthropist, and art patron. Now it's a private school for girls. ♦ 1 E 91st St (at Fifth Ave). 722.4745

23 Mrs. James A. Burden House

When Vanderbilt heiress Adele Sloane married James A. Burden, heir to a steel fortune, they moved into this freestanding mansion, which was built in 1902 by **Warren & Wetmore**. The spiral staircase under a stained-glass skylight is one of the city's grandest, and was called the "stairway to heaven." Not surprisingly, it is a favorite rental location for wedding receptions. ♦ 7 E 91st St (between Madison and Fifth Aves)

23 Mrs. John Henry Hammond House

When Hammond saw the plans for this house, designed in 1906 by **Carrère & Hastings**, he said that this gift from his wife's family made him feel "like a kept man." He moved in anyway, along with a staff of 16 full-time servants. The couple's musicales were legendary. Among the many noteworthy folk who visited, Benny Goodman came here frequently in the 1930s to play Mozart's clarinet works. ♦ 9 E 91st St (between Madison and Fifth Aves)

Jacob Walton, the owner of the Gracie Mansion area in 1770, was loyal to the King of England. When the Revolution began, he built a tunnel leading to the East River so he could escape to a waiting ship if necessary. The tunnel wasn't discovered until 1913.

The first recorded owner of the property on which Gracie Mansion stands was a Dutch farmer named Sybout Claessen, who acquired 106 acres and named it "Horn's Hook." In 1799, a subsequent owner, Archibald Gracie, built a handsome frame house on the property that he had acquired for $5,625.

24 Cooper-Hewitt National Design Museum

Historic and contemporary design are the focus of this branch of the Smithsonian. Its home, this splendidly decorated mansion designed in 1903 by **Babb, Cook & Willard**, was built on the northern fringe of the well-heeled stretch of Fifth Avenue mansions for industrialist Andrew Carnegie, who requested "the most modest, plainest, and most roomy house in New York City." The rather standard Renaissance-Georgian mix of redbrick and limestone trim on a rusticated base is most noteworthy for the fact that it is freestanding in an expansive garden. The richly ornamented rooms of the sumptuous mansion, which was renovated in 1977 by **Hardy Holzman Pfeiffer Associates**, sometimes compete with the exhibitions; the conservatory is particularly pleasant. Also notice the very low door to what was once the library at the west end—Carnegie was a short man, and this was his private room.

The permanent collection—built on the original early-20th-century collections of the Cooper and Hewitt families—encompasses textiles dating back 3,000 years, jewelry, 21st-century furniture, wallpaper, and metal-, glass-, and earthenware. It also includes the single largest group of architectural drawings in this country. The state-of-the-art **Design Resource Center** opened in 1998; it is a design student's—and a design professional's—reference paradise of picture collections, auction catalogs, 17th- and 18th-century architecture books, 20th-century product design, and more. Lectures, symposia, concerts (in the garden), and other events are held. A gift shop in the **Louis XV Music Room** sells design objects, catalogs, postcards, and museum publications. Café: May-Sept. ♦ Admission. M-Th, 10AM-5PM; F, 10AM-9PM; Sa, 10AM-6PM; Su, 12PM-6PM. 2 E 91st St (at Fifth Ave). 849.8400. www.cooperhewitt.org ♿

25 Eli's Vinegar Factory

Eli Zabar, of **E.A.T.** (and, yes, *that* Zabar family), turned an old mustard-and-vinegar factory into this grocery-store-and-more (good for produce, house-made delicacies, and Eli's bread). Weekend brunch is served until 4:30PM on the balcony above the selling floor; a café at ground level serves light fare. ♦ Daily. 431 E 91st St (between York and First Aves). 987.0885

26 Asphalt Green Sports & Fitness

Housed in part in what was once the **Municipal Asphalt Plant** (the immense concrete-coated parabola-shaped 1944 building was first converted to a general sports and arts center in 1982), this now 5 1/2-acre nonprofit sports and fitness complex houses the city's only Olympic-standard swimming pool; named the George Delacorte, it's a 50-meter beauty. Also on-site are a smaller exercise pool, steam and sauna rooms, basketball courts, a fully equipped gym, and indoor and outdoor running tracks. Since the Delacorte pool is sometimes used by local teams, it's best to call in advance for swim periods. ♦ Fee. Daily. 555 E 90th St (between East End and York Aves). AquaCenter entrance: 1750 York Ave (at E 90th St). 369.8890

27 National Academy Museum and School

Since its founding in 1825 by Samuel F.B. Morse, painter and inventor of the telegraph, this academy has been an artist-run museum, a fine-arts school, and an honorary organization of artists. Headquartered in a town house that was remodeled in 1915 by **Ogden Codman Jr.**, and located around the corner from its **School of Fine Arts**, it is the second-oldest museum school in the country. In addition to an annual exhibition (alternately open to member artists and all artists), the academy presents shows of mostly American artists, such as the Hudson River school, or landscapes by Frederic Edwin Church. Painters, sculptors, watercolorists, graphic artists, and architects number among its members today. ♦ Admission. Closed M, Tu. W, Th, noon-5PM; F-Su, 11AM-6PM. Gift shop: Tu-Su, noon-8PM. 1083 Fifth Ave (at E 89th St). 369.4880. School: 5 E 89th St. 996.1908. www.nationalacademy.org ♿

28 Guggenheim Museum

When Solomon R. Guggenheim wanted a museum that would "foster an appreciation of art by acquainting museum visitors with significant painting and sculpture of our time," he founded this repository, which has remained a testament to his personal taste. Guggenheim collected old masters at first, but in the 1920s he began acquiring the avant-garde work of painters such as Delaunay, Kandinsky, and Léger. Soon his apartment at The Plaza was bursting at the seams (the old masters were relegated to his wife's bedroom), and he began to look for other quarters for his burgeoning collection. During two sojourns in rented space, his new museum began to buy more of everything by both established and new talent. Finally, the need for a permanent home was realized in a building designed in 1959 by **Frank Lloyd Wright**. The museum is one of the architect's fantasies, first dreamed of in the mid-1940s. It is an extraordinary structure: A massive concrete spiral sits atop one end of a low horizontal base, expanding as it ascends, dominating not only its plinth and a counterweight block of offices at the other end, but the site itself and the blocks around it.

The display of art was clearly not Wright's main concern, however. The essence of architecture for the sake of architecture, the Guggenheim seems to evoke an opinion from most people who visit–some positive, many negative. To make matters worse, the first addition, built in 1968 by **Taliesin Associates**, was not up to snuff. That firm, Wright's successors and keepers-of-the-flame, never had the touch of the Master, who had personally handled all the details of the construction of the original building, right down to the Fifth Avenue sidewalk.

Construction of a second addition, by **Gwathmey Siegel & Associates**, was completed in 1992. Although it doubled the museum's gallery space and attendance increased, controversy continues over its questionable aesthetics. The refurbished exterior, which is nearing completion in 2008, is a happier matter.

The Wright-designed **Museum Café**, open daily for breakfast, lunch, and light dinner, makes for an excellent respite from museum trekking. ♦ Admission: pay-what-you-wish Friday, 5:45PM-7:45PM. Closed Thursday. Sa-W, 10AM-5:45PM; F, 10AM-7:45PM. 1071 Fifth Ave (between E 88th and E 89th Sts). Museum: 423.3500. Shop: 423.3615. Café: 427.5682. www.guggenheim.org

29 Elaine's

★$$$ Those whose idea of a good time is watching celebrities eat steamed mussels should be in heaven here. It's a kind of club for media celebrities, gossips, and literary types, but they don't necessarily come here for the food (although the spaghetti bolognese and grilled veal chops are decent). ♦ Italian ♦ Daily, dinner and late-night meals. Reservations required. 1703 Second Ave (between E 88th and E 89th Sts). 534.8103

Studio Shoo-Ins: How to Get TV Tickets

New York is headquarters for a variety of major TV shows and talk shows that the public—usually limited to those 18 years or older—can attend without charge. Although most tickets must be obtained in advance (four tickets per order is the common max), many programs offer standby seats. Lines for standby seats often form hours in advance, particularly when well-known guests are booked. You may find last-minute (fee-based) help at www.nytix.com

The Colbert Report (Comedy Central)

Advance tickets for Stephen Colbert's Monday-through-Thursday late-night show may be ordered online only, at **Comedy Central** (www.comedycentral.com). A limited batch of standby tickets are handed out in front of the studio at 513 W 54th St (between 10th and 11th Aves) at 4PM on show days.

The Daily Show with Jon Stewart (Comedy Central)

Tickets for *The Daily Show* (taped on Monday through Thursday) are available online only, on the **Comedy Central** web site (www.comedycentral.com). Occasional cancellations free up dates, so it's worth checking back if your preferred date was not available.

586.2477. Image Group Studios, 733 11th Ave, between 51st and 52nd Sts

Emeril Live

Emeril's an extremely tough ticket, granted only by lottery a few times a year. Interested viewers must subscribe online to the Food Network's newsletter to receive notification prior to the next lottery entry period. Food Network Studios, 75 Ninth Ave (at W 16th St). www.foodnetwork.com

Late Night with Conan O'Brien (NBC)

Use NBC's **Ticket Info Line** (664.3056) to reserve ahead—by at least two months—for Conan. The show is taped Tuesday through Friday at 5:30PM. A limited number of standby tickets (one per person) are distributed at 9AM on taping days at the NBC Studio's 49th Street entrance at 30 Rockefeller Plaza; entry isn't guaranteed, so get there earlier to have a shot at getting a seat. www.nbc.com

The Late Show with David Letterman (CBS)

The Late Show, usually taped Monday through Thursday is one of the hottest tickets in town. Advance tickets (two max) may be requested online—plan at least three

30 Church of the Holy Trinity

Built in 1897 by **Barney & Chapman**, this picturesque gold, brown, and red Victorian church modestly slipped into this side street encloses a charming garden. The sleek tower with its fanciful Gothic crown is rather nice, too. ♦ 316 E 88th St (between First and Second Aves). 289.4100

31 Gracie Mansion

The site was known to the Dutch as "Hoek Van Hoorn"; when the British captured it during the Revolutionary War, the shelling destroyed the farmhouse that was there. The kernel of the present house was built in 1799 by Scottish-born merchant Archibald Gracie as a country retreat. Acquired by the city in 1887, it served, among its many uses, as the first home of the **Museum of the City of New York**, a refreshment stand, and a storehouse. In 1942, at the urging of Parks Commissioner Robert Moses, Fiorello La-Guardia accepted it as the mayor's official residence. The 98 men who preceded him in the office had lived in their own homes. The 21st century has brought some new stay-at-homes (or away's . . .) like Rudolph Giuliani for the latter part of his time in office, and Mayor Michael Bloomberg. In 1966, an addition to the house was designed by **Mott B. Schmidt**. The Gracie Mansion Conservancy has restored the mansion to something better than its former glory, and conducts tours and special programs there. ♦ Fee. Tours by appointment only W, 10AM, 11AM, 1PM, 2PM. East End Ave (near the north end of Carl Schurz Park, at E 88th St). 570.4751, 570.4773. www.nyc.gov ♿

32 The Franklin Hotel

$$ Built in 1931, this 49-room hotel offers rooms that are small (even tiny, and that's by New York's already shrunken standards) but nicely decorated. Ask for a remodeled one. All have good beds and flat-screen TVs; the service is good, and the buffet breakfast is complimentary. East Side residents often book rooms for their guests here. Note the

o four months ahead. (You can also fill out a request orm at the theater.) You can also call the *Late Show*'s **Standby Line** (247.6497) around 11AM on show days. f you get a recording, the tickets are gone for that day. Ed Sullivan Theater, 1697 Broadway, between W 53rd and W 54th Sts. www.lateshowaudience.com

Live with Regis and Kelly (ABC)

This talk show broadcats Monday through Friday at 9AM. Advance mail-in requests are selected randomly; be prepared to wait—up to a year. You may request up to four tickets per postcard (mail to: Live Tickets, Ansonia Station, PO Box 230777, New York, NY 10023). Standby tickets are available after ticket-holders are seated each weekday; the line usually starts forming around 7AM at the studio, 7 Lincoln Square (West 67th Street and Columbus Avenue). www.bventertainment.go.com

The Martha Stewart Show (NBC)

Tickets to Martha's show may be requested online only, and only for the weeks posted on their site (there is usually a group of three consecutive weeks available, about 2 to 3 months in advance). The show tapes on 3 days per week, selected randomly, though you may state a preferred date when you apply. Chelsea Television Studios, 221 W 26th St (between Seventh and Eighth Aves). www.marthastewart.com

Saturday Night Live (NBC)

A ticket lottery is held but once each year, at the end of August; only e-mails (snltickets@nbcuni.com; two tickets each) sent in August will be added to the pool. Winners' seats will be for a randomly picked show date and time, and may be to either a dress rehearsal or a live taping. (Since the majority of each audience fills up with network associates, advertisers, and their families and friends, few seats make it to the lottery.) On Saturday mornings, single standby tickets for each seating are distributed at 7AM at NBC at the 49th Street entrance of 30 Rockefeller Plaza. Fans have been known to camp out overnight, although actually holding a ticket still does not guarantee admission. www.nbc.com

The View (ABC)

This show tapes Monday through Friday at 11AM at ABC studios (all but Friday's show are shown live). Apply online at least 12 weeks ahead for a specific date (your application will be canceled if you submit more than one date); the wait can be as much as one year. Arrive at *The View*'s audience entrance at 320 West 66th Street (at West End Avenue) between 8:30 and 10AM on the day of the show if you want a chance at a last-minute ticket. www.abc.go.com

swell period neon at the entrance. ♦ 164 E 87th St (between Third and Lexington Aves). 369.1000, 800/607.4009; fax 369.8000. www.franklinhotel.com

33 Henderson Place Historic District

These 24 remaining Queen Anne houses were commissioned by John C. Henderson, a fur importer and hat manufacturer, and designed by **Lamb & Rich** in 1882 as a self-contained community with river views. Symmetrical compositions tie the numerous pieces together below an enthusiastic profusion of turrets, parapets, and dormers. There are rumors that some of these houses are haunted. The ghosts may be looking for the eight houses from the group (originally 32) that were demolished to make room for an imposing apartment complex. ♦ Between East End and York Aves. 549-553 E 86th St, 552-558 E 87th St; 140-154 East End Ave; 6-16 Henderson Pl (at E 86th St)

CENTRAL PARK

"This different and many smiling presence" is how Henry James once referred to Central Park, bounded by **Fifth Avenue**, **Central Park West**, **Central Park South** and **Central Park North**. The completely man-made park, unlike any other urban park in the United States, certainly elicits smiles from the more than 14 million people who wander through it every year. It is an equally pleasing place to sky-borne creatures: nearly 250 species of birds are sighted here, with the best birding at **The Ramble**.

Not long after work began to clear the site on 12 August 1857, a friend suggested to journalist **Frederick Law Olmsted**, whose avocation was landscaping, that he should compete for the job of superintendent of the new Central Park. He found backers in newspaper editors Horace Greeley and William Cullen Bryant, and when writer Washington Irving added his name to the list, Olmsted got the job. Later that same year, the Parks Commission announced a design competition for the new park, and Olmsted's friend, landscape architect **Calvert Vaux**, suggested they join forces.

On 28 April 1858, after Olmsted and Vaux submitted their "Greensward" plan, Olmsted wrote: "Every foot of the Park's surface, every tree and bush, as well as every arch, roadway, and walk, has been placed where it is with a purpose." In the years since, buildings and monuments have been added, and playgrounds and roads have been constructed. But the original purpose is still well served.

The groundswell of support for the park had begun in 1844 when William Cullen Bryant warned that commerce was devouring Manhattan inch by inch. He pointed out that there were still unoccupied parts of the island, but that "while we are discussing the subject, the advancing population of the city is sweeping over them and covering them from our reach." In 1853, the state legislature authorized the city to buy the central site. The price tag was $5 million.

The land was no bargain. A swampy pesthole filled with pig farms and squatters' shacks, it was used as a garbage dump and served as a prime location for bone-boiling plants. But Olmsted succeeded in turning it into what New Yorkers today proudly call the "lungs of the city." Actual work began in 1857, and by the time the park was considered finished 16 years later, nearly five million cubic yards of stone and dirt had been rearranged and almost five million trees planted. Before construction started, 4[illegible] species of trees grew on the site; by the time it was completed, 402 kinds of deciduous trees thrived, along with 230 species of evergreens and 815 varieties of shrubs. There were also 58 miles of pedestrian walks, 6.5 miles of roads, and a bridle path 4.5 miles long. A reservoir was created in 1862, covering 106 acres, and a sprawling lake occupied another 22 acres. A series of smaller lakes and ponds was also created, and some 62 miles of pipe were installed to carry off unwanted water.

Fortunately, Central Park is alive and well in spite of countless schemes to "improve" it. In 1918, someone suggested digging trenches to give people an idea of what the doughboys were going through "over there." A year later, plans were submitted for an onsite airport. There have been proposals for housing projects, and plans for underground parking garages have been coming and going since the 1920s.

Like the rest of the city, Central Park suffered greatly during the fiscal crisis of the 1970s. But with the founding of the nonprofit **Central Park Conservancy** in 1980, restoration and renewal began in full force. By 2003, in time for the park's 150th birthday, the city working jointly with the conservancy could proudly celebrate their

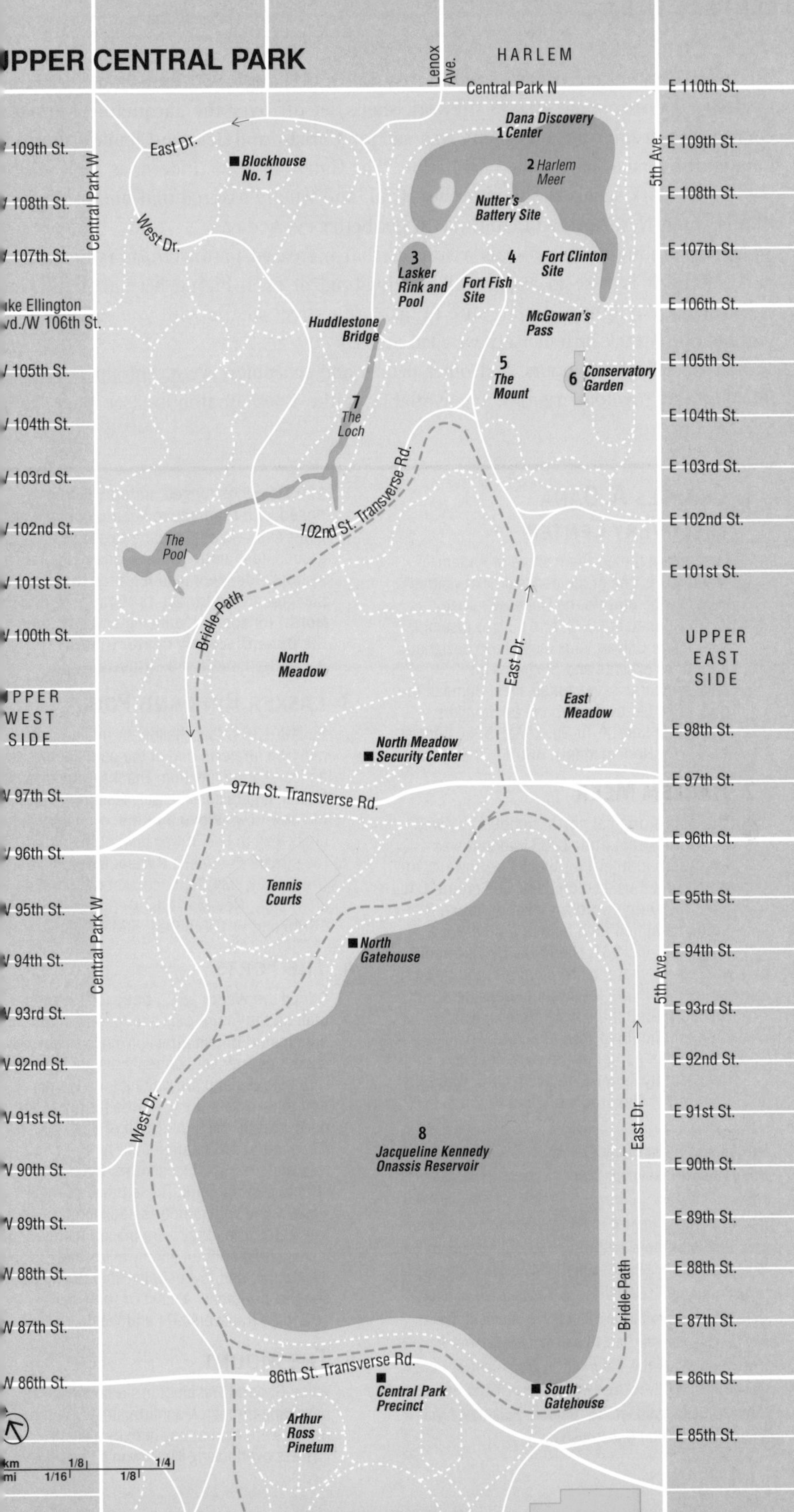
UPPER CENTRAL PARK
HARLEM
Lenox Ave.
Central Park N
E 110th St.
Dana Discovery Center
1
2 Harlem Meer
E 109th St.
5th Ave.
E 108th St.
Nutter's Battery Site
E 107th St.
3 Lasker Rink and Pool
4
Fort Clinton Site
Fort Fish Site
E 106th St.
McGowan's Pass
E 105th St.
5 The Mount
6 Conservatory Garden
E 104th St.
E 103rd St.
E 102nd St.
E 101st St.
UPPER EAST SIDE
East Dr.
East Meadow
E 98th St.
E 97th St.
E 96th St.
E 95th St.
E 94th St.
E 93rd St.
E 92nd St.
E 91st St.
E 90th St.
E 89th St.
E 88th St.
E 87th St.
E 86th St.
E 85th St.
Bridle Path
South Gatehouse
East Dr.
5th Ave.
East Dr.
Blockhouse No. 1
West Dr.
W 109th St.
W 108th St.
W 107th St.
Central Park W
Duke Ellington Blvd./W 106th St.
Huddlestone Bridge
W 105th St.
7 The Loch
W 104th St.
W 103rd St.
102nd St. Transverse Rd.
W 102nd St.
The Pool
W 101st St.
W 100th St.
Bridle Path
North Meadow
UPPER WEST SIDE
North Meadow Security Center
W 97th St.
97th St. Transverse Rd.
W 96th St.
Tennis Courts
W 95th St.
North Gatehouse
W 94th St.
Central Park W
W 93rd St.
W 92nd St.
West Dr.
W 91st St.
8 Jacqueline Kennedy Onassis Reservoir
W 90th St.
W 89th St.
W 88th St.
W 87th St.
W 86th St.
86th St. Transverse Rd.
Central Park Precinct
Arthur Ross Pinetum
km 1/8 1/4
mi 1/16 1/8

progress. Marking the occasion with artist Cai Guo-Qiang's 850-foot-diameter "Light Cycle"—a halo of some 10,000 firework shells set off over **the Jacqueline Kennedy Onassis Reservoir**—the precedent was set for Christo and Jeanne-Claude's glorious (and controversial) park-wide installation "The Gates" in 2005. Indeed, as each season passes, the park seems to get more beautiful, and we are assured that one of the best things about New York will continue to get better every day.

Note: Although city officials assure us that increased patrol efforts maintain the park safety, it is wise to avoid walking, jogging, or even biking here at night; and even during daylight hours, be sure to take your street smarts with you—especially if you head off-track into densely wooded areas.

For special events, hours, and other details and schedules: www.centralparknyc.org. Bicycle (and rowboat) rentals are available at the **Loeb Boathouse** (see page 267). 517.2233.

1 Charles A. Dana Discovery Center

Located on the northern shore of Harlem Meer, this is one of the park's official visitors' centers (the other is the Dairy; see page 270). Opened in 1993, and built to resemble a structure Calvert Vaux might have designed, it features exhibits and programs on environmental issues for all ages. Some of the park tours led by the Urban Park Rangers leave from here. ♦ Tu-Su, 10AM-5PM. Central Park N (at Harlem Meer). 860.1370 ♿

2 Harlem Meer

The park's original northern boundary was at 106th Street until 1863, when it was extended another four blocks northward, at which time this 11-acre lake was created. It uses the Dutch word for lake, although it hardly qualified as a lake or a meer for a long time. In 1941, the Parks Department altered its shoreline to eliminate the natural coves and inlets the original designers had placed there, and the whole lake was rimmed and lined with concrete. Fortunately, this corner of the park, long desperately in need of loving care, was fully restored to Olmsted's original vision in 1993. Now its rugged, natural shoreline—ringed with dramatic rock outcroppings and giant oaks—is again home to swans, grebes, lush native plants, and delighted visitors. The Meer also features two playgrounds, a terrace (at Central Park North) for summer dancing and jazz, and the **Dana Discovery Center** (above). ♦ Central Park N and Fifth Ave

Particularly evident from Central Park are a flurry of twin-towered buildings on Central Park West. Landmark luxury apartment complexes that are a favorite element in New York City's distinctive skyline, they were built from 1929 to 1931 during the peak of the Art Deco period, when zoning laws allowed taller buildings if setbacks and towers were used. That period's prolific architect, the eminent Emery Roth, designed the San Remo at 145 Central Park West as well as the Eldorado at 300 Central Park West and the Oliver Cromwell at West 72nd Street. The Art Deco gem at 55 Central Park West was featured in the film *Ghostbusters*.

3 Lasker Rink and Pool

Built in 1964, this shallow swimming pool near the far north end of the park doubles as an ice-skating rink from Thanksgiving through March. It gets considerably less traffic than the downtown **Wollman Rink**, even though it costs less to use. It was built at the mouth of the stream that feeds **Harlem Meer**. ♦ Pool: (free) daily, July-Sept. Ice-skating: (admission) daily, Nov-Mar. East Dr (between W 106th and W 108th Sts). 534.7639

4 The Forts

During the War of 1812, three forts were built on the future park site to fend off an anticipated British attack. None was actually used, but their now-barren sites are marked with plaques and are waiting for a history buff to re-create them. A little farther to the north stands the stone shell of Blockhouse #1, another fortification built for the 1812 war, and an 1814 blockhouse, the oldest structure in the park. These days, its thick walls, laced with gunports, look into groves of trees. But when they were placed there, men inside could spot an enemy miles away. None ever came, and few people climb the hill to see the site today. ♦ East Dr (between 102nd St Transverse Rd and West Dr)

5 The Mount

When General Washington's army was retreating through Manhattan in 1776, the British were held at bay here by a small fortress overlooking **McGowan's Pass**. The

Mount was named for a tavern on top of the hill, which in 1846 became, of all things, a convent. The sisters moved out when the park was created, and the building was converted back into a tavern. It was one of the city's better restaurants in the late 19th century, but was demolished on orders of Mayor John Purroy Mitchel in 1917. ♦ East Dr (between 102nd St Transverse Rd and West Dr)

6 Conservatory Garden

A park nursery was replaced in 1899 by a glass conservatory, which was removed in 1934 to create this series of three exquisite formal gardens, one of which is planted with seasonal flowers, another with perennials, and a third with grass surrounded by yew hedges and flowering trees and featuring a wisteria-covered pergola. Each is enhanced by a fountain. Near the head of Fifth Avenue's Museum Mile (**El Museo del Barrio** and **The Museum of the City of NY** are directly across the street; see page 254), it's a worthy stop in its own right—as the many folks who wed here can attest. ♦ Free. Daily, 8AM-dusk. Fifth Ave (between 102nd St Transverse Rd and Central Park N; enter from Fifth Ave at 105th St). 860.1382

7 The Loch

This natural pond, undisturbed by the original designers, has been left alone to the point of being silted almost out of existence. A brook leading from the north end forms a small waterfall near the **Huddleston Bridge**, which carries East Drive over it. ♦ Off East Dr (between 102nd St Transverse Rd and West Dr)

8 Jacqueline Kennedy Onassis Reservoir

Designed as part of the **Croton Water System** in 1862, this billion-gallon reservoir actively fed the city's thirst until 1994, when it was pulled out of service. Covering nearly 107 acres, it is better known for the soft-surface track that encircles it, providing a perfect amenity for serious runners—one of whom was the late **Jacqueline Kennedy Onassis**, after whom the reservoir was renamed in 1994. Once around is 1.58 miles. ♦ Bounded by East and West Drs, and 86th St Transverse and 97th St Transverse Rds

9 Great Lawn

The largest field in the park was formerly a rectangular reservoir that was drained just in time to provide a location for a Depression-driven collection of squatters' shacks known as **Hooverville**. By 1936 it was cleared again, and the oval-shaped lawn, with **Belvedere Lake** at the south end and two playgrounds to the north, was fenced off to create a cooling patch of green. It didn't stay that way long. It was surrounded by ball fields with their backstops where the lawn was, and overuse almost completely eliminated the grass. The lawn underwent a much-needed restoration in the late '90s, which has made it a verdant space once more. Grass or no, in 1980, Elton John drew 300,000 people here for a concert; in 1982, a "No Nukes" rally brought out 750,000; in 1993, Pavarotti sang before an audience of 500,000; and in 2003 the Dalai Lama delivered a message of peace to a crowd of 65,000. The **New York Philharmonic** and the **Metropolitan Opera** give several free performances here every summer, each of which attracts about 100,000 people who bring blankets and picnic dinners. ♦ Bounded by East and West Drs, and 79th St Transverse and 86th St Transverse Rds

10 The Obelisk (Cleopatra's Needle)

The Khedive of Egypt gave this obelisk to New York in 1879 and presented its mate to Queen Victoria, who had it placed on the Thames Embankment in London. When the 244-ton, 71-foot-tall granite shaft was delivered to New York, it was placed in a special cradle and rolled here from the Hudson River on cannonballs. Because it had stood for many centuries in front of a temple once believed to have been built by Cleopatra, New Yorkers immediately dubbed it Cleopatra's Needle. It was, however, built by Egypt's King Thutmosis III in 1500 BC. The hieroglyphics on its sides had survived for 3,500 years, but New York's air pollution rendered them unreadable in fewer than a hundred. Movie producer Cecil B. DeMille thoughtfully provided plaques translating the tales they told of Thutmosis III, Ramses II, and Osorkon I. ♦ It is just behind the **Metropolitan Museum of Art**, midway to the **Great Lawn**. East Dr (between 79th St Transverse and 86th St Transverse Rds)

11 Delacorte Theatre/ Shakespeare in the Park

A 1960 addition to the park provides a modern home for the late Joseph Papp's Shakespeare in the Park. Obtaining one of the 2,000 tickets (which are given out to the general public only on the day of the performance) is a summer ritual that begins when would-be audience members queue up for vouchers distributed at 1PM for that

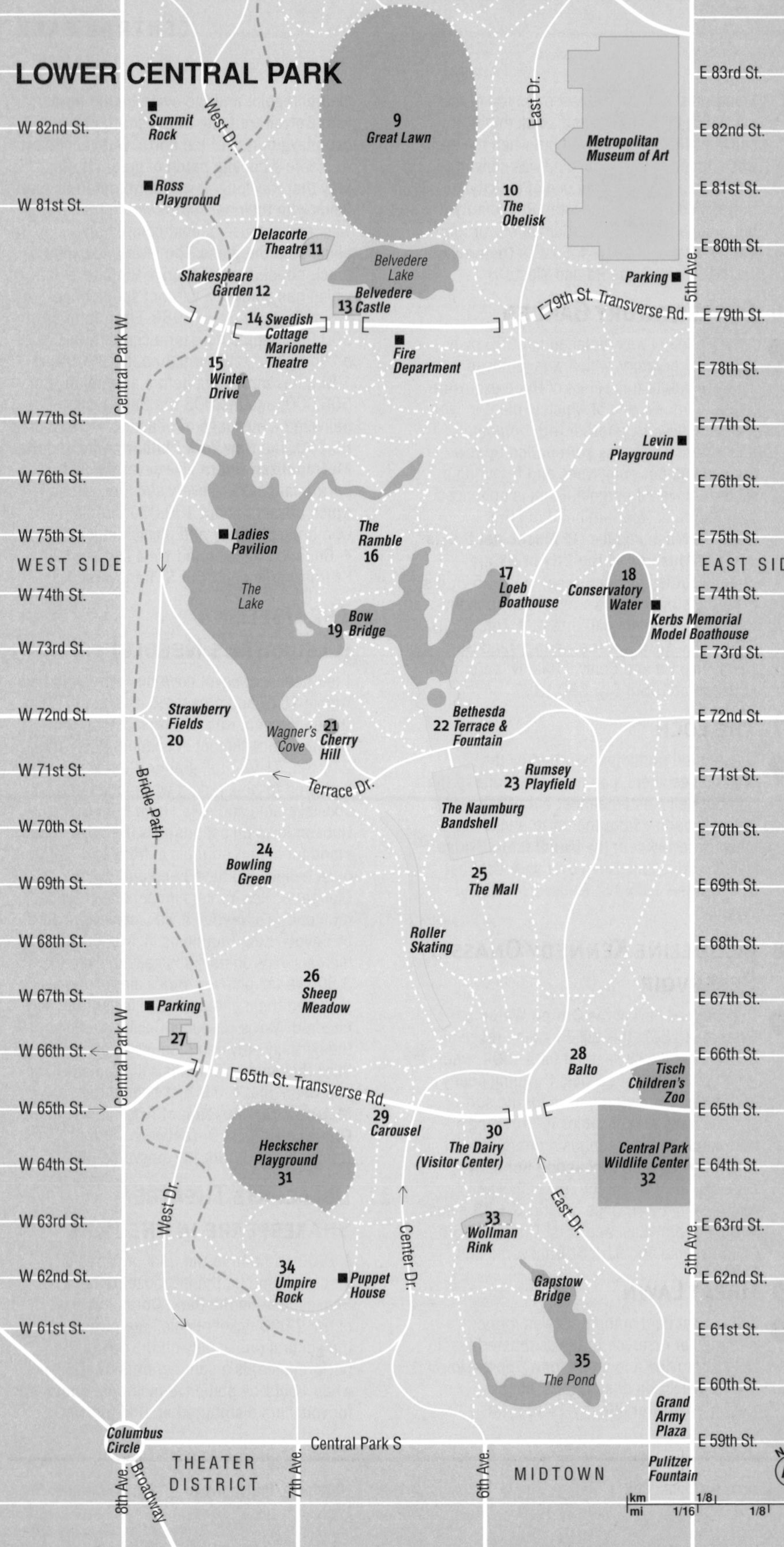
LOWER CENTRAL PARK
9 Great Lawn
Metropolitan Museum of Art
Summit Rock
Ross Playground
West Dr.
East Dr.
10 The Obelisk
Delacorte Theatre 11
Belvedere Lake
Shakespeare Garden 12
13 Belvedere Castle
14 Swedish Cottage Marionette Theatre
Fire Department
79th St. Transverse Rd.
Parking
15 Winter Drive
Levin Playground
Ladies Pavilion
The Ramble 16
The Lake
17 Loeb Boathouse
18 Conservatory Water
Kerbs Memorial Model Boathouse
19 Bow Bridge
Strawberry Fields 20
Wagner's Cove
21 Cherry Hill
22 Bethesda Terrace & Fountain
Terrace Dr.
23 Rumsey Playfield
The Naumburg Bandshell
24 Bowling Green
25 The Mall
Roller Skating
26 Sheep Meadow
Bridle Path
Parking
27
28 Balto
Tisch Children's Zoo
65th St. Transverse Rd.
29 Carousel
30 The Dairy (Visitor Center)
Heckscher Playground 31
Central Park Wildlife Center 32
33 Wollman Rink
Center Dr.
34 Umpire Rock
Puppet House
Gapstow Bridge
35 The Pond
Central Park W
5th Ave.
WEST SIDE
EAST SIDE
W 82nd St.
W 81st St.
W 77th St.
W 76th St.
W 75th St.
W 74th St.
W 73rd St.
W 72nd St.
W 71st St.
W 70th St.
W 69th St.
W 68th St.
W 67th St.
W 66th St.
W 65th St.
W 64th St.
W 63rd St.
W 62nd St.
W 61st St.
E 83rd St.
E 82nd St.
E 81st St.
E 80th St.
E 79th St.
E 78th St.
E 77th St.
E 76th St.
E 75th St.
E 74th St.
E 73rd St.
E 72nd St.
E 71st St.
E 70th St.
E 69th St.
E 68th St.
E 67th St.
E 66th St.
E 65th St.
E 64th St.
E 63rd St.
E 62nd St.
E 61st St.
E 60th St.
E 59th St.
Columbus Circle
Central Park S
Grand Army Plaza
Pulitzer Fountain
8th Ave.
Broadway
THEATER DISTRICT
7th Ave.
6th Ave.
MIDTOWN
km
mi
1/8
1/16
1/8
N

evening's performance. The line starts to form early, but with good friends and a picnic, it can be a pleasant experience. Tickets can also be picked up at the **Public Theater** (425 Lafayette St, between E Fourth St and Astor Pl), on the day of the performance. That line starts forming early also—while tickets are handed out starting at 1PM, don't expect to get any if you're not waiting by 10AM. Two plays are chosen for performance each summer. ♦ Free performances. Tu-Su, 8PM late June to early Sept. West Dr (between 79th St Transverse and 86th St Transverse Rds). 861.7277. www.publictheater.org ♿

12 Shakespeare Garden

In this lovely secluded garden, you'll find a series of pathways, pools, and cascades among trees and plants mentioned in the works of William Shakespeare. ♦ West Dr (between 79th St Transverse and 86th St Transverse Rds)

13 Belvedere Castle

A scaled-down version of a Scottish 19th-century castle was placed here to become part of the view. Its interior is just as impressive. The building serves as one of four visitor centers in the park and also houses a National Weather Service station and the **Henry Luce Nature Observatory**. ♦ Tu-Su, 10AM-5PM. 79th St Transverse Rd (between East and West Drs). 772.0210

14 Swedish Cottage Marionette Theatre

Moved here from Philadelphia after the 1876 Centennial Exposition, this building was used as a comfort station until Swedish-Americans mounted a protest. It was converted into a marionette theater in 1973. ♦ Admission. Call for show times. Reservations required. 79th St Transverse Rd and West Dr. 988.9093

15 Winter Drive

Evergreens were originally planted in all parts of the park to provide color in the winter months, but the heaviest concentration is here, where 19th-century gay blades entered the park for ice-skating. When the ice on **The Lake** was hard enough, a red ball was hoisted on the flagpole above Belvedere Castle, and horsecars on Broadway carried the message downtown by displaying special flags. At the time, parks commissioners estimated that as many as 80,000 people a day crowded the 20-acre slick. The **Arthur Ross Pinetum**, added in 1971 at the north end of the **Great Lawn**, enhances the original plantings with unusual species of conifers from all over the world. ♦ West Dr (between Terrace Dr and 79th St Transverse Rd)

16 The Ramble

This 37-acre wooded section of the park was conceived as a wild garden preserve for native plants and was also intended as a foreground for **Vista Rock** as viewed from the **Mall**. The garden has seen better days, but it is still a wild place, with a brook meandering through and tumbling over several small waterfalls, and it's a perfect place for bird-watching. One of the winding paths led to a man-made cave at the edge of the Lake, but the cave was walled up in the 1920s. There are few better places to get away from it all. Because this area can be relatively deserted, it may be best to share with a friend. ♦ Off East Dr (between Terrace Dr and 79th St Transverse Rd)

17 Loeb Boathouse

Besides seasonal rowboat (plus a kayak or two) and bicycle rentals, there is also an authentic Venetian gondola that holds six people. The Venetians gave a gondola to the park in 1862, but for lack of a gondolier, it rotted away. This one, a more recent gift, includes the services of an expert to pole it around the Lake. ♦ Fee Daily, Mar-Oct. **Gondola**: M-F, 5PM-10PM; Sa, Su, 2PM-10PM. Reservations required. Boats and bikes: No reservations taken. Credit card required. East Dr (between E 72nd St and 79th St Transverse Rd). 517.2233

Boathouse Restaurant

★★$$$ A seasonal "New American" menu accompanies the fantastic view of Central Park's boating pond (count on the view trumping the uneven grub; but how could it not?). There is also a more casual "bar & grill" menu and an Express Café with sandwiches and wraps. ♦ American ♦ M-F, lunch; Sa, Su, brunch; dinner Apr-Nov only, daily. Reservations recommended. Enter on E 72nd St. 517.2233

The first New York City Marathon took place in 1970, when 127 runners circled Central Park four times. The meager $1,000 budget left no room for extravagance: To save money, post-race sodas were purchased in Greenwich Village and lugged uptown, where soda was more expensive. In 2006, 38,000 people from all corners of the globe participated, and a remarkable 98 percent of them completed the 26.2-mile course.

18 Conservatory Water

The name for this pond comes from a conservatory that was never built. The space is occupied by the **Kerbs Memorial Model Boathouse**, designed by **Aymar Embury II** in 1954. It houses model yachts that race on the pond every Saturday in the summer. At the north end is **José de Creeft**'s fanciful ***Alice in Wonderland*** group, given to the park in 1960 by publisher George Delacorte. At the western edge is **George Lober**'s 1956 bronze statue of **Hans Christian Andersen**, a gift of the Danish people. During the summer, a storyteller appears here every Saturday at 11AM. A small snack bar with outdoor tables overlooks the water on the east side. ♦ Off Fifth Ave (between Terrace Dr and 79th St Transverse Rd)

19 Bow Bridge

Calvert Vaux designed most of the park's bridges, and no two are alike. This one, crossing the narrowest part of the Lake, is considered one of the most beautiful. When the cast-iron bridge was put in place, it was supposedly set on cannonballs to allow for expansion caused by temperature changes. But when it was restored in 1974, no cannonballs were found. ♦ The Lake (between Cherry Hill and the Ramble)

20 Strawberry Fields

This teardrop-shaped memorial grove has been sustained with funds provided by Yoko Ono in memory of her late husband, John Lennon. The former Beatle was assassinated in front of the **Dakota** apartment house, which overlooks this tranquil spot. You'll find many fans around the "Imagine" centerpiece mosaic. ♦ West Dr (at Terrace Dr)

21 Cherry Hill

Designed as a vantage point with a view of the **Mall**, the **Lake**, **Bethesda Terrace**, and the **Ramble**, this spot also provided a turnaround for carriages and a fountain for watering the horses. It was converted into a parking lot in 1934 but restored with 8,500 trees and shrubs and 23,000 square feet of sod in 1981. ♦ Terrace Dr (between East and West Drs)

22 Bethesda Terrace and Fountain

Located between the Lake and the Mall, Bethesda Terrace has always been considered the heart of Central Park. It was named for a pool in Jerusalem that the Gospel of St. John says was given healing powers by the annual visitation of an angel. *The Angel of the Waters,* Emma Stebbins's statue on top of the magnificent Bethesda Fountain, re-creates the event. (It should be familiar to viewers of *Angels in America*, in which it played a featured role.) It was unveiled in 1873; the terrace itself had opened in 1861. The basic design is the work of **Calvert Vaux**. But the arcade ceiling, tile floors, and elaborate friezes and other ornamentation are by **Jacob Wrey Mould**, whose early background was in Islamic architecture—which explains why the terrace is so much like a courtyard in a Spanish palace. ♦ Terrace Dr (between East and West Drs)

23 Rumsey Playfield

Now a spacious sand-surfaced space used mostly for school sports (in summer it hosts **Summerstage** concerts), the remnants of the field's past may be seen in the 1938 sculpture of Mother Goose by Frederick G.R. Roth and a wisteria-covered pergola at its western edge. Rumsey Playfield was built on the site of the **Central Park Casino**, a cottage originally designed as a ladies' house of refreshment. In the 1920s it was turned into a restaurant, designed by **Joseph Urban**, which became the most popular place in town for the likes of Gentleman Jimmy Walker, whose basic rule of life was that the only real sin was to go to bed on the same day that you got up. A decade or so later, under Mayor Fiorello LaGuardia's watch, Parks Commissioner Robert Moses leveled it and had **Rumsey Playground** built. It was never a success, and not long after a redesign in the '80s it was converted to the playfield it is today. ♦ East Dr (between Center and Terrace Drs)

24 Bowling Green

Lawn bowling and croquet were first played here in the 1920s. The folks who play today take their games very seriously, which explains why the greens are so well maintained. You can get a permit to join them by calling 360.8133. ♦ Games start at 1PM and 1:30PM Tu-Sa, 1 May-1 Nov. West Dr (between 65th St Transverse Rd and Terrace Dr)

25 The Mall

This formal promenade was largely the work of **Ignaz Anton Pilat**, a plant expert who worked with **Olmsted** and **Vaux** on the overall design of the park. He deviated from the romantic naturalism of the plan by

Before construction on Central Park began in 1856, Fifth Avenue from 59th to 120th Streets was called "Squatters' Sovereignty," where poor people lived in shacks made of wooden planks and flattened tin cans. When construction on the park started, the poor were evicted, and soon the area housed the city's richest and most powerful people.

The Best

Michael Boodro

Editor, *Martha Stewart Living*

The **Shakespeare Garden** in **Central Park**. Not far from the **Ramble**, the most serene, beautifully planted, and romantic spot in the park. And the views from **Belvedere Castle** are unsurpassed. Of course, hit the biggies, the **Metropolitan Museum of Art**, the **Museum of Modern Art**, the **Whitney**, and the **Guggenheim**. But don't forget the **Frick**, the **Pierpont Morgan Library**, or the **National Academy of Design**. The fantastic **Brooklyn Museum** is an easy subway ride away, and the **Brooklyn Botanic Garden** next door is spectacular.

After **Broadway** and **Lincoln Center**, check out the **Public Theater** and the innovative performance artists and drag theater **at PS 122** or **Dixon Place**. Any Balanchine piece being performed by **New York City Ballet** is a sure bet.

Window-shop if you must at the designer boutiques on **Madison Avenue** between **57th** and **80th Streets**, and in **SoHo**, but like real New Yorkers buy at **Barneys**, **Bergdorf**, **ABC Carpet**, the **Union Square Market**, and **Zabar's**.

In Midtown, soaring **Grand Central Station** and beautiful **Bryant Park** are both proof that the city still appreciates, and knows how to preserve, a few of its treasures.

planting a double row of elm trees along the length of the promenade, but in the process created a reminder of what country roads and New England villages were like a century ago. The walkway was placed on a northwest angle to provide a sightline directly to a high outcropping above 79th Street known as **Vista Rock**. Vaux designed a miniature castle for the top of the rock to create an impression of greater distance. The **Naumburg Bandshell** at the north end was designed in 1923 by **William G. Tachau** and donated by **Elkan Naumburg**, who presented concerts here for many years. It replaced an 1862 cast-iron bandstand that included a sky-blue cupola dotted with gold-leaf stars. Naumburg's legacy, the **Naumburg Orchestral Concerts**, take place here in summer. ♦ East and Center Drs (between 66th and 69th Sts)

26 Sheep Meadow

The original park design called for a meadow here to enhance the view from the gentle hill to the north. The 15-acre hill was resodded in 1980 after concerts and other crowd-pleasing events had reduced it to hardpan. On the first warm day of the year, New Yorkers flock here for picnicking, sunbathing, and quiet recreation. The view from the hill with the city skyline in the background is in some ways more breathtaking than the park's architects ever envisioned. ♦ 11AM to dusk, May–mid-Oct. West Dr (between W 66th and W 69th Sts).

27 Tavern on the Green

★★★$$$$ Designed by **Jacob Wrey Mould**, the building housing this lovely dining spot was erected in 1870 by Boss Tweed and his corrupt Tammany Hall city government over the strenuous objection of **Frederick Law Olmsted**, landscape architect and designer of Central Park. Originally called the **Sheepfold**, the structure housed the herd of Southdown sheep that grazed in Central Park until 1934, when they were exiled to **Prospect Park** in Brooklyn. The Sheepfold then became a restaurant, and was completely redesigned in 1976 by **James F. Floyd** and **Warner LeRoy**. The outdoor garden is a wonderful place to spend a summer evening and is spectacularly lit by twinkling lights in the trees from November through May. But any time of year the **Crystal Room**, dripping with chandeliers, is an unforgettable experience, especially for Sunday brunch. As always, it's more about atmosphere than food, but try the chef's warm house-smoked salmon with mushroom and potato salad in a chive aioli, grilled black Angus fillet of beef with wild mushrooms in a red-wine sauce, grilled porterhouse with bacon and cabbage mashed potatoes, or the Moroccan-style barbecued salmon on savoy cabbage. Desserts are terrific—especially the napoleon filled with ginger crème brûlée. There's an extensive wine list. ♦ American ♦ M-F, lunch and dinner; Sa, Su, brunch and dinner. Reservations required. Central Park W (at 65th St Transverse Rd). 873.3200

28 Balto

One of the most popular monuments in the park, this 1925 bronze portrait by **Frederick G.R. Roth** represents the husky (a compadre of **Togo**, memorialized in Chinatown's Seward Park) who led his team of dogs from Anchorage to Nome—a thousand miles—to deliver serum to stem a diphtheria epidemic. ♦ East Dr (just north of 65th St Transverse Rd)

29 The Carousel

There has been a merry-go-round here since 1871. The original was powered by real horses that walked a treadmill in an underground pit. The present one, built in 1908 at **Coney**

Island, was moved here in 1951. Its 58 horses were hand-carved by Stein & Goldstein, considered the best woodcarvers of their day. Don't just stand there—climb up and go for the ride of your life. ♦ Nominal admission. Daily, Apr-Nov; Sa, Su, Nov-Apr. 65th St Transverse Rd and Center Dr. 879.0244

30 The Dairy (Visitors' Center)

When this Gothic building was constructed in 1870, fresh milk was a relative luxury. The park's planners, following European models, added milkmaids and a herd of cows to enhance the sylvan setting and to provide children with a healthy treat. After the turn of the century, the cows were sent off to the country, the milkmaids retired, and the building became a storehouse. In 1981, it was restored and its wooden porch replaced and painted in Victorian colors. It is now the park's central **Visitors' Center**, with an information desk, exhibitions, and a gift shop. Weekend walking tours, led by the Urban Park Rangers, usually leave from here or from the **Dana Discovery Center**. ♦ Visitors' Center: Tu-Su, 10AM-5PM. 65th St Transverse Rd (between East and Center Drs). Urban Park Rangers (tour information), 794.6564

31 Heckscher Playground

The original park plan didn't include sports facilities, but this was one of three loosely connected areas for children who had secured the proper permits to play games like baseball and croquet. In the 1920s, adults wanted to get into the game and pressured the city into building them five softball diamonds with backstops and bleachers. At about the same time, the former meadow was converted into an asphalt-covered playground to give the kids something to do while the adults were running bases. It was the first formal playground in the park. The softball fields are available by permit only, and are used by teams from corporations, Broadway shows, and other groups. ♦ Call 794.6567 to see who's playing today; for a permit for your own team, call 397.3100. Off West Dr (between Center Dr and 65th St Transverse Rd)

32 The Arsenal

The 10 acres of land around this building we a park before Central Park was even a drean Designed by **Martin E. Thompson** and

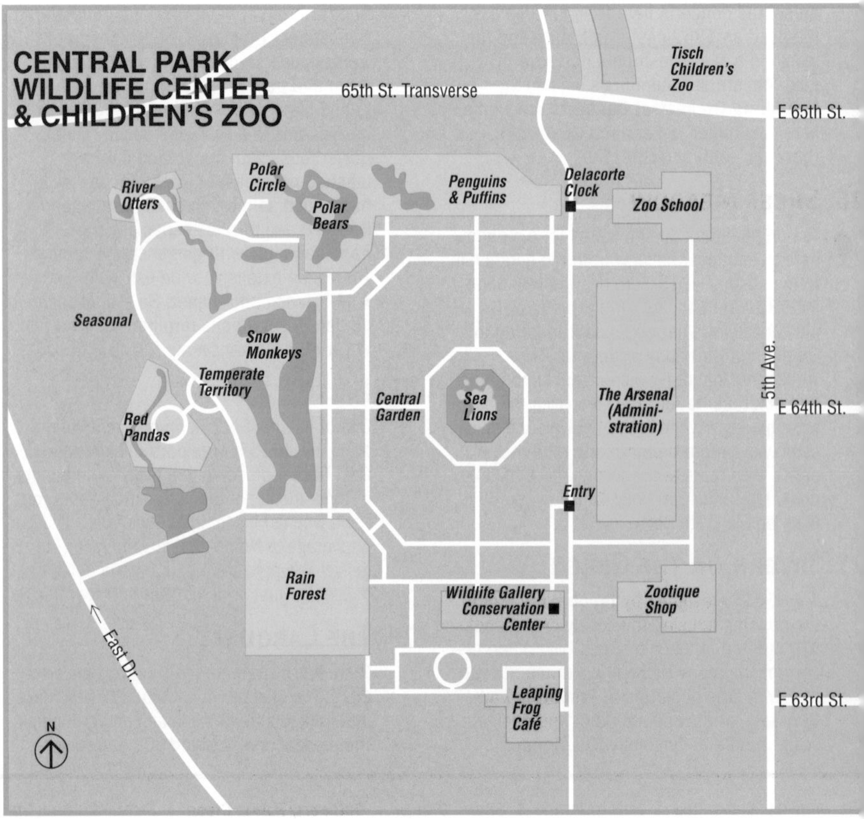

CENTRAL PARK WILDLIFE CENTER & CHILDREN'S ZOO

65th St. Transverse
Tisch Children's Zoo
E 65th St.
River Otters
Polar Circle
Polar Bears
Penguins & Puffins
Delacorte Clock
Zoo School
Seasonal
Snow Monkeys
Temperate Territory
Red Pandas
Central Garden
Sea Lions
The Arsenal (Administration)
5th Ave.
E 64th St.
Entry
Rain Forest
Wildlife Gallery Conservation Center
Zootique Shop
East Dr.
Leaping Frog Café
E 63rd St.
N

completed in 1851, the building's original use as a storehouse for arms and ammunition accounts for the iconography of cannons and rifles around the Fifth Avenue entrance. It became the citywide headquarters of the **Parks and Recreation Department** in 1934, following use as a police precinct, a weather bureau, a menagerie, and the first home of the **American Museum of Natural History**. A third-floor gallery contains, among other exhibits, the original Greensward plan, whose results are all around you. ♦ Free. M-F. Fifth Ave (at W 64th St). ♿

32 Central Park Zoo

This 5.5-acre complex—officially known as the **Central Park Wildlife Center**—is home to some 450 animals representing more than a hundred species. Opened in 1988 at the cost of $35 million, the zoo it replaced had elephants and other animals too large for such cramped quarters; they were given to other zoos with more hospitable facilities. The bears and sea lions have been given more natural homes here, and penguins cavort under a simulated ice pack in a pool with glass walls that allow you to watch their underwater antics. Monkeys swing in trees in a reproduction of an African environment, bats fly through a naturalistic cave, and alligators swim in the most comfortable swamp north of the Okefenokee. The center encompasses three climatic zones: tropical, temperate, and polar. **Leaping Frog Café** and the **Zootique** gift shop at the southern edge are accessible without entering the grounds. The zoo was designed by **Kevin Roche, John Dinkeloo & Associates**.The **Tisch Children's Zoo** is at the north end of the Wildlife Center, between the 65th Street Transverse and East 66th Street.

"In its influence as an educator, as a place of agreeable resort, as a source of scientific interest, and in its effect upon the health, happiness, and comfort of our people may be found its chief value."

—Frederick Law Olmsted,
Report of the Commissioners of Central Park, 1870

If you get lost in the park, find the nearest lamppost. The first two numbers signify the nearest numbered (east-west) street.

There are 22 playgrounds, 26 ball fields, and 30 tennis courts in Central Park.

♦ Admission. Daily. Fifth Ave (between E 63rd and E 65th Sts). 439.6500

33 Wollman Rink

Opened in 1950, the original rink lasted less than 30 years, and when the city attempted to rebuild it, the project became mired in so much red tape that it began to look as though it might take another 30 years to replace it. In 1986, real estate and casino tycoon Donald Trump took it upon himself to do the job—without the regulations the city imposes on itself—and finished it in record time. Ice-skating is generally from November through March, with roller-skating at other times. ♦ Admission; lockers and skate rental available. Daily, Nov-Mar. East Dr (between Grand Army Plaza and 65th St Transverse Rd). 439.6900

34 Umpire Rock

Central Park is laced with rocky outcrops like this one, left behind some 20,000 years ago by the Laurentian Glacier. The boulder on top is called an erratic, and was carried down with the ice from the Far North. The tracks on the face of the rock, called striations, were formed by the scraping of large stones embedded in the glacier as it moved southeast across Manhattan. Most of the rocky outcrops in the park are a type of mica-rich shale called Manhattan schist. About 400 million years ago, they formed the base of a mountain chain about as high as the present-day Rocky Mountains. ♦ Just south of Heckscher Playground

35 The Pond

A shot of the reflection of the nearby buildings, especially **The Plaza** hotel, in this crescent-shaped haven for ducks and other waterfowl may be among the best pictures you'll take home. The view is from the **Gapstow Bridge**, which crosses the northern end of the pond. The water pocket was created to reflect the rocks in what is now a bird sanctuary on its western shore, as well as a favorite lunch spot for nearby office workers. From the time the park opened until 1924, swan boats like the ones still used in the Boston Garden dodged real swans here. The Pond was reduced to about half its original size in 1951 when the **Wollman Memorial Skating Rink** was built. But in 2002 the 14-acre site was restored: an island habitat for the Pond's many birds and turtles, as well as a lovely cascading waterfall, now enhance the serene beauty of the re-landscaped shore. ♦ East Dr (between Grand Army Plaza and 65th St Transverse Rd)

WEST SIDE

Bisected by Broadway and its casual jumble of shops, delis, and restaurants, Manhattan's West Side is more relaxed and laid-back than its fashionable East Side counterpart across **Central Park.** The area was first settled by Eastern European Jews and other immigrants from the Lower East Side in the early part of the century. Today this vibrant neighborhood, bounded by **Central Park West**, the **Hudson River**, and We

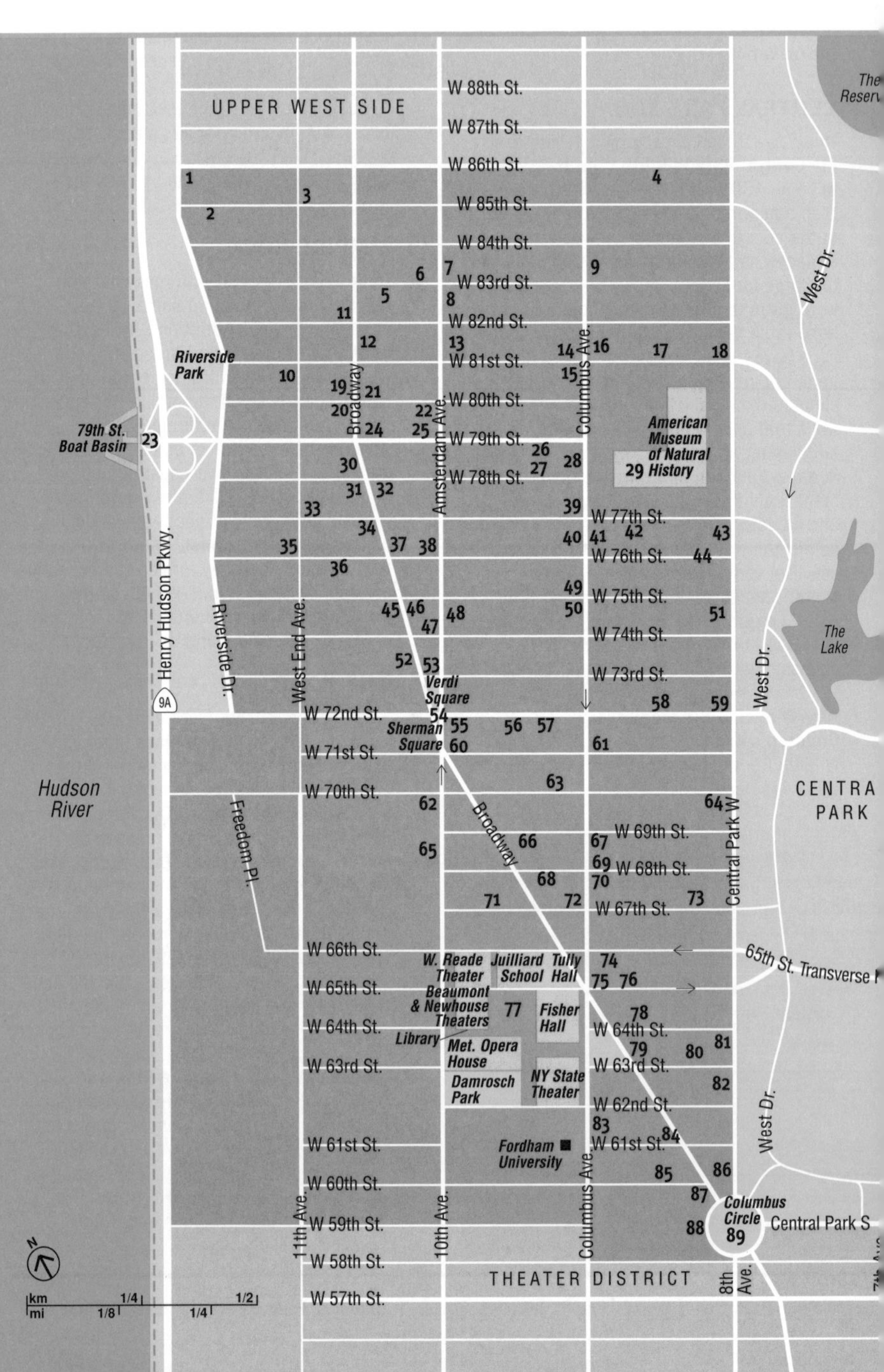

59th and West 86th Streets, is characterized by low-key locals—many in the literary and arts professions, mothers (and dads) pushing baby carriages, and well-dressed crowds pouring in and out of the concert halls and restaurants. Highlights include **Lincoln Center for the Performing Arts**, the **American Museum of Natural History**, the ever-changing mix of clothing stores and sidewalk cafés on **Amsterdam** and **Columbus Avenues, Riverside Park**, and numerous architecturally noteworthy buildings.

Riverside Drive, along the neighborhood's western edge, was originally a street of upper-middle-class town houses. Although it had spectacular river views, it lacked the cachet of Fifth Avenue, where "the 400" (Mrs. William Astor's most intimate circle, so called because her home could accommodate only that number) were erecting their palazzi and châteaux. Many of the private homes were replaced in the 1920s by the 15-story apartment buildings of today, their faces sometimes curving to follow the shape of the street.

Some argue that **Central Park West**, skirting the neighborhood's eastern edge, is finer than Fifth Avenue, because the buildings are more distinguished and the street wider. Most of the buildings on Central Park West were originally built as apartments rather than houses, including the chateaulike **Dakota** (the city's first luxury apartment house, built in 1884 by the same architect who would later design the **Plaza Hotel**) at **West 72nd Street**. Four twin-towered buildings, most notably the **San Remo** (145–146 Central Park West, at West 74th Street) and the Art Deco **Eldorado** (farther uptown, No. 300, at West 90th Street), the **Majestic** (No. 115), and the **Century** (No. 25) apartments, make Central Park West's skyline unique. The park blocks—the numbered cross-streets between Central Park West and Columbus Avenue—contain interesting collections of brownstones and apartments. Particularly noteworthy are the six buildings with artists' studios on **West 67th Street**, including the **Hotel des Artistes**, whose plush apartments have been home to many well-known artists, actors, and writers.

West End Avenue—once lined with Romanesque and Queen Anne–style row houses and now with apartment houses—was supposed to be the West Side's commercial street, while Broadway was slated to be the residential area; hence the avenue's generous width and the mall in the center. And while it is home to the irreplaceable **Apthorp Apartments** (at West 78th Street) and the Belle Epoque **Ansonia Hotel** (at West 73rd Street), mostly the reverse happened, and Broadway became—and has remained—the neighborhood's "Main Street."

1 The Clarendon

In 1908, publisher William Randolph Hearst moved his family into a 30-room apartment on the top three floors of this 1903 building designed by **Charles Birge**. In 1913, when the landlord refused to ask the residents on the other nine floors to leave so that Hearst, his family, and his art collection could spread out, Hearst simply purchased the building and forced them out himself. Faced with financial woes, he sold the property in 1938. ♦ 137 Riverside Dr (at W 86th St)

2 The Red House

Designed and built in 1904, and now on the National Register of Historic Places, this six-story terra-cotta-embellished apartment building is a cross between an Elizabethan manor and a redbrick row house. Note the dragon and crown near the top. ♦ 350 W 85th St (between West End Ave and Riverside Dr)

3 520 West End Avenue

Neighborhood residents vehemently defended their many-gabled "castle" when, in 1987, a misled developer proposed building an apartment house on this site. This survivor was built in 1892 to the designs of **Clarence F. True**. ♦ At W 85th St

4 The Bard Graduate Center Gallery

Housed in an elegant prewar town house near Central Park, **The Bard Graduate Center (BGC)** is dedicated to the study of the decorative and applied arts, as well as landscape design, all within a cultural and historical context. Founded in 1993 as a graduate institute of Bard College, the bonus for the public is the associated **BGC Gallery**. Always carefully curated and fastidiously presented, their shows are brilliant microcosms of whatever tradition they've chosen to focus on. Objects shown may be rare and fine or even commonplace, and range from a sweeping collection of ancient Roman glass miniatures to Marimekko fabrics and Hungarian ceramics. Publications, public programs, and tours are available. ♦ Admission. Tu-Su, 11AM-5PM; till 8PM on Th. 18 W 86th St (between Central Park W and Columbus Ave). 501.3001. www.bgc.bard.edu ♿

5 Children's Museum of Manhattan (CMOM)

This educational playground of interactive exhibitions and activity centers is all built around the museum's theme of self-discovery. On the second floor is the **Time Warner Media Center** where children can produce their own videotapes, newscasts, and public affairs programs. Exhibition interpreters are always on hand to provide assistance, and entertainers are stationed at key points to provide further understanding through song, dance, or puppetry. There is an art studio where classes in book- and paper-making and other studio arts are held, and a theater where performances are given by theater groups, dancers, musicians, puppeteers, and storytellers, as well as children participating in the museum's education and video programs and workshops. ♦ Admission. Tu-Su, 10AM-5PM. 212 W 83rd St (between Amsterdam Ave and Broadway). 721.1223. www.cmom.org ♿

"In Manhattan, there are gardens on roofs, gardens outside basement apartments, and minigardens on miniterraces. How do the gardens grow? Expensively. And what do they grow? Almost anything. Apparently, even cash crops. Wildflowers have been tamed on tiny balconies, and families fed on vegetables nurtured in the alien soil bordered by sidewalks."

—Ralph Caplan,
writer and design consultant

6 Cafe Lalo

★$ This dessert-only café with brick walls and a wooden floor has long French-style windows that open onto the street. During the day, it's quite pleasant to linger over a cappuccino and such desserts as cappuccino tart, Snicker's Bar cheesecake, lemon mousse cake, chocolate Vienna torte, and assorted fruit pies. At night, the café tends to attract young first-daters and can get crowded and loud. ♦ Café ♦ Daily until 2AM weeknights, 4AM weekends 201 W 83rd St (between Amsterdam Ave and Broadway). 496.6031

7 Good Enough to Eat

★★★$$ Breakfast and Sunday brunch are the best bets at this tiny Vermont-style outpost. But be ready to wait in line for pecan-flecked waffles, cinnamon-swirl French toast, or the lumberjack breakfast—it's as big as it sounds. Lunch and dinner are prepared with a homey, if less inventive, touch. Popular picks include a turkey dinner with gravy, stuffing, and cranberry sauce; meat loaf; and a turkey club sandwich. All breads, soups, and desserts are homemade and pasta and pizza specials change daily. ♦ American ♦ M-F, breakfast, lunch, and dinner Sa-Su, brunch and dinner. No reservations. 483 Amsterdam Ave (between W 83rd and W 84th Sts). 496.0163

8 Avventura

Gorgeous art glass and hand-painted pottery imported from all over the world, particularly Italy, is on display at this handsome store. The one-of-a-kind platters, bowls, and plates are absolute knockouts. ♦ Su-F. 463 Amsterdam Ave (between W 82nd and W 83rd Sts). 769.2510

9 April Cornell

For those who like the exotic look of hand silk screened or handblock-inspired fabrics, this is an oasis. The owners have asked their suppliers to make traditional patterns as well as totally untraditional ones, such as checks and Provençal-inspired florals, and to whip them up into well-made country-style kids' and adults' clothing and linens, like pillowcases, duvet covers, and tablecloths. Fabrics may also be purchased by the yard. ♦ Daily. 487 Columbus Ave (between W 83rd and W 84th Sts). 799.1110 ♿

10 Calhoun School

With two dark glass faces set in cream travertine, **Costas Machlouzarides**'s 1975 design for this progressive private school was said by some to resemble a giant television. An expansion by **FX Fowle Architects**, completed in 2004, added four stories above the original five, topped by a green roof with space for hands-on environmental studies.

Though the school is not open to the public, its performance center hosts cultural programs that are. ♦ 433 West End Ave (between W 80th and W 81st Sts). 497.6500. www.calhoun.org

11 Barnes & Noble

This multilevel space, like most B&Ns in the city, still has the late hours that helped build the chain's rep as a singles scene. (Of course, it also chased out most of the many indies that once ruled this neighborhood, so there's been a shortage of alt literary scenes in the decade or so since it landed.) Unfortunately, the once-plentiful chairs and tables that warmed up the place are long gone. ♦ Daily till late. 2289 Broadway (at W 82nd St). 362.8835. Also at numerous locations throughout the city ♿

12 The Yarn Co.

In addition to being one of the best sources for yarn and expert knitting instruction in the city, this is one of its most pleasant yarn shops, with a big wooden farm table and chairs in the center of the room and an abundant stock of high-quality yarns. ♦ Tu-Sa. 2274 Broadway (between W 81st and W 82nd Sts), second floor. 787.7878

Louie's WESTSIDE CAFÉ

13 Louie's Westside Café

★$$ Grand yet casual, this café with peach walls, subdued lighting, and French rattan chairs offers a basic but well-prepared American menu, with something for everyone. Try the crab cakes, spinach linguine with turkey bolognese, herb-roasted chicken, hanger steak, lamb chops with Tuscan white-bean stew, or pasta primavera. For dessert, have the mocha torte, chocolate velvet cake, or carrot cake. Brunch may be the best meal to have here; try the pecan waffles or Southwestern-style eggs. ♦ American ♦ M-F, breakfast, lunch, and dinner; Sa, Su, brunch and dinner. Reservations recommended. 441 Amsterdam Ave (at W 81st St). 877.1900 ♿

14 Greenstones & Cie

European clothing for children, including brightly colored French sportswear from Petit Boy and Maugin and dressy duds from Italy's Mona Lisa, are sold here. ♦ Daily. 442 Columbus Ave (between W 81st and W 82nd Sts). 580.4322. Also at 1184 Madison Ave (between E 86th and E 87th Sts). 427.1665; 1410 Second Ave (between W 73rd and W 74th Sts), 794.0530

14 Penny Whistle Toys

The Pustefix teddy bear out front is forever blowing bubbles to get your attention. If he could talk, he'd tell you all about the quality classics inside: board games, stuffed animals, dolls, cars, indoor gyms, table soccer games, rattles for infants, and—surprise—no electronic video games! ♦ Daily. 448 Columbus Ave (between W 81st and W 82nd Sts). 873.9090

15 Uno Chicago Grill

★$ The deep-dish, Chicago-style pizza at this chain outpost is a decent pie. This place also happens to be one of the very few near the **American Museum of Natural History** that is appropriate for children—the express lunch is ready in five minutes. ♦ Pizza ♦ Daily, lunch, dinner, and late-night meals. 432 Columbus Ave (at W 81st St). 595.4700. Also at numerous locations throughout the city

16 Maxilla & Mandible

When they say you can find anything in this city, they mean it. This shop specializes in selling all types of bones. Definitely worth a visit. ♦ Daily. 451 Columbus Ave (between W 81st and W 82nd Sts). 724.6173

17 Excelsior Hotel

$$ In a classy block across the street from the grounds of the **American Museum of Natural History**, this mid-priced hotel is a find. Comfy and freshened post an early-21st-century renovation, the hybrid French traditional décor and the mostly well-lit and decent-sized rooms (especially if you get a suite—and well over half of the 198 rooms here are actually single or double suites) offer a fine respite after a day of trekking around the city. The Excelsior maintains high-speed Internet access (including Wi-Fi) in all rooms and public spaces; there is a workout room, and breakfast is also available on-site. ♦ 45 W 81st St (between Central Park W and Columbus Ave). 362.9200, 800/368.4575; fax 721.2994. www.excelsiorhotelny.com

18 The Beresford

On a street of twin-towered landmarks, this deluxe 1929 apartment building designed by

> The New York City Landmarks Preservation Commission was established in 1965, two years after the demolition of the original Pennsylvania Station. The commission protects buildings of historic, cultural, and esthetic value to the city.

Emery Roth distinguishes itself by having three rather squat Baroque turrets that give it a double silhouette from two directions. Famous residents have included poet Sara Teasdale, underworld crime leader Meyer Lansky, Margaret Mead, Rock Hudson, tennis great John McEnroe, and newscaster Peter Jennings. ♦ 211 Central Park W (between W 81st St and W 82nd Sts)

19 Zabar's

This food bazaar is like no other in the world. Evolved from a small Jewish deli, it's now a block-long grocery and housewares store. Cookware and appliances (contained on their Housewares Mezzanine level), and packaged, prepared, and fresh foods from all over the world can be found here. On weekends, a long line forms for the Western Nova salmon (if you're lucky, the counter help will pass you a slice to taste-test). Though the crowded, narrow aisles can induce an attack of claustrophobia, take a deep breath and persevere: The reward is unrivaled quality at prices that beat the competition. ♦ Daily. 2245 Broadway (at W 80th St). 787.2000 ♿

20 H&H Bagels West

This bakery turns out 60,000 bagels a day, some of which are shipped as far as London! If you go for their large, airy style of bagel, you can count on getting one fresh from the oven around the clock. This also happens to be one of the last Manhattan bastions of the "baker's dozen" (buy 12, get 13). ♦ Daily, 24 hours. 2239 Broadway (at W 80th St). 595.8003, 800/692.2435 ♿. Also at 639 W 46th St (at 12th Ave). 595.8000 ♿

21 Westsider Rare & Used Books

No need to lament the old **Gryphon Book Shop**—this is still them, just under a different name, and we can confirm that a fascinating selection of used and rare books is still sold (and bought) here at decent prices. Look for general humanities, fiction, architecture, modern first editions, Asian and African-American titles, theater, performing arts, and children's books, especially the Oz series by L. Frank Baum. At their **Records** location you'll find a deeper collection of performing arts books, plus scores and LPs, CDs, and whatever other formats music comes in these days. ♦ Daily. 2246 Broadway (between W 80th and W 81st Sts). 362.0706. Also **Westsider Records**, 233 W 72nd St (between Broadway and West End Ave). 874.1588. www.westsiderbooks.com

22 Allan & Suzi

Halston, Prada, Marc Jacobs, Helmut Lang. This season's must-have skirt or a 1930s evening gown. If it is now or ever has been fabulous and fashionable, there's a good chance you'll find it at this amazing consignment shop, where the racks are packed with gorgeous garb—new and vintage, for men and women. Owners Allan Pollack and Suzi Kandel have costumed for film and TV, dressed an A-list of celebs, and still found time to stock more Jimmy Choos, platform boots, and Pucci hot pants than you ever thought you'd see in one place. ♦ Daily. 416 Amsterdam Ave (at W 80th St). 724.7745. www.allanandsuzi.net

23 West 79th Street Boat Basin Café

★★$ Run by the O'Neal's restaurant gang, this is a casual neighborhood joint with an all-too-rare water view. A cold beer or a pink lemonade on their open terrace is a great reward for actually finding it on a hot summer day (it's tucked under the West Side Highway overlooking the houseboats parked at the West 79th Street Boat Basin on the western fringe of **Riverside Park**). Stay for lunch or dinner—sandwiches trump salads here; grilled chicken or the burgers are the best bets—dining outside or in the sheltered area above. Either way, you can watch the urban mariners down at the boat basin, or enjoy the strollers and rollers on the lovely and ever-extending Riverside Park bikeway. The café draws a pretty dense after-work drink scene, and there's often live music. Quieter on weekday and weekend afternoons (the weekends are often accompanied by a classical or light jazz string band), there are worse ways to while away a couple of hours. ♦ American ♦ Mid-Apr through late Oct only. Daily, lunch and dinner. Riverside Park, 79th St Boat Basin. W 79th St (at the Hudson River). 496.5542 ♿

24 Dublin House Tap Room

At night, the area's younger, newer residents take over this former workingman's retreat, and the place gets lively indeed. The brilliant neon harp over the door beckons you to have a lager, and the separate back room makes you wish you'd invited the whole team. ♦ Daily. 225 W 79th St (between Amsterdam Ave and Broadway). 874.9528

24 Filene's Basement

Known for selling perfect and slightly damaged clothing and shoes for men and women from the country's best department stores at bargain prices, this Boston original gave rise to the expression "bargain basement." Now, of course, it's a chain of its own and the merchandise is all new and neatly hung, but the decent prices prevail. ♦ Daily. 2222 Broadway (at W 79th St). 873.8000. ♿ Also at numerous locations throughout the city

25 Nice Matin

★★★$$ If you're out and about not long after dawn, looking for more than a doughnut from the deli, this classy brasserie could make it a very, um, nice morning for you: it's open at 7AM every day of the year. Better still, it stays open through lunch and dinner, serving classics such as leeks vinaigrette, *pissaladière* (Niçoise pizza with olives and anchovies), and a tender *daube* of beef short ribs. In summer, you can sit outside, trading the buzz of the room for the hope of a breeze. ♦ French/Mediterranean. ♦ M-F, breakfast, lunch, and dinner; Sa, Su, breakfast, brunch, and dinner. 201 W 79th St (at Amsterdam Ave). 873.6423

26 Bag One Arts

Named after the interviews that John Lennon and Yoko Ono gave from the inside of a black bag, this gallery sells limited-edition graphics by the ex-Beatle. ♦ By appointment only. 110 W 79th St (between Columbus and Amsterdam Aves). 595.5537 ♿

27 121–131 West 78th Street

Built in 1886 by **Rafael Guastavino**, a Catalan mason famous for his vaults (see the **Oyster Bar** at **Grand Central Terminal**), these six red-and-white houses are unified by their symmetrical arrangement and cheery details. ♦ Between Columbus and Amsterdam Aves

28 Only Hearts

Silky lingerie, sweet-smelling sachets, jewelry, books about hearts and kissing, and heart-shaped waffle irons and fly swatters are sold in this pretty shop for the shameless romantic. ♦ Daily. 386 Columbus Ave (between W 78th and W 79th Sts). 724.5608. ♿ Also at 230 Mott St (between Prince and Spring Sts). 431.3694

29 American Museum of Natural History (AMNH)

This preeminent research institution is a big draw for families with small children, but its audience has grown broader as the museum aggressively revamps with new halls and exhibits that most successfully reflect both changes in the sciences and how that information is presented. Overall, the museum's extensive (now well over 34 million artifacts and specimens) collections are shown off to great advantage here and run a remarkable gamut from ethnography—or human culture—to dinosaurs, meteorites, butterflies, and more. Lots more.

Built in 1872 in the middle of a landscape of goats and squatters, the original building (designed by **Jacob Wrey Mould** and **Calvert Vaux**) can now be glimpsed only from Columbus Avenue. The body of the museum (built in 1899 by **J.C. Cady & Co.** and **Cady, Berg & See**, with later additions by **Charles Vos** and **Trowbridge & Livingston**), an example of Romanesque Revival at its grandest, can best be admired from West 77th Street. (That view will be even grander after a major cleaning and overhaul is completed in 2009.) The building itself is nothing if not a piecemeal reflection of changing tastes in style. In between the turreted extensions, a massive carriage entrance passes under a sweeping flight of stairs: The heavy red-brown brick and granite add to the medieval aura and positive strength typified by the seven-arch colonnade. The main façade of the museum these days is the one **John Russell Pope** designed in 1936, with its grand staircase rising from Central Park West, then opening into his dramatic **Theodore Roosevelt Rotunda**. The street-level entrance on Central Park West (now for staff only) opens into Pope's **Theodore Roosevelt Memorial Hall**.

The museum is widely recognized as having the greatest collection of fossil vertebrates in the world. The **Fossil Halls** reopened in 1995 as part of a seven-year, $45 million remodeling. Six exhibition halls (including Barosaurus, the world's tallest freestanding dinosaur exhibit, which stands majestically in the Theodore Roosevelt Rotunda at the museum entrance) now tell the story of the evolution of vertebrates.

The other fossil exhibits are grouped on the fourth floor and include extensive additional dinosaur mountings, reconfigured to reflect the latest scientific thinking. The hall's **Wallace Wing** displays an extraordinary assemblage of fossil mammals, including saber-toothed cats, woolly mammoths, giant sloths, and bizarre reptilelike creatures with three-foot sails on their backs. An interactive computer system allows visitors to explore different locations and time periods and the animals that inhabited them.

New exhibition halls in the same style, peppered with interactive video terminals and such, are continually being added. First-floor examples include the **Anne and Bernard Spitzer Hall of Human Origins** (formerly the Hall of Human Biology and Evolution), examining the heritage we share with other living things. The 10,000-square-foot hall, fully revamped and relaunched in 2007, now does its job of tracing the patterns of human evolution with the benefits of the latest work in genomic science. Here also are the **Hall of Biodiversity**, including a mockup of a Central African rain forest, and **Gottesman Hall of Planet Earth**, featuring computer simulations speeding up the inversion of Earth's magnetic

The Best

Cynthia Elliott

Executive Director, Symphony Space

SoHo on weekday mornings, when it feels like the old neighborhood of artists and families, and when you can really see the fabulous architecture.

Zabar's, where classical music plays on the P.A. system; where Saul, Stanley, and the rest of the family are ever-present; where you can see the great actors, writers, dancers, and musicians of our time picking over the cheeses alongside the rest of us; and where, by the way, you can buy the best food and coffee at the most reasonable prices.

Yankee Stadium on a warm summer evening, with a cold beer, a foot-long hotdog, and Jeter/Giambi/Clemens/Matsui/Rodriguez *et al.* in fine form.

The angels at Rockefeller Center at Christmastime—in fact, all the decorations around New York at Christmastime, even the cheesy star at 57th and Fifth.

The Messiah **at St. Thomas Church**—These outstanding performances, featuring their heavenly boys' choir, always put me in the Christmas spirit.

Symphony Space's annual 12-hour Wall to Wall marathons—a wonderful way to indulge in musical gluttony in the company of like-minded hordes (2008's **Wall to Wall Bach** is on May 17!).

field or the process of continental drift so you can watch the eons hurtle by in a couple of minutes. 2003 saw the return of the giant ceiling-suspended great blue whale. Spruced up (and tweaked for accuracy) after a two-year absence, it presides over the fully renovated **Milstein Hall of Ocean Life**. The **Ross Hall of Meteorites** was also relaunched in 2003. While the 34-ton Ahnighito (a little souvenir picked up by Admiral Perry from Greenland) is still the centerpiece, the entire installation benefits from the fresh interpretation.

There are always two or three large-scale temporary exhibits on at AMNH, some focusing on currently hot scientific topics; most charge an additional fee, including the famed **Butterfly Conservatory** (open early October through February). The museum has an ongoing program of lectures, films, plays, workshops, and concerts. Free Museum Highlights Tours assemble at the second-floor information desk approximately every hour.

Two gift shops, one just for children, and several more mini-stores all over the building offer an international assortment of crafts, microscopes, puppets, books, petrified wood, and other surprises. There are three restaurants: the **Under the Whale** (cocktails and snacks), the **Garden Cafe** (lunch and dinner in a greenhouse setting), and **Dinersaurus** (cafeteria). Limited paid parking is available in the museum lot on West 81st Street. ♦ Admission, plus additional fee for special exhibits, IMAX, and the Rose Center. Daily. Central Park W (at W 79th St). Note: You will be on the museum's second floor once you enter. 769.5100. www.amnh.org

29 Frederick Phineas and Sandra Priest Rose Center for Earth and Space

While the beloved old **Hayden Planetarium** (opened in 1935) was demolished to make way for the state-of-the-art **Rose Center**, few who visit the stunning facility (also known as the Hayden Planetarium) that replaced it in 2000 are heard to complain. Designed by **James Stewart Polshek & Partners**, the incredible glowing 95-foot-high glass cube that encases—and reveals—the 2,000-ton Hayden Sphere within is in fact the largest suspended glass curtain wall in the US. Star shows are provided by the Museum-designed Zeiss Universarium MkIX projector, with 9,000 fiber-optically projected stars and 84 deep-space objects, and computer-manipulated imagery to create displays of the latest discoveries in planetary and space science from unique perspectives. ♦ Admission. Daily. Call or check web for show schedule. W 81st St (between Central Park W and Columbus Ave). 769.5200. www.amnh.org ♿

30 Apthorp Apartments

Designed by **Clinton & Russell** and built in 1908, this is the best of the three big West Side courtyard buildings (the **Belnord** on West 86th Street and **Astor Court** on Broadway between West 89th and West 90th Streets are the others). The ornate ironwork here is especially wonderful; and if you can sneak a peak into the courtyard garden, a real treat awaits. The Apthorp was built by William Waldorf Astor, who owned much of the land in the area, and was named for the man who owned the site in 1763. ♦ 2207 Broadway (between W 78th and W 79th Sts)

31 La Caridad 78

★$ Since La Caridad expanded, you may not have to wait at this popular and inexpensive Cuban/Chinese eatery. Standards such as roasted pork, shredded beef, and roast chicken with black beans and yellow rice are the standouts. ♦ Cuban/Chinese ♦ Daily, lunch, dinner, and late-night meals. No credit cards accepted. 2199 Broadway (at W 78th St). 874.2780

32 Stand-Up NY

Up-and-coming and established merchants of the one-liner play this comedy club. ♦ Cover, minimum. Su-Th, show at 9PM; F, Sa, shows at 8PM, 10PM, and 12:30AM. Reservations required. 236 W 78th St (at Broadway). 595.0850 ♿

33 West End Collegiate Church/Collegiate School for Boys

Designed in 1892 by **Robert W. Gibson**, the original orange brick, tan terra-cotta, and red-tile structure here was built for use as a church and school for the Dutch Reformed church, which dates back in New York to 1625 and the founding days of New Amsterdam. A 17th-century butcher's guildhall in Holland served as the prototype for the striking stepped-gable structure. The school soon outgrew the site and gradually expanded to adjacent buildings, including a 1960s extension on West 78th Street and a 1914 polychrome apartment house at the corner of West 78th Street and West End Avenue. Arguably the oldest independent school in the US, it is today a highly regarded private institution for grades K-12, known as the Collegiate School for Boys. ♦ Church: 368 West End Ave (at W 77th St). 787.1566. School (entrance): 260 W 78th St (at West End Ave). 812.8500 ♿

34 Hotel Belleclaire

$ A young **Emery Roth** built this Art Nouveau landmark as one of New York's newly fashionable apartment hotels in 1903; Maxim Gorky scandalized it in 1906 when he checked in with a woman not his wife. Today, after a 2004 face-lift, it's a 189-room refuge with modern flair; some rooms include touches such as cushioned headboards upholstered in red leather. Rates start at reasonable but rise quickly; sharing a bath brings the price down. ♦ 250 W 77th St (at Broadway). 362.7700, 877/468.3522. www.hotelbelleclaire.com

35 343–357 West End Avenue

Built in 1891 and designed by **Lamb & Rich**, this complete block-front on West End and around both corners is a lively, well-ordered collection typical of Victorian town houses, and the only West Side block without high-rises between West End Avenue and Riverside Drive. (Rumor has it that Mayor Jimmy Walker's mistress lived at West 76th Street and Broadway, and the block was supposedly zoned to protect her river view.) The variety of shapes and materials—gables, bays, dormers, and limestone, red, and tan brick—is clearly under control, resulting in a stylish, humorous energy with no dissonance. ♦ Between W 76th and W 77th Sts

36 Milburn Hotel

$ Handsome prewar apartment buildings are common in this residential area, and the **Milburn** was one of them until a refurbishing converted it to a gracious 70-suite hotel. All the traditionally furnished rooms have high-speed Wi-Fi Internet access and fully equipped kitchens with microwaves. It ain't fancy (and it can be a bit frayed), but it's still an OK choice for businesspeople, families, and long-term visitors. There is an on-site exercise room and free use of a 25-meter indoor swimming pool nearby. ♦ 242 W 76th St (between Broadway and West End Ave). 362.1006, 800/833.9622; fax 721.5476. www.milburnhotel.com

37 Ruby Foo's

★ $$ Basically, this is an updated version of the old Trader Vic's concept: Asian food geared openly to American palates in an Oriental-fantasy décor. The bar area and upstairs dining room feature lacquered tables and walls, gilt Buddhas and mahjong tiles, all linked to the ground level by a grandiose staircase. The menu features sushi, dim sum, and some extravagant attempts at fusion: Thai basil-curried salmon with lemongrass risotto and Asian vegetables; wok-seared wasabi pork with stir-fried vegetables and black-bean sauce. Noise level: high; reservations recommended. ♦ Pan-Asian ♦ Daily, lunch, dinner, and late-night meals. 2182 Broadway (between W 76th and W 77th Sts). 724.6700. Also at 1626 Broadway (at W 49th St). 489.5600

38 Equinox Fitness Club

Ideal for visitors, this cutting-edge megagym opens its doors for one-time-use admission. A huge success since its 1991 debut, it is as famous for its social scene as for its unsurpassed fitness programs. A killer 10-week program is available for those who plan to stay on in New York. ♦ Daily. 344 Amsterdam Ave (between W 76th and W 77th Sts). 721.4200. Also at numerous locations throughout the city

39 Jacques-Imo's NYC

★★$$ Across from the American Museum of Natural History, a New Orleans legend has made itself comfortable and plans to stay awhile, to the satisfaction of Cajun aficionados and fried-chicken connoisseurs. Stop by after a visit to the Hall of North American Mammals to enjoy an insistently authentic menu (shrimp and alligator sausage), addictive appetizers (fried oysters in spicy garlic sauce), and a vibe virtually assured to let *les bon temps rouler*. ♦ Cajun/Creole. ♦ M, F, dinner; Sa, Su, brunch and dinner. 366 Columbus Ave (at W 77th St). 799.0150

40 GreenFlea Market

The emphasis at this giant indoor/outdoor Columbus Avenue market is on new, used, and vintage clothing and accessories, with a nice mix of antiques, collectibles, and furniture. Every Sunday the joint is packed with vendors (and visitors), purveying items you will surely need once you spy them. Favorites include Serita's fun vintage eyeglass frames; Michael Sheafe's classic toaster collection (all freshly rewired and ready to pop; www.toastercentral.com); Richard's "on-the-spot" hand-set letterpress cards (your choice of recycled cereal-box stock, wood, or good old card stock; www.usbcards.net); and Karin Grasso's jewelry enterprise (www.kjewels.com). GreenFlea markets are held on New York City public school grounds and the cool thing is, profits go to programs for the students of those schools. ♦ Free. Su, 10AM-6PM, year-round. IS 44, Columbus Ave (between W 76th and W 77th Sts). Also at Saturday location (11AM-7PM), outdoors/seasonal only: PS 41, Greenwich Ave (between W 10th and W 11th Sts). Free. GreenFlea: 239.3025. www.greenfleamarkets.com ♿

41 Isabella's

★★$$ Well-liked for its simple, pleasant décor and inviting sidewalk café, this place offers such Mediterranean-inspired New American dishes as sesame-crusted big-eye tuna with soba noodles; a selection of grilled dishes, including veal chops and chicken; and special pastas, like a nice asparagus ravioli, all of which are good. ♦ New American ♦ M-Sa, lunch and dinner; Su, brunch, lunch, and dinner. Reservations recommended. 359 Columbus Ave (at W 77th St). 724.2100

41 Kenneth Cole

Shoes and accessories by the witty, self-promoting designer are sold in this shop. Copies of his print ads–which address the political and social issues of the moment–are displayed along the right-hand wall as you enter. ♦ Daily. 353 Columbus Ave (between W 76th and W 77th Sts). 873.2061. Also at numerous locations throughout the city

42 Scaletta

★★$$$ A large dinner menu, fast and efficient service, and excellent pasta and antipasto (especially the prosciutto) are highlights of this lovely Northern Italian restaurant. Try the specials of the day, which might include risotto with wild mushrooms and veal *sorrentino* (sautéed with eggplant and mozzarella). Desserts are of the rich Italian variety, and the espresso is good, too. ♦ Northern Italian ♦ Daily, dinner. Reservations recommended. 50 W 77th St (between Central Park W and Columbus Ave). 769.9191

Broadway, originating in Lower Manhattan at Bowling Green and ending in Albany, is one of the world's longest streets, at 150 miles. It is officially designated as Highway 9.

43 New-York Historical Society

The Society is housed in a fine neoclassical French building, the central portion of which was designed by **York & Sawyer** in 1908, with unimaginative 1938 additions by **Walker & Gillette**. During the three-year tenure of Columbia University professor Kenneth T. Jackson as president (his term ended in 2004), the Society expanded significantly and took on a strong role in interpreting contemporary New York City history. Even before 9/11 it had focused on becoming the preeminent institution for the collection and display of items that help us grasp their economic and cultural as well as historic importance. (And if you're wondering about the hyphen in "New-York Historical Society," it's a point of pride for the museum: When it was founded in 1804, everybody spelled New York that way.)

In 2000, the **Henry Luce III Center for the Study of American Culture** was founded. Occupying the entire fourth floor, it is rich with such Americana as wall-to-wall silver, rare maps, antique toys, Tiffany lamps, watercolors by John James Audubon, and landscapes by the again-popular Frederic Church and the rest of the Hudson River boys; it also has stunning 17th-, 18th-, and 19th-century furniture arranged in chronological order. The Society beat out the New York Public Library in 2003 for the rights to house the important 40,000-document **Gilder-Lehrman Collection** of American history.

The main floors of the Society were home to a powerful series of shows on the building of the World Trade Center and the aftermath of its destruction. Changing exhibitions in recent years have often looked back, but with modern themes–like "Women Pioneers in Architecture and Design Photography," "Times Square in Pictures," or the architecture of Cass Gilbert–that often draw on their extensive photograph and prints collection. The Society's library is one of the major reference libraries of American history in this country; its gift shop is great fun and well-stocked with books, cards, and games. There are concerts, lectures, films, and walking tours. ♦ Admission. Museum and shop: Tu-Su, 1PM-6PM. 170 Central Park W (between W 76th and W 77th Sts). 873.3400. www.nyhistory.org ♿

44 CENTRAL PARK WEST/76TH STREET HISTORIC DISTRICT

This district, designated a historic area in 1973, comprises the blocks on Central Park West between West 75th and West 77th Streets and about half of West 76th Street. It includes a variety of row houses built at the turn of the century; the neo-Grecian **Nos. 21-31** by **George M. Walgrove** are the earliest, and the Baroque **Nos. 8-10** by **John H. Duncan** are the most recent. Of interest as well are the **Kenilworth** apartment building (151 Central Park W), designed in 1908 by **Townsend, Steinle & Haskell**, noteworthy for its convex mansard roof and highly ornamented limestone, and the Oxfordish **Universalist Church of New York** (W 76th St and Central Park W), designed in 1898 by **William A. Potter**. Also included in the designated area is **44 West 77th Street**, designed in 1909 by **Harde & Short**, a Gothic-style building used as artists' studios; much of the ornament was removed in 1944. ♦ Bounded by Central Park W and Columbus Ave, and W 75th and W 77th Sts

45 CITARELLA

This retail fish store hit the big-time with its elaborate fish-sculpture displays, which, in the boom-boom 1980s, took the art of window dressing to new heights. Though super-fresh fish are still the feature inside, the windows are no more, and the shop that Mike Citarella founded in 1912 up in Sugar Hill in Harlem is now more of an all-around high-end grocer. The take-out dishes are OK, and their breads are nice. ♦ Daily. 2135 Broadway (at W 75th St). 874.0383. Also at 1313 Third Ave (between E 75th and E 76th Sts). 874.0383; 424 Sixth Ave (between W Ninth and W 10th Sts). 874.0383; and 461 W 125th St (between Morningside and Amsterdam Aves)

45 FAIRWAY

Residents swear by this all-purpose market, which offers produce, excellent cheeses, charcuterie, coffee, chocolates, baked goods, breads, prepared foods, and smoked fish. Avoiding the crowds here is something of a local sport; the most promising strategy entails arriving early in the morning or after 8PM. You'll find the **Fairway Café** upstairs. It's a congenial neighborhood spot for breakfast and lunch. The white tablecloths come out in the evening, when the space becomes a steak house. ♦ Daily. 2127 Broadway (between W 74th and W 75th Sts). 595.1888. ♿ Also at 2328 12th Ave (at W 132nd St). 234.3883; and 480-500 Van Brunt St, Red Hook, Brooklyn. 718/694.6868 ♿

46 BEACON THEATRE

Special films, dance groups, and foreign performing arts groups, as well as mainstream soul and rock artists, are featured in this 1927 **Walter Ahlschlager** 2,700-seat theater. Some say the **Rambusch Studio**'s Greco-Deco interior—frayed and worn as it is—is second only to **Radio City**'s. ♦ 2124 Broadway (between W 74th and W 75th Sts). Info/Hotline: 465.6500. www.beacontheatrenyc.com

47 JOSIE'S

★★$$ This popular place serves food for the health conscious: The grains and produce are organic, the water is filtered, and all dishes are dairy-free. But healthful doesn't mean boring here—the creative cuisine features such dishes as ginger-grilled calamari with pineapple–red pepper salsa and sweet-potato ravioli with Gulf shrimp, sweet corn, and roasted peppers in white wine and leek sauce. There are a couple of unrepentantly sinful desserts, including lemon-ribbon ice-cream pie. ♦ American ♦ Daily, dinner. Reservations recommended. 300 Amsterdam Ave (at W 74th St). 769.1212. Also at 565 Third Ave (at E 37th St). 490.1558

48 SHARK BAR/RESTAURANT

★$$ Within a swanky setting—dark, split-level, candlelit—is a beautiful and well-dressed crowd, including more than a few models and music-industry types. Among the inventive appetizers that shouldn't be missed is the soul roll (pastry filled with vegetables, chicken, and rice). Otherwise, skip the Cajun side of the menu and stick to classic soul-food dishes—barbecued ribs, fried chicken, collard greens, black-eyed peas, macaroni and cheese, yams, and sweet potato pie. ♦ There's a satisfying mix on the bar menu as well. ♦ Soul food/Cajun ♦ Restaurant: M-Sa, dinner; Sa, Su, brunch and dinner. Reservations recommended. Bar: M, Tu, dinner; W-F, lunch and dinner; Sa, Su, brunch and dinner. 307 Amsterdam Ave (between W 74th and W 75th Sts). 874.8500

49 MUGHLAI

★$$ For Indian food that never errs on the too-spicy side, this is the place. The tandoori here is best, and the mango chutney served with the curry is quite good. Desserts are uninspired, except for the highly recommended rice pudding with rose water. ♦ Indian ♦ M-F, dinner; Sa, Su, brunch and dinner. Reservations recommended. 320 Columbus Ave (at W 75th St). 724.6363

50 Pappardella

★$$ This is a popular destination for pasta and *secondi piatti* (second, or main, dishes) with a Tuscan accent. Try a thin-crusted pizza with a glass of Chianti, ravioli with mushrooms, or *bistecca fiorentina* (grilled T-bone steak marinated in olive oil, rosemary, and a touch of garlic, served with sautéed vegetables), and relish the escape from the bustle of Columbus Avenue (or not: there's an outdoor seating area too). ♦ Italian ♦ M-F, lunch and dinner; Sa, Su, brunch and dinner. Reservations recommended. 316 Columbus Ave (at W 75th St). 595.7996

51 San Remo

In contrast to the streamlined **Century**, about 10 blocks south at West 63rd Street (see page 289), and **Majestic** (No. 115 Central Park West, at West 72nd Street) apartment buildings by **Irwin S. Chanin**, **Emery Roth**'s twin towers, constructed in 1930, are capped with Roman temples surmounted by finials. ♦ 145-146 Central Park W (between W 74th and W 75th Sts)

52 Ansonia Hotel

Designed by **Graves & Duboy** and built in 1904, this Belle Epoque masterpiece, bristling with ornament, balconies, towers, and dormers, is one of the great apartment buildings in New York. (As with the **Hotel des Artistes**, this was never a hotel at all; the appellation is from the French *hôtel de ville,* meaning town hall.) The thick walls and floors required for fireproofing have made the 16-story cooperative apartment building a favorite of musicians. Among those who have lived here are Enrico Caruso, Arturo Toscanini, Florenz Ziegfeld, Sol Hurok, Theodore Dreiser, and George Herman (Babe) Ruth. ♦ 2109 Broadway (between W 73rd and W 74th Sts)

53 2100 Broadway

A Florentine palazzo seems like an appropriate model for a bank. This one, an Apple branch, designed in 1928 by the masters **York & Sawyer** (who also designed the **Federal Reserve Bank of New York**), skillfully contains a proper rectangular banking hall within the trapezoidal building dictated by the site. The special decorative ironwork is by Samuel Yellin Studio. ♦ 2100 Broadway (between W 73rd and W 74th Sts) ♿

> **America's first patent was issued in New York City on 31 July 1790. It was granted to Samuel Hopkins for a process that involved the making and purifying of potash, an ingredient used in soap making. The patent was signed by President George Washington and Secretary of State Thomas Jefferson.**

54 Verdi Square/Sherman Square

Another one of those places where Broadway crosses the city grid to form a bow tie, not a square, the south end (**Sherman Square**) is occupied by an **IRT Subway Control House**, which was designed by **Heins & LaFarge** in 1904. This is one of two surviving ornate entrances to the original IRT subway line (the other is at the **Battery Park Control House** in Lower Manhattan). Note the stylish detailing of the neo-Dutch, somewhat Baroque shed. Now note the new shed on the north side (**Verdi Square**) of West 72nd Street. Long overdue for expansion, the much-trafficked subway stop finally got some additional space with this **Gruzen Samton** and **Richard Dattner**-designed period-sensitive (but oddly bloated-looking) structure—completed at last in 2003. ♦ Broadway and Amsterdam Ave

55 Gray's Papaya

$ Nowhere else does a dollar buy so much. A cast of characters frequents this supercheap round-the-clock hot-dog stand that brags its tube steaks are "tastier than filet mignon" and its papaya drink is "a definite aid to digestion." Unless you've got a cast-iron stomach, you'll need all the help you can get. The fruit-flavored refreshments are definitely worth a stop. ♦ Hot dogs ♦ Daily, 24 hours. 2090 Broadway (at W 72nd St). 799.0243. Also at 539 Eighth Ave (at W 37th St). 904.1588; 402 Sixth Ave (at W Eighth St). 260.3532; and other locations throughout the city

56 Acker Merrall & Condit

Experts on most any fermented fruit of the vine—or grain, for that matter—these established liquor merchants boast a reputation for good service. The elegant store has a wide-ranging stock of high-quality wine, sake, and whiskeys and more, from around the globe. Tastings and events. ♦ M-Sa. 160 W 72nd St (between Columbus and Amsterdam Aves). 787.1700 ♿

56 Blades Board & Skate

Rent a pair of rollerblades and protective gear, then set off for a day of blading in the park. The blades—as well as ice skates, skateboards, snowboards, helmets, and accessories—are also for sale. ♦ Daily. 156 W 72nd St (between Columbus and Amsterdam Aves). 787.3911. Also at 659 Broadway (between Bleecker and E Third Sts). 477.7350; and Manhattan Mall, 901 Sixth Ave (at W 33rd St). 646/733.2738

57 Fine & Schapiro

★$$ This long-established classic kosher delicatessen makes one nostalgic for the days before cholesterol counts. There's a salt-free corner on the menu, but if you need to consult it, you're probably in the wrong place. ♦ Jewish deli ♦ Daily, lunch and dinner. 138 W 72nd St (between Columbus and Amsterdam Aves). 877.2874

58 Dallas BBQ

★$ The barbecued ribs and chicken are decent enough for a quick fix, and who could argue with the price? But the big draw for many of the neighborhood fans of this large, informal, and noisy restaurant is the huge loaf of greasy onion rings. ♦ Barbecue ♦ Daily, lunch, dinner, and late-night meals. No reservations. 27 W 72nd St (between Central Park W and Columbus Ave). 873.2004. Also at numerous locations throughout the city

59 Dakota Apartments

Built in 1884, this was one of the first luxury apartment houses in the city (along with the **Osborne** on West 57th Street and **34 Gramercy Park East**). The building was christened when someone remarked to its owner, Edward Clark, president of the Singer Sewing Company, that it was so far out of town, "it might as well be in Dakota Territory." Clark, not without a sense of humor, went on to instruct the architect, **Henry J. Hardenbergh**, to embellish the building with symbols of the Wild West; arrowheads, sheaves of wheat, and ears of corn appear in bas-relief on the building's interior and exterior façades. (Hardenbergh later designed **The Plaza Hotel**.) The apartment building is a highly original masonry mass with echoes of Romanesque and German Renaissance architecture. A good cleaning has revealed the rich, creamy brownstone of the façade. Victorian details and miscellaneous pieces sprout at every turn—turrets, gables, oriels, dormers, and pinnacles. The top three floors, once servants' quarters and a playroom and gymnasium for children, are now some of the most prized apartments in Manhattan. The building, unfortunately synonymous with John Lennon's murder, had already gained notability as the setting for the film *Rosemary's Baby* and as the home of celebs past and present, including Boris Karloff, Judy Garland, Lauren Bacall, Leonard Bernstein, Rex Reed, Roberta Flack, Yoko Ono, and Kim Basinger. ♦ 1 W 72nd St (at Central Park W)

60 The Dorilton

When this Beaux Arts masterpiece, designed by **Janes & Leo**, was completed in 1902, critic Montgomery Schuyler was so displeased with its design that he wrote the following in *Architectural Record*: "The incendiary qualities of the edifice may be referred, first to violence of color, then to violence of scale, then to violence of 'thingness,' to the multiplicity and importunity of the details." When the Landmarks Preservation Commission granted this apartment building its landmark status in 1974, they described it as "exceptionally handsome." ♦ 171 W 71st St (at Broadway)

61 Harry's Burrito Junction

★$ If **Lincoln Center** tickets have busted your budget or if you happen to be in the market for some nachos, this is the place. A young crowd that fills the three-level space decorated with memorabilia from the 1960s seems to have a special fondness for the footlong bay burrito, oozing with black beans and shredded beef. ♦ Mexican ♦ Daily, lunch and dinner. 241 Columbus Ave (at W 71st St). 580.9494.

61 Café La Fortuna

★$ A mainstay of the neighborhood for decades, this pleasant, unassuming café serves excellent Italian coffees and a mouthwatering array of traditional Italian pastries and other sweets. The garden in the back is an ideal respite from summer heat. Sandwiches, antipasti, and salads are also available. ♦ Café ♦ Tu-Su, lunch, dinner, and late-night meals. No credit cards accepted. 69 W 71st St (between Central Park W and Columbus Ave). 724.5846

62 Café Luxembourg

★★★$$$ A people watcher's Art Deco brasserie, the zinc-topped bar here draws a stylish international crowd, and the menu is a carefully edited mix of French, Italian, and regional American offerings. Order marinated octopus, lemon risotto with fresh asparagus and Parmesan, Provençal vegetable tart, roasted leg of lamb, duck cassoulet, or striped bass with fresh herbs, garlic, and oil. For dessert, try the profiteroles with chocolate or vanilla ice cream. ♦ French bistro ♦ M-F breakfast, lunch, dinner, and late-night meals; Sa, Su, brunch, dinner, and late-night meals. Prix fixe available. Reservations recommended. 200 W 70th St (at Amsterdam Ave). 873.7411 ♿

63 Epices du Traiteur

★★$$ This tiny, friendly Tunisian restaurant hits the West Side like a beam of Mediterranean sunshine. Menu offerings, while diverse, are uniformly light and delicious, from the signature salade Epice, a tangy mélange of romaine, Caesar-style dressing, pine nuts, egg, and orange slices, to the flavorful pasta and seafood dishes. For dessert, opt for the homemade mousse au chocolat or a slice of the lighter but equally ambrosial mixed berry tart, flown in from France. ♦ Mediterranean ♦ Daily, dinner. 103 W 70th St (between Columbus Ave and Broadway). 579.5904

64 Congregation Shearith Israel

The oldest Jewish congregation in the US—and for 170 years the *only* one in New York City—is housed here in the fifth space it has occupied since its founding in 1654 by 23 settlers of mostly Spanish and Portuguese origin. Behind **Arnold W. Brunner**'s 1897 neoclassical façade, the interior is lit by Tiffany windows and fitted with several elements from the first synagogue building (built in 1730 on Mill Street in lower Manhattan), including the reader's desk and Sabbath lamp. ♦8 W 70th St (at Central Park W). 873.0300. www.shearithisrael.org

65 Lincoln Square Synagogue

Designed in 1970 by **Hausman & Rosenberg**, this is a mannered, curved building with fins and rectangular block attached, all clad in travertine, à la neighboring **Lincoln Center**. Begun as a small apartment nearby in the 1960s, the modern Orthodox congregation has grown rapidly—so much so that a new four-story, glass-fronted building (by **Cetra/ Ruddy Architects**), just a block to the south, was commissioned; it is expected to be completed by early 2009. ♦ 200 Amsterdam Ave (at W 69th St). 874.6100

66 Christ and St. Stephen's Church

This charming country church, built in 1880 to the designs of **William H. Day** and altered in 1897 by **J.D. Fouguet**, is holding up well in the big city. ♦ 120 W 69th St (between Columbus Ave and Broadway). 787.2755

67 Telepan

★★★$$$ Chef/owner Bill Telepan brings experience in a Michelin three-star kitchen, as well as stints at Le Bernardin, Le Cirque, and Judson Grill, to this soothing pale-green space where seasonal menus may feature house-smoked brook trout, foie gras doughnuts, or lemon-thyme-crusted cod. Telepan leans heavily on local producers, so you'll likely know which upstate farm yielded the sheep's milk ricotta for your blintzes at brunch. ♦ New American ♦ M, Tu, dinner; W-F, lunch and dinner; Sa, Su, brunch and dinner. Reservations recommended. 72 W 69th St (between Central Park W and Columbus Ave). 580.4300. www.telepan-ny.com

68 Loews Lincoln Square

Another New York multiplex, yes, but give them an "A" for effort. Each of the 10 screening rooms is meant to be reminiscent of an old-time movie palace (that would be in décor, not scale). Good-sized screens with decent sightlines are a draw, though the seating's gotten a bit tattered over time. The centerpiece of the complex is the 3-D IMAX theater with an eight-story-high screen (the largest in the US); reclining chairs and a sleek wraparound headset guarantee virtual immersion. ♦ Daily. Broadway and W 68th St. 336.5000 ♿

69 La Boîte en Bois

★★$$$ A few steps down and far from the madding crowd on Columbus Avenue, this charming (read: tiny) French bistro with a country atmosphere and Provençal menu offers fine fish soup, roast chicken with herbs, and roasted salmon glazed with honey mustard. ♦ French bistro ♦ M, dinner; Tu-Sa, lunch and dinner; Su, brunch and dinner. Pre-theater prix fixe available. Reservations required. No credit cards accepted. 75 W 68th St (between Central Park W and Columbus Ave). 874.2705

70 Vince & Eddie's

★★★$$ Locals pack this rustic-looking, intimate room—especially before a **Lincoln Center** performance. The menu changes seasonally, but such dishes as braised lamb shank with Michigan cherry sauce and pan-roasted chicken with spinach and lentils are available all year. Fish dishes—like grilled black bass with thyme pesto—are a favorite, and vegetable purées, including turnip and pumpkin, may sound humble but are silky and rich and not to be missed. ♦ American ♦ M-F, lunch and dinner; Sa, Su, brunch and dinner. Reservations recommended. 70 W 68th St (between Central Park W and Columbus Ave). 721.0068

70 67 Wine & Spirits

With its extensive selection of wines and spirits, this store is well known for its diversity, fair prices, and knowledgeable staff. A good place for half-bottles, it also offers a big selection of related paraphernalia—from wine and champagne glasses to books on wine, decanters, and even cooling units. ♦ M-Sa. 179 Columbus Ave (at W 68th St). 724.6767

71 Merkin Concert Hall

Concert series are held here within the Kaufman Center complex (which comprises the marvelous Merkin Hall and two music schools), including an eclectic range of ensemble programs and contemporary and chamber music. Fine acoustics and a timeless modern blond-wood interior design are the hallmarks of the 457-seat hall. The structure, known as the Goodman House, was built to an original 1978 Modernist design by **Ashok Bhavnani**; **Robert A.M. Stern** took the helm for a 2007-2008 renovation that served to enhance the façade, lobby area, and ADA accessibility, while preserving the acoustics and sprucing up the seating. ♦ 129 W 67th St (between Broadway and Amsterdam Ave). Closed for renovation until spring 2008. Box office: 501.3330. www.kaufman-center.org ♿

72 Reebok Sports Club/NY

This six-level megaclub is the most extravagant of urban country clubs. Over 140,000 square feet of tracks, courts, sun decks, pools, and locker rooms are outfitted with $55 million worth of state-of-the-art equipment. Membership is steep, but where else in town will you find a 45-foot rockclimbing wall or a downhill-skiing simulator? They don't offer day passes, but members may bring guests. Their street-level **Concept Store** carries all of Reebok's latest gear for feet and bod. ♦ Daily. 160 Columbus Ave (at W 67th St). 362.6800. Store: 160 Columbus Ave (between W 67th and W 68th Sts). 595.1480

73 Hotel des Artistes

An early studio building designed by **George Mort Pollard** in 1913 specifically for artists—duplexes with double-height main spaces—this is now one of the more lavish co-ops around. It has always attracted note-worthy tenants, among them Isadora Duncan, Alexander Woollcott, Norman Rockwell, Noël Coward, and Howard Chandler Christy. ♦ 1 W 67th St (between Central Park W and Columbus Ave)

Within the Hotel des Artistes:

Café des Artistes

★★★★$$$ The West Side's most charming and romantic restaurant was originally, as the name suggests, intended for artists. Light streams through the leaded-glass windows by day, and the six colorful murals of capricious female nudes, painted in 1934 by **Howard Chandler Christy**, are an enduring visual feast. The restaurant's serene trappings and legacy of quality have always drawn a high-powered crowd. Owner George Lang updates the menu and the well-chosen and well-priced wine list daily as well as seasonally—his renowned asparagus festival occurs every May and June. But regular dishes you shouldn't miss include the salmon four ways (smoked, poached, gravlax, and *tartare*), duck confit, fresh Dover sole meunière, and rack of lamb with basil crust. Save room for the hot fudge napoleon, or if your sweet tooth can take it, The Great Dessert Plate or "Chocolatissimo for Two." The famous weekend brunch is a must. ♦ French ♦ M-F, dinner; Sa, Su, brunch and dinner. Prix fixe available. Reservations required; jacket preferred after 5PM. 877.3500 ♿

74 First Battery Armory, New York National Guard/ American Broadcasting Company (ABC)

Today, some of **ABC**'s TV studios hide behind this fortress façade, designed in 1901 by **Horgan & Slattery** and altered in 1978 by **Kohn Pedersen Fox**. Kohn Pedersen is responsible as well for most of the other ABC offices and studios clustered in this neighborhood, including their overbearing 23-story headquarters at **No. 77** (just down the block) and the more pleasantly streamlined glass-and-brick **WABC Channel 7** building (around the corner on Columbus Avenue). ♦ 56 W 66th St (between Central Park W and Columbus Ave)

75 American Folk Art Museum/ Eva and Morris Feld Gallery at Lincoln Square

Until the **American Folk Art Museum** moved to its permanent building on West 53rd Street in 2001, this gallery was its sole presence in the city. The space is still run by the museum and tends to feature contemporary and historic quilt shows on changing themes, like African quilts or double-wedding-band designs. The gallery holds regular lectures and workshops and has an adjacent gift shop that's worth a visit. ♦ Voluntary contribution. Tu-Sa, noon-7:30PM; Su, noon-5PM. 2 Lincoln Sq (between W 65th and W 66th Sts). 595.9533. ♿ Main museum: 45 W 53rd St (between Fifth and Sixth Aves). 265.1040. www.folkartmuseum.org

76 Shun Lee West

★★★$$$ Long a favorite of the **Lincoln Center** crowd, this restaurant does many regional Chinese cuisines justice. Try the steamed dumplings, beggar's chicken (baked in clay), or prawns in black-bean sauce. The vast dining room is dramatic—black banquettes and brightly colored dragon lanterns—though not as fancy as the prices. In the second dining room, the lower-priced **Shun Lee Café** features dim sum. ♦ Chinese ♦ M-F, lunch and dinner; Sa, Su, brunch and dinner. Reservations required. 43 W 65th St (between Central Park W and Columbus Ave).

595.8895. Also at **Shun Lee Palace**, 155 E 55th St (between Third and Lexington Aves). 371.8844

77 Lincoln Center for the Performing Arts

Robert Moses, urban planner and New York powerbroker, initiated the idea of a center for the city's major performing arts institutions in the 1950s, and this conglomeration of travertine halls came slowly into existence. Massed on the **Jose Robertson Plaza** above the street, the buildings have been called an Acropolis, but the arrangement around the fountain is actually a static version of Michelangelo's Capitoline Hill in Rome. Although the main theaters all take their formal cues from images of classical architecture, critics claim they never really come together as a whole and remain, at best, individual *tours de trite.* Although **Wallace K. Harrison** coordinated the project and designed the master plan, individual architects designed the buildings in the 1960s. In 2004, Lincoln Center took a great leap south (to Columbus Circle) and built **Frederick P. Rose Hall** for their Jazz at Lincoln Center programming (see page 291). Today, great changes are afoot for the West 65th Street portion of the complex, affecting, most significantly, **Alice Tully Hall**, the **Walter Reade Theater**, and the **Juilliard School.** The concept, as designed by architects **Diller Scofidio + Renfro,** in collaboration with **FX Fowle Architects,** is to better integrate the venues on the north side of West 65th with the main campus. See Tour Information on page 288. ♦ Bounded by Columbus Ave, Broadway, Amsterdam Ave (10th Ave), and W 62nd and W 66th Sts. **CenterCharge**: 721.6500. www.lincolncenter.org

At Lincoln Center for the Performing Arts:

Avery Fisher Hall

Standing opposite the **State Theater**, this building was designed in 1966 by **Max Abramovitz**. Originally **Philharmonic Hall**, it has been reconstructed several times in the hopes of improving the sound, and a final touch-up in 1992 turned it into an acoustic gem. The stabile in the foyer is by Richard Lippold. **The New York Philharmonic** is in residence here from September through May. Music director Loren Maazel is the latest in an illustrious line that has included Kurt Masur, Zubin Mehta, Leonard Bernstein, Arturo Toscanini, and Leopold Stokowski. The informal Mostly Mozart concerts are held in July and August; Great Performances concerts are held September through May. Both are presentations of Lincoln Center Productions. The Philharmonic's Young People's Concerts have been letting kids in on the motives behind the music since 1898; performances take place four times a year. Don't miss the orchestra's regularly scheduled open rehearsals, which usually occur on Thursday a 9:45AM. In the lobby are a small gift shop (580.4356) and the **Espresso Bar.** ♦ Broadway and W 65th St. 875.5030 ♿

Within Avery Fisher Hall:

Panevino Ristorante

★$$ This is a pleasant place for dinner or just drinks. During the summer, the café spills out onto the plaza. For dinner, try carpaccio, mozza rella with roasted tomatoes, rigatoni with eggplant and mozzarella, grilled chicken paillard with balsamic vinegar, or grilled salmo with seasoned olive butter. ♦ Italian ♦ Lunch on Avery Fisher Hall matinée days; M-Sa, dinner. Reservations recommended. 874.7000

Metropolitan Opera House

Home to the **Metropolitan Opera Company**, the plaza's magnificent centerpiece (designed by **Wallace K. Harrison**) opened in 1966 with Samuel Barber's *Antony and Cleopatra.* Behin the thin, 10-story colonnade and sheer glass walls, two wonderful murals by Marc Chagall beam out onto the plaza. The interior is filled with a red-carpeted lobby, a dramatic staircas lit by exquisite Austrian crystal chandeliers, an an equally plush auditorium. The opera seaso from mid-September to April, leaves the stage available for visiting performers and companies, including the **American Ballet Theater**, during the rest of the year. Ticketholders may dine at the **Grand Tier** restaurant (799.3400. Contemporary American), Sa and matinée days, lunch; M-Sa, dinner and intermission. ♦ Off Columbus Ave (between W 62nd and W 65th Sts). 362.6000 ♿

Within the Metropolitan Opera House:

Metropolitan Opera Shop

Imaginative opera- and music-related gifts and clothing are sold here, most of them exclusive to this shop. Pick up hard-to-find books, records, posters, and libretti, with proceeds going to the **Metropolitan Opera**. ♦ Daily. Next to the Met box office. 580.4090

New York State Theater

Located on the plaza's south side, this theate was designed in 1964 by **Philip Johnson** anc **Richard Foster**. At the culmination of a serie of increasingly grand entrance spaces is a striking four-story foyer with balconies at ever level, a pair of large white marble sculptures by Elie Nadelman, and a gold-leaf ceiling. The rich red and gold auditorium was designed fo both ballet and musical theater. From 1964 t 1968, under the artistic directorship of Richard Rodgers of the **Music Theater of Lincoln Center**, revivals of musical classics were staged here. Now it's home to the **New York City Ballet** and the **New York City Oper**

The current artistic director is Paul Kellogg, who took the reins following the tenure of Christopher Keene (who in turn was preceded by the late, beloved Beverly Sills). The annually sold-out *Nutcracker* season runs the entire month of December. Note the diamond-shaped floodlights surrounding the building. When the NYC Opera is in the house, ticketholders may dine at the American bistro-style **Promenade Café** (877.1652); it's open then for dinner and intermission snacks only. ♦ Ballet: late Nov-Feb; Apr-June. **Opera:** July-Nov. Columbus Ave (between W 62nd and W 65th Sts). 870.5570 ♿

Damrosch Park Bandshell

South of the **Metropolitan Opera** within **Damrosch Park** (site of the annual Big Apple Circus), the bandshell is a beautiful space for free concerts. It was designed by **The Eggars Partnership** in 1969 and seats 2,500. ♦ Damrosch Park, W 62nd St (between Columbus and Amsterdam Aves). 875.5000

Vivian Beaumont Theater

Located north of the Metropolitan Opera House, behind a tree-studded plaza and reflecting pool (with a sculpture by Henry Moore), this theater was designed by **Eero Saarinen & Associates** and first opened in 1965. Its first season began under the direction of Robert Whitehead and Elia Kazan; an early highlight was Arthur Miller's *After the Fall*. During Joseph Papp's tenure in the 1970s, his New York Shakespeare Festival at Lincoln Center presented many innovative productions, David Rabe's *Streamers* and Miguel Piñero's *Short Eyes* among them. After Papp left in 1977, the Beaumont was dark for three years. But despite this bumpy start, by the turn of the 21st century the Beaumont had clearly found its stride, finding huge success with an Audra McDonald-led revival of *Carousel* in 1994, followed by the Susan Stroman-choreographed *Contact*, Tom Stoppard's *Arcadia*, and, in 2006, his *The Coast of Utopia*. ♦ 150 W 65th St (between Broadway and Amsterdam Ave). 239.6277 ♿

Mitzi E. Newhouse Theater

Directly below the **Vivian Beaumont Theater**, this smaller theater is for experimental and workshop productions, such as Mike Nichols's controversial *Waiting for Godot* starring Steve Martin, Robin Williams, and Bill Irwin. The Newhouse has been the stage for a number of Spalding Gray's memorable monologues and the opening production of *Six Degrees of Separation*. The 334-seat theater itself was designed by **Eero Saarinen & Associates** and opened in 1965. ♦ 150 W 65th St (between Broadway and Amsterdam Ave). 236.6277

Juilliard School

Located across a large terrace/bridge over West 66th Street is one of the nation's most acclaimed performing arts schools, founded in 1905 by Augustus D. Juilliard. Enrollment is limited to fewer than a thousand, making acceptance in itself a career achievement for gifted students of music, dance, and drama. The building, a Modernist contrast to Lincoln Center's classicism, was designed by **Pietro Belluschi** with **Eduardo Catalano** and **Westerman & Miller**, and opened in 1968. Theaters: **Juilliard Theater** (seats 933); **Drama Theater** (seats 206); **C. Michael Paul Recital Hall** (seats 278). ♦ 60 Lincoln Center Plaza. 799.5000

Alice Tully Hall

East of **Juilliard**, this recital hall is the most intimate and best of the auditoriums at Lincoln Center. Designed by **Pietro Belluschi** in 1969, it is being dramatically refurbished by **Diller Scofidio+Renfro,** with a planned reopen date of winter 2008-2009. Intended for chamber music and recitals, it is the home of the **Chamber Music Society of Lincoln Center** from October through May. Students of the Juilliard School perform here, too. Films from around the world are shown here (and at the upper-level **Walter Reade Theater**: see below) every late September and October at the **New York Film Festival.** ♦ 1941 Broadway (at W 65th St). 875.5050 ♿

Walter Reade Theater

Tenants on the first 10 floors of this tower, the **Samuel B. & Dave Rose Building** (designed by **Davis, Brody & Associates** and completed in 1990), include the superbly sightlined **Walter Reade Theater**—the premier repertory and New York Film Festival screening room, the **Film Society of Lincoln Center** (875.5610), and Lincoln Center, Inc. offices. Floors 12 to 29 are dormitories for students at **Juilliard** and the **School of American Ballet**. ♦ 165 W 65th St (between Broadway and Amsterdam Ave). Film info line: 875.5600; Tickets: 496.3809. www.filmlinc.com ♿

Library for the Performing Arts, NYPL/Dorothy and Lewis B. Cullman Center

Having undergone an extensive 3-year renovation, reopening in 2001, the library and its exhibition space are even grander than before. The original 1965 creation of **Skidmore, Owings & Merrill** was wholly transformed by **Polshek Partnership Architects** into a floodlit, technologically cutting-edge facility. The new galleries exhibit costume and set designs, music scores,

The Best

Anne Rosenzweig

Former Chef/Owner, Arcadia

An unusual perspective of Manhattan begins with an early-morning breakfast at **Sylvia's** (salmon cakes, grits, deep-fried slab bacon, and biscuits). This is the perfect start to a walking day. Then a stroll through the marvelous but crumbling architecture of **Harlem**, especially around **Mount Morris Park** . . . Then down to the **Conservatory Garden** at Fifth Avenue and 105th Street. The gardens are completely transformed every season. In spring, huge lilac bushes create an intoxicating aroma under which one can read the Sunday papers. During the summer, they are the setting of some of the most beautiful weddings in New York.

Sitting in the upper decks of **Shea Stadium** on a hot, hot summer night just to catch a good breeze. On the rare occasions when the city is under a deep, fresh blanket of snow—cross-country skiing in **Central Park** and getting hot roasted chestnuts afterward.

The Indian restaurants on **East Sixth Street** in summer—eating outside in back with a gang of friends on picnic tables for the cheapest sums possible.

Buying bags of flattened fortune cookies at one of the many bakeries in Chinatown—they're the ones that didn't make it.

Jazz cruises at night up the **Hudson River** and being able to see the skyline at twilight.

and other tools and tricks of the trade, as well as art. The updated 203-seat **Bruno Walter Auditorium** presents showcase productions and music recitals. In addition to the most extensive collection of books on the performing arts in the city, the library is equipped with state-of-the-art audio equipment and a vast collection of recordings. A convenient entrance is off the Plaza, betweeen the Metropolitan Opera House and Vivian Beaumont Theater. ♦ Tu-Sa. 111 Amsterdam Ave (between W 62nd and W 65th Sts). 870.1630 ♿

On the **Main Concourse** (access is from within the **Metropolitan Opera House**, **Avery Fisher Hall**, or the **New York State Theater**):

Lincoln Center Guided Tours

Take a tour to see the physical plant, hear the legends and history, and peek at whatever else is going on, perhaps a rehearsal of **The Philharmonic** or *Rigoletto.* Another plus: the expertise and enthusiasm of the tour guides, who are often performers themselves. Backstage tours of the **Metropolitan Opera** are also conducted by knowledgeable guides and provide a behind-the-scenes look at the opera. ♦ Fee. Hourly tours are offered daily; schedule varies, so call ahead. Main Concourse. 769.7020 ♿

The Gallery at Lincoln Center

This is the sales outlet for specially commissioned Lincoln Center prints and posters of works by such artists as Josef Albers, Marc Chagall, Robert Indiana, and Andy Warhol. ♦ M-Sa. Main Concourse. 875.5017 ♿

78 Picholine

★★★★$$$$ Chef/owner Terrance Brennan pays homage to the sunny foods of the Mediterranean, especially Provence. From the kitchen come dishes of great imagination and very heady flavor. Don't miss the signature grilled octopus with fennel, potato, and lemon pepper vinaigrette; Jamison Farm lamb three ways; tournedos of salmon with horseradish crust, cucumbers, and salmon caviar; licorice-glazed squab (with mission figs and baby turnips); and whole roasted fish (there's a different choice every day). Desserts are just as tempting, with homemade sorbets and warm caramel apple brioche leading the list. There's an excellent wine selection. ♦ Mediterranean ♦ Su-F dinner; Sa, lunch and dinner. Prix fixe available at lunch. Reservations required. 35 W 64th St (between Central Park W and Broadway). 724.8585

79 Cafe Fiorello

★★$$$ The location across from **Lincoln Center** is only one reason tables continue to fill up here. Pretheater, the place is a madhouse, but after 8PM the wood-paneled room, decorated with burgundy banquettes and Mark Kostabi paintings, is a calm place to sample the antipasto bar; such pastas as lamb *bolognese* and linguine with clams, calamari, and mussels; and main courses that include clay-pot-roasted chicken with rosemary, roasted bass with olives and sun-dried tomatoes, and lamb osso buco. A wide swath of sidewalk is devoted to outdoor seating in summer. ♦ Italian ♦ M-F, lunch and dinner; Sa, Su, brunch and dinner. Reservations required. 1900 Broadway (between W 63rd and W 64th Sts). 595.5330

80 West Side YMCA

$ In 1966, the city planned to raze this wonderful limestone and brick neo-Romanesque building, designed by **Dwight James Baum** and built in 1930, to clear the entire block up to Central Park West for a

The Best

George Vellonakis

Landscape Architect, NYC Department of Parks and Recreation
Designer of City Hall Park, Abingdon Square Park, and Dag Hammarskjöld Plaza

Grand New York parks where you might gladly while away some hours:

1. **Pelham Bay Park**, Bronx
2. **Greenbelt**, Staten Island
3. **Flushing Meadows–Corona Park**, Queens
4. **Van Cortlandt Park**, Bronx
5. **Central Park**, Manhattan
6. **Fresh Kills Park**, Staten Island
7. **Marine Park**, Brooklyn
8. **Bronx Park**, Bronx
9. **Alley Pond Park**, Queens
10. **Franklin D. Roosevelt Boardwalk, South and Midland Beaches**, Staten Island

Lincoln Center mall. Plans fell through when the **YMCA** refused to sell out. This hostelry offers 480 single and double rooms (all with shared baths, down the hall; the double rooms have bunk beds, and most rooms have color TVs) to both men and women. Two remarkable period swimming pools—one glazed with Italian tiles and graced with natural light from the tall windows around it, the other laid with deep cobalt-blue tiles from Andalusia—have been fully restored. They are a treasured complement to this Y's big and well-equipped fitness center. All gym facilities are free for guests lodging here; day passes may be purchased by anyone else. ♦ 5 W 63rd St (between Central Park W and Broadway). 787.4400; fax 875.4291. www.ymcanyc.org. ♿. Also at other locations throughout the city

81 New York Society for Ethical Culture

It's refreshing to find this example of Art Nouveau in New York. **Robert D. Kohn**, who was also the architect of **Temple Emanu-El**, was the president of the society—a group founded on the tenets of a "humanist religious" community—at the time he designed this building in 1910. The lovely 800-seat auditorium here (also known as **The Concert Hall**) hosts a broad spectrum of public musical events, from classical ensembles to solo acts, such as 12-string guitar wizard Leo Kottke; there is also a full roster of reading and speaking programs that are also open to the public, including film and book series on ethical themes. Regularly scheduled open discussion groups prevail in their **Socrates Café**. ♦ 2 W 64th St (at Central Park W). 874.5210. www.nysec.org

82 Century Apartments

Brother of the **Majestic** (**No. 115**, Central Park West, at West 72nd Street; designed in 1930), this is the southernmost pair of the sets of twin towers designed by the office of **Irwin S. Chanin** that make the skyline of Central Park West so distinctive. The structure was built in 1931, when Jacques Delamarre was the director of Chanin's office. The apartment house occupies the site of the resoundingly unsuccessful (but magnificent) **Century Theater**, a 1909 building by **Carrère & Hastings**, which first failed as a national theater, then as an opera house, and finally as a Ziegfeld vaudeville theater. ♦ 25 Central Park W (between W 62nd and W 63rd Sts).

83 45 Columbus Avenue

Designed by **Jardine, Hill & Murdock** in 1930, this 27-story building was originally the **Columbus Circle Automatic Garage**. It is a tremendous Art Deco sampler: All the walls are embellished with period ornament. ♦ Between W 61st and W 62nd Sts

84 Museum of Biblical Art (MOBIA)

True, this 2005-opened museum is under the wing of the American Bible Society, but the 2,700-square-foot space designed by **G and L Architects** has a mission to present religious art and objects with a broader view: to show an international spectrum of work specifically inspired by the Bible, and to explore its form and function. Housed on the second floor of **Fox & Fowle**'s 1998 innovative glass-and-steel addition to the Bible Society's original 1966 **Skidmore, Owings & Merrill** exposed-concrete construction, the museum features changing exhibitions ranging from 20th-century Guatemalan folk art to Romanov icons and African-American quilts. The Bible Society's Rare Scripture Collection may also be found here. ♦ Admission. Tu, W, F-Su, 10AM-6PM; Th, 10AM-8PM. 1865 Broadway (at W 61st St). 408.1500. www.mobia.org

The Best

Jimmy Breslin

Author and former *Newsday* columnist

Sit at night on **Shore Road** and watch the *Queen Elizabeth II* slide under the **Verrazano-Narrows Bridge**. The ship at first seems to be part of another shore. Then you see it moving so quickly. Coming from Queens to Manhattan at night over the **Queensboro Bridge**.

Living anywhere on the water in **Brooklyn Heights**, **Williamsburg**, **Long Island City**, or up on the hill in **Maspeth** and **Middle Village** in Queens and looking over at Manhattan. The people in Manhattan can only see Queens with its Pepsi-Cola signs. The smart people live in Queens and get a view that is unique in the world, even to photos, for the most sophisticated camera people don't know where these neighborhoods are.

The May Wave in the **Ramble** at **Central Park** and in the **Bird Sanctuary** at **Jamaica Bay**. The flocks come north again, and on 10 May the same birds are in the same places. For decades the same type of bird is in the same spot, in the Ramble or at the bird sanctuary. So many types that even the best books cannot have them all cataloged. They are en route to Canada and as far as the North Pole.

Third Avenue and **East 42nd Street** and all the sidewalks in every direction at 5PM. Crowds of such size that it is hard to think that one place can hold them.

85 Gabriel's

★★★$$$ Come here for arguably the best homemade pasta, risotto, grilled dishes, and desserts in the Lincoln Center area. Among the offerings are *pappardelle* with braised artichokes and mint, wood-grilled trout with fresh sautéed tomatoes and roasted peppers, and fettuccine with tomato, basil, and buffalo milk ricotta. If you need help deciding what to order, owner Gabriel Aiello is a great source for wine and food recommendations. ♦ Northern Italian ♦ M-F, lunch and dinner; Sa, dinner. Reservations required. 11 W 60th St (between Broadway and Columbus Ave). 956.4600

86 Trump International Hotel & Tower

$$$$ Developer Donald Trump combined forces with noted architects **Philip Johnson** and **Costas Kondylis** to transform the former **Gulf + Western Building** into a gleaming combination of hotel and residential condominiums. The hotel section is relatively small—there are 168 rooms and suites, which occupy the first 17 floors. Lavish condos fill the rest of the skyscraper. Hotel accommodations feature fresh flowers, a modern décor of wood accents, earthy tones of beige and brown, plush furnishings, plasma TV and entertainment center, marble bath, and a galley kitchen complete with fine crystal and china. In addition, there's a full-featured health club on the premises. ♦ 1 Central Park W (at Columbus Cir). 299.1000, 888/488.7867 (44 TRUMP); fax 299.1150. www.trumpintl.com ♿

Within the Trump International Hotel & Tower:

Jean Georges

★★★★$$$$ Yet another superchef Jean-Georges Vongerichten venture is this elegant room designed by Adam Tihany. Unlike his **Vong** and **JoJo** restaurants, this place is smallish (only 70 seats); it boasts a luxurious setting with marble and terrazzo floors with earthy shades of nutmeg, sage, and gray throughout. One factor remains constant: The food is uniquely prepared and beautifully presented. Look for such signature dishes as spit-roasted lobster with chanterelles and sautéed shrimp with orange zest and wild yarrow. Also, don't miss the broiled squab, rack of lamb, or Arctic char with potatoes and horseradish cream. Delicious endings include roasted pear spiked with vanilla beans and roasted apricot tart. There's an adjoining café (the more casual, and more favorably priced, **Nougatine** room), and in warm weather ask to sit on the terrace. ♦ French ♦ Jean Georges: M-F, lunch and dinner; Sa, dinner. Tasting menu available. Reservations required. Nougatine: M-F, breakfast, lunch, and dinner; Sa, lunch and dinner; Su, brunch. 299.3900

87 Mandarin Oriental Hotel

$$$$ A breathless elevator ride from street level takes you to the gracefully ovoid 35th-floor lobby of this five-star standout atop the northerly one of the **Time Warner Center**'s two towers, where every element of style is meant to evoke a feeling of peace and well-being. The theme builds on the ancient use of the ellipse form—good for *chi*, or energy flow—and is carried throughout the hotel's public and private spaces. From the silver-leaf cloud

To create Lincoln Center—six buildings devoted to theater, music, and dance in an area of 14 acres—it was necessary to demolish 188 buildings and relocate 1,600 people. These were the very slums in which Leonard Bernstein set his famous American musical *West Side Story.* He would later be instrumental in the development and creative organization of Lincoln Center.

motif found on the lobby's overhead lighting to the chain's signature fan (this one a crystal confection) by designer **Vivienne Tam**, to the silvered tree branches gracing the ceiling of the **Tony Chi**-designed French-Japanese fusion restaurant **Asiate**, the Mandarin is, if nothing else, utterly elegant. All 251 rooms (the best views are on floors 40 through 54, the highest) have tastefully opulent décor by Hirsch & Bedner and are wired for web access; some have flat-screen TV in the bathrooms (all bedrooms, of course, have them), though, oddly, no phones. Guest-pampering initiatives—and there are many—include **The Spa**, where your senses are duly challenged to attain complete relaxation, a lap pool, private yoga, and a complimentary Bedside Reading program; upper-floor suites come with binoculars, the better to view the sweeping vistas. The wide-open Lobby Lounge, with its floor-to-ceiling windows overlooking Central Park, is a fine spot for light meals, afternoon tea, or sipping from the sake menu; the darkly mod **MOBar** off the lobby pours drinks at a nickel bar with leather trim. ♦ 80 Columbus Circle (enter on W 60th St, at Broadway). 805.8800. www.mandarinoriental.com/newyork ♿

88 Time Warner Center

The memory of the old Coliseum that once stood so humbly—and unattractively—at the Time Warner World Headquarters site is fading fast as the 2003 **David M. Childs** (**Skidmore, Owings & Merrill**)-designed glass-faced double-tower, 2.8-million-square-foot (and $1.7 billion) extravaganza remakes the skyline on the west side of Columbus Circle. The five-star **Mandarin Oriental Hotel** (see page 290) was one of the first sections of this office-retail-restaurant-hotel-residence complex to open; following on its heels was a parade of ultra-exclusive restaurants with stunning views out onto Central Park, beginning with Asayoshi Takayama's **Masa** and **MasaBar** (823.9800. Japanese), Thomas Keller's **Per Se** (823.9335), Gray Kunz's long-anticipated **Café Gray** (823.6338), and Jean-Georges Vongerichten's already demised **V Steakhouse**. Later additions include the much more casual **Bouchon Bakery** (823.9366) and a branch of Marc Murphy's TriBeCa bistro-style restaurant, **Landmarc** (823.6123). **The Shops at Columbus Circle**, like the restaurants, are mostly clustered around the central atrium between the two towers. A small sampling of the boutiques joining a giant Borders bookstore and even more giant Williams-Sonoma here: Coach (581.4115), Thomas Pink (823.9650), Boss (485.1900), Bose (823.9314), Tumi (823.9390), and a Whole Foods market-*cum*-food hall. Who knew New York would welcome such a mall? ♦ Daily. Atrium: The Shops at Columbus Circle on Levels 1, 2, and 3; Restaurants on 3 and 4. Time Warner World Headquarters, South Tower; Mandarin Oriental Hotel, North Tower; Columbus Circle. Entrance for retail and restaurants through atrium, or from W 58th or W 60th St ♿

Within Time Warner Center:

Jazz at Lincoln Center

Finally Jazz at Lincoln Center has its own home, designed by architect **Rafael Viñoly** and tailored physically and acoustically to live jazz performance—the first and only such hall in the world. Starting with its inaugural season in fall 2004, the formally named **Frederick P. Rose Hall** established itself as an apt venue for America's musical heritage and the inspired programming of renowned artistic director Wynton Marsalis. Three intimate theaters (the flexibly planned 1,100-1,220-seat **Rose Theater**; amphitheater-like 300-600-seat **Allen Room**; and **Dizzy's Club Coca-Cola**, with 140 seats), plus recording and broadcasting space, education facilities, and a 1,200-square-foot **Jazz Hall of Fame** (by Broadway-set and restaurant designer David Rockwell) complete the 100,000-square-foot, $128 million landmark project. ♦ Fifth floor. Enter through atrium or on W 60th St at Columbus Circle. 258.9800; CenterCharge 721.6500. www.jalc.org ♿

89 Columbus Circle

This vast traffic circle was built after the commissioners of **Central Park** were empowered to develop the West Side from West 55th to West 155th Streets in 1887. An intensive two-year traffic-clogging renewal project was finally completed in 2005. The result is a gracious European-feeling open space and monument appropriate to the grand entrance to Central Park, at the circle's northeast perimeter. To the south stands a transformed version of the once loved—or loathed—modern white marble Moorish tower designed in 1962 by **Edward Durell Stone**. The **Museum of Art & Design** (see page 149) re-did it and took occupancy in 2008. To the west are the glass towers of the 2003 **Time Warner Center**, which obliterated the grayish lump of the Coliseum, designed in 1956 by **Leon & Lionel Levy**. And of course, to the north, there's the Trump Tower. All in all, a remarkable renaissance for a difficult space that planners have been trying to solve for years. At juncture of Eighth Ave, Broadway, Central Park S, and Central Park W, and bounded by W 58th and W 60th Sts

UPPER WEST SIDE

A neighborhood in transition, the Upper West Side is bordered by **Central Park** on the east, the **Hudson River** on the west, **West 86th Street** to the south, and **Cathedral Parkway/West 110th Street** on the north. Long a mix of brownstone homes sandwiched between apartment buildings on the avenues, the residential nature here was changed irrevocably in the late 1950s when city planning commissioner Robert Moses essentially divided it in half along the north-south axis of Amsterdam Avenue. Proclaiming it the Westside Urban Renewal Area, he had thousands of traditional single-family dwellings torn down on almost all of the cross-streets from West 97th through West 104th Street between Amsterdam and Central Park West. "Super blocks" with densely populated high-rise projects, like **Park West Village** and the **Frederick Douglass Houses**, replaced them.

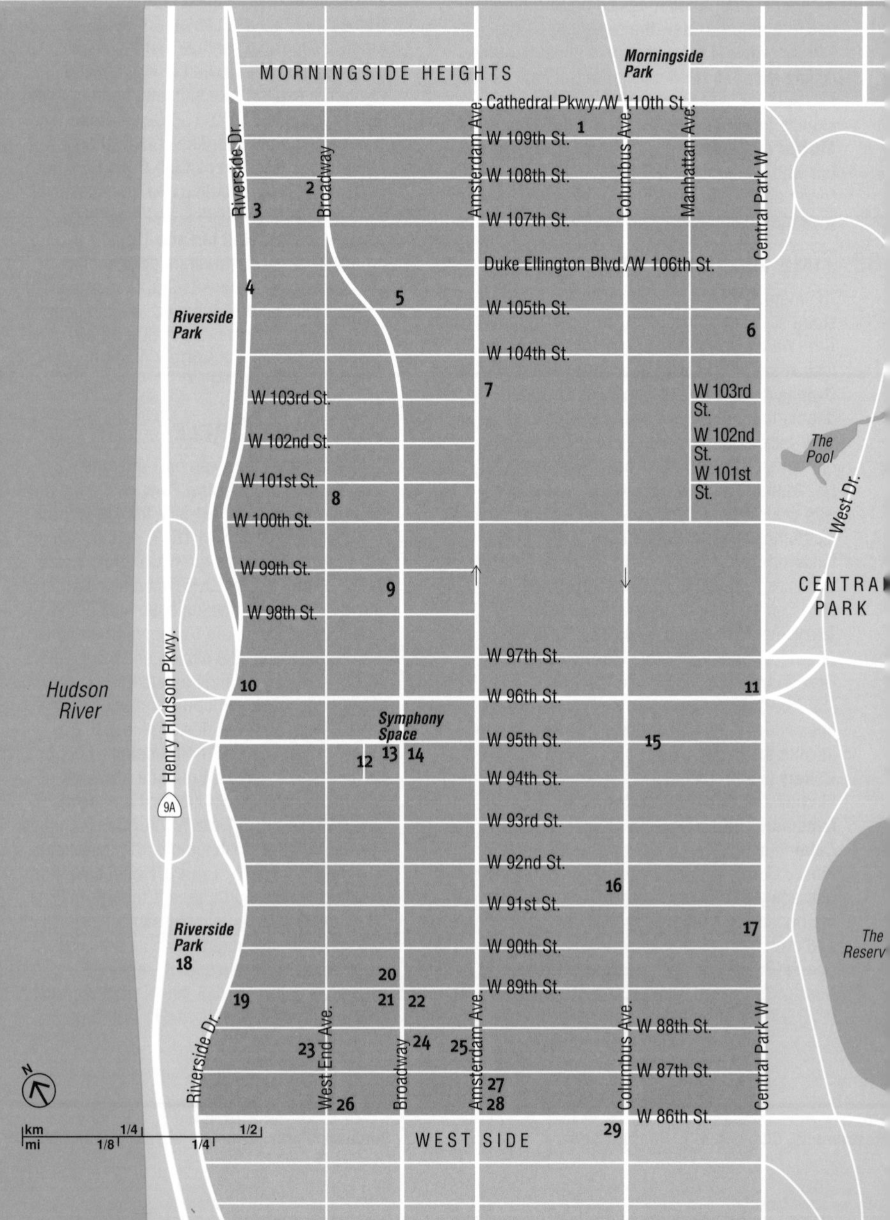

Along **Central Park West**, to the north and south of the projects, and along **Riverside Drive** and **West End Avenue** remain many of the striking and important apartment buildings that were built between the late 1800s and early 20th century. The twin-towered **Eldorado** at West 90th and the former **New York Cancer Hospital** at West 105th Street both grace Central Park West. Two enclaves on the way west side, the **Riverside–West End Historic District** and the **Riverside–West 105th Street Historic District**, offer special treats from Beaux Arts to Deco and more.

Columbia University, though a few blocks north of West 110th Street, has long impacted the northern fringe of the Upper West Side with its voracious need for housing stock—and campus space. Lower housing prices (and run-down properties) have also long made the area attractive to literati to and professorial and student types. An interesting phenomenon of late-20th-century gentrification is the melding up here—seen especially in the latest restaurants and shops—of an Amsterdam Avenue–centered Latino population with the Columbia crowd and folks of all stripes relocating here for the occasional housing find.

Revitalization is also a factor from the south, especially along the Broadway corridor. **Symphony Space** at West 95th Street has proven to be a community anchor like no other; whether the apartment buildings going up above West 96th Street will gain such favor remains to be seen. And **Riverside Park**, with its community gardens and bikeway along its entire extent, is a welcoming alternative to Central Park.

1 Cathedral Parkway Houses

These two massive apartment towers were carefully articulated in an attempt to accommodate them to the much smaller scale of the neighborhood. They were built in 1975 and designed by **Davis, Brody & Associates** and **Roger Glasgow**. ♦ 125 W 109th St (between Columbus and Amsterdam Aves). 749.1100

2 107 West

★$$ A mostly young, upscale crowd keeps this three-room establishment bustling. The overall tone is Cajun, but the menu throws a few Mexican and pasta specialties into the mix. The wine list offers decent selections at affordable prices. ♦ Eclectic ♦ Daily, dinner; Sa, Su, brunch. 2787 Broadway (between W 107th and W 108th Sts). 864.1555. Also at 811 W 187th St (between Fort Washington and Pinehurst Aves). 923.3311

3 Nicholas Roerich Museum

Roerich (1874–1947) was well known in his native Russia and throughout the world as an artist, philosopher, archeologist, and founder of an educational institution to promote world peace through the arts. This beautiful old town house, one unit of his **Master Institute**, overflows with his lovely landscapes, books, and pamphlets on art, culture, and philosophy. Classical music concerts (usually late Sunday afternoon) and poetry readings (often on Thursday evenings) also take place here. Donation suggested. Tu-Su, 2-5PM. 319 W 107th St (between Broadway and Riverside Dr). 864.7752. www.roerich.org

4 Riverside Drive/West 105th Street Historic District

Riverside Drive between West 105th and 106th Streets (plus some of West 105th Street) has an excellent collection of turn-of-the-century French Beaux Arts town houses. Architect teams **Hoppin & Koen** and **Mowbray & Uffinger** are well-represented, but it's the work of **Janes & Leo** that's most striking. Imagine contemplating the passersby from the grand bow windows on their 1899 row houses at 302-320 West 105th Street, or the fine river views from **331 Riverside Drive** (see below), which they designed in 1902 for actress Marion Davies.

4 New York Buddhist Church

Side-by-side buildings eras apart—**Janes & Leo**'s stately No. 331 (1902) and **Kelly & Gruzen**'s No. 332 (1963)—house the first Buddhist institution chartered in New York State. The bronze statue out front depicts 13th-century Japanese monk Shinran-Shonin, founder of the Jodoshinsu (True Pure Land) school of Buddhism. Even more resonant today, the statue first stood in Hiroshima; a survivor of that unfathomably horrific atomic blast, it was brought to New York in 1955 and dedicated here as a testament to that devastation and meant to forever symbolize a lasting hope for world peace. ♦ 331-332 Riverside Dr (between W 105th and W 106th Sts). www.newyorkbuddhistchurch.org

5 Métisse

★$$ Since the day it opened in the mid-'90s, this cozy bistro has been a neighborhood staple. Alas, the dining's uneven nowadays, and you can do much better in the city for authentic French. But it still has the chops to win folks over. Try sautéed sweetbreads with beurre blanc; the signature potato and goat-cheese terrine with arugula juice; duck breast with *pommes delices,* mushroom sauce, and confit of plum; or the fine steak frites. The wine list is small but well chosen and affordable. ♦ French ♦ Daily, dinner; Tu-F, Lunch; Sa, Su, brunch. Reservations recommended. 239 W 105th St (between Amsterdam Ave and Broadway). 666.8825

6 New York Cancer Hospital

Built in the 1880s by **Charles C. Haight** with five signature turrets (to avoid corners once thought to trap germs), this slate-roofed French Renaissance chateau—the first cancer hospital in the city—served as a nursing home, then sat empty for years, before conversion to condos overlooking Central Park. ♦ 455 Central Park W (between W 105th and W 106th Sts)

7 New York International American Youth Hostel (AYH)

$ Clean, safe, and inexpensive accommodations come in the form of 90 dorm-style rooms that sleep from 4 to 12; there is no curfew, and the hostel stays open all day long. Like other hostels, this one requires that guests be members of AYH (nonmembers can join here) and bring a sleeping bag or rent sheets. The huge red-brick building—designed by **Richard Morris Hunt**, and once a home operated by the Association for the Relief of Respectable Aged Indigent Females—is a Designated Landmark of the City of New York. The maximum stay is seven days, but you can apply for an extension. Bathrooms are shared. ♦ 891 Amsterdam Ave (between W 102nd and W 104th Sts). 932.2300. www.hinewyork.org ♿

8 839 West End Avenue

Covered with terra-cotta decoration, both in geometric patterns and stylized natural forms, this 12-story apartment building was designed by **George Blum** and **Edward Blum** in 1914. The brothers, both recent graduates of the École des Beaux-Arts in Paris, were pioneers in designing for the then-new taller buildings sprouting around the city. Instead of adapting traditional styles, as was then common, they rethought surface treatment and scale, and came up with some of the best buildings of the period. This one, the **Dallieu**, combined its terra-cotta façade with brick, and veered to Arts & Crafts style in the lobby. Their building at **780 West End Avenue**, three blocks down at West 98th Street, and also built in 1914, is particularly notable for its all-white surface of brick and terra-cotta, which is laid to an almost streamlined effect. ♦ At W 101st St

9 Health Nuts

Hypoallergenic vitamins, natural breads, and organic goods—grains, nuts, herbs, and honey—are sold here. ♦ Daily. 2611 Broadway (at W 99th St). 678.0054. Also at numerous locations throughout the city

10 Cliff Dwellers' Apartments

The façade is decorated with a frieze of mountain lions, snakes, swastikas, and buffalo skulls—as symbols of prehistoric cliff-dwelling people. Designed in 1914 by **Herman Lee Meader**, this unusual treatment predates the '20s and '30s Art Deco interest in Pueblo Indian art and culture (and was, of course, before swastikas were freighted with meaning other than the traditional one, good fortune). ♦ 243 Riverside Dr (at W 96th St)

11 1 West 96th Street

This building is, surprisingly, not particularly Beaux Arts, but more in the style of the English Renaissance, with a touch of Hawksmoor revealed in the energetic façade and steeple. The marble interiors—unfortunately not open to the public at this time—are quite impressive. **Carrère & Hastings**, who designed this structure in 1903 (the First Church of Christ, Scientist, used it in the late 20th century), were also responsible for the main **New York Public Library** building and the **Frick Residence**. ♦ At Central Park W.

12 Pomander Walk

A surprising little enclave, this double row of mock-Tudor town houses was named after a play that was produced in London and played on Broadway in 1911. The houses, designed in 1922 by **King & Campbell**, were meant to look like the stage set for the New York production. Tenants have included Rosalind Russell, Humphrey Bogart, and Lillian and Dorothy Gish. ♦ The buildings are not open to the public. Between Broadway and West End Ave, the walk runs north-south from W 95th to W 94th Sts

SYMPHONY SPACE

13 Symphony Space

Constructed during the first decade of the 20th century, this building began as the Crystal Carnival Skating Rink and was converted into a movie house in the 1920s. Founded by artistic directors Isaiah Sheffer and the late Allan Miller in 1978, it has become a vibrant performing arts center that has contributed greatly to a cultural renaissance on the Upper West Side. The Space underwent a complete renovation and redesign (by James Stewart Polshek/Polshek Associates) and re-emerged in 2002 with its formal name changed to **Peter Norton Symphony Space**. The forward-thinking redesign united the mainstream (now the 760-seat **Peter Jay Sharp Theatre**) with the old **Thalia** theater next door (old-timers will fondly remember its reverse rake and oddly placed columns). Reincarnated as the **Leonard Nimoy Thalia**, the informal 160-seater has both a repertory film program and live performances. In addition to a free-ranging program of music and dance events, Symphony Space is well known for its literary performances like "Selected Shorts: A Celebration of the Short Story," also broadcast on public radio. And, in a tradition begun in 1981, every 16 June they present Bloomsday on Broadway, a marathon event during which James Joyce's novel *Ulysses* is read aloud in its entirety. Also annually, usually in March, they present a free-of-charge 12-hour musical marathon featuring composers with such tributes as "Wall to Wall Sondheim," a free birthday salute to John Cage, and a glorious Aaron Copland celebration. Ticket holders and general public alike might enjoy a bite or a well-chosen bottle at their **UnWined Café** (daily, after 4PM. 646/403.3215). ♦ 2537 Broadway (between W 94th and W 95th Sts). 864.5400. www.symphonyspace.org ♿

14 Key West Diner

★$ The salmon-and-turquoise décor is straight out of the Sunshine State, just as the name suggests. Nevertheless, this place is just a well-kept and convenient New York coffee shop with standard fare such as decent burgers, sandwiches, salads, omelettes, bagels, and challah French toast. ♦ Diner ♦ Daily, breakfast, lunch, dinner, and late-night meals. 2532 Broadway (between W 94th and W 95th Sts). 932.0068

15 West 95th Street

These blocks of diverse row houses represent one aspect of the ongoing Upper West Side urban renewal effort. Between the housing projects on the avenues, side streets such as this one, which provide unique and charming character, are gradually being restored. ♦ Between Central Park W and Columbus Ave

16 Trinity School and Trinity House

The main building was built in 1894 to the designs of **Charles C. Haight**; the east building was designed by **William A. Potter** in 1892; and the apartment tower and school addition were designed by **Brown**, **Guenther**, **Battaglia**, **Seckler** in 1969. Straight, wonderful Romanesque Revival, now locked to an intricate 1960s tower, it is much better than average. ♦ House: 100 W 92nd St. School: 101 W 91st St (between Columbus and Amsterdam Aves). 873.1650

17 The Eldorado

The northernmost of the twin-towered silhouettes on Central Park West (see page 281), this apartment building, which was designed by **Margon & Holder** (**Emery Roth** consulted) and built in 1931, is characterized by its decorative metalwork and other Art Deco detailing. ♦ 300 Central Park W (at W 90th St)

18 Riverside Park

Originally designed by **Frederick Law Olmsted** (of **Central Park**) in 1875 and completed in 1910, this welcome strip of greenery stretches for three miles (blessedly covering a rail line below), with space for jogging, biking, tennis, and baseball. Local residents maintain a beautiful garden along the bench-lined median. When there's snow, people dig out their sleds and even cross-country ski here. Additions were made to the park in 1888 by **Calvert Vaux** and **Samuel Parsons Jr.** and in 1937 by **Clinton F. Lloyd**.

Not a monument in itself, as is Central Park, this piece of land is spattered with a few little memorials—most notably the **Soldiers' and Sailors' Monument** designed in 1902 by **Stoughton & Stoughton** and **Paul E.M. Duboy** at West 89th Street, modeled after the Choragic Monument of Lysicrates in Athens; the **Firemen's Memorial** at West 100th Street, designed in 1913 by sculptor

Attilio Piccirilli and architect **H. Van Buren Magonigle** and graced by statues of *Courage* and *Duty*; and the easy-to-overlook but not-to-be-forgotten **Carrère Memorial** (1916), a small terrace and plaque at West 99th Street honoring the great architect **John Merven Carrère**, designed by his partner **Thomas Hastings**. Carrère died in an automobile accident in 1911. The bike path along the Hudson extends through much of the park. ♦ Bounded by Riverside Dr and the Hudson River, and W 72nd and W 145th Sts. www.nycgovparks.org

19 346 West 89th Street

Isaac L. Rice had this house built in 1901 and named it Villa Julia for his wife, the founder of the now defunct **Society for the Suppression of Unnecessary Noise.** This (used in the late 1900s by Yeshiva Chofetz Chaim) and the former **Schinasi Residence** (351 Riverside Drive) are the only two mansions left from the days when Riverside Drive was lined with them. Note the slightly askew porte-cochere (a porch large enough for wheeled vehicles to pass through). The architects, **Herts & Tallant**, also designed the **Lyceum Theater**. ♦ 346 W 89th St (at Riverside Dr)

20 Docks Oyster Bar & Seafood Grill

★$$ Decent and reliable, if no longer wholly inspired, fresh seafood is featured in this neighborhood haunt. The catch of the day varies, but fried oysters coated in cornmeal are a good bet anytime, and the french-fried yams are an inspiration. Also worth trying are the crab cakes, grilled snapper, and fried calamari. Dessert specials include mud cake and Key lime pie. Stop in on Sunday or Monday night for a full New England clambake. ♦ Seafood ♦ M-Sa, lunch and dinner; Su, brunch and dinner. Reservations recommended. 2427 Broadway (between W 89th and W 90th Sts). 724.5588. Also at 633 Third Ave (between E 40th and E 41st Sts). 986.8080

20 Murray's Sturgeon Shop

For more than a half-century, the ultimate Jewish appetizing store has continued to live up to its reputation for high-quality sturgeon, herring, lox, whitefish, and other smoked fish items. The store also carries caviar, coffee beans, and dried fruit. ♦ Daily. 2429 Broadway (between W 89th and W 90th Sts). 724.2650

21 Gary Null's Uptown Whole Foods

A full selection of everything you need for a sound body and soul is available here: vitamins, grains, fresh fish, organic vegetables, kosher chicken and turkeys, cosmetics and an impressive assortment of books to explain what to do with all those things. ♦ Daily. 2421 Broadway (at W 89th St). 874.4000 ♿

22 Westside Judaica & Bookstore

Religious articles and a large stock of fiction and nonfiction covering all aspects of the Jewish experience are sold here, along with CDs, videos, and, for children, a nice selection of toys and games. ♦Daily. 2412 Broadway (between W 88th and W 89th Sts). 362.7846. www.westsidejudaica.com ♿

23 565 West End Avenue

Designed by **H.I. Feldman** in 1937, this is a neo-Renaissance building in Art Deco fabric—brick instead of stone, corner windows instead of quoins. At the bottom, banded brick represents the shadow of a traditional plinth, and the cornice is stainless steel. ♦ Between W 87th and W 88th Sts

24 Aix Brasserie

★★$$$ The first upscale, high-profile French restaurant to hit this part of town, Aix was a wonderment of fine food and fine service at steep downtown prices when it first opened in 2002. Now that opening chef Didier Virot is gone, and this stylish multilevel space has adopted more of a brasserie approach, the prices have come down a bit. Fitted out in the sunny colors of Provence, Aix serves up pleasing food to match the mood. Try an appetizer of peekytoe crab spring roll or crispy shrimp and basil brochette; your entrée might be a citrus-braised osso bucco, steamed wild striped bass, or prime hanger steak frites. Wines by the glass include some not-obvious selections: try a Corsican vin de pays or a 1993 Châteauneuf-du-Pape. ♦ French. ♦ M-Sa, dinner; Su, brunch and dinner. Reservations required, except in the bar. 2398 Broadway (at W 88th St). 874.7400

25 Ozu

★$ This simple, earthy room with exposed brick walls and wooden furniture serves good, if on the bland side, salmon teriyaki

Before the Ninth Avenue El was pushed uptown in 1879, the only "rapid" means of transportation on the Upper West Side were the Eighth Avenue horsecar line and a stage coach on the Bloomingdale Road (now Broadway).

and such macrobiotic fare as soba (buckwheat) noodle dishes; salads; a variety of grains, steamed vegetables, and seaweeds; and soups that include miso, pea, and carrot ginger. ♦ Japanese ♦ Daily, lunch and dinner. 566 Amsterdam Ave (between W 87th and W 88th Sts). 787.8316 ♿

26 Church of St. Paul & St. Andrew

Built in 1897 and designed by **R.H. Robertson**, this United Methodist church seems, some have said, inspired by the visionary perspective of 18th-century French Neoclassical architect Etienne-Louis Boullée, particularly in the octagonal tower. Note the angels in the spandrels. Call to arrange a tour ♦ 263 W 86th St (at West End Ave). 362.3179 ♿

27 Popover Café

★★$$ A cozy spot with white brick walls and plaid banquettes, this place has teddy bears scattered around the room for company. Breakfast is a popular meal here—the neighborhood piles in for freshly made popovers served with strawberry butter, raspberry jam, or apple butter; omelettes; and scrambled eggs with smoked salmon, cream cheese, and chives. There are also good salads and sandwiches at lunchtime, and at dinner more serious food is offered, including grilled prime rib, blackened swordfish, and duck breast with raspberry sauce. ♦American ♦M-F, breakfast, lunch, and dinner; Sa, Su, brunch and dinner. 551 Amsterdam Ave (between W 86th and W 87th Sts). 595.8555 ♿

27 Barney Greengrass (The Sturgeon King)

★★$ The Sturgeon King, "We've been a New York Tradition Since 1908," run by Barney's son Moe and grandson Gary, is folksier than **Zabar's**, though not as complete. On one side is a smoked fish counter with perfect smoked salmon, sturgeon, pickled herring, and chopped liver. On the other is an earthy dining room furnished with brown vinyl seats, fluorescent lighting that makes everyone look like they need to be hospitalized, and, inexplicably, a mural of New Orleans. It's well worth the wait for a table. ♦ Deli ♦ Tu-Su, breakfast and lunch. No reservations taken. No credit cards accepted. 541 Amsterdam Ave (between W 86th and W 87th Sts). 724.4707

28 West-Park Presbyterian Church

Originally the Park Presbyterian Church, this church was built in 1890 to the designs of **Henry F. Kilburn**. The rough-hewn red sandstone of the Richardsonian Romanesque mass is enlivened by the lightness of the almost Byzantine details of the capitals and doorways and the fineness of the colonettes in the tower. The church's boldness is emphasized by the asymmetrical massing, with the single tower holding the corner between two strong façades. As of 2007, West-Park was in poor condition; however, the expectation is that the developer who purchased adjacent land from them for a tower will, in turn, restore the church. ♦ 165 W 86th St (at Amsterdam Ave). 362.4890 ♿

29 La Mirabelle

★★$$$ Pleasant décor, efficient service, and food that is a notch above the ordinary keep this old-school French bistro busy. Good choices are escargots; soft-shell crabs cooked with lots of garlic and tomatoes; a pink, spicy rack of lamb; and the best steak frites on the West Side. However, we recommend going elsewhere to satisfy your sweet tooth. ♦ French ♦ Daily, dinner. Reservations required. 102 W 86th St (at Columbus Ave). 496.0458

> "New York had all the iridescence of the beginning of the world."
>
> —F. Scott Fitzgerald, *The Crack-up*

> "If I live in New York, it is because I choose to live here. It is the city of total intensity, the city of the moment."
>
> —Diana Vreeland

HEIGHTS/HARLEM

Located north of **Cathedral Parkway/West 110th Street**, the geographical peaks and valleys of the Heights and Harlem more or less define neighborhood boundaries all the way up to **Spuyten-Duyvil**, where the **Hudson** and **East Rivers** join. The predominant neighborhoods in this disparate swath of territory include, from south to north: the **Morningside Heights** enclave (on the west, up to West 123rd Street), with **Harlem** surrounding it to the east and north; **Washington Heights**, about where the island begins to narrow, near West 155th Street; and, sitting above Dyckman Street (about West 200th Street), **Inwood**.

The hilly terrain of Morningside Heights, was largely undeveloped until the opening of **Morningside Park** in 1887 and of **Riverside Drive** in 1891. World-renowned scholars began to settle in shortly thereafter, and today the area is dominated by educational giants. **Union Theological Seminary**, **Jewish Theological Seminary**, **Columbia University**, and **Barnard College** form the cornerstone of this outstanding academic community. Two other structures stand out in the landscape: the massive work-in-progress of the **Cathedral Church of St. John the Divine** and an important religious and cultural center in its own right, **Riverside Church**. While you're in the neighborhood, don't forget **Grant's Tomb**, set high on a hill above the river. **Broadway** is the main drag, just as it is on the Upper West Side, but here it's less prettied up, although Columbia University, a major property owner in the area, has been bringing in more chic—and consequently more expensive—stores and restaurants.

Harlem, which becomes **East Harlem** east of **Fifth Avenue**, is Manhattan's foremost historically residential black neighborhood, and a place where a multi-ethnic mix of immigrants from the Caribbean and Africa have often made their new home. Many people of Hispanic origin, mostly from Puerto Rico, settled in East Harlem, renaming it El Barrio ("the neighborhood" in Spanish).

This section of the island was covered with wooded hills and valleys inhabited by Indians when the Dutch started the settlement of **Nieuw Haarlem** in 1658. Black slaves owned by the West India Company helped build a road, later called Broadway and the Haarlem outpost grew. In the early 19th century, affluent Manhattanites, including James Roosevelt, built estates and plantations here. It was also a haven for the poor, with Irish immigrants among those who built shantytowns on the East River where they raised free-roaming hogs, geese, sheep, and goats. Harlem began to develop as a suburb for the well-to-do when the **New York and Harlem Railroad** started service from Lower Manhattan in 1837. More railway lines followed, and as handsome brownstones, schools, and stores went up, immigrant families who had achieved some degree of success, many of them German Jews, moved up from the Lower East Side.

The announcement that work was starting on the **IRT Lenox** subway line touched off another round of development, but this time the boom went bust. When the subway was completed in 1905, most of the buildings were still empty. Blacks began renting, often at inflated rates, after having been squeezed out of other parts of the city by commercial development. Eventually the only whites who remained were poor and lived on the fringes, and Harlem became an essentially all-black community. Although poverty was prevalent here in the 1920s and 1930s, arts and culture blossomed, so much so that the era has become known as the **Harlem Renaissance.** During this time, Harlem became a destination for intellectuals and artists—in dance, drama, literature, and music. Speakeasies flourished in the area during

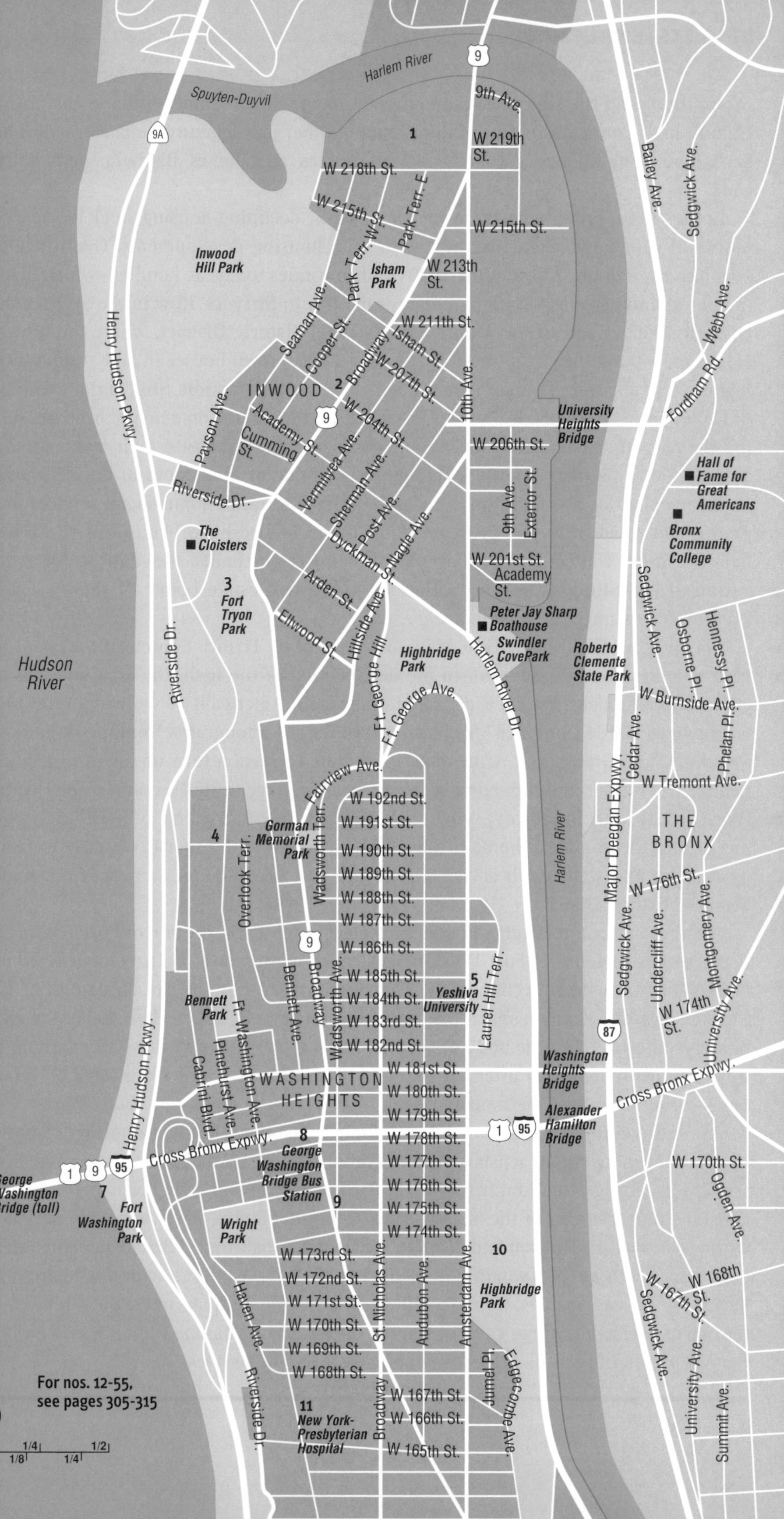

Harlem River
Spuyten-Duyvil
Inwood Hill Park
Isham Park
INWOOD
The Cloisters
Fort Tryon Park
Hudson River
Highbridge Park
Peter Jay Sharp Boathouse
Swindler CovePark
Roberto Clemente State Park
University Heights Bridge
Hall of Fame for Great Americans
Bronx Community College
Gorman Memorial Park
THE BRONX
Yeshiva University
Bennett Park
WASHINGTON HEIGHTS
Washington Heights Bridge
Alexander Hamilton Bridge
Cross Bronx Expwy.
George Washington Bus Station
George Washington Bridge (toll)
Fort Washington Park
Wright Park
Highbridge Park
New York-Presbyterian Hospital
Henry Hudson Pkwy.
Riverside Dr.
Broadway
Major Deegan Expwy.
Harlem River Dr.
For nos. 12-55, see pages 305-315

Prohibition, and the smart set came uptown to the **Sugar Cane Club** and the **Cotto Club** to hear Count Basie, Duke Ellington, and other jazz legends. Lena Horne got he start here, and literary giants Langston Hughes and James Baldwin were nativ sons.

In the 1950s, urban renewal made a dent in the declining housing stock by clearin blocks of slums and replacing them with grim housing developments. Gentrificatio began in Harlem in earnest in the 1970s and continues today, as families—white, blacl middle-and upper-class, straight and gay—move into **Strivers' Row** in the **St. Nichola Historic District** and to the **Mount Morris Park Historic District**, where the brown stones are among the city's finest. By the mid-2000s, town houses in and around thes historic districts were regularly selling for more than $2 million. Still, certain section of Harlem are less-than-ideal places to visit at night and, in some neighborhoods, dur ing the day. On the brighter side, venues for jazz are coming into their own again, a are upscale restaurants. In 1995, Harlem became one of nine zones in the US chose as the recipient of $100 million in federal aid for job training and social services pro grams, and in 2001, former President Bill Clinton moved his office to this revitalize neighborhood. The concomitant arrival of mainstream chains, the high-profile reno vation of **The Studio Museum** in Harlem, and a real-estate boom all signify a ne Harlem Renaissance in the works.

Washington Heights, marked at its south extent by **Trinity Cemetery**, was once a Irish neighborhood. In addition to the descendants of the Irish, the area now has a ethnic mix of blacks, Puerto Ricans and other Latin Americans (Broadway in the 14C is known as "Little Dominica" for its concentration of immigrants from the Dominica Republic), and Greeks and Armenians. **Audubon Terrace**, a turn-of-the-20th-centur Beaux Arts former museum complex, seems out of place in this section of the Heigh (**West 155th** and Broadway), where it's surrounded by housing projects and tene ments. But the complex—home to the **Hispanic Society of America**—is easy to reac by subway and well worth a visit. North and east of Audubon Terrace is the **Jum Terrace Historic District**.

Another important Heights landmark is **Fort Tryon Park**, the site of **Fort Tryon**, th northernmost defense of **Fort Washington**. Its crowning jewel is **The Cloisters**, whic houses the medieval collection of the **Metropolitan Museum of Art**. Just south of Th Cloisters is a little-known shrine, the **St. Frances Cabrini Chapel**. Here, under the alt in a crystal casket, lies the body of Mother Cabrini, the patron saint of all immigrant It is recorded that shortly after her death in 1917, a lock of her hair restored an infa boy's eyesight; he later became a priest.

As rents continue to rise all over Manhattan, **Inwood** has become a northern fronti in affordable housing for artists and young professionals. By the 2000s a nascent galler scene was getting attention. **Inwood Hill Park**, where Indian cave dwellers once live gives the northern end of the island a rural flourish. Playing fields and open parklan with views over the Hudson and down to the **George Washington Bridge** (and on a cle day as far north as the **Tappan Zee Bridge**) are highlights, along with a wilderness hackberry bushes, maples, Chinese white ash, and Oriental pine trees that stretches the end of the island, where you can wander the trails and imagine what it was like whe the Algonquin Indians had this forest paradise all to themselves.

1 Lawrence A. Wien Stadium

Columbia University's **Baker Field Athletics Complex** features Manhattan's only college football stadium. In 1984 the 17,000-seat Lawrence A. Wien replaced the venerable old Baker Field Stadium, which had been on this stunning site since 1923. The modern astro-turfed facility hosts lacrosse and track-and-field events as well as football (go Lions!); but whatever you come to watch is likely to be eclipsed by the views: Inwood Hill Park is just to the west, and the New Jersey Palisades lie beyond, barely a hop across the Hudson River; Spuyten-Duyvil, at the confluence of the Harlem River with the Hudson, is just beyond the northern end zone. ♦ 533 W 218th St (just west of Broadway). 567.0404. www.gocolumbialions.com ♿

2 Dyckman Farmhouse Museum

The only 18th-century Dutch farmhouse in Manhattan survives despite the inroads of 20th-century apartment houses and supermarkets. Built in 1783 and given to the city as a museum in 1915, the house has been restored and filled with original Dutch and English family furnishings, and gets high marks for authenticity and charm. An herb garden, smokehouse, and reproduction of a Revolutionary hut are further reminders of life on a farm in the colonies. It's worth a visit. ♦ Free. W-Sa, 11AM-4PM; Su, noon-4PM. 4881 Broadway (at W 204th St). 304.9422. www.dyckmanfarmhouse.org

3 Fort Tryon Park

This 62-acre park, with its sweeping views of the Hudson River, is beyond exquisite. Originally the C.K.G. Billings estate (whose entrance was the triple-arched driveway from Riverside Drive), the land was bought by John D. Rockefeller Jr. in 1909 and given to the city in 1930. (As part of the gift, the city had to agree to close off the ends of several streets above East 60th Street to create the site for **Rockefeller University**.) There are still signs of **Fort Tryon**, a Revolutionary War bulwark. Don't miss the magnificent flower gardens. The landscaping is by **Frederick Law Olmsted Jr.**, the son of **Central Park** designer Frederick Law Olmsted. ♦ Bounded by Broadway and Riverside Dr

Within Fort Tryon Park:

The Cloisters

Both the building and the contents of this branch of the **Metropolitan Museum of Art** were a gift of the munificent John D. Rockefeller Jr. Arranged among cloisters and other architectural elements from monasteries in southern France and Spain, this is very much a medieval ensemble, incorporating both Gothic and Romanesque elements dating from the 12th to 15th centuries. The complex was designed in the mid-1930s by Charles Collens to house the Met's medieval collection, and **The Fuentidueña Chapel**—a 12th-century wonder brought here from Spain—was added in 1962. The best way to see the pastiche of architectural and art fragments is in chronological sequence,

THE CLOISTERS

MAIN LEVEL

LOWER LEVEL

1 Gothic Chapel
2 Early Gothic Hall
3 Chapter House from Pontaut
4 Langon Chapel
5 West Terrace
6 Ramparts
7 St. Guilhem Cloister
8 Romanesque Hall
9 Fuentidueña Chapel
10 Books and Reproductions
11 Main Hall
12 Froville Arcade
13 Late Gothic Hall
14 Campin Room
15 Boppard Room
16 Unicorn Tapestries
17 Nine Heroes Tapestries
18 Cuxa Cloister
19 Gothic Chapel
20 Glass Gallery
21 Treasury
22 Trie Cloister
23 Bonnefont Cloister

Harlem's best-known dance hall during the Great Depression was the Savoy Ballroom, located at Lenox Avenue and West 140th Street. Notable talents, including Duke Ellington, Louis Armstrong, and Ella Fitzgerald, were regular performers.

discovering romantic gardens, ancient stained-glass windows, altarpieces, sculpture, and tapestries along the way. Highlights include the **Treasury**, where precious enamels, 13th- to 15th-century manuscripts, and ivories are on display, and the pièce de résistance, the celebrated **Unicorn Tapestries** from the late 15th and early 16th centuries. Recorded medieval music sets the mood. Special programs, including gallery talks, live musical performances, and demonstrations, are often scheduled. A special place to relax is the herb garden (in the **Bonnefont Cloister**), with a view of the Palisades as Henry Hudson might have seen them. (Rockefeller protected the view by also buying the land on the Palisades opposite and restricting development.) Visiting The Cloisters is an absolute must. Light meals, May through October only, are served at the **Trie Café.** Shop and bookstore. ♦ Admission. Tu-Su, 9:30AM-5:15PM (closes 4:45PM Nov-Feb). Concert reservations (fee includes museum admission): 650.2290. Free tours Tu-F, 3PM; Su, noon. Margaret Corbin Rd (off Ft. Washington Ave). 923.3700. www.metmuseum.org ♿

New Leaf Café

★★$$ In an original 1930s park building refitted by architect **Armand LeGuardeur**, this rustic, romantic spot is run by Bette Midler's not-for-profit New York Restoration Project. With dark woodwork and warm light, the room is a bigger draw than the food, but the menu has its highlights, including seared diver scallops and a satisfying duck confit panini. Best bets are Sunday brunch and drinks at the expertly staffed bar. ♦ American ♦ Tu-Th, lunch and dinner; F, Sa, breakfast, lunch, and dinner; Su, brunch and dinner. Reservations not taken for brunch, but are (and recommended) at all other times. 1 Margaret Corbin Dr (at Park Dr). 568.5323 ♿

4 Shrine of Saint Frances Xavier Cabrini

The remains of St. Frances Cabrini are enshrined in the glass altar here (above her neck is a wax mask; her head is in Rome). There is also a display of personal items belonging to the saint, the first American citizen ever to be canonized (in 1946) and patron saint of all immigrants. Mother Cabrini was born in Italy in 1850, became an American citizen in 1909, and died in the US in 1917. Tours by appointment only, Tu-Su. ♦ 701 Ft Washington Ave (at W 190th St). 923.3536 ♿

5 Yeshiva University

The oldest Jewish studies center in the country, this independent university celebrated its centennial in 1986. Offered here are both undergraduate and graduate degrees in programs ranging from Hebraic studies to biomedicine, law, and rabbinics. Also part of the university are the **Albert Einstein College of Medicine** in The Bronx; **Brookdale Center-Cardozo School of Law** Greenwich Village; and **Stern College for Women** in Midtown. The main building of its Washington Heights campus was built in 1928 by **Charles B. Meyers Associates**. It's characterized by a fanciful, romantic composition of institutional underpinnings overlaid with a Middle Eastern collection of turrets, towers and tracery, minarets, arches and balconies—all in an unusual orange, with marble and granite striping. The light in the auditorium is especially extraordinary, with mirrored chandeliers and orange and yellow windows. ♦ W 186th St (at Amsterdam Ave) 960.5400. www.yu.edu ♿

6 George Washington Bridge

In 1947, French architect and master of Modernism Le Corbusier said this spectacularly sited and magnificently elegant suspension bridge with its 3,500-foot span was "the most beautiful bridge in the world . . . it gleams like a reversed arch. It is blessed." If the original plans had been completed, architectural consultant **Cass Gilbert** would have encased the towers in stone. The work of master engineer **Othmar Ammann**, the bridge took four years to build and was completed in 1931. In 1962, it was expanded to become the world's first 14-lane suspension bridge. The roadway peaks at 212 feet above the water, and the towers rise 604 feet. Today the GW is considered the world's busiest bridge, with over 300,000 vehicles crossing it daily. For pedestrians, there is a good view of the bridge from West 181st Street, west of Fort Washington Avenue. But the real heart-thumper is a walk or bike ride across it. ♦ At W 178th St, spanning west across the Hudson River to Ft Lee (New Jersey)

7 Little Red Lighthouse

Overshadowed by the eastern tower of the **George Washington Bridge**, this 1880 lighthouse was moved here in 1921 to steer barges away from Jeffrey's Hook (its original location was at Sandy Hook, NJ). Because navigation lights were put on the bridge, the lighthouse was deactivated in 1947, then went up for auction, but the community's

All that remains of Revolutionary War-era Fort Washington is the outline of the foundation, marked by paving stones, in Bennett Park. Here at Fort Washington Avenue, between West 183rd and West 185th Streets, is the highest point in Manhattan, 267.75 feet above sea level.

support saved it. The pair is the subject of a well-known children's book by Hildegarde Hoyt Swift and Lynd Ward entitled *The Little Red Lighthouse and the Great Gray Bridge.* A 1990s restoration reopened it to visitors; a fresh coat of paint in 2007 spruced up the NYC Landmark in time for the 15th annual festival, held every September, in its honor. Scheduled tours are offered from spring through fall by the NYC Urban Park Rangers. Access is across the Hudson River Parkway via the 181st Street Walkway in **Fort Washington Park**. ♦ Fort Washington Park (at W 178th St and the Hudson River beneath the George Washington Bridge). Tour info: 304.2365. www.nycgovparks.org

8 George Washington Bridge Bus Station

This concrete butterfly is a noteworthy attempt at celebrating the bus station in the shadow of a grand bridge. It was constructed in 1963 by the Port Authority of New York in collaboration with architect/engineer **Pier Luigi Nervi**. ♦ 4211 Broadway (between W 178th and W 179th Sts). Bus info: 564.8484; 800/221.9903. www.panynj.gov

9 The United Palace

Erected in 1930 by **Thomas W. Lamb** as Loew's 175th Street Theater, this full-square-block Moorish edifice was movie-palace architecture at the height of its glory, dripping with rococo ornament. Christ Community United Church took it over in 1969 as a forum for the positive-thinking evangelism of Reverend Ike (Frederick Eikerenkoetter) and restored it to full brilliance. When services aren't in session, the building—with its vast gilded auditorium (it seats 3,293) and mammoth pipe organ—is a big-ticket venue for both mainstream and indie rock, as well as dance, lectures, and movie and TV shoots. ♦ 4140 Broadway (at W 175th St). 568.6700. www.theunitedpalace.com ♿

10 Highbridge Park/High Bridge/High Bridge Water Tower

A stroll through Highbridge Park, which parallels the Harlem River atop a vertiginous ridge, leads the unsuspecting to a striking sight: the eponymous footbridge itself, a soaring span of steel nearly 140 feet above the water, the oldest extant bridge connecting Manhattan to the mainland. As recently as 1970, you could still walk across it; by the late 2000s plans were afoot to make that possible again. Completed in 1848, the bridge carried water into the city via the Croton Aqueduct to its terminus at **The Gatehouse** (see page 308); originally, a stately Roman-style procession of masonry arches crossed the river, but in the 1920s the central section, considered a hazard to river traffic, was replaced with the single span. The massive granite tower, with a public swimming pool near its base (site of the former reservoir) and exceptional views from the top—opened to the public on special occasions—was added in 1872 to pump water to residents of northern Manhattan at elevations higher than the aqueduct's. ♦ Between University Ave (The Bronx) and Highbridge Park (at W 173rd St). Park bounded by W 155th St and Dyckman St, and Edgecombe and Amsterdam Aves and Harlem River Dr ♿

11 New York–Presbyterian Hospital/Columbia University Medical Center

Affiliated with **Columbia University**, this branch of the enormous hospital complex continues to grow. The hospital, with its renown in the field of vascular care, also enjoys a reputation as a top-notch teaching facility and working hospital, and it has stabilized the neighborhood it serves. ♦ 161 Fort Washington Ave (between W 165th and W 168th Sts). 305.2500. Also at **Weill Cornell Medical Center,** 525 E 68th St (at York Ave). 746.5454. www.nyp.org ♿

12 Carrot Top Pastries

Owner Renee Allen Mancino bakes the single best carrot cake in New York, as well as delicious pecan, sweet-potato, and pumpkin pies. Devoted customers can also enjoy the light café menu. It also serves pasta dishes and chicken, eggplant, and meatball parmigiana. ♦ M-Sa; Su, until 4PM. 3931 Broadway (between W 164th and W 165th Sts). 927.4800. Also at 5025 Broadway (at W 214th St). 569.1532

13 Morris-Jumel Mansion

Built in 1765 by **Roger Morris** as a summer residence on an estate that stretched from river to river, the mansion's two-story portico became the model for many houses built in Canada and the United States at the turn of the 19th century. During the Revolution, George Washington did sleep here, and even briefly used it as a headquarters, until New York City was taken over by the British. After housing a tavern, the mansion was bought and remodeled by French merchant **Stephen**

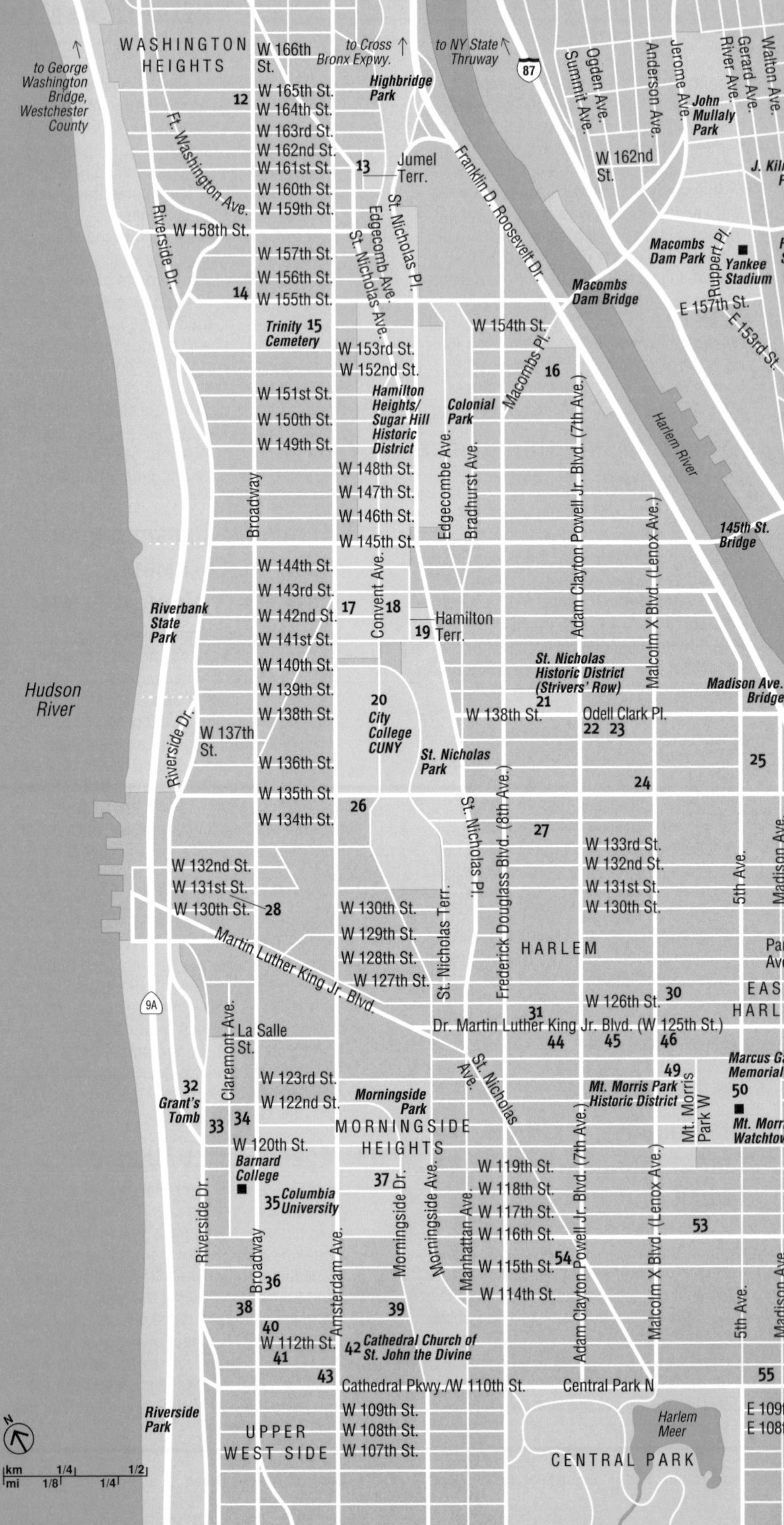

WASHINGTON HEIGHTS
to George Washington Bridge, Westchester County
to Cross Bronx Expwy.
to NY State Thruway
87
Highbridge Park
Ft. Washington Ave.
Riverside Dr.
W 166th St.
W 165th St.
W 164th St.
W 163rd St.
W 162nd St.
W 161st St.
W 160th St.
W 159th St.
W 158th St.
W 157th St.
W 156th St.
W 155th St.
Jumel Terr.
St. Nicholas Pl.
Edgecomb Ave.
St. Nicholas Ave.
Franklin D. Roosevelt Dr.
Ogden Ave.
Summit Ave.
Anderson Ave.
Jerome Ave.
River Ave.
Gerard Ave.
Walton Ave.
John Mullaly Park
W 162nd St.
Macombs Dam Park
Ruppert Pl.
Yankee Stadium
Macombs Dam Bridge
E 157th St.
E 153rd St.
Trinity Cemetery
W 154th St.
Macombs Pl.
W 153rd St.
W 152nd St.
W 151st St.
W 150th St.
W 149th St.
W 148th St.
W 147th St.
W 146th St.
W 145th St.
Hamilton Heights/ Sugar Hill Historic District
Colonial Park
Edgecombe Ave.
Bradhurst Ave.
Adam Clayton Powell Jr. Blvd. (7th Ave.)
Malcolm X Blvd. (Lenox Ave.)
Harlem River
145th St. Bridge
Broadway
W 144th St.
W 143rd St.
W 142nd St.
W 141st St.
W 140th St.
W 139th St.
W 138th St.
W 137th St.
W 136th St.
W 135th St.
W 134th St.
Convent Ave.
Hamilton Terr.
Riverbank State Park
Hudson River
St. Nicholas Historic District (Strivers' Row)
Madison Ave. Bridge
City College CUNY
St. Nicholas Park
W 138th St.
Odell Clark Pl.
St. Nicholas Pl.
Frederick Douglass Blvd. (8th Ave.)
W 133rd St.
W 132nd St.
W 131st St.
W 130th St.
W 132nd St.
W 131st St.
W 130th St.
Martin Luther King Jr. Blvd.
W 130th St.
W 129th St.
W 128th St.
W 127th St.
St. Nicholas Terr.
HARLEM
5th Ave.
Madison Ave.
Park Ave.
EAST HARLEM
W 126th St.
Dr. Martin Luther King Jr. Blvd. (W 125th St.)
9A
Claremont Ave.
La Salle St.
W 123rd St.
W 122nd St.
Grant's Tomb
Morningside Park
MORNINGSIDE HEIGHTS
St. Nicholas Ave.
Mt. Morris Park Historic District
Mt. Morris Park W
Marcus Garvey Memorial
Mt. Morris Watchtower
W 120th St.
Barnard College
Columbia University
W 119th St.
W 118th St.
W 117th St.
W 116th St.
W 115th St.
W 114th St.
Morningside Dr.
Morningside Ave.
Manhattan Ave.
Amsterdam Ave.
W 112th St.
Cathedral Church of St. John the Divine
Cathedral Pkwy./W 110th St.
Central Park N
W 109th St.
W 108th St.
W 107th St.
E 109th St.
E 108th St.
Riverside Park
UPPER WEST SIDE
Harlem Meer
CENTRAL PARK
N
km 1/4 1/2
mi 1/8 1/4
12
13
14
15
16
17
18
19
20
21
22
23
24
25
26
27
28
30
31
32
33
34
35
36
37
38
39
40
41
42
43
44
45
46
49
50
53
54
55

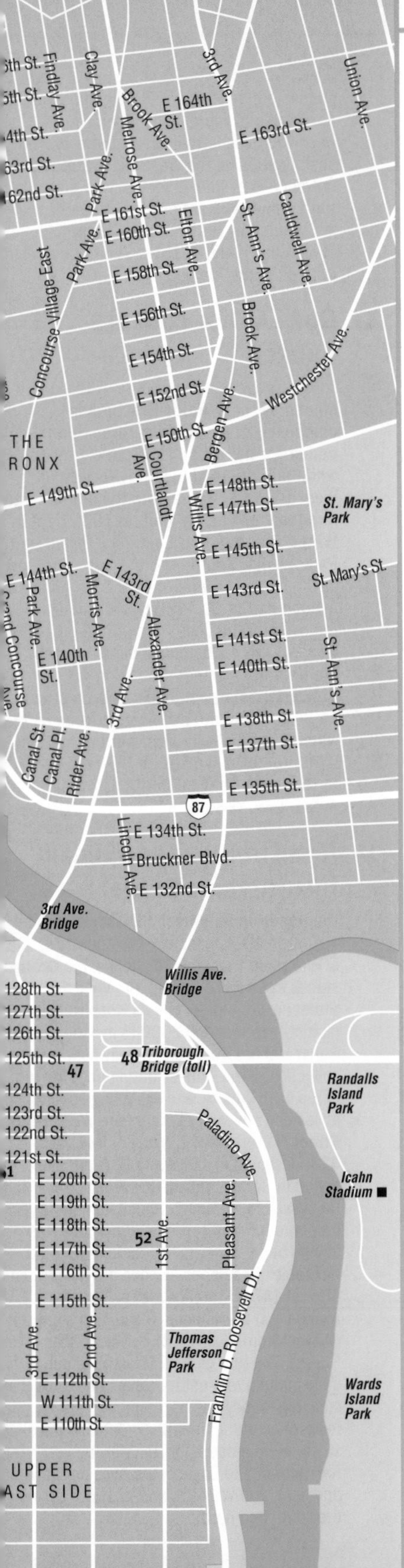

Jumel. The exterior of the house is Georgian Palladian, with some details added in the Federal period; note the conceit of the quoins—a stone form mimicked in wood.

Inside, the elegant home is decorated with excellent Georgian-, Federal-and French Empire-style furnishings, silver, and china. Some draperies were woven by master fabric-maker Franco Scalamandre using period patterns, and some of Napoleon's furniture is here. In 1833, Aaron Burr and the newly widowed Madame Jumel were married in the front parlor room (some accounts claim that her spirit still lingers about the place). Museum educators and volunteers now conduct guided tours of the house, and lectures and concerts are held here as well. Picnickers are welcome to use the colonial herb and rose gardens. Around the mansion is the **Jumel Terrace Historic District**, designated in 1970, a charming neighborhood of well-kept 19th-century row houses. ♦ Admission. W-Su, 10AM-4PM. 65 Jumel Terr (between W 160th and W 162nd Sts). 923.8008. www.morrisjumel.org

14 Audubon Terrace

This collection of classical buildings was first planned in 1908, and bankrolled by poet and scholar Archer M. Huntington. The master plan was created by **Charles Pratt Huntington**, his nephew, who also designed five of the buildings: the **Heye Foundation Museum of the American Indian** (now in Lower Manhattan, as part of the Smithsonian), built in 1916; the **American Geographic Society**, built in 1916; the **Hispanic Society of America** (north building constructed in 1916; south building between 1910 and 1926); the **American Numismatic Society**, built in 1908 (the ANS is now in Lower Manhattan as well); and the **Church of Our Lady of Esperanza**, built in 1912. The green-and-gold interior of the church is rather nice; the stained glass, skylight, and lamps were gifts of the king of Spain, who also knighted the architect. ♦ Broadway (between W 155th and W 156th Sts)

At Audubon Terrace:

Hispanic Society of America

The museum of the Hispanic Society is in a lavishly appointed Beaux Arts building lined with the paintings of old masters—El Greco, Goya, Velázquez—along with archeological finds, ceramics, and other decorative arts of the Iberian Peninsula as well as Latin America and the Philippines. Their library is an important research center, with an extensive collection of rare manuscripts dating back to the 11th and 12th centuries. There is an equally impressive Prints and Photographs division. Beginning in 2007, and running through 2010, visitors will find a special bonus: the **DIA Art Foundation** will be co-presenting projects by a rare selection of contemporary artists. ♦ Free. Tours: Sa, 2PM. Library: Tu-Sa, 10AM-4:15PM. Museum: Tu-Sa, 10AM-4:30PM; Su, 1PM-4PM; Galleries: Tu-Sa, 10AM-4PM; Su, 1:15PM-3:45PM. Audubon Terrace, Broadway (between W 155th and W 156th Sts). 926.2234. www.hispanicsociety.org

American Academy of Arts and Letters

View annual exhibitions of the work of members and nonmembers of this honor society for American writers, artists, and composers. ♦ Free. Exhibits: Th-Su, 1PM-4PM. 633 W 155th St (at Broadway). 368.5900. www.artsandletters.org

15 Trinity Cemetery

This hilly cemetery used to be part of the estate of naturalist J.J. Audubon, who is among those buried here. Others include many members of families that helped make New York, such as the Schermerhorns, Astors, Bleeckers, and Van Burens. The grave of Clement Clarke Moore draws special attention—he was, arguably, the scribe of *A Visit from St. Nicholas.* The boundary walls and gates date from 1876; the gatehouse and keeper's lodge were designed in 1883 by **Vaux & Redford**, and the grounds were laid out in 1881 by **Vaux & Co.** ♦ Daily, 8AM-dusk. Bounded by Amsterdam Ave and Riverside Dr, and W 153rd and W 155th Sts. 602.0787

At Trinity Cemetery:

Chapel of the Intercession

Built in 1914 by **Cram**, **Goodhue & Ferguson**, this chapel is essentially a large country church set in the middle of rural Trinity Cemetery. The cloister at the West 155th Street entrance is particularly nice, and the richly detailed interior is marvelous, highlighted by an altar inlaid with stones from the Holy Land and sites of early Christian worship. The ashes of architect **Bertram G. Goodhue** are entombed in a memorial in the north transept. ♦ Broadway and W 155th St. 283.6200

16 Harlem River Houses

This exemplary complex consisting of nine acres of public housing developed by the **Federal Administration of Public Works** was built in 1937 by **Archibald Manning Brown** with **Charles F. Fuller**, **Horace Ginsberg**, **Frank J. Forster**, **Will Rice Amon**, **Richard W. Buckley**, and **John L. Wilson**; **Michael Rapuano** was the landscape architect. An energetic variety of building shapes are arranged in three groups around a central plaza and landscaped courts, becoming less formal nearer the river. The sculpture inside the West 151st Street entrance is by Paul Manship, who also did the **Prometheus** at Rockefeller Center. ♦ Bounded by Harlem River Dr and Macombs Pl, and W 151st St and Colonel Charles Young Triangle

17 Our Lady of Lourdes Church

Truly a scavenger's monument, this 1904 church by the **O'Reilly Brothers** is composed of pieces from three other buildings: the Ruskinian Gothic gray-and-white marble and bluestone façade on West 142nd Street is from the old **National Academy of Design**, built in 1865 by **P.B. Wight**, that stood at East 23rd Street and Park Avenue South; and the apse and part of the east wall were once the Madison Avenue end of **St. Patrick's Cathedral**—removed for the construction of the **Lady Chapel**. The pedestals flanking the steps are from department-store king **A.T. Stewart**'s palatial mansion, which stood on 34th Street at Fifth Avenue from 1869, when it was built by **John Kellum**, until it was torn down in 1901. ♦ 467 W 142nd St (between Convent and Amsterdam Aves). 862.4380

18 Hamilton Heights/Sugar Hill Historic District

The **Hamilton Heights** area, first designated historic in 1974, was once the country estate of Alexander Hamilton. His house, the **Grange** stands at Convent Avenue and West 141st Street next to old **St. Luke's Hospital**. The district—expanded in 2000 to include the **Sugar Hill** area—has a generally high-quality collection of row houses dating from the turn of the 19th century and exhibiting a mixture of styles and a wealth of ornament. **West 144th Street** is exemplary. The row at **Nos. 413** to **423**, designed in 1898 by **T.H. Dunn**, has Venetian Gothic, Italian, and French Renaissance elements. Because there is very little through traffic, the neighborhood has always been somewhat secluded and desirable. Also especially fine are the stretch of West 147th Street between Convent Avenue and St. Nicholas Place, and along Convent from West 143rd to West 145th Streets. The turn of the 21st century saw a huge jump in real-estate values here, and it's clear big money has been spent in the restoration of the beautifully detailed housing stock. ♦ Bounded approximately by Amsterdam and Edgecombe Aves on the west and east, and W 140th and W 155th Sts on the south and north

19 Harlem School of the Arts (HSA)

In 1965, soprano Dorothy Maynor began teaching piano in the basement of the **St. James Presbyterian Church Community Center**. From that modest beginning, it has grown to 1,300 students and has gained national prominence as a performing arts school. Several former students and teachers now have active Broadway careers. The school teaches musical instrument study (piano, orchestral string, percussion), ballet and modern dance, and visual and dramatic arts. (The orchestral string department is especially noteworthy; the 23-member **Suzuki Ensemble**, made up of 8- to 17-year-olds, is known throughout the city.) Through the "Opportunities for Learning in the Arts" program, students from other schools are brought in to take classes during the day. The "Community and Culture in Harlem" program hosts concerts, art exhibitions, and readings. The school's award-winning building, a 1977 work of **Ulrich Franzen & Associates**, is a complex marriage of classrooms, practice studios, three large dance studios, auditoriums, offices, and an enclosed garden. An adjacent building holds the 200-seat **Harlem School of the Arts Theater**. ♦ 645 St. Nicholas Ave (at W 141st St). 926.4100. www.harlemschoolofthearts.org ♿

20 City College/City University of New York (CUNY)

A growing enrollment of some 11,000 students—over 75 percent of them minorities—attend classes at this 34-acre historic college. Bachelor's and master's degrees are offered in liberal arts, education, engineering, architecture, and nursing. The science programs are also noteworthy. The campus is an ornately costumed, energetic collection of white-trimmed neo-Gothic buildings constructed of Manhattan schist excavated during the construction of the IRT subway. The old campus, completed in 1905 by **George B. Post**, is especially wonderful in contrast to the more recent buildings that have grown up around it. The Romanesque south campus used to be **Manhattanville College of the Sacred Heart**, originally an academy and convent. ♦ Convent Ave (between Convent Hill and W 138th St). 650.7000. www.ccyn.cuny.edu ♿

21 Strivers' Row/St. Nicholas Historic District

In an unusual and highly successful 1891 venture, speculative builder David King chose three architects to design the row housing on these three blocks. **Nos. 202** to **250 West 138th Street** and **2350** to **2354 Adam Clayton Powell Jr. Boulevard** are by **James Brown Lord**, all in simple Georgian redbrick on a brownstone base. **Nos. 203** to **271 West 138th Street, 2360** to **2390 Adam Clayton Powell Jr. Boulevard**, and **Nos. 202** to **272 West 139th Street** are by **Bruce Price** and **Clarence S. Luce. Nos. 203** to **267 West 139th Street** and **1380** to **1390 Adam Clayton Powell Jr. Boulevard** are the finest—elegantly detailed, Renaissance-inspired designs by **McKim**, **Mead & White**. The harmony of the ensemble, achieved through similarity of scale and sensitive design despite the variety of styles and materials, is extraordinary. The area came to be known as **"Strivers' Row,"** the home of the area's young and professionally ambitious. It was designated a historic district in 1967 and has seen a growing interest in restoration ever since. The area is now a charming, well-established enclave for residents of all stripes—though ambition (and significant income) remains a constant. ♦ Bounded by Adam Clayton Powell Jr. and Frederick Douglass Blvds, and W 138th and W 139th Sts

22 Renaissance Ballroom & Casino

Landmark status eludes this 1920 cultural complex designed by **Harry Creighton Ingalls**, once a hub of the Harlem Renaissance and something of a Harlem rarity—it was built by black developers. It's lost a lot of spiff since the 1930s, when its signage promised "DANCING" and "FUN," but the Abyssinian Baptist Church next door is involved in a plan (envisioned for the 2010s) to restore part of the exterior, with its tapestry brick and colored tile, as the base for an apartment tower. ♦ 2341-2359 Adam Clayton Powell Jr. Blvd (between W 137th and W 138th Sts)

23 Abyssinian Baptist Church

Built in 1923 by **Charles W. Bolton**, this bluestone Gothic Tudor building is renowned for its late pastor, US Congressman Adam Clayton Powell Jr., and for its ongoing and historic role in social activism for the community it serves. Founded in 1808, it is New York's oldest black church. The rousing gospel services make it one of the most well-attended. ♦ Services: Su, 9AM and 11AM. Tours: Call for appointment. 132 Odell Clark Pl (formerly W 138th St, between Lenox Ave and Adam Clayton Powell Jr. Blvd). 862.7474. www.abyssinian.org

24 Schomburg Center for Research in Black Culture, NYPL

The largest library of black and African culture in the United States, collected by Puerto Rican black **Arthur A. (Arturo Alfonso) Schomburg** (1874-1938), is housed in this superbly appointed research center. As a young man, Schomburg was disturbed by the absence of information available on black heritage and history. The center—benefiting from an extensive 2007 renovation by **Dattner Architects**—hosts revolving exhibits and shows by African and black American artists. The gift shop offers items from the worldwide African diaspora, from hand-carved statues to postcards by Harlem's own African-American artists. ♦ Free. Tu-Sa, 10AM-6PM; Su, 10AM-5PM. 515 Malcolm X Blvd (at W 135th St). 491.2200. www.nypl.org

25 Riverbend Houses

This complex of 625 apartments for moderate-income families is respectful of context and use of material, while assembled with great style and imagination. Built in 1967 by **Davis**, **Brody & Associates**, the complex is a landmark in the recent tradition of publicly subsidized housing. ♦ Fifth Ave (between E 135th and E 138th Sts)

26 The Gatehouse

This 1890 brownstone-and-granite watchtower on the edge of the City College campus was reinvented in 2006 by **Ohlhausen DuBois Architects** for Harlem Stage's innovative programs in theater, dance, film, and music. (The company also uses **Aaron Davis Hall**, across the street.) The neo-Romanesque structure was originally a pumping station for the Croton Aqueduct, which terminated here after crossing the **High Bridge** (see page 303); from here, water was taken in pipes to West 119th Street, via aqueduct under Amsterdam Avenue to West 113th Street, then by pipe again to the city. ♦ 150 Convent Ave (at W 135th St). 281.9240. www.harlemstage.org ♿

27 P.S. 92

This 1965 work of **Percival Goodman** is elegantly articulated and warmly detailed. ♦ Not open to the public. 222 W 134th St (between Adam Clayton Powell Jr. and Frederick Douglass Blvds)

28 Dinosaur Bar-B-Que

★★$$ You may feel as if you've entered the Land of the Lost en route to this unlikely spot on the way west side of Harlem. But persevere and you'll reach an even more unlikely urban honky-tonk, this one straight from upstate Syracuse and a franchise begun by three bikers back in the '90s. Enter at the "Welcome Everyone" sign, and get ready for the finger-licking menu inside: classic apple-brined, pit-smoked pork ribs, brisket, chicken and more, with trimmings from mac and cheese to fried green tomatoes. There's a take-out option if you want your dino to go, but some nights you'll be missing live blues. ♦ Barbecue. Tu-Su, lunch and dinner, Reservations recommended. 646 W 131st St (between Broadway and Riverside Dr [12th Ave]). 694.1777

29 All Saints Church

This fine group of buildings shows the Gothic influence of architect **James Renwick Jr.** The firm he founded, **Renwick**, **Aspinwall & Russell**, built the church in 1894 and the rectory in 1889, and the school was built by **W.W. Renwick** in 1904. Some say this work is more pleasing than **St. Patrick's Cathedral**, also a Renwick creation. Especially worthwhile is the harmony of the terra-cotta tracery and buff, honey, and brown brick. ♦ 47 E 129th St (at Madison Ave). 534.3535

30 Sylvia's

★★$$ The most renowned soul-food restaurant in Harlem, and perhaps in New York City, opened back in 1962 and is still serving it up. Southern-fried and smothered chicken are standouts, as are the dumplings, candied sweets (yams), greens, and desserts—especially the cinnamony sweet potato pie. The atmosphere is homey and relaxed; there's a snow-scene mural on the wall and one of the best-stocked jukeboxes in town. ♦ Southern ♦ M-Sa, breakfast, lunch, and dinner; Su, gospel brunch and dinner. No reservations taken. 328 Lenox Ave (between W 126th and W 127th Sts). 996.0660

31 The Apollo

This former vaudeville house, designed by **George Keister** and built in 1914, became the entertainment center of the black community in the 1930s, and by the 1950s it was *the* venue for black popular music. A decade later, however, the theater fell on hard times as big-name acts began playing larger downtown houses. It wasn't until the early 1980s, when it was rescued by Inner City Broadcasting, that the faded theater was given a much-needed face-lift and turned into a showplace for black television productions as well as live entertainment. Stars who have performed here include such legends as B.B. King, Stevie Wonder, and James Brown. Wednesday amateur nights are always fun and packed with budding talents. ♦ 253 W 125th St (between Adam Clayton Powell Jr. and Frederick Douglass Blvds). 531.5305. www.apollotheater.org

32 Grant's Tomb/General Grant National Memorial

Now's the time to pose the infamous exam question: Who is buried in Grant's Tomb? The massive granite mausoleum, designed in 1897 by **John H. Duncan**, is set on a hill overlooking the Hudson River, thereby dominating its surroundings. The walk to the tomb is impressive: You pass along the terrace, up the stairs, through the colonnade and bronze doors, and find yourself under a high dome looking down on the identical black marble sarcophagi of the general and his wife in the center of a rotunda—an open crypt similar to Napoleon's tomb at the Hôtel des Invalides in Paris. It's surrounded by bronze busts of the general's comrades-in-arms and by allegorical figures between the arches representing scenes from his life. Photographs in two flanking rooms fill in with more realistic details. More fun, however, are the undulating benches on the outside, created in 1973 by Pedro Silva of the Cityarts Workshop. The bright Gaudí-like mosaic decorations were done by community residents. Make this trip in daytime only, as the tomb attracts some unsavory characters at night. Oh, yes, the answer: Ulysses S. Grant and his wife, Julia. ♦ Free. Daily. Riverside Dr (at W 122nd St). 666.1640. www.nps.gov/gegr

33 Riverside Church

This church was built in 1930 by **Allen & Collens**, **Henry C. Pelton**, and **Burnham Hoyt**, with a south wing added in 1960 by **Collens, Willis & Beckonert**. Funded by John D. Rockefeller Jr., it is a steel frame in a thin, institutional Gothic skin. The fine nave is almost overpowered by the tower, which rises 21 stories, and the 74-bell carillon is the largest in the world. Visit the **Observation Deck** in the tower, not only to look at the bells on the way up but for a splendid view of the Hudson, Riverside Park, and the surrounding institutions. ♦ 490 Riverside Dr (between W 120th and W 122nd Sts). 870.6700. **Tour info:** 870.6838. www.riversidechurchny.org. ♿

Billie Holiday called her home at 108 West 193rd Street "a combination YMCA, boardinghouse for broke musicians, soup kitchen for anyone with a hard luck story, community center, and after-hours joint where a couple of bucks would get you a shot of whiskey and the most fabulous fried chicken."

Within Riverside Church:

Theatre at Riverside Church

For more than a decade, dancers and choreographers tested their mettle on this tiny stage as part of the **Riverside Dance Festivals**. These days, the church no longer sponsors performances, but still opens its doors to various theater, music, video, and dance productions. ♦ Box office: 870.6784

34 Union Theological Seminary

In a landscape studded with institutions, this is one of the few that truly manage to keep the city at bay. Designed by **Allen & Collens** in 1910 with alterations by **Collens**, **Willis & Beckonert** in 1952, the building is an example of collegiate Gothic borrowed from Oxbridge and, in that tradition, has a secluded interior courtyard. ♦ Bounded by Broadway and Claremont Ave, and W 120th and W 122nd Sts. 662.7100

35 Columbia University

Founded in 1754, this historic Ivy League school has an enrollment of nearly 20,000. Historically famous for its graduate programs, such as journalism, Columbia offers undergraduates some hallowed choices as well: **Columbia College**, **School of General Studies**, and **School of Engineering and Applied Science**.

On the site of the **Bloomingdale Insane Asylum**, of which **Buell Hall** is a remnant, the original design and early buildings of the campus (the third one the university has occupied) were planned by **Charles Follen McKim** of **McKim**, **Mead & White** in a grand Beaux Arts tradition. Although only a segment of his plan was completed in 1897, most of its elements can be discerned. The Italian Renaissance-inspired institutional buildings—in redbrick with limestone trim and copper roofs—are arranged around a central quad on a terrace two stories above the street. There were to be six smaller side courts like the one between **Avery** and **Fayerweather Halls**

The Best

Howard J. Rubenstein

President, Rubenstein Associates, Inc.

Running around the **Central Park Reservoir** at sunrise with the morning glow of the sun peeking out behind New York's skyscrapers.

Savoring the steak at **Peter Luger**'s in **Brooklyn**—the nation's best steak house!

Cheering for the New York **Yankees** at **Yankee Stadium** on a warm summer night.

Enjoying a leisurely lunch at the **Helmsley Park Lane Hotel** while overlooking Central Park.

Ice skating at **Rockefeller Center** with your family.

Reading the delicious gossip in the newspaper columns of the *New York Post*—including Page Six, Cindy Adams, and Liz Smith.

Posing for a photo "ape-ortunity" with King Kong on the observation deck of the **Empire State Building**.

Watching the latest performance of a work of the Bard during **Shakespeare in the Park**.

Paying tribute to the courage and valor of our men and women in uniform while touring the ***Intrepid***.

Soaking up the incredible energy in **Times Square**.

Being as awestruck as your children (or grandchildren) by touring the **Museum of Natural History** and coming upon *Tyrannosaurus rex* looking for a snack.

Enjoying the fabulous music and rich history of **The Apollo** theater in **Harlem**.

(somewhat changed now due to the extension of **Avery Library**). McKim's dominant central element is the magnificent **Low Memorial Library** (1897), a monumental pantheon named after the father of university president Seth Low (who was also mayor of New York City from 1902 to 1903). No longer used as a library, Low remains the administrative and ceremonial center of the university. The statue of the Alma Mater on the front steps—made famous during the riots of 1968—was unveiled by Daniel Chester French in 1903. Other noteworthy buildings on the campus include **Butler Library**, a colonnaded box facing Low, completed in 1934 by James Gamble Rogers. The **Sherman Fairchild Center for the Life Sciences**, a 1977 **Mitchell/Giurgola** creation, is an interesting contextual essay in which a glass-and-metal building has been hidden behind a screen of quarry tile that resembles the ground pavers. The **Law School** and the **School of International Affairs** extension, built in 1963 and 1971 by **Harrison & Abramovitz**, forms a great white mass beyond a block-long bridge that spans Amsterdam Avenue. Charming and modest, the Byzantine/Renaissance **St. Paul's Chapel**, a 1907 work by **Howell & Stokes**, has a lovely, vaulted, and light interior. Tours of the campus, which originate at Low Library (854.4900), are conducted according to interest and the availability of guides. The main entrance is at 2960 Broadway at West 116th Street. ♦ Bounded by Morningside Dr and Broadway, and W 114th and W 122nd Sts. 854.1754. www.columbia.edu ♿

Within Columbia University:

Bancroft Hall

A stew of abstracted details—basically Beaux Arts Renaissance but with a touch of Spanish and a pinch of Art Nouveau—enliven the façade of this apartment house, designed in 1911 by **Emery Roth**. It is now a residence hall associated with **Teachers College**, which is part of **Columbia University**. ♦ 509 W 121st St (between Amsterdam Ave and Broadway)

Barnard College

The 2,200-student women's school, an undergraduate college of **Columbia University**, offers bachelor's degrees in 27 majors, with an emphasis on liberal arts. On the west side of Broadway, across from the elegant expanse of Columbia, the sister school's campus appears crowded but somehow more lively. The older buildings at the north end—**Milbank**, **Brinkerhoff**, and **Fiske Halls**—were designed by **Lamb & Rich** in the 1890s in a sort of New England academic style. More interesting is the heart of the campus today: the limestone counterpoints of **MacIntosh Center** and **Altschul Hall**, both built by Philadelphia architect **Vincent G. Kling** in 1969. In 1989, 400 students moved into **Sulzberger Hall**, a 17-story tower at the southern end of campus, designed by **James Stewart Polshek & Partners**. ♦ Bounded by Broadway and Claremont Ave, and W 116th and W 120th Sts. 854.5262

36 Miller Theatre

Executive director George Steel has a vision of how to best present the new music scene in New York, and no one who's had the opportunity to attend a show, like Steve Reich's seminal "Music for 21 Musicians," would argue with his approach. The 688-seat Miller, redesigned in 1988 and renamed after Kathryn Bache Miller (it had been the

McMillin), is part of **Columbia University**. Comfortable, with fine sight lines, and intimate in scale, this is a grand place to come for the latest in contemporary music, from updated interpretations of sacred and early music to the very modern poems of Ned Rorem. ♦ 2960 Broadway (at W 116th St). 854.1633: Box office: 854.7799. www.millertheatre.com ♿

37 Terrace in the Sky

★★$$$ Set atop **Columbia University**'s **Butler Hall**, the restaurant's sparkling wraparound views of the George Washington Bridge to the northwest and skyscrapers to the south are made even more romantic by the reflection of tabletop candles in the windows and harp music wafting in from the bar area. If only the food were as completely wonderful as the ambience, but perhaps that's an unmeetable challenge. The French-Mediterranean cuisine is beautifully presented, and although pricey, the wine list is very well chosen. Seasonal outdoor seating is available. ♦ French/Mediterranean ♦ Tu-F, lunch and dinner; Sa, dinner; Su, brunch. Reservations recommended. 400 W 119th St (at Morningside Dr). 666.9490

38 Morningside Bookshop

As **Papyrus Booksellers**, this shop has been a neighborhood establishment since the 1980s. While it changed hands in 2003, it is still a must-stop, not only for the **Columbia** students who buy their textbooks here (the university's just across the street), but for

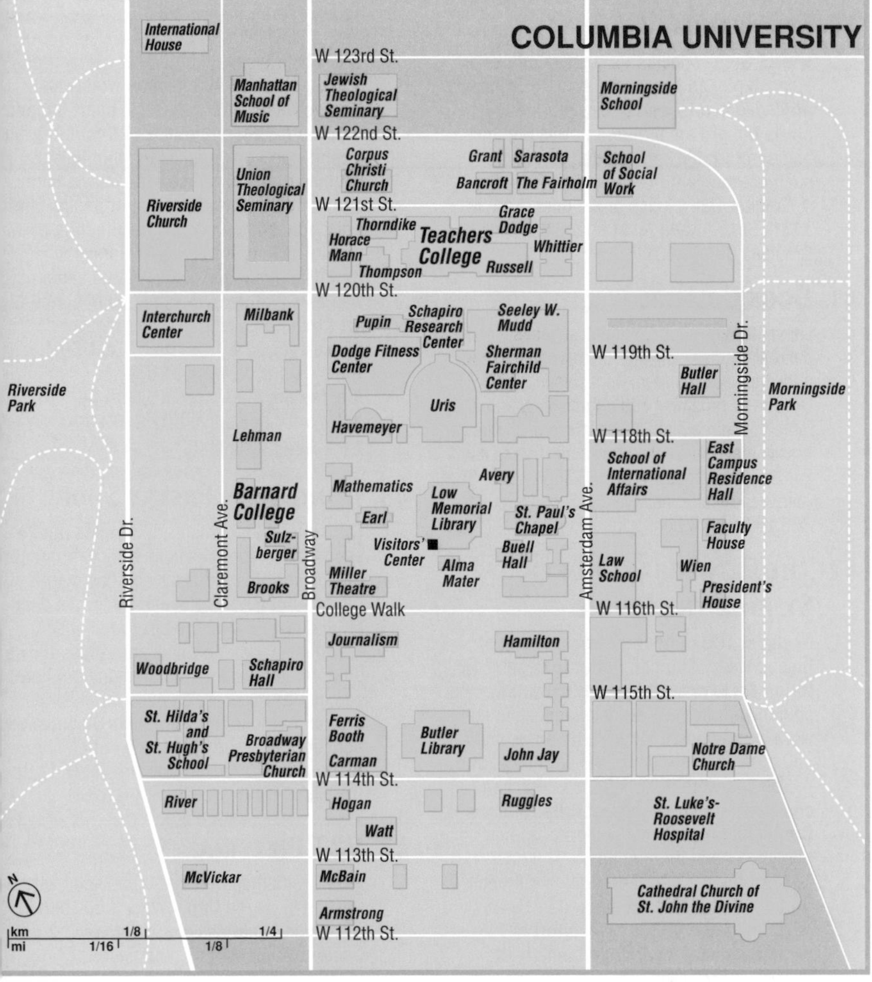

anyone who's interested in a deep selection of arts, literature, philosophy, politics, economics, and history. Computer books fill their lower level; general-interest paperback and hardcover editions are on the main level, along with a wealth of sale books and periodicals. ♦ Daily, till late. 2915 Broadway (at W 114th St). 222.3350. www.morningsidebookshop.com

39 St. Luke's-Roosevelt Hospital

At least the central entrance pavilion and east wing remain of **Ernest Flagg**'s Classical/Baroque composition. The 1896 building is charming, dignified, slightly busy, and certainly original. The St. Luke's cardio center is in one of the newer buildings on this campus. ♦ Morningside Dr (between W 113th and W 114th Sts). 523.4000

40 Symposium

★★★$ Greek specialties such as moussaka, spinach pie, and *exohiko* (lamb, feta cheese, artichoke hearts, and peas wrapped in phyllo dough) are featured at this popular and comfortable spot. During spring and summer, the garden is available for dining. ♦ Greek ♦ Daily, lunch and dinner. 544 W 113th St (between Amsterdam Ave and Broadway). 865.1011

41 Book Culture

Labyrinth Books fed Columbia scholars' cultural-studies crsavings on this site for years, until one of its founders went solo in 2007. Despite its renaming and refurbishing, and a bit more mainstream stock—bestsellers, children's books, magazines—the store stays true to its fine academic roots. ♦ Daily. 536 W 112th St (between Amsterdam Ave and Broadway). 865.1588. www.bookculture.com ♿

42 The Cathedral Church of St. John the Divine

Begun in 1892 under the sponsorship of Bishop Henry Codman Potter to designs by **Heins & LaFarge**, this giant, Byzantine church with Romanesque influences is still a work in progress. By 1911, the apse, choir, and crossing were done, the architects and the bishop were dead, and fashions had changed. Gothic enthusiast **Ralph Adams Cram** of **Cram & Ferguson** drew up new plans to complete the church. The nave and western façade are, therefore, fine French Gothic. Work was discontinued in 1941, but resumed in the 1980s in an effort to complete the cathedral, particularly the towers. In the stone yard in operation next to the church, two dozen artisans, many of them neighborhood youths, worked under a master mason from England to carve blocks in a centuries-old tradition until declaring bankruptcy in 1994; the cathedral has an ongoing major fund-raising campaign to resume building. When it is finished, this will be the largest cathedral in the world. The nave is 601 feet long and 146 feet wide; when completed, the transepts will be just as wide and span 320 feet. The floor area is greater than Chartres and Notre Dame together, and the towers will be 300 feet high. Although not entirely complete, four of the five portals have been fitted with Burmese teak doors; the bronze door of the central portal was cast in Paris by M. Barbedienne, who cast the Statue of Liberty. The interior is spectacular, with seven apsidal chapels in a variety of styles by a collection of prominent architects. The finest is that of **St. Ambrose**, a Renaissance-inspired composition by **Carrère & Hastings**. The eight granite columns that ring the sanctuary are 55 feet high and weigh 130 tons each. The dome over the crossing, intended to be temporary, was erected in 1909. Master woodworker George Nakashima's massive heart-shaped *Altar for Peace*, cut from a 125-foot English walnut tree from Long Island and finished with his trademark rosewood inlays, is the site of monthly meditations for peace. The Episcopal church, under the direction of its dean, The Very Reverend Dr. James A. Kowalski, hosts the visiting Dalai Lama as well as an impressive schedule of concerts, art exhibitions, lectures, and theater and dance events. ♦ Free. Daily, 7AM-6PM. Tours, Tu-Sa, 11AM; Su, 1PM. 1047 Amsterdam Ave. Enter at 112th St. 316.7540; box office 662.2133. www.stjohndivine.org ♿

43 Hungarian Pastry Shop

This venerable Morningside Heights pastry shop/coffee spot has held sway to students and neighborhood folks since Pamagiotis Binioris bought the place in 1976. It's dimly lit, and maybe a bit too cozy when it's crowded—which it often is—but those things do not deter anyone from hanging out here, sometimes for hours on end. The pastries are scrumptious (try something that involves apricot or raspberry jam), the coffee fine. ♦ Daily. 1030 Amsterdam Ave (at W 111th St), Morningside Heights. 866.4230

43 V&T Pizzeria

★$ Its fans maintain that this place has the best pizza on the Upper West Side—hefty, with fresh tomato sauce (it gets raves), whole-milk mozzarella, and flavorful toppings. ♦ Pizza ♦ Daily, lunch and dinner. No credit cards accepted. 1024 Amsterdam Ave (between Cathedral Pkwy and W 111th St). 666.8051

The Best

Betty Rollin

Author

Walking, walking, walking—and soaking up the diversity that is New York.

Hopping on a cool city bus on a hot day for a ride up or down the avenues.

Fairway: great, fresh, abundant/cheap (!) produce.

Wandering around the streets of **Murray Hill** (where the action isn't); then stopping at the **Morgan Library** with its lovely courtyard.

Getting exhausted at **Bloomingdale's**.

Dinner at the **Union Square Cafe**, where the food is divine and you don't have to trip the waiters to get their attention.

Playing hooky from work on a weekday and going to the **Botanical Gardens**.

The **New York Public Library**, starting with the lions.

The range of odd, beautiful, quirky, and occasionally peaceful places—apartments—in which people live.

44 M.A.C.

Right across the street from the **Apollo Theater** is the largest M.A.C. cosmetics shop in all New York, and, opened in 2003, it's at the forefront of the retail revitalization of Harlem. Much appreciated—by professional stylists and makeup dabblers alike—for the creative colors found in their well-made and recyclable cosmetics and other beauty products, they also seem to have as much fun giving you a makeover as you're having yourself. We're especially impressed with this location's semiprivate makeup stations. ♦ Daily. 202 W 125th St (between Adam Clayton Powell Jr. and Frederick Douglass Blvds). 665.0676

45 The Studio Museum in Harlem

With renewed dedication to contemporary art by artists of African descent, and work that's been influenced by African-American culture, big changes have been afoot at the compact Studio Museum. (Its permanent collection includes works by the likes of Romare Bearden, Robert Colescott, Richard Hunt, Loïs Mailou Jones, Jacob Lawrence, Betye Saar, Nari Ward, and Hale Woodruff; they also maintain the photo archives of that quintessential chronicler of 20th-century Harlem, James VanDerZee.) 2000 brought in a new director (Lowery S. Sims, formerly with the Met) and a new curator, Thelma Golden (who was with the Whitney)—both well-known for their expertise in modern art, 20th-century and beyond. The same year a major renovation began on the former **New York Bank for Savings** space they've occupied since 1982 (founded in 1968, the museum previously occupied a nearby loft). By 2003 their striking new glass façade and lobby and **Sculpture Garden** redo were all in place and attendance grew significantly, even as their exhibitions—in a range of media from photography to painting, sculpture, and video—began to achieve world-class status. The museum's permanent exhibition space is now almost twice its original size, and their many public programs—educational, music (like summer jazz and Uptown Fridays), lectures, and more—have a fresh new space and a café as well. Museum specialists **Rogers Marvel Architects** are responsible for the wonderfully inviting design changes to this intimate space. The diverse selection—books, CDs, jewelry, crafts—in The Studio's shop aptly reflects the museum's mission. ♦ Suggested admission; tours by appointment. Closed M, Tu. W-F, Su, noon-6PM; Sa, 10AM-6PM. 144 W 125th St (between Lenox Ave and Adam Clayton Powell Jr. Blvd). 864.4500. www.studiomuseum.org ♿

46 Lenox Lounge

★★★$$ A true survivor, this classic jazz club has been in continuous operation since 1941—back when the street was called Lenox Avenue—except for a few months for renovation in 2000. You can drink with locals in the bar up front, then dine on solid fare (the star rating here is for ambience more than food, but the salads, crab cakes, and soul-food standbys are fine) as a prelude to the main event—stepping into the storied high-Deco Zebra Room to hear swing, bebop, and modern jazz from big names and soon-to-bes, every night but Tuesday. ♦ American/Southern ♦ Cover in Zebra Room. Bar opens at noon. Daily, dinner till late. Call for schedule of shows. 288 Malcolm X Blvd (between W 124th and W 125th Sts). 427.0253

Child's Play

1 Feel like a shrimp under the 10-ton blue whale or watch lasers dance against a night sky. Or perhaps you'd rather travel the earth with T-Rex in the Dinosaur Hall. All are at the **American Museum of Natural History**.

2 Kids can indulge their dreams of being firefighters at the **New York City Fire Museum**.

3 The **New York City Ballet**'s *Nutcracker Suite* brings dancing toy soldiers, evil mice, and sugarplum fairies to **Lincoln Center**.

4 **The New York Philharmonic**'s Young People's Concerts at **Avery Fisher Hall** include talks to introduce kids to classical music.

5 Getting into the **Brooklyn Children's Museum** through a 180-foot tunnel and waterway is half the fun.

6 You can climb up on a mushroom and join Alice, the Cheshire Cat, and the Mock Turtle at José de Creeft's statue overlooking **Central Park's Conservatory Water**.

7 One of the best ways to enjoy **Lower Manhattan** is with a view from the deck of a 19th-century three-master on the river at the **South Street Seaport**.

8 Learn about the laws of physics in the futuristic playground of mazes and climb-friendly structures at the **New York Hall of Science** in **Flushing Meadows-Corona Park**.

9 Create your own animated cartoon, or pretend you're a famous movie star by looking into a "magic mirror," at the **American Museum of the Moving Image** in **Astoria**.

10 Produce your own newscasts and public affairs programs at the **Time Warner Center for Media** at the **Children's Museum of Manhattan**.

47 The Demolition Depot

Mantelpieces, light fixtures, stained-glass windows, saloon bars, even an elevator or two: if it can be torn down, ripped off, or pried loose, chances are you'll find it in this building-salvage emporium relocated from the East Village (where it was known as Irreplaceable Artifacts) to four floors and a backyard just a cornerstone's throw from the Triborough Bridge. ♦ M-Sa. 216 E 125th St (between Second and Third Aves). 860.1138

48 Triborough Bridge

A three-in-one for The Bronx, Queens, and Manhattan. From its Queens start, it crosses west over Randalls/Ward Island, forking along the way. Part lift bridge, part suspension, and part truss bridge, the impressive connector-collection was designed by **Othmar Ammann** (already recognized for his design of the **George Washington Bridge**) and **Aymar Embury II** in 1936. ♦Between Grand Central Pkwy (Queens), Bruckner Expwy (The Bronx), and E 125th St ♿

The Grand Central Parkway, which connects Long Island to Queens, was designed by Robert Moses as part of a network of parkways that was constructed in the 1940s and 1950s.

George Washington lost Queens to British troops during the Battle of Long Island in 1776. This was the first of several significant battles that led to the British occupation of New York City during the American Revolution.

49 Mount Morris Park Historic District

The charming Victorian character of this district, designated historic in 1971, was established during the speculative boom at the end of the 19th century, when it was urbanized by descendants of Dutch, Irish, and English immigrants. After 1900, it became a primarily German-Jewish neighborhood. The houses on Lenox Avenue between **120th** and **121st Streets**, designed by **Deimeuron & Smith** in 1888, are particularly captivating. The **Morris Apartments** at 81-85 East 125th Street, built just a year later by **Lamb & Rich**, were eventually converted to house **Mount Morris Bank and Safety Deposit Vaults**. The building is distinguished by Richardsonian Romanesque arches and stained glass. The district also has a fine collection of religious buildings. Dating from 1907, the neoclassical **Mount Olivet Baptist Church**, at 201 Lenox Avenue, was originally designed by **Arnold W. Brunner** as **Temple Israel**, one of the most prestigious synagogues in the city. **St. Martin's Episcopal Church**, on Lenox Avenue at 122nd Street, is a bulky, asymmetrical Romanesque 1888 composition by **William A. Potter** with a carillon of 40 bells, second in size only to that of **Riverside Church**. Built in 1889 by **Lamb & Rich**, the **Bethel Gospel Pentecostal**

Assembly, at 36 West 123rd Street, used to be the **Harlem Club**. The **Greater Bethel AME Church**, built in 1892 by **Lamb & Rich**, was originally the **Harlem Free Library**. Originally the **Dwight Residence**, **Frank H. Smith**'s 1890 building at 1 West 123rd Street is now the home of the **Ethiopian Hebrew Congregation**. It is a Renaissance mansion with an unusual round- and flat-bayed front that is a strong addition to the block of fine brownstones on West 123rd Street ♦Bounded by Mt. Morris Park W and Lenox Ave, and W 119th and W 124th Sts

50 Marcus Garvey Park

When the city purchased this craggy square of land in 1839, it was named **Mount Morris Park**. It was renamed in 1973 for Garvey, who was a brilliant orator and the founder of the Universal Negro Improvement Association and of the now-defunct newspaper *Negro World*. The highland in the center supports the **Mount Morris Fire Watchtower**; placed here in 1856, it's the only one surviving in the city. Its steel frame and sweeping spiral stairs, once practical innovations, are now nostalgic. ♦Bounded by Madison Ave and Mt Morris Park W, and E 120th and E 124th Sts. www.nycgovparks.org

51 Harlem Courthouse

Constructed with a mix of brick and stone, this Romanesque edifice was built in 1891 to the designs of **Thom & Wilson**. With its gables, archways, and corner tower, the dignified and delicate mass represents the American tradition of great "country" courthouses. It's of particular interest now, as this gem sits amidst a heap of modern block housing. ♦ 170 E 121st St (between Third and Lexington Aves)

52 Patsy's Pizzeria

★$ This location is the original Patsy's and it's well worth making the trip uptown for what connoisseurs say is the most delicious thin-crust pizza in the city. ♦ Pizza ♦ Daily, lunch, dinner, and late-night meals. No credit cards accepted. 2287 First Ave (between E 117th and E 118th Sts). 534.9783. Also at other locations throughout the city

53 Malcolm Shabazz Harlem Market

Traditional African art, crafts, clothing, and textiles, like authentic kenté cloth, are the centerpieces at this vibrant block-long partly covered, partly open-air market. While there's some of the run-of-the-mill street-fair stuff on hand—sneakers, handbags, electronic gadgetry—there's also a fine lot of all-cotton kenté yardage (look for **Arielle & Melissa** at booth #32), handmade jewelry (try **Fanta Sylla,** booth #95), imported Kenyan pottery (**Mame Diara,** #8), hair-braiding boutiques, and custom perfumes and oils. See **Harley the Buckleman** at the market's West 115th side for buckle bling. And, mostly on weekends, there's an ethnic potpourri of food choices. ♦Daily. Enter from W 115th or W 116th St. 102 W 116th St (between Fifth Ave and Malcolm X Blvd). 987.8131

54 115th Street Branch, NYPL

This 1908 Renaissance composition in limestone, a style favored by architects **McKim**, **Mead & White**, is one of the finest of the branch libraries. ♦ 203 W 115th St (between St. Nicholas Ave and Frederick Douglass Blvd). 666.9393. www.nypl.org

55 Arthur A. Schomburg Plaza

These 35-story octagonal apartment towers, completed in 1975 by **Gruzen & Partners** and **Castro-Blanco**, **Piscioneri & Feder**, are distinguished markers across from the northeast corner of **Central Park**. The pairing of the balconies creates an original rhythm in moderating the scale. ♦ 1295 Fifth Ave (between E 110th and E 111th Sts). 289.4465

New York's first subway (one car, seating 22 passengers) was fueled by a blast of air from a huge steam-driven fan, which would suck the car back when it reached the end of the line. It traveled 10 miles an hour and ran under Broadway from Warren to Murray Streets, a distance of 312 feet. It was conceived and constructed in 1870 by Alfred Ely Beach, a publisher and the inventor of the typewriter.

BOROUGHS

While Manhattanites refer to **Brooklyn, Queens, The Bronx,** and **Staten Island** as the "outer" boroughs, residents of these boroughs refer to Manhattan as "the city." A great deal of attitude is implied therein. They are outside the skyline's media limelight and inevitably play supporting roles to Manhattan. Their main contribution to the city is workforce: folks in every type of business—be it arts, corporate, or the service industry—have long found the boroughs more affordable (and even, shock, more pleasant) to live in. And they hold their own on many fronts, with their own high-caliber restaurants, museums, theaters, and architecture, and of course, world-class stadiums and sports arenas.

The Bronx

The Bronx not only stands as a study in contrasts, but also typifies the rapid succession of growth and decline experienced throughout New York City—a microcosm of American urban change squeezed into just over half a century. Today it is a mélange of tenements, suburban riverfront mansions, seaside cottages, massive housing superblocks, and fading boulevards of grand Art Deco apartment towers. Well past the low of the 1970s and '80s, when The Bronx had become a synonym for urban decay, much of the borough is stable now (even elegant and pastoral). Heavy philanthropic and governmental investment, as well as the energetic efforts of community-based groups, are to be credited in helping to restore some of the more run-down areas. Artists have discovered the South Bronx for both living and work space, it has some of the most beautiful—and oldest—parks and gardens in the city, the area around Arthur Avenue is the home of what some folks call the "real" Little Italy, and the mega-**Hunts Point Market** there is home to not only the largest wholesale produce market in the country, but a newly modern Fulton Fish Market as well. Hey, the Bronx *is* up!

For the latest information on Bronx arts and art initiatives, contact the **Bronx Council on the Arts** (718/931.9500, www.bronxarts.org). The **Bronx Historical Society** (718/881.8900, www.bronxhistoricalsociety.org) is an excellent source for tours and local research. Try the easy-on/-off **Bronx Trolley**, www.bronxtrolley.com, for a simple way to see the main sites.

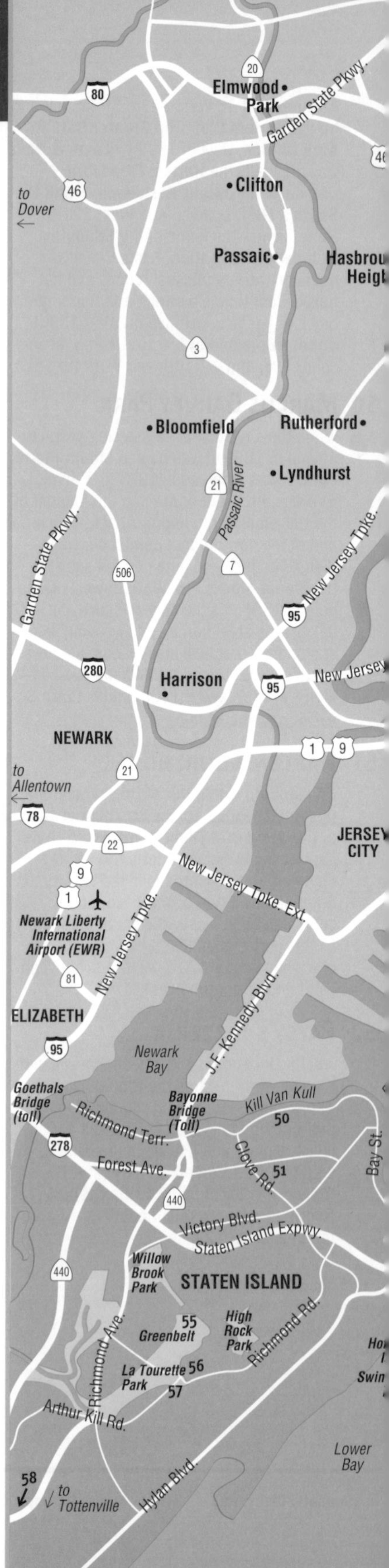

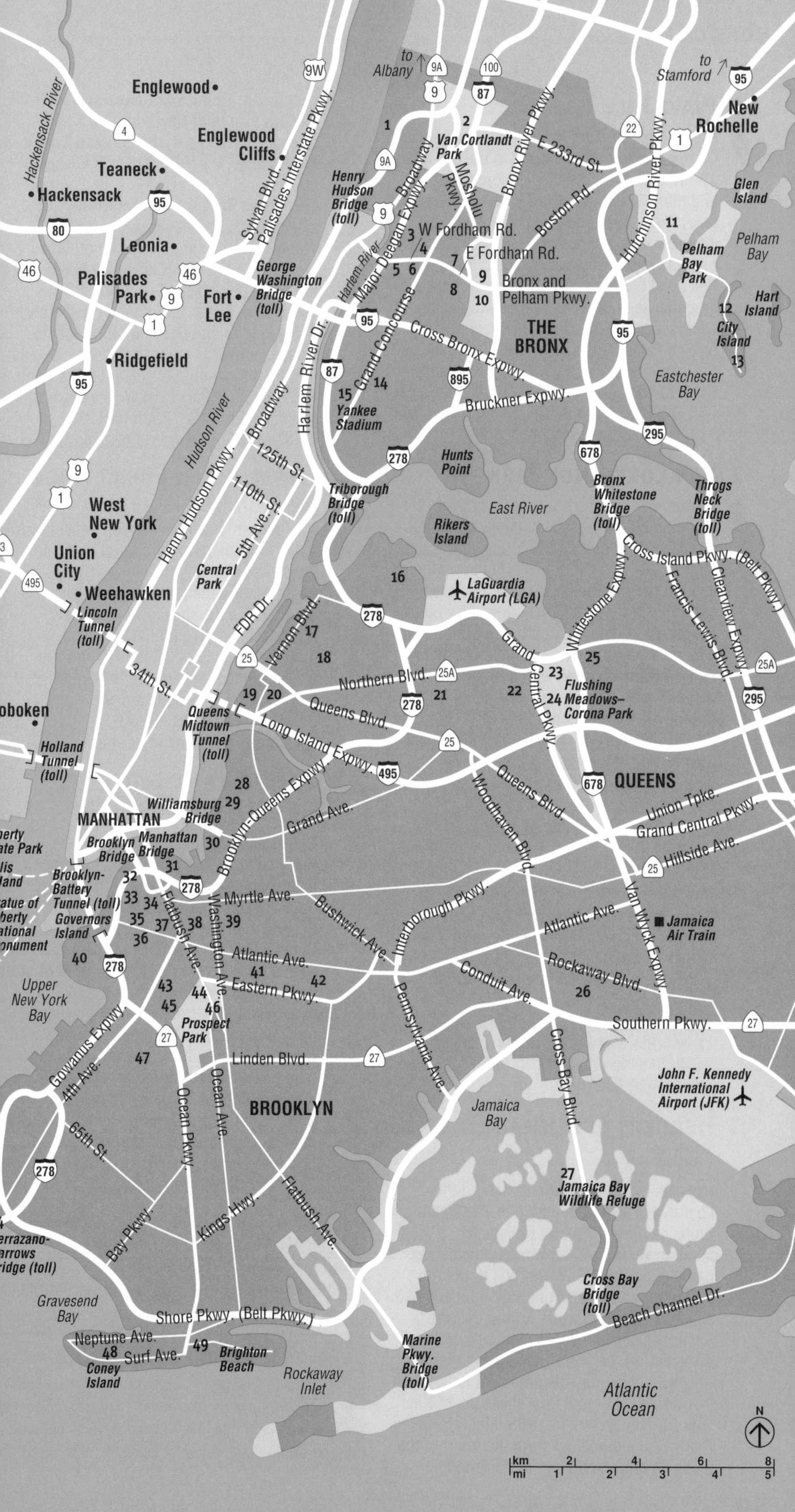

Englewood
Englewood Cliffs
Teaneck
Hackensack
Hackensack River
Leonia
Palisades Park
Fort Lee
Ridgefield
George Washington Bridge (toll)
Sylvan Blvd.
Palisades Interstate Pkwy.
to Albany
to Stamford
New Rochelle
Van Cortlandt Park
Henry Hudson Bridge (toll)
Broadway
Major Deegan Expwy.
Mosholu Pkwy.
Bronx River Pkwy.
E 233rd St.
Hutchinson River Pkwy.
Boston Rd.
Glen Island
Pelham Bay Park
Pelham Bay
Hart Island
City Island
W Fordham Rd.
E Fordham Rd.
Bronx and Pelham Pkwy.
Harlem River
Grand Concourse
Cross Bronx Expwy.
THE BRONX
Eastchester Bay
Bruckner Expwy.
Yankee Stadium
Harlem River Dr.
Hudson River
Hunts Point
Henry Hudson Pkwy.
125th St.
110th St.
5th Ave.
Triborough Bridge (toll)
Bronx Whitestone Bridge (toll)
Throgs Neck Bridge (toll)
West New York
Union City
Weehawken
East River
Rikers Island
Central Park
Cross Island Pkwy. (Belt Pkwy.)
Whitestone Expwy.
Francis Lewis Blvd.
Clearview Expwy.
LaGuardia Airport (LGA)
Lincoln Tunnel (toll)
FDR Dr.
Vernon Blvd.
Grand Central Pkwy.
34th St.
Northern Blvd.
Flushing Meadows–Corona Park
Hoboken
Queens Midtown Tunnel (toll)
Queens Blvd.
Long Island Expwy.
Holland Tunnel (toll)
QUEENS
Woodhaven Blvd.
Brooklyn-Queens Expwy.
Union Tpke.
Williamsburg Bridge
MANHATTAN
Grand Ave.
Brooklyn Bridge
Manhattan Bridge
Hillside Ave.
Brooklyn-Battery Tunnel (toll)
Myrtle Ave.
Interborough Pkwy.
Van Wyck Expwy.
Jamaica Air Train
Governors Island
Flatbush Ave.
Washington Ave.
Bushwick Ave.
Atlantic Ave.
Rockaway Blvd.
Upper New York Bay
Eastern Pkwy.
Conduit Ave.
Pennsylvania Ave.
Southern Pkwy.
Prospect Park
Gowanus Expwy.
Linden Blvd.
Cross Bay Blvd.
John F. Kennedy International Airport (JFK)
4th Ave.
Ocean Pkwy.
Ocean Ave.
BROOKLYN
Jamaica Bay
65th St.
Jamaica Bay Wildlife Refuge
Kings Hwy.
Bay Pkwy.
Cross Bay Bridge (toll)
Gravesend Bay
Shore Pkwy. (Belt Pkwy.)
Beach Channel Dr.
Neptune Ave.
Surf Ave.
Coney Island
Brighton Beach
Rockaway Inlet
Marine Pkwy. Bridge (toll)
Atlantic Ocean
N
km 2 4 6 8
mi 1 2 3 4 5

1 Wave Hill

The 28-acre Hudson River estate of financier George W. Perkins was given to the city in 1965. Arturo Toscanini, Theodore Roosevelt, and Mark Twain each lived here for a short time. The 19th-century mansion hosts a chamber music series and family-arts projects and presents vintage recordings of Toscanini concerts. The dazzling gardens and greenhouses put on an impressive display each season. Café, shop, and galleries. Tours on Sunday. ♦ Admission (free Tu, all day, and Sa, 9AM-noon). Tu-Su, 9AM-4:30PM (until 5:30PM 15 Apr-14 Oct); later on W in summer. 675 W 252nd St (at Sycamore Ave), Riverdale. 718/549.2055. www.wavehill.org ♿

2 Van Cortlandt Park

Wander deep enough into the city's fourth-largest park—with glacial ridges, wetlands, rare flora, and quite a few fauna—and you may forget you're in the city. Tamer features include trails, a cricket ground, and the country's first public golf course. From the southeast corner, look up to spot the ribbed-concrete Tracey Towers a few blocks away, built by **Paul Rudolph** with futuristic flair and very few right angles. ♦ Bounded by Broadway, Van Cortlandt Park S, W Gun Hill Rd, Jerome Ave, Van Cortlandt Park E, and the city line. www.vancortlandt.org ♿

Within Van Cortlandt Park:

Van Cortlandt House Museum

This Georgian-Colonial mansion is one of those where George Washington actually slept—it was his military headquarters on several occasions. Built in 1748, the mansion has been restored with Dutch, English, and Colonial furnishings. ♦ Admission. Tu-F, 10AM-3PM; Sa, Su, 11AM-4PM. Van Cortlandt Park, Broadway at 246th St within the park. 718/543.3344. www.vancortlandthouse.org

3 Herbert H. Lehman College, CUNY

More than 10,000 students attend this liberal arts school, founded in 1931 as the Bronx campus of Hunter College in Manhattan. Initially all-women, the school became co-ed after World War II, but not before it had served, for six months in 1946, as interim headquarters for the UN (the Security Council held its meetings in the gymnasium). Lehman—named for a former New York governor—became an independent institution within the City University of New York (CUNY) system in 1968. Finely detailed Tudor-Gothic buildings form the heart of the original campus; they were designed by **Thompson, Holmes & Converse** and **Frank Meyers** as one of New York State's WPA projects. In contrast, the **Lehman College Art Gallery** (718/960.8731) is housed in Lehman's Fine Arts Building, one of two here by modern Brutalist **Marcel Breuer.** The eclectic campus also includes **Rafael Viñoly**'s APEX, a sophisticated athletic facility. The **Lehman Center for the Performing Arts** (Box office: 718/960.8833) contains a 2,300-seat concert hall along with more intimate performance spaces. The complex attracts many of the same events that normally would play Manhattan only. ♦250 Bedford Park Blvd W (between Jerome and Goulden Aves), Bedford Park. 718/960.8000. www.lehman.cuny.edu ♿

4 Edgar Allan Poe Cottage

From 1846-1848 the writer and his dying wife lived in this little wooden house, which dates back to 1812. "Annabel Lee" and "The Bells" were among the works written here. Restored to period, the museum displays many of Poe's manuscripts and other memorabilia and contains some original furnishings, including his rocking chair. ♦ Admission. Sa, 10AM-4PM; Su, 1-5PM. E Kingsbridge Rd (at 193rd St), Grand Concourse. 718/881.8900. www.bronxhistoricalsociety.org

5 Hall of Fame for Great Americans

Bronze busts of nearly a hundred of America's greatest scientists, statesmen, and artists are on display in this handsome open-air colonnade designed in 1901 by **Stanford White**. Sculptures are by Daniel Chester French, Frederick MacMonnies, and James Earle Fraser. Set, appropriately, at the highest point in New York City, and overlooking the Bronx River, the sweeping neoclassical stone structure is adjacent to the gorgeously detailed (and Tiffany glass-bejeweled) **Gould Memorial Hall**, which is also by White. ♦ Free. Tours available. Daily 10AM-5PM. Bronx Community College, Hall of Fame Terr (between University and Sedgwick Aves), University Heights. 718/289.5161. www.bcc.cuny.edu ♿

The Bronx is the only borough that is part of mainland New York. Manhattan and Staten Island are islands, and Brooklyn and Queens are on the western end of Long Island. New York City is, in fact, an archipelago.

Flushing Meadows-Corona Park's Unisphere is the world's largest globe, at 140 feet high and 120 feet in diameter. Constructed for the 1964-1965 World's Fair, it was given landmark status by the Landmarks Preservation Commission in 1995.

6 Paradise Theater

When the Grand Concourse was grand, Loews Paradise Theater, built in 1929 by **John Eberson**, was an "atmospheric" movie-and-vaudeville palace where the auditorium's walls formed an Italian garden setting under a starry-sky ceiling. It fell into disuse before reopening in 2005, with its elaborate plasterwork and opulent fixtures lovingly restored from photos, as a setting for events from concerts to championship boxing (plus dining and nightlife). Tours, by appointment only. ♦ 2413 Grand Concourse (between 187th and 188th Sts). 718/220.6143. www.theparadisetheater.com ♿

7 Fordham University

One of the nation's foremost Jesuit schools, Fordham's **Rose Hill Campus** comprises 85 acres and has over 15,000 students enrolled in a traditional arts and sciences curriculum. **Rose Hill Manor** (1838), which now forms part of the **Administration Building**, was the home of the original school, **St. John's College**, begun in 1841 by John Hughes. Hughes later became New York State's first Catholic archbishop. This beautiful campus has a classic collection of Collegiate Gothic structures, most notably **Keating Hall**, designed in 1936 by **Robert J. Reiley**. **Fordham Law School** is located on its Lincoln Center campus. ♦ 441 E Fordham Rd (between Bathgate and Webster Aves), Fordham. 718/817.1000. www.fordham.edu ♿

8 Arthur Avenue Retail Market

This covered market is packed with stalls selling everything from high-quality Tuscan virgin olive oil to wheels of Parmigiano-Reggiano, fresh eggs, thinly sliced veal, baby eggplant, and zucchini. For the best cheese, stop by **Mike & Sons'** stall. ♦ M-Sa. 2344 Arthur Ave (between Crescent Ave and E 186th St), Fordham. 718/367.5686

8 Calabria Pork Store

Choose, if you can, among the 500 kinds of sausage dangling from the ceiling; all are delicious, many studded with peppercorns or garlic. ♦ M-Sa. 2338 Arthur Ave (between Crescent Ave and E 186th St), Fordham. 718/367.5145

8 Dominick's

★★$ Don't let the lines outside dissuade you from eating at this noisy and chaotic neighborhood favorite. Once inside, you'll be greeted with terrific home-style Southern Italian fare and a solicitous staff. Communal seating adds to the lively atmosphere. ♦ Italian ♦ M, W-Su, lunch and dinner. No reservations taken. No credit cards accepted. 2335 Arthur Ave (between E 184th and E 187th Sts), Fordham. 718/733.2807

9 New York Botanical Garden

Ⓟ One of the world's outstanding botanical gardens (and longstanding—it dates back to 1891), the National Historic Landmark's 250 acres include a 40-acre virgin hemlock forest, formal gardens, and the spectacular **Enid A. Haupt Conservatory**, a Victorian-style glass house modeled after the Great Palm House at Kew Gardens in England.

More than 3,000 exotic species are on show in the Conservatory, which, like much of the Garden, underwent an extensive renovation in 2001. Vibrant with changing plantings year-round, the gardens—both outdoors and in—also feature changing exhibits, such as the deliciously fragrant, color-kaleidoscope Caribbean Gardens, or Kiku, The Art of the Japanese Chrysanthemum. Dine in the delightful **Garden Café**, or even more casually in the Visitor Center café or in the picnic area. The Garden shop is a good source for planting advice for home-grown efforts. Coming via public transportation? Metro-North (from Grand Central) takes you to the door—that is, the main entrance at Moshulu Gate. ♦ Admission; advance ticketing available for special shows (additional fee). Tu-Su, hours change seasonally. Bounded by Bronx River Pkwy, Kazimiroff Blvd, and E Fordham Rd. 718/817.8700. www.nybg.org ♿

10 Bronx Zoo

Ⓟ Managed by the Wildlife Conservation Society, the zoo is home to almost 4,000 animals—650 species—on 265 acres, making it the largest metropolitan zoo in the United States. (See the map on page 320.) Near the north end is **Astor Court** (built from 1901 to 1922 to the Beaux Arts design of **Heins & LaFarge** and grandly restored in 2007), a collection of formal buildings that contains the **Zoo Center** (old elephant house), the renovated **Monkey House**, and the crowd-pleasing **Sea Lion Pool**. These structures, influenced by the 1893 Chicago World's Fair, were built as part of the original plan, which envisioned a formal central court area surrounded by natural park settings. The balance of the zoo's acreage is designed to re-create naturalistic habitats where African and Asian wildlife roam. 2003 brought the opening of **Tiger Mountain**, a spectacular setting (designed to re-create the Amur Valley environment between Russia and

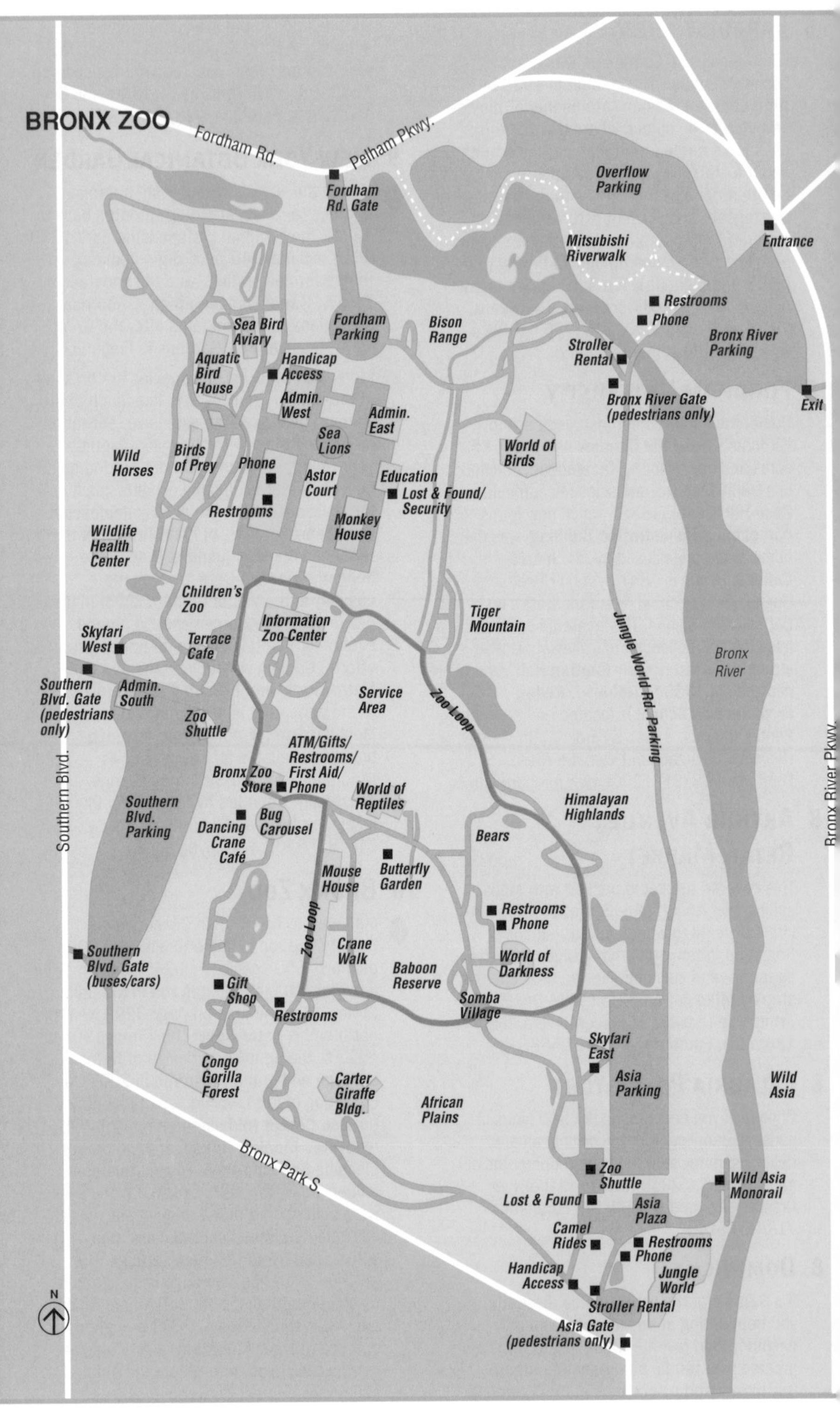
BRONX ZOO
Fordham Rd.
Pelham Pkwy.
Fordham Rd. Gate
Overflow Parking
Mitsubishi Riverwalk
Entrance
Restrooms
Phone
Bronx River Parking
Stroller Rental
Bronx River Gate (pedestrians only)
Exit
Sea Bird Aviary
Fordham Parking
Bison Range
Aquatic Bird House
Handicap Access
Admin. West
Admin. East
Sea Lions
World of Birds
Wild Horses
Birds of Prey
Phone
Astor Court
Education
Lost & Found/ Security
Restrooms
Monkey House
Wildlife Health Center
Children's Zoo
Tiger Mountain
Skyfari West
Terrace Cafe
Information Zoo Center
Jungle World Rd. Parking
Bronx River
Southern Blvd. Gate (pedestrians only)
Admin. South
Service Area
Zoo Loop
Zoo Shuttle
ATM/Gifts/ Restrooms/ First Aid/ Phone
Bronx Zoo Store
World of Reptiles
Himalayan Highlands
Bronx River Pkwy.
Southern Blvd.
Southern Blvd. Parking
Dancing Crane Café
Bug Carousel
Bears
Mouse House
Butterfly Garden
Restrooms
Phone
Zoo Loop
Crane Walk
World of Darkness
Southern Blvd. Gate (buses/cars)
Baboon Reserve
Gift Shop
Restrooms
Somba Village
Skyfari East
Congo Gorilla Forest
Carter Giraffe Bldg.
African Plains
Asia Parking
Wild Asia
Bronx Park S.
Zoo Shuttle
Wild Asia Monorail
Lost & Found
Asia Plaza
Camel Rides
Restrooms
Phone
Handicap Access
Jungle World
Stroller Rental
Asia Gate (pedestrians only)
N

China) for the 3-acre home of the largest of the big cats, Siberian tigers. That same year, a new baby was born at the zoo's hugely popular **Congo Gorilla Forest**. Young Zola joined the other lowland gorillas and other Congo wildlife, like mandrills and okapi, which were established here in 1999. Ever-updating, changes in the 2000s include a spectacular **Butterfly Garden** and an inspired **Bug Carousel** (a ride on one of its 64 species–praying mantis and more–is well worth the extra $2). There are shops and snack spots sprinkled about, but the largest space for year-round dining is the **Dancing Crane Café**, hard by the main **Bronx Zoo Store**. ♦ Admission. Free Wednesday, but expect a nominal fee at some individual habitats. Daily; hours change seasonally. Bounded by Bronx River Pkwy and Southern Blvd, and Bronx Park S and E Fordham Rd. 718/367.1010. www.bronxzoo.com ♿

Within the Bronx Zoo: ♿

Fordham Road Gate

Images of bears and deer decorate these imaginative Art Deco gates, created in 1934 by **Paul Manship.** Originally known as the Paul Rainey Memorial Gate (the prosaic name-change made, perhaps, due to Rainey's avocation as a big-game hunter), it was designed to open onto a 200-year-old Italian fountain donated by William Rockefeller. ♦ E Fordham Rd (at Bronx and Pelham Pkwy)

World of Birds

Visitors can observe more than 500 birds in the 25 environments of this well-designed aviary, with no bars or fences to obscure the view. It was designed in 1972 by **Morris Ketchum Jr. & Associates**. The recently opened **Aitken Aviary** is home to more than 100 Southern American sea birds (some were lost when the old aviary collapsed in 1995), including Inca terns and Magellanic penguins. ♦ Nominal admission. Daily

Children's Zoo

Children can explore prairie dog tunnels or hop like a wallaby in this hands-on zoo. Kids must be accompanied by an adult. The **Terrace Café** nearby stands ready to salve their hunger. ♦ Nominal admission. Last visitors admitted one hour before zoo closes.

Jungle World

This award-winning indoor rain forest has four habitats, five waterfalls, giant trees, and Asian animals separated from humans by bridges and small rivers. Look out for proboscis monkeys, silver-leaf langurs (monkey family), white-cheeked gibbons (ape family), and Indian gharials (a crocodilian relative that is believed to have lived 180 million years ago). ♦ Nominal admission Wednesday. Daily

World of Darkness

Day and night are reversed for the nocturnal animals who live here, so they are awake and active for daytime visitors. This fascinating exhibit was designed by **Morris Ketchum Jr. & Associates** in 1972. ♦ Nominal admission Wednesday. Daily

11 Bartow-Pell Mansion Museum

This Greek Revival home on beautifully manicured grounds, with views of the Long Island Sound and outstanding formal gardens, was built from 1836 to 1842. Fully restored to period, the early 19th-century furnishings, while not original, offer a fine survey of French and American Empire styles. This New York City landmark is a rare treat. Tours. ♦ Admission. W, Sa, Su, noon-4PM or by appointment. Pelham Bay Park, Pelham Bridge Rd (between City Island Rd and Park Dr). 718/885.1461. www.bartowpellmansionmuseum.org

12 City Island

A New England atmosphere persists on this small island that served as a US Coast Guard station in World War II. Located in the northeast reaches of The Bronx in Pelham Bay and attached to mainland New York by only one bridge, this picturesque 230-acre island is four blocks across at its widest point. It has the flavor of an island off the coast of Maine, not The Bronx, with marinas (four America's Cup yachts were built here), sea gulls, seafood restaurants, antiques shops, and atmosphere. The **New York Sailing School** (231 Kirby St, off King Ave, between Ditmars and Bowne Sts, 800/834.SAIL) offers boat rentals and sailing instruction from April through October. Like the island, the only museum is both charming and quirky. The **City Island Nautical Museum**, in the 1897-built PS 17 schoolhouse, features the library and archives of the City Island Historical Society, 1930s paintings of the island, and a Nautical Room packed with memorabilia from City Island's shipbuilding days, tracing the history of the island while offering a cache of old nautical curiosities. ♦ Museum: Su, 1PM-5PM, or by appointment. 190 Fordham St, over City Island Bridge. 710/885.0008. www.cityislandmuseum.org

12 Le Refuge Inn

$ Pierre Saint-Denis, proprietor/chef of Manhattan's East Side's popular

Le Refuge restaurant, also owns this seven-room inn in the beautifully restored 1876 **Samuel Pell House**, a New York City landmark. While none of the accommodations at the Inn's current location (for many decades they were down the street a bit, in another historic home) have private baths, the country-French décor is cozy and lovely—and the atmosphere is as gracious as ever. With fresh flowers everywhere, the occasional live jazz ensemble, and abundant antiques, this is a more-than-rare spot for New York City. While it's only a half hour by subway to Midtown Manhattan, it will seem light-years away. Continental breakfast is included. Prix-fixe lunch and dinner (Tu-Su; reservations required) are open to guests and visitors alike. ♦ 586 City Island Ave (between Cross St and City Island Bridge), City Island. 718/885.2478. www.lerefugeinn.com

13 Lobster Box

★$$$ The Masucchia family turned this small white 1812 house into a restaurant way back in 1946. The time shows in the service and décor, but pick from almost two dozen variations on the lobster theme—beginning with the simple steamed-and-split (lobsters here are never boiled)—or any of the fresh seafood, and simply enjoy watching the fleet of local boats glide by. ♦ Lobster/Seafood ♦ Daily, lunch and dinner Apr-Dec. 34 City Island Ave (between Belden and Rochelle Sts), City Island. 718/885.1952

14 The Bronx Museum of the Arts

Dedicated to 20th-century and contemporary art, the sleek and modern museum space is a terrific backdrop for the emerging and mid-career artists it often features. Changing solo and group shows range from traditional media to mixed-materials installations that might include just about anything from live performance to audio or video components, fashion, large-scale photography, and adornment. The museum's permanent holdings include the important **Stanley B. Burns Collection** of over 350 photographic portraits of African-Americans taken in the late 19th and early 20th centuries. Founded in 1971, the museum's current location in the heart of the historic **Grand Concourse** (not far from Yankee Stadium) makes it readily accessible to the diverse public the museum's mission strives to engage. Its exciting **Arquitectonica**-designed expanded (in 2006) facility makes a striking contribution to architectural diversity as well. Shows here often have a political- or issues-based subcontext; conceptual installations by Brazilian artist **Valeska Soares**, exquisite folk art–inspired paintings by Japan's **Tomie Arai**, and charcoals inspired by historic photographs by Bronx-born **Whitfield Lovell** are representative of the thought-provoking work that may often be found here. Bronx Museum's **Performance LAB** offers live stage performances, club nights, film and video screenings, music, new media, and dance. Shop. ♦ Suggested admission; free Friday. Closed M, Tu. 1-Th, Sa-Su, noon-6PM; F noon-8PM. 1040 Grand Concourse (at 165th St). 718/681.6000. www.bxma.org ♿

15 Yankee Stadium

Well over three-quarters of a century old, this iconic 57,545-seat horseshoe-shaped arena was designed in 1923 by Osborn Engineering Co. While remodeling over the years kept the home of the frequent World Series champs one of the most modern baseball facilities in the country, it finally reached its limits. Ground was broken in 2006 for their new 53,000-seat state-of-the-art facility (it's also planned to be a model of accessibility), located just to the north of this one. The new park—expected to open with the 2009 season—is designed to match the dimensions of the original: 11.6 acres, 3.5 of which are taken up by the field itself. Within the existing park are monuments to such Yankee greats as Lou Gehrig, Joe DiMaggio, Casey Stengel, and, of course, Babe Ruth; they will surely be relocated to the new grounds. ♦ E 161st St and River Ave, High Bridge. 718/293.4300; tours 718/579.4531. www.yankees.com ♿

Queens

This sprawling borough has always been a conglomeration of towns, villages, model communities, and real-estate developments. Suburban in spirit and design, it has grown far too dense to be anything but urban in essence, the type of immigrant staging ground that Manhattan, Brooklyn, and The Bronx used to be. Next to Athens, Queens has the world's largest Greek community in **Astoria**, while **Flushing**'s **Chinatown** rivals (if not surpasses) Manhattan's, and **Woodside**, **Elmhurst**, and **Jackson Heights** are home to ever-growing Indian, Asian, and Latino populations. The borough is also home to a growing arts—and museum—community. Queens is oriented toward the highways that lace it together, toward the airports (**Kennedy** and **LaGuardia**) that sit on either shore, and toward the suburban reaches of Nassau County. Things have changed considerably since the area of Queens was created in 1683 as one of the 12 counties in the province of New York. A destination for the earliest Quakers, this consummate melting pot was named for Queen Catherine of Braganza, the Portuguese-born wife of King Charles II of England.

For the latest information on the arts in Queens, contact the **Flushing Council on Culture and the Arts** at Flushing Town Hall, 137-35 Northern Boulevard (at Linden Pl), 718/463.7700, www.flushingtownhall.org. The **Queens Historical Society** (housed in historic Kingsland Cottage, 143-1135 37th Ave, Flushing) has exhibits and an extensive historical library. 718/939.0647, www.queenshistoricalsociety.org

16 Steinway Mansion

William Steinway was a great friend of President Grover Cleveland and presented him with a grand piano as a wedding gift. The Steinway home, built in 1856, was once a lively setting for fairy-tale social events. ♦ Not open to the public. 18-33 41st St (at 19th Ave), Astoria

17 The Noguchi Museum

Completed in 1985, and fully renovated and reopened in 2004, this is one of the few museums dedicated to the work of a single artist, created by that artist. Isamu Noguchi (1904-1988) had a controversial career filled with projects that ranged from immense sculpture gardens to akari lamps to set designs for choreographers Martha Graham and George Balanchine. Well-suited to the raw industrial space of this former photoengraving plant, some of the greatest examples of Noguchi's work are on display in the museum's 12 galleries and outdoor sculpture garden. A nice gift shop (with a small café) carries the full line of akari "light sculptures" and runs a video that explains how these special forms are made. *Note:* While you're here, **Socrates Sculpture Park**—where large-scale alfresco modernist sculpture complements the equally large-scale views back to Manhattan—is just a few blocks away (718/956.1819, www.socratessculpturepark.org). ♦ Admission; free first Friday of the month. Closed M, Tu. W-F, 10AM-5PM; Sa, Su, 11AM-6PM. 9-01 33rd Road (at Vernon Blvd), Long Island City. 718/204.7008. www.noguchi.org

18 Kaufman Astoria Studio

Rudolph Valentino and Gloria Swanson starred in silent films made here in the heyday of New York City's motion picture boom. Edward G. Robinson made the early talkie *Hole in the Wall* here, and the Marx Brothers used the studio for the filming of *The Cocoanuts.* After the studio's 1932 bankruptcy, the property passed through several hands. During World War II, it was used by the army for training and propaganda films done by Frank Capra. Now a historic landmark—not open to the public—the studio is back in business. It has been a favorite location of directors Sidney Lumet, Woody Allen, and others. ♦ 34-12 36th St (between 35th and 34th Aves), Astoria. 718/392.5600

18 Museum of the Moving Image

Opened in 1988 in one of the old Astoria Studio buildings (**Gwathmey Siegel & Associates** did the redesign), this museum is all that its name advertises and more, with extensive archives, special showings, and exhibitions. There are no snobbish distinctions between film and TV or technology and art, but it's not about junk culture, either. The artifacts displayed leave the visitor with an indelible impression of Pop history. Permanent exhibitions include "Behind the Scenes," an enlightening display on film production. Screenings—such as a Scorsese retrospective, or classic movie serials—take place in the **Red Grooms**-designed Tut's Fever Movie Palace. Rare and out-of-print scripts and some swell film doodads may be found in the book and gift shop; a small café provides sustenance . ♦ Admission; free Friday after 4PM. Most films (F evening; Sa, Su, afternoon and evening) are free with admission. Closed M, Tu. W, Th, 11AM-5PM; F, 11AM-8PM; Sa, Su, 11AM-6:30PM. 36-01 35th Ave (at 36th St), Astoria. 718/784.0077 www.movingimage.us ♿

19 Water's Edge

★★★$$$ Surrounded by glass walls on three sides, the tables in this swank riverside restaurant all have spectacular west-looking views of Midtown and Lower Manhattan. The creative menu includes items from fish to fowl, like bread-crusted French sea bass, pink snapper in filo, and sautéed mallard duck breast. A lighter (and less expensive) café menu is offered in their bar and lounge, and, seasonally, on the promenade. Manhattanites need not fret about transportation to and from Queens—the restaurant runs a complimentary dinner ferry from East 34th Street. ♦ Seafood ♦ M-F, lunch and dinner; Sa, dinner. Prix fixe available. Reservations required; jacket preferred. 44th Dr (between Vernon Blvd and the East River), Long Island City. 718/482.0033

Queens is the largest of New York City's five boroughs, covering 109 square miles.

Before 1929, the site now occupied by LaGuardia Airport was once an amusement park.

The New York Botanical Garden's conservatory is the largest Victorian glasshouse in the world.

20 Manducatis

★★$$ Family atmosphere and a cozy fireplace give this place an authentic trattoria feeling. Chef Ida's fine, straightforward touch with fresh ingredients brings people from all over town to this out-of-the-way spot. One of the best dishes on the menu is pappardelle with garlic and white beans, but most regulars don't even look at the menu; they simply ask their server what looks good that day. ♦ Italian ♦ M-F, lunch and dinner; Sa, Su, dinner. Reservations recommended. 13-27 Jackson Ave (at 47th Ave), Long Island City. 718/729.4602

20 P.S.1/MoMA

Since 2001 an official affiliate of the **Museum of Modern Art** (**MoMA**), this 19th-century school was adapted and reopened in 1976 as the P.S. 1 Contemporary Art Center, a venue for innovative installation art. Ever since, it has been used for exhibitions of new and established contemporary artists, most often of the cutting-edge variety. An extensive renovation and expansion, designed by Frederick Fisher, was completed in 1997. **The Clocktower Gallery**, P.S. 1's affiliate in Lower Manhattan, houses the museum's online radio station. **Le Rosier Café** is onsite. ♦ Suggested admission; free to MoMA ticket holders. Th-M, noon-6PM. 22-25 Jackson Ave (at 46th Ave), Long Island City. 718/784.2084. www.ps1.org ♿

20 Silvercup Studios

In 1983, the **Silvercup Bakery** was converted into a movie studio. Eighteen soundstages are contained within a mammoth three-block-long building. In addition to providing space for work on movies (*Garbo Talks, Street Smart, The Purple Rose of Cairo*), commercials (which account for most of the activity), and music videos, the studio rents screening rooms and production offices; some of the lucky tenants have windows overlooking the New York skyline. ♦ 42-22 22nd St (between 43rd Ave and Queens Plaza S), Long Island City. 718/784.3390

21 Little India

In **Jackson Heights**, this area is a solid, family-oriented neighborhood of Argentinians, Thais, Spaniards, Koreans, Italians, and Pakistanis. But the bold colors and pungent smells of India make it the most foreign and exotic to the curious visitor. Some 60,000 Indian immigrants in the New York City area either live on this one block of 74th Street north of Roosevelt Avenue or flock here regularly to shop, eat, and visit. Sari shops, aromatic grocery stores, jewelry stores whose windows are laden with 22K-gold wedding bands, and about a dozen authentic restaurants are part of the lively scene. ♦ 74th St (between Roosevelt and 37th Aves), Jackson Heights

In Little India:

Jackson Diner

★★$ This is the place to come for genuine, authentically spiced (read: hot!) Indian cuisine, with fare from both northern and southern India well represented. The ambience is nil, but the food is incredibly good—and incredibly well-priced. The menu includes lots of tandoori and vegetarian specials, as well as lamb, chicken, and shrimp; the weekend brunch buffet is a taste-tester's wonder. ♦ Indian ♦ M-F, lunch and dinner; Sa, Su, brunch and dinner. No reservations taken. No credit cards accepted. 37-47 74th St (between Roosevelt and 37th Aves), Jackson Heights. 718/672.1232

Delhi Palace

★★$ This is Queens's most elegant "Little India" dining choice, with crisp white tablecloths, fresh flowers, attentive service, and quiet background music. In addition to selections from the menu, choose from the extensive buffet that appears at both lunch and dinner. Don't miss the chicken with creamy cashew sauce or tandoori shrimp with *masala* (a mild creamy) sauce. ♦ Indian ♦ Daily, lunch and dinner. 37-33 74th St (between 37th Ave and 37th Rd) 718/507.0666

22 Louis Armstrong House & Archives

Queens College has been the longtime repository for the archives of jazz great Louis "Satchmo" Armstrong. While those materials—his writings, music, and rare home recordings—were opened to the public in 1994 (by appointment only; 718/996.3670) the comfortable brick house that he and his wife, Lucille, bought in 1943 was just opened for tours in late 2003. Located in this working-class neighborhood, Armstrong had barely been off the road a year to enjoy it when he died in 1971. **Platt Byard Dovell White** did the restoration after a master plan by **Rogers Marvel Architects.** The mid-century vintage paints, furnishings, and appliances that Lucille herself selected with New York decorator Morris Grossberg, along with striking color patterns throughout Satchmo's many radios, reel-to-reel tape decks, stereo, and of course his trumpet, are on display. Declared a National Historic Landmark in 1977, the sensitive restoration includes a visitor center and gift shop. ♦ Admission. By tour only, Tu-F, 10AM-5PM; Sa, Su, noon-5PM; last tour given at 4PM daily. 34-56 107th St (between 34th and 37th Aves), Corona. 718/478.8274. www.satchmo.net

23 Shea Stadium

Home of the **New York Mets**, this 55,300-seat stadium, designed by **Praeger-Kavanagh-Waterbury**, also hosted Pope John Paul II in 1979 and the history-making 1965 Beatles concert (the first of three they performed here). The stadium opened for the amazin' National League team's 1964 season, which coincided with the **World's Fair** next door at **Flushing Meadows-Corona Park**. Today, the big blue stadium's days are numbered: its replacement, the 45,000-seat **Citi Field** (set outside the current park, just beyond left and center field), is scheduled to open in time for the 2009 season. Until then, traffic around the stadium is quite congested before and after games; call for directions by public transportation. ♦ 126th St (between Roosevelt Ave and Northern Blvd), Flushing. Front office: 718/507.METS; tickets: 718/507.TIXX www.mets.com ♿

24 Flushing Meadows–Corona Park

Once a garbage dump, this triumph of reclamation, smack dab in the geographic center of New York City, was later chosen for the 1939-40 and 1964-65 **New York World's Fairs**. Among the few related structures still standing today are the 380-ton, 12-story-tall stainless steel **Unisphere** (designed by Peter Mueller-Munk) and Philip Johnson's futurist **New York State Pavilion** from the second fair, and the **New York City Pavilion** (now the **Queens Museum of Art**) from the first. **Meadow Lake**, at the center of the park, is also the center of a wealth of sports and special events, notably the annual **Hong Kong Dragon Boat Festival** in August. ♦ Bounded by Van Wyck Expwy, Grand Central Pkwy, and 111th St, Flushing. www.nycgovparks.org ♿

Within Flushing Meadows-Corona Park:

New York Hall of Science

Cutting-edge **Science City**, a major expansion for the Hall of Science, which includes a new **Rocket Park**, was completed in 2004. The additional 55,000 square feet of exhibit space was designed by **Polshek Partners Architects** and builds on the original space, which was designed by **Wallace K. Harrison** and built as a science pavilion for the 1964-65 **World's Fair**. This is New York's only hands-on science and technology museum. Besides those sparkling hallmarks of the early Space Age—an Atlas and a Titan 2 rocket, which were refurbished and reinstalled outside in 2003—the sophisticated collection includes 150 interactive exhibits focusing on color, light, microbiology, structures, feedback, and quantum physics. Outside, in the 30,000-square-foot **Science Playground**, kids can exercise both minds and bodies. Try the water play area, the construction zone, and the oversized teeter-totter that will balance 25 children at once. Science is made fun for youngsters, who learn centrifugal force on the Standing Spinner and kinetic energy from the enormous Pinball Machine. ♦ Admission. Tu-Su. 47-01 111th St (at 46th Ave). 718/699.0005. www.nyscience.org ♿

Queens Botanical Garden

Created in the shadow of the two World's Fairs, **The Unisphere** from the 1964-65 event may be seen from these verdant grounds just outside Flushing Meadows-Corona Park. About half of the tree-lined 39-acre gardens is devoted to native and exotic plants, with rich seasonal displays of flowering greenery. In the open space bounded by a circular rose garden, you're as likely to see a neighborhood tai chi demonstration as you are children frolicking. Reclaimed in the 1990s after a protracted fallow period, the Garden today is host to a wealth of programs and events and a welcome oasis from its urban surrounds. A foot bridge at its south end connects the Garden to the Park, or you may access it directly from Main Street. ♦ Free. Tu-Su; hours vary seasonally. 43-50 Main St (at Dahlia Ave), Flushing. 718/886.3800. www.queensbotanical.org ♿

Queens Museum of Art (QMA)

Highlights of this museum—housed in the only remaining building from the 1939 World's Fair—include art and photography shows, the important Neustadt Tiffany Art collection, and the world's largest scale model: a 9,225-square-foot panorama of New York City that is regularly brought up to date and includes just about every street, building, bridge, and park at a scale of one inch to 100 feet. **Rafael Viñoly**'s dramatic renovation of the interior galleries in 1994 complements the solid Art Deco-era building designed by **Aymar Embury II**. ♦ Suggested admission. W-Su. Off 49th Ave and 111th St, next to the Unisphere. 718/592.5555. www.queensmuseum.org

USTA National Tennis Center

Home to the US Open tennis championships since 1978, the center (built around the Singer Bowl from the 1964 World's Fair) now boasts the **Arthur Ashe Stadium**, the site of the annual August tournament. And for those who want to feel like champions, there are 27 outdoor courts and 9 indoor courts. Call to reserve play times. ♦ Fee. 111-51 Corona Ave. 718/760.6200. www.usta.com ♿

25 Joe's Shanghai

★★$ Don't ask for the usual Chinese fare here. This medium-size restaurant doesn't fit the mold of eateries that are now located in the area dubbed "New Chinatown." Among connoisseurs this place is known for its crabmeat steamed dumplings, which you first pierce in order to taste the savory crab-pork filling. Other tempting starters are shredded pork noodle soup, pork-and-chive fried dumplings, and scallion pancake. Among the best main dishes are crispy whole yellowfish, pan-fried noodles with chicken, fresh shiitake mushrooms with hearts of cabbage, and calamari with spicy black bean sauce. ♦ Chinese ♦ Daily, lunch and dinner. 136-21 39th Ave (between 138th and Main Sts), Flushing. 718/539.3838. Also in Manhattan at 9 Pell St (between Bosert and Doyers Sts), 212/233.8888; 24 W 56th St (between Fifth and Sixth Aves). 212/333.3868

26 Aqueduct

Thoroughbred racing takes place here. ♦ Oct-May. Rockaway Blvd (between 114th and 108th Sts), Ozone Park. 718/641.4700 ♿

27 Jamaica Bay Wildlife Refuge

Ⓟ Within the **Gateway National Recreation Area**, these sadly diminishing, once vast man-made tidal wetlands and uplands are still a haven for hundreds of species of birds and plants. The fall migratory season, starting in mid-August, is a particularly good time to come. Dress appropriately. ♦ Free. Daily. Visitor Center: Cross Bay Blvd (at First Rd), Broad Channel. 718/318.4340. www.nps.gov/gate ♿

Brooklyn

With over 300 years of history and more than 75 square miles of land, Brooklyn has always been a city in its own right. It has also been a step up the ladder for immigrant groups, an oceanfront resort, a shipping capital, a cultural mecca, a teeming slum, and the front-runner of an urban renaissance. Its national reputation is built on vaudeville jokes, a inimitable accent, urban conflict, and a host of famous and often comedic natives—George Gershwin, Woody Allen, Mel Brooks, Barbra Streisand and Beverly Sills among them. Impressive as it may be, this esteem doesn't begin to do justice to the diverse immensity of what would be, were it still autonomous, America's fourth-largest city. Independent until its annexation into New York City in 1898 (Brooklyn-born author Pete Hamill calls this the "great mistake"), Brooklyn has many of the earmarks of a major metropolis.

In a state of constant renewal, neighborhoods starting from **Park Slope** and **Brooklyn Heights**, to **Cobble Hill** and **Fort Greene**, and into the 2000s, Bushwick, **Bedford-Stuyvesant**, and even **Brooklyn Navy Yard** have seen development and growth. Arts communities have—as always—often led the way. **Red Hook** is the most recent such "settlement," and of course, **Williamsburg**, just across the East River, is the clearest example; **DUMBO** (Down Under the Manhattan Bridge Overpass) is another.

The borough is divided into many ethnic diversities, among them the Middle Eastern development along **Atlantic Avenue**, the Russian section of **Brighton Beach**, the Italian enclave **Bensonhurst**, Hasidim and Hispanics in **Crown Heights**, and the Asian center in **Sunset Park**. On any day, you'll see locals and visitors cramming the markets and stores in these vibrant communities. Much of the charm (and claustrophobia) of the Old Country can still be found in the heart of Brooklyn.

For the latest information on arts and culture in Brooklyn, contact **Brooklyn Information & Culture (BRIC)**, 718/855.7882; www.brooklynx.org. Additional Brooklyn information including walking tours, restaurants, lodging, and more may be found at the Brooklyn Tourism and Visitors' Center, 209 Joralemon Street, Brooklyn Heights. 718/802.3846. www.brooklyntourism.org. The **Brooklyn Historical Society** (see page 327) is another excellent borough resource.

28 Galapagos

This avant-garde venue, situated in the hull of a former mayonnaise factory, does triple duty as a bar, performance space, and screening room for foreign and experimental films. It's not as stark as it sounds: There are candles floating in a sculptured pond as you walk in, and more candles crawl up the exposed brick walls inside. Clever cabaret acts are known to enliven the bar scene at regular intervals throughout the night. ♦ Daily. 70 N 6th St, Williamsburg. 718/782.5188 ♿

29 Planet Thailand

★$ Owners David and Anna Popermhem add pizzazz to their restaurant's menu using fresh ingredients for their flavorful salads, lemony and tender squid, and charred beef with onions, chilies, and basil; just as fresh is the sushi on the expanded Japanese side of the menu. Best Thai-inspired entrées include chicken in a fragrant coconut curry and the grilled, moist marinated chicken. ♦ Thai/ Japanese ♦ Daily, lunch and dinner. Reservations recommended. No credit cards accepted. 133 N Seventh St (between Bedford Ave and Berry St), Williamsburg. 718/599.5758

30 Peter Luger

★★★★$$$ One of the oldest and still one of the better, more colorful steak houses in the city, this place is great for one thing only: well-charred porterhouse steak made from prime, aged, Iowa corn-fed beef. These hefty heifer parts, for two or more, are always cooked perfectly to order and come presliced unless you request otherwise. Potato side dishes are serviceable, but skip the other vegetables. For dessert, try cheesecake or ice cream. ♦ Steak house ♦ Daily, lunch and dinner. Reservations required. No credit cards accepted. 178 Broadway (at Driggs Ave), Williamsburg. 718/387.7400 ♿

31 St. Ann's Warehouse

St. Ann's established themselves as a cultural force back in the 1980s when they were based in **St. Ann's Church** in Brooklyn Heights. Their reputation for cutting-edge performance—theatrical, musical, film, and more—traveled with them to their current location in this adapted warehouse space in DUMBO, right near the waterfront. The larger space has allowed even more versatility; since they moved here in 2001, they've been host to pieces like an update of a perennial favorite, a raucous puppet-opera version of Rossini's *The Barber of Seville*, and the renowned Wooster Group's take on Chekhov. The lobby **Rice Bar** offers drinks from sake to microbrews, snacks from tamales to chocolates, and is open before and after performances. ♦ 38 Water St (between Main and Dock Sts), DUMBO. 718/254.8779. www.stannswarehouse.org

32 River Café

★★★$$$ The backdrop of this lovely dining spot—the towering, glittering Manhattan skyline seen from the foot of the Brooklyn Bridge—is unequaled. The menu is just as exciting, with such dishes as crisp duck breast with fresh rhubarb sauce, Taylor Bay scallop ceviche, and Colorado rack of lamb with golden fondant potatoes. And don't miss dessert. The chocolate mousse layer cake, shaped like the Brooklyn Bridge, will put a smile on your face—and a few inches around your middle. The wine list features the most extensive selection of California labels you'll find this side of the Golden Gate Bridge. ♦ American ♦ M-Sa, lunch and dinner; Su, brunch and dinner. Dinner is prix fixe; there's a 3- or 6-course option. Reservations required; jacket required. 1 Water St (between Furman and Old Fulton Sts), DUMBO. 718/522.5200

32 Grimaldi's Pizza

★★$ Patsy Grimaldi learned the art of pizza making from his late uncle (also named Patsy), owner of the famed **Patsy's** pizzeria in East Harlem. Fans of the pizza here say that it has surpassed even Uncle Patsy's. The fresh dough is charred in a brick oven and the mozzarella is made fresh, as is the tomato sauce. This may be as close to pizza heaven as you can get. It's also Sinatra heaven, with that most famous of the Grimaldi family friends heavily represented on the jukebox and in photos adorning the walls. ♦ Pizza ♦ M, W-Su, lunch and dinner. No credit cards accepted. 19 Old Fulton St (between Front and Water Sts), Brooklyn Heights. 718/858.4300 ♿

33 Brooklyn Historical Society

Housed in an immaculately restored 1881 landmark building, the Brooklyn Historical Society returned here in 2004 after an ambitious four-year restoration project was completed. The grand redbrick Romanesque structure is now even better suited to hold the diverse collections that so well reflect Brooklyn's wide-ranging heritage. Besides a huge library of books, maps, and photographs (now in a database, and available in digital format), their growing archives include many original paintings of the borough, and among Brooklyn Dodgers memorabilia, their 1955 World Series banner. ♦ Admission. W-Su, noon-5PM. 128 Pierrepont St (between Henry and Clinton Sts), Brooklyn Heights/ Downtown. 718/222.4111. www.brooklynhistory.org

34 Brooklyn Borough Hall

A palatial sweep of stairs rises to the entrance of this Greek Revival hall of government, designed by **Gamaliel King** and built in 1851. The building, originally fashioned after **Dr. William Thornton**'s competition-winning design, was supposed to mimic Manhattan's **City Hall**, but subsequent design changes dulled the effect. ♦ 209 Joralemon St (at Court St), Downtown. 718/802.3700 ♿

35 New York Transit Museum

Popular with both young and old transportation buffs, this small museum—located in a decommissioned subway station and reopened in fall 2003 after extensive renovations, just in time for the 2004 subway centennial—takes you back in time with one of the world's finest collections of mass transit artifacts, including vintage cars, signal equipment, turnstiles, mosaics, photographs, and an extensive collection of engineering drawings dating to the beginning of the century. ♦ Admission. Tu-F, 10AM-4PM; Sa, Su, noon-5PM. Schermerhorn St (at Boerum Pl), Brooklyn Heights. 718/694.1600. Also at Grand Central Terminal, Manhattan. 212/878.0106. www.mta.info ♿

36 Tripoli

★★$ Atlantic Avenue is the city's center for Middle Eastern cuisine, and among the numerous small restaurants, this family-run bi-level place, in business since the early 1970s, is probably the best and most authentic. Order any of the Lebanese dishes, including falafel, hummus, lamb kabobs, stuffed grape leaves, lamb stew, and one of the heavily honeyed desserts. On some Saturday nights there's live music and entertainment. ♦ Middle Eastern ♦ M, W-Su, lunch and dinner. Reservations recommended Friday and Saturday nights. 156 Atlantic Ave (at Clinton St), Brooklyn Heights. 718/596.5800

37 Junior's

★★$$ Some say the cheesecake at this vintage 1950 institution is the best in New York, and it just may be true. The rest of the food is standard deli/diner fare, however, including pastrami sandwiches and roasted chicken, distinguished only by the large portions. Weekend evenings the place jumps, and the cars are double- and triple-parked out front. ♦ Deli ♦ Daily, breakfast, lunch, dinner, and late-night meals. 386 Flatbush Ave (at DeKalb Ave), Downtown. 718/852.5257. Also at Grand Central Terminal (E 42nd St and Vanderbilt Ave), Manhattan. 212/983.5257; 1515 Broadway (at W 45th St). 212/302.2000

38 Brooklyn Academy of Music (BAM)

This splendidly eclectic, internationally recognized performing arts center, affectionately known as "BAM," was founded in 1859 on Montague Street and is now mostly housed in a 1908 **Herts & Tallant**-designed building on Lafayette Avenue. Among the superlative performers who have appeared here are Edwin Booth as Hamlet and Sarah Bernhardt as Camille. Pavlova danced and Caruso sang here.

During his tenure over the last three decades of the 20th century, executive director Harvey Lichtenstein has introduced many innovative programs in music and dance. His annual **Next Wave Festival** has been the launching pad for an international roster of artists like Philip Glass, Pina Bausch, Laurie Anderson, and choreographer Mark Morris. In 1987, the organization reopened the **Majestic** (now **Harvey**), an 83-year-old theater-turned-movie-house that had been lying dormant for nearly 20 years. The 874-seater was renamed the **Harvey Lichtenstein Theater** in 1999, when the gifted impresario retired. Interestingly, the shell of the theater was left intact—the wear and tear of the years showing—while two semicircular tiers of seats around a large stage were built, creating an intimate amphitheater-like space with an exciting medieval feel. The interior was designed by **Hardy Holzman Pfeiffer Associates**.

Besides being the primary performing home of the **Brooklyn Philharmonic**—in the 21,000-seat **Howard Gilman Opera House**—BAM has other vital programming. In 1997 **BAMcafé** opened (in the **Lepercq Space**) with a restaurant and live music, followed one year later by the four-screen **BAM Rose Cinemas**. **BAMcinématek** features repertory classics on one of these screens; the others offer first-run major releases as well as smaller independent films. ♦ A shuttle bus coordinated with scheduled performances at the Opera House and **Harvey Theater** departs one hour before curtain from the **Whitney Museum at Altria** (120 Park Ave at E 42nd St) in Manhattan. Harvey Theater, 651 Fulton St (between Ashland and Rockwell Pl); Howard Gilman Opera House, BAM Rose Cinemas, BAMcafé, Box Office: Peter Jay Sharp Building, 30 Lafayette Ave (between St. Felix St and Ashland Pl), Fort Greene. 718/636.4100. www.bam.org ♿

39 Pratt Institute

Architecture, business, science, and fine arts are the strong suits of this 3,200-student school established in 1887. The 25-acre main campus has a large outdoor **Sculpture Park** featuring changing shows of work from renowned American artists. ♦ 200 Willoughby Ave. Bounded by Taaffe Pl and Hall St, and DeKalb and Willoughby Aves (between Classon Ave and Hall St), Clinton Hill. 718/636.3600. Also at 144 W 14th St (between Sixth and Seventh Aves), Manhattan. 212/647.7775. www.pratt.edu ♿

40 Red Hook/Brooklyn Cruise Terminal

On a still-gritty slice of waterfront, you can drop into galleries, sample local beers, buy groceries at the fine **Fairway Market** (in a pre-Civil War cotton and coffee warehouse) off Van Brunt Street, or fish off a pier. Passenger ships such as the *Queen Mary 2* put in at the glossy **Brooklyn Cruise Terminal** amid the industrial buildings, brick row houses, and vacant lots. Before hopping a **Water Taxi** (www.nywatertaxi.com); Fairway's café is dockside to Manhattan, stop by the ball fields off Bay Street to sample the wares of vendors who dish up Honduran *baleadas* and Ecuadorean ceviche. ♦ Bounded by Hamilton Ave and the Gowanus Expwy

41 Brooklyn Children's Museum (BCM)

In this unusually comprehensive—and creative—children's museum, a unique underground structure built in 1976 to the designs of **Hardy Holzman Pfeiffer Associates**, kids visit a greenhouse, contemplate butterflies and fossils, and learn about how animals get energy from food. They can also participate in a dream sequence inside a 25-foot model of a sleeping head and use their five senses to unlock the mystery of objects, using as tools 20,000 cultural artifacts and natural history specimens from the museum's collection. Special events include films, workshops, field trips, concerts, and storytelling sessions. ♦ Expected to open in 2008, **Rafael Viñoly**'s daffodil-yellow, three-level redesign brings the 1899 institution aboveground for the first time in some 30 years at this site; not only that, it's the first LEED-certified "green" museum in New York City. ♦ Admission. W-Su. 145 Brooklyn Ave (at St. Mark's Ave), Crown Heights. 718/735.4400. www.brooklynkids.org ♿

42 Weeksville Heritage Center

In the mid-1800s, the Weeksville enclave was one of the nation's earliest free black communities—a center for commerce and culture, a haven for those fleeing slavery in the South and racial violence in the North. Today its past is compellingly preserved in four frame structures—the **Hunterfly Road Houses**, restored to showcase different eras—as well as an education center with exhibition and performance space, a library, and a café. ♦ Tu-Sa. 1698 Bergen St (between Utica and Ralph Aves). 718/756.5250. www.weeksvillesociety.org ♿

43 Santa Fe Grill

★$ At this popular spot for the young after-work crowd, the bar offers a variety of fancy concoctions and thirst-quenching margaritas. The serene Southwestern setting, rich in New Mexican artifacts, is lovely; the noise level, however, makes for a less-than-peaceful mood. The food is quite respectable for this far north—try the vegetable quesadilla, any of the burritos and enchiladas (including a spinach-and-cheese variety), or one of the decent burgers. ♦ Tex-Mex ♦ Daily, dinner. 62 Seventh Ave (at Lincoln Pl), Park Slope. 718/636.0279

43 Leaf & Bean

Approximately 50 types of coffee beans and 20 types of loose tea are offered here, along with other gourmet items, including truffle candies, fancy jams, and white cocoa. There's also a large supply of kitchen accessories—wineglasses, cookie jars, place mats, Italian ceramic plates, candles, cloth napkins, and of course, a variety of coffeemakers and teapots. ♦ Daily. 83 Seventh Ave (between Union St and Berkeley Pl), Park Slope. 718/638.5791

44 Grand Army Plaza

Monuments have been added since the plaza was first laid out in 1870 by **Frederick Law Olmsted** and **Calvert Vaux**. The Roman-style **Soldiers' and Sailors' Arch** was raised as a tribute to the Union Army in 1892 and was later encrusted with Frederick MacMonnies's massive sculptures and some less exuberant bas-relief forms. The **Bailey Fountain** was added in 1932 by architect **Edgerton Swarthout** and sculptor **Eugene Savage**. **Morris Ketchum Jr. & Associates** designed the 1965 **John F. Kennedy Memorial**. We think it's notable as well for its proximity to the superb **Brooklyn Public Library** (oddly, not part of the New York Public Library system); both the library and Prospect Park are just across the plaza. Library: 718/230.2100, www.brooklynpubliclibrary.org ♦ Flatbush Ave (between Prospect Park and Plaza St), Park Slope/Prospect Heights

44 PROSPECT PARK

The **Grand Army Plaza** is the official entrance to this 526-acre park, as loved by Brooklynites as the larger **Central Park** is by Manhattanites. In fact, these two parks share designers (landscape architects **Frederick Law Olmsted** and **Calvert Vaux**), and—not surprisingly—landscaping characteristics (meadowlands, footpaths, skating rink, and boating lake). The recipient of a multimillion-dollar face-lift, the 1866-vintage park is these days quite reminiscent of its original bucolic state. **Lefferts Homestead**, an 18th-century Dutch farmhouse relocated here to be used as a museum, the magnificently restored 1912 **Carousel**, the Beaux Arts **Boathouse** (now the nation's first urban **Audubon Center**), and the popular **Prospect Park Zoo** are just a few of the sites that make this park so special. ♦ Bounded by Ocean Ave, Flatbush Ave, Prospect Park SW, Prospect Park W, and Parkside Ave. 718/965.8900. www.prospectpark.org ♿

45 BED & BREAKFAST ON THE PARK

$ Former antiques-store owner Liana Paolella has meticulously restored this landmark 19th-century home-turned-inn. Her guests enjoy eight spacious, beautifully furnished rooms (two with shared baths) replete with wood-burning fireplaces, canopied beds, stained-glass windows, Oriental rugs, and an extensive collection of museum-quality paintings. A scrumptious breakfast further complements the inn's grand style. ♦ 113 Prospect Park W (between Sixth and Seventh Sts), Park Slope. 718/499.6115; fax 718/499.1385. www.bbnyc.com

46 BROOKLYN MUSEUM

This museum (briefly the **Brooklyn Museum of Art**), which broke ground in 1893, always seems to be undergoing construction to complete the original Beaux Arts design of **McKim**, **Mead & White**. Its grand **West Wing** was the first section to open to the public, in 1907. The museum's vast and growing collections of fine arts and antiquities—it became home to the world-renowned **Wilbour Library of Egyptology** in 1934—led to various renovations over the years. 1993 saw the completion of work by **Arata Isozaki** and **James Stewart Polshek & Partners** that included three floors of new galleries in the **West Wing**, the 460-seat **Iris and B. Gerald Cantor Auditorium** (which serves as the museum's first formal gathering place since the original auditorium was converted into the **Grand Lobby** in the early 1930s), and two floors of additional art storage space. Yet another round of changes, completed in 2004-05, introduced a dramatic **Entrance Pavilion and Public Plaza** (also by Polshek), a state-of-the-art **Library**, and the important **Luce Center for American Art** galleries and **Study Center**.

Excellent collections include the arts of Egypt, the classical Middle East, and Asia. Exhibitions of primitive arts come from Africa, the South Pacific, and the Americas; other displays feature Greek and Roman antiquities. Costumes, textiles, decorative arts, and period furniture dating from the late 17th century are all beautifully laid out for viewing. Contemporary art and photography, as well as design from the 19th and 20th centuries, are also well-represented. The permanent collection includes works by Rodin, Modigliani, Cassatt, Degas, Monet, Chagall, Gauguin, Toulouse-Lautrec, Homer, Sargent, and Bierstadt. The museum has a particularly good book and gift shop. ♦ Admission. W-F, 10AM-5PM; Sa, Su, 11AM-6PM. 200 Eastern Pkwy (at Washington Ave), Prospect Heights. 718/638.5000. www.brooklynmuseum.org ♿

46 BROOKLYN BOTANIC GARDEN

Although not as large or as famous as the **New York Botanical Garden** in The Bronx, this one has such celebrated plantings as **Takeo Shiota**'s **Japanese Hill-and-Pond Garden** (meticulously restored to its 1915 magnificence and reopened in 2000), an herb garden with over 300 specimens, exquisite displays of cherry blossoms, and one of the largest public rose collections in America. A conservatory houses the largest bonsai collection in the country. The 50 acres of flora include a fragrance garden for the blind. Built on a former ash dump, the concept for the garden was laid out by the **Olmsted Brothers** firm (Frederick Law Olmsted's two sons: Frederick Law Olmsted Jr. and his half-brother, John Charles Olmsted) to complement the orientation of the adjacent **Brooklyn Museum**. Landscape architect **Harold Caparn** stepped in after the garden opened in 1910, and between 1912 and 1945 he created the **Magnolia Plaza**, the **Cranford Rose Garden**, and many more of the areas beloved today. The **Steinhardt Conservatory**, which was designed by **Davis**, **Brody & Associates**, was completed in 1988. ♦ Parking fee. Admission, free all day Tuesday and 10AM-noon Saturday. Tu-Su. 1000 Washington Ave (between Empire Blvd and Eastern Pkwy), Prospect Heights. 718/623.7200. www.bbg.org ♿

48 Coney Island

Its golden days may be in the past, but who's to say there isn't more life in Coney yet? Not the developers who have their eye on it for a modern-day condo extravaganza, plans which set the premature demise of the beloved Astroland rides in motion at the end of 2007. But rattling over the tracks since 1927, the wooden Cyclone roller coaster still provides thrills, as does the Wonder Wheel, and a Nathan's hot dog with everything on it is still a treat. In the early 2000s, grafitti artists put their skills to work creating eye-popping new signage, the Coney Island Circus Sideshow Museum was reestablished (718/372.5159; www.coneyisland.com), the old Parachute Jump was restored (though not operational), and the annual Mermaid Parade (June) had become a fixture. Today the beach is still fine and it sure beats the tar beaches many a city-dweller settles for on the roofs of their apartment buildings on hot summer weekends. In the 1920s, however, this was the Riviera, the "World's Largest Playground" for generations of hardworking immigrants and native New Yorkers. Though faded now, it still provides fun for thousands. The **Coney Island History Project** (718/265.2100; www.coneyislandhistory.org) maintains an exhibition center in the shadow of the Cyclone; don't miss the horse salvaged from the famous ride that helped make the long-gone **Steeplechase Park** so unforgettable. Surf Ave (between Ocean Pkwy and W 37th St)

47 Green-Wood Cemetery

Ⓟ A sort of who's-who of the interment world, Green-Wood is actually not only about who's here, but also what. Established in 1838 on the highest point in Brooklyn, the views are grand and the grounds are an oasis of rolling landscape—and a virtual arboretum when it comes to their diverse plantings. A stroll through this National Historical Landmark is a walk through New York's history and culture; a visitor cannot help but be intrigued by the literary inscriptions along with the art and unusual detail of the headstones and individual mausoleums, many of which have original Tiffany-glass windows. Bird watchers flock here as well. So, who's buried here? Stars of culture and commerce like Leonard Bernstein, the Brooks Brothers, Jean Michel Basquiat, and F.A.O. Schwarz; and a few famed for their notoriety, like Joey Gallo and "Boss" Tweed. Green-Wood offers tours and concerts, as well as other events. ♦ Free. Daily. Main entrance: Fifth Ave (at 25th St), Sunset Park. 718/768.7300. www.greenwood.com

At Coney Island:

Nathan's Famous

★$ Indeed, this is probably the most famous and elaborate hot-dog stand in the world, having served spicy franks and fabulously greasy, crinkle-cut fried potatoes for nearly a century. Nowadays, there are branches all over, but this was the first. ♦ American ♦ Daily. Surf and Stillwell Aves. 718/946.2202. Also at numerous locations throughout the city

48 New York Aquarium

Native creatures of the Hudson River and dramatic denizens of the shark tank are on exhibit in the **Native Sea Life** building. Penguins and sea lions provide comic relief, and **Aquatheater** shows provide great entertainment: dolphins in the summer and whales, walruses, and sea lions in the winter. There's also a **Discovery Cove**, where kids can touch sea stars and horseshoe crabs. ♦ Admission; parking fee. Daily. Surf Ave (between Ocean Pkwy and W 10th St). 718/265.3400. www.nyaquarium.com ♿

48 Keyspan Park/Brooklyn Cyclones

In the shadow of **Coney Island**'s storied amusements, this minor-league park is home to the **Brooklyn Cyclones** (a Mets farm team named for the landmark wooden coaster down the boardwalk). Major rivals are the **Staten Island Yankees** across the Narrows; come prepared to take sides. ♦ 1904 Surf Ave (at W 16th St). 718/449.8497. www.brooklyncyclones.com. ♿

49 National Restaurant

★★$$ Known for its boisterous good times and late-night bonhomie, this Russian restaurant is the place to come with friends; the rivers of vodka and the live band will have you singing tunes from the motherland before you know it. The set dinners are huge, featuring a parade of cold appetizers, such as herring with potatoes or beet salad, and five main courses, including shish kebab or roasted chicken. ♦ Russian ♦ F-Su, dinner and late-night meals. Reservations recommended. 273 Brighton Beach Ave (between Third and Second Sts), Brighton Beach. 718/646.1225

Staten Island

Geographically distant from the rest of New York, Staten Island seems to be more a spiritual cousin to New Jersey, only a narrow stretch of water away. In fact, Staten Island's political ties to New York City are a historical accident: The island was ceded to Manhattan as a prize in a sailing contest sponsored by the Duke of York in 1687. For ages, though, access was possible only by ferry from Manhattan or by car through New Jersey. In 1964, the **Verrazano-Narrows Bridge** opened, tying Staten Island to Brooklyn. With a new frontier so close at hand, modern-day settlers poured over the bridge and changed the rugged face of the island forever. In 1990, tired of being ignored, residents of the "forgotten borough" voted to create a charter commission to provide for the separation of Staten Island from the rest of New York City. The attempt failed, but if it had succeeded, Staten Island would have become the second largest city in the state of New York.

For the latest information on the arts and culture on Staten Island, contact the **Council for the Arts & Humanities for Staten Island** at **Snug Harbor Cultural Center** (718/447.3329; www.statenislandarts.org).

50 Snug Harbor Cultural Center

Granted Smithsonian Affiliate status in 2005, this 83-acre center for the performing and visual arts—a retirement village for sailors from 1833 until the mid-1970s—is composed of 28 historic buildings, many of which are fine examples of Greek Revival, Beaux Arts, Italianate, and Victorian architecture. Stop by the Visitors' Center for historical exhibitions and information on current and upcoming events, including indoor and outdoor classical, pop, and jazz concerts. A historical tour is held every Saturday and Sunday at 2PM. ♦ Daily, dawn to dusk. 1000 Richmond Terr (between Tysen St and Snug Harbor Rd), Livingston. 718/448.2500. www.snug-harbor.org ♿

Within Snug Harbor Cultural Center:

Newhouse Center for Contemporary Art

New and emerging artists not often seen in Manhattan galleries are shown here. The center also hosts an indoor/outdoor sculpture exhibition in the summer. ♦ Donation suggested. W-Su, noon-5PM. 718/452.3560 ♿

Staten Island Children's Museum

Hands-on exhibits and related workshops and performances for 5- to 12-year-olds are featured. A recent program gave children the opportunity to study bugs from both the scientist's and the artist's perspective. ♦ Admission. Tu-Su, noon-5PM (opens at 10AM when school's out). 718/273.2060. www.statenislandkids.org ♿

Staten Island Botanical Garden

Located here are an English perennial garden; an herb and butterfly garden; a "White Garden" (all blooms in shades of gray and white) patterned after the famous English garden in Sissinghurst; a fully authentic classical **Chinese Scholar's Garden** that offers the formal tea ceremony at times, and is the only such garden in the US; and a greenhouse with a permanent display of tropicals, including the Neil Vanderbilt Orchid Collection. It's best to visit from May to October, when the flowers are in bloom. The **Café Botanica**—Asian-influenced design, with a mostly American menu—is adjacent to the Chinese Scholar's Garden. ♦ Chinese Scholar's Garden: Admission. T-Su, 10-5. Tours available Sa, Su. General admission: Free. Daily, dawn to dusk. 718/273.8200. www.sibg.org ♿

51 Staten Island Zoo

Popular attractions at this zoo, beloved by many for its small (8.5-acre) scale, include an animal hospital, a re-created tropical rain forest, an African savannah natural habitat, an aquarium, and an outstanding reptile collection, which features the country's largest collection of rattlesnakes. Children can feed domestic animals daily at the **Children's Center**, and there's also a special Saturday-morning program (requiring reservations) called "Breakfast with the Beasts." ♦ Admission. Daily, 10AM-4:45PM. 614 Broadway (between Forest Ave and Clove Rd), West New Brighton. 718/442.3100. www.statenislandzoo.org ♿

52 Alice Austen House Museum

This is one of the finest records of turn-of-the-twentieth-century American life from Alice Austen, a photographer whose work was first discovered in *Life* in 1949. ♦ Suggested donation. Th-Su, noon-5PM. 2 Hylan Blvd (at Edgewater St), Rosebank. 718/816.4506. www.aliceausten.org

52 Aesop's Tables

★$$ Emblematic of how Staten Island sees itself—closer at heart to the country than to the city—this rustic restaurant has country-garden wicker furniture, lots of dried flowers, and a patio for alfresco dining. The food can be a little uneven, but most dishes are interesting and flavorful; try the warm roasted pear salad, seafood risotto, or braised short ribs. ♦ American ♦ Tu-Sa, dinner; Su, brunch. No credit cards accepted. 1233 Bay St (at Maryland Ave), Rosebank. 718/720.2005

53 Fort Wadsworth

One of the oldest military installations in the US, it played a major role in American history. Pronounced a National Park site in 1997, this onetime vital fortification is now a part of the Gateway National Recreation area. The 226-acre facility near the Verrazano-Narrows Bridge has exhibits, a visitors' center, remaining fortifications with panoramic views, and guided tours by rangers. ♦ Free. W-Su, 10AM-5PM. Wadsworth Ave (at Bay St). 718/354.4500. www.nps.gov/gate ♿

54 Verrazano-Narrows Bridge

Built in 1964 and designed by **Othmar Ammann**, this exquisite 4,260-foot minimalist steel ribbon is the world's longest suspension bridge (San Francisco's Golden Gate comes in a close second). It flies across the entrance to New York Harbor and is especially beautiful when seen from the Atlantic, against the city's skyline. It is named for Giovanni da Verrazano, the first European explorer to see New York (1524). The bridge has become familiar as the starting point for the **New York City Marathon** every November. ♦ Between Gowanus Expwy (Brooklyn) and Staten Island Expwy

55 The Greenbelt

Even New Yorkers are amazed when told that the sprawling 843-acre **Central Park** is not the largest in the city. Measuring in at a remarkable 2,500 acres, this park located on Staten Island offers locals little-known proximity to a variety of landscapes, from shaded woodlands and freshwater swamps to hardwood forests with hiking trails and cross-country skiing in winter. Regular programs, talks, and walking tours are organized by the park service. Call for information and schedules. ♦ Daily. Visitors' Center: High Rock Park, 200 Nevada Ave (off Rockland Ave, between Richmond and Manor Rds), Egbertville. 718/667.2165. www.sigreenbelt.org ♿

56 Jacques Marchais Museum of Tibetan Art

Tucked away on a wooded hillside in the middle of the island (though just a few minutes from **Historic Richmond Town**) is this remarkable re-creation of a Tibetan mountain temple. Jacques Marchais established the site in the 1940s for her growing collections of Tibetan textiles and wall hangings, complex religious metalwork and stone statuary, and paintings, all dating from the 17th to 19th centuries. The terraced grounds include a lily and fish pond, as well as a serene sculpture garden. The Dalai Lama has visited here, and ongoing special events, lectures, and tours are offered. ♦ Gift shop. Admission. W-Su. 338 Lighthouse Ave. 718/987.3500. www.tibetanmuseum.com

57 Historic Richmond Town

New York City's answer to Colonial Williamsburg is a continuing restoration of 27 buildings that show a picture of 17th- through 19th-century village life. Fourteen are currently open to visitors, including the **Voorlezer House** (1695), the oldest surviving elementary school; the **General Store** (1840); and the **Bennet House** (1839), which is home to the **Museum of Childhood**. There are ongoing demonstrations of Early American trades and crafts, and working kitchens with cooking in progress. The **Museum Store** (in the **Historical Museum**) sells reproductions made by village craftspeople. ♦ Admission. W-Su, 1PM-5PM (may open earlier in summer). 441 Clarke Ave (at Old Mill Rd), Richmond Town. 718/351.1611. www.historicrichmondtown.org

58 The Conference House/ Billopp House

Built in the 1670s, this was the scene of the only peace conference held to try to prevent the Revolutionary War. Admiral Lord Howe, in command of the British forces, hosted the parley on 11 September 1776 for three Continental Congress representatives—Benjamin Franklin, John Adams, and Edward Rutledge. The house is now a National Historic Landmark. ♦ Admission. By tour only. F-Su, 1PM-4PM April through mid-Dec. 7455 Hylan Blvd (at Satterlee St), Tottenville. 718/984.2086, 718/984.0415. www.theconferencehouse.org

GAY NEW YORK CITY

The marvelous, maddening mix that is the Big Apple is home to the largest gay community in America and probably the most diverse in the world. Whatever your taste—from wildly conventional to outrageous—this city of 8 million has something (or someone) for you. Like bulging biceps? The designer tank-top-and-Prada-sport's-shoe herd in **Chelsea** will have your head spinning. Unimpressed with buffed bods? Try the **West Village**, home to a mix of older gym bods, black and Hispanic dudes, and friendly lesbians. In the **East Village**, youngsters are pierced, bleached, and shaved to the smallest detail, while the clean-cut **Upper West Side** and the more sedate and moneyed **Upper East Side** are veritable guppie havens. The **Meatpacking District**, with cutting-edge fashion boutiques, galleries, and eateries is the see-and-be-seen "it" area. Labeled the "New Chelsea," or "Hellsea," Midtown West's **Hell's Kitchen** area (officially renamed **Clinton**) is a hotbed of the freshest gay bars and clothing shops. The area clocks in with more hand-holding young gay couples per block than any other neighborhood. Leavening this local mix are a sprinkling of out-of-towners, "bridge-and-tunnel" types from the suburbs as well as tourists from all over the globe.

For most visitors—and for the purposes of this book—the borough of Manhattan is still what it's all about (for details on the scene in Brooklyn, Queens, The Bronx, or Staten Island, consult local rags like *HX* and *Next*, available in most gay venues). **Harlem** was the place to be for gays in the Roaring Twenties, the West Village in general and **Christopher Street** in particular have been the epicenter of gay New York for most of the decades through the '80s. Chelsea—a formerly less-than-chic West Side neighborhood roughly between 14th and 30th Streets—is still popular (though some say it peaked in the late '90s), particularly for theme bars and 30-something muscle cruising. Chelsea may not have the architectural character of the Village or the Upper West Side, but no one cares, because the sidewalks, shops, and restaurants of **Eighth Avenue** and, to a lesser extent, **Seventh Avenue** are hopping seven days a week with some of the country's hottest men. The gay hood with the most edge is Hell's Kitchen, with its slew of bars catering to the young and achingly fabulous.

There are some gay women in Chelsea, too, though lesbians tend to live and hang out in the West Village below Christopher Street and in the Brooklyn neighborhood of **Park Slope**, which reputedly has among the largest lesbian populations of any neighborhood in the world (see "A Slope with a Different Angle," on page 347).

In much of Manhattan, and in some pockets of New York's other boroughs, gays are accepted and flourish to a degree found in very few other US cities. In Chelsea and Hell's Kitchen, even the sandwich shops and dry cleaners sport rainbow flags—though that probably says more about homo buying power here than the enlightenment of local shopkeepers. Gays have won a significant measure of political power in this town, too (though far less than other minority groups), and the Empire State Building is swathed in lavender light for a weekend in the Gay Pride month of June.

In spite of its relative liberalism, diversity, and tolerance, however, New York City has its share of homophobia. Efforts to pass a citywide anti-discrimination bill were bitterly beaten back for years (it finally passed in 1986), and a heated debate over teaching tolerance of diverse sexualities in public schools continues to this day. In the fall of 2003, however, New York became the first city in the nation to open an accredited public high school targeted specifically at gay, lesbian, and transgender youth, the

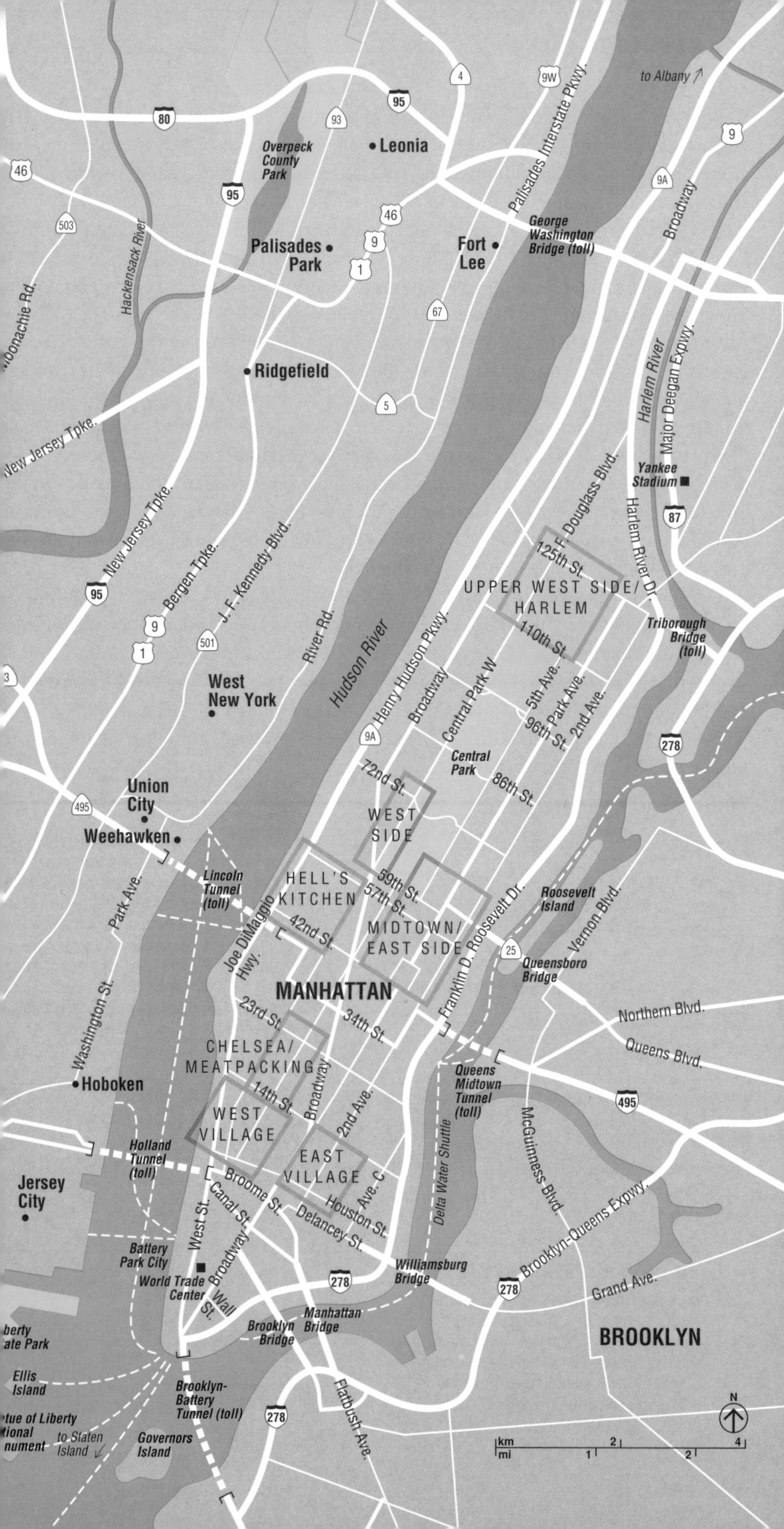

to Albany
Leonia
Overpeck County Park
Palisades Park
Fort Lee
George Washington Bridge (toll)
Palisades Interstate Pkwy.
Broadway
Hackensack River
Moonachie Rd.
Ridgefield
New Jersey Tpke.
Harlem River
Major Deegan Expwy.
Yankee Stadium
F. Douglass Blvd.
Harlem River Dr.
125th St.
UPPER WEST SIDE/ HARLEM
110th St.
Triborough Bridge (toll)
Bergen Tpke.
J. F. Kennedy Blvd.
River Rd.
Hudson River
Henry Hudson Pkwy.
Central Park W
5th Ave.
Park Ave.
2nd Ave.
96th St.
West New York
Central Park
86th St.
72nd St.
WEST SIDE
Union City
Weehawken
Lincoln Tunnel (toll)
HELL'S KITCHEN
59th St.
57th St.
MIDTOWN/ EAST SIDE
Roosevelt Island
Vernon Blvd.
Franklin D. Roosevelt Dr.
Queensboro Bridge
Park Ave.
Joe DiMaggio Hwy.
42nd St.
MANHATTAN
Washington St.
23rd St.
34th St.
Northern Blvd.
Queens Blvd.
CHELSEA/ MEATPACKING
Queens Midtown Tunnel (toll)
Hoboken
14th St.
WEST VILLAGE
2nd Ave.
McGuinness Blvd.
Holland Tunnel (toll)
EAST VILLAGE
Delta Water Shuttle
Jersey City
Broome St.
Canal St.
Houston St.
Ave. C
West St.
Delancey St.
Brooklyn-Queens Expwy.
Battery Park City
World Trade Center
Wall St.
Williamsburg Bridge
Grand Ave.
Manhattan Bridge
Brooklyn Bridge
BROOKLYN
Ellis Island
Brooklyn-Battery Tunnel (toll)
Flatbush Ave.
to Staten Island
Governors Island
N
km
mi

Harvey Milk High School in downtown Manhattan. From time to time particularly vicious gay bashings happen—local gay celeb Kevin Aviance was attacked in 2006 after a nightclub gig by four youths who were subsequently charged with a hate-crime assault. Occasionally murders occur, mostly in the outer boroughs but sometimes even in Greenwich Village and other parts of Manhattan, but, then, New York City is a big metropolis where crime can happen to anyone. So while same-sex smooching and hand-holding on Eighth Avenue, in Hell's Kitchen, or on Christopher Street are not uncommon, it's best not to let the old guard down—this is The Big City. All that said, it's safe to add that New York is in a league only with San Francisco in its variety of gay culture and social life. First of all, there is the numbing array of gay nightspots, which in recent years have strayed from standard New York–club style (small, industrial-looking, painted black) to encompass everything from futuristic discos to swanky cocktail lounges to *Cheers*-style neighborhood bars. Whatever your taste in music, entertainment, or companionship, you're sure to find a place to happily while away the evening (and early morning) here. (It should be noted, however, that Manhattan gay nightlife tends to be segregated; most clubs cater to and are frequented by either a male or a female clientele.)

Every day of the week also brings a wide selection of shows, cabarets, performance art, poetry and literary readings, experimental films, art and photography exhibitions, and fashion "happenings." (The cultural scene is so rich, and the gay influence on it so strong, that New York writer Fran Leibowitz once observed, "If you removed homosexuals and homosexual influence from what is generally regarded as American culture, you would be pretty much left with *Let's Make a Deal.*") In short, for our tribe there's just no place like New York, New York.

Symbols

♂ predominantly/exclusively gay-male-oriented

♀ predominantly/exclusively lesbian-oriented

♂♀ predominantly/exclusively gay-oriented, with a male and female clientele

Upper West Side & Harlem

The gay factor is subdued, but Harlem is beginning to garner a bit of buzz.

1 20 East 127th Street

On a stretch also known as **Langston Hughes Place**, this 1869 Italianate brownstone in Harlem was home during the Roaring Twenties to one of the leading lights of black American literature, poet and playwright Langston Hughes (1902-1967). In public, Hughes was never explicit about his sexual orientation, but he is believed by most historians to have been at least AC/DC. He was certainly an integral part of what he called the "queerly assorted throng" of black gays and lesbians who formed the core of that era's so-called Harlem Renaissance (see page 341). He later was the subject of the homoerotic 1989 film *Looking for Langston,* and had a US postage stamp created in his honor. The building is not open to the public. ♦ Between Madison and Fifth Aves

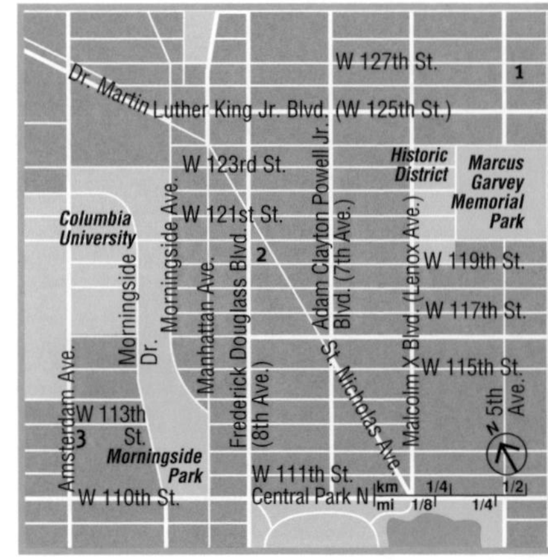

Out Magazine's 10 Must-Do's in New York City

By Bruce Shenitz

Executive Editor, *Out*

1. Dinner at **Lucky Cheng's**. The spectacle of Asian tranny waitresses must be experienced at least once! 24 First Ave (between Houston and 2nd Sts). 995.5500. www.planetluckychengs.com

2. Sunday brunch at **Jackson Diner**. Gorge on delicious Indian food to the point of near explosion. 37-47 74th St, Jackson Heights, Queens (located just north of Roosevelt Ave). 718/672.1232

3. Ride the **Staten Island Ferry**.

4. Walk across the **Brooklyn Bridge** at night.

5. Visit Christopher Park and check out the two George Segal sculptures, near the site of the beginning of the Stonewall riots.

6. Go to the legendary underground house party, Shelter, starting Saturday night through Sunday noon at **Club Shelter**. 20 W 39th St (between Fifth and Sixth Aves). 719.4479

7. See the gay penguins at the **Central Park Zoo**!

8. Shop for vintage clothes at boutiques in the **East Village** or **Williamsburg**, Brooklyn.

9. Check out all the hot shirtless guys sunbathing in Central Park's **Sheep Meadow**.

10. Score that Pair of Gucci sunglasses you've always wanted (or at least a decent-looking knockoff) in **Chinatown** for $10.

2 Billie's Black

**$$ In the heart of Harlem, this bar, lounge, and restaurant is touted as a "sensual and alluring space" at the forefront of the new Harlem Renaissance. Dinner faves include zesty fried catfish strips and Billie's Grand BBQ ribs. Lounge events include the Damn Happy Happy Hour, or Speed Dating (He Meets He or She Meets Her). ♦ Su, noon-8PM; Tu-Th, noon-midnight; F, Sa, noon-4AM. 271 W 119th St (between St. Nicholas Ave and Frederick Douglass Blvd). 280.2248

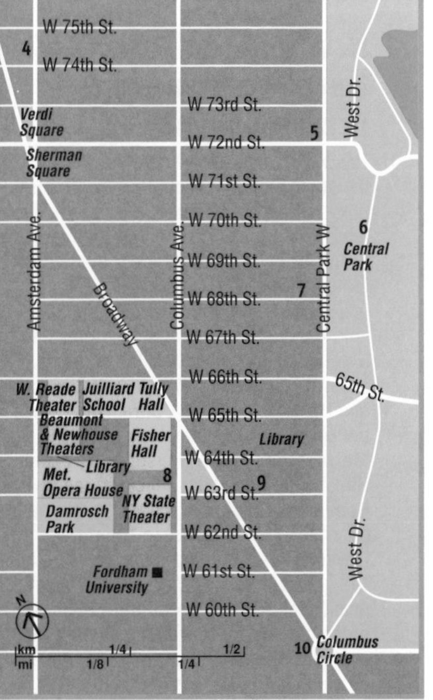

3 Cathedral of St. John the Divine/National AIDS Memorial

Begun in 1892 and still not finished, the huge, neo-Byzantine/Romanesque seat of New York's Episcopal diocese is famous for its annual St. Francis Day blessing of animals and for its liberal (and gay-supportive) bishop, Mark S. Sisk. Along the south nave, the fifth chapel from the entrance is the **Medical Bay**, containing the National AIDS Memorial, dedicated in 1985. Along with a stained-glass depiction of Christ healing the sick and medical greats such as Louis Pasteur, Father Damien, and Florence Nightingale, the memorial features a registry of AIDS victims called the Memorial Book of Remembrance, with more than 2,000 names inscribed. ♦ Donation requested. M-Sa, 7AM-6PM; Su, 7AM-7PM. 1047 Amsterdam Ave (between Cathedral Pkwy and W 113th St). 316.7540. Tours: 932.7347. www.stjohndivine.org ♿

West Side

Suit-and-tie yuppies dominate at the south end, but the farther north you push, strollers and literary types take over. The gay scene is secondary, but this is low-key, comfortable territory.

4 Candle Bar

♂ With soothing lighting and high ceilings, this friendly neighborhood gathering place appeals to a multiracial group of regulars, from your bashful bachelor postman to your ripped and hunky gym trainer, in addition to a few leatherish types. The bar got a 21st-century makeover to bring things up to cruising speed, adding theme nights like Cinema Sunday and wild '80s Mondays. ♦ Daily, 2PM-4AM. 309 Amsterdam Ave (between W 74th and W 75th Sts). 874.9155 ♿

5 Dakota Apartments

When this multi-gabled buff-and-brick structure was erected at the western fringe of **Central Park** in 1884, downtowners sniffed that it was so far uptown it might as well be in the Dakotas. The joke was ultimately on them, as this luxury apartment building, one of the city's first, has since become its most famous and exclusive. Apartments here run in the millions of dollars and may feature indoor pools, fabulous park views, and all manner of pricey accoutrements. The structure is familiar to many as the setting for Roman Polanski's film *Rosemary's Baby* and as the site of the 1980 murder of John Lennon. It has also been home to celebrities (Leonard Bernstein, Liberace) and beloved of queens (Judy Garland, Lauren Bacall). The building is not open to the public. ♦ 1 W 72nd St (at Central Park W)

6 Central Park

Popular with gay men almost from the beginning, this 840-acre expanse of meadow, lake, and woods laid out in the 1860s and 1870s in the very heart of Manhattan is twice the size of Monaco and probably more fun. The 1869 **Belvedere Castle** near West 77th Street was a same-sex cruising ground as far back as the turn of the 20th century, and 80 years ago the **Columbus Circle** entrance to the park at Central Park South became a popular meeting place as well. Future San Francisco supervisor Harvey Milk was arrested for indecent exposure here in 1947, and to this day the **Ramble**, a 37-acre wooded maze just north of the **Lake** and west of **The Boathouse** (517.2233), is known as an area not only for bird-watching but also for man-to-man cruising—largely but not exclusively during the warm-weather months. (But note, the post-Giuliani era has brought a spike in ticketing for hanky-panky in this area.) To the south, also on the Lake, is **Bethesda Terrace**, where a handsome 1870 fountain is crowned by lesbian sculptor Emma Stebbins's *Angel of the Waters*. (This dramatic statue was featured prominently in Tony Kushner's Pulitzer Prize–winning Broadway hit (and subsequent HBO film) *Angels in America: Millennium Approaches*.) Across the street from the park's southeast corner lurks the imposing **Plaza Hotel** (built in 1907), where in 1958 FBI director J. Edgar Hoover attended a suite party dolled up in a black dress, high heels, lace stockings, and a wig—and was introduced by fellow homophobic homo Roy Cohn to another guest as "Mary." (Amid some public grumblings, the hotel is planning to convert a chunk of its swanky rooms into condominiums.) History aside, the park today is a fun, vital part of daily life in New York, and the attractive weekend crowds of cyclists, sunbathers, and roller-bladers boggle the mind. Note: Avoid the park after dark whenever possible; if not, exercise caution and common sense, and stick to well-lighted, populated areas. ♦ Bounded by Fifth Ave and Central Park W, and Central Park S and Central Park N. Tours, 427.4040

7 19 West 68th Street

Fans of bi screen icon James Dean might want to stop for a look at the five-story, beige-brick town house where the legend lived, just a few paces from **Central Park** and not far from **Lincoln Center**. After acting in two Broadway plays, Dean was cast in *East of Eden* and moved out to Hollywood, but came back to this apartment off and on up till his fatal car accident at age 24. Walk up the curved sandstone steps and check out the graffiti in the foyer written by adoring fans. Sample: "To the little prince: You had class and you where [sic] a contender and you where the coolest cat that ever walked the streets." The building is not open to the public. ♦ Between Central Park W and Columbus Ave

8 New York State Theater/ Lincoln Center for the Performing Arts

This 2,792-seat glass-and-steel theater on the south side of **Lincoln Center**'s central plaza was designed in 1964 by world-renowned gay architect **Philip Johnson** as a venue for ballet and musicals. The theater features jewel-like lights and a mammoth spherical chandelier in the center of the gold-paneled ceiling. (Inside, look for the Numbers mural by painter Jasper Johns.) Today it is home to the **New York City Ballet** and the **New York City Opera**. Other parts of the Lincoln Center complex include the **Metropolitan Opera House**; **Avery Fisher Hall**, site of orchestral concerts; the **Vivian Beaumont Theater**, which stages dramatic plays; the **Mitzi Newhouse Theater**, featuring avant-garde productions; the **Alice Tully Recital Hall**, designed for chamber music and recitals; the **Juilliard School**, one of the nation's most acclaimed performing arts schools; and the **Library and Museum of the Performing Arts**. ♦ Columbus Ave (between W 62nd and W 66th Sts). Lincoln Center information 875.5000, tours 769.7020. www.lincolncenter.org ♿

9 West Side YMCA

$ A cross between a fortress, an apartment building, and a Romanesque church, this brick-and-limestone residential hotel just off Central Park was built in 1930 and is one of the reasons the Y has become part of gay folklore. A half-century before the Village People musically urged young men to "come and stay at the Y-M-C-A," songwriter Irving Berlin was already getting laughs in his World War I–era stage review *Yip, Yip, Yaphank* with a sailor's quip about having "lots of friends" at the Y. (Tennessee Williams, who lived at the Y before becoming famous, apparently had a few friends of his own here.) The place is still open for business, with 539 rooms that are clean and cheap if not chic, a cafeteria that's a good place for an inexpensive pit stop, and a gym that's popular with local homos. This frugal hostel does boast a concierge desk, two swimming pools, and a steam room for guests. And even if you don't stay, it's worth strolling down the street from Lincoln Center to take a look at the building's exotic façade, awash with fancy brickwork, columns, and arched windows. ♦ 5 W 63rd St (between Central Park W and Broadway). 875.4100, 875.4273. www.ymcanyc.org ♿

10 Time Warner Center

If the stunning, cathedral-height glass entryway to this posh shopper's paradise doesn't draw you, the 40 luxury stores that comprise "The Shops at Columbus Circle" will—everything from **Williams-Sonoma** (823.9750) to the man-centric **The Art of Shaving** shop (823.9410) or the booty-hugging **Calvin Klein Underwear** boutique (246.8200). Elegantly designed and very city-chic, the seven-level complex features dazzling views of Central Park, which get better the higher you go—which is a good reason to visit any of the center's top-line restaurants, all clustered on the third and fourth floors. **Per Se** (823.9335) holds just 15 tables, has a fireplace, and offers grand views of Central Park, while famed **Masa** (823.9800) offers some of the most elegant sushi in town and **Porter House New York** (923.9500) boasts hearty steaks and wrap-around windows overlooking Columbus Circle. ♦ 10 Columbus Circle (at W 59th St). 823.6300

Midtown/East Side

Unlike its Lower East Side sister 'hood, the farther upper East you go, the spottier the lavender attitude gets. There are a few relaxed-attitude bars and lounges worth a visit, though.

11 Frank E. Campbell Funeral Chapel

Judy Garland devotees on their way to or from the nearby museums might want to stop at the site of her memorial service on 26 June 1969. The line of grief-stricken queens went for blocks that day, and the police "restored order" on several occasions. Apparently the atmosphere created by La Judy's death played a role in sparking the Stonewall riots in the wee hours of the next morning (see page 345). Other celebrity funerals of gay interest held here include those of Tennessee Williams, Mae West, and Rudolph Valentino. Robert Kennedy, John Lennon, and James Cagney were also memorialized at this five-floor agglomeration of three town houses. ♦ 1076 Madison Ave (at E 81st St). 288.3500, 800/423.5928

12 570 Park Avenue

This distinguished redbrick and limestone apartment building on one of New York's toniest thoroughfares was home to American novelist Willa Cather (1873-1947). She lived here with her lover Edith Lewis from 1932 until her death in 1947. (Lewis stayed in the apartment until her own death 25 years later, not changing so much as a picture

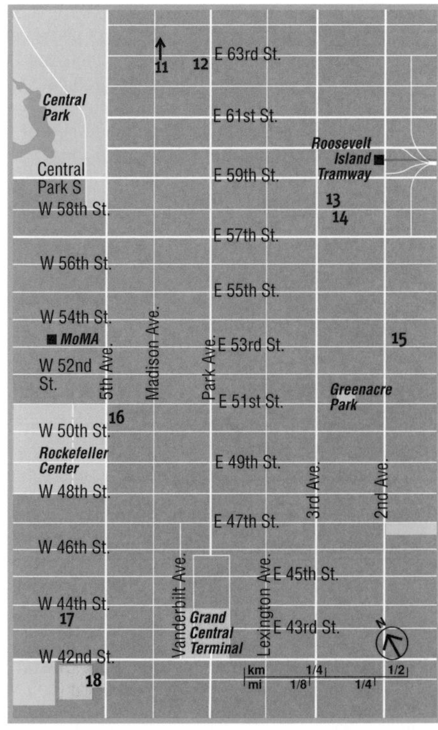

frame in all that time.) The building is not open to the public. ♦ At E 63rd St

13 O.W. Bar

Famous for its very long bar, very large patio, and killer jukebox, this is an Upper East Side classic. A fun, more low-key stop compared to its sister bars on the lower east part of town, its nightly live drag shows make it a fave of drag-hags. ♦ M-Sa, 4PM-4AM; Su, 2PM-4AM. ♦ 221 E 58th St (between Second and Third Aves). 355.3395. www.owbar.com

14 The Town House Bar

♂ A sea of jackets and ties (with the occasional T-shirt thrown in), this two-level, three-bar drinking establishment aspires to a "gentlemen's club" atmosphere: green walls, hunting prints, polished brass. Some might find it too sedate, but the piano sing-alongs in the back lounge have their moments, and the largely mature crowd does have its share of lookers. There are also a few youngsters in the crowd, who may or may not be hustlers. ♦ Daily. 236 E 58th St (between Second and Third Aves). 754.4649. www.townhouseny.com

15 Regents

♂ ★★$$ The regency referred to here is that of the British Raj in India, so there's an abundance of rattan and potted palms, and the tasteful tan walls are lined with photos of chaps in pith helmets. You might think you were in a Delhi officers' club had you not seen that hot bartender out last night at **Splash**. The latest entry from the owners of the **Town House Bar** (see above), this place offers two bars (including a popular jazz piano bar), an elegant dining area, and a most civilized evening out. The fare is neither British nor Indian, but rather Italian, and consistently high in quality. Jacket and tie requested. ♦ Italian ♦ Daily, lunch and dinner. 317 E 53rd St (between First and Second Aves). 593.3091

16 St. Patrick's Cathedral

Seat of the Roman Catholic archdiocese of New York and the 11th-largest church in the world, this 1879 Gothic Revival structure has been the backdrop to ongoing controversy since the late Cardinal John O'Connor took over in 1982. Gays and lesbians have demonstrated here against the Catholic Church's anti-gay ideology on many occasions, including the city's Gay Pride and St. Patrick's Day parades (both of which pass right in front of the cathedral). One of the most notorious protests occurred in 1989, when more than 5,000 ACT UP and WHAM (Women's Health Action Mobilization) demonstrators rallied outside, protesting the Church's opposition to safer-sex education (especially condom use) and abortion, and a handful of protestors went into the church and interrupted Mass. Sadly, the issues and the huge crowd are usually forgotten, and all that is remembered is that one participant crushed a communion wafer. ♦ Daily, 7AM-8PM. Fifth Ave (between E 50th and E 51st Sts). 753.2261. www.ny-archdiocese.org ♿

17 Hotel Royalton

$$$$ The block-long lobby of this gay-friendly hotel is dramatic indeed, designed by Philippe Starck and awash in Cognac mahogany and green-gray slate. The front desk is discreetly tucked away, as is the lobby bar, patterned after Hemingway's favorite at the Paris Ritz, it is forever full of networking hipsters. The 205 rooms, many with working fireplaces, are on the cutting edge of modern design and comfort, and extra amenities include daily newspaper delivery, Kiehl shampoos and bath cubes, and valet parking. The hotel is popular with fashion, publishing, and entertainment bigwigs, so you never know whom you might run into. The original structure, built in 1898 by **Ehrick Rossiter**, was renovated in 1988 by **Gruzen Samton Steinglass**. ♦ 44 W 44th St (between Fifth and Sixth Aves). 869.4400, 800/635.9013; fax 575.0012. www.royaltonhotel.com ♿

18 New York Public Library/ Humanities and Social Sciences Library

Opened in 1895, this grand building is completely dedicated to research, and none of its more than 6 million books or 17 million documents can be checked out; so vast is the collection that the original four floors of stacks beneath the building and behind the reading rooms have been supplemented by a space underneath **Bryant Park**, which can hold up to 92 miles of stacks. Still the repository of one of the largest research collections in the world, the **Carrère and Hastings** building remains one of the finest examples of Beaux Arts architecture.

Among the library's archives is the **International Gay Information Center**, a massive and ever-growing collection of books, magazines, correspondence, and audio- and videotapes. In 1994, the library mounted a highly acclaimed and somewhat controversial exhibit featuring materials drawn from this collection in honor of the 25th anniversary of the **Stonewall** riots. ♦ International Gay Information Center: Tu-Th, Sa. Main Reading Room: M-Sa. Tours: M-Sa, 11AM, 2PM. Free tours meet at the front desk; call ahead for schedule. Fifth Ave (between W 40th and W 42nd Sts). 661.7220, 930.0800. www.nypl.org/research

Gays and the Harlem Renaissance

'he Roaring Twenties saw the rise of a gay subculture in ;reenwich Village that has persisted to this day. For nany homosexuals, however, the hottest scene in Aanhattan at that time wasn't down in the Village, but vay uptown. The tolerance and cultural, social, and exual ferment of Jazz Age Harlem attracted black and vhite "sissies" and "bulldaggers" from all over the city, vho found heady liberation in its nightclubs, house arties, and ballrooms like the **Savoy**.

mong the giants of black culture who made the larlem Renaissance what it was were Langston Hughes nd Countee Cullen; bi blues singers Ma Rainey, Bessie mith, and cross-dressing Gladys Bentley; and an nterracial cast of gay and straight celebrities including)uke Ellington and Billy Strayhorn (the gay guy who gave the Duke his tunes), Josephine Baker, Fats Waller, Cab Calloway, Cole Porter, and Cary Grant.

The Great Depression put a damper on the party, though, and much of that "old black magic" had dissipated by 1935. The lavender magic, though, is making a comeback in Harlem, thanks in part to outrageous real-estate prices sending renters and buyers alike hunting the 'hood for a home.

Central Harlem has seen an increase in particular in gay residents. Case in point: a converted public school on West 126th Street and St. Nicholas Avenue has gay men occupying half of the 75 units (this reported in a *Village Voice* article as an estimate by residents). Could Harlem be the next Hell's Kitchen? Time will tell!

Hell's Kitchen

enamed Hellsea (aka the new Chelsea) by those in the now, this is a 'hood on the rise, and the true hot spot for e city's young, fresh, and frisky. There are tons of estaurants, shops, bars, and anything else rainbow. Enjoy now, while it's still on the true cutting edge.

19 Club H

A sleek, mod muscle entry to Hellsea, with all the necessary cute trainers, high-end equipment, and of course a ClubH20 offering of a chocolate almond crisp post-pump protein shake. ♦ M-Th, 5:30AM-11PM; F, 5:30AM-10PM; Sa, Su, 8AM-9PM. 423 W 55th St (between Ninth and 10th Aves). 245.5802

20 Xing

★★$$ Xing is an upscale take on a traditional Chinese restaurant with an elegant interior and a trendy gay crowd. A huge tropical fish tank lines one wall, highlighting a Postmodern décor. The expected egg roll is available, along with a few new items such as a smoked-tofu spring roll. ♦ 785 Ninth Ave (between W 52nd and W 53rd Sts). 289.3010

21 Therapy

♂ At first glance, this midtown spot looks like a chic sushi bar, and indeed the joint offers a menu of nibbling finger foods. Once inside, however, the vibe is all gay boy, cabaret shows, and dance fever. The two-level lounge is known for its entertainment, with jaw-dropping shows like the Electroshock Therapy Comedy Hour and an open-mike contest. ♦ 4PM-4AM. 348 W 52nd St (between Eighth and Ninth Aves). 397.1700

22 Bamboo 52

A sushi bar and lounge with an edgy Asian influence and a mix of Broadway divas and suited-up muscle boys. Features a back garden, popular DJs, and performances. ♦ Daily, 4PM-4AM. 344 W 52nd St (between Eighth and Ninth Aves). 888/640.CLUB.

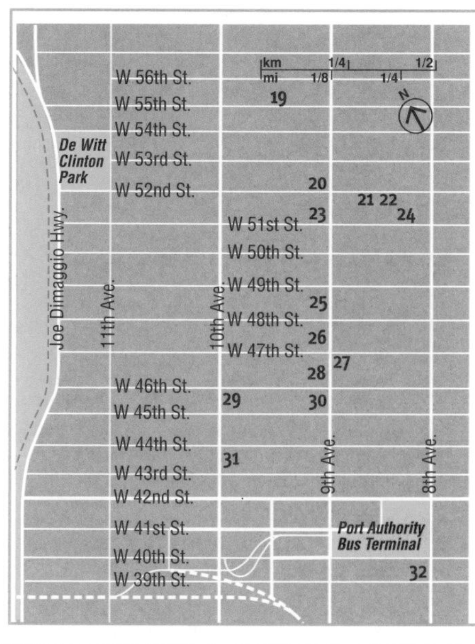

23 Posh

One of the first "hot" midtown gay bars that began to define Hell's Kitchen as the new Chelsea. Small, dark, and lean, the bar is like a long hallway with comfy sofas in back and a tiny patio out front where smokers and bawdier guests linger. Pulls in the tight and toned twenty-something set, along with a few Theater District sexy showboys. ♦ Daily, 4PM-4AM. 405 W 51st St (between Ninth and 10th Aves). 957.2222

24 Vlada

A two-floor lounge with an edge of Euro sophistication, a sexy young crowd, and performances by drag faves like the long-legged Edie! ♦ Daily, 4PM-4AM. 331 W 51st St (between Eighth and Ninth Aves). 974.8030

25 Kyotofu

★★$$ A hip Japanese eatery mixing unique desserts, teas, and cocktails. The sleek flow-through décor is said to incorporate elements of "Japan's hottest urban cafés" and the menu touts ginger-infused Japanese rice okay with sour cherry, kurmoitsu whipped cream, and ginger candy. Thirsty? Try sparkling sake or a guava and muddled ginger martini. ♦ Su, Tu, W, noon-12:30AM; Th-Sa, noon-1:30AM. 705 Ninth Ave (between W 48th and W 49th Sts). 979.6012

26 Tiny Thai

★★$ Designed by Peter Choptipan to be sexy, fresh, and stylish, this mod little gem is just another in the line of sassy gay-styled eateries dotting Ninth and 10th Avenues in Hell's Kitchen. Raw cement walls are the backdrop to popping cherry-red banquettes. Patrons can nosh on the fried dancing calamari with spicy plum sauce or rice molded into the shape of a star. ♦ Su-Tu, 11:30AM-11:00PM; Th-Sa, 11:30AM-midnight. 693 Ninth Ave (between W 47th and W 48th Sts). 265.2229. www.tinythainyc.com

27 Wear Me Out

A small but well-packed boutique that stays abreast of the latest trends and features casual clothing for the young gay dandy. From the latest G-Star Raw denim to chunky knock-off sunglasses or sexy Andrew Christian swimwear, it's perfect for shoppers not up to maneuvering the Fifth Avenue crowds. ♦ 353 W 47th St (between Eighth and Ninth Aves). 333.3047

28 Chelsea Grill of Hell's Kitchen

★$ This traditional, relaxed grill features burgers, homemade chili, wings, and cornmeal-dusted calamari. ♦ 675 Ninth Ave (between W 46th and W 47th Sts). 974.9002

29 XTH Ave. Lounge

This cute lounge features a stone-top bar, couches, and a clientele of models, actors, and a few neighborhood regulars. ♦ 642 10th Ave (between W 45th and W 46th Sts). 245.9088

30 Delphinium Home

One of the first gay shops to open in Hell's Kitchen, this is a tchotchke shop with an extra dollop of style. Pop in and browse for an adorable shower curtain, luxurious bath salts, or that perfect picture frame. Great fo last-minute gifts and home to the cutest coffee-table coasters in town—heavy stone versions featuring unique etchings by Studic Vertu. ♦ 653 Ninth Ave (between W 45th and W 46th Sts). 333.3213

31 44 & X

★★★$$ Floor-to-ceiling windows, a soft blond-wood interior, and creamy leather-lined banquettes make this friendly, chic little eate a neighborhood fave. They serve scrumptious comfort food—from a blueclaw crab fritter to buttermilk fried chicken or banana and white chocolate bread pudding. Brunch is super, the wait staff is model-cute, and the vibe is Hellsea now. ♦ M-F, 5:30PM-11:45PM; Su, 5:30PM-10:45PM; brunch, Sa, Su, 11:30AM. 622 10th Ave (at W 44th St). 977.1170 ♿

32 La Nueva Escuelita

When **La Escuelita**, the decades-old gay Hispanic dance club and cabaret, closed its doors in the mid-1990s, it seemed like the end of an era. Fortunately, an Israeli-owned successor opened in 1996 in the very same basement with the very same formula: a cockta lounge arranged around a dance floor/stage where Hispanic boys and their gringo buddies boogie to the salsa beat until hot male strippers and some of the most amazing female impersonators in the city take the stage. The Miss Escuelita Continental Pageant every April a must and Tea Dance Sunday ends with a sexy stripper contest, so grab your thong! Those who knew the old Escuelita should note

> Due to its historic status as a language of the oppressed, Yiddish is experiencing a somewhat surprising revival among young gay Jews in New York. The Klezmatics, a group (with a couple of openly gay members) that plays traditional Jewish klezmer music, has even titled one of its albums *Shvagyn = Toyt* (Yiddish for the famous ACT UP slogan "Silence = Death"). Or keep your eyes peeled for performances by The Isle of Klezbos; their leader, drummer Eve Sicular, also heads up New York's popular Metropolitan Klezmer.

that the entrance is now around the corner. Male or female, leave your guns and blades at home: This place will frisk you very thoroughly. ♦ Cover Tu, W, F-Su. Tu-F, Su, 9PM-5AM; Sa, 9PM-6AM. 301 W 39th St (at Eighth Ave). 631.0588

CHELSEA/MEATPACKING

ots of men with big pecs and little dogs, this area is anging on as New York's gay staple 'hood, and it's a great rst stop for tourists looking to get the city's vibe. While helsea may be losing the "it" factor, it's still packed to he pumps with gay-friendly stores, bars, and eateries.

33 THE EAGLE

The last reigning club for leather lovers in the city. Leave your polo shirt and khakis behind, this is the real thing—packed on weekends with cigar-smoking, beer-guzzling guys dressed in everything from chaps to motorcycle-cop gear. ♦ 554 W 28th St (between 10th and 11th Aves). 646/473.1866

34 DUSK

♂ Once **Dusk of London**, this Chelsea club now takes you to the hot and colorful Miami mindset. It's a swank hangout for those looking to have their rum drinks in a loungy

km 1/4 1/2
mi 1/8 1/4
N
←33
Fashion Institute of Technology (FIT)
W 29th St.
W 28th St.
W 27th St.
W 26th St.
W 25th St.
W 24th St.
W 23rd St.
W 22nd St.
W 21st St.
W 20th St.
W 19th St.
W 18th St.
W 17th St.
W 16th St.
W 15th St.
W 14th St.
W 13th St.
W 12th St.
8th Ave.
7th Ave.
6th Ave. (Avenue of the Americas)
34 35 36 37 38 39 40 41 42 43 44 45 46 47 48 49 50 51 52 53 54 55 56 57 58 59 60 61 62 63 64 65 66 ←67 68 69
Jackson Square
Horatio St.
Greenwich Ave.

setting. The feeling is hedonism, pure and simple. Check out the one-way reflecting surfaces in the bathrooms and enjoy a game of pool at the table up front. ♦ 147 W 24th St (between Sixth and Seventh Aves). 924.4490

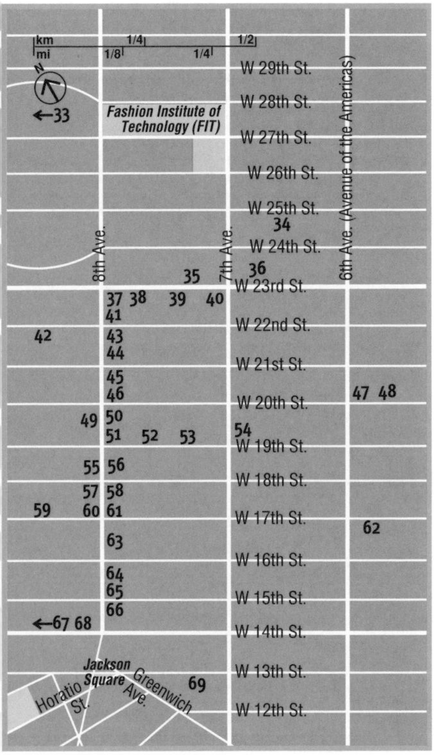

35 DAVID BARTON GYM

♂ ♀ The gay "it" gym, the multilevel workout space is laid out like a luxury loft and filled with the city's hottest boys. The aromatherapy locker room is elegantly designed, and the class schedule never fails to intrigue. ♦ M-F, 5AM-midnight; Sa, 8AM-9PM; Su, 9AM-11PM. 215 W 23rd St (between Seventh and Eighth Aves). 414.2022. Also at 30 E 85th St (between Madison and Fifth Aves), 517.7577. www.davidbartongym.com

36 XES LOUNGE

♂ ♀ This lounge hawks a host of weekly specials, from a $100 best butt contest on Thursdays to an "Out Professionals" mixer every fourth Tuesday. ♦ 157 W 24th St (between Sixth and Seventh Aves). 604.0212. xesnyc.com

37 CLEARVIEW CINEMA'S CHELSEA CLASSICS

The Clearview Cinema launched this campy series a few years back, and it's a bona fide hit. Local drag goddess Hedda Lettuce headlines a regular Thursday-night flick (everything from *Valley of the Dolls* to *Mommie Dearest*) featuring prizes and Hedda's own brand of wacky comedy pre-show. ♦ W 23rd St (between Seventh and Eighth Aves). 777.3456

38 EAST OF EIGHTH

★$$ This contemporary but warm and romantic dining room is a fine addition to an otherwise less-than-scintillating stretch of 23rd Street. The best thing about the place is unquestionably the charming back patio, landscaped and dolled up with an illuminated fountain, pond, and awning strung with small white lights. That and the smoothly executed and well-priced menu of sandwiches, pasta, pizza, and entrées make it a worthwhile candidate for a bite with friends or a hot date. The incredibly cute staff doesn't hurt either. Try the Tennessee chicken pot pie (with a country biscuit crust and a splash of Jack Daniel's) or the pecan-crusted salmon. The frisky brunch features guacamole Benedict poached eggs and Monte Cristo ciabatta French toast. ♦ American/Mediterranean ♦ Daily, lunch and dinner until 2AM along with pre-theater dinner specials; brunch Sa, Su, and holidays, 11AM-4PM. Bar: Daily, until 4AM. 254 W 23rd St (between Seventh and Eighth Aves). 352.0075

39 Hotel Chelsea

$$$ With its distinctive wrought-iron balconies, this massive Queen Anne–style apartment house dates from 1884, when this part of town was Manhattan's theater district. Converted to a 575-unit hotel two decades later, it subsequently was the residence at various times of Welsh poet Dylan Thomas, playwright Arthur Miller, authors O. Henry and Thomas Wolfe, gay composer Virgil Thomson, and punk rocker Sid Vicious. It was also the subject of Andy Warhol's film *Chelsea Girls* and was home to Viva and Edie Sedgwick, members of his Factory crowd in the 1960s. Although it has had an interesting past, the hotel is not recommended as a lodging place for most, since the premises are somewhat dingy. It remains, however, an edgy stop for strung-out fashionistas and punk wannabes. The gay-flavored **Star Bar** is just under the hotel. ♦ 222 W 23rd St (between Seventh and Eighth Aves). 243.3700. www.hotelchelsea.com

40 Chelsea Savoy

$$$ The first biggish hotel to open in Chelsea in years, this six-story brick cube dating from 1997 is perfectly clean and comfortable, but offers little in the way of frills (except for a small refrigerator in each of the 90 rooms). The reception area is so unobtrusive as to resemble the lobby of a modest apartment building, but why quibble over extras, when all the riches of gay Chelsea are right around the corner. ♦ 204 W 23rd St (at Seventh Ave). 929.9353; fax 741.6309. www.chelseasavoynyc.com ♿

41 Barracuda

♂ It might be dark, low of ceiling, and a tad claustrophobic, but this long, 1960s-style space is a popular hangout for a youngish crew that includes trendoids, boys-next-door, and everyone in between. The ambience is less glitzy than at **Splash** (see page 347). In addition to the main bar area, there's a laid-back lounge with sofas, a pool table, and an ever-changing décor (no dance floor, though). But wherever you are, you're never far enough from a blaring speaker. Come here for regular drag shows, comedy, and a weekly star search. ♦ Daily. 275 W 22nd St (between Seventh and Eighth Aves). 645.8613 ♿

41 Unicorn All-Male Erotica

♂ When the front door is closed, you might almost miss this brightly lit shop selling videos and bedroom supplies. A walk through the turnstile in the rear reveals a small, clean row of video booths where guys both hunky and skanky hang out waiting for quick dates. The place really gets rocking late at night, when a dark basement warren of booths opens up and the overflow crowd from **Barracuda** next door wanders in. ♦ Admission. M-Th, Su, noon-4AM; F, Sa, noon-6AM. 277C W 22nd St (between Seventh and Eighth Aves). 924.2921

42 Colonial House Inn

♂ ♀ $ Ensconced in a beautifully renovated 1880s brick town house that was the first home of the **Gay Men's Health Crisis** organization, this lodging place serves a primarily gay male clientele. Airy and cheerful, the guestrooms and public spaces feature bright white walls hung with colorful Impressionistic paintings by the owner. The 20 rooms are equipped with telephones, color TV, and air conditioning, and some also offer refrigerators, fireplaces, and private baths. The nifty rooftop sundeck is great for hanging out and catching rays (nude, if you like). There's no restaurant, but breakfast (with fresh-baked muffins) is included in the rate. Make reservations a month or more in advance. ♦ 318 W 22nd St (between Eighth and Ninth Aves). 243.9669, 800/689.3779 fax 633.1612. www.colonialhouseinn.com

43 The View

The best seat in this narrow little bar is in the front window. Formerly **The Works** bar, and situated in the heart of Chelsea, the big draw here (as the name suggests) is the glass-front window seat—perfect for cruising whatever wanders past on Eighth Avenue. A potted palm tree and a streamlined look give the spot a Miami feeling, and the crowd is laid back and a mixture of ages. ♦ 232 Eighth Ave (between W 21st and W 22nd Sts). 929.2243

44 Gallerie H

An actual haberdashery in Chelsea specializing in a slew of fun hats from the likes of Eugenia Kim, Stetson-Modern Collection, and Chrysty's of London. It also has Fred Perry bags, and everything from sunglasses to chic flip-flops. ♦ Daily, noon-10PM. 228 Eighth Ave (between W 21st and W 22nd Sts). 229.1975 ♿

45 Rawhide

♂ A holdout amid the snazzier nightspots of Chelsea, this neighborhood joint with a Western/biker motif and a lingering scent of stale beer has managed to hang on to a certain following. Here, the average age is a little higher, the average looks not modelesque, and the overall sensibility more down-to-earth than in other area spots. Dig the "Tom of Finland" and other macho posters spread across the walls, and the motorcycle suspended over the pool table. ♦ Daily, 8AM-4AM. 212 Eighth Ave (at W 21st St). 242.9332 ♿

The Stonewall Riots

Those still a bit hazy as to why Gay Pride is usually celebrated at the end of June should know that 27 June 1969 was probably the turning point in gay history. What started out as just another brutal vice squad raid on a gay bar gave birth to the homosexual liberation movement and an openness and pride in gay and lesbian life that was unimaginable to the generations that came before.

It all began at 1:20 AM on that warm June night. A then-routine raid on Greenwich Village's **Stonewall Inn** turned violent when the normally docile drag queens, "pansies," dykes, and other patrons, many upset by the recent death of Judy Garland, suddenly fought back against the police, who were forced to barricade themselves inside the bar until reinforcements arrived. The *New York Daily News* pooh-poohed this impertinence with the headline "Homo Nest Raided, Queen Bees Are Stinging Mad," but four subsequent nights of street protests in and around **Sheridan Square** eventually led to a 400-person protest march from **Washington Square Park** to Sheridan Square, the formation of the Gay Liberation Front, and the establishment of an annual Gay Pride March (later Parade). Such marches/parades and accompanying Gay Pride celebrations have since spread to more than 40 cities in the US and abroad.

46 The Blue Store

There's no sugar-coating this one: It's a porno shop smack in the heart of Chelsea. Racks of videos for sale (meant to tickle every taste) lead back to token-activated buddy booths. The frothy blue building front, and a slightly younger crowd, set this apart from similar joints in Midtown. ♦ 206 Eighth Ave (between W 20th and W 21st Sts). 924.8315

47 Avalon

All-gay on Sundays, expect a true New York disco experience with all the bells and whistles, including The Striptease Chapel hosted by Michael Formika Jones and regular Go-Go Idol competitions. ♦ Sa, 11PM-4AM. Sixth Ave (at W 20th St). 807.7780

48 West Side Club

♂ This clean, well-lighted Chelsea boys' bathhouse offers two floors of rooms big enough for a mattress and not much else; there's also a small steam room, a smaller sauna, an erotic-video lounge, and vending machines. The crowd peaks after midnight on weekends, and Sunday from mid-afternoon on. Expect a wait—and a divine amount of muscle-headed attitude—late weekend nights. The crowd is a crapshoot, but it's usually possible to find someone acceptable sooner or later. Under the same management is the less elaborate **East Side Club** (227 E 56th St, between Second and Third Aves, 753.2222), which attracts an older and heftier clientele. ♦ Daily, 24 hours. 27 W 20th St (between Fifth and Sixth Aves), second floor. 691.2700

The phallic Empire State Building goes gay for a weekend in June, when it's bathed in lavender light to celebrate Gay Pride.

"Recycling is nothing new to New York City's gay men. We've been reusing each other's tricks and lovers for years. Paper and plastic, that's how we separate them; the ones with the bills and the ones with the credit cards." —Drag queen Kenny Dash

49 The Dish

★★$ A fun and friendly spot, The Dish packs in everyone from muscle queens to neighborhood regulars. This comfy diner-style joint became so popular the owners expanded with more tables upstairs and a bench out front for patrons to sit and cruise the avenue while they wait to be seated. The food is good, if not extraordinary, though the potato-crusted chicken cutlet is an especially tasty treat. Cute waiters and a fun disco soundtrack make this a happening spot to dine, though definitely not a date restaurant. ♦ 201 Eighth Ave (between W 19th and W 20th Sts). 352.9800

50 Trois Canards

★★★$$ The pick of the flock for atmosphere, service, and food, the "Three Ducks" offers quality French bistro-style cuisine served amid fine mahogany, crystal, and silver appointments. The feel is casual, though, with customers in ties or T-shirts enjoying such specialties as crispy roast duckling with long-grain rice and fruit sauce, and lightly breaded rack of lamb with roasted vegetables. There's a reasonably priced wine list, too. ♦ French ♦ Daily, lunch and dinner. Reservations recommended on weekends.

184 Eighth Ave (between W 19th and W 20th Sts). 929.4320

50 Rainbows and Triangles

♂ ♀ Right in the thick of things on Eighth Avenue, this attractive little shop is a fun place to browse for greeting cards, mags, books and CDs, safe-sex supplies, Gay Pride doodads, and other assorted knickknacks. ♦ M-Sa, 11AM-10PM; Su, noon-9PM. 192 Eighth Ave (between W 19th and W 20th Sts). 627.2166 ♿

51 The Noose

♂ ♀ Here's a one-stop, mostly gay shop for bondage, leather, latex, and piercing enthusiasts. Where else in New York—or America, for that matter—could you just stroll in and put a real, honest-to-goodness straitjacket on your AmEx? ♦ Tu-F, 1PM-8PM; Sa, 11AM-8PM; Su, 1PM-6PM. 261 W 19th St (between Seventh and Eighth Aves). 807.1789 ♿

51 Nasty Pig

This tiny boutique has some vanilla gym wear, but mostly "play" gear like super-stretch nasty pig rubber short-shorts or a rubber tank top. ♦ M-Sa, noon-8PM; Su, 1PM-6PM. 265A W 19th St (between Seventh and Eighth Aves). 646/230.9423

52 The Starting Line

A sexy little storefront that carries the latest gay-boy trends (sought-after Puma shoe styles and leather bags, nappy hats, and Papi undergear), this place is current when it comes to buying and stocking up-to-the-minute head-turning gear. Check out an absolutely eye-popping T-shirt line from street-chic Label NY. Definitely for the younger set, though the underwear is surely timeless. ♦ 180 Eighth Ave (between W 19th and W 20th Sts). 691.4729

53 G

♂ Tagged the "original" Chelsea lounge, a nice spot to sit, sip, chat, and cruise, G features a striking oval steel bar and a dramatic glassed-in archway in front. The early evening scene (before the line forms) is best—it's fun, but less packed and with less attitude than later on at night. ♦ Daily, 4PM-4AM. 223 W 19th St (between Seventh and Eighth Aves). 929.1085. www.glounge.com

54 Le Singe Vert

★★★$$ This gorgeously charming French-style bistro (its name translates to The Green Monkey!) features a menu of stalwart favorites such as *gratinée à l'oignon, terrine de fois gras, moules frites, steak tartare, crème brûlée*, and many other mouth-watering delights, all given extra panache with flavors from Senegal incorporated into every dish. The décor recalls Lyon, and the waitstaff are not only stunning (this is Chelsea, after all) but—surprise!—courteous and friendly. The relaxed vibe is icing on the cake. ♦ French ♦ Daily, lunch and dinner. Reservations recommended. 160 Seventh Ave (between W 19th and W 20th Sts). 366.4100

55 Gym

♂ This brash little spot features shots of hunky rugby players on the walls, big-screen TV, video games, and a backyard patio. The bartenders look like that cute quarterback in high school. A mostly young and hunky crowd. ♦ 167 Eighth Ave between W 18th and W 19th Sts). 337.2439. www.gymsportsbar.com

56 Pink Berry

A frozen-yogurt dessert shop hawking no preservatives and low sugar, this colorful spot was a big hit on the West Coast before it came East. The Chelsea location caught on fast with the waist-conscious crowd. Get a fruit topping on the yogurt, or try a Green Tea smoothie or a fresh fruit shaved ice. The décor is meant to bring patrons "back to nature." ♦ M-Th, noon-11PM; F-Su, noon-11:30PM. 170 Eighth Ave (between W 18th and W 19th Sts). 488.2510 ♿

57 Food Bar

★$$ This Chelsea dining staple has become more intimate and less a scene, with a new owner and an updated everyman menu that includes items like mac and cheese, meat loaf, and a fried chicken sandwich. ♦ American ♦ M-F, lunch and dinner; Sa, Su, brunch and dinner. 149 Eighth Ave (between W 17th and W 18th Sts). 243.2020

58 Viceroy

♂ ♀ ★★$$ Large and bustling, this is one of Chelsea's prime "scene" (and be seen) spots, with a mostly male and rather pretty clientele in a cinematic Art Deco setting that's been used more than once for TV shoots. The menu—featuring an eclectic mix of Italian, Thai, and Japanese influences—is limited, but the food is well-prepared. The weekend brunch may be the week's most satisfying meal—try the cinnamon apple French toast. Enormous windows make the Eighth Avenue side of the room great for sipping and scoping. ♦ American/Continental ♦ M-W, lunch, dinner, and late-night menu until midnight; Th, F, lunch, dinner, and late-night menu until 1AM; Sa, brunch, dinner, and late-night menu until 1AM; Su, brunch and dinner. 160 Eighth Ave (at W 18th St). 633.8484

59 Energy Kitchen

★★★$ An ab-solutely essential addition to Chelsea (where measuring your body fat is a common pastime), this low-carb, high-protein

A Slope with a Different Angle

Top Spots for Lesbians in Park Slope, Brooklyn

By Winnie McCroy

Freelance arts and entertainment journalist

Brooklyn's famed **Prospect Park** offers the perfect patch of green to sun your buns or meet up with the girls for a pick-up game of softball. Also, take your pooch to the doggie beach, or enjoy the park's many amenities, and be sure not to miss **Brooklyn West Pride**, held at 15th Street and Prospect Park every year in mid-June.

Meander down to **The Tea Lounge** at 837 Union Street (718/789.2762) and pick up a latte. This casual neighborhood joint is packed with breast-feeding Slopies and yoga-mat-toting dykes during the day, and live music keeps the bar crowd moving at night.

Try the **PS 321 Flea Market** at Seventh Avenue and First Street for vintage threads and other digs, a nice contrast to some of the rather high-end boutiques that pepper this affluent 'hood.

Volunteer at **Dyke TV** (71 Fifth Ave, www.dyketv.org), a public-access program created by lesbians, for lesbians. Workshops will help you gain invaluable skills while you promote visibility of lesbian issues.

For lesbian nightlife, drop into **Ginger's** (363 Fifth Ave, 718/788.0924), a lesbian neighborhood bar with a phenomenal jukebox. Ladies gather to mingle, play pool, or enjoy the backyard patio, which sizzles in the summer. The after-party for Brooklyn Pride is a surefire winner.

On the first Sunday of the month, head to **Lucky 13 Saloon** (273 13th St, 718/499.3800, www.lucky13saloon.com) for the Atomic Reading Series, hosted by bisexual poet Cheryl B. Third. Wednesdays are lesbian night at this punk-rock/heavy metal/gay-friendly watering hole, which features PBR's for $2 and the White Trash Special (Rheingold and a shot of Wild Turkey) for $5.

For a great show, nothing in Park Slope comes close to **Southpaw** (125 Fifth Ave, 718/230.0236, www.spsounds.com), a 5,000-square-foot venue that has hosted such hotties as LP and Sahara Hotnight. The music is sweet and the beer is cheap and ice cold.

eatery offers a yummy selection of smoothies and main courses. Burgers are bunless and topped with egg whites. The fast-food-style tables are tiny, but the patrons are some of the buffest in town. ♦ 307 W 17th St (between Eighth and Ninth Aves). 645.5200

60 Nooch

★★$$ Designed by Karim Rashid, this new Japanese/Thai noodle spot in Chelsea features curvaceous furniture and a silk-screened glass façade. The menu offers a mix of sushi, pad Thai, and even a trendy little cocktail called the Tom Yumtini. ♦ 143 Eighth Ave (between W 17th and W 18th Sts). 691.8600

61 Cola's

★$ Here's an understated Italian gem in the very heart of Chelsea. The warm, yellow sponge-painted dining room is small but comfy and the consistently good fare combines cuisine from the north and south of the fair peninsula. A particular treat is the grilled Portobello mushroom salad with balsamic vinegar and shaved Parmesan, but it's tough to go wrong with any of the pastas, risottos, or entrées. ♦ Italian ♦ Daily, lunch and dinner. 148 Eighth Ave (between W 17th and W 18th Sts). 633.8020

62 Splash

♂ This loud, cavernous video/dance bar has been the reigning diva of Manhattan gay watering holes since opening in 1991, thanks in part to the jaw-droppingly hot "Splash Boy" bartenders. It was voted Best Gay Club 2003 by *HX Magazine*, after being refurbished (including a new sound system). Additions include a bigger dance floor, a small products boutique, and a basement cocktail bar swathed in stainless steel (a departure from the wood and mirrors upstairs). It's easier to hold a conversation downstairs, where jazz plays over the sound system. The clientele runs the age and looks gamut but is heavy on presentable guppies past their first jobs.

Before the 1850s, immigrants afflicted with diseases were kept on a remote spot on Staten Island. Many local residents became sick and died as a result, and others retaliated by setting fire to the quarantined buildings. This action prompted the state to build Hoffman and Swinburne Islands to house the afflicted. The islands are in Lower New York Bay off Staten Island and date from 1872. They were abandoned in the 1920s following the new immigration laws and serve no purpose today.

Besides cruising, entertainment takes the form of contests, shows, and comedy shtick on weekend nights and campy, clever videos along with endless pan shots of the Fire Island Pines (courtesy of co-owner Harry) the rest of the week. Do inspect the inspiring video installations over the urinals, too. ♦ Cover, F, Sa after 11PM. Daily, 5PM-4AM. 50 W 17th St (between Fifth and Sixth Aves). 691.0073. www.splashbar.com ♿

63 New York Sports Club (Chelsea)

Eyebrows furled when the New York Sports Club chain took over this West 16th Street gym location a few years back (formerly the very gay, very popular American Fitness Center), but the boys settled in when they realized little changed other than the name. For the record: The NY Sports Club has become perhaps the most gay-popular gym chain in the city (particularly the locations at 270 Eighth Ave between W 22nd and W 23rd Sts and at 34 W 14th St between Fifth and Sixth Aves), and the steam room is rumored to be quite…steamy. 128 Eighth Ave (between W 16th and W 17th Sts). 627.0065

64 Pad Thai

♂♀ ★★$$ Thai restaurants are rarely known for their hipness, but here's one that pulls it off, with plum-colored walls and black granite floors, wide-open windows overlooking the Eighth Avenue boy-show, and a youngish, comely, and very gay group of diners. The food's surprisingly good, too, from the refreshing green papaya salad through well-executed hot entrées like the ginger chicken. The eponymous dish, *pad thai*, is memorable, and for a little taste of everything, the "Thai box" is an excellent choice. ♦ Thai ♦ Daily, lunch and dinner. 114 Eighth Ave (between W 15th and W 16th Sts). 691.6226

65 Swich

★$ With a name that sounds like hips swaying, and signature-pressed sandwiches like the buffalo hot pants (chicken breast with hot sauce on French bread), this is destined to be a Chelsea classic. A mod fast-food-style eat-and-cruise spot. Try the homemade banana lemonade or the steak monster (sliced steak, caramelized onions) on a roll. ♦ Daily, 11:30AM-11PM. 104 Eighth Ave (between W 15th and W 16th Sts). 488.4800 ♿

66 Tour

★$$ A glass front reveals a peppy and fun dinner spot, right on the Chelsea strip. This replaced the slightly more upscale Diner 24. The menu is less pricey, the vibe young. A mixed menu features Mexican beef enchiladas, chicken fried chicken, and the Tour tomato soup. ♦ M-F, 11AM-midnight; Sa, Su, 9AM-midnight. 102 Eighth Ave (at W 15th St). 242.7773 ♿

67 Jeffrey

A chic menswear alternative to *über*-upscale Barneys NY, this one-level stomping ground for fashionistas in the Meatpacking District offers a seldom-found mix of high fashion and super-friendly service. It carries all the latest, from $300 denim to high-end skin-care items. ♦ 449 W 14th St (between Ninth Ave and Washington St). 206.3928

68 The Chelsea Pines

♂♀ $ With a convenient location straddling the border of Chelsea and the West Village, this 25-room inn set in an 1850 brick town house has become a more inviting place to roost after a recent refurbishing. Vintage movie posters (most of them camp) line the hallway walls, and the guestrooms feature telephones, refrigerators, color TV, and air conditioning (but not all have private baths). Complimentary breakfast is served in either the breakfast room or the pleasant garden patio out back. The staff is agreeable, the clientele youngish and about 80 percent male, and heterosexuals are discouraged from booking. Reservations are recommended one month in advance. ♦ 317 W 14th St (between Eighth and Ninth Aves). 929.1023; fax 645.9497. www.chelseapines.com

69 Lesbian, Gay, Bisexual & Transgender Community Center

♂♀ Set up in 1983 in an old four-story brickbuilding on West 13th Street that at one time housed the Food and Maritime Trade High School, the Center had a much-needed face-lift (including elevators and a great new front desk) in 2002. It is a busy beehive just about every night of the week, with activities ranging from ACT UP meetings to square dancing to gatherings of the Clann An Uabhair (a group of gay Scotspersons and wannabes) or the Grand Slam Bridge Group. It provides as good an introduction as any to New York homo life, hosting lectures, readings, art and photo exhibits, and well-attended weekend dances. Don't miss the explicit doodlings of the late gay graffiti artist Keith Haring that remain in the second-floor men's room. ♦ Daily, 9AM-11PM. 208 W 13th St (between Seventh and Greenwich Aves). 620.7310; hearing-impaired line, 800/662.1220, 800/421.1220. www.gaycenter.org ♿

West Village

Other than a small pocket of restaurants and shops that make up the very hot, model-favorite Meatpacking

District, the West Village has more baby-carriage-pushing brunch hetero couples than gays. Still, Christopher Street, the spot to cruise years back, draws a mature crowd at the city's oldest reliable gay watering holes and is home to Stonewall. Wander farther south, and you're in SoHo. Gay in sensibility, this is the area to cruise for art gallery lovers, celebrity watchers, and fans of super-high-end clothing boutiques and $5 lattes. Crowded on the weekends, its fun, colorful, and upscale artsy.

70 Lips

♂ ♀ ★★$$ Forget the outré neo-whorehouse décor, and even the gorgeous (and very convincing) "waitresses" who regularly drop what they're doing to swing into lip-synched production numbers. Surprisingly, Manhattan's best drag restaurant has food (prepared at **Artepasta** next door) that's pretty darn good. The only problem is figuring out what's what on a cutesy menu where the "Girlina" ("with the right buns, who cares about the meat!") is a veggie burger, and the "Mona Foot" ("knows just how to treat a sizeable and suitable zucchini") is the aforementioned squash stuffed with crabmeat and scallops in a citrus sauce. Straights and tourists have discovered the place, but there are still a few cute gay guys in attendance. ♦ American/Italian ♦ M-Sa, dinner; Su, brunch and dinner. 2 Bank St (at Greenwich Ave). 675.7710

71 Cubbyhole

♀ Overlooking the picturesque streets of Greenwich Village, this tiny corner barroom is certainly colorful, with sun-and-stars murals, Bugs Bunny and Daffy Duck bar stools, and all manner of thingies (Christmas ornaments, model airplanes, skeletons, Batman and Robin dolls, etc.) dangling from the ceiling. The clientele—mostly women and mostly in their thirties and up—is colorful, too, though generally more laid-back than the décor. Bands perform on weekends; otherwise the soundtrack is provided by a jukebox that hits all the bases from Cole Porter to Alanis Morisette. ♦ M-F, 4PM-4AM; Sa, Su, 2PM-4AM. 281 W 12th St (at W Fourth St). 243.9041

72 Incentra Village House

♂ $ The clientele is mostly male and mostly gay at this 1841 redbrick town house on Abingdon Square Park in the West Village, a skip and a hop from the Chelsea scene. The 10 rooms and two suites are furnished with Early American antiques, and all are equipped with telephones, air conditioning, private baths, and kitchenettes. Most also have fireplaces, and the **Garden Suite** even boasts a charming flower-filled patio. Other extras include an in-house masseur and a 1939 Steinway baby grand. It's best to reserve at least a month in advance. ♦ 32 Eighth Ave (between W 12th and Jane Sts). 206.0007; fax 604.0625. www.incentravillage.com

73 Julius

♂ The longest-running gay hangout in Greenwich Village is awash in history. The joint was originally a speakeasy for flappers and college kids in the Roaring Twenties, and was later written up by columnist Walter Winchell. A gay bar since the 1950s, it was the site of a 1965 incident that led to the tapering off of police entrapment of homosexuals in the city. These days the place, with its graffiti-carved wood bar and sawdust-covered floors, is more an archeological site than anything else, but it's still worth a look. And they do serve a good burger. ♦ M-F, 8AM-2AM; Sa, Su, 8AM-4AM. 159 W 10th St (at Waverly Pl). 929.9672 ♿

74 Oscar Wilde Memorial Bookshop

♂ ♀ The first gay bookstore in America, it was founded elsewhere in the Village in 1967 by the late Craig Rodwell. A pioneering homosexual rights activist, he also was a former lover of Harvey Milk. Today the bookstore is located in a somewhat cramped but comfy storefront room in an 1827 town house and boasts a wide-ranging selection of books and periodicals. A little back story: The bookstore nearly closed at the end of January 2003, but was saved in the eleventh hour when Deacon Maccubbin came to the rescue and made the historic outlet part of his **Lambda Rising** chain of gay and lesbian bookstores throughout the East Coast. ♦ Daily, 11AM-7PM. 15 Christopher St (between Greenwich Ave and Waverly Pl). 255.8097. www.oscarwildebooks.com

Visitors to Greenwich Village bemused by the sign boldly marking the intersection of Christopher and Gay Streets might be interested to know that the name "Gay Street" refers not to anyone's sexual orientation but to a family that lived in the area in the early 19th century. Not surprisingly, the sign has been swiped and replaced more than a few times.

75 Washington Square Hotel

$$ In 1961, the hostelry then called the **Hotel Earle** was the first New York home of Bob Dylan, who played neighborhood bars and coffeehouses. Today, its modest accommodations are still popular with arts and music types (Bo Diddley, to cite but one), as well as dollar-conscious grad students, young Europeans, and gay folks looking to be near the Chelsea and West Village action (and who don't mind the lack of porters or room service). The 170 rooms are smallish and not fancy, but nearly all have been renovated; ask for one overlooking Washington Square. The adjacent **North Square** (254.1200) restaurant and bar serves New American fare and drinks to a diverse, sometimes hip, crowd. ♦ 103 Waverly Pl (at MacDougal St). 777.9515, 800/222.0418; fax 979.8373. www.wshotel.com

76 Washington Square Park

Ⓟ A center of Greenwich Village life since 1828, this park is still a popular gathering place for straight and gay students, tourists, jugglers, drug dealers, and the occasional Village idiot. In the 1960s, the west side of the park was known as the "meat rack" because of the gay cruising here. The buildings that line the park, most of which now belong to **New York University**, are steeped in local history. At **3 Washington Square North** (currently student apartments), writer John Dos Passos (1896-1970) wrote his impressionistic novel of 1920s New York City life, *Manhattan Transfer*. In 1942, First Lady Eleanor Roosevelt moved to **29 Washington Square North** with her little black scottie, Fala, and stayed until 1949. Across the park, at **60 Washington Square South** (which is now occupied by New York University's **Kimmel Center**), was the boardinghouse where Stephen Crane wrote his classic tale *The Red Badge of Courage* in 1895; it was also home at one point to Willa Cather. Some of that sapphic scribe's modern-day admirers are undoubtedly to be found amid the veritable ocean of lesbians that fills the park when the Dyke March concludes here each Pride weekend (with the Lesbian Avengers giving new meaning to the words "hot dyke" by literally eating fire). ♦ Bounded by Washington Sq E and Washington Sq W, and Washington Sq S and Washington Sq N

77 The Duplex

♂ ♀ You can't miss this piano bar/cabaret set in an intriguing wedge of a building perched across the street from **Christopher Park**. French windows open up the small downstairs space, which offers fun, free entertainment and sing-alongs (attracting lots of straight tourists). Upstairs, the bar attracts a small but comely crowd, and a cabaret features stand-up comics and revues like "Talent!" and "Transsexuals on the Run" and even appearances by Joan Rivers, who started her career here. In summer there's sidewalk seating. ♦ Cover for cabaret. Daily, 4PM-4AM. 61 Christopher St (at Seventh Ave S). 255.5438. www.theduplex.com

77 Stonewall

♂ After the original **Stonewall Inn** (see sidebar on page 345) closed in 1969, the ground floor of the building housed, among other things, a bagel shop and a clothing store until a new gay bar opened here in 1994, piggybacking on its famous namesake. Downstairs has the feel of a neighborhood watering hole, while the second floor is a flashier video bar with a dance floor. The bar is low-key—an easygoing and casual multi-age mix of neighborhood guys and tourists, and regular guest-star go-go boys draw a crowd. ♦ Daily, 2:30PM-4AM. 53 Christopher St (between Waverly Pl and Seventh Ave S). 463.0950. www.stonewall-place.com ♿

78 Christopher Park

Ⓟ Smack in the heart of the West Village and enclosed by a black iron fence, the modest little park in front of the **Stonewall** bar (see above) is a great place to chill out on a warm evening. Take a look at George Segal's 1980 *Gay Liberation*, a white sculpture of two same-sex couples hanging out at one of the park's benches—they're not exactly inspiring (some would call them downright dreary), but at least they're visibly gay. The nearby intersection has been the site of many a traffic-blocking demonstration over the years, and the annual Gay Pride parade swings past here near the end of its colorful route in late June. ♦ Bounded by Grove, W Fourth, and Christopher Sts

79 The Monster

♂ At street level, a rambling, many-windowed cruise bar leads to a campy piano bar, while downstairs a dark dance floor keeps the boys jumping. A favorite of mature "friends of Judy," along with a younger generation of black and Hispanic guys. ♦ Cover F-Su. Daily, 4PM-4AM. 80 Grove St (at W Washington Pl). 924.3558. www.manhattan-monster.com ♿

80 Rubyfruit

♀ ★★$$ With a name right out of Rita Mae Brown, well-prepared gringo grub, multi-ethnic flourishes, and a romantic décor featuring ornate wooden chairs and tree branches festooned with tiny red lights, it's no wonder this West Village bar and restaurant is a fave with lesbians, especially on weekends. Sample the seared salmon over cucumber with oriental vinaigrette or the blackened pork chops with jalapeño dip. Rita Mae herself has stopped by on occasion, as have other lesbo luminaries such as Martina Navratilova and Melissa Etheridge. ♦ American ♦ M-Sa, dinner; Su, brunch. 531 Hudson St (between W 10th and Charles Sts). 929.3343

81 Boots and Saddle

♂ Despite the Western motif, and with the exception of the occasional Marlboro Man at the bar, this friendly one-room 1970s holdover attracts a fun and down-to-earth group of older Levi's lovers and tourists. (You definitely won't see any Chelsea glamour boys or muscle clones.) The funky car-shaped jukebox offers today's tunes along with a boogie down memory lane, and this is one of the relatively few gay places you'll find Spaten (Bavarian wheat beer) on tap. ♦ M-Sa, 8AM-4AM; Su, noon-4AM. 76 Christopher St (between Seventh Ave S and Bleecker St). 929.9684

82 Marie's Crisis

For show-tune queens only, this charming basement bar is a fun and friendly spot to lean on the piano and croon while you guzzle. (Next door is the similar **Rose's Turn**, so piano bar hopping is easy.) ♦ 59 Grove St (between Seventh Ave and Bleecker St). 243.9323

83 Hangar

♂ A West Village staple mostly for cruising and throwing a few back, with a mature crowd and a laid-back atmosphere. ♦ Daily, 1PM-4AM. 115 Christopher St (between Bleecker and Hudson Sts). 627.2044 ♿

84 The Factory Cafe

$ The setting, with its exposed brick walls, soothing jazz sound track, and cozy, mismatched chairs, invites lolling, and that's just what the patrons (most of whom are gay) do. Besides coffee, the menu offers fresh-squeezed juices, bagels and muffins, soups, salads, and sandwiches both simple (meat loaf, ham and Swiss) and chichi (brie, asparagus, and tomato). ♦ Coffeehouse ♦ Su-Th, 7AM-midnight; F, Sa, 7AM-1AM. 104 Christopher St (between Bleecker and Bedford Sts). 807.6900

85 Christopher Street

Named rather prosaically after the wealthy patron of one of Manhattan's first English settlers, this eight-block stretch of the West Village between **Sixth Avenue** and the **Hudson River** has become synonymous around the world with gay life and liberation.

Tops for Clubbing

Daniel Nardicio

Self-tagged "Willy Wonka of Queer NY Nightlife"

Pop into **Boysroom** (9 Ave A) to watch Tommy Grimaldi's Magic Touch, tough-guy dancers. The whole scene is surreal and a real bump-and-grind hoot.

Try out Cameron Dailey's kooky Sunday party, Easy, at **Metropolitan Bar** in Williamsburg, Brooklyn. The fete features a wild mix of arts and crafts . . . and sexy strip-off contests.

Lil Frankie's Pizzeria on First Avenue (between 1st and 2nd Sts). Heavenly pizza to keep your hangover less than wicked.

The **Juvenex Korean Spa** (24 hours!). Drop in at 5AM after a full night of clubbing. Dip into a lemon ginseng hot tub, or try the Jade Igloo fresh fruit and tons of teas and waters. 25 W 32nd St. 646/733.1330.

These days much of the parade has shifted northward to **Chelsea** and **Hell's Kitchen**, and eastward to the **East Village**, but there's still some spark to Christopher, with its old-time gay bars and restaurants such as **Boots and Saddle** (left). Then, of course, there's the **Stonewall** (see page 351), a drinking spot on the site of the eponymous bar where a few feisty dykes, drag queens, and "sissies" made history by fighting back against a brutal police raid on 27 June 1969 (see "The Stonewall Riots" on page 345). Farther west, between **Hudson Street** and the river, Christopher has more recently been reinvigorated by the gorgeous and very popular **Christopher Street Pier** in Hudson River Park. ♦ Between Sixth Ave and West St

85 Wings Theatre

♂♀ Lots of venues host gay-themed plays in New York City, but few do it quite so consistently as this 74-seat space, home to a small theater company brought to town in 1986 by artistic director Jeffrey Corrick. Not a week goes by that doesn't see something fruity here, mixed in with musicals, children's productions, and other fare. The popular Gay Plays series has included all manner of genres and different levels of quality, from *The Captain's Boy* (a gay pirate musical—oh, dear) to the wonderfully talented Georget Barthel's *The Naked Enemy* (about spies, intrigue, and World War II) to Clint Jefferies's award-winning play *The Jocker,* about runaways and hobos mingling during the Great Depression. ♦ 154 Christopher St (between Greenwich and Washington Sts). 627.2960, 627.2961 ♿

86 Cherry Lane Theatre

Housed in a onetime brewery built in 1836 on a picturesque little loop of Commerce Street, this early Off-Broadway theater is just around the corner from cofounder Edna St. Vincent Millay's Bedford Street playpen (see below). The rock musical *Godspell* and the avant-garde Samuel Beckett play *Waiting for Godot* had their debuts here, and more recent shows have included works by Edward Albee and Amiri Baraka, Beckett revivals, new playwright showcases, and appearances by the acclaimed drag performer Lypsinka. Oh, and Barbara Streisand was an usher here before she became Barbra. ♦ 38 Commerce St (between Bedford and Barrow Sts). 989.2020, tickets 239.6200. www.cherrylanetheatre.org

86 75½ Bedford Street

From 1923 to 1924, this step-gabled sliver of a building was the last New York City home of Pulitzer Prize–winning bisexual poet and playwright Edna St. Vincent Millay (1892-1950). The passionate woman who once wrote "what lips my lips have kissed, and where, and why, I have forgotten, and what arms have lain under my head till morning" was one of the many "artsy" types that helped build Greenwich Village's reputation for "decadence" and "deviance." Marked with a plaque citing her famous claim that "My candle burns at both ends," this three-story building dating from 1873 also has the distinction of being the narrowest house in the city—it is a mere 9½ feet wide. It is still a private residence. ♦ Between Morton and Commerce Sts

87 Henrietta Hudson

♀ Take the set from the old TV sitcom *Cheers*, fill it with fun and friendly dykes tending toward the young and the cute, throw in a handful of their guy friends, and you've got Henrietta's. A great bar, a great jukebox (heavy on Melissa and k.d., natch), and regular pool tournaments complete the picture. This is the place to go after the late-June Dyke March, but it's prized for its low attitude quotient all year round. Check out regular Henrietta speed-dating events and the city's hottest go-go girls. ♦ Daily, 3PM-4AM. 438 Hudson St (at Morton St). 924.3347 ♿

88 Sea Tea

♂♀ This Sunday-evening party restores a bit of the nautical sense to the term "cruising." A boatload of queens (and a handful of dykes) are ferried around Lower Manhattan in the three-deck paddle wheeler *Queen of Hearts*. The crowd is a mixed bag of ages and looks, but overall think Cherry Grove rather than Pines, and Key West instead of South Beach. Passengers boogie on the top deck after

The Best

Scott Hess

Writer/Actor

It wasn't hard to concoct a trés-gay day trip through New York; the difficulty came in narrowing it down to a mere 24 hours. The morning would start with a double espresso at **Bouchon Bakery** located at the city-chic **Time Warner Center** and shops overlooking Central Park.

From there, head east across 57th Street to Fifth Avenue. Then jog north a block to the city's most elegant men's fashion playground: **Bergdorf Goodman Men's** (745 Fifth Ave, at E 58th St, 753.7300). My vintage hand-woven sandals snapped up there are worth every hundred-dollar bill spent!

Have any shopping cash left after Bergdorf? Then backtrack to East 57th Street, stopping at such gorgeous flagship stores as **Louis Vuitton** (1 E 57th St, at Fifth Ave, 752.4730) and **Jil Sander** (11 E 57th St, between Fifth and Madison Aves, 838.6321).

Twirling downtown, stop by Greenwich Village's **Washington Square Park** for a quick dip in the park's huge central fountain (you can really jump in—during the summer, that is). To date, this little watery bit of relief is uncrowded and very cool, one of the only spots in the city where visitors can literally frolic under surging fountain jets.

A midafternoon very-deep tissue massage with wunderkind therapist **Rob Pinter** (www.hometown.aol.com/massageace) would lead to dinner at Hell's Kitchen's **44 & X** (62 10th Ave, at W 44th St, 977.1170), where the only thing sweeter than the fabulous banana and white chocolate bread pudding is the super-friendly and cute waiter staff. Of course, a day of luxury demands a trashy nightcap: take the F train to the end of the line and visit the campy-kitschy **Coney Island Amusement Park**—and hurry, since 2007 is the final summer before a major renovation of the park begins. Scream your head off on the infamous Cyclone Roller Coaster (ranked number one in the world), nosh on a **Nathan's** chili-cheese-smothered hot dog, and peek at the ocean before leaving the isle of Coney. End the evening with a real nightcap at the boy-toy East Village hangout **The Urge** bar (33 Second Ave, at E Second St, 533.5757), which features some of the hottest go-go boys in town.

The next day: rinse and repeat.

partaking of the high school cafeteria-quality buffet downstairs. Remember, there is no escape, so consider hanging out a bit before the ship sails, just to be sure it's your cup of tea. ♦ Cover. Su, 6PM-10PM mid-June through September. Pier 40, West St (just south of Clarkson St). 675.4357. www.seatea.com

89 Leslie-Lohman Gay Art Foundation

♂♀ This gallery in a SoHo basement is New York City's only regular venue for homoerotic fine art, with permanent and rotating exhibitions (among them an annual photography show and a biannual show of lesbian works). Though the quality of the art can be uneven, the exhibits are usually thought-provoking. Among the artists represented are Delmas Howe, Avital Greenberg, and Bruce Kamerling. They also feature the Queer Men's Erotic Art drawing workshop. ♦ Tu-Sa, 1PM-6PM. 127-B Prince St (between Wooster St and W Broadway). 673.7007. www.leslielohman.org

90 SoHo Grand Hotel

$$$$ Rising 17 stories, the first major upscale hostelry located between Midtown and the Financial District kicked up a lot of controversy when it opened in 1996, but it has since become a favorite of folks in the art and fashion worlds and other chic and gay types. With exposed beams, faux sandstone walls, and bronze lanterns, the lobby does a stylish take on the industrial/cast-iron look of the neighborhood (unfortunately, the huge windows overlook an unsightly parking lot across the street). The 367 rooms are also stylish, decorated in tones of gray and beige with blocky custom-designed furniture and photos of old New York on the walls. The four penthouse suites boast marble baths and terraces with spectacular skyline views. Also on the premises are the **Grand Bar**, **The Gallery** restaurant, and a fitness center. There's even a classy little "dog bar" out front with water for thirsty pooches (the place is owned by the maker of Hartz flea collars). Extras for human guests include round-the-clock room service and valet parking. ♦ 310 W Broadway (between Canal and Grand Sts). 965.3000, 800/965.3000; fax 965.3200 www.sohogrand.com ♿

East Village

When Gap opened in this edgy 'hood, it seemed the end of an era. The East Village, however, remains one of the most fun, sexy, and artsy areas to hang, with an ever-flowing crop of bouncy young gays (students, performance artists, filmmakers, and writers). The bars are packed on weekends and the vibe is young.

91 Nowhere

Another low-down pub: dark, cheap drinks, hot juke box, hotter boys. ♦ Daily, 3PM-4AM.

West Village (Best of the West)

David Drake

Obie Award-winning playwright/performer of *The Night Larry Kramer Kissed Me*

Chelsea and Hell's Kitchen may be the epicenter of the Gay Apple now, but with its charming tree-lined streets, vintage brownstones, and roots in queer history, downtown's West Village still holds my heart.

Best Battleground Toast: Pay homage to those who started the riots on 27 June 1969 at the **Stonewall** (53 Christopher St, at Seventh Ave S). Friendly neighborhood crowd, with go-go boys and a wee dance floor on weekends. Across the street in **Christopher Park**, check out the same-sex paired statues. Like ghosts, they gently remind us of the warriors who came before us.

Best Window Display: **Pleasure Chest** (156 Seventh Ave S). Always a scandalously camp scene. Inside, it's FAO Schwarz for grown-ups, with everything from cocoa-flavored lube to kicky vibrators.

Best Slice: **Two Boots** (corner of Seventh Ave S and Greenwich Ave). Crispy crust, oven-baked fresh. And for $3.95, the Big Maybelle—dolloped with chicken, pepperoni, garlic, and bread crumbs—is a nutritious and cheap lunch.

Best Hot Cider: Queer scribes William F. Burroughs, Willa Cather, and Allen Ginsberg lifted their glasses at **Chumleys**, and you should too. The former 1920s speakeasy at 86 Bedford Street (with a secret entrance at 58 Barrow St) retains its bookish, table-nooked aura.

Best Bookstore: The tiny but vital **Oscar Wilde Bookshop** (15 Christopher St, www.oscarwildebooks.com) has been serving readers of our stories since 1967. Also helpful with locating rare and out-of-print stuff.

Best All-Night Eats: The Meatpacking District's gay-owned and -operated **Florent** (69 Gansevoort St, www.restaurantflorent.com). Open 24/7, the steak frites are abfab at any hour.

Best Piano Bar: Sing Out, Louise, at **Rose's Turn!** (Seventh Ave at Grove St). This well-trodden, split-level cabaret is housed in the original Duplex cabaret location, where Joan Rivers got her start in the '60s!

322 E 14th St (between First and Second Aves). 477.4744.

92 Rapture

Christened by très-gay *Village Voice* columnist Michael Musto with a cover story in *Next* magazine, this highly literate and equally arousing café/bookshop is the percolated brainchild of downtown wunderkind Joe Birdsong and drag legend Hattie Hathaway. Muscled-up java and light treats are on the menu, along with the city's most eclectic and titillating collection of high- and low-brow literature. Page through Jean Genet, Charles Dickens, or Edmund White or eyeball a copy of *Honcho*, *Latin Inches*, or *Bark, The Modern Dog Culture Magazine*. Regular readings and events. ♦ Daily, 10AM-10PM. 200 Ave A (between E 12th and E 13th Sts). 228.1177 ♿

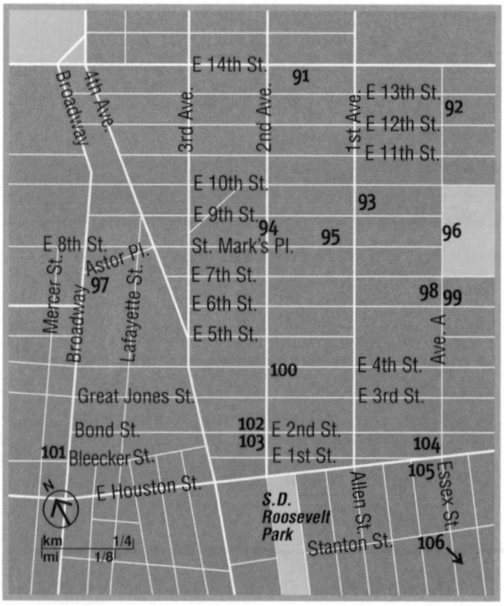

93 Performance Space 122 (PS 122)

The name of this theater and arts center is an allusion to the building's original identity as a New York public school. Since 1979, it has hosted a wide variety of avant-garde and experimental work—much of it queer—in its two small theaters. The legendary gay-themed Ridiculous Theater Company has taken the stage here, as have drag performer/writer Linda Simpson and cross-dressing, Tony-nominated British comedian Eddie Izzard. ♦ 150 First Ave (between E Ninth and E 10th Sts). 477.5288, 477.5029. www.ps122.org

94 St. Mark's Place

A distillation of what the neighborhood is all about, this East Village street was the hippie capital of the East in the 1960s. In the 1970s and early 1980s it was home to the legendary-among-gay-men **St. Mark's Baths** (at **No. 6** St. Mark's Pl), which were closed during the initial AIDS scare of the mid-1980s. The years since have brought bikers, punks with Mohawks, grunge kids, and a horde of nonconformists too far out there to be classified. The street somehow hangs on to its funky, gritty edge (with stores like **Religious Sex** and holiday

The Best

Hattie Hathaway & Joe Birdsong

Owners, Rapture Café & Books (East Village)

Hattie and Joe share what they consider the "East Village Crème de la Crème of Everything Gay!"

Nowhere Bar (322 E 14th St, between First and Second Aves, 477.4744). Simply the best folksy neighborhood gay watering hole south of 14th Street, run by our good friend and former Calvin Klein model/ Clit Club NYC promoter, Tjet Clark. Includes unique offerings like the paw-fully jolly Max Scott's Bear Essentials every Tuesday night.

Lost Shoe Productions Art & Fashion Boutique (168 Ludlow St, between Houston and Stanton Sts, 529.2537). Rocker clothing and accessories and original artwork by East Village musical legends such as Kembra Pfahler make Ann Hanavan's little store a standout on the Ludlow Street Strip.

Mo' Pitkins House of Satisfaction (34 Avenue A, between E Second and E Third Sts, 777.5660). From soup to nuts, and brunch too, this place provides amazing entertainment. Of note: Murray Hill's Monday Night Bingo, the hilarious Poo Poo Platter, Little Annie's Annual Christmas Show (get your reservations now), and the Borscht Belt Brunch!

Eastern Bloc (505 E Sixth St, between Aves A and B, 777.2555). Gabe and Darren are the hosts with the most at this little out-of-the-way cheap drinks hideaway on the site of the old, well-worn Wonderbar.

Tokyo 7 (64 E Seventh St, between First and Second Aves, 353.8443). Cajun, Mex, and Southern Soul vittles that're too good to be true. Try the spicy Eggs Oaxaca and say hi to the ruling server, Merideth.

Christine's (208 First Ave, between Stanton and Rivington Sts, 254.2474). Authentic and filling Polish cuisine with the Solidarity-inspired no-frills waitresses and décor to match. Note the "Bear Pride" sticker on the door.

Ninth Street Barber (439 E Ninth St, between Ave A and First Ave, 777.0798). A fave of hipsters looking for a trim, namely due to hair cutter Eric, who is known as the "Sweeney Todd of the East Village." Watch him safely and stunningly wield a straight razor and you'll see why.

Dinosaur Hill (306 E Ninth St, between First and Second Aves, 473.5850). This store truly makes visitors feel like they are in fairyland. Features everything from hand puppets (the real kind) and tiny harmonicas to vintage toys from granddad's day.

Tribal Sounds (340 E Sixth St, between First and Second Aves, 673.5992). This shop's unique native instruments from around the world, from thumb pianos to talking drums and beyond, always astound.

signs wishing passersby "Season's Beatings"). ♦ Between Ave A and Third Ave

95 77 St. Mark's Place

The renowned Anglo-American poet W.H. Auden (1907-1973) and his male lover lived on the second floor of this five-story brick town house between 1953 and 1957. It is still a private residence.♦ Between First and Second Aves

96 Tompkins Square Park

This 16-acre park began as a parade ground in the 1830s. The site of America's first labor demonstration—it came to a bloody end when club-wielding police went in to break it up—in 1874, the park would become known as a more peaceful place during the 1960s, when it drew crowds for "love-ins" and "be-ins."

On a gayer note, in 1985 the park hosted the first **Wigstock**, one of the most outrageous drag events in the world and the subject of a 1994 movie. The outdoor festival was held here on Labor Day, almost every year through 1993, ultimately attracting crowds of more than 25,000 revelers.

In 1988 radical squatters (including a politicized HIV-positive contingent), and others protesting a park curfew, became embroiled in a violent confrontation with the police. The police then left Tompkins—and its shantytown of homeless people—alone until 1991, when the park was closed for renovations, and some 200 people were evicted.

A $2.1 million renovation later, the park is popular with the whole neighborhood. The dog run is always friendly (and cruisy) and on warm, sunny days, shirtless boys gather here to soak up the rays and check each other out. As for Wigstock, it began an intermittent return to Tompkins in 2003, as part of the (also on-and-off) **Howl! Festival** (www.howlfestival.com). But the wiggy event continues to evolve and venues can change annually—some say according to organizer Lady Bunny's mood (ladybunny.net).
♦ Bounded by Aves A and B, and E Seventh and E 10th Sts. nycgovparks.org

Open-Air New York

Justin Ocean

Editor-in-Chief, Next Magazine

Add up all the time you spend riding the subway, taking cabs, shopping, eating out, and immersing yourself in any of New York's world-class museums and it can seem as if your entire trip is spent indoors. But when the weather is warm and the concrete canyons are breezy, nothing beats taking a big gulp of hearty city air in the parks, pavilions, and open-air spaces secreted around the city.

1. **Worldwide Plaza** (W 50th St, between Eighth and Ninth Aves). Smack in the center of gay nabe Hell's Kitchen, this Euro-style piazza has 24-hour seating and security, sporadic concerts, and $3 margaritas at low-key Mexican restaurant **Blockheads** (noon-11PM, 307.7029) to fuel a hopping people-watching scene.

2. **Christopher Street, Pier 45** (dawn-1AM. Christopher St, at the West Side Highway). Sunshine means plenty of Speedos at this cruisy yet relaxed, grass-covered sunbathing area on the Hudson. When the gay skin parade becomes too hot, cool off in the icily refreshing mister.

3. **Shake Shack** (spring through fall, 11AM-11PM. 889.6600, shakeshacknyc.com. Southeast corner of Madison Square Park, Madison Ave at E 23rd St). Pack in thick 'n' juicy Shack Burgers, loaded-up Chicago Dogs, or triple-thick milk shakes before lolling about with wine or beer from the counter or corner deli in a verdant oasis by the Flatiron Building.

4. **Rooftop Film Series** (rooftopfilms.com). from June till the end of September, hipsters and cinephiles gather for over 30 different series showcasing predominantly New York-based independent and underground short and feature films on rooftops throughout Brooklyn and Manhattan.

5. **Spiegeltent** (Pier 17, South Street Seaport. spiegelworld.com). From early July through the end of September, old-world opulence comes to the East River with dramatic, drunken flair. Cavort with friends in the European-style beer garden that boasts stunning riverside views of the Brooklyn, Manhattan, and Williamsburg Bridges before, after, and between the packed schedule of concerts, cabarets, and Cirque du Soleil-esque shows Absinthe and La Vie taking place in the opulent Art Deco wood-and-mirror traveling tent.

6. **Le Petit Versailles** (346 E Houston St, between Aves B and C. www.alliedproductions.org). Gay artists and Alphabet City community members have transformed this lush public garden into a sanctuary for meditation, relaxation, and ever-changing public arts and performance events.

7. **McCarren Park Pool** (Lorimer St, between Driggs Ave and Bayard St, Greenpoint, Brooklyn. mccarrenpark.com). Williamsburg hipsters have reclaimed a massive, dilapidated WWII-era public swimming pool and turned it into one of summer's premier outdoor venues with indie and mainstream concerts, free pool parties (concerts, beer, and slip 'n' slide! 2pm-sunset, Sundays mid-June-mid-August, www.thepoolparties.com) and free film screenings by Summer Screen (7PM, Tuesdays late July-late August. www.summerscreen.org).

8. **The Cloisters** (Fort Tryon Park, 99 Margaret Corbin Dr. 923.3700, www.metmuseum.org). When the city bustle is too much, take the A train to the upper tip of Manhattan (W 190th St) and relax amid the densely wooded, primeval forest (the last remaining on the island) of Fort Tryon Park before taking in a one-of-a-kind collection of medieval European art and relics at the sleepy, historic museum and gardens.

9. **Rooftop Pools**: If you tend to meet the elite in bars, have some cash to burn on a membership, or choose to bed down in any of these locations, a day working on your tan and social status at the très chic rooftop pools at the **Gansevoort** (18 Ninth Ave, at W 13th St. 206.6700, www.hotelgansevoort.com), **Soho House** (29-35 Ninth Ave, at W 14th St. 627.9800, www.sohohouseny.com), or **Gramercy Park Hotel** (2 Lexington Ave, at E 21st St. 920.3300, www.gramercyparkhotel.com) is the height of haute traveling.

10. **Gay Bar Patios**: Whether for a smoke or an afternoon and evening spent tossing back a few, gay bars with outdoor space are always a hoppin' bet. **O.W. Bar** (221 E 58th St, between Second and Third Aves. 355.3395, www.owbar.com), **The Eagle** (554 W 28th St, at Eleventh Ave. 646/473.1866, www.eagleny.com), **XES Lounge** (157 W 24th St, between Sixth and Seventh Aves. 604.0212, www.xeslounge.com), **Bamboo 52** (344 W 52nd St, between Eighth and Ninth Aves. 315.2777, www.bamboo52nyc.com).

97 Hetrick-Martin Institute/ Harvey Milk High School

The Harvey Milk School made national headlines in June of 2002 when the New York City Board of Education approved a $3.2 million expansion grant, making it the world's first accredited four-year high school devoted to the needs of lesbian, gay, bisexual, transgender, and "questioning" youth. Prior to nabbing the grant and loads of CNN headlines, the school had been run at the same East Village location, but on a smaller scale (50 students as opposed to the current 170 admit limit). Since hitting the news, the school's guest roster has gone glam, and the ongoing list of visitors includes actress Susan Sarandon in a stint as a "principal for the day," as well as visits from actress Hillary Swank and Senator Hillary Rodham Clinton. The school is but one of many programs for gay young people (age 21 and under) run by the **Hetrick-Martin Institute**, which is also based here. The institute serves some 8,000 New York City youths, offering family counseling, a drop-in center, outreach programs for the homeless, job training, and other assistance. ♦ 2 Astor Pl (between Lafayette St and Broadway). 674.2400. www.hmi.org

98 Pyramid

♂ Possibly the most joyous gay dance party of the week goes down at this East Village mainstay every Friday night, when "1984" brings together a good-looking mix of nostalgic thirtysomethings with NYU students and other fresh-faced youngsters (expect to wait on line to get in, though). The space is a very basic black-painted saloon with a no-frills dance area at the rear. But nobody minds, and it's a kick to see boys who were practically in diapers in the 1980s literally jump for joy to "Karma Chameleon" and "Rock the Casbah." Historical note: This was the birthplace of the early-1980s New York City drag revival that spawned **Wigstock** (see **Tompkins Square Park**, page 355) and unleashed its many divas on the world. ♦ Cover. F, 10PM-4AM. 101 Ave A (between E Sixth and E Seventh Sts). 462.9077

99 Eastern Bloc

The quintessential East Village hangout: a small, dark bar with cute boys, drink specials, abstract images on a junky-looking TV screen, and fresh music. Dirty and fun. ♦ Daily, 4PM-4AM. 505 E Sixth St. (between Aves B and A). 777.2555.

100 2 by 4

♂ A refreshing alternative to Chelsea glitz and attitude, this dim old one-room East Village saloon, once simply known as The Bar, is a real slice of the 1970s, but with a groovily updated jukebox. The crowd is a mix of ages and kinds, including cute NYU students, "alternative types," and older guys. Larry Mitchell's classic East Village gay novel *The Terminal Bar* is set here. ♦ Daily. 68 Second Ave (at E Fourth St). 254.5766 ♿

100 The Boiler Room

♂ ♀ With a décor that lives up to the name, this East Village hot spot is not much to look at inside or out, but the steam can certainly rise on weekends, when a fun, eclectic, and youngish flock (liberally seasoned with New York University students and endearingly scruffy locals) packs the place. Boys usually outnumber the girls, but Sunday's "women's night" draws a happening mix of womanhood. Most people bop back and forth all night between here and **2 by 4** (see above). ♦ Daily. 86 E Fourth St (between First and Second Aves). 254.7536 ♿

101 Mr. Black

A mixed crowd of hipsters and hard-bodied gays, this popular dance den regularly features DJ Larry Tee and gay icon Johnny McGovern (who landed a spot on Logo TV's *Big Gay Sketch Comedy Show*). ♦ Tu-Su, 10PM-6AM. 643 Broadway (at Bleecker St). 253.2560

102 The Urge

A long, narrow East Village hangout with all the action literally on top of the circular bar. Incredibly hot and friendly go-go boys gingerly strut the bar, bending down to chat up customers. While showing off their assets, these boys are known to also share their thoughts (discussing the rigors of college mid-terms while tweaking their nipples). ♦ Daily, 4PM-4AM. 33 Second Ave (at E Second St). 533.5757

103 The Cock

♂ The name says it all: This is a sassy, sleazy East Village bar with a rock 'n' roll attitude. The late-night weekend crowd gets wild and rowdy. ♦ 29 Second Ave (between First and Second Sts)

104 Boysroom

♂ Boysroom offers two floors of down-and-dirty go-go boys, lots of special events, and a true trashy vibe. ♦ 9 Ave A (between First and Second Sts). 995.8684. www.tripwithus.com

105 Element

One of a fresh crop of East Village dance clubs drawing a hot and young crowd. This tri-level "nightlife playground" features three full-service bars, a V.I.P. mezzanine, lounge spaces, and popular DJs. ♦ Sa only, 10PM-6AM. 225b E Houston St (between Ludlow and Essex Sts). 254.2200

106 Wessel + O'Connor Fine Art

This pleasant, gay-owned gallery exhibits and sells the works of many gay artists and photographers, including Andy Warhol, Robert Mapplethorpe, John Dugdale, Bruce of Los Angeles, and Baron Wilhelm von Gloeden, a 19th-century German photographer who specialized in studies of lithe Sicilian youths. Keeping a finger on the camp factor, the gallery has also featured a series of vintage photographic hairdressing studies from the 1940s produced by the National Beauty Service of Chicago. Annual historical shows are also held. ♦ W-Sa, 11AM-6PM. 111 Front St (between Washington and Adams Sts), 2nd floor, DUMB. Brooklyn. 718/596.1700. wesseloconnor.com ♿

HISTORY

1524 Italian explorer Giovanni da Verrazano sails into New York Harbor.

1609 British captain Henry Hudson, in search of a shortcut to India for the Dutch West India Company, sails up the river that will bear his name.

1621 The city's history begins with a permanent Dutch settlement named **Nieuw Amsterdam**.

1625 The first black settlers are brought as slaves to build the city.

1626 Peter Minuit, the first governor, buys **Manhattan Island** from the Indians for a trunkful of relatively worthless trinkets.

1664 Nieuw Amsterdam becomes **New York** when Stuyvesant cedes control to Charles II of England and his brother, James, Duke of York.

1765 The British impose taxes, the harshest of which is the Stamp Act.

1774 The New York Tea Party takes place when the Sons of Liberty board the *London* and dump 18 cases of tea into the **East River**.

1776 The American Revolution starts, and General George Washington sets up quarters in Lower Manhattan . . . As the Declaration of Independence is adopted by Congress, the Revolutionary forces are driven out of Manhattan by Lord Howe.

1789 New York City becomes capital of the United States. George Washington is inaugurated in front of **Federal Hall**.

1804 Aaron Burr, the vice president of the US, kills Alexander Hamilton, the first secretary of the treasury, in a duel.

1812 War is declared when the British blockade Manhattan. The new **City Hall** opens.

1829 William Cullen Bryant becomes editor in chief of the *New York Evening Post*, a newspaper launched by Alexander Hamilton.

1830 With the arrival of new German immigrants throughout the previous decade, the population rises to 202,000.

1835 Samuel F.B. Morse develops a working model of the telegraph.

1841 Horace Greely founds the *New York Tribune.*

1850 Irish immigrants, escaping the famine in their homeland, arrive in the city.

1851 The *New York Times* publishes its first edition.

1858 Calvert Vaux and Frederick Law Olmsted design **Central Park**.

1869 Infamous Black Friday rocks the financial world.

1870 A city charter approved by the state legislature gives the notorious William Marcy "Boss" Tweed financial control over New York City. Incredible sums of money disappear from city coffers.

When the first burials took place in St. Paul's and Trinity churchyards, at the end of the 17th century, they provided employment for gentlemen licensed by the city as Inviters to Funerals. Dressed in somber black, with long black streamers attached to their stovepipe hats, they marched in pairs from house to house extolling the virtues of the recently deceased. As they walked through the streets, one tolled a bell and the other pounded the pavement with a long black pole. They served as masters of ceremonies at the funeral itself, and their fee was determined by the turnout. At the gravesite, the 12 pallbearers were given souvenir spoons engraved with figures of the 12 apostles, which were usually so badly cast they were known as monkey spoons. Female relatives were given a mourning brooch or ring, which had a compartment containing strands of the deceased's hair. (If they were burying a bald man, it was the hair of his nearest male relative.) Spoons, brooches, and rings were all sold by the Inviters, who also earned a fee for supervising the party that followed every funeral. The quality of the wine served was a tribute in itself, and many people stored away the best they could afford to be used at their own funerals. When a person became mortally ill, a different pair of licensed professionals, known as Comforters of the Sick, were hired by relatives to spend as many hours as were needed reading Scriptures, singing hymns, and otherwise preparing the doomed soul for an easy entry into Heaven.

1873 **Wall Street** panics as banks fail.

1883 The **Brooklyn Bridge**, considered the structural wonder of the age, opens.

1885 Southern Europeans, including large numbers of Italians, begin to arrive.

1886 The **Statue of Liberty** is unveiled . . . Samuel Gompers organizes the American Federation of Labor (AFL).

1890 Jewish immigrants begin to arrive from Eastern Europe, many settling on the Lower East Side.

1891 **Carnegie Hall** opens with a concert featuring Peter Tchaikovsky as conductor.

1892 **Ellis Island** becomes the city's immigration depot.

1898 The five boroughs unite to form **Greater New York**. The population is now over three million, making New York City the largest city in the world.

1904 The first subway system begins operation.

1911 The **New York Public Library** opens at **42nd Street** and **Fifth Avenue** . . . The Triangle Shirtwaist Company sweatshop fire leads to new labor laws and public safety measures.

1925 Playboy James Walker is elected mayor by popular vote.

1927 Charles A. Lindbergh returns to New York City after his solo flight to France . . . Babe Ruth becomes baseball's home-run king, scoring 60 homers in one year . . . The **Holland Tunnel**, the first **Hudson River** vehicular tunnel, opens and connects Manhattan with Jersey City, NJ.

1929 The stock market crashes as banks fail . . . The **Chrysler Building** and the **Museum of Modern Art** open.

1931 The **Empire State Building**, the **George Washington Bridge**, and the new **Waldorf-Astoria Hotel** are completed.

1932 Mayor James Walker resigns after it is learned that he and his administration are involved in municipal corruption.

1933 Fiorello La Guardia is elected mayor.

1937 The **Lincoln Tunnel** opens, connecting Midtown with Weehawken, NJ.

1940 The **Queens-Midtown Tunnel** opens . . . After the fall of France, New York City becomes home to many European artists–Mondrian, Léger, Ernst, Moholy-Nagy, and Breton among them.

1941 Mayor La Guardia initiates work on a giant air terminal in **Queens** (first called Idlewild, it was later renamed **John F. Kennedy International Airport**).

1945 William O'Dwyer is elected mayor . . . On 28 July, a US Army plane strikes the 79th floor of the **Empire State Building**, causing 14 deaths and a million dollars' worth of damage.

1946 The **United Nations** establishes headquarters in Manhattan on 17 acres donated by the Rockefeller family.

1950 The **Brooklyn Battery Tunnel** and the **Port Authority Bus Terminal** open . . . William O'Dwyer resigns as mayor after disclosures of scandal and fraud in his administration.

1953 Robert F. Wagner is elected mayor.

1956 **Ebbets Field** is sold for a housing site after the **Brooklyn Dodgers** leave for Los Angeles.

1959 The **Guggenheim Museum** opens.

1964 The **Verrazano-Narrows Bridge** connects Staten Island and Brooklyn . . . The **World's Fair** opens in **Flushing Meadow–Corona Park**.

1965 New York City is paralyzed by a power blackout . . . John V. Lindsay is elected mayor.

1970 The **World Trade Center** is topped off and its first tenants move in.

1974 Abraham D. Beame is elected mayor.

1978 Edward I. Koch is elected mayor . . . A four-month strike deprives New Yorkers of their newspapers.

1981 A ticker-tape parade salutes 52 American hostages held captive in Iran for 444 days . . . Former Beatle John Lennon is killed outside the **Dakota** apartments.

1982 Over half a million demonstrators against nuclear arms march to Central Park.

1986 Developer Donald Trump revamps **Wollman Rink** in Central Park . . . The Statue of Liberty renovation is completed.

1987 The stock market crashes on 19 October . . . Andy Warhol, the Father of Pop, dies in **New York Hospital**.

1989 David Dinkins wins the mayoral campaign to become the first black mayor in New York City history.

1990 Ellis Island reopens after a $156 million renovation.

1991 Carnegie Hall celebrates its 100th anniversary.

1993 On 26 February, a terrorist bombing in the parking garages at **One World Trade Center** kills six people and injures thousands more.

1994 Democrat David Dinkins is ousted in a bitter mayoral race by Rudolph Giuliani, a former federal prosecutor. Giuliani becomes the first Republican to defeat an incumbent mayor in 60 years and the first Republican to head City Hall since 1974.

1995 New York City helps commemorate the 50th anniversary of the United Nations on 24 October.

1997 *Cats* becomes the longest-running show on **Broadway**, with 6,138 performances.

1998 The City of New York celebrates its 100th birthday.

2001 The population of New York City tops eight million . . . On September 11, two passenger jets hijacked by terrorists fly into and destroy both towers of the World Trade Center, killing thousands, in the worst act of terrorism in US history . . . Republican Michael R. Bloomberg is elected mayor, the first to pay for his campaign entirely out of his own pocket.

2003 New York's economy—hurt by the Wall Street downturn and 9/11—begins to rebound.

2004 New York City Subway Centennial, 1904-2004 . . . The Republican National Convention takes place at the **Jacob Javits Center**.

2005 Christo and Jeanne-Claude install "The Gates" in Central Park, drawing huge crowds and international acclaim. New York has the lowest crime rate of major cities in the nation. Mayor Michael R. Bloomberg is overwhelmingly reelected to a second term.

2007 Ground is broken (again) for the much-needed Second Avenue subway line. Funding didn't materialize at the first attempt in 1972; East Siders are more hopeful the plan will come to fruition this time around.

2008–09 Parks, greenways, and other bicycle routes are the byword for city development. Greenways now circumvent Manhattan Island, and cover much of the boroughs as well; Hudson River Park—extending from the Battery to West 59th Street—is about complete. And, building on the fact that city cycling had grown 75% from 2000 to 2006, over 600 miles of an 1,800-mile bike route master plan will be completed in 2009.

INDEX

N

T

U

V

W

RESTAURANTS

Only restaurants with star ratings are listed below. All restaurants are listed alphabetically in the main (preceding) index. Always call in advance to ensure a restaurant has not closed, changed its hours, or booked its tables for a private party. The restaurant price ratings are based on the average cost of an entrée for one person, excluding tax and tip.

★★★★ An Extraordinary Experience
★★★ Excellent
★★ Very Good
★ Good

★

HOTELS

The hotels listed below are grouped according to their price ratings; they are also listed in the main index. The hotel price ratings reflect the base price of a standard room for two people for one night during the peak season.

$$$$ Big Bucks ($500 and up)
$$$ Expensive ($300-$500)
$$ Reasonable ($200-$300)
$ The Price is Right (less than $200)

$$$$

$$$

$$

$

FEATURES

BESTS

MAPS

New York City Subways
215th St.
Inwood 207th St.
207th St.
Dyckman St.
Dyckman St.
191st St.
190th St.
181st St.
181st St.
175th St.
168th St. Washington Heights
168th St. Washington Heights
Amsterdam Ave. 163rd St.
157th St.
155th St.
155th St.
Harlem River
Harlem 148th St.
145th St.
145th St.
145th St.
137th St. City College
135th St.
135th St.
125th St.
125th St.
125th St.
116th St. Columbia University
116th St.
116th St.
Cathedral Pkwy. 110th St.
Cathedral Pkwy. 110th St.
110th St. Central Park North
103rd St.
103rd St.
96th St.
96th St.
86th St.
86th St.
81st St.– Museum of Natural History
79th St.
72nd St.
72nd St.
66th St. Lincoln Center
Hudson River
Central Park
Fordham Rd.
Fordham Rd.
183rd St.
182nd-183rd Sts.
Burnside Ave.
Tremont Ave.
176th St
174th-175th Sts.
Mt. Eden Ave.
170th St
170th St.
167th St.
167th St.
161st St. Yankee Stadium
149th St.– Grand Concourse
3rd Ave. 149th St.
138th St. Grand Concourse
3rd Ave. 138th St.
125th St.
116th St.
110th St.
103rd St.
96th St.
86th St.
77th St.
68th St. Hunter College
59th St. Lexington Ave.

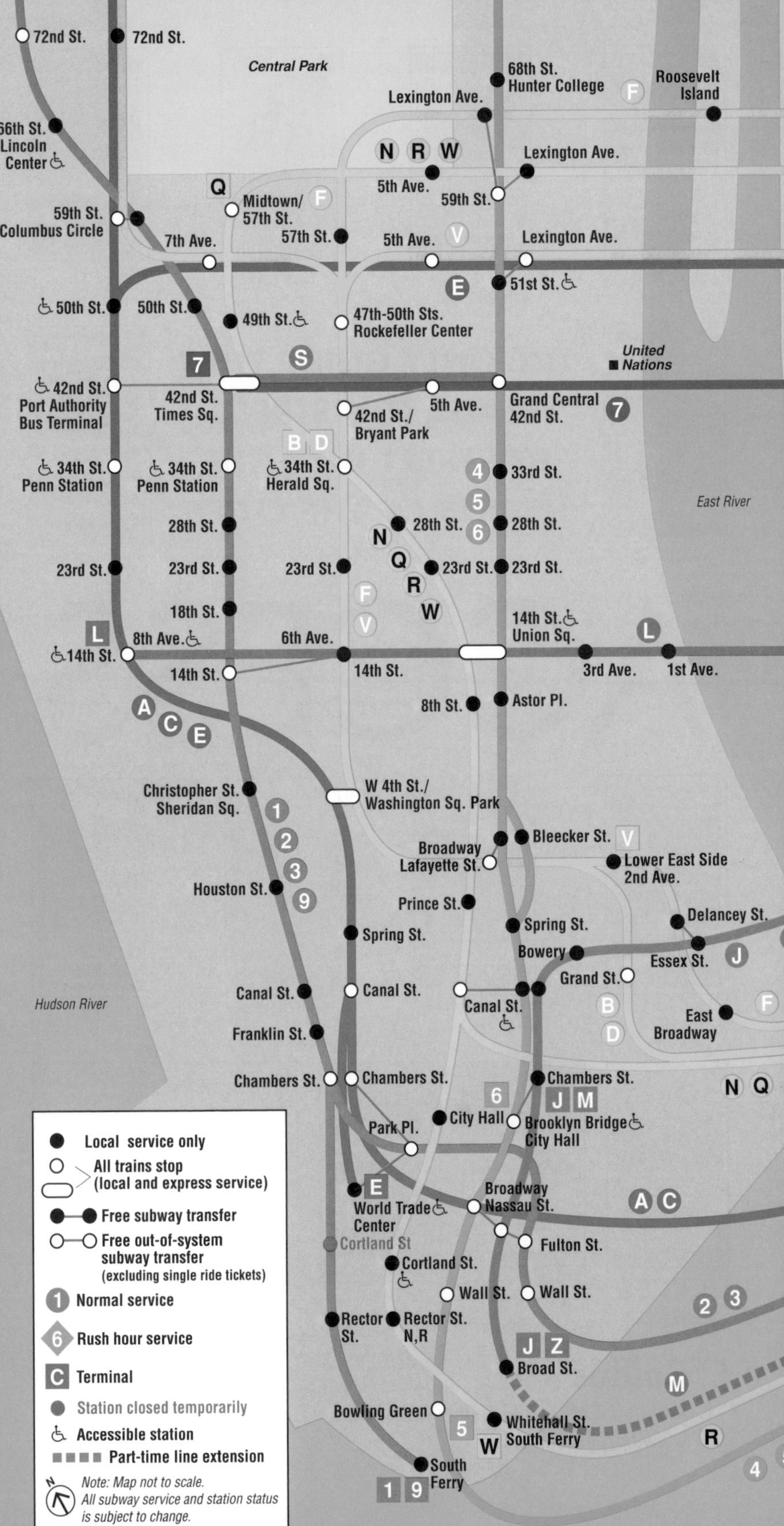

72nd St.
72nd St.
Central Park
68th St.
Hunter College
Roosevelt Island
Lexington Ave.
66th St.
Lincoln Center
N R W
Lexington Ave.
5th Ave.
59th St.
Q
Midtown/
57th St.
F
59th St.
Columbus Circle
57th St.
5th Ave.
V
Lexington Ave.
7th Ave.
E
51st St.
50th St.
50th St.
49th St.
47th-50th Sts.
Rockefeller Center
7
S
United Nations
42nd St.
Port Authority
Bus Terminal
42nd St.
Times Sq.
5th Ave.
42nd St./
Bryant Park
Grand Central
42nd St.
7
B D
34th St.
Penn Station
34th St.
Penn Station
34th St.
Herald Sq.
4
33rd St.
5
6
East River
28th St.
28th St.
28th St.
N
Q
R
W
23rd St.
23rd St.
23rd St.
23rd St.
23rd St.
F
V
18th St.
L
8th Ave.
6th Ave.
14th St.
Union Sq.
L
14th St.
14th St.
14th St.
3rd Ave.
1st Ave.
8th St.
Astor Pl.
A C E
Christopher St.
Sheridan Sq.
W 4th St./
Washington Sq. Park
1 2 3 9
Bleecker St.
V
Broadway
Lafayette St.
Lower East Side
2nd Ave.
Houston St.
Prince St.
Spring St.
Spring St.
Delancey St.
Bowery
Essex St.
J
Grand St.
Canal St.
Canal St.
Canal St.
Hudson River
B D
F
East Broadway
Franklin St.
Chambers St.
Chambers St.
Chambers St.
6
J M
N Q
City Hall
Brooklyn Bridge
City Hall
Park Pl.
E
World Trade Center
Broadway
Nassau St.
A C
Cortland St
Fulton St.
Cortland St.
Wall St.
Wall St.
2 3
Rector St.
Rector St.
N,R
J Z
Broad St.
M
Bowling Green
5
Whitehall St.
South Ferry
W
R
South Ferry
1 9
4 5
Local service only
All trains stop
(local and express service)
Free subway transfer
Free out-of-system
subway transfer
(excluding single ride tickets)
1 Normal service
6 Rush hour service
C Terminal
Station closed temporarily
Accessible station
Part-time line extension
N
Note: Map not to scale.
All subway service and station status
is subject to change.